Methods in Behavioral Research

FOURTEENTH EDITION

PAUL C. COZBY

California State University, Fullerton

SCOTT C. BATES

Utah State University

Mc
Graw
Hill

METHODS IN BEHAVIORAL RESEARCH, FOURTEENTH EDITION

Published by McGraw-Hill Education, 2 Penn Plaza, New York, NY 10121. Copyright ©2020 by McGraw-Hill Education. All rights reserved. Printed in the United States of America. Previous editions ©2018, 2015, and 2012. No part of this publication may be reproduced or distributed in any form or by any means, or stored in a database or retrieval system, without the prior written consent of McGraw-Hill Education, including, but not limited to, in any network or other electronic storage or transmission, or broadcast for distance learning.

Some ancillaries, including electronic and print components, may not be available to customers outside the United States.

This book is printed on acid-free paper.

1 2 3 4 5 6 7 8 9 LCR 24 23 22 21 20 19

ISBN 978-1-260-20558-9 (bound edition)
MHID 1-260-20558-4 (bound edition)
ISBN 978-1-260-38005-7 (loose-leaf edition)
MHID 1-260-38005-X (loose-leaf edition)

Product Development Manager: *Dawn Groundwater*
Senior Marketing Manager: *Augustine Laferrera*
Marketing Manager: *Olivia Kaiser*
Content Project Managers: *Sandy Wille, Jodi Banowetz*
Senior Buyer: *Susan K. Culbertson*
Designer: *Egzon Shaqiri*
Senior Content Licensing Specialist: *Gina Oberbroeckling*
Cover Image: *rzeszutek/Getty Images*
Compositor: *SPi Global*

All credits appearing on page or at the end of the book are considered to be an extension of the copyright page.

Library of Congress Cataloging-in-Publication Data

CIP has been applied for

The Internet addresses listed in the text were accurate at the time of publication. The inclusion of a website does not indicate an endorsement by the authors or McGraw-Hill Education, and McGraw-Hill Education does not guarantee the accuracy of the information presented at these sites.

mheducation.com/highered

Contents

Preface xii
About the Authors xx

1. SCIENTIFIC UNDERSTANDING OF BEHAVIOR 1

Consuming Research 2
Ways of Knowing 3
Goals of Behavioral Science 7
Basic and Applied Research 11
Review Questions 18
Study Terms 18
Check Your Learning: Answers 18

2. WHERE TO START 19

Research Questions, Hypotheses, and Predictions 20
Sources of Ideas 21
Types of Journal Articles 25
Exploring Past Research 32
Review Questions 43
Study Terms 43
Check Your Learning: Answers 44

3. ETHICS IN BEHAVIORAL RESEARCH 45

Milgram's Obedience Experiment 46
Historical Context of Current Ethical Standards 48
APA Ethics Code 49
Assessment of Risks and Benefits 50
Informed Consent 52
The Importance of Debriefing 57
Institutional Review Boards 58
Research with Nonhuman Animal Subjects 61
Being an Ethical Researcher: The Issue of Misrepresentation 62
Conclusion: Risks and Benefits Revisited 66
Review Questions 70
Study Terms 71
Check Your Learning: Answers 71

4. FUNDAMENTAL RESEARCH ISSUES 72

Validity: An Introduction 73

Variables 73

Operational Definitions of Variables 74

Relationships Between Variables 76

Nonexperimental Versus Experimental Methods 79

Experimental Methods: Additional Considerations 86

Evaluating Research: Summary of the FOUR Validities 89

Review Questions 94

Study Terms 94

Check Your Learning: Answers 95

5. MEASUREMENT CONCEPTS 96

Reliability of Measures 97

Construct Validity of Measures 101

Reactivity of Measures 105

Variables and Measurement Scales 105

Review Questions 111

Study Terms 112

Check Your Learning: Answers 112

6. OBSERVATIONAL METHODS 113

Quantitative and Qualitative Approaches 114

Naturalistic Observation 114

Systematic Observation 117

Case Studies 119

Archival Research 120

Review Questions 125

Study Terms 125

Check Your Learning: Answers 125

7. ASKING PEOPLE ABOUT THEMSELVES: SURVEY RESEARCH 126

Why Conduct Surveys? 127

Constructing Questions to Ask 128

Responses to Questions 131

Finalizing the Survey Instrument 135

Administering Surveys 136

Survey Designs to Study Changes Over Time 138

Sampling From a Population 139

Sampling Techniques 141

Evaluating Samples 144

Reasons for Using Convenience Samples 145

Review Questions 149

Study Terms 149

Check Your Learning: Answers 150

8. EXPERIMENTAL DESIGN 151

Confounding and Internal Validity 152

Basic Experiments 153

Assigning Participants to Experimental Conditions 157

Review Questions 165

Study Terms 166

Check Your Learning: Answers 166

9. CONDUCTING EXPERIMENTS 167

Selecting Research Participants 168

Manipulating the Independent Variable 168

Measuring the Dependent Variable 173

Additional Controls 176

Final Planning Considerations 179

Analyzing and Interpreting Results 181

Communicating Research to Others 181

Review Questions 185

Study Terms 186

Check Your Learning: Answers 186

10. COMPLEX EXPERIMENTAL DESIGNS 187

Increasing the Number of Levels of an Independent Variable 188

Increasing the Number of Independent Variables: Factorial Designs 189

Outcomes of a 2 × 2 Factorial Design 194

Assignment Procedures and Factorial Designs 197

Increasing the Number of Levels of an Independent Variable 198

Factorial Designs with Three or More Independent Variables 200

Review Questions 204

Study Terms 204

Check Your Learning: Answers 205

11. SINGLE-CASE, QUASI-EXPERIMENTAL, AND DEVELOPMENTAL RESEARCH 206

Single-Case Experimental Designs 207

Quasi-Experimental Designs 210

Developmental Research Designs 218

Review Questions 224

Study Terms 225

Check Your Learning: Answers 225

12. UNDERSTANDING RESEARCH RESULTS: DESCRIPTION AND CORRELATION 227

Scales of Measurement: A Review 228

Describing Results 229

Frequency Distributions 230

Descriptive Statistics 233

Graphing Relationships 234

Correlation Coefficients: Describing the Strength of Relationships 235

Effect Size 240

Regression Equations 241

Multiple Correlation/Regression 241

The Third-Variable Problem 243

Structural Equation Modeling 244

Review Questions 247

Study Terms 247

Check Your Learning: Answers 248

13. UNDERSTANDING RESEARCH RESULTS: STATISTICAL INFERENCE 249

Samples and Populations 250

Inferential Statistics 251

Null and Research Hypotheses 251

Probability and Sampling Distributions 252

Group Differences: The t and F Tests 254

Type I and Type II Errors 260

Choosing a Significance Level 263

Interpreting Nonsignificant Results 264

Choosing a Sample Size: Power Analysis 265

The Importance of Replications 266

Significance of a Pearson r Correlation Coefficient 266

Statistical Analysis software 267

Selecting the Appropriate Statistical Test 267

Review Questions 271

Study Terms 272

Check Your Learning: Answers 272

14. GENERALIZATION 274

Generalizing to Other Populations 275

Generalizing Across Methods 280

Supporting Good External Validity 282

Using Research to Improve Lives 288

Review Questions 290

Study Terms 290

Check Your Learning: Answers 291

APPENDIX A: REPORTING RESEARCH 292

Introduction 292

Writing Your Report 293

Formatting Your Report 299

Organization of the Report 300

The Use of Headings 312

Citing and Referencing Sources 312

Abbreviations 320

Reporting Numbers and Statistics 321

Paper and Poster Presentations 323

Sample Paper 325

APPENDIX B: ETHICAL PRINCIPLES OF PSYCHOLOGISTS AND CODE OF CONDUCT 344

General Principles 344

Standard 8: Research and Publication 345

APPENDIX C: STATISTICAL TESTS 346

Descriptive Statistics 346

Statistical Significance and Effect Size 349

Illustrative Articles

Chapter 1: Introduction

Chapter 2: Laptops in Class

Chapter 3: Replication of Milgram

Chapter 4: Studying Behavior

Chapter 5: Measurement Concepts

Chapter 6: Observational Methods

Chapter 7: Conducting Experiments

Chapter 8: Experimental Design

Chapter 9: Conducting Experiments

Chapter 10: Complex Experimental Designs

Chapter 11: Longitudinal Study

Chapter 14: Generalizing Results

Glossary 369

References 380

Index 397

APA Formatting Checklist 412

Preface

Methods in Behavioral Research featuring updates from the Publication Manual of the American Psychological Association (7th ed.) guides students toward success by helping them study smarter and more efficiently. Supported by SmartBook®, McGraw-Hill Education's adaptive and personalized reading experience, Cozby and Bates provide helpful pedagogy, rich examples, and clear voice in their approach to methodological decision making.

IN THE FOURTEENTH EDITION, we strive for an accessible presentation and continue looking for opportunities to drive home foundational concepts and reinforce students' understanding of the material. We have reimagined end-of-chapter content. We chose concepts that students have traditionally found most challenging and designed exercises that ask them to reflect, recall, and organize the material. We have also aligned the fourteenth edition with the newly released the Publication Manual of the American Psychological Association (7th ed.). Focused organization combined with clear and direct writing remains a hallmark of *Methods in Behavioral Research*. Chapters follow the arc of a research investigation from planning through conducting and presenting.

ORGANIZATION

Methods in Behavioral Research moves carefully through the major concepts in behavioral research from the foundations of scientific study through practical issues in research design and implementation.

"Scientific Understanding of Behavior" grounds students in the scientific approach, emphasizing the distinction between basic and applied research. "Where to Start" discusses sources of ideas for research and the importance of library research. "Ethics in Behavioral Research" focuses on research ethics; ethical issues are covered in depth here and emphasized throughout the book. "Fundamental Research Issues" introduces validity and examines psychological variables and the distinction between experimental and nonexperimental approaches to studying relationships among variables. "Measurement Concepts" focuses on measurement issues, including reliability and validity. Nonexperimental research approaches—including naturalistic observation, cases studies, and content analysis—are described in "Observational Methods." "Asking People About Themselves: Survey Research" covers sampling as well as the design of questionnaires and interviews. "Experimental Design" and "Conducting Experiments" present the basics of designing and conducting experiments. Factorial designs are emphasized in "Complex Experimental Designs." "Single-Case, Quasi-Experimental, and Developmental Research" discusses the designs for special applications: single-case experimental designs, developmental research designs, and quasi-experimental designs. "Understanding Research Results: Description and Correlation" and "Understanding Research Results: Statistical Inference" focus on the use of statistics to help students understand research results. These chapters include material on effect size and confidence intervals. Finally, "Generalization" discusses generalization issues, meta-analyses, and the importance of replications.

FEATURES

Methods in Behavioral Research includes the following features to enhance learning:

NEW! Critical Thinking: Consumer of Research. These exercises are designed to get students out of the textbook and out of their classrooms and into the broader world in which we all move. These exercises ask students to look at examples of research—such as studies on the predictors of happiness and the causes and effects of sitting in the front of the classroom—to compare what they've learned in class or the text with what they see. Applying the concepts they have learned will help them expand their understanding of the content.

NEW! Fully updated according to the Publication Manual of the American Psychological Association (7th ed.): This edition includes and supports new guidelines on ethical and bias-free writing, adopted the new standard for in-text citations, updated rules for manuscript formatting, and adopted APA's final resolution to the eternal question: One space or two after a period? (Answer: One!)

NEW! Updated to align with 2019 federal guidelines that govern IRBs, including new categories of exempt review.

UPDATED! Check Your Learning: Practice Exercises. In previous editions, these Check Your Learning boxes were placed within the body of the chapter. We found that students often found this placement distracting and preferred to be able to control when to complete the exercises. We now include an in-text callout to place the content; the actual exercises and answers are at the end of the chapter.

Illustrative articles. These boxes include published journal articles with questions and exercises designed to focus on chapter-related material. In addition, the articles help students become familiar with the structure and language of journal articles in psychology. We have several new articles in this edition. Most important, we have provided links to online copies of the articles whenever possible.

Solid pedagogy. Each chapter opens with a set of learning objectives that serve as reading guides and ends with a review of major concepts and key terms.

Practical examples. Thought-provoking examples help students interpret challenging concepts and complex research designs. The concept of diversity of ideas is examined through the lens of biases regarding rap music. Theory article formats are introduced though a recent study on suicide.

Decision-making emphasis. Distinguishing among a variety of research designs helps students understand when to use one type of design over another.

FLEXIBLE

Chapters are designed to work independently, so that they can be adapted to any curriculum or syllabus. Sections are clearly defined and relevant practice exercises called out within each, making it easy to reorder or skip topics.

In addition, three appendices related to communicating research findings, ethical standards, and conducting statistical analyses can be used any time throughout the course. Appendix A includes an annotated version of a published paper and provides firm instructions for organizing research. Students can easily refer to the APA Ethics Code in Appendix B, and Appendix C includes a bank of statistical tests that can be applied to a variety of research designs.

Methods in Behavioral Research is available to instructors and students in traditional print format as well as online within McGraw Hill Connect, a digital assignment and assessment platform. Connect includes assignable and assessable videos, quizzes, exercises, and interactive activities, all associated with learning objectives for *Methods in Behavioral Research.* These online tools make managing assignments easier for instructors, and learning and studying more motivating and efficient for students.

Power of Process, available in Connect for Research Methods, guides students through the process of critical reading, analysis, and writing. Faculty can select or upload their own content, such as journal articles, and assign analysis strategies to gain insight into students' application of the scientific method. For students, Power of Process offers a guided visual approach to exercising critical thinking strategies to apply before, during, and after reading published research.

BETTER DATA, SMARTER REVISIONS, IMPROVED RESULTS

For this new edition, data were analyzed to identify the concepts students found to be the most difficult, allowing for expansion upon the discussion, practice, and assessment of challenging topics. The revision process for a new edition used to begin with gathering information from instructors about what they would change and what they would keep.

Experts in the field were asked to provide comments that pointed out new material to add and dated material to review. Using all these reviews, authors would revise the material. But today a new tool has revolutionized that model.

McGraw-Hill Education authors now have access to student performance data to analyze and inform their revisions. These data are anonymously collected from the many students who use SmartBook, the adaptive learning system that provides students with individualized assessment of their own progress. Because virtually every text paragraph is tied to several questions that students answer while using SmartBook, the specific concepts with which students are having the most difficulty are easily pinpointed through empirical data in the form of a "heat map" report.

New to this edition, SmartBook is now optimized for mobile and tablet and is accessible for students with disabilities. Content-wise, it has been enhanced with improved learning objectives that are measurable and observable to improve student outcomes.

POWERFUL REPORTING

Whether a class is face-to-face, hybrid, or entirely online, McGraw-Hill Connect provides the tools needed to reduce the amount of time and energy instructors spend administering their courses. Easy-to-use course management tools allow instructors to spend less time administering and more time teaching, while reports allow students to monitor their progress and optimize their study time.

- The **At-Risk Student Report** provides instructors with one-click access to a dashboard that identifies students who are at risk of dropping out of the course due to low engagement levels.
- The **Category Analysis Report** details student performance relative to specific learning objectives and goals, including APA learning goals and outcomes and levels of Bloom's taxonomy.
- **Connect Insight** is a one-of-a-kind visual analytics dashboard—now available for both instructors and students—that provides at-a-glance information regarding student performance.
- **The SmartBook Reports** allow instructors and students to easily monitor progress and pinpoint areas of weakness, giving each student a personalized study plan to achieve success.

ADDITIONAL RESOURCES

Achieve simplicity in assigning and engaging your students with course materials. Craft your teaching resources to match the way you teach! With McGraw-Hill Create, you can easily rearrange chapters, combine material from other content sources, and quickly upload content you have written, such as your course syllabus or teaching notes. Find the content you need in Create by searching through thousands of leading McGraw-Hill textbooks. Arrange your book to fit your teaching style. Create even allows you to personalize your book's appearance by selecting the cover and adding your name, school, and course information. Order a Create book and you'll receive a complimentary electronic review copy (eComp) via email in about an hour. Experience how McGraw-Hill Create empowers you to teach your students *your* way: http://create.mheducation.com

McGraw Hill **Campus**

McGraw-Hill Campus provides faculty with true single sign-on access to all of McGraw-Hill's course content, digital tools, and other high-quality learning resources from any LMS. This innovative offering allows for secure and deep integration, enabling seamless access for faculty and students to any of McGraw-Hill's course solutions, such as McGraw-Hill Connect (all-digital teaching and learning platform) and McGraw-Hill Create (state-of-the-art custom-publishing platform McGraw-Hill Campus includes access to McGraw-Hill's entire content library, including eBooks, assessment tools, presentation slides, multimedia content, and other resources. McGraw-Hill Campus provides instructors with open, unlimited access to prepare for class, create tests/quizzes, develop lecture material, integrate interactive content, and more: http://www.mhcampus.com

CHANGES TO THE FOURTEENTH EDITION

The fourteenth edition of *Methods in Behavioral Research* includes numerous updates and new references. Here is a list of major changes as they appear by chapter.

Chapter 1

- Added discussion on the importance of becoming a savvy consumer of research.
- Added discussion of risky outcomes that result from researcher overreach.
- Critical Thinking: Read editorials from large national newspapers and evaluate for intuition, appeals to authority, and supporting evidence. Consider both sides of two arguments about major assertions about behavioral research studies as a discipline. Sift through data presented in an online article about eating disorders to identify cause and effect and explanation.

Chapter 2

- New discussion added to "Source of Ideas" offers clues to where one might find inspiration for a new research study.
- Added example of how practical problems in everyday life can stimulate research studies.
- New analysis of biases toward rap music within the framework of diversity of ideas.
- Refined discussion of literature reviews, where to find them and how to use them.
- New example of a recent theory article about suicide.
- New example of an article search using Web of Science.
- New Critical Thinking box: Review four different articles related to behavioral science that have recently appeared in the popular press including stress in teens and happy memories as health boosters.

Chapter 3

- Added emphasis on the exempt review of minimal risk research.
- Deeper discussion of the functions of an IRB.
- New Critical Thinking box: Consider the ethics behind three controversial research studies including Milgram. Read your college's student code of conduct and consider ways to improve upon the plagiarism section.

Chapter 4

- A fourth validity added: statistical validity.
- New Critical Thinking box: Review operational definitions and why they are important. Work through the components of research including hypothesis (both experimental and nonexperimental method) variable, cause and effect.

Chapter 5

- New study added to illustrative article on measurement concepts that aimed to reduce bias in STET ratings by adjusting language on the form.
- New Critical Thinking box: Review two personality assessments to determine their reliability and consider ways to assess construct validity.

Chapter 6

- New Critical Thinking box: Develop a research question that can best be used addressed through qualitative techniques. Locate and summarize two reviews of a recent book about Henry Molaison by his grandson.

Chapter 7

- Updated Figure 1 includes new data on annual prevalence of teenage marijuana use.
- Section of nonverbal scales has been expanded to include adult populations.
- Explanation of recently developed *Prime Panels*, a recruiting tool for unique samples.
- New Critical Thinking box: Work through a survey from evaluating the questions to analyzing the results. Briefly plan an online survey with an adult population regarding family, professional, and life satisfaction.

Chapter 8

- New Critical Thinking box: Review two different experimental designs and share ideas for how they could be improved or how specific problems could be addressed.

Chapter 9

- Refined discussion on quantifying observed behaviors.
- New illustrative article: "Conducting Experiments."
- New Critical Thinking box: Consider sample scenario in a pilot study and work through questions about the manipulations, variables, controls, and outcomes.

Chapter 10

- Revised illustrative article: "Complex Experimental Designs."
- New Critical Thinking box: Work through a 2 × 2 with independent groups and consider the effects as variables are adjusted. In a second experiment, identify the design, variables, conditions and possible interactions.

Chapter 11

- New illustrative article: "A Longitudinal Study."
- New Critical Thinking box: Look for problems and explain outcomes in five different sample research scenarios.

Chapter 12

- New Critical Thinking box: Create your own sample by asking students on campus to ask a question about the courses they are taking. Think of three variables that use a nominal scale

Chapter 13

- Added discussion on choosing a sample size.
- New Critical Thinking box: Plan parts of a research design. Analyze research on attitudes toward individuals in wheelchairs.

Chapter 14

- Added an in-depth note on the Open Science initiative and the replication crisis in psychology.
- New Critical Thinking box: Think through a sample of college students and consider what makes it a unique population.

INSTRUCTOR RESOURCES

Methods in Behavioral Research also includes the following instructor resources:

Instructor's Manual: Designed to provide a wide variety of resources for presenting the course, the instructor's manual includes learning objectives, ideas for lectures and discussions, laboratory demonstrations, and activities aligned specifically to facilitate a clearer knowledge of research methods.

Test Bank: By increasing the rigor of the test bank development process, McGraw-Hill has raised the bar for student assessment. A coordinated team of subject-matter experts methodically vetted each question and each set of possible answers for accuracy, clarity, and effectiveness. Each question is further annotated for level of page difficulty, Bloom's taxonomy, APA learning outcomes, and corresponding coverage in the text. Structured by chapter, the questions are designed to test students' conceptual, applied, and factual understanding.

Test Builder: New to this edition and available within Connect, Test Builder is a cloud-based tool that enables instructors to format tests that can be printed or administered within a Learning Management System. Test Builder offers a modern, streamlined interface for easy content configuration that matches course needs, without requiring a download.

Test Builder enables instructors to:

- Access all test bank content from a particular title
- Easily pinpoint the most relevant content through robust filtering options
- Manipulate the order of questions or scramble questions and / or answers
- Pin questions to a specific location within a test
- Determine your preferred treatment of algorithmic questions
- Choose the layout and spacing
- Add instructions and configure default settings

Lecture Presentation: Accessibility compliant, PowerPoint slides are provided that present key points of the chapter, along with supporting visuals. All of the slides can be modified to meet individual needs.

Image Gallery: The complete set of figures and tables from the text are available for download and can be easily embedded into PowerPoint slides.

ACKNOWLEDGMENTS

Many individuals helped to produce this and previous editions of this book. The portfolio manager at McGraw-Hill was Nancy Welcher; we are also indebted to the editors of previous editions, Franklin Graham, Ken King, Mike Sugarman, and Krista Bettino, for their guidance. We are extremely grateful for the input from numerous students and instructors, including the following individuals, who provided detailed reviews for this edition:

Marina Bornovalova
University of South Florida

Kristy Boyce
The Ohio State University

Blaine Browne
Valdosta State University

Robert Christman
Mohawk Valley Community College

Emily Cohen-Shikora
Washington University at St. Louis

Paul Curran
Grand Valley State University

Robert O. Deaner
Grand Valley State University

Christopher Dickinson
Appalachian State University

Dana S. Dunn
Moravian College

Mario Fific
Grand Valley State University

Stephen Gabbard
Wright State University, Dayton

Leslie A. Gill
Eastern New Mexico University

Suzanne Helfer
Adrian College

Charles M. Huffman
Georgia Southwestern State University

Christopher Howard
Husson University

Ashley Jordan
University of Arizona

Jeff Kibler
Nova Southeastern University

Cecile Lardon
University of Alaska Fairbanks

Mindy Ma
Nova Southeastern University

Hajime Otani
Central Michigan University

Mary K. Radeke
Central Washington University

Theodore M. Singelis
California State University, Chico

Lynda Villaneuva
University of Houston

About the Authors

Paul C. Cozby is Emeritus Professor of Psychology at California State University, Fullerton. Dr. Cozby was an undergraduate at the University of California, Riverside, and received his Ph.D. in psychology from the University of Minnesota. He is a fellow of the American Psychological Association and a member of the Association for Psychological Science, and he served as an officer of the Society for Computers in Psychology and as Executive Officer of the Western Psychological Association. He is the author of *Using Computers in the Behavioral Sciences* and co-editor with Daniel Perlman of *Social Psychology*.

Scott C. Bates is a Professor and Department Head of the Psychology Department at Utah State University in Logan, Utah. He earned a B.S. in Psychology from Whitman College, an M.S. in Psychology from Western Washington University, and a Ph.D. in social psychology from Colorado State University. His research interests and experiences are varied. He has conducted research in areas as wide-ranging as adolescent problem behavior and problem-behavior prevention, teaching and learning in higher education, and the psychological consequences of growing and tending plants in outer space.

We are always interested in receiving comments and suggestions from students and instructors. Please email us at scott.bates@usu.edu or cozby@fullerton.edu.

1 Scientific Understanding of Behavior

Meiwphotographer/Shutterstock

LEARNING OBJECTIVES

- Describe why it is important to understand research methods.
- Describe the scientific approach to understanding behavior, and contrast it with a pseudoscientific approach.
- Define and give examples of the four goals of scientific research: description, prediction, determination of cause, and explanation of behavior.
- Discuss the three elements for inferring causation: temporal order, covariation of cause and effect, and elimination of alternative explanations.
- Define, describe, compare, and contrast basic and applied research.

Do social media sites like Facebook and Instagram impact our relationships? What causes alcoholism? How do our early childhood experiences affect our later lives? How do we remember things, what causes us to forget, and how can memory be improved? Why do we procrastinate? Why do some people experience anxiety so extreme that it disrupts their lives, while others—facing the same situation—seem to be unaffected? How can we help people who suffer from depression? Why do we like certain people and dislike others? How can employers nurture employee well-being in a high-stress workplace?

Curiosity about questions like these is probably the most important reason many students decide to take courses in the behavioral sciences. Science is the best way to explore and answer these sorts of questions. In this book, we will examine the methods of scientific research in the behavioral sciences. In this introductory chapter, we will focus on ways in which knowledge of research methods can be useful in understanding the world around us. Further, we will review the characteristics of a scientific approach to the study of behavior and the general types of research questions that concern behavioral scientists.

CONSUMING RESEARCH

We are continuously bombarded with research results: The *New York Times* runs many articles with titles like "Parents Should Avoid Comments on a Child's Weight," "Abortion Is Found to Have Little Effect on Women's Mental Health," and "Insomniacs Are Helped by Online Therapy." The *Washington Post* declared, "Large study supports 'weekend warrior' approach to lifetime fitness." Meanwhile, over on cable news, CNN reports that "Facebook can actually make us more narrow-minded," while Fox News notes that "Alcohol ads should be banned from sporting events, says study." MSNBC told us to buy a pet—"Kids with pets have less anxiety"—but *People Magazine* tells us, hold on, "Your Beloved Cat Could Be Making Your PMS Worse!" Even Buzzfeed gets into the act, letting the bookstore owners among us know that a "New Study Finds That Filling Bookstores with the Scent of Chocolate Makes You Shop Longer," and Buzzfeed also wondered, "Is America Having a 'Friendship Slump'?"

Articles, books, websites, and social media posts make claims about the beneficial or harmful effects of particular diets or vitamins on one's sex life, personality, or health. There are frequent reports of survey results that draw conclusions about our views on a variety of topics—who we will vote for, what we think about a product, where we stand on political hot topics of the day.

The key question is: How do you evaluate such reports? Do you simply accept the findings because they are supposed to be scientific? A background in research methods will help you read these reports critically, evaluate the methods employed, and decide whether the conclusions are reasonable. Learning about research methods will help you think critically; learning about research methods will help you be a skilled consumer of research.

Why Learn About Research Methods?

Beyond learning to think critically about research findings, there are many ways that research impacts today's society, and many reasons why learning about research methods is important.

First, many occupations require the use of research findings. For example, mental health professionals must make decisions about treatment methods, assignment of clients to different types of facilities, medications, and testing procedures. Such decisions are made on the basis of research; to make good decisions, mental health professionals must be able to read the research literature in the field and apply it to their professional lives. Similarly, people working in business environments frequently rely on research to make decisions about marketing strategies, ways of improving employee productivity and morale, and methods of selecting and training new employees. Educators must keep up with research on topics such as the effectiveness of various teaching strategies or programs to deal with special student problems. It is useful to have a knowledge of research methods and the ability to evaluate research reports in many fields.

It is also important to recognize that scientific research has become increasingly prominent in public policy decisions. Legislators and political leaders at all levels of government frequently take political positions and propose legislation based on research findings. Research may also influence judicial decisions: A classic example of this is the *Social Science Brief* that was prepared by psychologists and accepted as evidence in the landmark 1954 case *Brown v. Board of Education,* in which the U.S. Supreme Court banned school segregation in the United States. One of the studies cited in the brief was conducted by Clark and Clark (1947), who found that when allowed to choose between light-skinned and dark-skinned dolls, both Black and White children preferred to play with the light-skinned dolls (see Stephan, 1983, for a further discussion of the implications of this study).

Behavioral research on human development has influenced U.S. Supreme Court decisions related to juvenile crime. In 2005, for instance, the Supreme Court decided that juveniles could not face the death penalty (*Roper v. Simmons*), and the decision was informed by neurological and behavioral research showing that in juveniles, the level of development of their brains, social relationships, and character make juveniles less culpable than adults for the same crimes. Similarly, in 2010, in *Graham v. Florida*, the U.S. Supreme Court decided that juvenile offenders could not be sentenced to life in prison without parole for nonhomicide offenses. This decision was influenced by research in developmental psychology and neuroscience. The Court majority pointed to this research in their conclusion that assessment of blame and standards for sentencing should be different for juveniles and adults because juveniles lack adults' maturity, ability to resist pressures from peers and others, and personal sense of responsibility (Clay, 2010).

Research is also important when developing and assessing the effectiveness of programs designed to achieve certain goals—for example, to increase retention of students in school, influence people to engage in behaviors that reduce their risk of contracting HIV, or teach employees how to reduce the effects of stress. We need to be able to determine whether these programs are successfully meeting their goals.

Finally, research methods are important because they can provide us with the best answers to questions like those we posed at the outset of this chapter. Research methods can be the way to satisfy our native curiosity about ourselves, our world, and those around us.

WAYS OF KNOWING

We opened this chapter with several questions about human behavior and suggested that scientific research is a valuable means of answering them. How does the scientific approach differ from other ways of learning about behavior? People have always observed the world around them and sought explanations for what they see and experience. However, instead of using a scientific approach, many people rely on *intuition* and *authority* as primary ways of knowing.

Intuition and Anecdote

Most of us either know or have heard about a couple in a relationship who, after years of trying to conceive, adopt a child. Then very soon after adopting, the woman becomes pregnant. This observation leads to a belief that adoption increases the likelihood of pregnancy for couples who are having difficulties conceiving a child.

People usually go one step further and offer an explanation for this effect—such as, that the adoption reduces a major source of marital stress, and the stress reduction in turn increases the chances of conception (see Gilovich, 1991).

This example illustrates the use of intuition and anecdotal evidence to draw general conclusions about the world around us. When you rely on intuition, you accept unquestioningly what your own personal judgment or a single story (anecdote) about one person's experience tells you. The intuitive approach takes many forms. Often it involves finding an explanation for our own behaviors or the behaviors of others. For example, you might develop an explanation for why you keep having conflicts with your roommate, such as "He hates me" or "Having to share a bathroom creates conflict." Other times, intuition is used to explain events that you observe, as in the case of concluding that adoption increases the chances of conception among couples having difficulty conceiving a child.

A problem with intuition is that numerous cognitive and motivational biases affect our perceptions, and so we may draw erroneous conclusions about cause and effect (cf. Fiske & Taylor, 1984; Gilovich, 1991; Nisbett & Ross, 1980; Nisbett & Wilson, 1977). Gilovich points out that there is in fact no relationship between adoption and subsequent pregnancy, according to scientific research investigations. So why do we hold this belief? Most likely it is because of a cognitive bias called *illusory correlation* that occurs when we focus on two events that stand out and occur together. When an adoption is closely followed by a pregnancy, our attention is drawn to the situation, and we are biased to conclude that there must be a causal connection. Such illusory correlations are also likely to occur when we are highly motivated to believe in the causal relationship. Although this is a natural thing for us to do, it is not scientific. A scientific approach requires much more evidence before conclusions can be drawn.

Authority

The philosopher Aristotle said: "Persuasion is achieved by the speaker's personal character when the speech is so spoken as to make us think him credible. We believe good men more fully and readily than others." Aristotle would argue that we are more likely to be persuaded by a speaker who seems prestigious, trustworthy, and respectable than by one who appears to lack such qualities.

Many of us might accept Aristotle's arguments simply because he is considered a prestigious authority—a convincing and influential source—and his writings remain important. Similarly, many people are all too ready to accept anything they learn from the internet, news media, books, government officials, celebrities, religious figures, or even a professor! They believe that the statements of such authorities must be true. The problem, of course, is that the statements may not be true. The scientific approach rejects the notion that one can accept *on faith* the statements of any authority; again, more evidence is needed before we can draw scientific conclusions.

Empiricism

The scientific approach to acquiring knowledge recognizes that intuition, anecdote, and authority can be sources of ideas about behavior. However, scientists do not unquestioningly accept anyone's intuitions—including their own. Scientists recognize that *their* ideas are just as likely to be wrong as anyone else's. Also, scientists do not accept on faith anyone's pronouncements, regardless of that person's prestige or authority. Thus, scientists are very skeptical about what they see and hear. Scientific skepticism means that ideas must be evaluated on the basis of careful logic and results from scientific investigations.

If scientists reject intuition and blind acceptance of authority as ways of knowing about the world, how do they go about gaining knowledge? The fundamental characteristic of the scientific method is **empiricism**—the idea that knowledge comes from observations. Data are collected that form the basis of conclusions about the nature of the world. The scientific method embodies a number of rules for collecting and evaluating data; these rules will be explored throughout this book.

The Scientific Approach

The power of the scientific approach can be seen all around us. Whether you look at biology, chemistry, medicine, physics, anthropology, or psychology, you will see amazing advances over the past 5, 25, 50, or 100 years. We have a greater understanding of the world around us, and the applications of that understanding have kept pace. Goodstein (2000) describes an "evolved theory of science" that defines the characteristics of scientific inquiry. These characteristics are summarized below.

- **Data play a central role.** For scientists, knowledge is primarily based on observations. Scientists enthusiastically search for observations that will verify or reject their ideas about the world. They develop theories, argue that existing data support their theories, and conduct research that can increase our confidence that the theories are correct. Observations can be criticized, alternatives can be suggested, and data collection methods can be called into question. But in each of these cases, the role of data is central and fundamental. Scientists have a "show me, don't tell me" attitude.

- **Scientists are not alone.** Scientists make observations that are accurately reported to other scientists and the public. You can be sure that many other scientists will follow up on the findings by conducting research that replicates and extends these observations.

- **Science is adversarial.** Science is a way of thinking in which ideas do battle with other ideas in order to move ever closer to truth. Research can be conducted to test any idea; supporters of the idea and those who disagree with the idea can report their research findings, and these can be evaluated by others. Some ideas, even some very good ideas, may prove to be wrong if research fails to provide support for them. Good scientific ideas are testable. They can be supported or they can be falsified by data—the latter concept is called **falsifiability** (Popper, 2002). If an idea is falsified when it is tested, science is thereby advanced because this result will spur the development of new and better ideas.

- **Scientific evidence is peer reviewed.** Before a study is published in a top-quality scientific journal, it is reviewed by other scientists who have the expertise to carefully evaluate the research. This process is called **peer review.** The role of these reviewers is to recommend whether the research should be published. This review process ensures that research with major flaws will not become part of the scientific literature. In essence, science exists in a free market of ideas in which the best ideas are supported by research, and scientists can build upon the research of others to make further advances.

Integrating Intuition, Anecdote, and Authority With Skepticism

The advantage of the scientific approach over other ways of knowing about the world is that it provides an objective set of rules for gathering, evaluating, and reporting information. It is an open system that allows ideas to be refuted or supported by others. This does not mean that intuition, anecdote, and authority are unimportant, however. As noted previously, scientists often rely on intuition and assertions of authorities for ideas for research. Moreover, there is nothing wrong with accepting the assertions of an authority as long as we do not accept them as scientific evidence. In many cases scientific evidence is not obtainable—for example, when a religious figure or text asks us to accept certain beliefs on faith. Some beliefs cannot be tested and thus are beyond the realm of science. In science, however, ideas must be evaluated on the basis of available evidence that can be used to support or refute the ideas.

There is also nothing wrong with having opinions or beliefs as long as they are presented simply as opinions or beliefs. However, we should always ask whether the opinion can be tested scientifically or whether scientific evidence exists that relates to the opinion. For example, opinions on whether exposure to violent movies, TV, and video games increases aggression are only opinions until scientific evidence on the issue is gathered.

As you learn more about scientific methods, you will become increasingly skeptical of the research results reported in the media and the assertions of scientists as well. You should be aware that scientists often become authorities when they express their ideas. When someone claims to be a scientist, should we be more willing to accept what he or she has to say? First, ask about the individual's credentials. It is usually wise to pay more attention to someone with an established reputation in the field and attend to the reputation of the institution represented by the person. It is also worthwhile to examine the researcher's funding source; you might be a bit suspicious when research funded by a drug company supports the effectiveness of a drug manufactured by that company, for example. Similarly, when an organization with a particular social-political agenda funds the research that supports that agenda, you should be skeptical of the findings and closely examine the methods of the study.

You should also be skeptical of pseudoscientific research. **Pseudoscience** is the use of seemingly scientific terms and demonstrations to substantiate claims that have no basis in scientific research. The claim may be that a product or procedure will enhance your memory, relieve depression, or treat autism or post-traumatic stress disorder. The fact that these are all worthy outcomes makes us very susceptible to believing pseudoscientific claims and forgetting to ask whether there is a valid scientific basis for the claims.

A good example comes from a procedure called *facilitated communication* that has been used by therapists working with children with autism. These children lack verbal skills for communication; to help them communicate, a facilitator holds the child's hand while the child presses keys to type messages on a keyboard. This technique produces impressive results, indicating that the children are now able to express themselves. Of course, well-designed studies revealed that the facilitators, not the children, controlled the typing. The problem with all pseudoscience is that hopes are raised and promises will not be realized. Often the techniques can be dangerous as well. In the case of facilitated communication, a number of facilitators typed messages accusing a parent of physically or sexually abusing the child. Some parents were actually convicted of child abuse. In these legal cases, the scientific research on facilitated communication was used to help the defendant parent. Cases such as this have led to a movement to promote the exclusive use of evidence-based therapies—therapeutic interventions grounded in scientific research findings that demonstrate their effectiveness (Brown, 2016; cf. Lilienfeld et al., 2004).

So how can you tell if a claim is pseudoscientific? It is not easy. In fact, a philosopher of science noted that "the boundaries separating science, nonscience, and pseudoscience are much fuzzier and more permeable than ... most scientists ... would have us believe" (Pigliucci, 2010). Here are a few things to look for when evaluating claims:

- Claims that are untestable and therefore cannot be refuted
- Claims that rely on imprecise, biased, or vague language
- Evidence that is based on anecdotes and testimonials rather than scientific data
- Evidence that is from "experts" who have only vague qualifications and do not support their claims with sound scientific evidence
- Claims based only on confirmatory evidence, ignoring conflicting evidence
- Reliance on "scientific" evidence that cannot be independently verified because the methods used to establish that evidence have not been described

Finally, we are all increasingly susceptible to false reports of scientific findings circulated via the internet. Many of these reports claim to be associated with a reputable scientist or scientific organization, and then they take on a life of their own. A recent widely covered report, supposedly from the World Health Organization, claimed that the gene for blond hair was being selected out of the human gene pool. Blond hair would be a disappearing trait! General rules to follow when reading internet sites: (1) Be highly skeptical of scientific assertions that are supported by only vague or improbable evidence, and (2) Take the time to do an internet search for supportive evidence. At internet sites like **snopes.com**, **truthorfiction.com**, and **factcheck.org/asksc icheck/** you can check many of the claims that are on the internet.

Being a Skilled Consumer of Research

How much trust we should place in a study depends upon the methods that were used to conduct the study. Sometimes study authors overreach, coming to conclusions that are not justified. Four questions can be asked of any research study that will reveal a lot about how much the study should be trusted. The better the answers to these questions, the more confident you can be of the study:

1. **"What was measured?"** All studies in the behavioral sciences start with measurement: identifying the important concepts to be studied, and figuring out how to measure them. This is related to the concept of construct validity, which will be covered in depth in later chapters.

2. **"How do they know that one thing caused another?"** Often—particularly in popular media—there will be the claim that one thing causes another. A good question to ask here is: How do they know? This is related to the concept of internal validity, which will be covered in later chapters.

3. **"To what or whom can we generalize the results?"** This is related to the concept of external validity, which will be covered in later chapters.

4. **"Have other researchers found similar results?"** A single study can be interesting, but scientific progress involves the accumulation of studies. We can be more confident in a study if other studies have found the same thing.

GOALS OF BEHAVIORAL SCIENCE

Scientific research on behavior has four general goals: (1) to describe behavior, (2) to predict behavior, (3) to determine the causes of behavior, and (4) to understand or explain behavior.

Description of Behavior

The scientist begins with careful observation, because the first goal of science is to describe behavior—which can be something directly observable (such as running speed, eye gaze, or loudness of laughter) or something less observable (such as self-reports of perceptions of attractiveness). Using a written questionnaire, researchers at the Kaiser Family Foundation (Rideout et al., 2010) collected data on the use of media (e.g., television, cell phones, movies) by more than 2,000 8- to 18-year-olds. One section of the questionnaire asked about computer use. **Figure 1** shows the percentage of time spent on various recreational computer activities in a typical day. As you can see, social networking and game playing are the most common activities. This is the sort of study that benefits from replication every few years to reveal changes that occur with new technologies and attitudes.

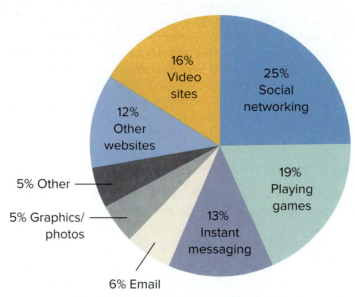

FIGURE 1   Time spent on recreational computer activities by 8-18 year olds

Researchers are often interested in describing the ways in which events are systematically related to one another. If parents place limits on their children's recreational computer use, do their children perform better in school? Do jurors judge attractive defendants more leniently than unattractive defendants? Are people more likely to be persuaded by a speaker who has high credibility? In what ways do cognitive abilities change as people grow older? Do students who study with a television set on score lower on exams than students who study in a quiet environment? Do taller people make more money than shorter people?

Prediction of Behavior

A second goal of behavioral science is to predict behavior. Once it has been observed with some regularity that two events are related to one another (e.g., that greater attractiveness is associated with more lenient sentencing), it becomes possible to make predictions. We can anticipate events. If you read about an upcoming trial of a very attractive defendant, you can predict that the person will likely receive a lenient sentence. Further, the ability to make accurate predictions can help us make better decisions. For example, if you study the behavioral science research literature on attraction and relationships, you will learn about factors that predict long-term relationship satisfaction. You may be able to then use that information when predicting the likely success of your own relationships. You can even complete a questionnaire designed to measure a number of predictors of relationship success. Measures such as RELATE, FOCCUS Pre-Marriage Inventory, and PREPARE can be completed by yourself, with a partner, or with the help of a professional counselor (Larson et al., 2002).

Determining the Causes of Behavior

A third goal of science is to determine the *causes* of behavior. Although we might accurately predict the occurrence of a behavior, we might not correctly identify its cause. Research shows that a child's aggressive behavior can be predicted by knowing how much violence the child views on television. Unfortunately, unless we know that exposure to television violence is a *cause* of behavior, we cannot assert that aggressive behavior can be reduced by limiting scenes of violence on television. A child who is highly aggressive may prefer to watch violence when choosing television programs. We are now confronting questions of cause and effect: To know how to *change* behavior, we need to know the *causes* of behavior.

Cook and Campbell (1979) describe three types of evidence (drawn from the work of philosopher John Stuart Mill) used to identify the cause of a behavior. It is not enough to know that two events occur together, as in the case of knowing that watching television violence is a predictor of actual aggression. To conclude causation, three things must hold true (see **Figure 2**):

1. There is a temporal order of events in which the cause *precedes* the effect. This is called **temporal precedence.** Thus, we need to know that television viewing occurred first and aggression followed.

2. When the cause is present, the effect occurs; when the cause is not present, the effect does not occur. This is called **covariation of cause and effect.** We need to know that children who watch television violence behave aggressively and that children who do not watch television violence do not behave aggressively.

3. Nothing other than a causal variable could be responsible for the observed effect. This is called elimination of **alternative explanations.** There should be no other plausible alternative explanation for the relationship. This third point about alternative explanations is very important: Suppose that the children who watch a lot of television violence are left alone more than are children who do not view television violence. In this case, the increased aggression could have an alternative explanation: lack of parental supervision. Causation will be discussed again in the chapter **"Fundamental Research Issues."**

Explanation of Behavior

A final goal of science is to explain the events that have been described. The scientist seeks to understand *why* the behavior occurs. Consider the relationship between playing violent video games and aggression (APA Task Force on Violent Media, 2015). Even if we know that playing violent video games is a cause of aggressiveness, we still need to explain this relationship. Is it due to imitation or "modeling" of the game violence? Is it the result of psychological desensitization to violence and its effects? Does playing violent video games lead to a belief that aggression is a normal response to frustration and conflict? Further research is necessary to shed light on possible explanations of what has been observed. Usually additional research like this is carried out by testing theories that are developed to explain particular behaviors.

Description, prediction, determination of cause, and explanation are all closely intertwined. Determining cause and explaining behavior are particularly closely related because it is difficult ever to know the true cause or all the causes of any behavior. An explanation that appears satisfactory may turn out to be inadequate when other causes are identified in subsequent research. For example, when early research showed that speaker credibility is related to attitude change, the researchers explained the finding by stating that people are more willing to believe what is said by a person with high credibility than by one with low credibility. However, this explanation has given way to a more complex theory of attitude change that takes into account many other factors that are related to persuasion (Cooper et al., 2016; Petty et al., 2003). In short, there is a certain amount of ambiguity in the enterprise of scientific inquiry. New research findings almost always pose new questions that must be addressed by further research; explanations of behavior often must be discarded or revised as new evidence is gathered. Such ambiguity is part of the excitement and fun of science.

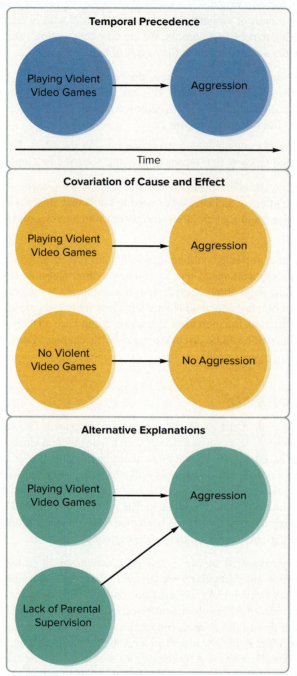

FIGURE 2   Determining cause and effect

Check Your Learning: Practice Exercise #1 gives you a chance to test your understanding of the distinctions among these four goals of science.

BASIC AND APPLIED RESEARCH

In addition to identifying the goals of scientific research (describe, predict, determination of cause, explanation), it is useful to categorize behavioral research investigations as primarily basic research or applied research. In this section we will explore the differences and similarities between basic and applied research.

Basic Research

Basic research tries to answer fundamental questions about the nature of behavior. Studies are often designed to address theoretical issues concerning phenomena such as cognition, emotion, motivation, learning, personality, development, and social behavior. Here are descriptions of a few journal articles that pertain to some basic research questions:

Brothers, T., & Traxler, M. J. (2016). Anticipating syntax during reading: Evidence from the boundary change paradigm. *Journal of Experimental Psychology: Learning, Memory, and Cognition, 42*(12), 1894–1906. https://doi.org/10.1037/xlm0000257

When reading, you focus on text in the center of your visual field. However, you may also "pre-process" words that are just beyond the central focus; this is called the parafovea. This effect occurs even though the text lacks the clarity of the text in the center of the field of vision. The Brothers and Traxler (2016) study demonstrated that participants process not just the words in the parafovea but also their meaning. For example, sentences with valid syntax in the parafovea, such as "The admiral would not confess," were read more quickly than sentences with invalid syntax, such as "The admiral would not surgeon."

Butler, L. P., Schmidt, M. F. H., Tavassolie, N. S., & Gibbs, H. M. (2018). Children's evaluation of verified and unverified claims. *Journal of Experimental Child Psychology, 176*(1), 73–83. https://doi.org/10.1016/j.jecp.2018.07.007

Do children as young as 3 to 5 years old distinguish between claims based on verified evidence and claims that have no supporting evidence? In their research, Butler et al. (2018) presented male and female children with a story involving two animal characters. In one of three test conditions, the characters discover a container outside their homes. One character looks inside the container and announces what's in the container; the other character declares the contents without looking in the container. The children then rated the claims on an acceptability scale ranging from "okay" to "not okay." For all the 3- to 5-year-old children, the evidence-based claim was rated more acceptable. This effect was greater for 4-year-olds than for 3-year-olds and greater still for the 5-year-olds.

Mace, J. H., McQueen, M. L., Hayslett, K. E., Staley, B. J. A., & Welch, T. J. (2019). Semantic memories prime autobiographical memories: General implications and implications for everyday autobiographical remembering. *Memory & Cognition, 47*(2), 299–312. https://doi.org/10.3758/s13421-018-0866-9

The researchers studied whether activation of a semantic memory (general knowledge) will activate related autobiographic memories (memories of personal experiences). In the first part of the experiment, participants were presented with a word familiarity task in which they might see a word such as *summer.* Later, they completed an autobiographical memory task with no limits on the topic of the memories. Compared to a control group that did not take part in the word familiarity task, the semantic priming word (e.g., *summer*) did influence the participants' autobiographical memories (summer-related personal memories).

Applied Research

The research articles listed above were concerned with basic processes of behavior and cognition rather than any immediate practical implications. In contrast, **applied research** is conducted to address issues in which there are practical problems and potential solutions. To illustrate, here are a few summaries of journal articles about applied research:

Rosen, C. C., Simon, L. S., Gajendran, R. S., Johnson, R. E., Lee, H. W., & Lin, S.-H. (Joanna). (2019). Boxed in by your inbox: Implications of daily e-mail demands for managers' leadership behaviors. *Journal of Applied Psychology*, *104*(1), 19–33. https://doi.org /10.1037/apl0000343

A common source of work stress is the overwhelming demands of incoming email messages. This study measured email demands among 48 managers enrolled in a university Executive Master of Business Administration program. Using the Experience Sampling Method (EMS), the researchers asked participants to complete two surveys each day for 10 consecutive workdays. The first survey arrived at the end of the morning and asked about the morning email demands and the manager's progress in meeting work goals up to that point in the day. Another survey at the end of the day measured the extent to which managers had engaged in behaviors reflecting outstanding leadership. As predicted, higher morning email demands were related to perceptions of lower goal progress. And the end-of-day surveys revealed that the morning demands were associated with fewer leadership behaviors.

Tauber, S. K., Witherby, A. E., Dunlosky, J., Rawson, K. A., Putnam, A. L., & Roediger, H. L., III. (2018). Does covert retrieval benefit learning of key-term definitions? *Journal of Applied Research in Memory and Cognition*, *7*(1), 106–115. https://doi.org/ 10.1016/j.jarmac.2016.10.004

Past research demonstrated that practicing recall of material results in superior recall in contrast with simply re-reading the same material. This study used the key-term definitions that are often found at the end of textbook chapters. The researchers were interested in whether the type of recall practice had an effect on actual recall later (as in a class exam). One group of participants studied the definitions and then used overt practice (typing the definitions). A second group used covert practice (mentally rehearsing the definitions). Another group did not practice recall; instead they simply restudied the definitions. On the final recall test taken later, participants using overt practice had higher scores than those in either of the other conditions. Typing the definitions proved superior to mental practice or restudy.

Guzzo, K. B., & Hayford, S. R. (2018). Adolescent reproductive and contraceptive knowledge and attitudes and adult contraceptive behavior. *Maternal and Child Health Journal*, *22*(1), 32–40. https://doi.org /10.1007/s10995-017-2351-7

Is knowledge about reproduction and contraception in adolescence related to adult contraceptive behavior? The researchers examined this question by using data from the National Longitudinal Survey of Adolescent to Adult Health, which surveyed the same individuals as adolescents in 1995 and as adults in 2007–2008. The adolescents who had more accurate knowledge of reproduction and contraception were found to be using more effective contraception methods as adults, and they were using contraceptives more consistently. The researchers recommend providing adolescents with more comprehensive sex education.

A major area of applied research is called **program evaluation,** which assesses the social reforms and innovations that occur in government, education, the criminal justice system, industry, health care, and mental health institutions. In an influential paper on "reforms as experiments," Campbell (1969) noted that social programs are really experiments designed to achieve certain outcomes. He argued persuasively that social scientists should evaluate each program to determine whether it is having its intended effect. If it is not, alternative programs should be tried. This is an important point that people in all organizations too often fail to remember when new ideas are implemented; the scientific approach dictates that new programs should be evaluated. Here are two sample journal articles about program evaluation:

Peterson, K., Sharps, P., Banyard, V., Powers, R. A., Kaukinen, C., Gross, D., ... & Campbell, J. (2018). An evaluation of two dating violence prevention programs on a college campus. *Journal of Interpersonal Violence*, *33*(23), 3630–3655. https://doi.org/10.1177/0886260516636069

Alarm over dating violence on college campuses has led to the development of programs designed to raise awareness and provide skills that might reduce the incidence of violence. This study compared two dating violence prevention programs presented to first-year college students. One was a 90-minute bystander education program designed to provide bystanders of violence with motivation and skills to intervene. The other program was a traditional education program focused on awareness of the problem. In addition, there was a no education control group. All students completed measures of rape myth acceptance, beliefs about the effectiveness of bystanders, and intentions to help in a dating violence situation. Both programs were superior to no education in changing attitudes and intentions; the bystander education program was superior to the traditional education program.

Schwinn, T. M., Schinke, S. P., Hopkins, J., Keller, B., & Liu, X. (2018). An online drug abuse prevention program for adolescent girls: Posttest and 1-year outcomes. *Journal of Youth and Adolescence*, *47*(3), 490–500. https://doi.org/10.1007/s10964-017-0714-4

Because drug abuse among early adolescent girls is increasing, an online program was designed to reduce drug use in this population. The program was presented online to a national sample of 788 13- and 14-year-old girls. The girls were assigned to participate in the program or a control condition with no intervention. The program consisted of nine sessions with particular attention paid to gender-specific aspects of drug use. A variety of measures were completed prior to the program, immediately after completion, and at a 1-year follow-up. These included drug/alcohol use, self-esteem, stress coping skills, and ability to refuse drug offers. The program had positive effects as measured immediately and one year later.

Much applied research is conducted in settings such as large business firms, marketing research companies, government agencies, and public polling organizations and is not published but instead is used within the company or by clients of the company. Whether or not such results are published,

however, they are used to help people make better decisions concerning problems that require immediate action.

Comparing Basic and Applied Research

Both basic and applied research are important, and neither can be considered superior to the other. In fact,
progress in science is dependent on an interconnection between basic and applied research. Much applied
research is guided by the theories and findings of basic research investigations. For example, one of the most
effective treatment strategies for specific phobia—an anxiety disorder characterized by extreme fear reactions
to specific objects or situations—is called *exposure therapy* (Chambless et al., 1996). In exposure therapy,
people who suffer from a phobia are exposed to the object of their fears in a safe setting while a therapist
trains them in relaxation techniques in order to counterprogram their fear reaction. This behavioral treatment
emerged from the work of Pavlov and Watson, who studied the processes by which animals acquire, maintain, and, critically, lose reflexive reactions to stimuli (Wolpe, 1982). Today this work has been extended even
further, as the use of virtual reality technologies to treat anxiety disorders has been studied and found to be
as effective as traditional exposure treatment (Opris et al., 2012).

In recent years, many in our society, including legislators who control the budgets of research-granting agencies of the government, have demanded that research be directly relevant to specific social issues. The problem with this attitude toward research is that we can never predict the ultimate applications of basic research.
Psychologist B. F. Skinner, for example, conducted basic research in the 1930s on operant conditioning,
which carefully described the effects of reinforcement on such behaviors as bar pressing by rats. Years later
this research led to many practical applications in therapy, education, and industry. Research with no apparent practical value ultimately can be very useful. The fact that no one can predict the eventual impact of basic
research leads to the conclusion that support of basic research is necessary both to advance science and to
benefit society.

At this point, you may be wondering if there is a definitive way to know whether a study should be considered
basic or applied. The distinction between basic and applied research is a convenient typology but is probably
more accurately viewed as a continuum. Notice in the listing of applied research studies that some are more
applied than others. The study on adolescent smoking is very much applied—the data will be valuable for people who are planning smoking prevention and cessation programs for adolescents. The research on studying
could be immediately used in advisement materials for students visiting a learning resource center on campus. All of these studies are grounded in applied issues and solutions to problems, but they differ in how
quickly and easily the results of the study can actually be used.

> **Check Your Learning:** In Practice Exercise #2, test your understanding of the distinction between basic
> and applied research.

Behavioral research is important in many fields and has significant applications to public policy. This chapter
has introduced you to the major goals and general types of research. All researchers use scientific methods,
whether they are interested in basic research, applied research, or program evaluation. The themes and concepts in this chapter will be expanded in the remainder of the book. They will be the basis on which you
evaluate the research of others and plan your own research projects.

ILLUSTRATIVE ARTICLE: INTRODUCTION

Most chapters in this book include a chapter-closing feature called Illustrative Article, which is designed to relate some of the key points in the chapter to a published journal article. In each case, you will be asked to obtain a copy of the article using some of the skills that will be presented in our discussion in the chapter **"Where to Start."** Then, you will be asked to read the article and answer some questions that are closely aligned with the material in the chapter.

For our first illustrative article, acquire and read this article. Tip: You will find a pre-publication copy of the article using this link: https://openaccess.city.ac.uk/20979/1/FictionalMemories 19-04-18.pdf

Akhtar, S., Justice, L. V., Morrison, C. M., & Conway, M. A. (2018). Fictional first memories. *Psychological Science, 29*(10), 1612–1619. https://doi.org/10.1177/0956797618778831

After reading the article, answer the following questions (which will be familiar to you from earlier in this chapter!):

1. **"What was measured?"** All studies in the behavioral sciences start with measurement: identifying the important concepts to be studied, and figuring out how to measure them. This is related to the concept of construct validity, which will be covered in depth in later chapters.

2. **"How do they know that one thing caused another?"** Many times—particularly in popular media—there will be the claim that one thing causes another. It's always important to ask: How do they know? This is related to the concept of internal validity, which will be covered in later chapters.

3. **"To what or whom can we generalize the results?"** This is related to the concept of external validity, which will be covered in later chapters.

4. **"Have other researchers found similar results?"** A single study can be interesting, but scientific progress involves the accumulation of studies. We can be more confident in a study if other studies have found the same thing.

5. Finally, answer the following questions:

    a. Would you describe this study being applied research or basic research? Why?

    b. Which goal of science (description, prediction, causation, explanation) do you think is primarily targeted by this article? Why?

CRITICAL THINKING: BEING A SKILLED CONSUMER OF RESEARCH

1. Read several editorials in the *New York Times, Wall Street Journal, USA Today, Washington Post,* or another major metropolitan news publication and identify the sources used to support the assertions and conclusions. Did the writer use intuition, appeals to authority, scientific evidence, or a combination of these? Give specific examples.

2. Imagine a debate on the following statement: "Behavioral scientists should only conduct research that has immediate practical applications." Develop "pro" and "con" arguments—arguments that support or oppose the assertion.

3. Imagine a debate on the following statement: "Knowledge of research methods is unnecessary for students who intend to pursue careers in clinical and counseling psychology." Develop "pro"

and "con" arguments—arguments that support or oppose the assertion.

4. You read an article online that says, "Eating disorders may be more common in warm regions." It also says that a researcher found that the incidence of eating disorders among female students at a university in Florida was higher than at a university in Pennsylvania. Assume that this study accurately describes a difference between students at the two universities. Discuss the finding in terms of the issues of identification of cause and effect and explanation.

Check Your Learning: Practice Exercises

Practice Exercise #1

For the five studies briefly described below, identify the primary goal of science that seems designed to achieve: (a) description, (b) prediction, (c) determination of cause, or (d) understand/ explain.

Study	Primary Goal of Science			
	Description	Prediction	Determination of Cause	Understand / Explain
1. A researcher studies sleep habits of college students in order to identify those who will graduate in four years and those who will not.				
2. A researcher uses a survey to collect information about the sleeping habits of college students in order to see if sleep has an impact on grades.				
3. A researcher conducts interviews of college students about their sleep habits in order to figure out why				

Study	Primary Goal of Science			
	Description	Prediction	Determination of Cause	Understand / Explain
college students struggle to get enough sleep.				
4. A researcher uses a survey to collect information about the sleeping habits of college students.				
5. A researcher has some college students drink a caffeinated soda at 11 p.m. and has others drink a decaffeinated version of the same soda, in order to see if sleep is affected by caffeine intake.				

Practice Exercise #2

Basic and Applied Research		
Examples of research questions	Basic	Applied
1. What is the impact of being observed by others on a performance task like math problems?		
2. Do violent video games increase aggression among children and young adults?		
3. How do neurons generate neurotransmitters?		
4. Do we process visual images and sound simultaneously?		
5. How can a city increase recycling by residents?		
6. Which strategies are best for coping with climate change?		

(Answers are provided at the end of this chapter.)

CHAPTER REVIEW

Review Questions

1. Why is it important for anyone in our society to have knowledge of research methods?
2. Why is scientific skepticism useful in furthering our understanding of behavior?
3. How does the scientific approach differ from other ways of gaining knowledge about behavior?
4. Provide (a) definitions and (b) examples of description, prediction, determination of cause, and explanation as goals of scientific research.
5. Describe the three elements for inferring causation. Describe the characteristics of scientific inquiry, according to Goodstein (2000).
6. How does basic research differ from applied research?

Study Terms

Alternative explanations

Applied research

Authority

Basic research

Covariation of cause and effect

Empiricism

Falsifiability

Goals of behavioral science

Intuition

Peer review

Program evaluation

Pseudoscience

Skepticism

Temporal precedence

Check Your Learning: Answers

Practice Exercise #1

1. b; 2. c; 3. d; 4. a; 5. c

Practice Exercise #2

basic = 1, 3, 4; applied = 2, 5, 6

Where to Start

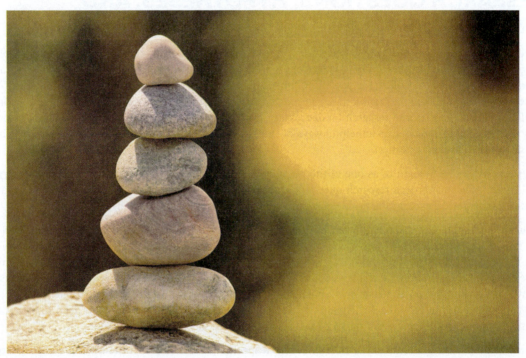

Don Hammond/Design Pics

LEARNING OBJECTIVES

- Discuss how research questions, hypotheses, and predictions are related.
- Describe the different sources of ideas for research, including common sense, observation, theories, past research, and practical problems.
- Identify the two functions of a theory.
- Describe the three kinds of research reports.
- Summarize the information included in the abstract, introduction, method, results, and discussion sections of research articles.
- Summarize the fundamentals of exploring past research in psychology, including the use of PsycINFO.

The motivation to conduct scientific research comes from a natural curiosity about the world. Most people have their first experience with research when their curiosity leads them to ask, "I wonder what would happen if ..." or "I wonder why ...," followed by an attempt to answer the question. What are the sources of inspiration for such questions? How do you find out about other people's ideas and past research? In this chapter, we will explore some sources of scientific ideas. We will also consider the nature of research reports published in professional journals.

RESEARCH QUESTIONS, HYPOTHESES, AND PREDICTIONS

Curiosity is expressed in the form of questions. A **research question** is the first and most general step in designing and conducting a research investigation. A good research question must be specific so that it can be answered with a research project. So, you might initially be motivated to want to answer a question like "What causes depression?" This question is much too general, given the complexity of the topic. After becoming familiar with the theories and research on depression, your interest might focus on a more specific question, such as "Is depression related to unhelpful ways of thinking about the causes of success and failure?" That is a more specific, testable question.

A hypothesis can be thought of as one of the possible answers to a research question. In research, a **hypothesis** is a tentative answer to a research question. Once a hypothesis is proposed, data must be gathered and evaluated in terms of whether the evidence is consistent or inconsistent with the hypothesis.

In our example, the hypothesis might be: "Depression is related to the types of attributions made about success and failure experiences." More specifically, the hypothesis might be that individuals who are diagnosed with depression will attribute success to good luck but will attribute failure to their personal shortcomings. Once the hypothesis is stated, the researcher can design a study to test it. This will require making decisions about how to choose the people who will participate, the nature of the tasks that they might work on, and how to devise a way to have the participants experience success or failure. There would need to be a way to measure attributions of luck versus personal factors as the cause of the success or failure.

Once the study is designed, the researcher can make a specific prediction about the outcome of the study. A **prediction** follows directly from a hypothesis, is directly testable, and includes specific variables and methodologies. The prediction in our example might be: "In comparison to those with minimal or mild depression, participants categorized as having moderate or severe depression, based on the Beck Depression Inventory score, will score higher on luck when responding to a success experience and higher on personal causes when responding to a failure experience."

If a prediction is confirmed by the results of the study, the hypothesis is supported. If the prediction is not confirmed, the researcher will either reject the hypothesis or conduct further research using different methods to study the hypothesis. It is important to note that when the results of a study confirm a prediction, the hypothesis is only supported, not proven. Researchers study the same hypothesis using a variety of methods, and each time this hypothesis is supported by a research study, we become more confident that the hypothesis is correct.

Figure 1 shows the relationships among research questions, hypotheses, and predictions, using an actual study of cell phone use. Cramer et al. (2007) had general questions about use of cell phones while driving, such as "What impact do passengers have on cell phone use while driving?" The researchers developed some specific hypotheses, such as "Having a passenger in the car reduces cell phone use." They then designed a procedure for observing student driving on campus and made predictions about the outcome. For example, "Drivers with a passenger in the car will be less likely to be using a cell phone than those driving alone."

FIGURE 1   Relationships among research questions, hypotheses, and predictions

> **Check Your Learning:** Practice Exercise #1 will help you tease apart question, hypothesis, and prediction.

SOURCES OF IDEAS

Each day seems to bring us some type of information about a phenomenon related to human behavior. This information may arrive on an internet news site, a tweet or Facebook post, a television program, or even a printed magazine. The topic might be a description of an individual's experience of trauma with a discussion of possible effects, the potential benefits of delaying age of first marriage, or an assertion that a vegetarian diet improves cognitive functioning. It is not easy to say where good ideas come from. Many people are capable of coming up with worthwhile ideas but find it difficult to verbalize the process by which they are generated. Cartoonists know this—they show a brilliant idea as a lightbulb flashing over the person's head. But where does the electricity come from? Let's consider five sources of ideas: common sense, practical problems, observation of the world around us, theories, and past research.

Common Sense

One source of ideas that can be tested is the body of knowledge called common sense—the things we all believe to be true. Do "opposites attract"? Do "birds of a feather flock together"? If you "spare the rod," do you "spoil the child"? Is "a picture worth a thousand words"? Asking questions such as these can lead to research programs studying attraction, the effects of punishment, and the role of visual images in learning and memory.

Testing a commonsense idea can be valuable because such notions do not always turn out to be correct, or research may show that the real world is much more complicated than our commonsense ideas would have it. For example, pictures can aid memory under certain circumstances, but sometimes pictures detract from learning (see Levin, 1983). Conducting research to test commonsense ideas often forces us to go beyond a commonsense theory of behavior.

Practical Problems

Research is also stimulated by practical problems that can have immediate applications. On a larger scale, researchers have guided public policy by conducting research on obesity and eating disorders, as well as other social and health issues. Such problems may be local and highly specific; for example, groups of city planners and citizens might survey bike riders to determine the most desirable route for a bike path. Other problems may be applicable to much larger problems and populations such as early childhood education, substance abuse, domestic violence, and suicide prevention.

Observation of the World Around Us

Observations can provide many ideas for research. The curiosity sparked by your observations and experiences can lead you to ask questions about all sorts of phenomena. In fact, this type of curiosity is what drives many students to engage in their first research project.

Have you ever had the experience of storing something away in a "special place" where you were sure you could find it later (and where no one else would possibly look for it), only to later discover that you could not recall where you had stored it? Such an experience could lead to systematic research on whether it is a good idea to put things in special places. In fact, Winograd and Soloway (1986) conducted a series of experiments on this very topic. Their research demonstrated that people are likely to forget where something is placed when two conditions are present: (1) The location where the object is placed is judged to be highly memorable *and* (2) the location is considered a very unlikely place for the object. Thus, although it may seem to be a good idea at the time, storing something in an unusual place is generally not a good idea.

A more recent example demonstrates the diversity of ideas that can be generated by curiosity about things that happen around you. Case in point: biases about rap music. Dunbar et al., (2016) were interested in how rap lyrics were perceived; specifically, they asked if evaluations of rap lyrics are subject to biases from stereotypes. In other words, do some people think of rap lyrics as being more offensive because they are rap lyrics? The researchers asked subjects what they thought about a set of lyrics that were labeled as being rap lyrics, as opposed to being labeled as country music lyrics. They found that when the lyrics were labeled as rap, subjects rated them as more literal and offensive, and in greater need of regulation, than when they were labeled as country.

Observations of the world around us may even lead to an academic career. When he was an undergraduate, psychologist Michael Lynn worked in restaurants, and much of his compensation consisted of tips from customers. That experience sparked an interest in studying tipping. For many years Lynn has studied tipping behavior in restaurants and hotels in the United States and in other countries (Tipping Expert, 2013). He has looked at factors that increase tips, such as posture, touching, and phrases written on a check, and his research has had an impact on the hotel and restaurant industry. If you have ever worked in restaurants, you have undoubtedly formed many of your own hypotheses about tipping behavior. Lynn went one step further and took a scientific approach to testing his ideas. His research illustrates that taking a scientific approach to a problem can lead to new discoveries and important applications.

Finally, we should mention the role of serendipity—sometimes the most interesting discoveries are the result of accident or sheer luck. Ivan Pavlov is best known for discovering what is called *classical conditioning*, wherein a neutral stimulus (such as a tone), if paired repeatedly with an unconditioned stimulus (such as food) that produces a reflex response (such as salivation), will eventually produce the response when presented alone. Pavlov did not set out to discover classical conditioning. Instead, he was studying the digestive system in dogs by measuring their salivation when given food. He accidentally discovered that the dogs were salivating prior to the actual feeding and then studied the ways in which the stimuli preceding the feeding could produce a salivation response. Of course, such accidental discoveries are made only when viewing the world with an inquisitive eye.

Theories

Much research in the behavioral sciences tests theories of behavior. A **theory** consists of a systematic body of ideas about a particular topic or phenomenon. Psychologists have theories relating to human behavior, learning, memory, and personality, for example. These ideas form a coherent and logically consistent structure that serves two important functions.

First, theories *organize and explain* a variety of specific facts or descriptions of behavior. Such facts and descriptions are not very meaningful by themselves, and so theories are needed to impose a framework on them. This framework makes the world more comprehensible by providing a few abstract concepts around which we can organize and explain a variety of behaviors. As an example, consider how Charles Darwin's theory of evolution organized and explained a variety of facts concerning the characteristics of animal species. Similarly, in psychology one classic theory of memory asserts that there are separate systems of short-term memory and long-term memory. This theory accounts for a number of specific observations about learning and memory, including such phenomena as the different types of memory deficits that result from a blow to the head versus damage to the hippocampus area of the brain and the rate at which a person forgets material he or she has just read.

Second, theories *generate new knowledge* by focusing our thinking so that we notice new aspects of behavior—theories guide our observations of the world. The theory generates hypotheses about behavior, and the researcher conducts studies to test the hypotheses. If the studies confirm the hypotheses, the theory is supported. As more and more evidence accumulates that is consistent with the theory, we become more confident that the theory is correct.

Sometimes people describe a theory as "just an idea" that may or may not be true. We need to separate this use of the term—which implies that a theory is essentially the same as a hypothesis—from the scientific meaning of *theory*. A scientific theory consists of much more than a simple "idea." A scientific theory is grounded in actual data from prior research as well as numerous hypotheses that are consistent with the theory. These hypotheses can be tested through further research. Such testable hypotheses are falsifiable—the data can either support or refute the hypotheses. As a theory develops with more and more evidence that supports the theory, it is wrong to say that it is "just an idea." Instead, the theory becomes well established as it enables us to explain a great many observable facts. It is true that research may reveal a weakness in a theory when a hypothesis generated by the theory is not supported. When this happens, the theory can be modified to account for the new data. Sometimes a new theory will emerge that accounts for both new data and the existing body of knowledge. This process defines the way in which science continually develops with new data that expand our knowledge of the world around us.

Evolutionary theory has influenced our understanding of sexual attraction and mating patterns (Buss, 2011). For example, Buss describes a well-established finding that males experience more intense feelings of jealousy when a partner has a sexual relationship with someone else (sexual infidelity) than when the partner has developed an emotional bond only (emotional infidelity); females, in contrast, are more jealous when the partner has engaged in emotional infidelity rather than sexual infidelity. This finding is consistent with evolutionary theory, which asserts that males and females have evolved different strategies for mate selection. All individuals have an evolutionary interest in passing their genes on to future generations. However, females have relatively few opportunities to reproduce, have a limited age range during which to reproduce, and traditionally have had to assume major child-care responsibilities. Males, in contrast, can reproduce at any time and have a reproductive advantage in that they can produce more offspring than a given female can. Because of these differences, the theory predicts that females and males will have different perspectives on infidelity. Females will be more threatened if the partner might no longer provide support and resources for childrearing by developing an emotional bond with another partner. Males are more distressed if it is possible that they will be caring for a child who does not share their genes. Although research supports evolutionary theory, alternative theories can be developed that may better explain the same findings.

Levy and Kelly (2010) suggest that attachment theory may provide a better explanation. They point out that males and females differ in their level of attachment in relationships. Also, females in general show greater attachment than males do. From the perspective of attachment theory, the amount of attachment will be related to the distress experienced by an instance of emotional infidelity. Research by Levy and Kelly found that high-attachment individuals were most upset by emotional infidelity; individuals with low attachment to the relationship were more distressed by sexual infidelity. These findings will lead to more research to test the two theoretical perspectives.

Theories are usually modified as new research defines the scope of the theory. The necessity of modifying theories is illustrated by the theory of short-term versus long-term memory. In the original conception, the long-term memory system was described as a storehouse of permanent, fixed memories. However, now-classic research by cognitive psychologists, including Loftus (1979), has shown that memories are easily reconstructed and reinterpreted. In one study, participants watched a film of an automobile accident and later were asked to tell what they saw in the film. Loftus found that participants' memories were influenced by the way they were questioned. For example, participants who were asked whether they saw "the" broken headlight were more likely to answer yes than were participants who were asked whether they saw "a" broken headlight. Results such as these have required a more complex theory of how long-term memory operates.

Past Research

Another source of ideas is past research. Becoming familiar with a body of research on a topic is perhaps the best way to generate ideas for new research. Because the results of research are published, researchers can use the body of past literature on a topic to continually refine and expand our knowledge. Virtually every study raises questions that can be addressed in subsequent research. The research may lead to an attempt to apply the findings in a different setting, to study the topic with a different age group, or to use a different methodology to replicate the results. In the Cramer et al. (2007) study on cell phone use while driving, trained observers noted cell phone use of 3,650 students leaving campus parking structures during a 3-hour period on two different days. They reported that 11% of all drivers were using cell phones. Females were more likely than males to be using a cell phone, and drivers with passengers were less likely than solitary drivers to be talking on a phone. Knowledge of this study might lead to research on ways to reduce students' cell phone use while driving.

In addition, as you become familiar with the research literature on a topic, you may see inconsistencies in research results that need to be investigated, or you may want to study alternative explanations for the results. Also, what you know about one research area often can be successfully applied to another research area.

Let's look at a concrete example of a study that was designed to address methodological flaws in previous research. Recall from the chapter **"Scientific Understanding of Behavior"** the procedure called "facilitated communication." Facilitated communication was intended to help children who are diagnosed with autism spectrum disorder (ASD). Autism spectrum disorder is characterized by a number of symptoms. In some cases, children diagnosed with ASD show severe impairments in language and communication. Parents and care providers were greatly encouraged by facilitated communication, which allowed a child with ASD to communicate with others by pressing keys on a keyboard showing letters and other symbols. A facilitator held the child's hand to facilitate the child's ability to determine which key to press. With this technique, many autistic children seemed to begin communicating their thoughts and feelings and answering questions posed to them. Most people who saw facilitated communication in action regarded the technique as a miraculous breakthrough.

The conclusion that facilitated communication was effective was based on a comparison of the child with ASD's ability to communicate with and without the facilitator. The difference is impressive to most observers. Recall, however, that scientists are by nature skeptical. They examine all evidence carefully and ask whether claims are justified. In the case of facilitated communication, Montee et al., (1995) noted that the facilitator might have been unintentionally guiding the child's fingers to type meaningful sentences. In other words, the facilitator, and not the autistic individual, might be controlling the communication. Montee et al. conducted a study to test this idea. In one condition, both the facilitator and the autistic child were shown a picture, and the child was asked to indicate what was shown in the picture by typing a response with the facilitator. This was done on a number of trials. In another condition, only the child saw the pictures. In a third condition, the child and facilitator were shown different pictures (but the facilitator was unaware of this fact). Consistent with the hypothesis that the facilitator is controlling the child's responses, the pictures were correctly identified only in the condition in which both saw the same pictures. Moreover, when the child and facilitator viewed different pictures, the child never made the correct response, and usually the picture the facilitator had seen was the one identified.

As you can see, previous research and thinking on a topic can be a critical source of ideas for a study. So, then, the next questions are: What does published work look like? What sorts of research reports are there?

TYPES OF JOURNAL ARTICLES

There are many types of journal articles (APA, 2020), but most fall into three categories: literature reviews that summarize research, theory articles that describe theories, and empirical articles that describe specific research projects.

Literature Reviews

Literature reviews provide summaries of previous research on a particular topic. The journal *Psychological Bulletin* and the *Annual Review of Psychology* specialize in publishing literature reviews. However, you will now find reviews in many different publications in all areas of research. Traditionally, literature reviews were narrative descriptions of individual research investigations along with conclusions, controversies, and directions for future research. This is one such review:

Storer, H. L. et al., (2016). Efficacy of bystander programs to prevent dating abuse among youth and young adults: A review of the literature. *Trauma, Violence, & Abuse, 17*(3), 256–269. https://doi.org/10.1177/1524838015584361

These authors review research on "bystander" programs that are designed to prevent dating violence and abuse. Bystander programs focus on developing skills for people to intervene when they witness dating abuse or behaviors that can lead to dating abuse. This article describes bystander programs and attempts to summarize their impact on bystander attitudes and behaviors.

Today you are likely to see the terms *systematic review* or *systematic literature review* in the titles of literature review articles. These terms signify that the author used specific methods for searching past literature along with criteria for including a study in the review. Systematic reviews often use published "preferred reporting items" that provide consistency across reviews and allow others to replicate the procedures (Moher et al., 2009).

García-Vera, M. P., Sanz, J., & Gutiérrez, S. (2016). A systematic review of the literature on posttraumatic stress disorder in victims of terrorist attacks. *Psychological Reports, 119*(1), 328–359. https://doi.org/10.1177/0033294116658243

These researchers reviewed the literature on post-traumatic stress disorder (PTSD) among victims of terrorist attacks. Having identified 35 studies of PTSD among such victims, they report that across studies, 33% to 39% of direct victims of a terrorist attack developed PTSD. They also reported rates for others (e.g., community members, emergency workers, and relatives and friends of victims). They discussed their results in the context of treatment for victims of terrorism.

Because literature reviews summarize research across many studies, they are an important part of the research landscape. A more quantitative type of review method for comparing a large number of studies in a specific research area is called **meta-analysis** (Borenstein et al., 2009). In meta-analysis, researchers analyze the results of a number of studies using statistical procedures. Thus, rather than relying solely on judgments obtained in a narrative literature review, meta-analysis allows researchers to draw statistical conclusions. In short, with meta-analysis researchers attempt to determine if a research finding is the same across multiple studies. Here is one example of a meta-analysis:

Credé, M., Roch, S. G., & Kieszczynska, U. M. (2010). Class attendance in college: A meta-analytic review of the relationship of class attendance with grades and student characteristics. *Review of Educational Research, 80*(2), 272–295. https://doi.org/10.1016/0749-5978(91)90020-T

These authors used meta-analytic techniques to look at the relationship between college class attendance and college grades. They identified 52 published studies and 16 unpublished dissertations from 1927 to 2009 on the topic. In sum, these studies included data from 28,034 college students. You may be shocked by what they found: "Attendance is a better predictor of class grades than any other known predictor (including high school GPA, SAT scores, and study habits)."

Theory Articles

Some published research reports are the culmination of work that describes a theory. A theory, as we described earlier, consists of a systematic body of ideas about a particular topic or phenomenon. While literature reviews summarize, theory articles generally summarize and integrate research to provide a new framework for understanding a phenomenon.

The following three articles are examples of theory articles:

Ajzen, I. (1991). The theory of planned behavior. *Organizational Behavior and Human Decision Processes, 50*(2), 179–211.

Ajzen's very influential theory of planned behavior has been cited in other articles more than 10,000 times. The article describes the theory of planned behavior, which links behavior to attitudes toward a given behavior, the social norms surrounding the behavior, and intention to engage in the behavior. Thus, an attitude like "College is good" and a social norm like "All of my friends to go college" predict intention to go to college, which in turn predicts applying to college.

Bandura, A. (1977). Self-efficacy: Toward a unifying theory of behavioral change. *Psychological Review, 84*(2), 191–215. https://doi.org/10.1037/0033-295X.84.2.191

Bandura's equally influential theory article defined self-efficacy as our belief in our own ability to be successful and hypothesized that self-efficacy would predict many behavioral outcomes. If I believe that I can lose 20 pounds or stop smoking, I am more likely to be able to successfully do so.

Klonsky, E. D., & May, A. M. (2015). The Three-Step Theory (3ST): A new theory of suicide rooted in the "ideation-to-action" framework. *International Journal of Cognitive Therapy, 8*(2), 114–129. https://doi.org/10.1521/ijct.2015.8.2.114

This more-recent theory article is related to suicide. The authors theorize that suicide ideation—as opposed to a suicide attempt—is the result of psychological pain and hopelessness, and that for people who are experiencing pain and hopelessness, connections to other people are critical to keeping them safe.

Empirical Research Articles

The empirical research article is a report of a study in which data were gathered to help answer a research question.

Empirical research articles usually have five sections: (1) an *Abstract,* such as the ones found in PsycINFO; (2) an *Introduction or literature review* that explains the problem under investigation and the specific hypotheses being tested; (3) a *Method* section that describes in detail the exact procedures used in the study; (4) a *Results* section in which the findings are presented; and (5) a *Discussion* section in which the researcher may speculate on the broader implications of the results, propose alternative explanations for the results, discuss reasons that a particular hypothesis may not have been supported by the data, and/or make suggestions for further research on the problem. In addition to the five major sections, you will find a list of all the references that were cited. Review the summary of the sections in **Figure 2** as you read about each section in greater detail.

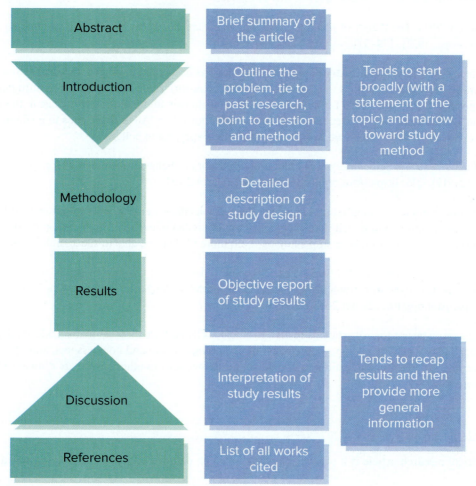

FIGURE 2   Major sections of a research article

Abstract

The *Abstract* is a summary of the research report and typically runs between 150 and 250 words in length. It includes information about the hypothesis, the procedure, and the broad pattern of results. Generally, little information is abstracted from the Discussion section of the paper.

Introduction

In the *Introduction,* the researcher outlines the problem that has been investigated. Past research and theories relevant to the problem are described in detail. The researcher's specific expectations are noted, often as formal hypotheses. In other words, the investigator introduces the research in a logical format that shows how past research and theory are connected to the current research problem and the expected results.

Method

The *Method section* is divided into subsections, with the number of subsections determined by the author and dependent on the complexity of the research design. Sometimes the first subsection presents an overview of the design to prepare the reader for the material that follows. The next subsection describes the characteristics of the participants. What was the gender composition of the participants? What was the ethnic composition of the participants? What was the average age? How many participants were included? If the study used human participants, some mention of how participants were recruited for the study would be needed. The next subsection details the procedure used in the study. In describing any stimulus materials presented to the participants, the way the behavior of the participants was recorded, and so on, it is important that no potentially crucial detail be omitted. Such detail allows the reader to know exactly how the study was conducted, and it provides other researchers with the information necessary to replicate the study. Other subsections may be necessary to describe in detail any equipment or testing materials that were used.

We have been using the term *participants* to refer to the individuals who are studied in research projects. An equivalent term in psychological research is *subjects*. The *Publication Manual of the American Psychological Association* (APA, 2020) allows the use of either *participants* or *subjects* when describing humans who are studied in psychological research. You will see both terms when you read about research; both terms will be used in this book. Other terms that you may encounter include *respondents* and *informants*. The individuals who take part in survey research are often called *respondents*. *Informants* are the people who help researchers understand the dynamics of particular cultural and organizational settings—this term originated in anthropological and sociological research, and is now being used by psychologists as well. Many research reports will use more specific descriptions of the participants—such as *employees* in an organization, *students* in a classroom, or *residents* of an assisted living facility.

Results

In the *Results section,* the researcher presents the findings, usually in three ways. First, there is a description in narrative form—for example, "The location of items was most likely to be forgotten when the location was both judged to be highly memorable and an unusual place for the item to be stored." Second, the results are described in statistical language. Third, the material is often depicted in tables and graphs.

The statistical terminology of the Results section may appear formidable. However, lack of knowledge about the calculations is not really a deterrent to understanding the article or the logic behind the statistics. Statistics are only a tool the researcher uses in evaluating the outcomes of the study.

Discussion

In the *Discussion section,* the researcher reviews the research from various perspectives. Do the results support the hypothesis? If they do, the author should give all possible explanations for the results and discuss why one explanation is superior to another. If the hypothesis has not been supported, the author should suggest potential reasons. What might have been wrong with the methodology, the hypothesis, or both? The researcher may also discuss how the results compare with past research results on the topic. This section may also include suggestions for possible practical applications of the research and for future research on the topic.

You should familiarize yourself with some actual research articles. **Appendix A** ends with an entire article in manuscript form. An easy way to find more articles in areas that interest you is to visit the websites of the American Psychological Association (APA) at **www.apa.org** and the Association for Psychological Science (APS) at **www.psychologicalscience.org**. All the APA journals listed in **Table 1** have links that you can find by going to **www.apa.org/journals**. When you select a journal that interests you, you will go to a page that allows you to read the abstracts—and sometimes the full text—of recent articles published in the journal. Read articles to become familiar with the way information is presented in reports. As you read, you will develop ways of efficiently processing the information in the articles. It is usually best to read the abstract first, then skim the article to decide whether you can use the information provided. If you can, go back and read the article carefully. Note the hypotheses and theories presented in the introduction, write down anything that seems unclear or problematic in the method, and read the results in view of the material in the introduction. Be critical when you read the article; students often generate the best criticism. Most important, as you read more research on a topic, you will become more familiar with the questions being studied, the methods used to study the variables, the important theoretical issues being considered, and the problems that need to be addressed by future research. In short, you will find yourself generating your own research ideas and planning your own studies.

TABLE 1   Some major journals in psychology

General	
American Psychologist * (articles on a variety of topics)	*Psychological Methods* *
Psychological Science **	*Advances in Methods and Practices in Psychological Science* **
Psychological Bulletin * (literature reviews)	*Current Directions in Psychological Science* **
Psychological Review * (theoretical articles)	*Psychological Science in the Public Interest* **
Perspectives on Psychological Science **	*History of Psychology* *
Clinical and counseling psychology	
Journal of Abnormal Psychology *	*Journal of Clinical Psychology*
Journal of Consulting and Clinical Psychology *	*Behavior Therapy*
Clinical Psychological Science **	*Journal of Abnormal Child Psychology*
Journal of Counseling Psychology *	*Clinical Psychology Review*
Behavior Analysis: Research and Practice *	*Professional Psychology: Research and Practice* *
Experimental areas of psychology	
Journal of Experimental Psychology:	*Memory & Cognition*
General *	*Cognitive Psychology*
Applied *	*Cognition*
Learning, Memory, and Cognition *	*Cognitive Science*
Human Perception and Performance *	*Decision* *
Animal Learning and Cognition *	*Journal of the Experimental Analysis of Behavior*
Animal Behavior Processes *	*Applied Cognitive Psychology*
Behavioral Neuroscience *	

Motivation Science*	*Neuropsychology**
Psychonomic Bulletin & Review	*Emotion**
Learning and Motivation	*Applied Cognitive Psychology*

Developmental psychology

Developmental Psychology*	*Journal of Applied Developmental Psychology*
Psychology and Aging*	*Developmental Review*
Child Development	*Infant Behavior and Development*
Journal of Experimental Child Psychology	*Experimental Aging Research*

Personality and social psychology

Journal of Personality and Social Psychology*	*Social Psychology Quarterly*
Personality and Social Psychology Bulletin	*Journal of Applied Social Psychology*
Journal of Experimental Social Psychology	*Basic and Applied Social Psychology*
Journal of Research in Personality	*Journal of Social and Personal Relationships*
Journal of Social Issues	

Applied areas of psychology

Journal of Applied Psychology*	*American Journal of Community Psychology*
Journal of Educational Psychology*	*Evaluation and Program Planning*
Journal of Applied Behavior Analysis	*Environment and Behavior*
Health Psychology*	*Journal of Environmental Psychology*
Psychological Assessment*	*Journal of Consumer Research*
Psychology, Public Policy, and Law*	*Journal of Marketing Research*
Law and Human Behavior*	*Psychology of Popular Media Culture**
Educational and Psychological Measurement	*Rehabilitation Psychology**
American Educational Research Journal	*Journal of Business and Psychology*
Psychology of Violence*	*Journal of Economic Psychology*
Psychology of Religion and Spirituality*	

Family studies and sexual behavior

Journal of Family Psychology*	*Journal of Marital and Family Therapy*
Families, Systems and Health*	*Journal of Sex Research*
Journal of Marriage and the Family	*Journal of Sexual Behavior*

Ethnic, gender, and cross-cultural issues	
Cultural Diversity and Ethnic Minority Psychology*	*Psychology of Sexual Orientation and Gender Diversity**
Journal of Latinx Psychology	*Sex Roles*
Hispanic Journal of Behavioral Sciences	*Psychology of Women Quarterly*
Journal of Black Psychology	*Psychology of Men and Masculinities**
Journal of Cross-Cultural Psychology	*International Perspectives in Psychology: Research, Practice, Consultation**
Some Canadian and British journals	
Canadian Psychology	*British Journal of Psychology*
Canadian Journal of Experimental Psychology	*British Journal of Social and Clinical Psychology*
Canadian Journal of Behavioural Science	

* Published by the American Psychological Association. ** Published by the Association for Psychological Science.

As you can see, previous research and thinking on a topic can be a critical source of ideas for a study. So, then, the next question is: How can you find previously published research?

EXPLORING PAST RESEARCH

For most of us, accessing information has never been easier. Google alone searches as many as 50 billion websites (van den Bosch et al., 2016). Of course, having access to information is different from being able to assess its quality. Searching online for the answer to questions like "What has the impact of marijuana legalization been?" or "Is climate change real?" will generate lists of every conceivable answer, and probably some inconceivable ones, too! Anybody looking at such a list could cherry-pick the sources that they want, to tell the story that they want, and start writing—perhaps publishing what they write on the Web and contributing to the Internet's noise on a topic. So, how do you evaluate the quality of a source? How do you conduct a research project that is connected to other research?

Before conducting any research project, an investigator must have a thorough knowledge of previous research findings. Even if the researcher formulates the basic idea, a review of past studies will help the researcher clarify the idea and design of the study. Thus, it is important to know how to search the literature on a topic and how to read research reports in professional journals. In this section, we will discuss only the fundamentals of conducting library research; for further information, you should go to your college library and talk with a librarian (large libraries may have a librarian devoted to providing assistance in psychology and other behavioral sciences). Librarians have specialized training and a lot of practical experience in conducting library research.

Journals

There is an enormous number of psychology journals in which researchers publish the results of their investigations. After a research project has been completed, the study is written as a report, which then may be submitted to the editor of an appropriate journal. The editor solicits reviews from other scientists in the same field and then decides whether the report is to be accepted for publication; this is the process of peer review, in which experts in the field assess the quality of the research. Because each journal has a limited amount of space and receives many more papers than it has room to publish, many papers are not accepted; rejection may be based on many factors, including overall study quality, potential impact on the field, a small or biased sample size, inappropriate analyses of results, or not the right fit for that particular journal. Papers that are accepted are published about a year later, although sometimes online editions are published more quickly.

Most psychology journals specialize in one or two topic areas. Even so, the number of journals in many areas is so large that it is almost impossible for anyone to read them all. **Table 1** lists some of the major journals in several areas of psychology; the table does not list any journals that are published only on the internet, and it does not include the many journals that publish in areas closely related to psychology or in highly specialized areas within psychology.

Clearly, it would be difficult to read all of the journals listed, even if you restricted your reading to a single research area in psychology, such as learning and memory. If you were seeking research on a single specific topic, it would be impractical to look at every issue of every journal in which relevant research might be published. Fortunately, you do not have to.

Online Scholarly Research Databases

You are probably thinking that you should be able to find information on your topic with an internet search tool such as Google. Instead of looking through printed journals and books, you already have access to a very large database of information. Unfortunately, a search of websites may find some scholarly information but it will also likely access information that is not relevant and may even be inaccurate. In this section we will explore search tools that specialize in access to databases of scholarly research in psychology and related fields. These include PsycINFO, Web of Science, and SCOPUS. We also describe a specialized Google search tool for scholarly information called Google Scholar.

PsycINFO

The American Psychological Association began the monthly publication of *Psychological Abstracts,* or *Psych Abstracts,* in 1927. The abstracts are brief summaries of articles in psychology and related disciplines indexed by topic area. Today the abstracts are maintained in a digital database called **PsycINFO,** which is accessed via the internet and is updated weekly. The exact procedures you will use to search PsycINFO will depend on how your library has arranged to obtain access to the database. In all cases, you will obtain a list of abstracts that are related to your particular topic of interest. You can then find and read the articles in your library or, in many cases, link to full text that your library subscribes to. If an important article is not available in your library, ask a librarian about services to obtain articles from other libraries.

Conducting a PsycINFO Search

The exact look and feel of the system you will use to search PsycINFO will depend on your library website. Your most important task is to specify the search terms that you want the database to use. These are typed into a search box. How do you know what words to type in the search box? Most commonly, you will want to use standard psychological terms. The *Thesaurus of Psychological Index Terms* lists all the standard terms that are used to index the abstracts, and it can be accessed directly with most PsycINFO systems.

Suppose you are interested in the topic of academic performance in STEM courses (Science, Technology, Engineering, Math). A search on the terms *academic performance* and *STEM* will result in a listing of articles that used these terms. The reference citation for one of the articles (Herrmann et al., 2016) is shown in **Figure 3**. Note that we have identified the elements of a reference in this figure. The reference citation provides everything you need to know about a given source.

FIGURE 3   Anatomy of a standard reference

Go to **Check Your Learning:** Practice Exercise #2 to see if you can identify the parts of a citation.

Below is the PsycINFO output for this article. The exact appearance of the output you receive will depend on your library's search system. The default output includes the citation information you will need, along with the abstract itself. Notice that the output is organized into "fields" of information. The full name of each field is included here; many systems allow abbreviations. You will almost always want to see the *title, author, source/publication title,* and *abstract*. Note that you also have fields such as publication type, keywords to briefly describe the article, and age group. When you do the search, some fields will appear as hyperlinks to lead you to other information in your library database or to other websites. Systems are continually being upgraded to enable users to more easily obtain full-text access to the articles and find other articles on similar topics. The *digital object identifier* (DOI) is particularly helpful in finding full-text sources of the article and is now provided with other publication information when journal articles are referenced.

PsycINFO output for Herrmann et al. (2016) appears as follows:

Title:	**The effects of a female role model on academic performance and persistence of women in STEM courses.**

Authors:	Herrmann, Sarah D., Arizona State University, Tempe, AZ, US, sarah.herrmann@asu.edu
	Adelman, Robert Mark, Arizona State University, Tempe, AZ, US
	Bodford, Jessica E., Arizona State University, Tempe, AZ, US
	Graudejus, Oliver, Arizona State University, Tempe, AZ, US
	Okun, Morris A., Arizona State University, Tempe, AZ, US
	Kwan, Virginia S. Y., Arizona State University, Tempe, AZ, US
Address:	Herrmann, Sarah D., Department of Psychology, Arizona State University, 950 South McAllister Avenue, P.O. Box 871104, Tempe, AZ, US, 85287-1104, sarah.herrmann@asu.edu

Source:	Basic and Applied Social Psychology, Vol 38(5), Sep, 2016. pp. 258–268.
Page Count:	11
Publisher:	United Kingdom: Taylor & Francis
Other Publishers:	US: Lawrence Erlbaum
ISSN:	0197-3533 (Print)
	1532-4834 (Electronic)
Language:	English
Keywords:	female role model, academic performance, STEM courses

Abstract:	Women are more likely to leave science, technology, engineering, and mathematics compared to men, in part because they lack similar role models such as peers, teaching assistants, and instructors. We examined the effect of a brief, scalable online intervention that consisted of a letter from a female role model who normalized concerns about belonging, presented time spent on academics as an investment, and exemplified overcoming challenges on academic performance and persistence. The intervention was implemented in introductory psychology (Study 1, N = 258) and chemistry (Study 2, N = 68) courses. Relative to the control group, the intervention group had higher grades and lower failing and withdrawal rates. (PsycINFO Database Record (c) 2016 APA, all rights reserved)

Subjects:	*Academic Achievement; *Human Females; *Role Models; *STEM
PsycINFO Classification:	Academic Learning & Achievement (3550)
Population:	Human
	Female

Location:	US
Age Group:	Adulthood (18 yrs & older)
Grant Sponsorship:	Sponsor: US Department of Education, Institute of Education Sciences, US Grant Number: R305A160023 Other Details: To Arizona State University
Methodology:	Empirical Study; Quantitative Study
Format Covered:	Electronic
Publication Type:	Journal; Peer Reviewed Journal
Document Type:	Journal Article
Publication History:	First Posted Date: Aug 27, 2012; Accepted Date: Feb 3, 2012; Revised Date: Feb 2, 2012; First Submitted Date: Apr 29, 2011
Release Date:	20161013
Copyright:	Taylor & Francis. 2016
Digital Object Identifier:	**http://dx.doi.org/10.1080/01973533.2016.1209757**
Accession Number:	2016-45061-002
Database:	PsycINFO

When you do a simple search with a single word or a phrase such as *academic performance,* the default search yields articles that have that word or phrase anywhere in any of the fields listed. Often you will find that this produces too many articles, including articles that are not directly relevant to your interests. One way to narrow the search is to limit it to certain fields. Your PsycINFO search screen will allow you to limit the search to one field, such as the title of the article. You can also learn how to type a search that includes the field you want. For example, you could specify *academic performance in TITLE* to limit your search to articles that have the term in the title of the article. Your search screen will also allow you to set limits on your search to specify, for instance, that the search should find only journal articles (not books or dissertations) or include participants from certain age groups.

Most PsycINFO systems have advanced search screens that enable you to use the Boolean operators AND, OR, and NOT. These can be typed as discussed below, but the advanced search screen uses prompts to help you design the search. Suppose you want to restrict the *academic performance in TITLE* search to studies that also examined STEM. You can do this by asking for *(academic performance in TITLE) AND (STEM).* The AND forces both conditions to be true for an article to be included. The parentheses are used to separate different parts of your search specification and are useful when your searches become increasingly complicated.

The OR operation is used to expand a search that is too narrow. Suppose you want to find articles that discuss romantic relationships on the internet. A PsycINFO search for *internet AND romance* in any field produces

189 articles; changing the specification to *internet AND (romance OR dating OR love)* yields 773 articles. Articles that have the term *internet* and any of the other three terms specified were included in the second search.

The NOT operation will exclude sources based on a criterion you specify. The NOT operation is used when you anticipate that the search criteria will be met by some irrelevant abstracts. In the internet example, it is possible that the search will include articles on *child predators*. To exclude the term *child* from the results of the search, the following adjustment can be made: *internet AND (romance OR dating OR love) NOT child*. When this search was conducted, 685 abstracts were found instead of the 773 obtained previously.

Another helpful search tool is the "wildcard" asterisk (*). The asterisk stands for any set of letters in a word and so it can expand your search. Consider the word *romance* in the search above—by using *roman**, the search will expand to include both *romance* and *romantic*. The wildcard can be very useful with the term *child** to find *child, children, childhood,* and so on. You have to be careful when doing this, however; the *roman** search would also find *Romania* and *romanticism*. In this case, it might be more efficient to simply add *OR romantic* to the search. These and other search strategies are summarized in **Figure 4**.

General Strategies

- Use several databases—for example, both PsycINFO and Google Scholar. Become familiar with the databases available in your library to expand the range of information available to you.
- Record your search terms and repeat your searches to find updates.
- Do not restrict yourself to full-text articles, as this introduces a bias in your results.
- Try a variety of key words: *angry driving* and *road rage* generate two sets of results that do not completely overlap.
- Consider using the words *review* and *meta-analysis* in the title of an article to find literature reviews.
- Look for the perfect key article and then use that one to identify additional articles. Use the results that you do find to generate new results.
- Use the "times cited in this database" information from PsycINFO or the "related articles" information in Google Scholar.
- Use the "cited references" information provided by PsycINFO and Google Scholar.

PsycINFO Search Strategies

- Use fields such as the TITLE and AUTHOR. Example: Typing *divorce* in TITLE requires that the term appear in the title.
- Use AND, OR, and NOT. AND limits the search. Example: Typing *divorce AND child* requires both terms to be included.
- Use OR to expand search. Example: Typing *divorce OR breakup* includes either term.
- Use NOT to exclude search terms. Example: Typing *shyness NOT therapy* excludes any shyness articles that have the term *therapy*.

- Use the wildcard asterisk (*). Example: Typing *child** finds any word that begins with *child* (childhood, child's, etc.).
- Find the procedure for restricting the search to peer-reviewed articles.
- Review and use keywords that were selected by article authors (in PsycINFO, these are found in the more detailed result output).

Google Search Strategies

- Use advanced search (**http://www.google.com/advanced_search**) to
  - Search for a specific phrase
  - Specify a set of "AND" words or phrases so that each of the results of your search will include all the words or phrases
  - Specify a set of "OR" words or phrases to expand your search
  - Specify a set of "NOT" words or phrases to limit your search

FIGURE 4   Some strategies for searching research databases

It is a good idea to give careful thought to your search terms. Consider the case of a student who decided to do a paper on the topic of road rage. She wanted to know what might cause drivers to become so angry at other drivers that they become physically aggressive. A search on the term *road rage* led to a number of interesting articles. However, when looking at the output from the search, she noticed that the major keywords included *driving behavior* and *anger* but not *road rage*. When she asked about this, we realized that she had only found articles that included the term *road rage* in the title or abstract. This term has become popular, but it might not be used in many academic studies of the topic. She then expanded the search to include *driving AND anger*. The new search yielded many articles not found in the original search.

As you review the results of your search, you can print, save, or send information to your email address. Other options, such as printing a citation in APA style, may also be available.

Now, go to **Check Your Learning:** Practice Exercise #3 and do some of your searching in the literature.

Web of Science & Scopus

Web of Science and Scopus are similar databases that allow searches of authors, titles, and psychological terms; in addition they let users perform searches for citations in a specific article. The most important feature of both resources is the ability to use the "key article" method. Here you need to first identify a key article on your topic that is particularly relevant to your interests. Choose an article that was published sufficiently long ago to allow time for subsequent related research to be conducted and reported. You can then search for the subsequent articles that cited the key article. This search will give you a bibliography of articles relevant to your topic. To provide an example of this process, we chose the following article:

Krahé, B., & Möller, I. (2010). Longitudinal effects of media violence on aggression and empathy among German adolescents. *Journal of Applied Developmental Psychology, 31*(5), 401–409. https://doi.org/10.1016/j.appdev.2010.07.003

When we did an article search using Web of Science, we found 62 articles that had cited the Krahé and Möller paper since it was published in 2010. Here is one of them:

Khurana, A., Bleakley, A., Ellithorpe, M. E., Hennessy, M., Jamieson, P. E., & Weitz, I. (2019). Media violence exposure and aggression in adolescents: A risk and resilience perspective. *Aggressive Behavior, 45*(1), 70–81. https://doi.org/10.1002/ab.21798

This article as well as the others on the list might then be retrieved. It may then turn out that one or more of the articles might become new key articles for further searches.

Other Electronic Search Resources

The American Psychological Association (APA) maintains several databases in addition to PsycINFO. These include PsycARTICLES, consisting of full-text scholarly articles, and PsycBOOKS, a database of full-text books and book chapters published by APA. Other major databases include Sociological Abstracts, PubMed, and ERIC (Educational Resources Information Center). In addition, services such as LexisNexis Academic and Factiva allow you to search general media resources such as newspapers. A reference librarian can help you use these and other resources available to you.

Internet Searches

The most widely available information resource is the wealth of material that is available on the internet and located using search services such as Google, Bing, and DuckDuckGo. The internet is a wonderful source of information; any given search may help you find websites devoted to your topic, articles that people have made available to others, book reviews, and even online discussions. Although it is incredibly easy to search, you can improve the quality of your searches by learning (1) the differences in the way each service finds and stores information; (2) advanced search rules, including how to narrow your searches and how to find exact phrases; and (3) ways to critically evaluate the quality of the information that you find. You also need to make sure that you carefully record the search service and search terms you used, the dates of your search, and the exact location of any websites that you will be using in your research; this information will be useful as you provide documentation in the papers that you prepare.

Google Scholar

Google Scholar is a specialized scholarly search engine that can be accessed at **https://scholar.google.com**. When you do a search using Google Scholar, you find articles, theses, books, abstracts, and court opinions from a wide range of sources, including academic publishers, professional societies, online repositories, universities, and other websites. Both Google and Google Scholar rank the output of searches. In the case of Google Scholar, search output is ranked by the contents of the article (i.e., did the article contain the keywords that were used in the search?) along with an article's overall prominence based on author, journal, and how often it is cited in other articles.

Google Scholar operates like any other Google search. Access Google Scholar at **https://scholar.google.com** and type in a keyword as you would in a basic PsycINFO search. The key difference is that whereas the universe of content for PsycINFO comes from the published works in psychology and related sciences, the universe for Google Scholar includes the entire internet. This can be both a strength and a weakness. If your topic is broad—for example, if you are interested in doing a search for *depression* or *ADHD* or *color perception*—Google Scholar will generate many more hits than PsycINFO would, and many of those hits will not be from the scientific literature. On the other hand, if you have a narrow search (e.g., *adult ADHD treatment*; *color perception and reading speed*), then Google Scholar will generate a set of results more closely aligned with your intentions.

Google Scholar is powerful. It will be worth your while to explore its excellent documentation (https://scholar.google.com/intl/en/scholar/about.html) and learn about its more advanced features, including email alerts for searches and its reference management capabilities.

ILLUSTRATIVE ARTICLE: LAPTOPS IN CLASS

Ravizza et al., (2017) studied computer use in college classrooms by having students in an introductory psychology class log into a proxy server that monitored all online activity during class. They were specifically interested in the relationship between internet use and classroom performance.

First, search for the article in PsycINFO and acquire a full-text version. (Note: The article is available at https://journals.sagepub.com/doi/pdf/10.1177/0956797616677314.) Read the article:

> Ravizza, S. M., Uitvlugt, M. G., & Fenn, K. M. (2017). Logged in and zoned out: How laptop internet use relates to classroom learning. *Psychological Science, 28*(2), 171–180. https://doi.org/10.1177/0956797616677314

After you have a full copy of the article:

1. Read the introduction:
   a. Summarize the authors' purpose for conducting the study; note that their purpose is supported by other references.
   b. Identify the research question or questions that are being explored by this study. In some studies, research questions are clearly labeled as such.
   c. Identify the hypotheses that are being tested by this study. As with research questions, in some studies hypotheses are clearly labeled as such.
2. Read the Method section:
   a. To whom can we generalize the results? How many participants did they invite to participate? How many participants did they collect data from? What was the breakdown of the students' class-rank?
   b. What was measured? How did they record internet use?
3. Read the Results section:
   a. How much time, on average, did their participants spend on non-class-related purposes during class?
   b. How did the authors measure academic use versus nonacademic use of the internet?
4. Read the Discussion section: How do they know that one thing caused another? What are the key points in the discussion section? Are their findings similar to or different from the findings of others?
5. Read the Abstract: How well did the abstract summarize the entire article?

6. Review the references. Pick a reference and try to find it using only its title via (a) a standard Google search, (b) Google Scholar, and (c) PsycINFO. What did you notice about the results of these three search strategies?

CRITICAL THINKING: BEING A SKILLED CONSUMER OF RESEARCH

Below are four examples of recent articles related to behavioral science in the popular press. For each one: (1) use PsycINFO or Google Scholar to find the original published article, (2) read the article, and (3) compare and contrast what the published article says and the popular media article says.

1. Your choice in utensils can change how food tastes: https://www.npr.org/sections/thesalt/2013/0 6/30/196708393/from-farm-to-fork-to-plate-how-utensils-season-your-meal

2. Social media is making you spend money: https://www.washingtonpost.com/us-policy/2019/02/1 9/your-friends-social-media-posts-are-making-you-spend-more-money-researchers-say/?noredir ect=on

3. Happy childhood memories may boost physical and mental health as adult: https://www.usatoda y.com/videos/news/health/2018/11/05/happy-childhood-memories-may-boost-physical-and-ment al-health-adult/38403451/

4. Stress and mindset among teens: https://www.dallasnews.com/life/better-living/2016/10/07/ne w-strategy-managing-teen-stress-believe-power-change

Check Your Learning: Practice Exercises

Practice Exercise #1

There are many common sayings or cliches about behavior, such as "Laughter is the best medicine" and "Beauty is only skin deep." For each of the two common sayings in this exercise, interpret the meaning, develop a hypothesis that is suggested by the saying, and form a research prediction that follows from the hypothesis.

Hypotheses and Predictions
Spare the rod, spoil the child
Interpret the saying:
Write a hypothesis:
Make a prediction:
Absence makes the heart grow fonder
Interpret the saying:
Write a hypothesis:
Make a prediction:
Source: Based on Gardner, 1988.

Practice Exercise #2

Below are three articles published in 2019 in major journals. For each reference, identify:

1. The authors
2. The title of the article
3. The name of the journal
4. The pages in that journal that contain the article
5. The journal volume
6. The journal issue number
7. The digital object identifier
8. Then, find that article using PsychINFO or google scholar and list the first three words of the abstract

> O'Brien, E. (2019). Enjoy it again: Repeat experiences are less repetitive than people think. *Journal of Personality and Social Psychology, 116*(4), 519–540. https://doi.org/10.1037/pspa0000147

> Rodriguez-Seijas, C., Eaton, N. R., & Pachankis, J. E. (2019). Prevalence of psychiatric disorders at the intersection of race and sexual orientation: Results from the National Epidemiologic Survey of Alcohol and Related Conditions–III. *Journal of Consulting and Clinical Psychology, 87*(4), 321–331. https://doi.org/10.1037/ccp0000377

> Yechiam, E., Ashby, N. J. S., & Hochman, G. (2019). Are we attracted by losses? Boundary conditions for the approach and avoidance effects of losses. *Journal of Experimental Psychology: Learning, Memory, and Cognition, 45*(4), 591–605. https://doi.org/10.1037/xlm0000607

Practice Exercise #3

Conduct your own PsychINFO Search. There are so many articles, books, and book chapters that are indexed (collected, sorted, and identified) in databases like PsychINFO.

1. First, let's take a standard topic and just see how many things are published:

    a. In PsychINFO, search on the term "Stress and College Students." How many total hits in search results did you find? When we ran this search, we had 10,950 total hits.

    b. Now, specify that you'd like only articles that have been published since 2010. How many hits? Our search resulted in 4,197 articles.

    c. Now, specify articles that are peer reviewed. How many hits? Our search resulted in 3,224 hits.

    d. Now, limit the search to 2019. How many hits? Our search resulted in 76 articles.

2. Now, search for whatever interests you. Start with some keywords (if you can't think of any, use the PsychINFO thesaurus, which indexes all keywords).

    a. Now do this process again, using Google Scholar—first using the terms "Stress" and "College Students," and then your own topic.

(Some answers are provided at the end of this chapter.)

CHAPTER REVIEW

Review Questions

1. What is a hypothesis? What is the distinction between a hypothesis and a prediction?
2. What are the two functions of a theory?
3. Distinguish between literature reviews, theory articles, and empirical research articles.
4. Describe the differences in the ways past research is found when you use PsycINFO versus the "key article" method of the Web of Science or Scopus.
5. What information does the researcher communicate in each of the sections of a research article?

Study Terms

Hypothesis	PsycINFO
Meta-analysis	Research questions
Literature review	Theory
Prediction	

Check Your Learning: Answers

Practice Exercise #1

Spare the rod, spoil the child

- Interpret the idiom: Generally, a way of saying that children need to be disciplined when misbehaving. Otherwise, they will become spoiled and will always act out to get their own way. A more literal interpretation is that physical punishment (use of the "rod") is an effective way of changing behavior in children.
- Write a hypothesis: Parental use of physical punishment is related to less antisocial behavior in adolescence and adulthood.
- Make a prediction: Adolescents who indicate that their parents used higher amounts of punishment for misbehaving will be described by their teacher as less aggressive and disruptive in the classroom and when interacting with peers.

Absence makes the heart grow fonder

- Interpret the idiom: Physical separation enhances romantic emotional feelings.
- Write a hypothesis: Physical and psychological separation of romantic partners is related to romantic attraction.
- Make a prediction: Romantic partners who have been together for more than a year will report higher levels of romantic attraction when isolated from one another for one week.

Practice Exercise #2

1. The author(s): O'Brien, E
2. The title of the article: Enjoy it again: Repeat experiences are less repetitive than people think
3. The name of the journal: *Journal of Personality and Social Psychology*
4. The pages in that journal that contain the article: 519–540
5. The journal volume: 4
6. The journal issue number: 116
7. The digital object identifier (doi): **https://doi.org/10.1037/pspa0000147**
8. First three words of the abstract (the abstract may be found using the doi): What would it

3 Ethics in Behavioral Research

Mikkel Bigandt/Shutterstock

LEARNING OBJECTIVES

- Summarize the ethical principles in the APA Ethics Code concerning research with human research participants.
- Discuss how potential risks and benefits of research are evaluated.
- Describe the function of an Institutional Review Board.
- Contrast the categories of risk involved in research activities: exempt, minimal risk, and greater than minimal risk.
- Summarize the ethical issues concerning research with nonhuman animals.
- Understand the concept of research fraud and its connection to ethics and the ethical code.
- Understand plagiarism and describe how to avoid it.

Ethical practice is fundamental to the conceptualization, planning, execution, and evaluation of research. Researchers who do not consider the ethical implications of their projects risk harming individuals, communities, and behavioral science. This chapter provides a historical overview of ethics in behavioral research, reviews core ethical principles for researchers, describes relevant institutional structures that protect research participants, and concludes with a discussion of what it means to be an ethical researcher.

MILGRAM'S OBEDIENCE EXPERIMENT

Stanley Milgram **Figure 1** conducted a series of studies (1963, 1964, 1965) to study obedience to authority. He placed an ad in the local newspaper in New Haven, Connecticut, offering a small sum of money to men to participate in a "scientific study of memory and learning" being conducted at Yale University. The volunteers reported to Milgram's laboratory at Yale, where they met a scientist dressed in a white lab coat and another volunteer in the study, a middle-aged man named "Mr. Wallace." Mr. Wallace was actually a confederate (an accomplice) of the experimenter, but the participants did not know this. The scientist explained that the study would examine the effects of punishment on learning. One person would be a "teacher" who would administer the punishment, and the other would be the "learner." Mr. Wallace and the volunteer participant then drew slips of paper to determine who would be the teacher and who would be the learner. The drawing was rigged, however—Mr. Wallace was always the learner and the actual volunteer was always the teacher.

The scientist attached electrodes to Mr. Wallace and then placed the "teacher" in front of an impressive-looking shock machine that was located in an adjoining room. The shock machine had a series of levers that, the individual was told, when pressed would deliver shocks to Mr. Wallace. The first lever was labeled 15 volts, the second 30 volts, the third 45 volts, and so on up to 450 volts. The levers were also labeled "Slight Shock," "Moderate Shock," and so on up to "Danger: Severe Shock," followed by red X's above 400 volts.

Mr. Wallace was instructed to learn a series of word pairs. Then he was given a test to see if he could identify which words went together. Every time Mr. Wallace made a mistake, the teacher was to deliver a shock as punishment. The first mistake was supposed to be answered by a 15-volt shock, the second by a 30-volt shock, and so on. Each time a mistake was made, the learner received a greater shock.

The learner, Mr. Wallace, never actually received any shocks, but the participants in the study did not know that. In the experiment, Mr. Wallace made mistake after mistake. When the teacher "shocked" him with about 120 volts, Mr. Wallace began screaming in pain and eventually yelled that he wanted out. What if the teacher wanted to quit? This happened—the volunteer participants became visibly upset by the pain that Mr. Wallace seemed to be experiencing. The experimenter told the teacher that he could quit but urged him to continue, using a series of verbal prods that stressed the importance of continuing the experiment.

To each volunteer, the study was purportedly an experiment on memory and learning, but Milgram really was interested in learning whether participants would continue to obey the experimenter by administering ever higher levels of shock to the learner. What happened? Approximately 65% of the participants continued to deliver shocks all the way to 450 volts.

Milgram went on to conduct several variations on this basic procedure with 856 subjects. The study received a great deal of publicity, and the results challenged many of our beliefs about our ability to resist authority. The Milgram study is important, and the results have implications for understanding obedience in real-life situations, such as the Holocaust in Nazi Germany and the Jonestown mass suicide (see Miller, 1986).

But the Milgram study is also an important example for discussing the problem of ethics in behavioral research. How should we make decisions about whether the Milgram study or any other study is ethical? The

Milgram study was one of many that played an important role in the development of ethical standards that guide our ethical decision making.

In this chapter, we work through some of these issues, and more. First, let us turn to an overview of the history of our current standards to help frame your understanding of ethics in research.

FIGURE 1   The Milgram obedience experiment is one of the most important studies in behavioral science.

Jan Rieckhoff/ullstein bild/Getty Images

HISTORICAL CONTEXT OF CURRENT ETHICAL STANDARDS

Before we can delve into current ethical standards, it is useful to briefly talk about the origin of ethics codes related to behavioral research. Generally speaking, modern codes of ethics in behavioral and medical research have their origins in three important documents.

The Nuremberg Code, the Declaration of Helsinki, and the Belmont Report

Following World War II, the Nuremberg Trials were held to hear evidence against the Nazi doctors and scientists who had committed atrocities while forcing concentration camp inmates to be research subjects. The legal document that resulted from the trials contained what became known as the **Nuremberg Code:** a set of 10 rules of research conduct that would help prevent future research atrocities (see **https://history.nih.gov/research/downloads/nuremberg.pdf**).

The Nuremberg Code was a set of principles without any enforcement structure or endorsement by professional organizations. Moreover, it was rooted in the context of the Nazi experience and not generally seen as applicable to general research settings. Consequently, the World Medical Association developed a code that is known as the **Declaration of Helsinki.** This 1964 document is a broader application of the Nuremberg Code that was produced by the medical community and included a requirement that journal editors ensure that published research conform to the principles of the Declaration.

The Nuremberg Code and the Helsinki Declaration did not explicitly address behavioral research and were generally seen as applicable to medicine. In addition, by the early 1970s, news about numerous ethically questionable studies forced the scientific community to search for a better approach to protect human research subjects. Behavioral scientists were debating the ethics of the Milgram studies and the world was learning about the Tuskegee Syphilis Study, in which 399 African American men in Alabama were not treated for syphilis in order to track the long-term effects of this disease (Reverby, 2000). This study, supported by the U.S. Public Health Service, took place from 1932 to 1972, when the details of the study were made public by journalists investigating the study. The outrage over the fact that this study was done at all and that the subjects were African Americans spurred scientists to overhaul ethical regulations in both medical and behavioral research. The fact that the Tuskegee study was not an isolated incident was brought to light in 2010 when documentation of another syphilis study done from 1946 to 1948 in Guatemala was discovered (Reverby, 2011). Men and women in this study were infected with syphilis and then treated with penicillin. Reverby describes the study in detail and focuses on one doctor who was involved in both the Guatemala study and the Tuskegee study.

As a result of new public demand for action, a committee was formed that eventually produced the **Belmont Report,** the third critical document in the development of ethical standards in behavioral science. Current ethical guidelines for both behavioral and medical researchers have their origins in *The Belmont Report: Ethical Principles and Guidelines for the Protection of Human Subjects of Research* (National Commission for the Protection of Human Subjects of Biomedical and Behavioral Research, 1979). This report defined the principles and applications that have guided more detailed regulations developed by the American Psychological Association and other professional societies and U.S. federal regulations that apply to both medical and behavioral research investigations.

The three basic ethical principles of the Belmont Report are:

- **Principle of Beneficence:** Research should confer benefits and risks must be minimal. The associated application is the necessity to conduct a risk-benefit analysis.

- **Principle of Respect for Persons (Autonomy):** Participants are treated as autonomous; they are capable of making deliberate decisions about whether to participate in research. The associated application is informed consent—potential participants in a research project should be provided with all information that might influence their decision on whether to participate.

- **Principle of Justice:** There must be fairness in receiving the benefits of research as well as bearing the burdens of accepting risks. This principle is applied in the selection of subjects for research.

APA ETHICS CODE

The American Psychological Association (APA) has provided leadership in formulating ethical principles and standards for behavioral research. The *Ethical Principles of Psychologists and Code of Conduct*—known as the **APA Ethics Code**—is amended periodically with the current version always available online at **http://apa.o rg/ethics/code**. The Ethics Code applies to psychologists in their many roles, including teachers, researchers, and practitioners. The Ethics Code presents five general principles that guide the conduct of psychologists. These are followed by specific standards that apply to each of the major activities of psychologists including research and publication (Standard 8). A summary of the Ethics Code principles and the Standard 8 sections are included in Appendix B.

The preamble to the APA Ethics Code states: "Psychologists are committed to increasing scientific and professional knowledge of behavior and people's understanding of themselves and others and to the use of such knowledge to improve the condition of individuals, organizations and society." Ethical principles support and nurture a healthy science.

APA Ethics Code: Five Principles

The APA Ethics Code includes five general ethical principles, many of which are echoes of the Belmont Report: beneficence and nonmaleficence, fidelity and responsibility, integrity, justice, and respect for rights and responsibilities. Next, we will discuss the ways that these principles relate to research practice.

Principle A: Beneficence and Nonmaleficence

As in the Belmont Report, the **principle of beneficence** refers to the need for research to maximize benefits and minimize any possible harmful effects of participation. The Ethics Code specifically states: "Psychologists strive to benefit those with whom they work and take care to do no harm. In their professional actions, psychologists seek to safeguard the welfare and rights of those with whom they interact professionally and other affected persons and the welfare of animal subjects of research."

Principle B: Fidelity and Responsibility

The **principle of fidelity and responsibility** states: "Psychologists establish relationships of trust with those with whom they work. They are aware of their professional and scientific responsibilities to society and to the specific communities in which they work." For researchers, such trust is primarily applicable to relationships with research participants.

Researchers make several implicit contracts with participants during the course of a study. For example, if participants agree to be present for a study at a specific time, the researcher should also be there. If researchers promise to send a summary of the results to participants, they should do so. If participants are to receive course credit for participation, the researcher must immediately let the instructor know that the person took part in the study. These may seem to be minor details, but they are very important in maintaining trust between participants and researchers.

Principle C: Integrity

The **principle of integrity** states: "Psychologists seek to promote accuracy, honesty and truthfulness in the science, teaching and practice of psychology. In these activities psychologists do not steal, cheat or engage in fraud, subterfuge or intentional misrepresentation of fact." Later in this chapter, we will cover the topic of integrity in the context of being an ethical researcher.

Principle D: Justice

As in the Belmont Report, the **principle of justice** refers to fairness and equity. Principle D states: "Psychologists recognize that fairness and justice entitle all persons to access to and benefit from the contributions of psychology and to equal quality in the processes, procedures and services being conducted by psychologists."

Consider the Tuskegee Syphilis study, or the similar study conducted in Guatemala. In both cases a cure for syphilis (i.e., penicillin) was withheld from participants. This is a violation of principle D of the APA Ethics Code and a violation of the Belmont Report's principle of justice.

Principle E: Respect for People's Rights and Dignity

The last of the five APA ethical principles builds upon the Belmont Report's **principle of respect for persons.** It states: "Psychologists respect the dignity and worth of all people, and the rights of individuals to privacy, confidentiality, and self-determination. Psychologists are aware that special safeguards may be necessary to protect the rights and welfare of persons or communities whose vulnerabilities impair autonomous decision making. Psychologists are aware of and respect cultural, individual, and role differences, including those based on age, gender, gender identity, race, ethnicity, culture, national origin, religion, sexual orientation, disability, language, and socioeconomic status, and consider these factors when working with members of such groups. Psychologists try to eliminate the effect on their work of biases based on those factors, and they do not knowingly participate in or condone activities of others based upon such prejudices."

One of the ethical dilemmas in the Milgram obedience study was the fact that participants did not know that they were participating in a study of obedience. This limited participants' rights to self-determination. Later, we will explore this issue in depth.

With these principles in mind, we will consider the ways in which research subjects—humans and animals—are protected in behavioral research.

ASSESSMENT OF RISKS AND BENEFITS

The **principle of beneficence**—maximizing benefits and minimizing harms—leads us to examine potential risks and benefits that are likely to result from the research; this is called a *risk-benefit analysis.*

Potential risks to participants include factors like psychological or physical harm and loss of confidentiality; we will discuss these in detail. The benefits of a study include direct benefits to the participants, such as an educational benefit, acquisition of a new skill, or treatment for a psychological or medical problem. There may also be material benefits such as a monetary payment, some sort of gift, or even the possibility of winning a prize in a raffle. Other less tangible benefits include the satisfaction gained through being part of a scientific investigation and the potential beneficial applications of the research findings (e.g., the knowledge gained through the research might improve future educational practices, psychotherapy, or social policy). As we will see when discussing the review boards that regulate research in universities and research centers, a risk-benefit analysis with a determination of the level of risk must be completed before research can be approved. We will discuss this later in this chapter.

Risks in Behavioral Research

Let's return to a consideration of Milgram's research. The risk of experiencing stress and psychological harm is obvious. It is not difficult to imagine the effect of delivering intense shocks to an obviously unwilling learner. A film that Milgram made shows participants protesting, sweating, and even laughing nervously while delivering the shocks. You might ask whether subjecting people to such a stressful experiment is justified, and you might wonder whether the experience had any long-range consequences for the volunteers. For example, did participants who obeyed the experimenter feel continuing remorse or begin to see themselves as cruel, inhumane people? Let's consider some common risks in behavioral research.

Physical Harm

Procedures that could conceivably cause physical harm to participants are rare but possible. Many medical procedures—for example, administering a drug such as alcohol or caffeine—fall into this category. Other studies might expose subjects to physical stressors such as loud noise, extreme hot or cold temperatures, or deprivation of sleep for an extended period. The risks in such procedures require that great care be taken to make them ethically acceptable. Moreover, the research would have to offer clear benefits that would outweigh the potential risks.

Stress and Distress

More common than physical stress is psychological stress. The participants in the Milgram study were exposed to a high level of stress; they believed that they were delivering fatal doses of electricity to another person. Milgram described one of his participants:

> While continuing to read the word pairs with a show of outward strength, she mutters in a tone of help-lessness to the experimenter, "Must I go on? Oh, I'm worried about him. Are we going all the way up there (pointing to the higher end of the generator)? Can't we stop? I'm shaking. I'm shaking. Do I have to go up there?" She regains her composure temporarily but then cannot prevent periodic outbursts of distress. (Milgram, 1974, p. 80)

There are other examples. For instance, participants might be told that they will receive some extremely intense electric shocks. They never actually receive the shocks; it is the fear or anxiety during the waiting period that is the variable of interest. Research by Schachter (1959) employing a procedure like this showed that the anxiety produced a desire to affiliate with others during the waiting period.

In another procedure that produces psychological stress, participants are given unfavorable feedback about their personalities or abilities. Researchers may administer a test that is described as a measure of social intelligence and then told that they scored very high or very low. The impact of this feedback can then be studied. Asking people about traumatic or unpleasant events in their lives might also cause stress for some participants. Thus, research that asks people to think about the deaths of a parent, spouse, or friend, or their memories of living through a disaster, could trigger a stressful reaction.

When using procedures that may create psychological distress, the researcher must ask whether all safeguards have been taken to help participants deal with the stress. Usually a debriefing session following the study is designed in part to address any potential problems that may arise during the research.

Confidentiality and Privacy

The loss of expected privacy and confidentiality is another important risk to consider. **Confidentiality** is an issue when the researcher has assured subjects that the collected data are accessible only to people with permission, generally only the researcher. This becomes particularly important when studying sensitive topics. For example, asking participants about sexual behavior, or personal questions about family history, or illegal activity ("Have you ever stolen something worth more than $50?"), may leave them vulnerable if their answers became known to others. Or consider a study that obtained information about employees' managers. It is extremely important that responses to such questions be confidential; revealing their responses could result in real harm to the individual. In most cases, researchers will attempt to avoid confidentiality problems by making sure that the responses are completely anonymous—that there is no way to connect any person's identity with the data. This happens, for example, when questionnaires are administered to groups of people and no information is asked that could be used to identify an individual (such as name, taxpayer identification number, email address, or phone number). However, in other cases, such as a personal interview in which the identity of the person might be known, the researcher must carefully plan ways of coding data, storing data, and explaining the procedures to participants to ensure the confidentiality of responses.

Privacy becomes an issue when, without the subject's permission, the researcher collects information under circumstances that the subject ordinarily believes are private—free from unwanted observation by others. In some studies, researchers make observations of behavior in public places without informing the people being observed. Observing people as they are walking in a public space, stopped at a traffic light, or drinking in a bar does not seem to present any major ethical problems. However, what if a researcher wishes to observe behavior in more private settings or in ways that may violate individuals' privacy? For example, would it be ethical to rummage through people's trash or watch people in public restrooms like Laud Humphreys did in the 1960s or Borchgrevink et al. (2013) did to study hand-washing?

The internet has posed other issues of privacy. Every day, thousands of people post messages on websites. The messages can potentially be used as data to understand attitudes, disclosure of personal information, and expressions of emotion. Many messages are public postings, much like a letter sent to a newspaper or magazine. But consider websites devoted to psychological and physical problems that people seek out for information and support. Many of these sites require registration to post messages. Consider a researcher interested in using one of these sites for data. What ethical issues arise in this case? Buchanan and Williams (2010) address these and other ethical issues that arise when doing research using the internet.

INFORMED CONSENT

Recall Principle E of the APA Ethics Code (**Respect for People's Rights and Dignity**)—research participants are to be treated as autonomous; they are capable of making deliberate decisions about whether to participate in research. The key idea here is **informed consent**—potential participants in a research project should be provided with all information that might influence their active decision of whether or not to participate in a study (Standard 8.02). Thus, research participants should be informed about the purposes of the study, the risks and benefits of participation, and their rights to refuse or terminate participation in the study. They can then freely consent or refuse to participate in the research.

Informed Consent Form

Participants are usually provided with some type of informed consent form that contains the information that participants need to make their decision. Most commonly, the form is presented for the participant to read and agree to. There are numerous examples of informed consent forms available on the internet. Your college may have developed examples through the research office. **Figure 2** summarizes critical parts of the informed consent form in terms of both content anf format. The content will typically cover (1) the purpose of the research, (2) procedures that will be used including time involved (remember that you do not need to tell participants exactly what is being studied), (3) risks and benefits, (4) any compensation, (5) confidentiality, (6) assurance of voluntary participation and permission to withdraw, and (7) contact information for questions.

Check to make sure the informed consent form is in the correct format and includes the necessary information:

Creating the Form

- Form is printed in no smaller than 11-point type (no "fine print").
- Form is free of technical jargon and written at sixth- to eighth-grade level.
- Form is not written in the first person (statements such as "I understand ..." are discouraged).
- Contact information is provided for questions about the study (usually phone and email contacts for the researcher, faculty advisor, and the Institutional Review Board office).

Description of the Study

- Explanation of the purposes of the research in clear language.
- Expected duration of the subject's participation.
- Description of the procedures.

Description of the Risks and Benefits

- Description of any reasonably foreseeable risks or discomforts and safeguards to minimize the risks.
- Description of any benefits to the individual or to others that may reasonably be expected from the research.

- Description of the extent, if any, to which confidentiality or records identifying the individual will be maintained.
- If applicable, a disclosure of appropriate alternative procedures or courses of treatment, if any, that might be advantageous to the individual.

Request for Consent

- Statement that participants are being asked to participate in a research study.
- Statement that participation is voluntary; refusal to participate will involve no penalty or loss of benefits to which the subject is otherwise entitled, and the subject may discontinue participation at any time without penalty for loss of benefits to which the individual is otherwise entitled.
- If an incentive is offered, a description of the incentive and requirement to obtain it; also, a description of the impact of a decision to discontinue participation.

FIGURE 2   Creating the informed consent form: Format and content

The form must be written so that participants understand the information in the form. In some past cases, the form was so technical or loaded with legal terminology that it is very unlikely that the participants fully realized what they were signing. In general, consent forms should be written in simple and straightforward language that avoids jargon and technical terminology (generally at a sixth- to eighth-grade reading level; most word processors provide grade-level information with the Grammar Check feature). To make the form easier to understand, it should not be written in the first person. Instead, information should be provided as if the researcher were simply having a conversation with the participant. Thus, the form might say *Participation in this study is voluntary. You may decline to participate without penalty,* instead of *I understand that participation in this study is voluntary. I may decline to participate without penalty.* The first statement is providing information to the participant in a straightforward way using the second person ("you"), whereas the second statement has a legalistic tone that may be more difficult to understand. Finally, a participant cannot give informed consent if the consent form itself is not in a language the participant can read; researchers should provide each participant with a consent form in that participant's primary language.

Autonomy Issues

Informed consent seems simple enough; however, there are important issues to consider. The first concerns lack of autonomy. What happens when the participants lack the ability to make a free and informed decision to voluntarily participate? Special populations such as minors, patients in psychiatric hospitals, or adults with cognitive impairments require special precautions. When minors are asked to participate, for example, a written consent form signed by a parent or guardian is generally required in addition to agreement by the minor; this agreement by a minor is formally called *assent*. The Society for Research on Child Development has established guidelines for ethical research with children (see **http://www.srcd.org/about-us/ethical-standards-research**).

Coercion is another threat to autonomy. Any procedure that limits an individual's freedom to consent is potentially coercive. For example, a supervisor who asks employees to fill out a survey during a staff meeting or a professor who requires students to participate in a specific study in order to pass the course is applying considerable pressure on potential participants. The employees may believe that the supervisor will somehow punish them if they do not participate; they also risk embarrassment if they refuse in front of co-workers. Sometimes the promise of benefits can also be coercive (Standard 8.06). Researchers often offer an incentive with the request to participate. Monetary incentives (actual money or gift cards) are usually small and must not be so great to induce people to discount any risks. Another incentive used is a chance to win a drawing for a larger prize. Again, the prize cannot be so valuable that potential subjects would fail to consider all the other risks and benefits of the research. Many institutions have specific guidelines for researchers to use when designing incentives.

Withholding Information and Deception

It may have occurred to you that providing all information about the study to participants might be unwise. Providing too much information could potentially invalidate the results of the study; for example, researchers usually will withhold information about the hypothesis of the study or the particular condition an individual is participating in (see Hertwig & Ortman, 2008; Sieber, 2009). It is generally acceptable to withhold information when the research is designated as minimal risk, the information would not affect the decision to participate, and when the information will later be provided, usually in a debriefing session when the study is completed. Most people who volunteer for psychology research do not expect full disclosure about the study prior to participation. However, they do expect a thorough debriefing after they have completed the study. Debriefing will be described after we consider the more problematic issue of deception (Standard 8.07).

It may also have occurred to you that there are research procedures in which informed consent is not necessary or even possible. If you choose to observe the number of same-sex and mixed-sex study groups in your library, you probably do not need to announce your presence or obtain anyone's permission. If you study the content of the self-descriptions that people write for an online dating service, do you need to contact each person in order to include their information in your study? When planning research, it is important to make sure that you either acquire informed consent, or have very good reasons not to obtain informed consent.

In research, **deception** is defined as active misrepresentation of information about the nature of a study. The Milgram experiment illustrates two types of deception. First, participants were deceived about the purpose of the study. Participants in the Milgram experiment agreed to take part in a study of memory and learning, but they actually took part in a study on obedience. Who could imagine that a memory and learning experiment (that title does sound tame, after all) would involve delivering high-intensity, painful electric shocks to another person? Participants in the Milgram experiment did not know what they were letting themselves in for.

The Milgram study was conducted before it was routine to obtain informed consent; however, you can imagine that Milgram's consent form would deceptively have participants agree to be in a memory study. They would also be told that they are free to withdraw from the study at any time. Is it possible that the informed consent procedure would affect the outcome of the study? If they had known that the research was designed to study obedience, participants likely would have behaved differently. Few of us like to think of ourselves as obedient, and we would probably go out of our way to prove that we are not.

Research indicates that providing informed consent may in fact bias participants' responses, at least in some research areas. For example, research on stressors such as noise or crowding has shown that a feeling of "control" over a stressor reduces its negative impact. If you know that you can terminate a loud, obnoxious noise, the noise produces less stress than when the noise is uncontrollable. Studies by Gardner (1978) and Dill,

Gilden et al. (1982) have demonstrated that informed consent procedures do increase perceptions of control in stress experiments and therefore can affect the conclusions drawn from the research.

It is also possible that the informed consent procedure may bias the sample. In the Milgram experiment, if participants had prior knowledge that they would be asked to give severe shocks to the other person, some might have declined to be in the experiment. Therefore, we might limit our ability to generalize the results only to those "types" who agreed to participate. If this were true, anyone could say that the obedient behavior seen in the Milgram experiment occurred simply because the people who agreed to participate were sadists in the first place!

Second, the Milgram study also illustrates a type of deception in which participants become part of a series of events staged for the purposes of the study. A confederate of the experimenter played the part of another participant in the study; Milgram created a reality for the participant in which obedience to authority could be observed. Such deception has been most common in social psychology research; it is much less frequent in areas of experimental psychology such as human perception, learning, memory, and motor performance. Even in these areas, researchers may use a cover story to make the experiment seem plausible and involving (e.g., telling participants that they are reading actual newspaper stories for a study on readability when the true purpose is to examine memory errors or organizational schemes).

The problem of deception is not limited to laboratory research. Procedures in which observers conceal their purposes, presence, or identity are also deceptive. In a study famous for its ethical dilemmas and intricacies, Humphreys (1970) studied the sexual behavior of men who frequented public restrooms (often referred to as "tearooms" in this context). Humphreys did not directly participate in sexual activities, but he served as a lookout who would warn the others of possible intruders. In addition to observing the activities in the tearoom, Humphreys wrote down license plate numbers of tearoom visitors. Later, he obtained the addresses of the men, disguised himself, and visited their homes to interview them. Humphreys' procedure is certainly one way of finding out about anonymous sex in public places, but it employs considerable deception.

Is Deception a Major Ethical Problem in Psychological Research?

Many psychologists believe that the problem of deception has been exaggerated (Bröder, 1998; Kimmel, 1998; Korn, 1998; Smith & Richardson, 1985). Bröder argues that the extreme examples of elaborate deception cited by these critics are rare.

In the decades since the Milgram experiments, some researchers have attempted to assess the use of deception to see if elaborate deception has indeed become less common. Because most of the concern over this type of deception arises in social psychological research, attempts to address this issue have focused on social psychology. Gross and Fleming (1982) reviewed 691 social psychological studies published in the 1960s and 1970s. Although most research in the 1970s still used deception, the deception primarily involved false cover stories.

Has the trend away from deception continued? Sieber et al. (1995) examined the studies published in the *Journal of Personality and Social Psychology* in 1969, 1978, 1986, and 1992. The number of studies that used some form of deception decreased from 66% in 1969 to 47% in 1978 and to 32% in 1986 but increased again to 47% in 1992. The large drop in 1986 may be due to an increase that year in the number of studies on such topics as personality that require no deception to carry out. Also, informed consent was more likely to be explicitly described in 1992 than in previous years, and debriefing was more likely to be mentioned in the years after 1969. However, false cover stories are still frequently used. Korn (1997) has also concluded that use of deception is decreasing in social psychology.

There are three primary reasons for a decrease in the type of elaborate deception seen in the Milgram study. First, more researchers have become interested in cognitive variables rather than emotions and so use methods that are similar to those used by researchers in memory and cognitive psychology. Second, the general level of awareness of ethical issues as described in this chapter has led researchers to conduct studies in other ways. Third, ethics committees at universities and colleges now review proposed research more carefully, and elaborate deception is likely to be approved only when the research is important and there are no alternative procedures available (ethics review boards are described later in this chapter).

THE IMPORTANCE OF DEBRIEFING

Debriefing occurs after the completion of a study, and includes an explanation of the purposes of the research that is given to participants following their participation (Standard 8.08). It is an opportunity for the researcher to deal with issues of withholding information, deception, and potential harmful effects of participation. Debriefing is one way that researchers can follow the guidelines in the APA Ethics Code, particularly Principles B (Fidelity and Responsibility), C (Integrity), and E (Respect for People's Rights and Dignity).

If participants were deceived in any way, the researcher needs to explain why the deception was necessary. If the research altered a participant's physical or psychological state in some way—as in a study that produces stress—the researcher must make sure that the participant has calmed down and is comfortable about having participated. If a participant needs to receive additional information or to speak with someone else about the study, the researcher should provide access to these resources. The participants should leave the experiment without any ill feelings toward the field of psychology, and they may even leave with some new insight into their own behavior or personality.

Debriefing also provides an opportunity for the researcher to explain the purpose of the study and tell participants what kinds of results are expected and perhaps discuss the practical implications of the results. In some cases, researchers may contact participants later to inform them of the actual results of the study. Thus, debriefing has both an educational and an ethical purpose.

The Milgram study can also teach us something about the importance of debriefing. Milgram described a very thorough debriefing. However, an examination of original records and interviews with subjects by Perry (2013) reveals that often the debriefing was little more than seeing that Mr. Wallace was indeed not harmed. Many subjects were rushed from the lab; some did not even learn that no shocks were actually administered but only found that out when Milgram mailed a report of his research findings to the subjects 6 months after data collection was completed (and some never received the letter). Today we would consider Milgram's less than thorough debriefing immediately following the experiment to be a real problem with his research procedure.

Despite all the problems of the stress of the procedure and the rather sloppy debriefing, most of the subjects in the Milgram studies were positive about their experience. The letter that Milgram sent with a detailed report of the study included a questionnaire to assess subjects' reactions to the experiment; 92% of the subjects returned the questionnaire. The responses showed that 84% were glad that they had participated, and 74% said they had benefited from the experience. Only 1% said they were sorry they had participated (Blass, 2004). Other researchers who have conducted further work on the ethics of the Milgram study reached the same conclusion (Ring et al., 1970).

More generally, research on the effectiveness of debriefing indicates that debriefing is an effective way of dealing with deception and other ethical issues that arise in research investigations (Oczak, 2007; Smith, 1983; Smith & Richardson, 1983). There is some evidence that at least in some circumstances, the debriefing needs to be thorough to be effective. In a study on debriefing by McFarland et al. (2007), participants were given false feedback about their ability to accurately judge whether suicide notes were genuine; after making a judgment, they were told that they had succeeded or failed at the task. The researchers then gave different types of debriefing. A minimal debriefing only mentioned that the feedback they received was not based on their performance at all. A more thorough debriefing also included information that the suicide notes were not real. Participants with the additional information had a more accurate assessment of their ability than did subjects receiving the minimal debriefing procedure.

INSTITUTIONAL REVIEW BOARDS

Although the Belmont Report provided an outline for issues of research ethics, and the APA Ethics Code provides guidelines as well, the actual rules and regulations for the protection of human research participants were issued by the U.S. Department of Health and Human Services (HHS). Under these regulations (HHS, 2018), every institution that receives federal funds must have an **Institutional Review Board (IRB)** that is responsible for the review of research conducted within the institution (also see Standard 8.01). IRBs are local review agencies composed of at least five individuals; at least one member of the IRB must be from outside the institution. Every college and university in the United States that receives federal funding has an IRB; in addition, most psychology departments have their own research review committee (Chastain & Landrum, 1999). All research conducted by faculty, students, and staff associated with the institution is reviewed in some way by the IRB. This includes research that may be conducted at another location such as a school, community agency, or hospital, or via the internet.

The federal regulations for IRB oversight of research continue to evolve. For example, all researchers must now complete specified educational requirements. Most colleges and universities require students and faculty to complete one or more online tutorials on research ethics to meet these requirements.

The HHS regulations also categorized research according to the amount of risk involved in the research. This concept of risk was later incorporated into the Ethics Code of the American Psychological Association.

Federal agencies that regulate IRBs define research as a "systematic investigation, including research development, testing, and evaluation designed to develop or contribute to generalizable knowledge" (HHS, 2009). There are two important parts of this definition:

- Systematic: The Belmont Report defined research as "an activity designed to test a hypothesis and permit conclusions to be drawn ... Research is usually described in a formal protocol that sets an objective and a sequence of procedures to reach that objective" (National Commission, 1979). This means that for a project or data collection to be considered research, it must be purposefully and intentionally designed.

- Generalizable knowledge: This means that for a project to be considered research, a person must have intent to create new knowledge with the results. For instance, a project wherein students watch parking behavior in a parking lot in order to learn how to measure parking behavior is not research, because the point of the data collection is not the creation of new knowledge. On the other hand, if a research team wanted to watch parking behavior in a parking lot to address a hypothesis about parking behavior, then it would be research. Finally, generalizable knowledge typically is created to share with others via presentation, publication, or another form of dissemination.

Researchers planning to conduct an investigation are required to submit an application to the IRB. The application requires a description of risks and benefits, procedures for minimizing risk, the exact wording of the informed consent form (in all languages in which the form will be used), how participants will be debriefed, and procedures for maintaining confidentiality. The IRB may specify procedures for continuing review. If it is a long-term project, it will be reviewed at least once each year. If there are any changes in procedures, researchers are required to obtain approval from the IRB.

Determining Type of IRB Review

For purposes of IRB review, research with human subjects is classified as either **minimal risk** or *greater than minimal risk*. Minimal risk means that the risks of harm to participants are no greater than risks encountered in daily life or in routine physical or psychological tests. If the research procedures are judged by the IRB as no greater than minimal risk, the study qualifies for one of three levels of review: exempt review, expedited review, or limited review. If a project is judged to be greater than minimal risk, then a full board review is required. **Figure 3** shows this process.

Exempt Review of Minimal Risk Research

Exempt review research is exempt from the more rigorous review requirements of the federal regulations. Such research must fall into one of several exempt research categories. Examples of exempt research include:

- Research conducted in educational settings that does not have an adverse effect on learning opportunities. This includes research that focuses on comparisons of educational strategies, curriculum, and classroom management techniques.
- Research that only involves cognitive tests, surveys, interviews, or observation of public behavior. The identity of the subjects of such research cannot be ascertained. Research with children that only involves observation of public behavior with no contact with the researchers is included.
- Research using "benign behavior interventions" with adult participants who are able to provide their consent to participate. Examples of benign interventions include performing a cognitive or behavioral task and manipulation of the physical or social environment. The intervention must be brief in duration, harmless, and very unlikely to cause discomfort or embarrassment. Data collection is limited to self-report by the subjects themselves and observation of the subjects. Observation may not include wearing physical measurement devices but can involve audiovisual recording. Except as approved by the IRB, the data collected should be anonymous.
- Use of secondary data. Secondary data include information that already exists and was collected either for nonresearch purposes or as part of a research investigation in which informed consent was obtained. The data must be publicly available, and the identity of participants cannot be ascertained. An example of a secondary data source is the General Social Survey or GSS (**https://www.norc.org**), a series of surveys conducted regularly since 1972. Each survey covers a range of topics, such as attitudes, life satisfaction, health, religion, education, age, and marital status.

The IRB at each institution develops procedures to allow researchers to apply for exempt status and to evaluate whether the research is given the exemption. Researchers cannot decide by themselves that the research is exempt.

Expedited Review of Minimal Risk Research

Expedited review applies to research that is minimal risk research but does not match the exempt research categories. Much expedited review research is biological/medical (e.g., blood samples, collection of hair samples, or saliva); it also includes research procedures frequently used by behavioral researchers. These procedures include (U.S. Department of Health and Human Services, 1998):

- Blood samples with limitations of the amount taken, frequency of taking samples, characteristics of participants.
- Taking "biological specimens" such as hair, saliva, sweat, and skin cells.
- Common physical measures made using healthy adults, such as heart rate, muscle tension, blood pressure. Further, participants may be asked to wear devices that record such measures.
- Data from voice, video, digital, or image recordings.
- "Research on individual or group characteristics or behavior (including, but not limited to, research on perception, cognition, motivation, identity, language, communication, cultural beliefs or practices, and

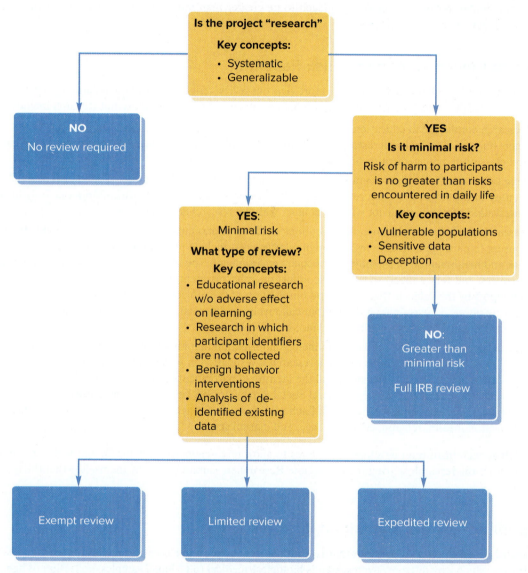

FIGURE 3   IRB decision tree. In order to determine which type of review is required, answer the questions in this decision tree.

social behavior) or research employing survey, interview, oral history, focus group, program evaluation, human factors evaluation, or quality assurance methodologies. (NOTE: Some research in this category may be exempt from the HHS regulations for the protection of human subjects. 45 CFR 46.10 1(b)(2) and (b)(3). This listing refers only to research that is not exempt.)"

The IRB develops a procedure for determining that proposed research should receive expedited review. The proposal will be reviewed by a subcommittee identified by the IRB. This review is less extensive and time-consuming than a full review, requiring meetings of the entire IRB.

Limited Review of Minimal Risk Research

The third category of IRB review for minimal risk research is called **limited review.** Studies that can be subject to limited review are those that include benign behavioral interventions for which sensitive data are collected from adult participants under the circumstance where participates would need to be identified.

Every IRB develops procedures for determining that proposed research should receive limited review. This review is less extensive and less time-consuming than full IRB review and does not require meetings of the entire IRB. Limited review is usually carried out by a member of the IRB. This person may approve the research as exempt or recommend further review.

Full Review of Greater Than Minimal Risk Research

Any research procedure that places participants at greater than minimal risk is subject to thorough full review by the IRB. Such review is more extensive and time-consuming than the exempt and expedited levels of review. The IRB will carefully consider the proposed informed consent procedure, the nature of the sample and plans for recruiting participants, potential risks, and whether there are alternative procedures available to the researcher. Changes in the methods may be required.

> Now, head to **Check Your Learning:** Practice Exercise #1, to tests your skills in identifying the risks involved in research scenarios.

RESEARCH WITH NONHUMAN ANIMAL SUBJECTS

Although much of this chapter has been concerned with the ethics of research with humans, you are no doubt well aware that psychologists sometimes conduct research with animals (Akins et al., 2005). Animals are used in behavioral research for a variety of reasons. Researchers can carefully control the environmental conditions of the animals, study the same animals over a long period, and monitor their behavior 24 hours a day if necessary. Animals are also used to test the effects of drugs and to study physiological and genetic mechanisms underlying behavior.

About 7% of the articles in *Psychological Abstracts* (now *PsycINFO*) in 1979 described studies involving nonhuman animals (Gallup & Suarez, 1985), and data indicate that the amount of research done with animals has been steadily declining (Thomas & Blackman, 1992). Most commonly, psychologists work with rats and mice and, to a lesser extent, birds (usually pigeons); according to surveys of animal research in psychology journals, over 95% of the animals used in research are rats, mice, and birds (see Gallup & Suarez, 1985; Viney et al., 1990). Some of the decline in animal research is attributed to increased interest in conducting cognitive research with human participants (Viney et al., 1990). This interest in cognition is now extending to research with dogs, horses, and other nonhuman species. Canine cognition labs have been growing at universities in the United States, Canada, and around the world (e.g., Yale, Harvard, Duke, Barnard, University of Florida, University of Western Ontario; see, for example, dogcognition.com and the journal *Animal Cognition*). Typically the subjects are family pets that are brought to the lab by their owners.

In recent years, groups opposed to animal research in medicine, psychology, biology, and other sciences have become more vocal and active. Animal rights groups have staged protests at conventions of the American Psychological Association, animal research laboratories in numerous cities have been vandalized, and researchers have received threats of physical harm.

Scientists argue that animal research benefits humans and point to many discoveries that would not have been possible without animal research (Carroll & Overmier, 2001; Miller, 1985). Also, animal rights groups often exaggerate the amount of research that involves any pain or suffering whatsoever (Coile & Miller, 1984).

Plous (1996a, 1996b) conducted a national survey of attitudes toward the use of animals in research and education among psychologists and psychology majors. The attitudes of both psychologists and psychology students were quite similar. In general, there is support for animal research: 72% of the students support such research, 18% oppose it, and 10% are unsure (the psychologists "strongly" support animal research more than the students, however). In addition, 68% believe that animal research is necessary for progress in psychology. Still, there is some ambivalence and uncertainty about the use of animals: When asked whether animals in psychological research are treated humanely, 12% of the students said "no" and 44% were "unsure." In addition, research involving rats or pigeons was viewed more positively than research with dogs or primates unless the research is strictly observational. Plous concluded that animal research in psychology will continue to be important for the field but will likely continue to decline as a proportion of the total amount of research conducted.

Animal research is indeed very important and will continue to be necessary. It is crucial to recognize that strict laws and ethical guidelines govern both research with animals and teaching procedures in which animals are used. Such regulations deal with the need for proper housing, feeding, cleanliness, and health care. They specify that the research must avoid any cruelty in the form of unnecessary pain to the animal. In addition, institutions in which animal research is carried out must have an *Institutional Animal Care and Use Committee (IACUC)* composed of at least one scientist, one veterinarian, and a community member. The **IACUC** is charged with reviewing animal research procedures and ensuring that all regulations are adhered to (see Holden, 1987).

The APA Ethics Code (Standard 8.09) addresses the ethical responsibilities of researchers when studying nonhuman animals. APA has also developed a more detailed *Guidelines for Ethical Conduct in the Care and Use of Nonhuman Animals* (**http://www.apa.org/science/leadership/care/guidelines.aspx**). Clearly, psychologists are concerned about the welfare of animals used in research. Nonetheless, this issue likely will continue to be controversial.

BEING AN ETHICAL RESEARCHER: THE ISSUE OF MISREPRESENTATION

Principle C of the APA Ethics Code focuses on integrity—the promotion of accuracy, honesty, and truthfulness. The ethical researcher acts with integrity and in so doing does not engage in misrepresentation. Specifically, we will explore two specific types of misrepresentation: fraud (Standard 8.10) and plagiarism (Standard 8.11).

Fraud

Making up data–fabrication–is **fraud.** We must be able to believe the reported results of research; otherwise, the entire foundation of the scientific method as a means of knowledge is threatened. In fact, although fraud may occur in many fields, it probably is most serious in two areas: science and journalism. This is because science and journalism are both fields in which written reports are assumed to be accurate descriptions of actual events. There are no independent accounting agencies to check on the activities of scientists and journalists.

Instances of fraud in the field of psychology are considered to be very serious (see, for instance, Hostetler, 1987; Riordan & Marlin, 1987), but fortunately, they are very rare (Murray, 2002). Perhaps the most famous case is that of Sir Cyril Burt, who reported that the IQ scores of identical twins reared apart were highly similar. The data were used to support the argument that genetic influences on IQ are extremely important. However, Kamin (1974) noted some irregularities in Burt's data. A number of correlations for different sets of twins were exactly the same to the third decimal place, virtually a mathematical impossibility. This observation led to the discovery that some of Burt's presumed co-workers had not in fact worked with him or had simply been fabricated. Ironically, though, Burt's "data" were close to what has been reported by other investigators who have studied the IQ scores of twins.

In most cases, fraud is detected when other scientists cannot replicate the results of a study. Suspicions of fabrication of research data by social psychologist Karen Ruggiero arose when other researchers had difficulty replicating her published findings. The researcher subsequently resigned from her academic position and retracted her research findings (Murray, 2002). Sometimes fraud is detected by a colleague or by students who worked with the researcher. For example, Stephen Breuning was guilty of faking data showing that stimulants could be used to reduce hyperactive and aggressive behavior in children (Byrne, 1988). In this case, another researcher who had worked closely with Breuning had suspicions about the data; he then informed the federal agency that had funded the research.

A recent case of extensive fraud that went undetected for years involves a social psychologist at Tilburg University in the Netherlands (Verfaellie & McGwin, 2011). Diederik Stapel not only created data that changed the outcome of studies that were conducted, he also reported results of studies that were never conducted at all. His studies were published in prestigious journals and often reported in popular news outlets because his research reported intriguing findings (e.g., that being in a messy, disorderly environment results in more stereotypical and discriminatory thoughts). Students eventually reported their suspicions to the university administration, but the fact that Stapel's misconduct continued for so long is certainly troublesome. According to a committee that investigated Stapel, one cause was the fact the professor was powerful, prestigious, and charismatic. He would work closely with students to design studies but then collect the data himself. He would invite a colleague to take his existing data set to analyze and write a report. These are highly unusual practices but his students and colleagues did not question him.

Fraud is not a major problem in science in part because researchers know that others will read their reports and conduct further studies, including replications. They know that their reputations and careers will be seriously damaged if other scientists conclude that the results are fraudulent. In addition, the likelihood of detection of fraud has increased in recent years as data accessibility has become more open: Regulations of most funding agencies require researchers to make their data accessible to other scientists (Standard 8.14).

Why, then, do researchers sometimes commit fraud? For one thing, scientists occasionally find themselves in jobs with extreme pressure to produce impressive results. This is not a sufficient explanation, of course, because many researchers maintain high ethical standards under such pressure. Another reason is that researchers who feel a need to produce fraudulent data have an exaggerated fear of failure, as well as a great need for success and the admiration that comes with it. Every report of scientific misconduct includes a discussion of motivations such as these.

One final point: Allegations of fraud should not be made lightly. If you disagree with someone's results on philosophical, political, religious, or other grounds, it does not mean that they are fraudulent. Even if you cannot replicate the results, the reason may lie in aspects of the methodology of the study rather than deliberate fraud. However, the fact that fraud could be a possible explanation of results stresses the importance of careful record keeping and documentation of the procedures and results.

Plagiarism

Plagiarism refers to misrepresenting another's work as your own. Writers must give proper citation of sources. Plagiarism can take the form of submitting an entire paper written by someone else; it can also mean including a paragraph or even a sentence that is copied without using quotation marks and a reference to the source of the quotation. Plagiarism also occurs when you present another person's ideas as your own rather than properly acknowledging the source of the ideas. Thus, even if you paraphrase the actual words used by a source, it is plagiarism if the source is not cited.

Although plagiarism is certainly not a new problem, access to internet resources and the ease of copying material from the internet may be increasing its prevalence. In fact, Szabo and Underwood (2004) report that more than 50% of a sample of British university students believe that using internet resources for academically dishonest activities is acceptable. It is little wonder that many schools are turning to computer-based mechanisms of detecting plagiarism.

Word-for-Word Plagiarism

It is useful to further distinguish between plagiarism that is "word for word" and plagiarism that is "paraphrased." A writer commits **word-for-word plagiarism** when he or she copies a section of another person's work word for word without placing those words within quotation marks to indicate that the segment was written by somebody else, and without citing the source of the information. As an example, consider the following paragraph from Burger (2009):

> Milgram's obedience studies have maintained a place in psychology classes and textbooks largely because of their implications for understanding the worst of human behaviors, such as atrocities, massacres, and genocide. (p. 10)

A writer who wrote the following in his or her work without attributing it to Burger (2009) would be committing word-for-word plagiarism:

> Since they were conducted in the 1960s, Milgram's obedience studies have maintained a place in psychology classes and textbooks largely because of their implications for understanding the worst of human behaviors, including atrocities, massacres, and genocide.

The highlighted text in this example is plagiarized. Note that adding a few words, or changing a few words, does not change the fact that much of the text is taken from another source, without attribution.

An ethical writer would put quotation marks around sentences that were directly taken from the original source and would include a citation. For instance:

> Burger (2009) concluded that since they were conducted in the 1960s "Milgram's obedience studies have maintained a place in psychology classes and textbooks largely because of their implications for understanding the worst of human behaviors, such as atrocities, massacres, and genocide" (p. 10).

Paraphrasing Plagiarism

When a writer expresses the meaning of a passage from a source text without using the actual words of that text, she or he is paraphrasing. In **paraphrasing plagiarism,** instead of the words being directly copied without attribution, the ideas are copied without attribution. Note that there is not a "number or percentage of words" that moves writing from paraphrasing to plagiarism, but rather it is the underlying idea.

Supplying an example of paraphrasing plagiarism is more difficult. Let us use the same passage:

> Milgram's obedience studies have maintained a place in psychology classes and textbooks largely because of their implications for understanding the worst of human behaviors, such as atrocities, massacres, and genocide (Burger, 2009, p. 10).

One example of paraphrasing plagiarism would be:

> Humans are capable of many vile and reprehensible acts. The reality is that Milgram's studies have remained important to psychology because they seem to explain these behaviors.

Here the basic idea presented is directly related to the passage in Burger (2009). In this case, ethical writing may be:

> Humans are capable of many vile and reprehensible acts. The reality is that Milgram's studies have remained important to psychology because they seem to explain these behaviors (Burger, 2009).

The flowchart in **Figure 4** can help you evaluate your own writing for plagiarism by using two key questions: Did I write the words? Did I think of the idea?

Plagiarism is wrong and can lead to many severe consequences, including academic sanctions such as a failing grade or expulsion from the school. Finally, it is interesting to note that some students believe that citing sources weakens their paper—that they are not being sufficiently original. But in fact, Harris (2002) notes that student papers are actually strengthened when sources are used and properly cited.

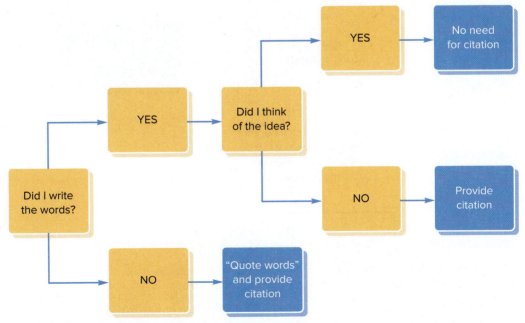

FIGURE 4   Guide for avoiding plagiarism in writing

Visit **Check Your Learning:** Practice Exercises #2 and #3. Both are targeted on one of the most essential topics of the chapter: plagiarism.

CONCLUSION: RISKS AND BENEFITS REVISITED

You are now familiar with the ethical issues that confront researchers who study human and animal behavior. When you make decisions about research ethics, you need to consider the many factors associated with risk to the participants. Are there risks of psychological harm or loss of confidentiality? Who are the research participants? What types of deception, if any, are used in the procedure? How will informed consent be obtained? What debriefing procedures are being used? You also need to weigh the direct benefits of the research to the participants, as well as the scientific importance of the research and the educational benefits to the students who may be conducting the research for a class or degree requirement (see **Figure 5**).

These are not easy decisions. Consider a study in which a confederate posing as another subject insults the participant (Vasquez et al., 2013). The subject wrote an essay expressing attitudes on a controversial topic; subsequently, the subject heard the confederate evaluate the essay as unclear, unconvincing, and "one of the worst things I have read in a long time." The subject could then behave aggressively in choosing the amount of hot sauce that the other person would have to consume in another part of the experiment. The insult did

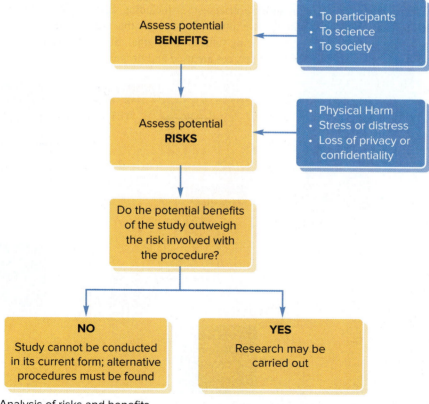

FIGURE 5   Analysis of risks and benefits

lead to choosing more hot sauce, particularly if the subject was given an opportunity to ruminate about it rather than being distracted by other tasks. Instances of aggression following perceived insults are common so you can argue that this is an important topic. Do you believe that the potential benefits of the study to society and science outweigh the risks involved in the procedure?

Obviously, an IRB reviewing this study concluded that the researchers had sufficiently minimized risks to the participants such that the benefits outweighed the costs. If you ultimately decide that the costs outweigh the benefits, you must conclude that the study cannot be conducted in its current form. You may suggest alternative procedures that could make it acceptable. If the benefits outweigh the costs, you will likely decide that the research should be carried out. Your calculation might differ from another person's calculation, which is precisely why having ethics review boards is such a good idea. An appropriate review of research proposals makes it highly unlikely that unethical research will be approved.

Ethical guidelines and regulations evolve over time. The APA Ethics Code and federal, state, and local regulations may be revised periodically. Researchers need to always be aware of the most current policies and procedures. In the following chapters, we will discuss many specific procedures for studying behavior. As you read about these procedures and apply them to research you may be interested in, remember that ethical considerations are always paramount.

In the time when Stanley Milgram was conceptualizing his obedience experiments, there were no institutional review boards. If there had been, it might have been difficult to get his study approved. Participants were not informed of the purpose of the study (indeed, they were deceived into thinking that it was a study of learning), and they were also deceived into thinking that they were harming another person. The struggle is, of course, that if participants had known the true nature of the study, or that they were not really delivering electric shocks, the results would not have been as meaningful.

The Milgram study was partially replicated by Burger in 2009. That study is included as the Illustrative Article for this chapter.

ILLUSTRATIVE ARTICLE: REPLICATION OF MILGRAM

Burger (2009) conducted a partial replication of the classic Stanley Milgram obedience studies.

First, acquire and read the article (available at **https://www.apa.org/pubs/journals/releases/amp-6 4-1-1.pdf**):

> Burger, J. M. (2009). Replicating Milgram: Would people still obey today? *American Psychologist, 64*(1), 1–11. https://doi.org/10.1037/a0010932

Then, after reading the article, consider the following:

1. Key Questions
   a. What was measured?
   b. How do they know that one thing caused another?
   c. To whom can we generalize the results?
   d. Have other researchers found similar results?
2. Conduct an informal risk-benefit analysis. What are the risks and benefits inherent in this study as described?

3. Do you think that the study is ethically justifiable, given your analysis? Why or why not?

4. How did Burger screen participants in the study? What was the purpose of the screening procedure?

5. Burger paid participants $50 for two 45-minute sessions. Could this be considered coercive? Why or why not?

6. Describe the risks to research participants in Burger's study.

7. Burger uses deception in this study. Is it acceptable? Do you believe that the debriefing session described in the report adequately addresses the issues of deception?

CRITICAL THINKING: BEING A SKILLED CONSUMER OF RESEARCH

1. What do you think about the ethical aspects of the Milgram obedience study? Do you think that the study should have been allowed? Were the potential risks to Milgram's participants worth the knowledge gained by the outcomes? If you were a participant in the study, would you feel okay with having been deceived into thinking that you had harmed someone? What if the person you were "shocking" was a younger sibling? Or a grandparent? Would that make a difference? Why or why not?

2. Consider the following experiment, similar to one that was conducted by Smith et al. (1978). Each participant interacted for an hour with another person who was actually an accomplice of the researcher. After this interaction, both persons agreed to return one week later for another session with each other. When the real participants returned, they were informed that the person they had met the week before had died. The researchers then measured reactions to the death of the person.

   a. Discuss the ethical issues raised by the experiment.

   b. What alternative methods for studying this problem (reactions to death) might you suggest?

   c. Would your reactions to this study be different if the participants had played with an infant and then later been told that the infant had died?

3. Dr. Alucard conducted a study to examine various aspects of college students' drug use. The students filled out a questionnaire in a classroom on the campus; about 50 students were tested at a time. The questionnaire asked about prior experience with various illegal substances. If a student had experience with a drug, a number of other detailed questions were asked. However, if the student did not have any prior experience with a drug, they skipped the detailed questions and simply went on to answer another general question about a drug use. What ethical issues arise when conducting research such as this? What problems might arise because of the "skip" procedure used in this study?

4. Find your college's code of student conduct online and review the section on plagiarism. How would you improve this section? What would you tell your professors to do to help students avoid plagiarism?

Check Your Learning: Practice Exercises

Practice Exercise #1

Levels of Risk for Research Scenarios

Scenario	No risk	Minimal risk	Greater than minimal risk
1. Researchers conducted a study on a college campus examining perceptions of physical attractiveness within peer groups by taking pictures of students on campus and then asking students at another college to rate the attractiveness of each student in the photos.			
2. A group of researchers plans to measure differences in depth perception accuracy with and without perceptual cues. In one condition participants could use both eyes and in another condition one eye was covered with an eye patch.			
3. Researchers conducted an anonymous survey on attitudes toward gun control among shoppers at a local mall.			
4. College students watched a 10-minute video of either a male or a female newscaster presenting the same news content. While the video played, a device that recorded eye movement tracked the amount of time the students actually looked at the video.			

Practice Exercise #2

Below is a direct passage from Burger (2009):

> "I cannot say with absolute certainty that the present participants would have continued to the end of the shock generator's range at a rate similar to Milgram's participants. Only a full replication of Milgram's procedure can provide such an unequivocal conclusion. However, numerous studies have demonstrated the effect of incrementally larger requests." (Burger, 2009, p. 9)

a. First—and hopefully the first and last time you are ever told to do this—commit word-for-word plagiarismof the passage above
b. Second—and hopefully this is the last time that you will ever do this—commit paraphrasing plagiarism of the passage above
c. Finally—and hopefully this is the beginning of a lifetime of ethical writing: paraphrase the passage and correctly cite the source

Practice Exercise #3

Indiana University created an excellent online resource called "How to Recognize Plagiarism." You can find it here: **https://www.indiana.edu/~academy/firstPrinciples/index.html**.

This practice exercise is simple: First, complete their training program, then complete the test to earn a certificate.

(Some answers are provided at the end of this chapter.)

CHAPTER REVIEW

Review Questions

1. Discuss the major ethical issues in behavioral research, including risks, benefits, deception, debriefing, informed consent, and justice. How can researchers weigh the need to conduct research against the need for ethical procedures?
2. Why is informed consent an ethical principle? What are the potential problems with obtaining fully informed consent?
3. What alternatives to deception are described in the text?
4. Summarize the principles concerning research with human participants in the APA Ethics Code.
5. What is the difference between "no risk" and "minimal risk" research activities?
6. What is an Institutional Review Board?
7. Summarize the ethical procedures for research with animals.
8. What constitutes fraud, what are some reasons for its occurrence, and why does it not occur more frequently?
9. Describe how you would proceed to identify plagiarism in a writing assignment.

Study Terms

APA Ethics Code

Belmont Report

Confidentiality

Debriefing

Deception

Declaration of Helsinki

Exempt review research

Expedited review

Fraud

IACUC

Informed consent

Institutional Review Board (IRB)

Limited review

Minimal risk research

Nuremberg Code

Paraphrasing plagiarism

Plagiarism

Principle of Beneficence (Belmont Report)

Principle of Fidelity and Responsibility

Principle of Integrity

Principle of Justice (Belmont Report)

Principle of Respect for Persons (Autonomy) (Belmont Report)

Privacy

Risk

Risk-benefit analysis

Word-for-word plagiarism

Check Your Learning: Answers

Practice Exercise 1

1. greater than minimal risk; 2. minimal risk; 3. no risk; 4. minimal risk

Practice Exercise 2

Example passages

a. I cannot say with absolute certainty that the present participants would have continued to the end of the shock generator's range at a rate similar to Milgram's participants. Only a full replication of Milgram's procedure can provide such an unequivocal conclusion. However, numerous studies have demonstrated the effect of incrementally larger requests.

b. Milgram study—that would require perfect replication.

c. Burger pointed out that it was unclear if the participants in his study would have gone as far as participants in the original Milgram study. Determining this would require perfect replication (Burger, 2009).

4   Fundamental Research Issues

Piotr Kuczek/Shutterstock

LEARNING OBJECTIVES

- Define and distinguish among *construct validity, internal validity, external validity,* and *statistical validity.*
- Define *variable* and describe the *operational definition* of a variable.
- Describe the different relationships between variables: positive, negative, curvilinear, and no relationship.
- Compare and contrast nonexperimental and experimental research methods.
- Distinguish between an independent variable and a dependent variable.
- Discuss the strengths and limitations of laboratory experiments and the advantage of using multiple methods of research.

In this chapter, we explore some of the basic issues and concepts that are necessary for understanding the scientific study of behavior. We will focus on the nature of variables and the relationships between variables. We also examine general methods for studying these relationships. Most importantly, we introduce the concept of validity in research.

VALIDITY: AN INTRODUCTION

You are likely aware of the concept of validity, even if you cannot precisely define what it means. You use the term when asking whether the information that you found on a website is valid. A juror must decide whether the testimony given in a trial is valid. Someone on a diet may wonder if the weight shown on the bathroom scale is valid. Behavioral scientists use the term "validity" to refer to the extent to which, given everything that is known, a conclusion is reasonably accurate–that is, the extent to which it approaches what we would call truth. Should you conclude that the information on the website is true, given what you know about its source and the evidence used to support the claims made on the site? Does the testimony reflect what actually happened; are there sources of bias or error that lead you to doubt the validity of the testimony? Is the scale really showing your actual weight? In all these cases, someone is confronted with information and must draw a conclusion about the extent to which that information is accurate, true, or valid.

Scientists constantly evaluate the validity of their own research and of research conducted by others. Are the conclusions made on the basis of the research reasonable? Validity is a key concept in research methods. In fact, scientific research focuses on several aspects of validity. In this chapter, we introduce four types of validity:

- **Construct validity:** the extent to which the measurement or manipulation of a variable accurately represents the theoretical variable being studied. In the case of measurement, is the measure that is used an accurate representation of the variable?

- **Internal validity:** the accuracy of conclusions drawn about cause and effect.

- **External validity:** the extent to which a study's findings can accurately be generalized to other populations and settings.

- **Statistical validity:** the accuracy or the statistical conclusions drawn from the results of a research investigation (sometimes called *statistical conclusion validity*).

These issues will be described in greater depth in this and subsequent chapters. Before exploring issues of validity, we need to have a fundamental understanding of variables and the operational definition of variables.

VARIABLES

A **variable** is something that changes. A variable can be a behavior, thought, feeling, situation, characteristic, or an event. Anything that varies and can be measured is a variable. Any variable must have two or more levels or values. Consider the following examples of variables that you might encounter in research and your own life. As you read a book, you encounter the variable of *word length,* with values defined by the number of letters of each word. You can take this one step further and think of the *average word length* used in paragraphs in the book. One book you read may use a longer average word length than another. When you think about yourself and your friends, you might categorize the people on a variable such as *extraversion*. Some people can be considered relatively low on the extraversion variable (or introverted); others are high on extraversion. You might volunteer at an assisted living facility and notice that the residents differ in their *subjective well-being:* Some of the people seem much more satisfied with their lives than others. When you are driving and the car in front of you brakes to slow down or stop, the period of time before you apply the brakes in your own car is called *response time.* You might wonder if response time varies depending on the driver's age or whether the driver is talking to someone using a cell phone. In your biology class, you are studying for a final exam that is very important and you notice that you are experiencing the variable of *test anxiety.* Because the test is important, everyone in your study group says that they are very anxious about it. You might remember that you never felt anxious when studying for quizzes earlier in the course. As you can see, we all encounter variables continuously in our lives even though we do not usually call them that. Researchers, however, systematically study variables.

Examples of variables a psychologist might study include cognitive task performance, depression, intelligence, reaction time, rate of forgetting, aggression, speaker credibility, attitude change, anger, stress, age, and self-esteem. For some variables, the values will have true numeric, or quantitative, properties. Values for the number of free throws made, number of words correctly recalled, and the number of symptoms of major depression would all range from 0 to an actual value. The values of other variables are not numeric, but instead simply identify different categories. You might be asked to indicate your gender, eye color, major, or marital status. In all cases, your answer will be a category—for example, you may be a psychology major and the person seated next to you might major in computer science. These are different, but they do not differ in amount or quantity.

OPERATIONAL DEFINITIONS OF VARIABLES

A variable such as *aggression, cognitive task performance, pain, self-esteem,* or even *word length* must be defined in terms of the specific method used to measure or manipulate it. The **operational definition** of a variable is the set of procedures used when you measure or manipulate the variable.

A variable must have an operational definition to be studied empirically. The variable *bowling skill* could be operationalized as a person's average bowling score over the past 20 games, or it could be operationalized as the number of pins that fall in a single roll. Such a variable is concrete and easily operationalized in terms of score or number of pins. But things become more complicated when studying behavior. For example, a variable such as *pain* is very general and more abstract. Pain is a subjective state that cannot be directly observed, but that does not mean that we cannot create measures to infer how much pain someone is experiencing. A common pain measurement instrument in both clinical and research settings is the McGill Pain Questionnaire, which has both a long form and a short form (Melzack, 2005). The short form includes a 0 to 5 scale with descriptors *no pain, mild, discomforting, distressing, horrible, excruciating.* There is also a line with end points of *no pain* and *worst possible pain;* the person responds by making a mark at the appropriate place on the line. In addition, the questionnaire offers sensory descriptors such as *throbbing, shooting,* and *stabbing;* each of these descriptors has a rating of *none, mild, moderate,* or *severe.* This is a relatively complex set of questions and is targeted for use with adults.

When working with children over 3, a better measurement instrument would be the Wong-Baker FACES Pain Rating Scale (**http://wongbakerfaces.org/**). The FACES scale consists of a series of six faces with expressions described as ranging from "no hurt" to "hurts worst." To illustrate, the face indicating "no hurt" is similar to this:

Using the FACES scale, a researcher could ask a child, "How much pain do you feel? Point to how much it hurts." These examples illustrate that the same variable of pain can be studied using different operational definitions.

There are two important benefits in operationally defining a variable. First, the task of developing an operational definition of a variable forces scientists to discuss abstract concepts in concrete terms. The process can result in the realization that the variable is too vague to study. This realization does not necessarily indicate that the concept is meaningless; it might simply mean that systematic research is not possible until the concept can be operationally defined.

In addition, operational definitions help researchers communicate their ideas with others. If someone wishes to tell me about aggression, I need to know exactly what is meant by this term, because there are many ways of operationally defining it. For example, aggression could be defined as (1) the number and duration of shocks delivered to another person, (2) the number of times a child punches an inflated toy clown, (3) the number of times a child fights with other children during recess, (4) homicide statistics gathered from police records, (5) a score on a personality measure of aggressiveness, or even (6) the number of times a pitcher hits a batter with a pitch during baseball games. Communication with another person will be easier if we agree on exactly what we mean when we use the term *aggression* in the context of our research.

Of course, a very important question arises once a variable is operationally defined: How good is the operational definition? How well does it match up with reality? How well does my average bowling score really represent my skill?

> Now do the **Check Your Learning:** Practice Exercise #1 that will test your skills at creating operational definitions.

Construct Validity

Construct validity refers to the accuracy of our operational definitions: Does the operational definition of a variable actually reflect the true theoretical meaning of the variable? If you wish to scientifically study the variable *extraversion,* you need some way to measure extraversion. Psychologists have developed measures that ask people whether they like to socialize with strangers or whether they prefer to avoid such situations. Do the answers on such a measure provide a good or "true" indication of the underlying variable of extraversion? If you are studying anger, will telling college students that judges have rated them unattractive create feelings of anger? Researchers are able to address these questions when they design their studies and examine the results.

RELATIONSHIPS BETWEEN VARIABLES

Many studies investigate the relationship between two variables: Do the levels of the two variables vary together? For example, does playing violent video games result in greater aggressiveness? Is a speaker's perceived credibility related to how fast she or he talks? As age increases, does well-being increase as well?

Recall that some variables have true numeric values whereas the levels of other variables are simply different categories (e.g., female versus male; being a student-athlete versus not being a student-athlete). For the purposes of describing relationships among variables, we will begin by discussing relationships in which both variables have true numeric properties.

When both variables have values along a numeric scale, many different "shapes" can describe their relationship. We begin by focusing on the four most common relationships found in research: the **positive linear relationship,** the **negative linear relationship,** the **curvilinear relationship,** and, of course, the situation in which there is *no relationship* between the variables. These relationships are best illustrated by line graphs that show the way changes in one variable are accompanied by changes in a second variable. The four graphs in **Figure 1** show these four types of relationships.

Positive Linear Relationship

In a positive linear relationship, an increase in the value of one variable is accompanied by an increase in the value of the second variable. To illustrate, consider the variable of the rate of speech when delivering a persuasive message. Are "fast talkers" more persuasive? Research suggests that the answer is "yes" (Guyer et al., 2019; Smith & Shaffer, 1991). In the Smith and Shaffer (1991) study, students listened to a speech delivered at a slow (144 words per minute), intermediate (162 wpm), or fast (214 wpm) speech rate. The speaker advocated a position favoring legislation to raise the legal drinking age; the students initially disagreed with this position. Graph A in **Figure 1** shows the positive linear relationship between speech rate and attitude change that was found in this study. That is, as the rate of speech increased, attitude change also increased. In a graph like this, we see a horizontal and a vertical axis, termed the *x-axis* and *y-axis*, respectively. Values of the first variable are placed on the horizontal axis, labeled from low to high. Values of the second variable are placed on the vertical axis. Graph A shows that higher speech rates are associated with greater amounts of attitude change.

Negative Linear Relationship

Variables can also be negatively related. In a negative linear relationship*,* an *increase* in the value of one variable is accompanied by a *decrease* in the value of the other variable. Latané et al. (1979) were intrigued with reports that increasing the number of people working on a task may actually reduce group effort and productivity. The researchers designed an experiment to study this phenomenon, which they termed "social loafing" (which you may have observed in group projects!). The researchers asked participants to clap and shout to make as much noise as possible. They did this alone or in groups of two, four, or six people. Graph B in **Figure 1** illustrates the negative relationship between number of people in the group and the amount of noise made by each person. As the size of the group *increased,* the amount of noise made by each individual *decreased.* The two variables are systematically related, just as in a positive relationship; only the direction of the relationship is reversed.

Curvilinear Relationship

In a curvilinear relationship, increases in the values of one variable are accompanied by systematic increases and decreases in the values of the other variable. In other words, the direction of the relationship changes at least once. This type of relationship is sometimes referred to as a *nonmonotonic function* (as opposed to a *monotonic function* like a positive or negative relationship, a relationship that does not change direction).

Graph C in **Figure 1** shows a curvilinear relationship. This particular relationship is called an *inverted-U*. A number of inverted-U relationships are described by Grant and Schwartz (2011). Graph C depicts the relationship between the complexity of a visual stimulus and liking of that stimulus. Having a complex visual stimulus—one with a lot of detail—is associated with more visual attractiveness, but only up to a point. With too many details, the relationship becomes negative as visual attractiveness diminishes. Of course, it is also possible to have a U-shaped relationship. Research on the relationship between age and happiness indicates that adults in their 40s are less happy than younger and older adults (Blanchflower & Oswald, 2008). A U-shaped curve results when this relationship is graphed.

FIGURE 1   Four types of relationships between variables

No Relationship

When there is no relationship between the two variables, the graph is simply a flat line. Graph D in **Figure 1** illustrates the relationship between crowding and task performance found in a series of studies by Freedman et al. (1971). Unrelated variables vary independently of one another. Increases in crowding were not associated with any particular changes in performance; thus, a flat line describes the lack of relationship between the two variables.

You rarely hear about variables that are *not* related. In large U.S. surveys such as the General Social Survey (**http://gss.norc.org/**), the size of the community in which a person lives is not related to reported health problems or amount of internet use. Usually such findings are just not as interesting as results that do show a relationship, so there is little reason to focus on them (although research that does not support a widely assumed relationship may receive attention, as when a common medical procedure is found to be ineffective). We will examine "no relationship" findings in greater detail in the chapter **"Understanding Research Results: Statistical Inference."**

Remember that these are general patterns. Even if, in general, a positive linear relationship exists, it does not necessarily mean that everyone who scores high on one variable will also score high on the second variable. Individual deviations from the general pattern are likely. In addition to knowing the general type of relationship between two variables, it is also necessary to know the strength of the relationship. That is, we need to know the size of the correlation between the variables. Sometimes two variables are strongly related to each other and show little deviation from the general pattern. Other times the two variables are not highly correlated because many individuals deviate from the general pattern. A numerical index of the strength of relationship between variables is called a **correlation coefficient.** Correlation coefficients are very important because we need to know how strongly variables are related to one another. Correlation coefficients are discussed in detail in the chapter **Understanding Research Results: Description and Correlation**.

> **Check Your Learning:** Practice Exercise #2 provides you with an opportunity to review types of relationships—for each example, identify the shape of the relationship as positive, negative, or curvilinear.

Relationships and Reduction of Uncertainty

When we detect a relationship between variables, we reduce uncertainty by increasing our understanding of the variables we are examining. The term *uncertainty* implies that there is randomness in events; scientists refer to this as *random variability* in events that occur. Research can reduce random variability by identifying systematic relationships between variables.

Identifying relationships between variables seems complex but is much easier to see in a simple example. For this example, the variables will have no quantitative properties—we will not describe *increases* in the values of variables but only differences in values—in this case whether a person is an active user of Instagram. Suppose a researcher has permission to ask 200 teens in your town whether they use Instagram frequently. Now suppose that 104 of them said *Yes* and the remaining 96 said *No*. What do you do with this information? You know only that there is variability in people's use of Instagram—some people are frequent users and some are not.

This variability is called *random variability*. If you tried to guess if a teen was a user of Instagram, you would have to make a random guess—you would be right about half the time and wrong half the time (because we know that about 50% of the teens are users and 50% are not, any guess you make will be right about half the time). However, if we could explain the variability, it would no longer be random. How can the random variability be reduced? The answer is to see if we can identify variables that are related to Instagram use.

Suppose the researcher also included a question (with space to write an answer) on gender: Do you most identify as male, female, or other? Now let's look at what happens when you examine whether gender is related to Instagram use. **Table 1** shows one possible outcome (to simplify, only those indicating male or female are included). Note that there are 100 males and 100 females in the study. The important thing, though, is that 44 of the males say they frequently use Instagram compared to 61 females. Have we reduced the random variability? We clearly have. Before you had this information, there would be no way of predicting whether a given person would be a regular Instagram user. Now that you have the research finding, you can predict the likelihood that any female would use Instagram and any male would not use it. Now you will be right about 60% of the time; this is a big increase from 50% when everything was random.

TABLE 1   Instagram use by gender: Teens ages 13–17

		Participant gender	
		Males	**Females**
Frequent Instagram user?	Yes	44	61
	No	56	39
	Number of participants	100	100

Source: Pew Research Center, 2015.

Is there still random variability? The answer is clearly yes. You will be wrong about 40% of the time, and you do not know when you will be wrong. For unknown reasons, many males will say they are frequent users of Instagram and many females will not. Can you reduce this remaining uncertainty? The quest to do so motivates additional research. With further studies, you may be able to identify other variables that are also related to Instagram use. For example, variables such as income or extraversion may also be related to Instagram use.

This discussion underscores once again that relationships between variables are rarely perfect: There are males and females who do not fit the general pattern. The relationship between the variables is stronger when there is less random variability—for example, if 90% of females and 10% of males were Instagram users, the relationship would be much stronger (with less uncertainty or randomness).

Next, we will discuss a central concept in our efforts to reduce uncertainty in a study: Nonexperimental versus experimental methods.

NONEXPERIMENTAL VERSUS EXPERIMENTAL METHODS

How can we determine whether variables are related? There are two general approaches to the study of relationships among variables: the *nonexperimental method* and the *experimental method.* With the **nonexperimental method,** relationships are studied by observing variables of interest. This may be done by asking people to describe their behavior, directly observing behavior, recording physiological responses, or even examining various public records such as census data. In all these cases, variables are observed as they occur naturally. A relationship between variables is established when the two variables vary together. For example, the relationship between class attendance and course grades can be investigated by obtaining measures of these variables in college classes. A review of many studies that did this concluded that attendance is indeed related to grades (Credé et al., 2010).

The second approach to the study of relationships, the **experimental method,** involves direct manipulation and control of variables. The researcher manipulates the first variable of interest and then observes the response. For example, Ramirez and Beilock (2011) were interested in the anxiety produced by important "high-stakes" examinations. Because such anxiety may impair performance, it is important to find ways to reduce the anxiety. In their research, Ramirez and Beilock tested the hypothesis that writing about testing worries would improve performance on the exam. In their study, they used the experimental method. All students took a math test and were then given an opportunity to take the test again. To make this a high-stakes test, students were led to believe that the monetary payout to themselves and their partner was dependent on their performance. The writing variable was then manipulated. Some students spent 10 minutes before taking the test writing about what they were thinking and feeling about the test. The other students constituted a control group; these students simply sat quietly for 10 minutes prior to taking the test. Next, the new, important test was then administered. The researchers found that students in the writing condition improved their scores; the control group's scores actually decreased. With the experimental method, the two variables do not merely vary together; one variable is introduced first to determine whether it affects the second variable.

Nonexperimental Method

Suppose a researcher is interested in the relationship between exercise and anxiety. How could this topic be studied? Using the nonexperimental method, the researcher would devise operational definitions to measure both the amount of exercise that people engage in and their level of anxiety. There could be a variety of ways of operationally defining either of these variables; for example, the researcher might simply ask people to provide self-reports of their exercise patterns and current anxiety level. Now suppose that the researcher collects data on exercise and anxiety from a number of people and finds that exercise is negatively related to anxiety—that is, the people who exercise more also have lower levels of anxiety. The two variables covary, or correlate, with each other: Observed differences in exercise are associated with amount of anxiety. Because the nonexperimental method allows us to observe covariation between variables, another term that is frequently used to describe this procedure is the *correlational method.* With this method, we examine whether the variables correlate or vary together.

The nonexperimental method seems to be a reasonable approach to studying relationships between variables such as exercise and anxiety. A relationship is established by finding that the two variables vary together—the variables covary or correlate with each other. However, this method is not ideal when we ask questions about cause and effect. We know the two variables are related, but what can we say about the causal impact of one variable on the other? There are two problems with making causal statements when the nonexperimental method is used: (1) It can be difficult to determine the direction of cause and effect, and (2) researchers face the third-variable problem—that is, extraneous variables may be causing an observed relationship. These problems are illustrated in **Figure 2**. The arrows linking variables depict direction of causation.

Direction of Cause and Effect

The first problem involves *direction of cause and effect*. With the nonexperimental method, it is difficult to determine which variable causes the other. In other words, it cannot really be said that exercise causes a reduction in anxiety. Although there are plausible reasons for this particular pattern of cause and effect, there are also reasons the opposite pattern might occur (both causal directions are shown in **Figure 2**). Perhaps high anxiety causes people to reduce exercise. The issue here is one of temporal precedence, which is very important in making causal inferences (see the chapter **"Scientific Understanding of Behavior"**). Knowledge of the correct direction of cause and effect in turn has implications for applications of research findings: If exercise reduces anxiety, then undertaking an exercise program would be a reasonable way to lower one's anxiety. However, if anxiety causes people to stop exercising, simply forcing someone to exercise is not likely to reduce the person's anxiety level.

The problem of direction of cause and effect is not the most serious drawback to the nonexperimental method, however. Scientists have pointed out, for example, that astronomers can make accurate predictions even though they often cannot manipulate variables in an experiment. In addition, often the direction of cause and effect is not crucial because, for some pairs of variables, the causal pattern may operate in both directions. For instance, there seem to be two causal patterns in the relationship between the variables of similarity and liking: (1) Similarity causes people to like each other, and (2) liking causes people to become more similar. In general, the third-variable problem is a much more serious fault of the nonexperimental method.

The Third-Variable Problem

When the nonexperimental method is used, there is the danger that no direct causal relationship exists between the two variables. Exercise might not influence anxiety, and anxiety might have no causal effect on exercise; this would be known as a spurious relationship. Instead, there may be a relationship between the two variables because some other variable causes both exercise *and* anxiety. This is known as the **third-variable problem.**

A **third variable** is any variable that is extraneous to the two variables being studied; this is why these variables are sometimes referred to as **extraneous variables.** Any number of other third variables may be responsible for an observed relationship between two variables. In the exercise and anxiety example, one such third variable could be income level. Perhaps high income allows people more free time to exercise (and the ability to

Directionality Problem

Exercise causes anxiety reduction.

Exercise → Anxiety

Anxiety causes a reduction in exercise.

Anxiety → Exercise

Third-Variable Problem

Higher income leads to both lower anxiety and more exercise.

Third Variable: Income → Exercise
→ Anxiety

FIGURE 2 Causal possibilities in a nonexperimental study afford a health club membership!) and also lowers anxiety. Income acting as a third variable is illustrated in **Figure 2**. If income is the determining variable, there is no direct cause-and-effect relationship between exercise and anxiety; the relationship was caused by the third variable, income level. The third variable is an alternative explanation for the observed relationship between the variables. Recall from the chapter **"Scientific Understanding of Behavior"** that the ability to rule out alternative explanations for the observed relationship between two variables is another important factor when we try to infer that one variable causes another.

The fact that third variables could be operating is a serious problem because third variables introduce alternative explanations that reduce the overall validity of a study. The fact that income could be related to exercise means that income level is an alternative explanation for an observed relationship between exercise and anxiety. The alternative explanation is that high income reduces anxiety level, so exercise has nothing to do with it.

When we know that an uncontrolled third variable is operating, we can call the third variable a **confounding variable.** If two variables are confounded, they are intertwined so you cannot determine which of the variables is operating in a given situation. If income is confounded with exercise, income level will be an alternative explanation whenever you study exercise. Fortunately, there is a solution to this problem: The experimental method provides us with a way of controlling for the effects of third variables.

As you can see, direction of cause and effect and potential third variables are serious limitations of the nonexperimental method. Often they are not considered in media reports of research results. For instance, a newspaper may report the results of a nonexperimental study that found a positive relationship between amount of coffee consumed and likelihood of a heart attack. Obviously, there is not necessarily a cause-and-effect relationship between the two variables. Numerous third variables (e.g., occupation, personality, or genetic predisposition) could cause both a person's coffee-drinking behavior and the likelihood of a heart attack. In sum, the results of such studies are ambiguous and should be viewed with skepticism.

Experimental Method

The experimental method reduces ambiguity, and thus uncertainty, in the interpretation of results. With the experimental method, one variable is manipulated and the other is then measured. The manipulated variable is called the **independent variable** and the variable that is measured is termed the **dependent variable.** If a researcher used the experimental method to study whether exercise reduces anxiety, exercise would be manipulated—perhaps by having one group of people exercise each day for a week and another group refrains from exercise for a week. Anxiety would then be measured. Suppose that people in the exercise group have less anxiety than the people in the no-exercise group. The researcher could now say something about the direction of cause and effect: In the experiment, exercise came first in the sequence of events. Thus, level of anxiety could not influence the amount of exercise that the people engaged in.

Another characteristic of the experimental method is that it attempts to eliminate the influence of all potential confounding third variables on the dependent variable. This is generally referred to as control of extraneous variables. Such control is usually achieved by making sure that every feature of the environment except the manipulated variable is held constant. Any variable that cannot be held constant is controlled by making sure that the effects of the variable are random. Through randomization, the influence of any extraneous variables is equal in the experimental conditions. Both procedures are used to ensure that any differences between the groups are due to the manipulated variable.

Experimental Control

In a perfect experiment, all extraneous variables are controlled by being held constant. This is called **experimental control.** If a variable is held constant—that is, the variable is not allowed to vary during the experiment—it cannot be responsible for the results of the experiment. In other words, any variable that is held constant cannot be a confounding variable. In the experiment on the effect of exercise, the researcher would want to make sure that the only difference between the exercise and no-exercise groups is the exercise. For example, because people in the exercise group are removed from their daily routine to engage in exercise, the people in the no-exercise group should be removed from their daily routine as well. Otherwise, the lower anxiety in the exercise condition could have resulted from the "rest" from the daily routine rather than from the exercise.

Experimental control is accomplished by treating participants in all groups in the experiment identically; the only difference between groups is the manipulated variable. In the Loftus (1979) experiment on memory (discussed in the chapter **"Where to Start"**), individuals in both groups witnessed the same accident, the same experimenter asked the same questions in both groups, the lighting and all other conditions were the same, and so on. When a difference occurred between the groups in reporting memory, researchers could be sure that the difference was the result of the method of questioning rather than of some other variable that was not held constant.

Randomization

The number of potential confounding variables is infinite, and sometimes it is difficult to keep a variable constant. The most obvious such variable is any personal characteristic of the participants. Consider an experiment in which half the research participants are in the exercise condition and the other half are in the no-exercise condition; the participants in the two conditions might be different on some extraneous, third variable such as income. This difference could cause an apparent relationship between exercise and anxiety. How can the researcher eliminate the influence of such extraneous variables in an experiment?

The experimental method eliminates the influence of such variables by **randomization.** Randomization ensures that an extraneous variable is just as likely to affect one experimental group as it is to affect the other group. To eliminate the influence of individual characteristics, the researcher assigns participants to the two groups in a random fashion. In actual practice, this means that assignment to groups is determined using a list of random numbers. To understand this, think of the participants in the experiment as forming a line. As each person comes to the front of the line, a random number is assigned, much like random numbers are drawn for a lottery. If the number is even, the individual is assigned to one group (e.g., exercise); if the number is odd, the subject is assigned to the other group (e.g., no exercise). By using a random assignment procedure, the researcher is confident that the characteristics of the participants in the two groups will be virtually identical. In this "lottery," for instance, people with low, medium, and high incomes will be distributed equally in the two groups. In fact, randomization ensures that the individual characteristic composition of the two groups will be virtually identical in every way. This ability to randomly assign research participants to the conditions in the experiment is an important difference between the experimental and nonexperimental methods.

To make the concept of random assignment more concrete, you might try an exercise like this one: Suppose you have a box full of old baseball cards. The box contains cards of 50 American League players and 50 National League players. The cards are thoroughly mixed up. Select 32 of the cards and assign them to "groups" using a sequence of random numbers obtained from a website that generates random numbers (www.randomizer.org). As each card is drawn, use the following decision rule: If the random number is even, the player is assigned to Group 1, and if the number is odd, the player is assigned to Group 2. Then check to see whether the two groups differ in terms of league representation. A likely outcome would be something like this: Group 1 has nine American League players and seven National League players, whereas Group 2 has an equal number of players from the two leagues. These two groups are virtually identical in terms of league representation!

Any other variable that cannot be held constant is also controlled by randomization. For instance, many experiments are conducted over a period of several days or weeks, with participants arriving for the experiment at various times during each day. In such cases, the researcher uses a random order for scheduling the sequence of the various experimental conditions. This procedure prevents a situation in which one condition is scheduled during the first days of the experiment whereas the other is studied during later days. Similarly, participants in one group will not be studied only during the morning and the others only in the afternoon.

Direct experimental control and randomization eliminate the influence of any extraneous variables (keeping variables constant across conditions). Thus, the experimental method allows a relatively unambiguous interpretation of the results. Any difference between groups on the observed variable can be attributed to the influence of the manipulated variable.

Internal Validity and the Experimental Method

Internal validity is the ability to draw conclusions about causal relationships from the results of a study. A study has high internal validity when strong inferences can be made that one variable caused changes in the other variable. We have seen that strong causal inferences can be made more easily when the experimental method is used.

Inferences of cause and effect require three elements. So, strong internal validity requires an analysis of these three elements:

- **Temporal precedence:** First, there must be temporal precedence: The causal variable should come first in the temporal order of events and be followed by the effect. The experimental method addresses temporal order by first manipulating the independent variable and then observing whether it has an effect on the dependent variable. In other situations, you may observe the temporal order or you may logically conclude that one order is more plausible than another.

- **Covariation:** Second, there must be covariation between the two variables. Covariation is demonstrated with the experimental method when participants in an experimental condition (e.g., an exercise condition) show the effect (e.g., a reduction in anxiety), whereas participants in a control condition (e.g., no exercise) do not show the effect.

- **Eliminate plausible alternative explanations:** Third, there is a need to eliminate plausible alternative explanations for the observed relationship. An alternative explanation is based on the possibility that some confounding third variable is responsible for the observed relationship. When designing research, a great deal of attention is paid to eliminating alternative explanations, because doing so brings us closer to truth. Indeed, eliminating alternative explanations is fundamental to internal validity. The experimental method begins by attempting to keep such variables constant through random assignment and experimental control.

Other issues of control will be discussed in later chapters. The main point here is that inferences about causal relationships are stronger when there are fewer alternative explanations for the observed relationships.

Independent and Dependent Variables

When researchers study the relationship between variables, the variables are usually conceptualized as having a cause-and-effect connection. That is, one variable is considered to be the cause and the other variable the effect. Thus, rate of speech is viewed as a cause of attitude change, and exercise is viewed as having an effect on anxiety. Researchers using both experimental and nonexperimental methods view the variables in this fashion, even though there is less ambiguity about the direction of cause and effect when the experimental method is used. As we have seen, researchers use the terms **independent variable** and **dependent variable** when referring to the variables being studied. The variable that is considered to be the cause is called the independent variable, and the variable that is the effect is called the dependent variable. It is often helpful to actually draw a relationship between the independent and dependent variables using an arrow as we did in **Figure 2**. The arrow always indicates your hypothesized causal sequence:

In an experiment, the manipulated variable is the independent variable. After manipulating the independent variable, the researchers measure a second variable, called the dependent variable. The basic idea is that the researchers make changes in the independent variable and then see if the dependent variable changes in response.

One way to remember the distinction between the independent and dependent variables is to relate the terms to what happens to participants in an experiment. First, the participants are exposed to a situation, such as watching a violent versus a nonviolent program or exercising versus not exercising. This is the manipulated variable. It is called the independent variable because the participant has nothing to do with its occurrence; the researchers vary it independently of any characteristics of the participant or situation.

In the next step of the experiment, the researchers want to see what effect the independent variable had on the participant; to find this out, they measure the dependent variable. In this step, the participant is responding to what happened to him or her; whatever the participant does or says, the researcher assumes must be caused by—or be dependent on—the effect of the independent (manipulated) variable. The independent variable, then, is the variable manipulated by the experimenter, and the dependent variable is the participant's measured behavior, which is assumed to be caused by the independent variable.

When the relationship between an independent and a dependent variable is plotted in a graph, the independent variable is always placed on the horizontal axis and the dependent variable is always placed on the vertical axis. If you look back to **Figure 1**, you will see that this graphing method was used to present the four relationships. In Graph B, for example, the independent variable, "Group Size," is placed on the horizontal axis; the dependent variable, "Amount of Noise," is placed on the vertical axis.

Note that some research focuses primarily on the independent variable, with the researcher studying the effect of a single independent variable on numerous behaviors. Other researchers may focus on a specific dependent variable and study how various independent variables affect that one behavior. To make this distinction more concrete, consider a study of the effect of jury size, the independent variable, on the outcome of a trial, the dependent variable. One researcher studying this issue might be interested in the effect of group size on a variety of behaviors, including jury decisions and risk taking among business managers. Another researcher, interested solely in jury decisions, might study the effects of many aspects of trials, such as jury size and the judge's instructions, on juror behavior. Both emphases lead to important research.

It is important to know the difference between a dependent and an independent variable. This can be challenging. To see if you understand these basic types of variables, complete the **Check Your Learning:** Practice Exercise #3.

EXPERIMENTAL METHODS: ADDITIONAL CONSIDERATIONS

The advantages of the experimental method for studying relationships between variables have been emphasized. You may be asking yourself, Why isn't every study an experiment? There *are* disadvantages to experiments and many good reasons for using methods other than experiments. Let's examine some of the issues that arise when choosing a method.

Experiments Are Tightly Controlled, Unlike the Real World

The **external validity** of a study is the extent to which the results can be generalized to other populations and settings. In thinking about external validity, several questions arise: Can the results of a study be replicated with other operational definitions of the variables? Can the results be replicated with different participants? Can the results be replicated in other settings?

The goal of designing a study that has high internal validity may require placing less importance on external validity. Consider a researcher interested in establishing that there is a causal relationship between variables is most interested in internal validity. An experiment would be designed in which the independent variable is manipulated and other variables are kept constant (experimental control).

This is most easily done in a laboratory setting, often with a highly restricted sample such as college students drawn from introductory psychology classes. This procedure permits relatively unambiguous inferences concerning cause and effect and reduces the possibility that extraneous variables could influence the results. These unambiguous inferences are another way of saying "strong internal validity." Laboratory experimentation is an extremely valuable way to study many problems. However, the high degree of control and the laboratory setting may sometimes create an artificial atmosphere that may limit the external validity of the results. So, although laboratory experiments often have strong internal validity, they may often have limited external validity. For this reason, researchers may decide to use a nonexperimental procedure to study relationships among variables.

Another alternative is to try to conduct an experiment in a field setting. In a **field experiment,** the independent variable is manipulated in a natural setting. As in any experiment, the researcher attempts to control extraneous variables via either randomization or experimental control. As an example of a field experiment, consider the Lee et al. (2010) study on the impact that public sneezing had on perceptions of risk resulting from flu. On a day when swine flu received broad media attention, students on a university campus were exposed to a confederate who either sneezed and coughed, or did not, as participants passed. Afterward, participants were asked to complete a measure of perceived risks in order to help on a "class project." The researchers then conducted similar studies at shopping malls and local businesses. In all cases, they found that participants who were exposed to sneezing and coughing reported feeling more risks to their health, including risks such as contracting a serious disease, having a heart attack prior to age 50, and dying from a crime or accident.

Many other field experiments take place in public spaces such as street corners, shopping malls, and parking lots. Ruback and Juieng (1997) measured the amount of time drivers in a parking lot took to leave their space under two conditions: (1) when another car (driven by the experimenter) waited a few spaces away or (2) when no other car was present. As you might expect, drivers took longer to leave when a car was waiting for the space. Apparently, the motive to protect a temporary territory is stronger than the motive to leave as quickly as possible!

The advantage of the field experiment is that the independent variable is investigated in a natural context. The disadvantage is that the researcher loses the ability to directly control many aspects of the situation. For instance, in the parking lot, there are other shoppers in the area and security guards that might drive by. The laboratory experiment permits researchers to more easily keep extraneous variables constant, thereby eliminating their influence on the outcome of the experiment. Of course, it is precisely this control that leads to the artificiality of the laboratory investigation. Fortunately, when researchers have conducted experiments in both lab and field settings, the results of the experiments have been very similar (Anderson et al., 1999).

Some Variables Cannot Be—or Should Not Be—Manipulated

Sometimes the experimental method is not a feasible alternative because experimentation would be either unethical or impractical. Child-rearing practices would be impractical to manipulate with the experimental method, for example. Further, even if it were possible to randomly assign parents to two child-rearing conditions, such as using withdrawal of love versus physical types of punishment, the manipulation would be unethical. Instead of manipulating variables such as child-rearing techniques, researchers usually study them as they occur in natural settings. Many important research areas present similar problems—for example, studies of the effects of alcoholism, divorce and its consequences, or the impact of corporal punishment on children's aggressiveness. Such problems need to be studied, and generally the only techniques possible are nonexperimental.

When such variables are studied, people are often categorized into groups based on their experiences. When studying corporal punishment, for example, one group would consist of individuals who were spanked as children and another group would consist of people who were not. This is sometimes called an *ex post facto* design. Ex post facto means "after the fact"—the term was coined to describe research in which groups are formed on the basis of some actual difference rather than through random assignment as in an experiment. It is extremely important to study these differences. However, it is important to recognize that this is nonexperimental research because there is no random assignment to the groups and no manipulation of an independent variable.

Participant variables (also called *subject variables* and *personal attributes*) are characteristics of individuals, such as age, gender, ethnic group, nationality, birth order, personality, or marital status. These variables are by definition nonexperimental; they cannot be manipulated, they must only be measured. For example, to study a personality characteristic such as extraversion, you might have people complete a personality test that is designed to measure this variable. Such variables may be studied in experiments along with manipulated independent variables (see the chapter **"Complex Experimental Designs"**).

Some Questions Are Not Answerable by an Experiment

A major goal of science is to provide an accurate description of events. Thus, the goal of much research is to describe behavior; in those cases, causal inferences are not relevant to the primary goals of the research. A classic example of descriptive research in psychology comes from the work of Jean Piaget, who carefully observed the behavior of his own children as they matured. He described in detail the changes in their ways of thinking about and responding to their environment (Piaget, 1952). Piaget's descriptions and his interpretations of his observations resulted in an important theory of cognitive development that greatly increased our understanding of this topic. Piaget's theory had a major impact on psychology that continues today (Flavell, 1996).

A more recent example of descriptive research in psychology is Meston and Buss's (2007) study on the motives for having sex. The purpose of the study was to describe the "multitude of reasons that people engage in sexual intercourse" (p. 496). In the study, 444 male and female college students were asked to list the reasons they had engaged in sexual intercourse in the past. The researchers combed through the answers and identified 237 reasons, including "I was attracted to the person," "I wanted to feel loved," "I wanted to make up after a fight," and "I wanted to defy my parents." The next step for the researchers was to categorize the reasons their participants reported for having sex, including physical reasons (such as attraction) and goal attainment reasons (such as revenge). In this case, as with some of Piaget's work, the primary goal was to describe behavior rather than to understand its causes.

In many real-life situations, a major concern is to make a successful prediction about a person's future behavior—for example, success in school, ability to learn a new job, or probable interest in various major fields in college. In such circumstances, there may be no need to be concerned about issues of cause and effect. It is possible to design measures that increase the accuracy of predicting future behavior. School counselors can give tests to decide whether students should be in "enriched" classroom programs, employers can test applicants to help determine whether they should be hired, and college students can take tests that help them decide on a major. These types of measures can lead to better decisions for many people. When researchers develop measures designed to predict future behavior, they must conduct research to demonstrate that the measure does, in fact, relate to the behavior in question. This research will be discussed in the chapter **"Measurement Concepts."**

Advantages of Multiple Methods

Perhaps most important, a complete understanding of any phenomenon requires study using multiple methods, both experimental and nonexperimental. No method is perfect, and no single study is definitive. To illustrate, consider a hypothesis developed by Frank and Gilovich (1988). They were intrigued by the observation that the color black represents evil and death across many cultures over time, and they wondered whether this has an influence on our behavior. They noted that several professional sports teams in the National Football League and National Hockey League wear black uniforms and hypothesized that these teams might be more aggressive than other teams in the leagues.

They first needed an operational definition of "black" and "nonblack" uniforms; they decided that a black uniform is one in which 50% or more of the uniform is black. Using this definition, five NFL and five NHL teams had black uniforms. They first asked people who had no knowledge of the NFL or NHL to view each team's uniform and then rate the teams on "malevolent" adjectives such as "mean" and "aggressive." Overall, the black-uniform teams were rated as being more malevolent. They then compared the penalty yards of NFL black-uniform and nonblack-uniform teams and the penalty minutes of NHL teams. In both cases, black-uniform teams were assessed more penalties. But is there a causal pattern? Frank and Gilovich discovered that two NHL teams had switched uniforms from nonblack to black, so they compared penalty minutes before and after the switch; consistent with the hypothesis, penalties did increase for both teams. They also looked at the penalty minutes of a third team that had changed from a nonblack color to another nonblack color and found no change in penalty minutes. Note that none of these studies used the experimental method. In an experiment to test the hypothesis that people perceive black uniform teams as being more aggressive, students watched videos of two plays from a staged football game in which the defense was wearing either black or white. Both plays included an aggressive act by the defense. On these plays, the students penalized the black-uniform team more than the nonblack-uniform team. In a final experiment to see whether being on a black-uniform team would increase aggressiveness, people were brought into the lab in groups of three. The groups were told they were a "team" that would be competing with another team. All members of the team were given either white or black clothing to wear for the competition; they were then asked to choose the games they would like to have for the competition. Some of the games were aggressive ("dart gun duel") and some were not ("putting contest"). As you might expect by now, the black-uniform teams chose more aggressive games.

The important point here is that no study is a perfect test of a hypothesis. However, when multiple studies using multiple methods all lead to the same or a similar conclusion—as has been the case with "black is bad" (see Alter et al., 2016)—our confidence in the findings and our understanding of the phenomenon are greatly increased.

EVALUATING RESEARCH: SUMMARY OF THE FOUR VALIDITIES

The key concept of validity was introduced at the outset of this chapter. *Validity* refers to the idea that, given everything that is known, a conclusion is reasonably accurate. Research can be described and evaluated in terms of four types of validity:

- **Construct validity:** the extent to which the measurement or manipulation of a variable accurately represents the theoretical variable being studied.

- **Internal validity:** the accuracy of conclusions drawn about cause and effect.

- **External validity:** the extent to which findings of a study can be accurately generalized to other populations and settings.

- **Statistical validity:** the accuracy or the statistical conclusions drawn from the results of a research investigation (sometimes called *statistical conclusion validity*).

Each gives us a different perspective on any particular research investigation, and every research study should be evaluated on these aspects of validity.

At this point, you may be wondering how researchers select a methodology to study a problem. A variety of methods are available, each with advantages and disadvantages. Researchers select the method that best enables them to address the questions they wish to answer. No method is inherently superior to another. Rather, the choice of method is made after considering the problem under investigation, ethics, cost and time constraints, and issues associated with the three types of validity. In the remainder of this book, many specific methods will be discussed, all of which are useful under different circumstances. In fact, all are necessary to understand the wide variety of behaviors that are of interest to behavioral scientists. Complete understanding of any problem or issue requires research using a variety of methodological approaches.

ILLUSTRATIVE ARTICLE: STUDYING BEHAVIOR

Many people have had the experience of anticipating something bad happening to them: "I'm not going to get that job" or "I'm going to fail this test" or "She'll laugh in my face if I ask her out!" Do you think that anticipating a negative outcome means that a person is less distressed when a negative outcome occurs? That is, is it better to think "I'm going to fail" if, indeed, you may fail?

In a study published by Golub et al. (2009), two experiments and a field study were conducted in an effort to determine whether this negative expectation is a good thing or a bad thing.

In the two laboratory studies, participants were asked to complete a personality assessment and were then led to have either positive, negative, or no expectations about the results. Participants' affective (emotional) state was assessed prior to—and directly after—hearing a negative (in the case of study 1a) or positive (in the case of study 1b) outcome. In the field study, participants were under-graduate introductory psychology students who were asked about their expectations of their per-formance in an upcoming exam. Then, a day after the exam, positive and negative emotions were assessed. Taken together, the results of these three studies suggest that anticipating bad outcomes may be an ineffective path to positive emotion.

First, acquire and read the article (available at **http://coglab.wjh.harvard.edu/~dtg/GOLUB%20GIL BERT%20WILSON%20(2009).pdf**):

> Golub, S. A., Gilbert, D. T., & Wilson, T. D. (2009). Anticipating one's troubles: The costs and benefits of negative expectations. *Emotion, 9*, 227–281. https://doi.org/10.1037/a0014716

Then, after reading the article, consider the following:

1. For each of the studies, how did Golub et al. (2009) operationally define the *positive expectations*? How did they operationally define *affect*?
2. In experiments 1a and 1b, what were the independent variable(s)? What were the dependent variable(s)?
3. This article includes three different studies. In this case, what are the advantages to answering the research question using multiple methods?
4. On what basis did the authors conclude, "Our studies suggest that the affective benefits of negative expectations may be more elusive than their costs" (p. 280)?
5. Evaluate the external validity of the two experiments and one field study that Golub et al. (2009) conducted.
6. How good was the internal validity?

CRITICAL THINKING: BEING A SKILLED CONSUMER OF RESEARCH

1. The dictionary definition of shy is "being reserved or having or showing nervousness or timidity in the company of other people." Create three different operational definitions of shyness and provide a critique of each one. Example: An operational definition of shyness could be the number of new people that a person reports meeting in a given day. Critique: What if an outgoing person has a job that requires them to meet very few people? They might (incorrectly) be considered shy by this operational definition.

2. People who identify as male and people who identify as female might differ in their approaches to helping others. For example, males may be more likely to help a person having car trouble, and females may be more likely to bring dinner to a sick friend. Develop two operational definitions for the concept of helping behavior, one that emphasizes the "male style" and the other the "female style." How might the use of one or the other lead to different conclusions from experimental results regarding who helps more, males or females? What does this tell you about the importance of operational definitions?

3. Consider the hypothesis that stress at work causes family conflict at home.

    a. What type of relationship is proposed (e.g., positive linear, negative linear)?

    b. Graph the proposed relationship.

    c. Identify the independent variable and the dependent variable in the statement of the hypothesis.

    d. How might you investigate the hypothesis using the experimental method?

    e. How might you investigate the hypothesis using the nonexperimental method (recognizing the problems of determining cause and effect)?

    f. What factors might you consider in deciding whether to use the experimental or nonexperimental method to study the relationship between work stress and family conflict?

4. You observe that classmates who get good grades tend to sit toward the front of the classroom, and those who receive poorer grades tend to sit toward the back. What are three possible cause-and-effect relationships for this nonexperimental observation?

5. Identify the independent and dependent variables in the following descriptions of experiments:

    a. Students watched a cartoon either alone or with others and then rated how funny they found the cartoon to be.

    b. A comprehension test was given to students after they had studied textbook material either in silence or with the television turned on.

    c. Some elementary school teachers were told that a child's parents were college graduates, and other teachers were told that the child's parents had not finished high school; they then rated the child's academic potential.

    d. Workers at a company were assigned to one of two conditions: One group completed a stress management training program; another group of workers did not participate in the training. The number of sick days taken by these workers was examined for the two subsequent months.

6. A few years ago, newspapers reported a finding that Americans who have a glass of wine a day are healthier than those who have no wine (or who have a lot of wine or other alcohol). What are some plausible alternative explanations for this finding? That is, what variables other than wine could explain the finding? (Hint: What sorts of people in the United States are most likely to have a glass of wine with dinner?)

7. The limitations of nonexperimental research were dramatically brought to the attention of the public by the results of an experiment on the effects of postmenopausal hormone replacement therapy (part of a larger study known as the Women's Health Initiative). An experiment is called a *clinical trial* in medical research. In the clinical trial, participants were randomly assigned to receive either the hormone replacement therapy or a placebo (no hormones). Hormone replacement therapy consisted of estrogen plus progestin. In 2002 the investigators concluded that women taking the hormone replacement therapy had a higher incidence of heart disease than did women in the placebo (no hormone) condition. At that point, they stopped the experiment and informed both the participants and the public that they should talk with their physicians about the advisability of this therapy. The finding dramatically contrasted with the

results of nonexperimental research in which women taking hormones had a lower incidence of heart disease; in these studies, researchers compared women who were already taking the hormones with women not taking hormones. Why do you think the results were different with the experimental research and the nonexperimental research?

Check Your Learning: Practice Exercises

Practice Exercise #1

Identifying Variables

Think of five different variables. Then, describe two operational definitions for each variable.

Here are two examples:

Variable: age

- **Operational Definition 1:** What is your age (in years)? _____
- **Operational Definition 2:** What is your age? Check one: _____ 25 or younger _____ 26 or older

Variable: happiness

- **Operational Definition 1:** Response to the question "How happy would you describe yourself" on a scale ranging from 1 (not at all happy) to 10 (very happy)
- **Operational Definition 2:** Count the number of positive and negative words in a 5-minute period after an interviewer asks a person to "tell me about yourself"

Practice Exercise #2

Identify the Type of Relationship

Read the following examples and identify the relationship by placing a check mark in the appropriate box.

	Positive	Negative	Curvilinear
1. Increased caloric intake is associated with increased body weight.			
2. As people gain experience speaking in public, their anxiety level decreases.			
3. Performance of basketball players increases as crowd noise increases from low to moderate levels, then decreases as crowd noise becomes extremely high.			
4. Increased partying behavior is associated with decreased grades.			
5. A decrease in the number of headaches is associated with a decrease in the amount of sugar consumed per day.			
6. Amount of education is associated with higher income.			
7. Liking for a song increases the more you hear it, but then after a while, you like it less and less.			
8. The more you exercise your puppy, the less your puppy chews on things in your house.			

Practice Exercise #3

Types of Variables

Read the following and answer the questions below. Researchers conducted a study to examine the effect of music on exam scores. They predicted that scores would be higher when students listened to soft music compared to nomusic during the exam. One hundred (50 male, 50 female) students were randomly assigned to either the soft-music or no-music conditions. Students in the soft-music condition listened to music using headphones during the exam. Students in the no-music condition completed the exam as they normally would. As predicted, exam scores were significantly higher in the soft-music condition compared to the no-music condition.

1. The independent variable is : _____
2. The dependent variable is : _____
3. A potential confounding variable is : _____

(Some answers are provided at the end of this chapter.)

CHAPTER REVIEW

Review Questions

1. What is a variable?
2. Define "operational definition" of a variable.
3. Distinguish among positive linear, negative linear, and curvilinear relationships.
4. What is the difference between the nonexperimental method and the experimental method?
5. What is the difference between an independent variable and a dependent variable?
6. Distinguish between laboratory experiments and field experiments.
7. What is meant by the problem of direction of cause and effect and the third-variable problem?
8. How do direct experimental control and randomization influence the possible effects of extraneous variables?
9. What are some reasons for using the nonexperimental method to study relationships between variables?

Study Terms

Alternative explanation

Confounding variable

Construct validity

Correlation coefficient

Covariation

Curvilinear relationship

Dependent variable

Experimental control

Experimental method

External validity

Extraneous variable

Field experiment

Independent variable

Internal validity

Negative linear relationship

Nonexperimental method (correlational method)

Operational definition

Participant (subject) variable

Positive linear relationship

Randomization

Statistical validity

Temporal precedence

Third variable

Third-variable problem

Variable

Check Your Learning: Answers

Practice Exercise #2

1. positive; 2. negative; 3. curvilinear; 4. negative; 5. positive; 6. positive; 7. curvilinear; 8. negative

Practice Exercise #3

1. Independent variable = music condition
2. Dependent variable = exam score
3. Potential confounding variables = use of headphones (headphones were worn only by participants in the soft-music condition)

5 Measurement Concepts

Dennis Wise/Photodisc/Getty Images

LEARNING OBJECTIVES

- Define *reliability* of a measure of behavior and describe the difference between test-retest, internal consistency, and interrater reliability.
- Define *construct validity* and discuss ways to establish construct validity.
- Distinguish between face validity, content validity, predictive validity, concurrent validity, convergent validity, and discriminant validity.
- Describe the problem of reactivity of a measure of behavior and discuss ways to minimize reactivity.
- Describe the properties of the four scales of measurement: nominal, ordinal, interval, and ratio.

We learn about behavior through careful measurement. Behavior can be measured in many ways. Perhaps the most common measurement strategy is to ask people to tell you about themselves: How would you rate your overall happiness? How many times have you argued with your partner in the past week? How fair was the professor's grading system? Of course, you can also directly observe behaviors. You can count the number of errors someone makes on a task, whether or not people who you approach in a shopping mall give you change for a dollar, or how many times a person smiled during an interview. Physiological and neurological responses can be measured as well. How much did the subject's heart rate change while working on the problems? Did the subject's muscle tension increase during the interview? Did the part of the brain involved in emotion "light up" on the fMRI? There is an endless supply of fascinating variables that can be studied. We will describe many methods of measuring variables throughout this book. In this chapter we explore the technical aspects of measurement. We need to consider reliability, validity, and reactivity of measures. We will also consider scales of measurement.

RELIABILITY OF MEASURES

Reliability refers to the consistency or stability of a measure. Your everyday definition of reliability is quite close to the scientific definition. For example, you might say that Professor Fuentes is "reliable" because she begins class exactly at 10 a.m. each day; in contrast, Professor Fine might be called "unreliable" because, although she sometimes begins class exactly on the hour, on any given day she may appear anytime between 10:00 a.m. and 10:20 a.m.

Similarly, a reliable measure of a psychological variable like intelligence will yield the same result each time you administer the intelligence test to the same person. The test would be unreliable if it measured the same person as average 1 week, low the next, and bright the next. Put simply, a reliable measure does not fluctuate from one reading to the next. If the measure does fluctuate, there is error in the measurement device; it is, to some extent, unreliable.

An Intelligence Quotient (IQ) test is a measure of intelligence. Another way to think about the reliability of a measure is to think about the concepts of true score and measurement error. A **true score** is someone's real, "true" value on a given variable: true intelligence, true reaction time, true happiness, true memory. If we consider intelligence, a person's true score is the correct answer to the question: How smart are they? A true score cannot be directly measured; we cannot know a person's true intelligence, we can only know their score on an IQ test. But IQ tests are not perfect measures of intelligence any more than the thermostat in your bedroom is a perfect measure of temperature. The difference between a true score and a measured score is **measurement error.** You can think of measurement error as the distance between an unobservable true state (the true score) and a measured (observed) score. Here, then, is the connection between true scores, measurement error, and reliability. An unreliable measure of intelligence contains considerable measurement error. Thus, it cannot reflect an individual's true intelligence. In contrast, a reliable measure of intelligence—one that contains little measurement error—will yield an identical (or nearly identical) intelligence score each time the same individual is measured. Another way to think about reliability is that reliability is measurement that is free from measurement error.

To further illustrate the concept of reliability, imagine that you know someone whose true score for intelligence is 100. Now suppose that you administer an unreliable intelligence test to this person each week for a year. After the year, you calculate the person's average score on the test based on the 52 scores you obtained. Now suppose that you test another friend who also has a true intelligence score of 100; however, this time you administer a highly reliable test. Again, you calculate the average score. What might your data look like? Typical data are shown in **Figure 1.** In each case, the average score is 100. However, scores on the unreliable test range from 85 to 115, whereas scores on the reliable test range from 97 to 103. The *measurement error* in the unreliable test is revealed in the greater variability shown by the person to whom you administered the unreliable test.

When conducting research, you can measure each person only once; you cannot give the measure 50 or 100 times to discover a true score. Thus, it is very important that you use a reliable measure. Your single administration of the measure should closely reflect the person's true score.

The importance of reliability is obvious. An unreliable measure of length would be useless in building a table; an unreliable measure of a variable such as intelligence is equally useless in studying that variable. Researchers cannot use unreliable measures to systematically study variables or the relationships among variables. Trying to study behavior using unreliable measures is a waste of time because the results will be unstable and unable to be replicated.

Reliability is most likely to be achieved when researchers use careful measurement procedures. In some research areas this might involve carefully training observers to record behavior; in other areas it might mean paying close attention to the way questions are phrased or the way recording electrodes are placed on the body to measure physiological reactions. In many areas, reliability can be increased by making multiple measures. This is most commonly seen when assessing personality traits and cognitive abilities. A personality measure, for example, will typically have 10 or more questions (called *items*) designed to assess a trait. Responses on the items are then combined for a total score. Reliability is increased when the number of items increases.

How can we assess reliability? We cannot directly observe the true score and error components of an actual score on the measure. However, we can assess the statistical stability of measures using correlation coefficients. A correlation coefficient is a number that tells us how strongly two variables are related to each other. There are several ways of calculating correlation coefficients; the correlation coefficient most commonly referred to when discussing reliability is the **Pearson product-moment correlation coefficient.** The Pearson correlation coefficient (symbolized as r) can range from 0.00 to +1.00 and 0.00 to −1.00. A correlation of 0.00 tells us that the two variables are not related at all. The closer a correlation is to 1.00, either +1.00 or −1.00, the stronger is the relationship. The positive and negative signs provide information about the direction of the relationship. When the correlation coefficient is positive (a plus sign), there is a positive linear relationship—high scores on one variable are associated with high scores on the second variable. A negative linear relationship is indicated by a minus sign—high scores on one variable are associated with low scores on

FIGURE 1   Comparing data of a reliable and unreliable measure

the second variable. The Pearson correlation coefficient is discussed further in the chapter **"Understanding Research Results: Description and Correlation."**

To assess the reliability of a measure, we will need to obtain at least two scores on the measure from many individuals. If the measure is reliable, the two scores should be very similar; a Pearson correlation coefficient that describes the relationship between the scores should be a high positive correlation. When you read about reliability, the correlation will usually be called a *reliability coefficient.* Let's examine specific methods of assessing reliability.

Test-Retest Reliability

Test-retest reliability is assessed by measuring the same individuals at two points in time. For example, the reliability of a test of intelligence could be assessed by giving the measure to a group of people on one day and again a week later. We would then have two scores for each person, and a correlation coefficient could be calculated to determine the relationship between the first test score and the retest score. Recall that high reliability is indicated by a high correlation coefficient showing that the two scores are very similar. If many people have very similar scores, we conclude that the measure reflects true scores rather than measurement error. It is difficult to say how high the correlation should be before we accept the measure as reliable, but for most measures the reliability coefficient should probably be at least .80.

Given that test-retest reliability requires administering the same test twice, the correlation might be artificially high because the individuals remember how they responded the first time. **Alternate forms reliability** is sometimes used to avoid this problem; it requires administering two different forms of the same test to the same individuals at two points in time. A drawback to this procedure is that creating a second equivalent measure may require considerable time and effort.

Intelligence is a variable that can be expected to stay relatively constant over time; thus, we expect the test-retest reliability for intelligence to be very high. However, some variables may be expected to change from one test period to the next. For example, a mood scale designed to measure a person's current mood state is a measure that might easily change from one test period to another, and so test-retest reliability might not be appropriate. On a more practical level, obtaining two measures from the same people at two points in time may sometimes be difficult. To address these issues, researchers have devised methods to assess reliability without two separate assessments.

Internal Consistency Reliability

It is possible to assess reliability by measuring individuals at only one point in time. We can do this because most psychological measures are made up of a number of different questions, called *items*. An intelligence test might have 100 items, a measure of extraversion might have 15 items, or a multiple-choice examination in a class might have 50 items. A person's test score would be based on the total of his or her responses on all items. In the class, an exam consists of a number of questions about the material, and the total score is the number of correct answers. An extraversion measure might ask people to agree or disagree with items such as "I enjoy lively parties." An individual's extraversion score is obtained by finding the total number of such items that are endorsed. Recall that reliability increases with increasing numbers of items.

Internal consistency reliability is the assessment of reliability using responses at only one point in time. Because all items measure the same variable, they should yield similar or consistent results.

One indicator of internal consistency is **split-half reliability;** this is the correlation of the total score on one half of the test with the total score on the other half. The two halves are created by randomly dividing the items into two parts. The actual calculation of a split-half reliability coefficient is a bit more complicated because the final measure will include items from both halves. Thus, the combined measure will have more items and will be more reliable than either half by itself. This fact must be taken into account when calculating the reliability coefficient; the corrected reliability is termed the *Spearman-Brown split-half reliability coefficient.*

Split-half reliability is relatively straightforward and easy to calculate, even without a computer. One drawback is that it is based on only one of many possible ways of dividing the measure into halves. The most commonly used indicator of reliability based on internal consistency, called **Cronbach's alpha,** provides us with the average of all possible split-half reliability coefficients. To actually perform the calculation, scores on each item are correlated with scores on every other item. A large number of correlation coefficients are produced; you would only want to do this with a computer! The value of Cronbach's alpha is based on the average of all the inter-item correlation coefficients and the number of items in the measure. Again, you should note that more items will be associated with higher reliability.

It is also possible to examine the correlation of each item score with the total score based on all items. Such **item-total correlations** are very informative because they provide information about each individual item. Items that do not correlate with the total score on the measure are actually measuring a different variable; they can be eliminated to increase internal consistency reliability. This information is also useful when it is necessary to construct a brief version of a measure. Even though reliability increases with longer measures, a shorter version can be more convenient to administer and still retain acceptable reliability.

Interrater Reliability

In some research, raters observe behaviors and make ratings or judgments. To do this, a rater uses instructions for making judgments about the behaviors—for example, by rating whether a child's behavior on a playground is aggressive and how aggressive the behavior is. You could have one rater make judgments about aggression, but the single observations of one rater might be unreliable. That is, one rater's scores may contain a lot of measurement error. The solution to this problem is to use at least two raters who observe the same behavior. **Interrater reliability** is the extent to which raters agree in their observations. Thus, if two raters are judging whether behaviors are aggressive, high interrater reliability is obtained when most of the observations result in the same judgment. A commonly used indicator of interrater reliability is called *Cohen's kappa.*

The methods of assessing reliability are summarized in **Figure 2**.

Test-Retest Reliability

- A measure is taken two times. The correlation of a score at time 1 with the score at time 2 represents *test-retest reliability.* The correlation between two versions of a measure is called *alternative forms reliability.*

Internal Consistency Reliability

- *Cronbach's Alpha:* Correlation of each item on the measure with every other item on the measure is the Cronbach's Alpha reliability coefficient.
- *Split-Half Reliability:* The correlation of total score on one half of a measure with the total score on the other half of the measure presents split-half reliability.

Interrater Reliability

- Evidence for reliability is present when multiple raters agree in their observations of the same thing. *Cohen's kappa* is a commonly used indicator of *interrater reliability*.

FIGURE 2   Three strategies for assessing reliability

Reliability and Accuracy of Measures

Reliability is clearly important when researchers develop measures of behavior. But reliability is not the only characteristic of a measure or the only thing that researchers worry about. Reliability tells us about measurement error, but it does not tell us whether we have a good measure of the variable of interest. To use a silly example, suppose you want to measure intelligence and the measure you develop looks remarkably like the device that is used to measure shoe size at your local shoe store. You ask your best friend to place one foot in the device, and you use the gauge to measure their intelligence. Numbers on the device provide a scale of intelligence so you can immediately assess a person's intelligence level. Will these numbers result in a reliable measure of intelligence? The answer is that they will! Consider what a test-retest reliability coefficient would be. If you administer the "foot intelligence scale" on Monday, it will be almost the same the following Monday; the test-retest reliability is high. But is this an accurate measure of intelligence? Obviously, the scores have nothing to do with intelligence; just because the device is labeled an intelligence test does not mean that it is a *good* measure of intelligence or that it is a measure of intelligence at all.

Let's consider a less silly example. Suppose your neighborhood gas station pump puts the same amount of gas in your car every time you purchase a gallon (or liter) of fuel; the gas pump gauge is reliable. However, the issue of accuracy is still open. The only way you can know about the accuracy of the pump is to compare the gallon (or liter) you receive with some standard measure. In fact, states have inspectors responsible for comparing an exact gallon measure with the amount that the pump says is a gallon. A pump with a gauge that does not deliver what it says it delivers must be repaired or replaced. This difference between the reliability and accuracy of measures leads us to a consideration of the validity of measures.

CONSTRUCT VALIDITY OF MEASURES

If something is valid, it is "true" in the sense that it is supported by available evidence. The amount of gasoline that the gauge indicates should match some standard measure of liquid volume; a measure of a personality characteristic such as shyness should be an accurate indicator of that trait. **Construct validity** refers to the adequacy of the operational definition of variables. To what extent does the operational definition of a variable actually reflect the true theoretical meaning of the variable? In terms of measurement, construct validity is a question of whether the measure that is employed actually measures the construct it is intended to measure. Applicants for some jobs are required to take a Clerical Ability Test; this measure is supposed to predict an individual's clerical ability. The validity of such a test is determined by whether it actually does measure this ability. A measure of shyness is an operational definition of the shyness variable; the validity of this measure is determined by whether it does measure this construct.

How do we know that a measure is valid? Evidence for construct validity takes many forms.

Indicators of Construct Validity

Face Validity

The simplest way to argue that a measure is valid is to suggest that the measure appears to accurately assess the intended variable. This is called **face validity**—the evidence for validity is that the measure appears "on the face of it" to measure what it is supposed to measure. Face validity is not very sophisticated; it involves only a judgment of whether, given the theoretical definition of the variable, the content of the measure appears to actually measure the variable. That is, do the procedures used to measure the variable appear to be an accurate operational definition of the theoretical variable? Thus, a measure of a variable such as shyness will usually appear to measure that variable. A measure of shyness called the Shy Q (Bortnik et al., 2002) includes items such as "I often feel insecure in social situations" but does not include an item such as "I learned to ride a bicycle at an early age"—the first item appears to be more closely related to shyness than does the second one. Note that the assessment of validity here is a very subjective, intuitive process. A way to improve the process somewhat is to systematically seek out experts in the field to make the face validity determination.

In either case, face validity is not sufficient to conclude that a measure is in fact valid. Appearance is not a very good indicator of accuracy. Some very poor measures may have face validity; for example, most personality measures that appear in popular magazines typically have several questions that look reasonable but often do not tell you anything meaningful. The interpretations of the scores may make fun reading, but there is no empirical evidence to support the conclusions that are drawn in the article. In addition, many good measures of variables do not have obvious face validity. For example, is it obvious that rapid eye movement during sleep is a measure of dreaming?

Content Validity

Content validity is based on comparing the content of the measure with the universe of content that defines the construct. For example, a measure of depression would have content that links to each of the symptoms that define the depression construct. Or consider a measure of "knowledge of psychology" that could be administered to graduating seniors at your college. In this case, the faculty would need to define a universe of content that constitutes this knowledge. The measure would then have to reflect that universe. Thus, if classical conditioning is one of the content areas that defines knowledge of psychology (it is!), then questions relating to this topic will be included in the measure.

Both face validity and content validity focus on assessing whether the content of a measure reflects the meaning of the construct being measured. Other indicators of validity rely on research that examines how scores on a measure relate to other measures of behavior. In validity research, the behavior is termed a *criterion*. These validity indicators are predictive validity, concurrent validity, convergent validity, and discriminant validity.

Predictive Validity

Research that uses a measure to predict some future behavior is using **predictive validity.** Thus, with predictive validity, the criterion measure is based on future behavior or outcomes. Predictive validity is clearly important when studying measures that are designed to improve our ability to make predictions. A Clerical Ability Test is intended to provide a fast way to predict future performance in a clerical position. Similarly, many college students take the Graduate Record Exam (GRE), which was developed to predict success in graduate programs, or the Law School Admissions Test (LSAT), developed to predict success in law school. The construct validity of such measures is demonstrated when scores on the measure predict the future behaviors. For example, predictive validity of the LSAT is demonstrated when research shows that people who score high on the test do better in law school than people who score low on the test (i.e., when there is a positive relationship between the test score and grades in law school). The measure can be used to advise people on whether they are likely to succeed in law school or to select applicants for law school admission.

Concurrent Validity

Concurrent validity is demonstrated by research that examines the relationship between the measure and a criterion behavior at the same time (concurrently). Research using the concurrent validity approach can take many forms. A common method is to study whether two or more groups of people differ on the measure in expected ways. Suppose you have a measure of shyness. Your theory of shyness might lead you to expect that salespeople whose job requires making cold calls to potential customers would score lower on the shyness measure than salespeople in positions in which potential customers must make the effort to contact the company themselves.

Another approach to concurrent validity is to study how people who score either low or high on the measure behave in different situations. For example, you could compare a group of people who score high on the shyness score with another group consisting of low scorers. People in each group might be asked to describe themselves to a stranger while you measure their level of anxiety. Here you would expect that the people who score high on the shyness scale would exhibit higher amounts of anxiety.

Convergent Validity

Any given measure is a particular operational definition of the variable being measured. Often there will be other operational definitions—other measures—of the same or similar constructs. **Convergent validity** is the extent to which scores on the measure in question are related to scores on other measures of the same construct or similar constructs. Measures of similar constructs should converge—for example, one measure of shyness should correlate highly with another shyness measure or a measure of a similar construct such as social anxiety. In actual research on a shyness scale, the convergent validity of a measure of shyness called the Shy Q was demonstrated by showing that Shy Q scores were highly correlated (.77) with a scale called the Fear of Negative Evaluation (Bortnik et al., 2002). Because the constructs of shyness and fear of negative evaluation have many similarities (such fear is thought to be a component of shyness), the high correlation is expected and increases our confidence in the construct validity of the Shy Q measure.

Discriminant Validity

When the measure is *not* related to variables with which it should not be related, **discriminant validity** is demonstrated. The measure should discriminate between the construct being measured and other unrelated constructs. In other words, evidence for construct validity can be found when a measure is unrelated to other variables and constructs that it should be unrelated to. In research on the discriminant validity of their shyness measure, Bortnik et al. (2002) found no relationship between Shy Q scores and several conceptually unrelated interpersonal values such as being forceful with others.

Ways in which we can assess validity are summarized in **Table 1.**

TABLE 1 Indicators of Construct Validity of a Measure

Validity	Definition	Example
Face validity	The content of the measure appears to reflect the construct being measured.	If the new measure of depression includes items like "I feel sad" or "I feel down" or "I cry a lot," this would be evidence that the measure has face validity.
Content validity	The content of the measure is linked to the universe of content that defines the construct.	Depression is defined by a mood and by cognitive and physiological symptoms. If the new measure of depression has content validity, it will include items from each of these domains.
Predictive validity	Scores on the measure predict behavior on a criterion measured at a future time.	If the measure of depression predicts future diagnosis of depression, this is evidence that the measure has predictive validity.
Concurrent validity	Scores on the measure are related to a criterion measured at the same time (concurrently).	If two groups of participants were given the measures, and they differed in predictable ways (e.g., if those in therapy for depression scored higher than those in therapy for an anxiety disorder), then this would be evidence for concurrent validity.
Convergent validity	Scores on the measure are related to other measures of the same construct.	If scores from the new measure, collected at the same time as other measures of depression (e.g., Beck Depression Inventory or Duke Anxiety-Depression Scale), were related to scores from those other measures, then it could be said to have evidence for convergent validity.
Discriminant validity	Scores on the measure are not related to other measures that are theoretically different.	If the new measure, collected at the same time as other measures of anxiety (e.g., state/trait anxiety), was unrelated to those measures, then it could be said to have evidence for discriminant validity because it would indicate that what was being measured was *not* anxiety.

> Now do the **Check Your Learning:** Practice Exercise #1 to help solidify your understanding of indicators of construct validity.

REACTIVITY OF MEASURES

A potential problem when measuring behavior is **reactivity.** A measure is said to be reactive if awareness of being measured changes an individual's behavior. A reactive measure tells what the person is like when he or she is aware of being observed, but it does not tell how the person would behave under natural circumstances. Simply having various devices such as electrodes and blood pressure cuffs attached to your body may change the physiological responses being recorded. Knowing that a researcher is observing you or recording your behavior on tape might change the way you behave. Measures of behavior vary in terms of their potential reactivity. There are also ways to minimize reactivity, such as allowing time for individuals to become used to the presence of the observer or the recording equipment.

A book by Webb et al. (1981) has drawn attention to a number of measures that are called *nonreactive* or *unobtrusive.* Many such measures involve clever ways of indirectly recording a variable. For example, an unobtrusive measure of preferences for paintings in an art museum is the frequency with which floor tiles near each painting must be replaced—the most popular paintings are the ones with the most tile wear. Levine (1990) measured the pace of life in cities, using indirect measures such as the accuracy of bank clocks and the speed of processing standard requests at post offices. Some of the measures described by Webb et al (1981) are simply humorous. For instance, in 1872 Sir Francis Galton studied the efficacy of prayer in producing long life. Galton wondered whether British royalty, who were frequently the recipients of prayers by the populace, lived longer than other people. He checked death records and found that members of royal families actually led shorter lives than other people, such as "men of literature and science." The book by Webb and his colleagues is a rich source of such nonreactive measures. More importantly, it draws attention to the problem of reactivity and sensitizes researchers to the need to reduce reactivity whenever possible. We will return to this issue at several points in this book.

VARIABLES AND MEASUREMENT SCALES

Every variable that is studied must be operationally defined. The operational definition is the specific method used to manipulate or measure the variable. There must be at least two values or levels of the variable. The values may be quantitatively different or they may reflect categorical differences. In actuality, the world is a bit more complex. The levels can be conceptualized as a scale that uses one of four kinds of measurement scales: nominal, ordinal, interval, and ratio.

Nominal Scales

Nominal scales have no numerical or quantitative properties. Instead, categories or groups simply differ from one another (sometimes nominal variables are called "categorical" variables). An obvious example is the variable of handedness. A person is classified as either left-handed, right-handed, or ambidextrous. Being right-handed does not imply a greater amount of "handedness" than being left-handed or ambidextrous; the three levels are merely different. This is called a nominal scale because we simply assign names to different categories. Another example is the classification of undergraduates according to major. A psychology major would not be entitled to a higher number than a history major, for instance. Even if you were to assign numbers to the different categories, the numbers would be meaningless, except for identification.

In an experiment, the independent variable is often a nominal or categorical variable. For example, Hölzel et al (2011) studied the effect of meditation on brain structures using magnetic resonant imaging (MRI). They found that after participants underwent an 8-week mindfulness meditation-based stress-reduction program, there was an increase in the density of gray matter in specific areas of their brains, as compared with other participants who did not take part in the program. The independent variable in this case (participating in the program or not) was clearly nominal because the two levels are merely different; participants either did, or did not, participate in the stress reduction program.

Ordinal Scales

Ordinal scales allow us to rank order the levels of the variable being studied. Instead of having categories that are simply different, as in a nominal scale, the categories can be ordered from first to last. Letter grades are a good example of an ordinal scale. Another example of an ordinal scale is provided by the movie rating system used on a movie review website, where movies are given one to four stars, based on these descriptions:

★ ★ ★ ★	Great! New or old, a classic
★ ★ ★	Good! First rate
★ ★	Flawed, but may have some good moments
★	Poor! Desperation time

The rating system is not a nominal scale, because the number of stars is meaningful in terms of a continuum of quality. However, the stars allow us only to rank order the movies. A four-star movie is better than a three-star movie; a three-star movie is better than a two-star movie; and so on. Although we have this quantitative information about the movies, we cannot say that the difference between a one-star and a two-star movie is always the same or that it is equal to the difference between a two-star and a three-star movie. No particular value is attached to the intervals between the numbers used in the rating scale.

Interval and Ratio Scales

One problem with ordinal scales is that while they provide rank-ordered categories, they do not provide any information about the distance between the categories. All four-star movies are equally good, all one-star movies are equally bad. In an **interval scale,** the difference between the numbers on the scale is meaningful. Specifically, the intervals between the numbers are equal in size. The difference between 1 and 2 on the scale, for example, is the same as the difference between 2 and 3. Interval scales generally have five or more quantitative levels.

A household thermometer (Fahrenheit or Celsius) measures temperature on an interval scale. The difference in temperature between 40° and 50° is equal to the difference between 70° and 80°. However, there is no absolute zero on the scale that would indicate the *absence* of temperature. The zero on an interval scale is only an arbitrary reference point. (Note that the zero point on the Celsius scale was chosen to reflect the temperature at which water freezes; this is the same as 32° on the Fahrenheit scale. The zero on both scales is arbitrary, and there are even negative numbers on the scale.) Without an absolute zero point on interval scales, we cannot form ratios of the numbers. That is, we cannot say that one number on the scale represents twice as much (or three times as much, and so forth) temperature as another number. You cannot say, for example, that 60° is twice as warm as 30°.

An example of an interval scale in the behavioral sciences might be a personality measure of a trait such as extraversion. If the measurement is an interval scale, we cannot validly claim that "the person who scored 20 is twice as extraverted as the person who scored 10," because there is no absolute zero point that indicates an absence of the trait being measured.

Ratio scales do have an absolute zero point that indicates the absence of the variable being measured. Examples include many physical measures, such as length, weight, or time. With a ratio scale, it is possible to make true claims such as "a person who weighs 220 pounds weighs twice as much as a person who weighs 110 pounds" or "participants in the experimental group responded twice as fast as participants in the control group."

Ratio scales are used in the behavioral sciences when variables that involve physical measures are being studied—particularly time measures such as reaction time, rate of responding, and duration of response. However, many variables in the behavioral sciences are less precise and therefore use nominal, ordinal, or interval scale measures. It should also be noted that the statistical tests for interval and ratio scales are the same. **Table 2** summarizes the four kinds of measurement scales.

TABLE 2   Scales of measurement

Scale	Description	Examples	Distinction
Nominal	• Categories with no numeric scales	• Lefty/righty • Eye color • College major	• Impossible to define any quantitative values and/or differences between/across categories
Ordinal	• Rank ordering Numeric values limited	• Two-, three-, and four-star restaurants • Ranking TV programs by popularity	• Intervals between items not known
Interval	• Numeric properties are literal • Assume equal interval between values	• A measure of intelligence • Aptitude test score • Temperature (Fahrenheit or Celsius)	• No true zero

Scale	Description	Examples	Distinction
Ratio	• Zero indicates absence of variable measured	• Reaction time • Age • Frequencies of behaviors	• Can form ratios (someone weighs twice as much as another person)

The Importance of the Measurement Scales

When you read about the operational definitions of variables, you will recognize the levels of the variable in terms of these types of scales. The conclusions one draws about the meaning of a particular score on a variable depend on which type of scale was used. With interval and ratio scales, you can make quantitative distinctions that allow you to talk about amounts of the variable. With nominal scales, there is no quantitative information. To illustrate, suppose that after reading a review of the research on math anxiety by Chang and Beilock (2016), you decide to do your own research on math anxiety and performance on a statistics test. For your study, you will need a measure of math anxiety. You might ask participants to report how anxious they are about math. You could use a nominal scale such as:

_____ Not Anxious About Math   _____ Anxious About Math

These scale values allow participants to state whether they are anxious about math, but does not allow you to know about the amount of anxiety. As an alternative, you could use a scale that asks participants to rate their anxiety when thinking about doing math problems:

Very Anxious ___ ___ ___ ___ ___ Not at All Anxious

This rating scale provides you with quantitative information about anxiety levels because you can assign numeric values to each of the response options on the scale; in this case, the values would range from 1 to 5.

The scale that is used also determines the types of statistics that are appropriate when the results of a study are analyzed. For now, we do not need to worry about statistical analysis. However, we will return to this point in the chapter **"Understanding Research Results: Description and Correlation."**

Now do the **Check Your Learning:** Practice Exercise #2 to help solidify your understanding of scales of measurement.

We are now ready to consider methods for measuring behavior. A variety of observational methods are described in the chapter **"Observational Methods."** We focus on questionnaires and interviews in the chapter **"Asking People About Themselves: Survey Research."**

ILLUSTRATIVE ARTICLE: MEASUREMENT CONCEPTS

Every term, millions of students complete student evaluation of teaching (SET) forms in an effort to assess the quality and performance of their instructors. The specific measurement instrument can vary from campus to campus, but the overall goal is the same. Course evaluations are used to inform hiring decisions, promotion decisions, and classroom instruction decisions, and they are also used by individual instructors to improve the courses they teach. However, they are also biased against female instructors, who are evaluated more negatively than male instructors.

Peterson et al. (2019) were interested in reducing bias in SET ratings by using language intended to reduce that bias. Using four college classes with large enrollments, and two male instructors and two female instructors, students were randomly assigned the standard SET form or a form that had been modified to reduce bias. They found that students who completed a form with anti-bias language rated female instructors higher than students who were given the standard form; no differences were found among the male instructors.

For this exercise, acquire and read the following article (available at **https://doi.org/10.1371/journal.pone.0216241**):

> Peterson, D. A. M., Biederman, L. A., Andersen, D., Ditonto, T. M., & Roe, K. (2019). Mitigating gender bias in student evaluations of teaching. *PLOS ONE, 14*(5), e0216241. https://doi.org/10.1371/journal.pone.0216241

After reading the article, consider the following:

1. What was measured?
   a. The authors don't report any evidence for reliability or validity. How would you test their measure for reliability? How would you test it for validity?
   b. Do you think that SET measures teaching quality at all? That is, even if we are able to reduce bias, do you think that we are still measuring good teaching with instruments like the one that Peterson et al (2019) used?
2. How do they know that one thing caused another?
   a. A. We will explore various aspects of experimental methodology in other chapters. The key question is this: Can you think of any other explanation of their results?
3. To what or whom can we generalize the results?
   a. Do you think that their findings would be the same if they used courses in psychology? Or mathematics? Why or why not?
   b. Do you think that their findings would be generalizable to all college courses, including courses that are offered online? Why or why not?
4. Have other researchers found similar results?
   a. Are the findings of this study similar to the findings of other studies on the same topic?
5. What do you think would happen if this intervention were used widely at your college? Do you think that bias would be decreased? Why or why not?

CRITICAL THINKING: BEING A SKILLED CONSUMER OF RESEARCH

1. Take a personality test on the internet (you can find such tests by searching the internet). Based on the information provided, what can you conclude about the test's reliability, construct validity, and reactivity?

2. The "five-factor" or "Big 5" model of personality describes five fundamental personality traits: Extraversion, Agreeableness, Conscientiousness, Emotional stability (Neuroticism), and Openness to experience. You can assess yourself on the Big 5 using this link: **https://projects.fi vethirtyeight.com/personality-quiz/#personality**. For this exercise, choose one of the Big 5 factors and then:

    a. provide a definition,

    b. describe how you might measure the personality trait, and

    c. describe a method that you might use to assess construct validity.

3. Few concepts are more important to behavioral science—or to any science!—than measurement. Consider the following three broad categories of behavioral research and the ways in which measurement impacts what we understand. For each, consider: (1) How reliable would each of your strategies be? (2) How might the measurement strategy be biased (i.e., how valid would your strategy be)?

    a. **Emotional experience.** Few things are more important to humans than our emotions. Of course, emotions are difficult to measure. For this exercise, think of two ways you could measure a specific emotion. For example, you could measure grief by interviewing people at a funeral (consider the ethical implications of this strategy before you implement it!).

    b. **Parenting practice.** Parenting practices can be difficult to directly measure because when you are a parent you are always parenting! (Likewise, when you are a child, you are always being parented.) Think of two ways you could measure a specific parenting practice. For example, you could ask teenagers about their parents' parenting practices related to curfew.

    c. **Racism.** A microaggression is an act of casually degrading any marginalized group (Sue et al., 2007). For example, asking a co-worker who appears to be Asian or Latinx where they are from is a microaggression because it implies that they are "not from here." For this exercise, think of two ways you could measure occurrences of microaggressions in a workplace (for example, you could conduct face-to-face interviews with employees and ask them if they have observed microaggressions).

Check Your Learning: Practice Exercises

Practice Exercise #1

Dr. Shattuck has created a new measure of social anxiety for teens. The measure has 10 items that present social scenarios, such as "going to a party with 10 people, none of whom you know" and "having dinner with a friend and the friend's parents," and asks how "appealing" each scenario is on a scale of 1 (highly unappealing) to 10 (highly appealing). For each of the following, identify the correct type of validity.

1. Dr. Shattuck administers the new measure and the obsessive-compulsive inventory; the two measures are not highly related.
2. Dr. Shattuck administers the new measure and the Beck Anxiety Inventory to groups of research participants. Both measures are related.
3. Dr. Shattuck's new measure is predictive of a diagnosis of social anxiety disorder.
4. The new measure uses only ratings of "unappealing - appealing" as indicators of social anxiety about each situation. A suggestion was made to include other indicators (e.g., ratings of "not anxious - anxious").
5. After reviewing all of the questions in the new measure of social anxiety for teens, Dr. Roy, an expert on social anxiety, finds the measure valid.
6. Dr. Shattuck administers the new measure and the Wilson Social Anxiety Inventory to groups of research participants; the measures are related.

Practice Exercise #2

Scales of Measurement

For each of the following, identify whether a nominal, ordinal, interval, or ratio scale is being used:

1. The type of programming on each radio station in your city (e.g., KPSY plays jazz, KSOC is talk radio).
2. The number of hours you spent studying each day during the past week.
3. Ethnic group categories of people in a neighborhood.
4. Your friend's score on an intelligence test.
5. The temperatures in various U.S. cities that are listed in most U.S. newspapers.
6. The number of votes received by the Republican and Democratic candidates for Congress in your district in the last election.
7. The cell phone listed as third best on an online electronics review website.
8. The birth weights of babies who were born at Wilshire General Hospital last week.
9. Connecticut's listing as the number one team in a poll of sportswriters, with Kansas listed number two.
10. Yellow walls in your office and white walls in your boss's office.
11. The amount of the tip left after each meal at a restaurant during a 3-hour period.

(Answers are provided at the end of this chapter.)

CHAPTER REVIEW

Review Questions

1. What is meant by the reliability of a measure? Distinguish between true score and measurement error.
2. Describe the methods of determining the reliability of a measure.
3. Discuss the concept of construct validity. Distinguish among the indicators of construct validity.

4. Why isn't face validity sufficient to establish the validity of a measure?
5. What is a reactive measure?
6. Distinguish between nominal, ordinal, interval, and ratio scales.

Study Terms

Alternate forms reliability

Concurrent validity

Construct validity

Content validity

Convergent validity

Cronbach's alpha

Discriminant validity

Face validity

Internal consistency reliability

Interrater reliability

Interval scale

Item-total correlation

Measurement error

Nominal scale

Ordinal scale

Pearson product-moment correlation coefficient

Predictive validity

Ratio scale

Reactivity

Reliability

Split-half reliability

Test-retest reliability

True score

Check Your Learning: Answers

Practice Exercise #1

1. discriminant; 2. concurrent; 3. predictive; 4. content; 5. face; 6. convergent

Practice Exercise #2

1. nominal; 2. ratio; 3. nominal; 4. interval; 5. interval; 6. ratio; 7. ordinal; 8. ratio; 9. ordinal; 10. nominal; 11. ratio

Observational Methods

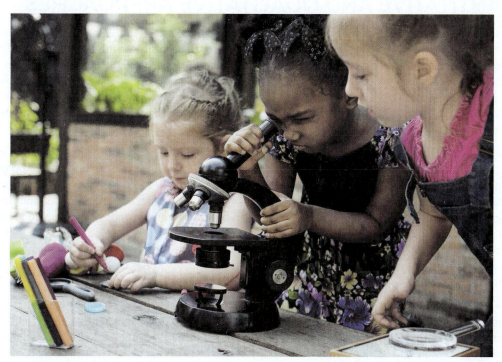

Rawpixel.com/Shutterstock

LEARNING OBJECTIVES

- Compare quantitative and qualitative methods of studying behavior.
- Describe naturalistic observation and discuss methodological issues such as participation and concealment.
- Describe systematic observation and discuss methodological issues such as the use of equipment, reactivity, reliability, and sampling.
- Describe the features of a case study.
- Describe archival research and the sources of archival data: statistical records, survey archives, and written records.

All scientific research requires careful observation. In this chapter we will explore a variety of observational methods, including naturalistic observation, systematic observation, case studies, and archival research. Because so much research involves surveys using questionnaires or interviews, we cover the topic of survey research in the chapter **"Asking People About Themselves: Survey Research."** Before we describe these methods in detail, it will be helpful to understand the distinction between quantitative and qualitative methods of describing behavior.

QUANTITATIVE AND QUALITATIVE APPROACHES

Research based on observational methods can be broadly classified as primarily quantitative or qualitative. Quantitative research tends to focus on specific behaviors that can be easily quantified (e.g., counted); qualitative research focuses on people behaving in natural settings and describing their world in their own words. Quantitative investigations generally include large samples; qualitative researchers generally emphasize collecting in-depth information on a relatively few individuals or within a very limited setting. The conclusions in quantitative research are based upon statistical analysis of data; the conclusions of qualitative research are based on interpretations drawn by the investigator.

To more concretely understand the distinction, imagine that you are interested in describing the ways in which their lives are affected when teenagers have a paying job. You might take a quantitative approach by developing a questionnaire that you would ask a sample of teenagers to complete. You could ask about the number of hours they work, the type of work they do, their levels of stress, their school grades, and their relationships with family and friends. After assigning numerical values to the responses, you could subject the data to a quantitative, statistical analysis. A quantitative description of the results would focus on such things as the percentage of teenagers who work and the way this percentage varies by age. There might also be an examination of whether the number of work hours is related to school grades, use of drugs and alcohol, and sleep problems.

Suppose, instead, that you take a qualitative approach to describing behavior. You might conduct a series of focus groups, each consisting of 8–10 teenagers, and engage them in a discussion about their perceptions and experiences with the world of work. You would ask them to tell you about the topic using their own words and their own ways of thinking about the world. To record the focus group discussions, you might use a video or audio recorder and have a transcript prepared later, or you might have observers take detailed notes during the discussions. A qualitative description of the findings would focus on the themes that emerge from the discussions and the manner in which the teenagers conceptualized the issues. Such description is qualitative because it is expressed in nonnumerical terms.

Other methods, both quantitative and qualitative, could also be used to study teenage employment. For example, a quantitative study could examine data collected from the state Department of Economic Development; a qualitative researcher might work in a fast-food restaurant as a management trainee. Keep in mind the distinction between quantitative and qualitative approaches to describing behavior as you read about other specific observational methods discussed in this chapter. Both approaches are valuable and provide us with different ways of understanding behavior.

NATURALISTIC OBSERVATION

Naturalistic observation is sometimes called *field work* or simply *field observation* (see Lofland et al., 2006). In a study using **naturalistic observation,** the researcher makes observations of individuals in their natural environments (the field). This research approach has roots in anthropology and the study of animal behavior and is currently widely used in the social sciences to study many phenomena in all types of social and organizational settings. Thus, you may encounter naturalistic observation studies that focus on employees in a business organization, members of a sports team, patrons of a bar, students and teachers in a school, or prairie dogs in a colony in Arizona.

Sylvia Scribner's (1997) research on "practical thinking" is a good example of naturalistic observation research in psychology. Scribner studied ways people in a variety of occupations make decisions and solve problems. She describes the process of this research: "My colleagues and I have driven around on a 3 a.m. milk route, helped cashiers total their receipts and watched machine operators logging in their production for the day. . . . We made detailed records of how people were going about performing their jobs. We collected copies of all written materials they read or produced—everything from notes scribbled on brown paper bags to computer printouts. We photographed devices in their working environment that required them to process other types of symbolic information—thermometers, gauges, scales, measurement instruments of all kinds (Scribner, 1997, p. 223)." One aspect of thinking that Scribner studied was how workers make mathematical calculations. She found that milk truck drivers and other workers make complex calculations that depend on their acquired knowledge. For example, a delivery invoice might require the driver to multiply 32 quarts of milk by $.68 per quart. To arrive at the answer, drivers use knowledge acquired on the job about how many quarts are in a case and the cost of a case; thus, they multiply 2 cases of milk by $10.88 per case. In general, the workers whom Scribner observed employed complex but very efficient strategies to solve problems at work. More important, the strategies used could often not be predicted from formal models of problem solving. Scribner's research had a particular emphasis on people making decisions in their everyday environment. Scribner has since expanded her research to several more occupations and many types of decisions.

Other naturalistic research may examine a narrower range of behaviors. For example, Graham and her colleagues observed instances of aggression that occurred in bars in a large city late on weekend nights (Graham, et al., 2006). The Scribner study and the Graham study are both instances of naturalistic research because the observations were made in natural settings and the researchers did not attempt to influence what occurred in the settings.

Description and Interpretation of Data

The goal of naturalistic observation is to provide a complete and accurate picture of what occurred in the setting, rather than to test hypotheses formed prior to the study. To achieve this goal, the researcher must keep detailed field notes—that is, write or dictate on a regular basis (at least once each day) everything that has happened. Field researchers rely on a variety of techniques to gather information, depending on the particular setting. In the Graham et al. (2006) study in bars, the observers were alert to any behaviors that might lead to an incident of aggression. They carefully watched and listened to what happened. They immediately made notes on what they observed; these were later given to a research coordinator. In other studies, the observers might interview key "informants" to provide inside information about the setting, talk to people about their lives, and examine documents produced in the setting, such as newspapers, newsletters, or memos. In addition to taking detailed field notes, researchers conducting naturalistic observation usually use audio or video recordings.

The researcher's first goal is to describe the setting, events, and persons observed. The second, equally important goal is to analyze what was observed. The researcher must interpret what occurred, essentially generating hypotheses that help explain the data and make them understandable. Such an analysis is done by building a coherent structure to describe the observations. The final report, although sensitive to the chronological order of events, is usually organized around the structure developed by the researcher. Specific examples of events that occurred during observation are used to support the researcher's interpretations.

A good naturalistic observation report will support the analysis by using multiple confirmations. For example, similar events may occur several times, similar information may be reported by two or more people, and several different events may occur that all support the same conclusion.

The data in naturalistic observation studies are primarily *qualitative* in nature; that is, they are the descriptions of the observations themselves rather than *quantitative* statistical summaries. Such qualitative descriptions are often richer and closer to the phenomenon being studied than are statistical representations. However, it is often useful to also gather quantitative data. Depending on the setting, data might be gathered on income, family size, education levels, age, or sex of individuals in the setting. Such data can be reported and interpreted along with qualitative data gathered from interviews and direct observations.

Participation and Concealment

Two related issues facing the researcher are whether to be a participant or nonparticipant in the social setting and whether to conceal his or her purposes from the other people in the setting. Recall the discussion related to reactivity of a measure from the chapter **"Measurement Concepts"** and ask yourself: Do you become an active participant in the group, or do you observe from the outside? Do you conceal your purposes or even your presence, or do you openly let people know what you are doing?

A nonparticipant observer is an outsider who does not become an active part of the setting. In contrast, a participant observer assumes an active, insider role. Because **participant observation** allows the researcher to observe the setting from the inside, he or she may be able to experience events in the same way as natural participants. Friendships and other experiences of the participant observer may yield valuable data. A potential problem with participant observation, however, is that the observer may lose the objectivity necessary to conduct scientific observation. Remaining objective may be especially difficult when the researcher already belongs to the group being studied or is a dissatisfied former member of the group. Remember that naturalistic observation requires accurate description and objective interpretation with no prior hypotheses. If a researcher has some prior reason to either criticize people in the setting or give a glowing report of a particular group, the observations will likely be biased and the conclusions will lack objectivity.

Should the researcher remain concealed or be open about the purposes of the research? Concealed observation may be preferable because the presence of the observer may influence and alter the behavior of those being observed. Imagine how a nonconcealed observer might alter the behavior of high school students in many situations at a school. Thus, concealed observation is less reactive than nonconcealed observation because people are not aware that their behaviors are being observed and recorded. Still, nonconcealed observation may be preferable from an ethical viewpoint: Consider the invasion of privacy when researchers hid under beds in dormitory rooms to discover what college students talk about (Henle & Hubbell, 1938)! Also, people often quickly become accustomed to the observer and behave naturally in the observer's presence. This fact allows documentary filmmakers to record very private aspects of people's lives, as was done in the 2009 British documentary *Love, Life, and Death in a Day.* For the death segments, the filmmaker, Sue Bourne, contacted funeral homes to find families willing to be filmed throughout their grieving over the death of a loved one.

The decision of whether to conceal one's purpose or presence depends on both ethical concerns and the nature of the particular group and setting being studied. Sometimes a participant observer is nonconcealed to certain members of the group, who give the researcher permission to be part of the group as a concealed observer. Often a concealed observer decides to say nothing directly about his or her purposes but will completely disclose the goals of the research if asked by anyone. Nonparticipant observers are also not concealed when they gain permission to "hang out" in a setting or use interview techniques to gather information. In actuality, then, there are degrees of participation and concealment: A nonparticipant observer might not become a member of the group, for example, but might over time become accepted as a friend or simply part of the ongoing activities of the group. In sum, researchers who use naturalistic observation to study behavior must carefully determine what their role in the setting will be.

You may be wondering about informed consent in naturalistic observation. Recall from the chapter **"Ethics in Behavioral Research"** that observation in public places when anonymity is not threatened may be considered exempt research. In these cases, informed consent may not be necessary. Moreover, in nonconcealed observation, informed consent may be given verbally or in written form. Nevertheless, researchers must be sensitive to ethical issues when conducting naturalistic observation. Of particular interest is whether the observations are made in a public place with no clear expectations that behaviors are private. For example, should a neighborhood bar be considered public or private?

Limits of Naturalistic Observation

Naturalistic observation obviously cannot be used to study all issues or phenomena. The approach is most useful when investigating complex social settings in order to both understand the settings and develop theories based on the observations. It is less useful for studying well-defined hypotheses under precisely specified conditions or phenomena that are not directly observable by a researcher in a natural setting (e.g., color perception, mood, response time on a cognitive task).

Field research is also very difficult to do. Unlike a typical laboratory experiment, field research data collection cannot always be scheduled at a convenient time and place. In fact, field research can be extremely time-consuming, often placing the researcher in an unfamiliar setting for extended periods. In the Graham et al. (2006) investigation of aggression in bars, observers spent more than 1,300 nights in 118 different bars (74 pairs of observers were required to accomplish this feat).

Also, in more carefully controlled settings, such as laboratory research, the procedures are well defined and the same for each participant and the data analysis is planned in advance. In naturalistic observation research, however, there is an ever-changing pattern of events, some important and some unimportant; the researcher must record them all and remain flexible in order to adjust to them as research progresses. Finally, the process of analysis that follows the completion of the research is not simple (imagine the task of sorting through the field notes of every incident of aggression that occurred on more than 1,300 nights). The researcher must repeatedly sort through the data to develop hypotheses to explain the data, and then make sure all data are consistent with the hypotheses. Although naturalistic observation research is a difficult and challenging scientific procedure, it yields invaluable knowledge when done well.

SYSTEMATIC OBSERVATION

Systematic observation refers to the careful observation of one or more specific behaviors in a particular setting. This research approach is much less global than naturalistic observation research. The researcher is interested in only a few very specific behaviors, the observations are quantifiable, and often the researcher has developed prior hypotheses about the behaviors. We will focus on systematic observation in naturalistic settings; these techniques may also be applied in laboratory settings.

Bakeman and Brownlee (1980; also see Bakeman, 2000), for instance, were interested in the social behavior of young children. Three-year-olds were videotaped in a room in a "free play" situation. Each child was taped for 100 minutes; observers viewed the videotapes and coded each child's behavior every 15 seconds, using the following coding system:

Unoccupied: Child is not doing anything in particular or is simply watching other children.

Solitary play: Child plays alone with toys but is not interested in or affected by the activities of other children.

Together: Child is with other children but is not occupied with any particular activity.

Parallel play: Child plays beside other children with similar toys but does not play with the others.

Group play: Child plays with other children, including sharing toys or participating in organized play activities as part of a group of children.

Bakeman and Brownlee were particularly interested in the sequence or order in which the different behaviors were engaged in by the children. They found, for example, that the children rarely went from being unoccupied to engaging in parallel play. However, they frequently went from parallel to group play, indicating that parallel play is a transition state in which children decide whether to interact in a group situation.

Coding Systems

Numerous behaviors can be studied using systematic observation. The researcher must decide which behaviors are of interest, choose a setting in which the behaviors can be observed, and most importantly, develop a **coding system,** such as the one described above, to measure the behaviors. In another example, Rhoades and Stocker (2006) describe the use of the Marital Interaction Video Coding System. Couples are recorded for 10 minutes as they discuss an area of conflict; they then discuss a positive aspect of their relationship for 5 minutes. The video is later coded for hostility and affection displayed during every 5 minutes of the interaction. To code hostility, the observers rated the frequency of behaviors such as "blames other" and "provokes partner." Affection behaviors that were coded included "expresses concern" and "agrees with partner."

Methodological Issues

We should briefly mention several methodological issues in systematic observation.

Equipment

The first issue concerns equipment. You can directly observe behavior and code it at the same time; for example, you could use paper-and-pencil measures to directly observe and record the behavior of children in a classroom or couples interacting on campus. However, it is becoming more common to use video and audio recording equipment to make such observations because they provide a permanent record of the behavior observed that can be coded later.

An interesting method for audio recording is called the *Electronically Activated Recorder* (EAR), which was used to compare sociability behaviors of Americans and Mexicans (Ramírez-Esparza et al., 2009). The EAR is a small audio recorder that a subject wears throughout the day. It is set to turn on periodically to record sounds in the subject's environment. The study examined frequency of sociable behaviors. Previous research had found that Americans score higher than Mexicans on self-report measures of sociability, contradicting stereotypes that Mexicans are generally more sociable. Coders applied the *Social Environment of Sound Inven-*

tory to code the recorded sounds as: alone, talking with others in a public environment, or on the phone. When sociability was measured this way, the Mexican subjects were in fact more sociable than the American subjects.

Reactivity

A second issue is **reactivity**–the possibility that the presence of the observer will affect people's behaviors (see the chapter **"Measurement Concepts"**). Reactivity can be reduced by concealed observation. Using small cameras and microphones can make the observation unobtrusive, even in situations in which the participant has been informed of the recording. Also, reactivity can be reduced by allowing time for people to become accustomed to the observer and equipment.

Reliability

Recall from the chapter **"Measurement Concepts"** that reliability refers to the degree to which a measurement reflects a true score rather than measurement error. Reliable measures are stable, consistent, and precise. When conducting systematic observation, two or more raters are usually used to code behavior. Reliability is indicated by a high agreement among the raters. Very high levels of agreement (generally 80% agreement or higher) are reported in virtually all published research using systematic observation. For some large-scale research programs in which many observers will be employed over a period of years, observers are first trained using videotapes, and their observations during training are checked for agreement with results from previous observers.

Sampling

For many research questions, samples of behavior taken over an extended period provide more accurate and useful data than single, short observations. Consider a study on the behaviors of nursing home residents and staff during meals (Stabell et al., 2004). The researchers were interested in the frequency of different resident behaviors such as independent eating, socially engaged eating, and dependent eating in which help is needed. The staff behaviors included supporting the behaviors of the residents (e.g., assisting, socializing). The researchers could have made observations during a single meal or two meals during a single day. However, such data might be distorted by short-term trends–the particular meal being served, an illness, a recent event such as the death of a resident. The researchers instead sampled behaviors during breakfast and lunch over a period of 6 weeks. Each person was randomly chosen to be observed for a 3-minute period during both meals on 10 of the days of the study. A major finding was that the staff members were most frequently engaged in supporting dependent behavior with little time spent supporting independent behaviors such as socializing. Interestingly, part-time nursing student staff were more likely to support independence.

CASE STUDIES

A **case study** is an observational method that provides a detailed description of an individual. This individual is usually a person, but it may also be a setting such as a business, school, or neighborhood. A naturalistic observation study is sometimes called a case study, and in fact the naturalistic observation and case study approaches sometimes overlap. We have included case studies as a separate category in this chapter because case studies do not necessarily involve naturalistic observation. Instead, the case study may be a description of a patient by a clinical psychologist or a historical account of an event such as a model school that failed.

A **psychobiography** is a type of case study in which a researcher applies psychological theory to explain the life of an individual, usually an important historical figure (Schultz, 2005). Thus, case studies may use such techniques as library research and telephone interviews with persons familiar with the case but no direct observation at all (Yin, 2014).

Depending on the purpose of the investigation, the case study may present the individual's history, symptoms, characteristic behaviors, reactions to situations, or responses to treatment. Typically a case study is done when an individual possesses a particularly rare, unusual, or noteworthy condition. One famous case study involved a man with an amazing ability to recall information (Luria, 1968). The man, called "S.," could remember long lists and passages with ease, apparently using mental imagery for his memory abilities. Luria also described some of the drawbacks of S.'s ability. For example, he frequently had difficulty concentrating because mental images would spontaneously appear and interfere with his thinking.

Another example of a case study, involving a child called "Genie," concerns language development. Genie was kept isolated in her room, tied to a chair, and never spoken to until she was discovered at the age of 13½ (Curtiss, 1977). Genie had not developed any language skills. Her case gave psychologists and linguists the opportunity to attempt to teach her language skills. Apparently Genie was able to acquire some rudimentary language skills, such as forming childlike sentences, but she never developed full language abilities, perhaps because she had missed a critical period of language acquisition.

Individuals with particular types of brain damage can allow researchers to test hypotheses. For example, Stone et al. (2002) studied an individual, R.M., who had extensive damage to the limbic system. The researchers were interested in studying people's ability to detect cheaters in social exchange relationships. Social exchange is at the core of our relationships: One person provides goods or services for another person in exchange for some other resource. Stone et al. were seeking evidence that social exchange can evolve in a species only when there is a biological mechanism for detecting cheaters—that is, those who do not reciprocate by fulfilling their end of the bargain. R.M. completed two types of reasoning problems. One type involved detecting violations of social exchange rules (e.g., you must fulfill a requirement if you receive a particular benefit); the other type focused on nonsocial precautionary action rules (e.g., you must take this precaution if you engage in a particular hazardous behavior). Individuals with no brain injury do equally well on both types of measures. However, R.M. performed very poorly on the social exchange problems but did well on the precautionary problems, as well as other general measures of cognitive ability. This finding supports the hypothesis that our ability to engage in social exchange relationships is grounded in the development of a biological mechanism—specifically, one related to the limbic system—that differs from general cognitive abilities.

Case studies are valuable sources of information regarding conditions that are rare or unusual, and they can provide unique data about some psychological phenomena, such as memory, language, or social exchange. Insights gained through a case study may also lead to the development of hypotheses that can be tested using other methods.

ARCHIVAL RESEARCH

Archival research involves using previously compiled information to answer research questions. In an archival research project, the researcher does not actually collect the original data (thus, it may be referred to as secondary research data). Instead, he or she analyzes existing data, such as statistics that are part of publicly accessible records (e.g., the number of texting-related traffic accidents; the number of children born in a given state or county), reports of anthropologists, the content of letters to the editor, or information contained in databases (e.g., tweets, Facebook or Instagram posts, census data), or original data made available from prior research studies (see the **"Open Science"** box).

Open Science and Data Accessibility

The U.S. Office of Science and Technology Policy (2013) published a memorandum about data accessibility. The memorandum, titled "Expanding Public Access to the Results of Federally Funded Research," further energized the open science movement by declaring that "the direct results of federally funded scientific research are made available to and useful for the public, industry, and the scientific community."

One of the organizations at the forefront of the open science movement is the Center for Open Science (**https://cos.io/**), a nonprofit group dedicated to "increasing the openness, integrity and reproducibility of scientific research." We will come back to the idea of reproducibility in the chapter **"Generalization."** Here, we will focus on the idea of openness and accessibility as it relates to archival research.

The Center for Open Science envisions a "future scholarly community in which the process, content, and outcomes of research are openly accessible by default." One of the things this would mean is that data would be accessible to other researchers as well as consumers of research. If a researcher publishes a paper in the context of Open Science, a data set is made available so that others can evaluate a project or use the data in their own projects (e.g., a **meta-analysis**). As you can imagine, this will create a lot of opportunities for archival research now and in the future.

Judd et al. (1991) described three types of archival research data: statistical records, survey archives, and written records.

Statistical Records

Statistical records are collected by many public and private organizations. The U.S. Census Bureau maintains the most extensive set of statistical records available, but state and local agencies also maintain such records. In a study using public records, Bushman et al. (2005) examined the relationship between temperature and aggression. They used temperature data in Minneapolis that had been recorded in 3-hour periods in 1987 and 1988; data on assaults were available through police records. They found that higher temperature is related to more aggression; however, this effect was limited to data recorded between 9:00 p.m. and 3:00 a.m.

There are also numerous less-obvious sources of statistical records, including public health statistics, test score records kept by testing organizations such as the Educational Testing Service, and even sports organizations. Major League Baseball is known for the extensive records that are kept on virtually every aspect of every game and every player. Abel and Kruger (2010) took advantage of this fact to investigate the relationship between positive emotions and longevity. They began with photographs of 230 Major League players published in 1952. The photographs were then rated for smile intensity to provide a measure of emotional positivity. The longevity of players who had died by the end of 2009 was then examined in relation to smile intensity. The results indicated that these two variables are indeed related. In the same study, they also found that ratings of attractiveness were unrelated to longevity.

Survey Archives

Survey archives consist of data from surveys that are stored digitally and available to researchers who wish to analyze them. Major polling organizations make many of their surveys available. Also, many universities are part of the Inter-university Consortium for Political and Social Research (ICPSR; http://www.icpsr.umich.edu/), which makes survey archive data available. One very useful data set is the General Social Survey (GSS; see their website at https://www.norc.org), a series of surveys of the U.S. population conducted since 1972. Each survey includes over 200 questions covering a range of topics such as attitudes, life satisfaction, health, religion, education, age, gender, and race.

Survey archives are now becoming available online at sites that enable researchers to analyze the data online. Survey archives are extremely important because most researchers do not have the financial resources to conduct surveys of randomly selected national samples; the archives allow them to access such samples to test their ideas. A study by Robinson and Martin (2009) illustrates how the GSS can be used to test hypotheses. The study examined whether internet users differed from nonusers in their social attitudes. Clearly, the findings would have implications for interpreting the results of surveys conducted via the internet. The results showed that although internet users were somewhat more optimistic, there were no systematic differences between those who used the internet and those who did not.

Written and Mass Communication Records

Written records are documents such as diaries and letters that have been preserved by historical societies, ethnographies of other cultures written by anthropologists, and public documents as diverse as speeches by politicians or discussion board messages left by internet users. Mass communication records include books, tweets, Instagram or Facebook posts, magazine articles, movies, television programs, newspapers, and blog posts.

An example of archival research using such records is a study of Twitter posts. Golder and Macy (2011) analyzed 509 million tweets from 2.4 million individuals from all over the world, classifying each tweet as having positive affect (e.g., enthusiasm, delight, activeness, and alertness) or negative affect (distress, fear, anger, guilt, and disgust). They found that people across the world generally wake up in a good mood, but that their moods get worse over the course of the day. They also found, unsurprisingly, that on weekends people tweeted happier tweets.

Content analysis is the systematic analysis of existing documents. Like systematic observation, content analysis requires researchers to devise coding systems that raters can use to quantify the information in the documents. Sometimes the coding is quite simple and straightforward; for example, it is easy to code whether the addresses of the applicants on marriage license applications are the same or different. More often the researcher must define categories in order to code the information. In a study of 487 anti-smoking ads that was conducted by Rhodes et al. (2009), the researchers defined categories to describe the ads—for example, *attacks tobacco companies* or *causes cancer.* Similar procedures would be used in studies examining archival documents such as speeches, magazine articles, television shows, and reader comments on articles published on the internet.

The use of archival data allows researchers to study interesting questions, some of which could not be studied in any other way. Archival data are a valuable supplement to more traditional data collection methods. There are at least two major problems with the use of archival data, however. First, the desired records may be difficult to obtain: they might have been placed in long-forgotten storage places, or they may have been destroyed. Second, we can never be completely sure of the accuracy of information collected by someone else.

Visit **Check Your Learning:** Practice Exercise #1 and see if you can distinguish among various observational methods.

This chapter has provided a great deal of information about important qualitative and quantitative observational methods that can be used to study a variety of questions about behavior. In the chapter **"Asking People About Themselves: Survey Research"** we will explore a very common way of finding out about human behavior—simply asking people to tell us about themselves.

ILLUSTRATIVE ARTICLE: OBSERVATIONAL METHODS

Happiness, according to Aristotle, is the most desirable of all things. In the past few decades many researchers have been studying predictors of happiness in an attempt to understand the construct.

Mehl et al. (2010) conducted a naturalistic observation on the topic of happiness using electronically activated recorders (devices that unobtrusively record snippets of sound at regular intervals, for a fixed amount of time). In this study, 79 undergraduate students wore a recorder for 4 days; 30-second recordings were made every 12.5 minutes. Each snippet was coded as having been taken while the participant was alone or with other people. If the participant was with somebody, the recordings were also coded for "small talk" and "substantial talk." Other measures administered were well-being and happiness.

First, acquire and read this article (available at **https://www.researchgate.net/publication/4334825 4_Eavesdropping_on_Happiness_Well-Being_Is_Related_to_Having_Less_Small_Talk_and_M ore_Substantive_Conversations**):

> Mehl, M. R., Vazire, S., Holleran, S. E., & Clark, C. S. (2010). Eavesdropping on happiness: Well-being is related to having less small talk and more substantive conversations. *Psychological Science, 21*(4), 539–541. https://doi.org/10.1177/0956797610362675

Then, after reading the article, consider the following:

1. What was measured?
   a. How did the researchers operationally define small talk, substantive talk, well-being, and happiness? What do you think about the quality of these operational definitions?
   b. Do you think that participants would be reactive to this data collection method?
   c. How reliable were the coders? How did the authors assess their reliability?

2. How do they know that one thing caused another?
   a. Does this study suffer from the third-variable problem? How so?
   b. Do you think that this study included any confounding variables? Provide examples.
   c. Does this study suffer from the problem involving the direction of causation? How so?

3. To what or whom can we generalize the results?
   a. Do you think that this study would generalize across cultures, age groups, or other sorts of demographic variables? Why or why not?

4. Have other researchers found similar results?
   a. Do the results of this study line up with other studies on the same topic?

5. Finally, answer the following questions:
   a. Is the basic approach in this study qualitative or quantitative?
   b. Given the topic of this study, what other ways can you think of to conduct this study using an observational method?

c. Is this study an example of concealed or nonconcealed observation? What are the ethical issues present in this study?

CRITICAL THINKING: BEING A SKILLED CONSUMER OF RESEARCH

1. Some questions are more readily answered using quantitative techniques, and others are best addressed through qualitative techniques or a combination of both approaches. Suppose you are interested in how an adolescent's life is affected by their parent's alcoholism. Develop a research question best answered using quantitative techniques and another research question better suited to qualitative techniques. An example of a quantitative question is "Are adolescents with alcoholic parents more likely to have criminal records?" and an example of a qualitative question is "What issues can arise in an adolescent's peer relationships due to their parent's alcoholism?"

2. One of the most important case studies ever conducted was about Henry Molaison (H.M.), who suffered from epilepsy and, as the result of surgery, lost his normal memory functioning. H.M. was studied from the 1950s until his death in 2008. A recent book, written by his grandson, sheds some light on H.M.'s experiences as one of the quintessential case studies in the history of psychology (Dittrich, 2016). Search for and summarize at least two reviews of this book.

Check Your Learning: Practice Exercise

Practice Exercise #1

Read each scenario below and determine whether a case study, naturalistic observation, systematic observation, or archival research was used.

1. Researchers conducted an in-depth study with certain 9/11 victims to understand the psychological impact of the attack on the World Trade Center in 2001.

3. Researchers recorded the time it took drivers in parking lots to back out of a parking stall. They also measured the age and gender of the drivers, and whether another car was waiting for the space.

4. The researcher spent more than a year meeting with and interviewing Aileen Wuornos, the infamous female serial killer who was the subject of the film *Monster*, to construct a psychobiography.

5. Researchers examined unemployment rates and the incidence of domestic-violence police calls in six cities.

6. A group of researchers studied recycling behavior at three local parks over a 6-month period. They concealed their presence and kept detailed field notes.

(Answers are provided at the end of this chapter.)

CHAPTER REVIEW

Review Questions

1. What are the differences between qualitative and quantitative approaches to studying behavior?
2. What is naturalistic observation? How does a researcher collect data when conducting naturalistic observation research?
3. Why are the data in naturalistic observation research primarily qualitative?
4. Distinguish between participant and nonparticipant observation; between concealed and nonconcealed observation.
5. What is systematic observation? Why are the data from systematic observation primarily quantitative?
6. What is a coding system? What are some important considerations when developing a coding system?
7. What is a case study? When are case studies used? What is a psychobiography?
8. What is archival research? What are the major sources of archival data?
9. What is content analysis?

Study Terms

Archival research

Case study

Coding system

Content analysis

Naturalistic observation

Participant observation

Psychobiography

Reactivity

Systematic observation

Check Your Learning: Answers

Practice Exercise #1

1. case study; 2. systematic observation; 3. archival research; 4. case study; 5. archival research; 6. naturalistic observation

7

Asking People About Themselves: Survey Research

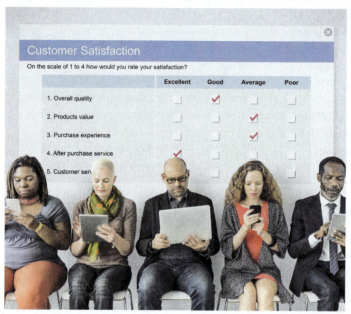

On the scale of 1 to 4 how would you rate your satisfaction?

Rawpixel.com/Shutterstock

LEARNING OBJECTIVES

- Discuss reasons for conducting survey research.
- Identify factors to consider when writing questions for interviews and questionnaires.
- Describe different ways to construct questionnaire responses, including closed-ended questions, open-ended questions, and rating scales.
- Compare the two ways to administer surveys: written questionnaires and oral interviews.
- Distinguish between probability and nonprobability sampling techniques, including simple random sampling, stratified random sampling, and cluster sampling; convenience (or haphazard) sampling, purposive sampling, and quota sampling.
- Describe how samples are evaluated for potential bias, including sampling frame and response rate.

Survey research involves using questionnaires and interviews to ask people to provide information about themselves—their attitudes and beliefs, demographics (age, gender, income, marital status, and so on), and past or intended future behaviors. In this chapter we will explore methods of designing and conducting surveys. We will also introduce sampling techniques.

WHY CONDUCT SURVEYS?

Surveys are a way to collect data directly from research participants by asking them questions. Surveys have become extremely important as society demands data about people's behavior and what people think about issues.

Surveys are being conducted all the time. Just look at your daily newspaper, local TV news broadcast, or the internet. From the Centers for Disease Control and Prevention comes a report on the results of a survey of new mothers asking about breast-feeding. A college survey center is reporting the results of a telephone survey asking about political attitudes. If you look around your campus, you will find academic departments conducting surveys of seniors or recent graduates. If you make a major purchase, you will likely receive a request to complete a survey that asks about your satisfaction. Each year since 2007, the American Psychological Association has conducted an online survey that focuses on topics related to stress. You can download the *Stress in America* reports from their website at **https://www.apa.org/news/press/releases/stress/index**.

Clearly, surveys are a common and important method of studying behavior. Every university needs data from graduates to help determine changes that should be made to the curriculum and student services. Auto companies want data from buyers to assess and improve product quality and customer satisfaction. Without the collection of such data, we are totally dependent upon stories we might hear or letters that a graduate or customer might write. Other surveys can be important to lawmakers and public agencies when they are making public policy decisions. In research, many important variables—including attitudes, current emotional states, and self-reports of behaviors—are most easily studied using questionnaires or interviews.

We often think of survey data as providing a snapshot of how people think and behave at a given point in time. However, the survey method is also an important way for researchers to study relationships among variables and ways that attitudes and behaviors change over time. For example, the *Monitoring the Future* project (**https://monitoringthefuture.org**) has been conducted every year since 1975—its purpose is to monitor the behaviors, attitudes, and values of American high school and college students. Each year, 50,000 8th-, 10th-, and 12th-grade students participate in the survey. **Figure 1** shows a typical finding: Each line on the graph represents the percentage of survey respondents who reported using marijuana in the past 12 months. Note the trend that shows the peak of marijuana popularity occurring in the late 1970s and the least reported use in the early 1990s. After some increases in the late 1990s, use has been relatively stable: 20% to 25% of 12th-grade students, 15% to 20% of 10th-grade students, and 5% to 10% of 8th-grade students report using marijuana in the past year.

Survey research is also important as a complement to experimental research findings. Recall from the chapter **Where to Start** that Winograd and Soloway (1986) conducted experiments on the conditions that lead to forgetting where we place something. To study this topic using survey methods, Brown and Rahhal (1994) asked both younger and older adults about their actual experiences when they hid something and later forgot its location. They reported that older adults take longer than younger adults to find the object and that older adults hide objects from potential thieves, whereas younger people hide things from friends and relatives. Interestingly, most lost objects are eventually found, usually by accident in a location that had been searched previously. This research illustrates a key point: Multiple methods are needed to understand any behavior.

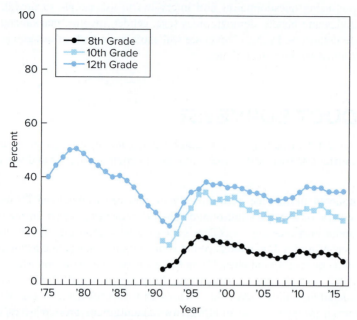

FIGURE 1   Percentage of survey respondents who reported using marijuana in the past 12 months, over time

An assumption that underlies the use of questionnaires and interviews is that people are willing and able to provide truthful and accurate answers. Researchers have addressed this issue by studying possible biases in the way people respond. A **response set** is a tendency to respond to all questions from a particular perspective rather than to provide answers that are directly related to the questions. Thus, response sets can affect the usefulness of data obtained from self-reports. Response sets include a tendency to express agreement or disagreement with anything that is asked. But the most common response set is called **social desirability,** or "faking good." The social desirability response set leads the individual to answer in the most socially acceptable way—the way that person perceives "most people" to respond or the way that would reflect most favorably on the person. Thus, a social desirability response set might lead a person to underreport undesirable behaviors (e.g., alcohol or drug use, fighting with partners, cheating) and overreport positive behaviors (such as amount of exercise, vegetable intake, amount of time spent studying for an upcoming exam). However, it should not be assumed that people consistently misrepresent themselves. If the researcher openly and honestly communicates the purposes and uses of the research, promises to provide feedback about the results, and ensures confidentiality, then the participants can reasonably be expected to give honest responses.

We turn now to three major considerations when designing a survey research project or conducting survey research: constructing the questions that are asked, choosing the methods for presenting the questions, and sampling the individuals taking part in the research.

CONSTRUCTING QUESTIONS TO ASK

A great deal of thought must be given to writing questions for questionnaires and interviews. This section describes some of the most important factors to consider when constructing questions.

Defining the Research Objectives

When constructing questions for a survey, the first thing the researcher must do is explicitly determine the research objectives: What is it that they want to know? The survey questions must be tied to the research questions that are being addressed. Too often, surveys get out of hand when researchers begin to ask any question that comes to mind about a topic without considering exactly what useful information will be gained by doing so. This process will usually require the researcher to decide on the type of questions to ask. There are three general types of survey questions (Judd et al., 1991).

Facts and Demographics

Factual questions ask people to indicate things they know about themselves and their situation. In most studies, asking some demographic information is necessary to adequately describe your sample; thus, questions about age, gender, and ethnicity are typically asked. Depending on the topic of the study, questions on marital status, employment status, and number of children might be included. Obviously, if you are interested in making comparisons among groups, such as those with incomes under $50,0000 per year compared to those with incomes over $50,000, you must ask the relevant information about income. You may also need such information to adequately describe the sample. However, you should not ask questions for which you have no legitimate reason to collect the information.

Other factual information you might ask will depend on the topic of your survey. Each year *Consumer Reports* magazine asks readers to tell them about the repairs that have been necessary on many of the products the readers own, such as cars and dishwashers. Factual questions about illnesses and other medical information would be asked in a survey of health and quality of life.

Behaviors

Other survey questions can focus on past behaviors or intended future behaviors. How many days last week did you exercise for 20 minutes or longer? How many children do you plan to have? Have you ever been so depressed that you called in sick to work?

Attitudes and Beliefs

Questions about attitudes and beliefs focus on the ways people evaluate and think about issues. Should more money be spent on mental health services? Are you satisfied with how the police responded to your call? How do you evaluate this instructor? Next we look at question wording generally and bias in question wording.

Question Wording

A great deal of care is necessary to write the very best questions for a survey. After all, the validity of a study that is based on a survey is dependent on the quality of the questions on the survey. Cognitive psychologists have identified a number of potential problems with question wording (see Graesser et al., 1999). Many of the problems stem from a difficulty with understanding the question, including (a) unfamiliar technical terms, (b) vague or imprecise terms, (c) ungrammatical sentence structure, (d) phrasing that overloads working memory, and (e) embedding the question with misleading information. Here is a question that illustrates some of the problems identified by Graesser et al.:

Did your mother, father, full-blooded sisters, full-blooded brothers, daughters, or sons ever have a heart attack or myocardial infarction?

This example has many problems. First, this is an example of memory overload because of the length of the question and the need to keep track of all those relatives while reading the question. The respondent must also worry about two different diagnoses with regard to each relative. Further, the term *myocardial infarction* may be unfamiliar to most people.

So, how do you write questions to avoid such problems? The following items are important to consider when you are writing questions.

Simplicity

The questions asked in a survey should be relatively simple. People should be able to easily understand and respond to the questions. Avoid jargon and technical terms that people will not understand. Sometimes, however, you have to make the question a bit more complex—or longer—to make it easier to understand. Usually this occurs when you need to define a term or describe an issue prior to asking the question. Thus, before asking whether someone approves or disapproves of "Ballot Proposition A" in the November election, you will probably want to provide a brief description of the content of this ballot measure. Likewise, if you want to know about the frequency of alcohol use in a population, asking, "Have you had a drink of alcohol in the past 30 days?" may generate a slightly different answer than "One drink of alcohol is one full can of beer, one shot of liquor, or one glass of wine. Have you had a drink of alcohol in the past 30 days?" The latter case is probably closer to what you would be interested in knowing.

Double-Barreled Questions

Avoid double-barreled questions that ask two things at once. A question such as "Should senior citizens be given more money for recreation centers and food assistance programs?" is difficult to answer because it taps two potentially very different attitudes. If you are interested in both issues, ask two questions.

Loaded Questions

A loaded question is written to lead people to respond in one way. For example, the questions "Do you favor eliminating the wasteful excesses in the public school budget?" and "Do you favor reducing the public school budget?" will likely elicit different answers. Or consider that women are less likely to say they have been raped than to say that they have been forced to have unwanted sex (Hamby & Koss, 2003). Questions that include emotionally charged words such as *rape, waste, immoral, ungodly,* or *dangerous* influence the way that people respond and thus lead to biased responses; more neutral, behavior-based terminology is preferable.

Negative Wording

Avoid phrasing questions with negatives. This question is phrased negatively: "Do you feel that the city should not approve the proposed women's shelter?" Agreement with this question means disagreement with the proposal. This phrasing can confuse people and result in inaccurate answers. A better format would be: "Do you believe that the city should approve the proposed women's shelter?"

"Yea-Saying" and "Nay-Saying"

When you ask several questions about a topic, a respondent may employ a response set to agree or disagree with all the questions. The tendency to agree consistently is referred to as **yea-saying** (also called *acquiescence* response set). The tendency to disagree consistently is termed **nay-saying.** The problem here is that the respondent may, in fact, be expressing true agreement, but alternatively may simply be agreeing with anything you say. One way to detect this response set is to word the questions so that consistent agreement is unlikely. For example, a study of family communication patterns might ask people how much they agree with the following statements: "The members of my family spend a lot of time together" and "I spend most of my weekends with friends." Similarly, a measure of loneliness could phrase some questions so that agreement means the respondent is lonely ("I feel isolated from others") and others with the meaning reversed so that disagreement indicates loneliness (e.g., "I feel part of a group of friends"). Although it is possible that someone could legitimately agree with both items, consistently agreeing or disagreeing with a set of related questions phrased in both standard and reversed formats is an indicator that the individual is "yea-saying" or "nay-saying."

Graesser et al., (2006) have developed a computer program called *QUAID* (Question Understanding Aid) that analyzes question wording. Researchers can try out their questions online at the QUAID website (**https://quaid.cohmetrix.com/**).

> You can test your own analysis of question wording using the examples in **Check Your Learning:** Practice Exercise #1.

RESPONSES TO QUESTIONS

You have undoubtedly completed (or at least started) many surveys and observed many different types of questions on those surveys. Next, we will consider the many varieties of responses to questions.

Closed-Versus Open-Ended Questions

First, questions may be either closed- or open-ended. With **closed-ended questions**, a limited number of response alternatives are given; with **open-ended questions**, respondents are free to answer in any way they like. Thus, you could ask a person, "What is the most important thing children should learn to prepare them for life?" followed by a list of answers from which to choose (a closed-ended question), or you could leave this question open-ended for the person to provide the answer.

Closed-ended questions provide a more structured approach; they make it easier to assign values to responses because the response alternatives are the same for everyone. Open-ended questions require time to categorize and code the responses and are therefore more costly to conduct and more difficult to interpret. Sometimes a respondent's response cannot be categorized at all because the response does not make sense or the person could not think of an answer. Still, an open-ended question can yield valuable insights into what people are thinking. Open-ended questions are most useful when the researcher needs to know what people are thinking and how they naturally view their world; closed-ended questions are more likely to be used when the dimensions of the variables are well defined.

Schwarz (1999) points out that the two approaches can sometimes lead to different conclusions. He cites the results of a survey question about preparing children for life. When "To think for themselves" was one alternative in a closed-ended list, 62% chose this option; however, only 5% gave this answer when the open-ended format was used. This finding points to the need to have a good understanding of the topic when asking closed-ended questions.

Number of Response Alternatives

With closed-ended questions, there is a fixed number of response alternatives. In public opinion surveys, a simple "yes or no" or "agree or disagree" dichotomy is often sufficient. In other research, it is often preferable to provide more quantitative distinctions—for example, a 5- or 7-point scale ranging from *strongly agree* to *strongly disagree* or *very positive* to *very negative*. Such a scale might appear as follows:

Strongly agree ____ ____ ____ ____ ____ ____ ____ Strongly disagree

Rating Scales

Rating scales such as the one shown above are very common in many areas of research. Rating scales ask people to provide "how much" judgments on any number of dimensions—amount of agreement, liking, or confidence, for example. Rating scales can have many different formats. The format that is used depends on factors such as the topic being investigated. Perhaps the best way to gain an understanding of the variety of formats is simply to look at a few examples. The simplest and most direct scale presents people with five or seven response alternatives with the endpoints on the scale labeled to define the extremes. The response choices might be lines to mark on a paper questionnaire, check boxes, or radio buttons in an online survey form. For example,

Students at the university should be required to pass a comprehensive examination to graduate.

Strongly agree □□□□□□ Strongly disagree

How confident are you that the defendant is guilty of attempted murder?

Not at all confident □□□□ Very confident

Graphic Rating Scale

A **graphic rating scale** requires a mark along a continuous 100-millimeter line that is anchored with descriptions at each end.

How would you rate the movie you just saw?

Not very enjoyable _____ Very enjoyable

A ruler is then placed on the line to obtain the score on a scale that ranges from 0 to 100.

Semantic Differential Scale

The **semantic differential scale** is a measure of the meaning of concepts that was developed by Osgood and his associates (Osgood et al., 1957). Respondents are asked to rate any concept—persons, objects, behaviors, ideas—on a series of bipolar adjectives using 7-point scales, as follows:

Smoking cigarettes

Good	_____ _____ _____ _____ _____ _____ _____	Bad
Strong	_____ _____ _____ _____ _____ _____ _____	Weak
Active	_____ _____ _____ _____ _____ _____ _____	Passive

Research on the semantic differential shows that virtually anything can be measured using this technique. Ratings of specific things (marijuana), places (the student center), people (the governor, accountants), ideas (death penalty, marriage equality), and behaviors (attending church, using public transit) can be obtained. A large body of research shows that the concepts are rated along three basic dimensions: the first and most important is *evaluation* (e.g., adjectives such as good-bad, wise-foolish, kind-cruel); the second is *activity* (active-passive, slow-fast, excitable-calm); and the third is *potency* (weak-strong, hard-soft, large-small).

Nonverbal Scales

Researchers sometimes study populations with problems understanding the types of scales we have just described, but they are able to give ratings. Such populations may include young children, or adults with specific cognitive deficits. In such cases, a nonverbal scale may be appropriate.

Think back to the example that uses drawings of faces to aid in the assessment of the level of pain a child is experiencing. Similar face scales can be used to ask children to make ratings of other things, such as a toy.

Source: Wong-Baker FACES Foundation (2015). Wong-Baker FACES® Pain Rating Scale

Labeling Response Alternatives

The examples thus far have labeled only the endpoints on the rating scale. Respondents decide the meaning of the response alternatives that are not labeled. This is a reasonable approach, and people are usually able to use such scales without difficulty. Sometimes researchers need to provide labels to more clearly define the meaning of each alternative. Here is a fairly standard alternative to the *agree-disagree* scale shown above:

○   ○   ○   ○   ○

Strongly agree   Agree   Undecided   Disagree   Strongly disagree

This type of scale assumes that the middle alternative is a "neutral" point halfway between the endpoints. Sometimes, however, a perfectly balanced scale may not be possible or desirable. Consider a scale asking a college professor to rate a student for a job or graduate program. This particular scale asks for comparative ratings of students:

In comparison with other graduates, how would you rate this student's potential for success?

○   ○   ○   ○   ○

Lower 50%   Upper 50%   Upper 25%   Upper 10%   Upper 5%

Notice that more of the alternatives ask people to make a rating within the top 25% of students. This is done because students who apply for such programs tend to be very bright and motivated, and so professors rate them favorably. The wording of the alternatives attempts to force the raters to make finer distinctions among generally very good students.

Labeling alternatives is particularly interesting when asking about the frequency of a behavior. For example, you might ask, "How often do you exercise for at least 20 minutes?" What kind of scale should you use to let people answer this question? You could list (1) never, (2) rarely, (3) sometimes, (4) frequently. These terms convey your meaning but they are vague. Here is another set of alternatives with greater specificity (Schwarz et al., 2008):

○ less than twice a week
○ about twice a week
○ about four times a week
○ about six times a week
○ at least once each day

A different scale might be:

○ less than once per month
○ about once a month
○ about once every 2 weeks
○ about once a week
○ more than once per week

Schwarz et al. (2008) call the first scale a *high-frequency scale* because most alternatives indicate a high frequency of exercise. The other scale is referred to as low frequency. Schwarz et al. point out that the labels should be chosen carefully because people may interpret the meaning of the scale differently, depending on the labels used. If you were actually asking the exercise question, you might decide on alternatives different from the ones described here. Moreover, your choice should be influenced by factors such as the population you are studying. If you are studying people who generally exercise a lot, you will be more likely to use a higher-frequency scale than you would if you were studying people who generally do not exercise a great deal.

FINALIZING THE SURVEY INSTRUMENT

Once questions are written and responses to questions are finalized, it is time to make final adjustments to the survey. Formatting, question sequence, and survey pilot-testing are critical steps before submitting your survey project to an Institutional Review Board, and then administering the survey to a sample of research participants.

Formatting

A questionnaire is the set of questions in a survey designed to be administered using a printed or a web-based instrument (in contrast to questions posed in a face-to-face or telephone interview). The questionnaire should appear attractive and professional. It should be neatly designed and free of spelling errors. Respondents should find it easy to identify the questions and the response alternatives to the questions. Leave enough space between questions so people do not become confused when reading the questionnaire. If you have a particular scale format, such as a 5-point rating scale, use it consistently. Do not change from 5- to 4- to 7-point scales, for example.

Sequence of Questions

It is also a good idea to carefully consider the sequence in which you will ask your questions. In general, it is best to ask the most interesting and important questions first to capture the attention of your respondents and motivate them to complete the survey. Roberson and Sundstrom (1990) obtained the highest return rates in an employee attitude survey when important questions were presented first and demographic questions were asked last. In addition, it is a good idea to group questions together when they address a similar theme or topic. Doing so will make your survey appear more professional, and your respondents will be more likely to take it seriously.

Refining Questions: Pilot Testing the Survey

Before actually administering a survey, it is a good idea to give the questions to a small group of people and have them think aloud while answering them. The participants might be chosen from the population being studied, or they could be friends or colleagues who can give reasonable responses to the questions. For the think-aloud procedure, you will need to ask the individuals to tell you how they interpret each question and how they respond to the response alternatives. This procedure can provide valuable information that can make it easier to identify and correct problems like negative wording, overly complex language, and double-barreled or loaded questions. (The importance of pilot studies such as this is discussed further in the chapter **"Conducting Experiments."**)

ADMINISTERING SURVEYS

There are two ways to administer surveys. One is to use a written questionnaire, either printed or online, wherein respondents read the questions and indicate their responses on a form. The other way is to use an interview format. An interviewer asks the questions and records the responses in a personal verbal interaction. Both questionnaires and interviews can be presented to respondents in several ways. Let's examine the various methods of administering surveys.

Questionnaires

With questionnaires the questions are presented in written format and respondents write their answers. There are several benefits to using questionnaires. First, they generally cost less than interviews, as questionnaires can be administered in person to groups or individuals, through the mail, on the internet, and with other technologies. Second, they also allow the respondent to be completely anonymous as long as no identifying information (e.g., name, Social Security number, or driver's license number) is asked for. However, questionnaires require that the respondents be able to read and understand the questions. In addition, many people find it boring to sit by themselves reading questions and then providing answers; thus, a problem of motivation may arise.

Administration to Groups or Individuals

Often researchers are able to distribute questionnaires to groups of individuals. This might be a college class, parents attending a school meeting, people attending a new employee orientation, or students waiting for an appointment with an advisor. An advantage of this approach is that you have a captive audience of individuals who are likely to complete the questionnaire once they start it. Also, the researcher is present, so people can ask questions if necessary.

Mail Surveys

A mail survey can be mailed to individuals at a home or business address. This is a very inexpensive way of contacting the people who were selected for the sample. However, the mail format is a drawback because of potentially low response rates (response rate is the percentage of people who are asked to complete a survey who actually complete a survey). The questionnaire can easily be placed aside and forgotten among all the other tasks that people must attend to at home and work. Even if people start to fill out the questionnaire, something may happen to distract them, or they may become bored and simply throw the survey in the trash. Some of the methods for increasing response rates are described later in this chapter. Another drawback is that no one is present to help if the person doesn't understand some of the questions.

Online Surveys

Online surveys are increasingly being used by academic researchers (Buchanan & Hvizdak, 2009; Sue & Ritter, 2012). There are many benefits to conducting survey research online. It is very easy to design a questionnaire for online administration using one of several online survey software services. Both open- and closed-ended questions can be included. After users complete the questionnaire, their responses are immediately available to the researcher.

On the other hand, there are some drawbacks to consider. The first one is how to identify people to take the survey. That is, how does the researcher provide people with a link to the online survey? Major polling organizations have built databases of people interested in participating in surveys. Online survey software services have mailing lists that can be purchased. There are online special interest groups for people with a particular illness or of a particular age that may allow the researcher to post a recruitment message. An easily accessible method of recruiting participants for online data collection is *Amazon Mechanical Turk (MTurk)*, a method for people to be compensated to perform tasks that can be completed via the internet. Buhrmester et al. (2011) described this resource and concluded that it is an inexpensive and efficient method of recruiting diverse samples for psychology research. MTurk has expanded with a new recruitment tool, *Prime Panels*. Prime Panels is designed to assist researchers studying unique samples with particular characteristics (e.g., men over 50 with a particular medical condition). More information is available at **https://www.mturk.com/** and **https://www.turkprime.com/**.

As researchers increasingly use online research strategies, it is important to consider ethical implications. The ethical issues of internet research are described in detail by Buchanan and Hvizdak (2009), Buchanan and Williams (2010), and Hoerger and Currell (2012).

Interviews

The fact that an interview requires an interaction between people has important implications. First, people are often more likely to agree to answer questions for a real person than to answer a mailed questionnaire. Good interviewers become quite skilled in convincing people to participate. Thus, response rates tend to be higher when interviews are used. The interviewer and respondent often establish a rapport that helps motivate the person to answer all the questions and complete the survey. People are more likely to leave questions unanswered on a written questionnaire than in an interview. An important advantage of an interview is that the interviewer can clarify any problems the person might have in understanding questions. Further, an interviewer can ask follow-up questions if needed to help clarify answers.

One potential problem in interviews is called **interviewer bias.** This term describes all of the biases that can arise from the fact that the interviewer is a unique human being interacting with another human. Thus, one potential problem is that the interviewer could subtly bias the respondent's answers by inadvertently showing approval or disapproval of certain answers. Interviewer characteristics such as race, sex, or age can influence responses, especially when asking about sensitive topics. Imagine how you might respond differently if a male or female interviewer is asking about your sexual history. Another problem is that interviewers may have expectations that could lead them to "see what they are looking for" in the respondents' answers. Such expectations could bias their interpretations of responses or lead them to probe further for an answer from certain respondents but not from others—for example, when questioning Whites but not people from other groups or when testing boys but not girls. Careful screening and training of interviewers help to limit such biases.

We can now examine three methods of conducting interviews: face-to-face, telephone, and focus groups.

Face-to-Face Interviews

Face-to-face interviews require that the interviewer and respondent meet to conduct the interview. Usually the interviewer travels to the person's home or office, although sometimes the respondent goes to the interviewer's office. Such interviews tend to be quite expensive and time-consuming. Therefore, they are most likely to be used when the sample size is fairly small and there are clear benefits to a face-to-face interaction.

Telephone Interviews

Almost all interviews for large-scale surveys are done via telephone. *Telephone interviews* are less expensive than face-to-face interviews, and they allow efficient data collection because many respondents can be contacted quickly with no need for travel. There are two forms of the telephone interview. The first is a live interview in which an interviewer asks the questions and records responses. This is usually conducted using a *computer-assisted telephone interview (CATI)* system—the interviewer's questions are prompted on the computer screen, and the data are entered directly into the computer for analysis. More recently, *interactive voice response (IVR)* technology has been adapted for survey data collection. With IVR, respondents listen to questions and respond via the telephone keypad or a speech recognition system. Both methods lower the cost of telephone surveys by reducing labor and data analysis costs. IVR surveys may be particularly useful when asking sensitive questions about topics such as drug use or sexual behaviors (Midanik & Greenfield, 2008). It is also possible to combine the methods—the interviewer can switch to IVR for a portion of the interview.

Focus Group Interviews

An interview strategy that is often used by businesses is the focus group interview. A **focus group** is an interview with a group of about 6 to 10 individuals brought together for a period of usually 2–3 hours. Virtually any topic can be explored in a focus group. Often the group members are selected because they have a particular knowledge of or interest in the topic. Because the focus group requires people to both spend time and incur some costs traveling to the focus group location, participants usually receive some sort of monetary or gift incentive.

The questions in a focus group tend to be open-ended, and they are asked of the whole group. An advantage here is that group interaction is possible: People can respond to one another, and one comment can trigger a variety of responses. The interviewer must be skilled in working with groups both to facilitate communication and to deal with problems that may arise, such as one or two persons trying to dominate the discussion or hostility between group members.

The group discussion is usually recorded and may be transcribed. The recordings and transcripts are then analyzed to find themes and areas of group consensus and disagreement. Sometimes the transcripts are analyzed with a computer program to search for certain words and phrases. Researchers usually prefer to conduct multiple discussion groups on a given topic to make sure that the information gathered is not unique to one group of people. However, because each focus group is time-consuming and costly and provides a great deal of information, researchers do not conduct very many such groups on any one topic.

SURVEY DESIGNS TO STUDY CHANGES OVER TIME

Surveys most frequently study people at one point in time. On many occasions, however, researchers wish to make comparisons over time. For example, local newspapers often hire firms to conduct an annual random survey of county residents. Because the questions are the same each year, it is possible to track changes over time in such variables as satisfaction with the area, attitudes toward the school system, and perceived major problems facing the county. Similarly, a large number of first-year students are surveyed each year at colleges throughout the United States to study changes in the composition, attitudes, and aspirations of this group (Eagan et al., 2015). First-year college students today, for instance, come from more ethnically diverse backgrounds than those in the 1970s (90.9% of respondents in 1971 were White whereas in 2015, 68.2% were). Political attitudes have also shifted over time among this group: Trends in opinions about paying taxes and abortion rights can be seen. And the percentage of new students who think that their "emotional health" is above average or in the "top 10%" has decreased from 64% in 1985 to 51% in 2015.

Another way to study changes over time is to conduct a **panel study** in which the same people are surveyed at two or more points in time. In a two-wave panel study, people are surveyed at two points in time; in a three-wave panel study, three surveys are conducted; and so on. Panel studies are particularly important when the research question addresses the relationship between one variable at "time 1" and another variable at some later "time 2." For example, Schmiedeberg et al., (2017) analyzed five waves of data from a study of more than 5,000 German respondents to examine whether changes in frequency of sexual intercourse in one wave of data are related to changes in ratings of life satisfaction in the next wave. Does an increase in sexual frequency result in an increase in life satisfaction, and does a decrease in sexual frequency result in a decrease in life satisfaction? This was indeed the result of the study, and it was consistent for both women and men.

SAMPLING FROM A POPULATION

Most research projects involve selecting a **sample** of participants from a population of interest. The **population** is composed of all individuals of interest to the researcher. One population of interest in a large public opinion poll, for instance, might be all eligible voters in the United States. This implies that the population of interest does not include people under the age of 18, convicted prisoners, visitors from other countries, and anyone else not eligible to vote. You might conduct a survey in which your population consists of all students at your college or university. With enough time and money, a survey researcher could conceivably contact everyone in the population. The United States attempts to do this every 10 years with an official census of the entire population. With a relatively small population, however, you might find it relatively easy to study the entire population.

Let's use another example. What if you asked every single student at your college or university to tell you whether they prefer to study at home or at school and you found that 64% preferred studying at home. In this case, you would be very certain of the answer to your question—after all, you asked everybody. That, of course, would be quite costly; you would likely have to hire a team of research assistants to track down every student. But suppose you are not independently wealthy (or you have better uses for your wealth). In that case, you could randomly select a subgroup of students at your university and ask them the question. With proper sampling, we can use information obtained from the participants (or "respondents") who were sampled to estimate characteristics of the population as a whole. Statistical theory allows us to use data obtained from a sample to estimate what the entire population is like.

Confidence Intervals

When researchers make inferences about a population from a sample, they do so with a certain degree of confidence. Here is a statement that you might see when you read the results of a survey based on a sample of a population: "The results from the survey are accurate within ±3 percentage points, using a 95% level of confidence." What does this tell you?

To extend our example above, suppose you asked a small sample of students at your college to tell you whether they prefer to study at home or at school, and in that case the survey results from the sample indicate that 61% prefer to study at home. Using the same degree of confidence, you would now know that the actual population value is probably between 58% (61% − 3%) and 64% (61% + 3%). This is called a **confidence interval**—you can have 95% confidence that the true population value lies within this interval around the obtained sample result. Indeed, in our example we know the population value (64%). Your best estimate of the population value is the sample value. However, because you have only a sample and not the entire population, your result may be in error. The confidence interval gives you information about the likely amount of the error. The formal term for this error is **sampling error,** although you are probably more familiar with the term *margin* *of error.* Recall the concept of measurement error discussed in the chapter **"Measurement Concepts."** When you measure a single individual on a variable, the obtained score may deviate from the true score because of measurement error. Similarly, when you study one sample, the obtained result may deviate from the true population value because of sampling error.

The surveys you often read about in newspapers and the previous example deal with percentages. What about questions that ask for more quantitative information? The logic in this instance is very much the same. For example, if you also ask students to report how many hours and minutes they studied during the previous day, you might find that the average amount of time was 76 minutes. A confidence interval could then be calculated based on the size of the sample; for example, the 95% confidence interval is 76 minutes plus or minus 10 minutes. It is highly likely that the true population value lies within the interval of 66 to 86 minutes.

Sample Size

It is important to note that a larger sample size will reduce the size of the confidence interval—the closer you get to receiving responses from every member of a population, the more accurate the estimate of that answer can be! Although the size of a confidence interval is determined by several factors, the most important is sample size. Larger samples are more likely to yield data that accurately reflect the true population value. This statement should make intuitive sense to you; a sample of 200 people from your school should yield more accurate data about your school than a sample of 25 people.

How large should the sample be? The sample size can be determined using a mathematical formula that takes into account the size of the confidence interval and the size of the population you are studying. **Table 1** shows the sample size needed for a sample percentage to be accurate within plus or minus 3%, 5%, and 10%, given a 95% level of confidence. Note first that you need a larger sample size for increased accuracy. With a population size of 10,000, you need a sample of 370 for accuracy within ±5%; the needed sample size increases to 964 for accuracy within ±3%. Note that sample size is *not* a constant percentage of the population size. Many people believe that proper sampling requires a certain percentage of the population; these people often complain about survey results when they discover that a survey of an entire state was done with "only" 700 or 1,000 people. However, you can see in the table that the needed sample size does not change much, even as the population size increases from 5,000 to 100,000 or more. As Fowler (2014) notes, "a sample of 150 people will describe a population of 1,500 or 15 million with virtually the same degree of accuracy" (p. 38).

TABLE 1   Sample size and precision of population estimates (95% confidence level)

Size of population	Precision of estimate		
	±3%	±5%	±10%
2,000	696	322	92
5,000	879	357	94
10,000	964	370	95
50,000	1,045	381	96
100,000	1,055	383	96
Over 100,000	1,067	384	96

Note: The sample sizes were calculated using conservative assumptions about the nature of the true population values.

SAMPLING TECHNIQUES

There are two broad categories of techniques for sampling individuals from a population: probability sampling and nonprobability sampling.

- **Probability sampling:** Each member of the population has a specifiable probability (chance) of being chosen.

- **Nonprobability sampling:** The probability (chance) of any particular member of the population being chosen is unknown.

Probability sampling is required when you want to make precise statements about a specific population on the basis of the results of your survey. Although nonprobability sampling is not as sophisticated as probability sampling, we shall see that nonprobability sampling is quite common and useful in many circumstances.

Probability Sampling

Simple Random Sampling

With **simple random sampling,** every member of the population has an equal probability of being selected for the sample. If the population has 1,000 members, each has one chance out of a thousand of being selected. Suppose you want to sample students who attend your school. A list of all students would be needed; from that list, students would be chosen at random to form the sample.

When conducting telephone interviews, researchers commonly have a computer generate phone numbers used in the area of the sample. This will produce a random sample of the population because most people have phones (if many people do not have phones, the sample would be biased).

Stratified Random Sampling

A somewhat more complicated probability sampling procedure is **stratified random sampling.** The population is divided into subgroups (also known as *strata*), and random sampling techniques are then used to select sample members from each stratum. Any number of dimensions could be used to divide the population, but the dimension (or dimensions) chosen should be relevant to the problem under study. For instance, a survey of political attitudes might stratify on the basis of age, gender, and amount of education because these factors are related to political attitudes. Stratification on the basis of height or hair color would be ridiculous for this survey as these variables are likely to be unrelated to a survey of political attitudes.

Stratified random sampling has the advantage of a built-in assurance that the sample will accurately reflect the numerical composition of the various subgroups. This kind of accuracy is particularly important when some subgroups represent very small percentages of the population. For instance, if African Americans make up 5% of a city of 100,000, a simple random sample of 100 people might not include any African Americans; a stratified random sample would include five African Americans chosen randomly from the population. In practice, when it is important to represent a small group within a population, researchers will "oversample" that group to ensure that a representative sample of the group is surveyed; a large enough sample must be obtained to be able to make inferences about the population. Thus, if your campus's distribution of students is similar to that of the city described here and you need to compare attitudes of African Americans and Whites, you will need to sample a large percentage of the African American students and only a small percentage of the White students to obtain a reasonable number of respondents from each group.

Cluster Sampling

It might have occurred to you that obtaining a list of all members of a population might be difficult. What if officials at your school decide that you cannot have access to a list of all students? What if you want to study a population that has no list of members, such as people who work in county health care agencies? In such situations, a technique called **cluster sampling** can be used to create a probability sample. Rather than randomly sampling from a list of individuals, the researcher can identify "clusters" of individuals and then sample from these clusters. After the clusters are chosen, all individuals in each cluster are included in the sample. For example, you might conduct the survey of students using cluster sampling by identifying all classes being taught—the classes are the clusters of students. You could then randomly sample from this list of classes and have all members of the chosen classes complete your survey (making sure, of course, that no one completes the survey twice).

Most often, use of cluster sampling requires a series of samples from larger to smaller clusters—a multistage approach. For example, a researcher interested in studying county health care agencies might first randomly determine a number of states to sample and then randomly sample counties from each state chosen. The researcher would then go to the health care agencies in each of these counties and study the people who work in them. Note that the main advantage of cluster sampling is that the researcher does not have to sample from lists of individuals to obtain a truly random sample of individuals.

Nonprobability Sampling

In contrast to probability sampling, where the probability of every member is knowable, in nonprobability sampling, the probability of being selected is not known. Nonprobability sampling techniques are quite arbitrary. A population may be defined, but little effort is expended to ensure that the sample accurately represents the population. However, among other things, nonprobability samples are cheap and convenient. Three types of nonprobability sampling are convenience sampling, purposive sampling, and quota sampling.

Convenience Sampling

One common form of nonprobability sampling is **convenience sampling,** also called "haphazard" sampling. Convenience sampling could be called a "take-them-where-you-find-them" method of obtaining participants. Thus, you would select a sample of students from your school in any way that is convenient. You might stand in front of the student union at 9 a.m. and interview passersby, ask people who sit around you in your classes to participate, or visit a couple of fraternity and sorority residences. Unfortunately, such procedures are likely to introduce biases into the sample so that the sample may not be an accurate representation of the population of all students. Thus, if you selected your sample from students walking by the student union at 9 a.m., your sample excludes students who do not frequent this location, and it may also eliminate afternoon and evening students. At many colleges this sample would differ from the population of all students by being younger, working fewer hours, and being more likely to belong to a fraternity or sorority. Sample biases such as these limit your ability to use your sample data to estimate the actual population values. Your results may not generalize to your intended population but instead may describe only the biased sample that you obtained.

Purposive Sampling

A second form of nonprobability sampling is **purposive sampling.** The *purpose* is to obtain a sample of people who meet some predetermined criterion. Sometimes at a large movie complex, you may see researchers asking customers to fill out a questionnaire about one or more movies. They are always doing purposive sampling. Instead of sampling anyone walking toward the theater, they take a look at each person to make sure that they fit some criterion—under the age of 30 or an adult with one or more children, for example. This is a good way to limit the sample to a certain group of people. However, it is not a probability sample, because selection was determined by convenience.

Quota Sampling

A third form of nonprobability sampling is **quota sampling.** A researcher who uses this technique chooses a sample that reflects the numerical composition of various subgroups in the population. Thus, quota sampling is similar to the stratified sampling procedure previously described; however, random sampling does not occur when you use quota sampling. To illustrate, suppose you want to ensure that your sample of students includes 19% first-year students, 23% sophomores, 26% juniors, 22% seniors, and 10% graduate students because these are the percentages of the classes in the total population. A quota sampling technique would make sure you have these percentages, but you would still collect your data using convenience techniques. If you did not get enough graduate students in front of the student union, perhaps you could go to a graduate class to complete the sample. Although quota sampling is a bit more sophisticated than convenience sampling, the problem remains that no restrictions are placed on how individuals in the various subgroups are chosen. The sample does reflect the numerical composition of the whole population of interest, but respondents within each subgroup are selected in a haphazard manner. These techniques are summarized in **Table 2.**

TABLE 2   **Advantages and disadvantages of sampling techniques**

Sample technique	Example	Advantages	Disadvantages
Probability sampling techniques			
Simple random sampling	A computer program randomly chooses 100 students from a list of all 10,000 students at College X.	Representative of population.	May cost more. May be difficult to get full list of all members of any population of interest.
Stratified random sampling	The names of all 10,000 College X students are sorted by major, and a computer program randomly chooses 50 students from each major.	Representative of population.	May cost more. May be difficult to get full list of all members of any population of interest.
Cluster sampling	Two hundred clusters of psychology majors are identified at schools all over the United States. Out of these 200 clusters, 10 clusters are chosen randomly, and every psychology major in each cluster is sampled.	Researcher does not have to sample from lists of individuals in order to get a full, random sample.	May cost more. May be difficult to get full list of all members of any randomly chosen cluster.

Sample technique	Example	Advantages	Disadvantages
Nonprobability sampling techniques			
Convenience sampling	Ask students around you at lunch or in class to participate.	Inexpensive, efficient, convenient.	Likely to introduce bias into the sample; results may not generalize to intended population.
Purposive sampling	In an otherwise haphazard sample, select individuals who meet a criterion (e.g., an age group).	Sample includes only types of individuals you are interested in.	Likely to introduce bias into the sample; results may not generalize to intended population.
Quota sampling	Collect specific proportions of data representative of percentages of groups within population, then use haphazard techniques.	Inexpensive, efficient, convenient.	Likely to introduce bias into the sample; results may not generalize to intended population; no method for choosing individuals in subgroups.

EVALUATING SAMPLES

Samples should be representative of the population from which they are drawn. A completely unbiased sample is one that is highly representative of the population. How do you create a completely unbiased sample? First, you would use a probability sampling technique and randomly sample from a population that contains *all* individuals in the population. Second, you would contact and obtain completed responses from *all* individuals selected to be in the sample. Unfortunately, such standards are rarely achieved. Even if random sampling is used, bias can be introduced from two sources: the sampling frame used and poor response rates. Moreover, even though nonprobability samples have more potential sources of bias than probability samples, there are many reasons (summarized in **Table 2**) why they are used and should be evaluated positively.

Sampling Frame

The **sampling frame** is the *actual* population of individuals (or clusters) from which a random sample will be drawn. Rarely will this perfectly coincide with the population of interest—some biases will be introduced. Suppose you want to know what doctors think about a new state law that impacts patient rights. A reasonable sampling frame would be all doctors listed in your telephone directory. Immediately you can see that you have limited your sample to a particular geographical area. More important, you have also limited the sample to doctors who have private practices—doctors who work only in clinics and hospitals have been excluded. At this point, you may want to find out if the state medical board lists doctors by name and address—this might produce a better sampling frame. When evaluating the results of the survey, you need to consider how well the sampling frame matches the population of interest. Often the biases introduced are quite minor; however, they could be consequential to the results of a study.

Response Rate

The **response rate** in a survey is simply the percentage of people who were selected in the sample who actually completed the survey. Thus, if you mail 1,000 questionnaires to a random sample of adults in your community and 500 are completed and returned to you, the response rate is 50%.

Response rate is important because it indicates how much bias there might be in the final sample of respondents. Nonrespondents may differ from respondents in any number of ways, including age, income, marital status, and education. The lower the response rate, the greater the likelihood that such biases may distort the findings and in turn limit the ability to generalize the findings to the population of interest (i.e., reduce the external validity of the results).

In general, mail surveys have lower response rates than telephone surveys. With both methods, however, steps can be taken to maximize response rates. With mail surveys, an explanatory postcard or letter can be sent a week or so prior to mailing the survey. Follow-up reminders and even second mailings of the questionnaire are often effective in increasing response rates. It often helps to have a personally stamped return envelope rather than a business reply envelope. Even the look of the cover page of the questionnaire can be important (Dillman et al., 2014; Guiding Principles for Mail and Internet Surveys, 2012).

With telephone surveys, respondents who are not home can be called again, and people who cannot be interviewed today can be scheduled for a call at a more convenient time. Sometimes an incentive may be necessary to increase response rates. Such incentives can include cash, a gift, or a gift certificate for agreeing to participate. A crisp dollar bill "thank you" can be included with a mailed questionnaire. Other incentives include a chance to win a prize drawing or a promise to contribute money to a charity. Finally, researchers should attempt to convince people that the survey's purposes are important and their participation will be a valuable contribution.

> Now, try organizing your own nonprobability sampling technique in **Check Your Learning:** Practice Exercise #2.

REASONS FOR USING CONVENIENCE SAMPLES

Much of the research in psychology uses nonprobability sampling techniques to obtain participants for either surveys or experiments. The advantage of these techniques is that the investigator can obtain research participants without spending a great deal of money or time on selecting—or collecting data from—the sample. For example, it is common practice to select participants from students in introductory psychology classes. Often these students are asked to participate in studies being conducted by faculty and their students; the introductory psychology students can choose which studies they wish to participate in.

Even in studies that do not use college students, the sample is often based on convenience rather than concern for obtaining a random sample. One of our colleagues studies children, but they are almost always from one particular elementary school. You can guess that this is because our colleague has established a good relationship with the teachers and administrators; thus, obtaining permission to conduct the research is fairly easy. Even though the sample is biased because it includes only children from one neighborhood that has certain social and economic characteristics, the advantages outweigh the sample concerns for the researcher.

Why aren't researchers more worried about obtaining random samples from the "general population" for their research? Most psychological research is focused on studying the relationships between variables even though the sample may be biased (e.g., the sample will have more college students, be younger, etc., than the general U.S. population). But to put this in perspective, remember that even a random sample of the general population of U.S. residents tells us nothing about citizens of other countries. So our research findings provide important information even though the data cannot be strictly generalized beyond the population defined by the sample that was used. For example, the findings of Brown and Rahhal (1994) regarding experiences of younger and older adults when they hid an object but later forgot the location are meaningful even though the actual sample consisted of current students (younger adults) and alumni (older adults) of a particular university who received a mailed questionnaire.

In the chapter **"Generalization"** we will emphasize that generalization in science is dependent upon replicating the results. We do not need better samples of younger and older adults; instead, we should look for replications of the findings using multiple samples and multiple methods. The results of many studies can then be synthesized to gain greater insight into the findings (cf. Albright & Malloy, 2000).

These issues will be explored further in the chapter **"Generalization."** For now, it is also important to recognize that some nonprobability samples are more representative than others. Introductory psychology students, for instance, are fairly representative of college students in general, and most college student samples are fairly representative of young adults. So there are not many obvious biases, particularly if you are studying basic psychological processes.

On the other hand, other samples might be much less representative of an intended population. When local news programs, 24-hour news channels, or websites ask viewers to vote on a topic, the resulting samples are not representative of the population to which they are often trying to generalize. First, their viewers may be different from the U.S. population in meaningful ways (e.g., more Fox News viewers are conservative, more MSNBC viewers are liberal). Second, these programs and websites often ask about hot-button topics, things that people care passionately about, because that is what drives viewers and visitors to tune in. Questions about abortion, taxes, and wars tend to drive certain types of viewers to these informal "polls." The results, whatever they may be, are biased because the sample consists primarily of people who have chosen to watch the program or visit the website, and they have chosen to vote because they are deeply interested in a topic.

You now have a great deal of information about methods for asking people about themselves. If you engage in this type of research, you will often need to design your own questions by following the guidelines described in this chapter and consulting sources such as Groves et al. (2009) and Fowler (2014). However, you can also adapt questions and entire questionnaires that have been used in previous research. Consider using previously developed questions, particularly if they have proven useful in other studies (make sure you do not violate any copyrights, however). A variety of measures of social, political, and occupational attitudes developed by others have been compiled by Robinson and his colleagues (Robinson et al., 1969; Robinson et al., 1968; Robinson et al., 1991, 1999).

ILLUSTRATIVE ARTICLE: CONDUCTING EXPERIMENTS

Student alcohol use and abuse is a major concern on many college campuses. Of course, some populations of college students use alcohol more than others. Indeed, varsity student athletes have been observed to be such a population—using alcohol more often, and more often to drunkenness, than students who are not varsity athletes. Few studies, however, have examined alcohol consumption by other types of university athletes.

Barry et al., (2015) analyzed data from the 2011 National College Health Assessment, which surveyed nearly 30,000 college students from all over the United States in order to understand differences in alcohol use (and its consequences) among intercollegiate athletes, club-sport athletes, intramural athletes, and non-athlete college students.

First, acquire and read the following article (available at **https://www.researchgate.net/publication/ 268529429_Alcohol_Use_among_College_Athletes_Do_Intercollegiate_Club_or_Intramural_S tudent_Athletes_Drink_Differently**) :

> Barry, A. E., Howell, S. M., Riplinger, A., & Piazza-Gardner, A. K. (2015). Alcohol use among college athletes: Do intercollegiate, club, or intramural student athletes drink differently? *Substance Use & Misuse, 50*(3), 302–307. https://doi.org/10.3109/10826084.2014.977398

Then, after reading the article, consider the following:

1. What kinds of questions were included in the survey? Identify examples.
2. How and when was the survey administered? Was the survey conducted via an internet-based survey or a paper-based survey?
3. What was the nature of the sampling strategy? Did the researchers use probability sampling or nonprobability sampling? What was the final sample size?
4. Describe the demographic profile of the sample.
5. Evaluate the sampling strategy: Do you think that sample can be generalized to the entire population of U.S. college students? Why or why not?

CRITICAL THINKING: BEING A SKILLED CONSUMER OF RESEARCH

1. As we noted at the beginning of this chapter, surveys are being conducted all the time. Many survey reports are not published in peer-reviewed journals. Identify a survey report of interest to you and answer the questions below. Survey reports can be found on the internet. Here are some examples: Youth Risk Behavior Survey Surveillance: **https://www.cdc.gov/healthyyouth/d ata/yrbs/index.htm**; Pew Religious Landscape Study: **https://www.pewforum.org/religious-lan dscape-study/**; National Crime Victimization Survey (NCVS): **https://www.bjs.gov/index.cfm?t y=dcdetail&iid=245**; Behavioral Risk Factor Surveillance System: **https://cdc.gov/brfss/**

   a. What kinds of questions were included in the survey? Identify examples of each.
   b. How were the questions developed?
   c. How and when was the survey administered?
   d. What was the nature of the sampling strategy? What was the final sample size?
   e. What was the response rate for the survey?
   f. What was the confidence interval for the survey findings?
   g. Describe at least one survey finding that you found particularly interesting or surprising.

2. Suppose you want to study the relationships between ratings of family satisfaction, job satisfaction, and life satisfaction. Describe how you might conduct an online survey of adults to obtain your data. What would be the reason to conduct a two-wave panel study rather than a one-wave-only procedure?

Check Your Learning: Practice Exercises

Practice Exercise #1

	Question Wording: What Is the Problem?			
Read each of the following questions and identify the problems for each.				
	Negative wording	Simplicity	Double-barreled	Loaded
1. Professors should not be required to take daily attendance. 1 = (Strongly Disagree) and 5 = (Strongly Agree)				
2. I enjoy studying and spending time with friends on weekends.				
3. Do you support the legislation that would unfairly tax hardworking farmers?				
4. I would describe myself as funny and intelligent.				
5. Do you believe the relationship between cell phone behavior and consumption of fast food is orthogonal?				
6. Restaurants should not have to be inspected each month.				
7. Are you in favor of the boss's whim to cut lunchtime to 30 minutes?				

Practice Exercise #2:

Suppose you want to know how many books in a bookstore have only male authors, only female authors, or male and female co-authors (assume that the "bookstore" is a retail store located in or near your city). Because there are many hundreds of books in the store, you decide to study a sample of the books rather than examine every book there. Describe a possible sampling procedure using a nonprobability sampling technique. Then describe how you might sample books using a probability sampling technique. Now speculate on how the outcomes of your research might differ using the two techniques. You might think about an additional complication: What if you want to conduct your study with a sample of books available from an online bookseller?

(Some answers are provided at the end of this chapter.)

CHAPTER REVIEW

Review Questions

1. What is a survey? Describe some research questions you might address with a survey.
2. What are some factors to take into consideration when constructing questions for surveys (including both questions and response alternatives)?
3. What are the advantages and disadvantages of using questionnaires versus interviews in a survey?
4. Compare the different questionnaire, interview, and internet survey administration methods.
5. Define interviewer bias.
6. What is a social desirability response set?
7. How does sample size affect the interpretation of survey results?
8. Distinguish between probability and nonprobability sampling techniques. What are the implications of each?
9. Distinguish between simple random, stratified random, and cluster sampling.
10. Distinguish between convenience (haphazard) sampling and quota sampling.
11. Why don't researchers who want to test hypotheses about the relationships between variables worry a great deal about random sampling?

Study Terms

Closed-ended questions

Cluster sampling

Confidence interval

Convenience sampling

Focus group

Graphic rating scale

Interviewer bias

Mail survey

Nonprobability sampling

Online survey

Open-ended questions

Panel study

Population

Probability sampling

Purposive sampling

Quota sampling

Rating scale

Response rate

Response set

Sample

Sampling error

Sampling frame

Semantic differential scale

Simple random sampling

Social desirability

Stratified random sampling

Survey research

Yea-saying and nay-saying

Check Your Learning: Answers

1. negative wording; 2. double-barreled; 3. loaded; 4. double-barreled; 5. simplicity; 6. negative wording; 7. loaded

8 Experimental Design

mikser45/Shutterstock

LEARNING OBJECTIVES

- Provide a definition of a confounding variable and describe how confounding variables are related to internal validity.
- Describe the posttest-only design and the pretest-posttest design, including the advantages and disadvantages of each design.
- Contrast an independent groups (between-subjects) design with a repeated measures (within-subjects) design.
- Summarize the advantages and disadvantages of using a repeated measures design. Explain how counterbalancing provides a way of addressing the order effects problem.
- Describe a matched pairs design, including reasons to use this design.

In the experimental method, the researcher attempts to control all extraneous variables. Suppose you want to test the hypothesis that exercise affects mood. To do this, you might put one group of people through a 1-hour aerobics workout and put another group in a room where they are asked to watch a video of people exercising for an hour. All participants would then complete the same mood assessment. Now suppose that the people in the aerobics class rate themselves as happier than those in the video-viewing condition. Can the difference in mood be attributed to the difference in the exercise? Yes, *if* there is no other difference between the groups. However, what if the aerobics group was given the mood assessment in a room with windows but the video-only group was tested in a room without windows? In that case, it would be impossible to know whether the better mood of the participants in the aerobics group was due to the exercise or to the presence of windows.

CONFOUNDING AND INTERNAL VALIDITY

Recall from the chapter **"Fundamental Research Issues"** that the experimental method has the advantage of allowing a relatively unambiguous interpretation of results. To conduct a true experiment, the researcher manipulates the independent variable to create groups (an experimental group and a comparison or control group). All other variables are kept constant, either through *experimental control* or through *randomization,* including random assignment to groups. The groups are then compared on the dependent variable. If the groups differ on the dependent variable, the researcher can conclude that the independent variable caused the results, because the only difference between the groups is the manipulated independent variable.

Although the task of designing an experiment is logically elegant and exquisitely simple, you should be aware of possible pitfalls. In the hypothetical exercise experiment just described, the variables of exercise and window presence are confounded. The window variable was not kept constant. A **confounding variable** is a variable that varies along with the independent variable. Confounding occurs when the effects of the independent variable and an uncontrolled variable are intertwined so that you cannot determine which of the variables is responsible for the observed effect on the dependent variable. If the window variable had been held constant, both the exercise and the video condition would have taken place in identical rooms. That way, the effect of windows would not be a factor to consider when interpreting the difference between the groups.

In short, both rooms in the exercise experiment should have had windows or both should have been windowless. Because one room had windows and one room did not, any difference in the dependent variable (mood) cannot be attributed solely to the independent variable (exercise). An alternative explanation can be offered: The difference in mood may have been caused, at least in part, by the window variable.

Good experimental design requires eliminating all possible confounding variables that could result in alternative explanations. A researcher can claim that the independent variable caused the results only by eliminating competing, alternative explanations. When the results of an experiment can confidently be attributed to the effect of the independent variable, the experiment is said to have **internal validity.** (Remember that internal validity refers to the accuracy of conclusions drawn about cause and effect; see the chapter **"Fundamental Research Issues."**) To achieve a high degree of internal validity, the researcher must design and conduct the experiment so that only the independent variable can be the cause of the results (Campbell & Stanley, 1966). This chapter will focus on true experimental designs, which provide the highest degree of internal validity.

BASIC EXPERIMENTS

The simplest possible experimental design has two variables: the independent variable and the dependent variable. The independent variable has a minimum of two levels, an experimental group and a control group. Researchers must make every effort to ensure that the only difference between the two groups is the manipulated (independent) variable.

Remember, the experimental method involves control over extraneous variables, through either keeping such variables constant (experimental control) or using randomization to make sure that any extraneous variables will affect both groups equally. The basic, simple experimental design can take one of two forms: a posttest-only design or a pretest-posttest design.

Posttest-Only Design

A researcher using a **posttest-only design** must (1) obtain two equivalent groups of participants, (2) manipulate the independent variable, and (3) measure the effect of the independent variable on the dependent variable. The posttest-only design looks like this:

Thus, the first step is to choose the participants and assign them to the two groups. The procedures used must achieve equivalent groups to eliminate any potential **selection differences:** The people selected to be in the conditions cannot differ in any systematic way. For example, you cannot select high-income individuals to participate in one condition and low-income individuals for the other. The groups can be made equivalent by randomly assigning participants to the two conditions or by having the same participants participate in both conditions. Recall from the chapter **"Fundamental Research Issues"** that random assignment is done in such a way that each participant is assigned to a condition randomly without regard to any personal characteristics. The R in the diagram means that participants were randomly assigned to the two groups.

Next, the researcher must choose two levels of the independent variable, such as an experimental group that receives a treatment and a control group that does not. Thus, a researcher might study the effect of reward on motivation by offering a reward to one group of children before they play a game and offering no reward to children in the control group. A study testing the effect of a treatment method for reducing smoking could compare a group that receives the treatment with a control group that does not. Another approach would be to use two different amounts of the independent variable—that is, to use more reward in one group than the other or to compare the effects of different amounts of relaxation training designed to help people quit smoking (e.g., 1 hour of training compared with 10 hours). Another approach would be to include two qualitatively different conditions; for example, one group of test-anxious students might write about their anxiety and the other group could participate in a meditation exercise prior to a test. All of these approaches would provide a basis for comparison of the two groups. (Of course, experiments may include more than two groups; for example, we might compare two different smoking cessation treatments along with a no-treatment control group—these types of experimental designs will be described in the chapter **"Complex Experimental Designs."**)

Finally, the effect of the independent variable is measured. The same measurement procedure is used for both groups, so that comparison of the two groups is possible. Because the groups were equivalent prior to the introduction of the independent variable and there were no confounding variables, any difference between the groups on the dependent variable must be attributed to the effect of the independent variable. This elegant experimental design has a high degree of internal validity. That is, we can confidently conclude that the independent variable caused the dependent variable. In actuality, a statistical significance test would be used to assess the difference between the groups. However, we do not need to be concerned with statistics at this point. An experiment must be well designed, and confounding variables must be eliminated before we can draw conclusions from statistical analyses.

Pretest-Posttest Design

The only difference between the posttest-only design and the **pretest-posttest design** is that in the latter a pretest is given before the experimental manipulation is introduced:

This design makes it possible to ascertain that the groups were, in fact, equivalent at the beginning of the experiment. However, this precaution is usually not necessary if participants have been randomly assigned to the two groups. With a sufficiently large sample of participants, random assignment will produce groups that are virtually identical in all respects.

You are probably wondering how many participants are needed in each group to make sure that random assignment has made the groups equivalent. The larger the sample, the less likelihood there is that the groups will differ in any systematic way prior to the manipulation of the independent variable. In addition, as sample size increases, so does the likelihood that any difference between the groups on the dependent variable is due to the effect of the independent variable. There are formal procedures for determining the sample size needed to detect a statistically significant effect, but as a rule of thumb you will probably need a minimum of 50 participants per condition (Simmons et al., 2013). In some areas of research, many more participants may be necessary. However, fewer participants may be appropriate when conducting exploratory research. Further issues in determining the number of participants needed for an experiment are described in the chapter **"Understanding Research Results: Statistical Inference."**

Comparing Posttest-Only and Pretest-Posttest Designs

Each of these two experimental designs has advantages and disadvantages that influence the decision whether to include or omit a pretest. The first decision concerns the equivalence of the groups in the experiment. Although randomization is likely to produce equivalent groups, it is possible that, with small sample sizes, the groups will not be equal. Thus, a pretest enables the researcher to tell whether the groups are in fact equivalent to begin with.

The pretest-posttest design immediately makes us focus on the *change* from pretest to posttest. This emphasis on change is incorporated into the analysis of the group differences. Also, the extent of change in each individual can be examined. If a smoking reduction program appears to be effective for some individuals but not others, attempts can be made to find out why.

A pretest is also useful whenever there is a possibility that participants will drop out of the experiment; this is most likely to occur in a study that lasts over a long time period. The dropout factor in experiments is called **attrition** or **mortality.** People may drop out for reasons unrelated to the experimental manipulation, such as illness; sometimes, however, attrition is related to the experimental manipulation. Even if the groups are equivalent to begin with, different attrition rates can make them nonequivalent. How might mortality affect a treatment program designed to reduce smoking? One possibility is that the heaviest smokers in the experimental group might leave the program. Therefore, when the posttest is given, only the light smokers would remain, so that a comparison of the experimental and control groups would show less smoking in the experimental group even if the program had no effect. In this way, attrition (mortality) becomes an alternative explanation for the results. Use of a pretest enables you to assess the effects of attrition; you can look at the pretest scores of the dropouts and know whether their scores differed from the scores of the individuals completing the study. Thus, with the pretest, it is possible to examine whether attrition is a plausible alternative explanation—an advantage in the experimental design.

One disadvantage of a pretest, however, is that it may be time-consuming and awkward to administer in the context of the particular experimental procedures being used. Perhaps most important, a pretest can sensitize participants to what you are studying, enabling them to figure out what is being studied and (potentially) why. They may then react differently to the manipulation than they would have without the pretest. When a pretest affects the way participants react to the manipulation, it is very difficult to generalize the results to people who have not received a pretest. That is, the independent variable may not have an effect in the real world, where pretests are rarely given. We will examine this issue more fully in the chapter **"Generalization."**

However, if awareness of the pretest is a problem, the pretest can be disguised. One way to do this is by administering it in a completely different situation with a different experimenter. Another approach is to embed the pretest in a set of irrelevant measures so it is not obvious that the researcher is interested in a particular topic.

It is also possible to assess the impact of the pretest directly with a combination of both the posttest-only and the pretest-posttest design. In this design, half the participants receive only the posttest, and the other half receive both the pretest and the posttest (see **Figure 1**). This is formally called a **Solomon four-group design.**

If there is no impact of the pretest, the posttest scores will be the same in the two control groups (with and without the pretest) and in the two experimental groups. Garvin and Damson (2008) employed a Solomon four-group design to study the effect of viewing female fitness magazine models on a measure of depressed mood. Female college students spent 30 minutes viewing either the fitness magazines or magazines such as *National Geographic*. Two possible outcomes of this study are shown in **Figure 2**. The top graph illustrates an outcome in which the pretest has no impact on the outcome of the study: The fitness magazine viewing results in higher depression in both the posttest-only and the pretest-posttest condition. This is what Garvin and Damson (2008) found in their study. The lower graph shows an outcome in which taking the pretest does affect the results of the study. There is a difference between the treatment and control groups when there is a pretest, but there is no group difference when the pretest is absent.

FIGURE 1   Solomon four-group design

FIGURE 2   Examples of outcomes of Solomon four-group design

ASSIGNING PARTICIPANTS TO EXPERIMENTAL CONDITIONS

Recall that there are two basic ways of assigning participants to experimental conditions. In one procedure, participants are randomly assigned to the various conditions so that each participates in only one group. This is called an **independent groups design.** It is also commonly known as a **between-subjects design** because comparisons are made between different groups of participants (you may also see this called a *between-persons design*). In the other procedure, all participants are in all conditions. In an experiment with two conditions, for example, each participant is assigned to both levels of the independent variable. This is called a **repeated measures design,** because each participant is measured after receiving each level of the independent variable. You will also see this called a **within-subjects design** or a *within-person design*; in this design, comparisons are made within the same participants (subjects, persons). In the next two sections, we will examine each of these designs in detail.

Independent Groups Design

In an independent groups design, different participants are assigned to each of the conditions using **random assignment.** This means that the decision to assign an individual to a particular condition is completely random and beyond the control of the researcher. For example, you could ask for the participant's month of birth; individuals born in odd-numbered months would be assigned to one group and those born in even-numbered months would be assigned to the other group. In practice, researchers use a sequence of random numbers to determine assignment. Such numbers come from a random number generator such as Research Randomizer, available online at **http://www.randomizer.org** or QuickCalcs at **http://www.graphpad.com/quickcalcs/randomize1.cfm**. Excel can also generate random numbers. These programs allow you to randomly determine the assignment of each participant to the various groups in your study.

Random assignment will prevent any systematic biases, and the groups can be considered equivalent in terms of participant characteristics such as income, intelligence, age, personality, and political attitudes. In this way, participant differences cannot be an explanation for results of the experiment. Thus, in our experiment on the effects of exercise on mood, more positive mood levels in the exercise group than in the no-exercise group cannot be explained by saying that people in the groups somehow differ in characteristics such as income, education, or personality.

An alternative procedure is to have the *same* individuals participate in all of the groups. This is called a repeated measures experimental design.

Repeated Measures Design

Consider an experiment investigating the relationship between the meaningfulness of material and the learning of that material. In an independent groups design, one group of participants is given highly meaningful material to learn and another group receives less meaningful material. Meaningfulness refers to the ease with which new material can be related to something that is already known. For example, new material might be more meaningful if it is connected to a story about a familiar real-life event. In a repeated measures design, the same individuals participate in both conditions. Thus, participants might first read low-meaningful material and take a recall test to measure learning; the same participants would then read high-meaningful material and take the recall test. You can see why this is called a repeated measures design; participants are repeatedly measured on the dependent variable after being in each condition of the experiment.

Advantages and Disadvantages of Repeated Measures Design

The repeated measures design has several advantages. An obvious one is that fewer research participants are needed, because each individual participates in all conditions. When participants are scarce or when it is costly to run each individual in the experiment, a repeated measures design may be preferred. In much research on perception, for instance, extensive training of participants is necessary before the actual experiment can begin. Such research often involves only a few individuals, who participate in all conditions of the experiment.

An additional advantage of repeated measures designs is that they are extremely sensitive to finding statistically significant differences between groups. This is because we have data from the same people in both conditions. To illustrate why this is important, consider possible data from the recall experiment. Using an independent groups design, the first three participants in the high-meaningful condition had scores of 68, 81, and 92. The first three participants in the low-meaningful condition had scores of 64, 78, and 85. If you calculated an average score for each condition, you would find that the average recall was a bit higher when the material was more meaningful. However, there is a lot of variability in the scores in both groups. You certainly are not finding that everyone in the high-meaningful condition has high recall and everyone in the other condition has low recall. The reason for this variability is that people differ—there are individual differences in recall abilities, so there is a range of scores in both conditions. This is part of "random error" in the scores that we cannot explain.

However, if the same scores were obtained from the first three participants in a repeated measures design, the conclusions would be much different. Let's line up the recall scores for the two conditions:

	High meaning	Low meaning	Difference
Participant 1	68	64	+4
Participant 2	81	78	+3
Participant 3	92	85	+7

With a repeated measures design, the individual differences can be seen and explained. It is true that some people score higher than others because of individual differences in recall abilities, but now you can much more clearly see the effect of the independent variable on recall scores. It is much easier to separate the systematic individual differences from the effect of the independent variable: Scores are higher for every participant in the high-meaningful condition. As a result, we are much more likely to detect an effect of the independent variable on the dependent variable.

The major problem with a repeated measures design stems from the fact that the different conditions must be presented in a particular sequence. For instance, suppose that there is greater recall in the high-meaningful condition. Although this result could be caused by the manipulation of the meaningfulness variable, the result could also simply be an **order effect**—the order of presenting the treatments affects the dependent variable. Thus, greater recall in the high-meaningful condition could be attributed to the fact that the high-meaningful task came second in the order of presentation of the conditions.

There are a variety of types of order effects. For instance, performance on the second task might improve merely because of the practice gained on the first task. This improvement is in fact called a **practice effect,** or learning effect. It is also possible that a **fatigue effect** could result in a deterioration in performance from the first to the second condition as the research participant becomes tired, bored, or distracted. It is also possible for the effect of the first treatment to carry over to influence the response to the second treatment—this is known as a **carryover effect.** Suppose the independent variable is severity of a crime. After reading about the less severe crime, the more severe one might seem much worse to participants than it normally would. In addition, reading about the severe crime might subsequently cause participants to view the less severe crime as much milder than they normally would. In both cases, the experience with one condition carried over to affect the response to the second condition. In this example, the carryover effect was a psychological effect of the way that the two situations contrasted with one another.

A carryover effect may also occur when the first condition produces a change that is still influencing the person when the second condition is introduced. Suppose the first condition involves experiencing failure at an important task. This may result in a temporary increase in stress responses. How long does it take before the person returns to a normal state? If the second condition is introduced too soon, the stress may still be affecting the participant.

There are two approaches to dealing with order effects. The first is to employ counterbalancing techniques. The second is to devise a procedure in which the interval between conditions is long enough to minimize the influence of the first condition on the second.

Counterbalancing

Because of the problem that order-effects present, in a repeated measures design it is very important to counterbalance the order of the conditions.

Complete Counterbalancing

With complete **counterbalancing,** all possible orders of presentation are included in the experiment. In the example of a study on learning high- and low-meaningful material, half of the participants would be randomly assigned to the low-high order, and the other half would be assigned to the high-low order. This design is illustrated below:

By counterbalancing the order of conditions, it is possible to determine the extent to which order is influencing the results. In the hypothetical memory study, you would know whether the greater recall in the high-meaningful condition is consistent for both orders; you would also know the extent to which a practice effect is responsible for the results.

Counterbalancing principles can be extended to experiments with three or more groups. With three groups, there are 6 possible orders ($3! = 3 \times 2 \times 1 = 6$). With four groups, the number of possible orders increases to 24 ($4! = 4 \times 3 \times 2 \times 1 = 24$); you would need a minimum of 24 participants to represent each order, and you would need 48 participants to have only two participants per order. Imagine the number of orders possible in an experiment by Shepard and Metzler (1971). In their basic experimental paradigm, each participant is shown a three-dimensional object along with the same figure rotated at 1 of 10 different angles ranging from

0 degrees to 180 degrees (see the sample objects illustrated in **Figure 3**). Each time, the participant presses a button when it is determined that the two figures are the same or different. The dependent variable is reaction time—the amount of time it takes to decide whether the figures are the same or different. The results show that reaction time becomes longer as the angle of rotation increases away from the original. In this experiment with 10 conditions, there are 3,628,800 possible orders! Fortunately, there are alternatives to complete counterbalancing that still allow researchers to draw valid conclusions about the effect of the independent variable without running some 3.6 million tests.

Latin Squares

A technique to control for order effects without having all possible orders is to construct a **Latin square:** a limited set of orders constructed to ensure that (1) each condition appears at each ordinal position and (2) each condition precedes and follows each condition one time. Using a Latin square to determine order controls for most order effects without having to include all possible orders. Suppose you replicated the Shepard and Metzler (1971) study using only 4 of the 10 rotations: 0, 60, 120, and 180 degrees. A Latin square for these four conditions is shown in **Figure 4**. Each row in the square is one of the orders of the conditions (the conditions are labeled A, B, C, and D). The number of orders in a Latin square is equal to the number of conditions; thus, if there are four conditions, there are four orders. When you conduct your study using the Latin square to determine order, you need at least one participant per row. Usually, you will have two or more participants per row; the number of participants tested in each order must be equal.

FIGURE 3   Example of the three-dimensional figures used by Shepard and Metzler (1971)

Order of Conditions

	1	2	3	4
Row 1	A (60)	B (0)	D (120)	C (180)
Row 2	B (0)	C (180)	A (60)	D (120)
Row 3	C (180)	D (120)	B (0)	A (60)
Row 4	D (120)	A (60)	C (180)	B (0)

FIGURE 4   A Latin square with four conditions

Note: The four conditions were randomly given letter designations. A = 60 degrees, B = 0 degrees, C = 180 degrees, and D = 120 degrees. Each row represents a different order of running the conditions.

Now, design your own repeated measures by completing **Check Your Learning:** Practice Exercise #1.

Time Interval Between Treatments

In addition to counterbalancing the order of treatments, researchers need to carefully determine the time interval between presentation of treatments and possible activities between them. A rest period may counteract a fatigue effect; attending to an unrelated task between treatments may reduce the possibility that participants will contrast the first treatment with the second. If the treatment is the administration of a drug that takes time to wear off, the interval between treatments may have to be a day or more. Lane et al., (2005) used a repeated measures design to study the effect of marijuana on risk taking. The subjects came to the lab in the morning and passed a drug test. They were then given one of three marijuana doses. The dependent variable was a measure of risk taking. Subjects were tested in this way for each dosage. Because of the time necessary for the effects of the drug to wear off, the three conditions were run on separate days at least 5 days apart. A similarly long time interval would be needed with procedures that produce emotional changes, such as heightened anxiety or anger. You may have noted that introduction of an extended time interval may create a separate problem: Participants will have to commit to the experiment for a longer period of time. This can make it more difficult to recruit volunteers, and if the study extends over 2 or more days, some participants may drop out of the experiment altogether. And for the record, increased marijuana doses did result in making riskier decisions.

Choosing Between Independent Groups and Repeated Measures Designs

Repeated measures designs have two major advantages over independent groups designs: (1) a reduction in the number of participants required to complete the experiment and (2) greater control over participant differences and thus greater ability to detect an effect of the independent variable. As noted previously, in certain areas of research, these advantages are very important. However, the disadvantages of repeated measures designs and the precautions required to deal with them are usually sufficient reasons for researchers to use independent groups designs.

A very different consideration in whether to use a repeated measures design concerns generalization to conditions in the "real world." Greenwald (1976) has pointed out that in actual everyday situations, we sometimes encounter independent variables in an independent groups fashion: We encounter only one condition without a contrasting comparison. However, some independent variables are most frequently encountered in a repeated measures fashion: Both conditions appear, and our responses occur in the context of exposure to both levels of the independent variable. Thus, for example, if you are interested in how a defendant's characteristics affects jurors, an independent groups design may be most appropriate because actual jurors focus on a single defendant in a trial. However, if you are interested in the effects of a job applicant's characteristics on employers, a repeated measures design would be reasonable because employers typically consider several applicants at once. Whether to use an independent groups or repeated measures design may be partially determined by these generalization issues.

Finally, any experimental procedure that produces a relatively permanent change in an individual cannot be used in a repeated measures design. Examples include a psychotherapy treatment or a surgical procedure such as the removal of brain tissue.

Matched Pairs Design

A somewhat more complicated method of assigning participants to conditions in an experiment is called a **matched pairs design:** Instead of simply randomly assigning participants to groups, the goal is to first match people on a participant variable such as age or a personality trait. The matching variable will be either the dependent measure or a variable that is strongly related to the dependent variable. For example, in a learning experiment, participants might be matched on the basis of scores on a cognitive ability measure or even grade point average. If cognitive ability is not related to the dependent measure, however, matching would be a waste of time. The goal is to achieve the same equivalency of groups that is achieved with a repeated measures design without the necessity of having the same participants in both conditions. The design is shown below:

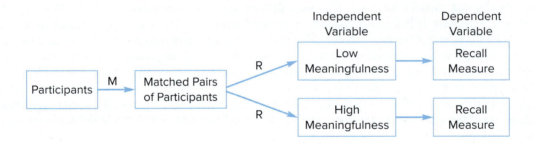

When using a matched pairs design, the first step is to obtain a measure of the matching variable from each individual. The participants are then rank ordered from highest to lowest based on their scores on the matching variable. Now the researcher can form matched pairs that are approximately equal on the characteristic (the highest two participants form the first pair, the next two form the second pair, and so on). Finally, the members of each pair are randomly assigned to the conditions in the experiment. (Note that there are methods of matching pairs of individuals on the basis of scores derived from multiple variables; these methods are described briefly in the chapter **"Single-Case, Quasi-Experimental, and Developmental Research."**)

A matched pairs design ensures that the groups are equivalent (on the matching variable) prior to introduction of the independent variable manipulation. This assurance could be particularly important with small sample sizes because random assignment procedures are more likely to produce equivalent groups as the sample size increases. Matching, then, is most likely to be used when only a few participants are available or when it is very costly to run large numbers of individuals in the experiment—as long as there is a strong relationship between a dependent measure and the matching variable. The result is a greater ability to detect a statistically significant effect of the independent variable because it is possible to account for individual differences in responses to the independent variable, just as we saw with a repeated measures design. (The issues of variability and statistical significance are discussed further in the chapter **"Understanding Research Results: Statistical Inference"** and in **Appendix C.**)

> Assess your understanding of the designs discussed in this chapter by completing the **Check Your Learning**: Practice Exercise #2.

However useful they are, matching procedures can be costly and time-consuming, because they require measuring participants on the matching variable prior to the experiment. Such efforts are worthwhile only when the matching variable is strongly related to the dependent measure and you know that the relationship exists prior to conducting your study. For these reasons, matched pairs is not a commonly used experimental design. However, we will discuss matching again in the chapter **"Single-Case, Quasi-Experimental, and Developmental Research"** when describing quasi-experimental designs that do not have random assignment to conditions. You now have a fundamental understanding of the design of experiments. In the chapter **"Conducting Experiments"** we will consider issues that arise when you decide how to actually conduct an experiment.

ILLUSTRATIVE ARTICLE: EXPERIMENTAL DESIGN

Mobile phones are ubiquitous, and they have become an ever-present feature of today's college classroom. So far there has been little research on the impact of cell-phone use. Instructors have tried everything from integrating cell phones into their instruction (e.g., texting-based polls) to forbidding their use in the classroom.

A study by Lee et al. (2017) explored the impact of cell phone policies on learning, and on emotion regulation. (Imagine being denied your cell phone for 60 minutes; what would your emotional experience be?)

For this exercise, acquire and read the following article (available at **https://www.researchgate.net/publication/316169063_The_Effects_of_Cell_Phone_Use_and_Emotion-regulation_Style_on_College_Students'_Learning**):

> Lee, S., W. Kim, M., Mcdonough, I., Mendoza, J., & Kim, M. (2017). The Effects of Cell Phone Use and Emotion-regulation Style on College Students' Learning. *Applied Cognitive Psychology* *31*(3), 360–366. https://doi.org/10.1002/acp.3323

What was measured?

a. How did Lee et al. measure student learning? Do you believe that their measure of learning has good construct validity?

How do they know that one thing caused another?

a. What were the independent variables in this study?

b. What were the levels of the independent variable for this study? Why was each level important?

c. Why did they used a video-recorded lecture? Why not use a live lecturer?

To what or whom can we generalize the results?

a. Who were the participants in the study? Do you think that the findings would be the same if the content of the course was different? What if it was a course in biology? Or mathematics?

b. Do you think that their findings would be generalizable to courses with very few students? What about courses with many students? (Some lecture courses have more than 1,000 students in them!)

Have other researchers found similar results? Are the findings of this study similar to other studies of the same topic? Is there any other evidence about the use of technology in a college classroom and the impact of that technology on student learning?

CRITICAL THINKING: BEING A SKILLED CONSUMER OF RESEARCH

1. Professor Foley conducted a cola taste test. Each participant in the experiment first tasted 2 ounces of Coca-Cola, then 2 ounces of Pepsi, and finally 2 ounces of Sam's Choice Cola. A rating of the cola's flavor was made after each taste. What are the potential problems with this experimental design and the procedures used? Revise the design and procedures to address these problems. You may wish to consider several alternatives and think about the advantages and disadvantages of each.

2. Dr. Kim wanted to study the impact of different volumes of music on dart-throwing performance. She hypothesized that distraction would affect dart-throwing skills. She decided to design a repeated measures experiment with three conditions: no music, soft music, and loud music. Answer these two questions:

   a. Why would she choose a repeated measures design?

   b. Her participants threw darts in a room with music volume set to none, soft, or loud. All subjects started in the no-music room, and then proceeded to the soft-music room and finally to the loud-music room. How could her study results be affected by these three order effects—practice, fatigue, carryover? How could Dr. Kim address these problems?

Check Your Learning: Practice Exercises

Practice Exercise #1

Design a repeated measures experiment that investigates the effect of report presentation style on the grade received for the report. Use two levels of the independent variable: a "professional style" presentation (correct spelling and grammar) and a "nonprofessional style" (spelling and grammar mistakes). Discuss the necessity for using counterbalancing. Create a table illustrating the experimental design.

Practice Exercise #2

Match the design on the left with the definition on the right

Design	Definition
1. Posttest-Only Design	A method of assigning subjects to groups in which pairs of subjects are first matched on some characteristic and then individually assigned randomly to groups.
2. Pretest-Posttest Design	An experiment in which different subjects are assigned to each group. Also called independent groups design.

3. Solomon Four-Group Design	A true experimental design in which the dependent variable (posttest) is measured only once, after manipulation of the independent variable.
4. Between-Subjects Design	An experiment in which the same subjects are assigned to each group.
5. Within-Subjects Design (also known as Repeated Measures Design)	A true experimental design in which the dependent variable is measured both before (pretest) and after (posttest) manipulation of the independent variable.
6. Matched Pairs Design	Experimental design in which the experimental and control groups are studied with and without a pretest.

(Some answers are provided at the end of this chapter.)

CHAPTER REVIEW

Review Questions

1. What is a confounding variable?
2. What is meant by the internal validity of an experiment?
3. How do the two true experimental designs eliminate the problem of selection differences?
4. Distinguish between the posttest-only design and the pretest-posttest design. What are the advantages and disadvantages of each?
5. What is a repeated measures design? What are the advantages of using a repeated measures design? What are the disadvantages?
6. What are ways of dealing with the problems of a repeated measures design, including counterbalancing?
7. When would a researcher decide to use the matched pairs design? What would be the advantages of this design?
8. The procedure used to obtain your sample (i.e., random or nonrandom sampling) is not the same as the procedure for assigning participants to conditions; distinguish between random sampling and random assignment.

Study Terms

Attrition (also mortality)

Between-subjects design (also independent groups design)

Carryover effect

Confounding variable

Counterbalancing

Fatigue effect

Independent groups design (also between-subjects design)

Internal validity

Latin square

Matched pairs design

Mortality (also attrition)

Order effect

Posttest-only design

Practice effect (also learning effect)

Pretest-posttest design

Random assignment

Repeated measures design (also within-subjects design)

Selection differences

Solomon four-group design

Within-subjects design (also repeated measures design)

Check Your Learning: Answers

Practice Exercise #2

1. A true experimental design in which the dependent variable (posttest) is measured only once, after manipulation of the independent variable.

2. A true experimental design in which the dependent variable is measured both before (pretest) and after (posttest) manipulation of the independent variable.

3. Experimental design in which the experimental and control groups are studied with and without a pretest.

4. An experiment in which different subjects are assigned to each group. Also called independent groups design.

5. An experiment in which the same subjects are assigned to each group.

6. A method of assigning subjects to groups in which pairs of subjects are first matched on some characteristic and then individually assigned randomly to groups.

Conducting Experiments

Guennadi Iakoutchik/Shutterstock

LEARNING OBJECTIVES

- Distinguish between straightforward and staged manipulations of an independent variable.
- Describe the three types of dependent variables: self-report, behavioral, and physiological.
- Discuss sensitivity of a dependent variable, contrasting floor effects and ceiling effects.
- Describe ways to control participant expectations and experimenter expectations.
- List the reasons for conducting pilot studies.
- Describe the advantages of including a manipulation check in an experiment.

The previous chapters have laid the foundation for planning a research investigation. In this chapter, we will focus on some very practical aspects of conducting research: How do you select the research participants? What should you consider when deciding how to manipulate an independent variable? What should you worry about when you measure a variable? What do you do when the study is completed?

SELECTING RESEARCH PARTICIPANTS

The focus of your study may be children, college students, elderly adults, employees, rats, pigeons, or even cockroaches or flatworms; in all cases, the participants or subjects must somehow be selected. The method used to select participants can have a profound impact on the external validity of your study. Remember that external validity is defined as the extent to which results from a study can be generalized to other populations and settings.

Most research projects involve sampling research participants from a population of interest. The population is composed of all of the individuals of interest to the researcher. Samples may be drawn from the population using probability sampling or nonprobability sampling techniques. When it is important to accurately describe the population, you must use probability sampling. This is why probability sampling is so crucial when conducting scientific polls. Much research, on the other hand, is more interested in testing hypotheses about behavior: attempting to detect whether *X* causes *Y* rather than describing a population. Here, the study focuses on the relationships between the variables being studied and tests of predictions derived from theories of behavior. In such cases, the participants may be found in the easiest way possible using nonprobability sampling methods such as convenience sampling. You might ask students in introductory psychology classes to participate, obtain permission to distribute questionnaires to employees during their break time, or recruit participants using Amazon Mechanical Turk or MTurk (Chandler, 2017). Nothing is wrong with such methods as long as you recognize that they affect the ability to generalize your results to some larger population. In the last chapter of this text, **"Generalization,"** we examine the issues of generalizing from the rather atypical samples of college students and other conveniently obtained research participants.

Researchers also need to determine sample size. How many participants will they need in their study? In general, increasing the sample size increases the likelihood that your results will be statistically significant, because larger samples provide more accurate estimates of population values (see the chapter **"Asking People About Themselves: Survey Research," Table 2**). A more formal approach to determine sample size, called power analysis, is discussed in the chapter **"Understanding Research Results: Description and Correlation."**

MANIPULATING THE INDEPENDENT VARIABLE

To manipulate an independent variable, you have to construct an operational definition of the variable. That is, you must turn a conceptual variable into a set of operations—specific instructions, events, and stimuli to be presented to the research participants. The manipulation of the independent variable, then, is when a researcher changes the conditions to which participants are exposed. In addition, the independent and dependent variables must be introduced within the context of the total experimental setting. This has been called *setting the stage* (Aronson et al., 1985).

Setting the Stage

In setting the stage, you usually have to supply the participants with the information necessary for them to provide their informed consent to participate (informed consent is covered in the chapter **"Ethics in Behavioral Research"**). This generally includes information about the underlying rationale of the study. Sometimes the rationale given is completely truthful, although only rarely will you want to tell participants the actual hypothesis. For example, you might say that you are conducting an experiment on memory, when in fact you are studying a specific aspect of memory (your independent variable). If participants know what you are studying, they may try to confirm (or even deny) the hypothesis, or they may try to look good by behaving in the most socially acceptable way. If you find that deception is necessary, you have a special obligation to address the deception when you debrief the participants at the conclusion of the experiment.

There are no clear-cut rules for setting the stage, except that the experimental setting must seem plausible to the participants, nor are there any clear-cut rules for translating conceptual variables into specific operations. Exactly how the variable is manipulated depends on the variable and the cost, practicality, and ethics of the procedures being considered.

Types of Manipulations

Straightforward Manipulations

Researchers are usually able to manipulate an independent variable with relative simplicity by presenting written, verbal, or visual material to the participants. Such **straightforward manipulations** manipulate variables with instructions and stimulus presentations. Stimuli may be presented verbally, in written form, via videotape, or with a computer. Let's look at a few examples.

Goldstein et al. (2008) were interested in the influence of signs that hotels leave in their bathrooms encouraging guests to reuse their towels. In their research, they simply printed signs that were hooked on towel shelves in the rooms of single guests staying at least two nights. In a standard message, the sign read "HELP SAVE THE ENVIRONMENT. You can show your respect for nature and help save the environment by reusing towels during your stay." In this case, 35% of the guests reused their towels on the second day. Another condition invoked a social norm that other people are reusing towels: "JOIN YOUR FELLOW GUESTS IN HELPING TO SAVE THE ENVIRONMENT. Almost 75% of guests who are asked to participate in our new resource savings program do help by using their towels more than once. You can join your fellow guests in this program to save the environment by reusing your towels during your stay." This sign resulted in 44% reusing their towels. As you might expect, the researchers have extended this research to study ways that the sign can be even more effective in increasing conservation.

Most memory research relies on straightforward manipulations. For example, Coltheart and Langdon (1998) displayed lists of words to participants and later measured recall. The word lists differed on phonological similarity: Some lists had words that sounded similar, such as *cat, map,* and *pat,* and other lists had dissimilar words such as *mop, pen,* and *cow.* They found that lists with dissimilar words are recalled more accurately.

Educational programs are most often straightforward. Pawlenko et al. (2013) examined the effectiveness of three educational training programs designed to improve jurors' ability to evaluate eyewitness testimony. Subjects viewed one of three 15-minute slide presentations on a computer screen. The Interview-Identification-Eyewitness training focused on three steps to analyze eyewitness evidence: Ask if the eyewitness interviews were done properly, ask if identification methods were proper, and evaluate if the conditions of the crime scene allowed for an accurate identification. A second presentation, *Biggers* Training, was a presentation of five eyewitness factors that the U.S. Supreme Court determined should be used (developed in a case called *Neil v. Biggers*). The Jury Duty presentation was a summary of standard information provided to jurors, such as the need to be fair and impartial and the importance of hearing all evidence before reaching a verdict. After viewing the presentations, subjects read a trial transcript that included problems with the eyewitness identification procedures. The subjects in the Interview-Identification-Eyewitness conditions were most likely to use these problems in reaching a verdict.

As a final example of a straightforward manipulation, consider a study by Mazer et al. (2009) on the effect of college teacher self-disclosure (via Facebook) on students' perceptions of teacher effectiveness. For this study, students read one of three Facebook profiles that were created for a volunteer teacher, one for each of the high-, medium-, and low-disclosure conditions. Level of disclosure was manipulated by changing the number and nature of photographs, biographical information, favorite movies/books/quotes, campus groups, and posts on "the wall." After viewing the profile to which they were assigned, participants rated the teacher on several dimensions. Higher disclosure resulted in perceptions of greater caring and trustworthiness; however, disclosure was not related to perceptions of teacher competence.

You will find that most manipulations of independent variables in all areas of research are straightforward. Researchers vary in a straightforward manner the difficulty of material to be learned, motivation levels, the way questions are asked, characteristics of people to be judged, and a variety of other factors.

Staged Manipulations

Other manipulations are less straightforward. Sometimes it is necessary to stage events during the experiment in order to manipulate the independent variable successfully. When this occurs, the manipulation is called a **staged manipulation** or *event manipulation*.

Staged manipulations are most frequently used for two reasons. First, the researcher may be trying to create some psychological state in the participants, such as frustration, anger, or a temporary lowering or raising of self-esteem. For example, Zitek and her colleagues studied what is termed a *sense of entitlement* that occurs when a person has been unfairly treated (Zitek et al., 2010). The sense of entitlement leads to behaving more selfishly with others. In their study, all participants played a computer game. The researchers programmed the game so that some participants would lose when the game crashed. This is an unfair outcome because the participants lost for no good reason. Participants in the other condition also lost, but they thought it was because the game itself was very difficult. The participants experiencing the broken game did in fact behave more selfishly after the game; they later allocated themselves more money than deserved when competing with another participant.

Second, a staged manipulation may be necessary in order to simulate some situation that occurs in the real world. In the Milgram obedience study, an elaborate procedure—ostensibly to study learning—was constructed to actually study obedience to an authority (see the chapter **"Ethics in Behavioral Research"**). Or consider a study on computer multitasking conducted by Bowman et al. (2010), wherein students read academic material presented on a computer screen. In one condition, the participants received and responded to instant messages while they were reading. Other participants did not receive any messages. Student performance on a test was equal in the two conditions. However, students in the instant message condition took longer to read the material (after the time spent on the message was subtracted from the total time working on the computer).

Staged manipulations frequently employ a **confederate** (sometimes termed an "accomplice"). Usually the confederate appears to be another participant in an experiment but is actually part of the manipulation. A confederate may be useful to create a particular social situation. For example, Hermans et al. (2010) studied whether food intake by males is affected by the amount of food consumed by a companion. Participants were recruited for a study on evaluation of movie trailers. The participant and a confederate sat in a comfortable setting in which they viewed and evaluated three trailers. They were then told that they needed a break before viewing the next trailers; snacks were available if they were interested. In one condition, the confederate ate a large serving of snacks. In the second condition, the confederate ate a small serving; in the third condition, the confederate did not eat. The researchers then measured the amount consumed by the actual participants; would the participants model the eating behavior of the confederate? Contrary to previous findings, only very hungry participants consumed amounts similar to the amounts consumed by the confederate. The authors suggested reasons for this finding that could be studied in the future.

The classic Asch (1956) conformity experiment provides another example of how confederates may be used. Asch gathered people into groups and asked them to respond to a line judgment task such as the one in **Figure 1.** Which of the three test lines matches the standard? Although this appears to be a simple task, Asch made it more interesting by having several confederates announce the same incorrect judgment prior to asking the actual participant; this procedure was repeated over a number of trials with different line judgments. Asch was able to demonstrate how easy it is to produce conformity—participants conformed to the unanimous majority on many of the trials even though the correct answer was clear.

Finally, confederates may be used in field experiments as well as laboratory research. As described in the chapter **"Fundamental Research Issues,"** Lee et al. (2010) studied the impact of public sneezing on the perception of unrelated risks by having an accomplice either sneeze or not sneeze (control condition) while walking by someone in a public area of a university. A researcher then approached those people with a request to complete a questionnaire, which they described as a "class project." The questionnaire measured participants' perceptions of average Americans' risk of contracting a serious disease. The researchers found that, indeed, being around a person who sneezes increases self-reported perception of risk.

As you can see, staged manipulations demand a great deal of creativity, ingenuity, and even some acting ability. They are used to involve the participants in an ongoing social situation that the individuals perceive not as an experiment but as a real experience. Researchers assume that the result will be natural behavior that truly reflects the feelings and intentions of the participants. However, such procedures allow for a great deal of subtle interpersonal communication that is hard to put into words; this may make it difficult for other researchers to replicate the experiment. Also, a complex manipulation is difficult to interpret. If many things happened during the experiment, what *one* thing was responsible for the results? In general, it is easier to interpret results when the manipulation is relatively straightforward. However, the nature of the variable you are studying sometimes demands complicated procedures.

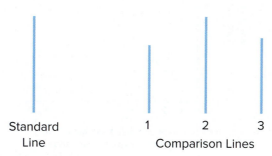

FIGURE 1   Example of the Asch line judgment task

Now, test your understanding of staged versus straightforward manipulation by completing
Check Your Learning: Practice Exercise #1 at the end of the chapter.

Strength of the Manipulation

The simplest experimental design has two levels of the independent variable. In planning the experiment, the researcher has to choose these levels. A general principle to follow is to make the manipulation as strong as possible; the **strength of manipulation** matters. A strong manipulation maximizes the differences between the two groups and increases the chances that the independent variable will have a statistically significant effect on the dependent variable.

To illustrate, suppose you think that there is a positive linear relationship between attitude similarity and liking ("birds of a feather flock together"). In conducting the experiment, you could arrange for participants to encounter a person who is a confederate. In one group, the confederate and the participant would share similar attitudes; in the other group, the confederate and the participant would have dissimilar attitudes. Similarity, then, is the independent variable, and liking is the dependent variable. Now you have to decide on the amount of similarity. **Figure 2** shows the hypothesized relationship between attitude similarity and liking at 10 different levels of similarity. Level 1 represents the least amount of similarity, with no common attitudes, and level 10 the greatest amount of similarity (all attitudes are similar). To achieve the strongest manipulation, the participants in one group would encounter a confederate of level 1 similarity; those in the other group would encounter a confederate of level 10 similarity. This would result in the greatest difference in the liking means—a 9-point difference. A weaker manipulation—using levels 4 and 7, for example—would result in a smaller mean difference.

A strong manipulation is particularly important in the early stages of research, when the researcher is most interested in demonstrating that a relationship does, in fact, exist. If the early experiments reveal a relationship between the variables, subsequent research can systematically manipulate the other levels of the independent variable to provide a more detailed picture of the relationship.

The principle of using the strongest manipulation possible should be tempered by at least two considerations. The first concerns the external validity of a study: The strongest possible manipulation may entail a situation

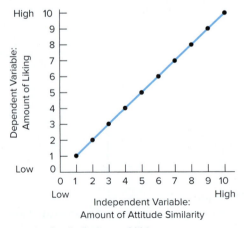

FIGURE 2   Relationship between attitude similarity and liking

that rarely, if ever, occurs in the real world. For example, an extremely strong crowding manipulation might involve placing so many people in a room that no one could move—a manipulation that might significantly affect a variety of behaviors. However, we would not know if the results were similar to those occurring in more common, less crowded situations, such as many classrooms or offices.

A second consideration is ethics: A manipulation should be as strong as possible within the bounds of ethics. A strong manipulation of fear or anxiety, for example, might not be possible because of the potential physical and psychological harm to participants.

Cost of the Manipulation

Cost is another factor in the decision about how to manipulate the independent variable. Researchers with limited monetary resources may not be able to afford expensive equipment, salaries for confederates, or payments to participants in long-term experiments. Also, a manipulation in which participants must be run individually requires more of the researcher's time than a manipulation that allows running many individuals in a single setting. In this respect, a manipulation that uses straightforward presentation of written or verbal material is less costly than a complex, staged experimental manipulation. Some government and private agencies offer grants for research; because much research is costly, continued public support of these agencies is very important.

MEASURING THE DEPENDENT VARIABLE

In previous chapters we have discussed various aspects of measuring variables, including reliability, validity, and reactivity of measures; observational methods; and the development of self-report measures for questionnaires and interviews. In this section, we will focus on measurement considerations that are particularly relevant to experimental research.

Types of Measures

The dependent variable in most experiments is one of three general types: self-report, behavioral, or physiological.

Self-Report Measures

Self-reports can be used to measure attitudes, liking for someone, judgments about someone's personality characteristics, intended behaviors, emotional states, attributions about why someone performed well or poorly on a task, confidence in one's judgments, and many other aspects of human thought and behavior. The most commonly used rating scales are those with descriptive anchors (endpoints). For example, Funk and Todorov (2013) studied the impact of a facial tattoo on impressions of a man accused of assault. The man, Jack, had punched another man in a bar following a dispute over a spilled drink. A description of the incident included a photo of Jack with or without a facial tattoo. After viewing the photo and reading the description, subjects responded to several questions on a 7-point scale that included the following:

How likely is it that Jack is guilty?

Very unlikely ☐☐☐☐☐☐ Very likely

Behavioral Measures

Behavioral measures are direct observations of behaviors. As with self-reports, it is possible to measure an almost endless number of behaviors. Sometimes the researcher might record whether a given behavior occurs—for example, whether an individual responds to a request for help, makes an error on a test, or chooses to engage in one activity rather than another. Often the researcher needs to quantify observed behaviors:

- Rate of a behavior—how many times the behavior occurs in a given time period
- Reaction time—how quickly a response occurs after a stimulus (e.g., a sound, a light, a word)
- Duration—how long a behavior persists

The decision about which aspect of behavior to measure depends on which aspect is most theoretically relevant for the study of a particular problem or which measure logically follows from the independent variable manipulation.

As an example, consider a study on eating behavior while viewing either a food-related or a nature television program (Bodenlos & Wormuth, 2013). Participants had access to chocolate-covered candies, cheese curls, and carrots; all snacks were weighed before and after the session. More candy was consumed during the food-related program; there were no differences for the other two foods.

Sometimes the behavioral measure is not an actual behavior but a behavioral intention or choice. In a study on aggression after being provoked by another subject, participants decided how much hot sauce the other subject would have to consume later in the study (Vasquez et al., 2013). They did not actually pour the hot sauce, but they did commit to an action rather than simply indicate their feelings about the other subject.

Physiological Measures

Physiological measures are recordings of responses of the body. Many such measurements are available; examples include the **galvanic skin response (GSR), electromyogram (EMG)**, and **electroencephalogram (EEG)**. The GSR is a measure of general emotional arousal and anxiety; it measures the electrical conductance of the skin, which changes when sweating occurs. The EMG measures muscle tension and is frequently used as a measure of tension or stress. The EEG is a measure of electrical activity of brain cells. It can be used to record general brain arousal as a response to different situations, such as activity in certain parts of the brain as learning occurs or brain activity during different stages of sleep.

The GSR, EMG, and EEG have long been used as physiological indicators of important psychological variables. Measures are available for many other physiological variables, including temperature, heart rate, and analysis of blood or urine (see Cacioppo & Tassinary, 1990). In recent years, **MRI (magnetic resonance imagery)** has become an increasingly important tool for researchers in behavioral neuroscience. An MRI provides an image of an individual's brain structure. It allows scientists to compare the brain structure of individuals with a particular condition (e.g., a cognitive impairment, schizophrenia, attention deficit hyperactivity disorder) with the brain structure of people without the condition. In addition, a **functional MRI (fMRI)** allows researchers to scan areas of the brain while a research participant performs a physical or cognitive task. The data provide evidence for what brain processes are involved in these tasks. For example, a researcher can see which areas of the brain are most active when performing different memory tasks. In one study using fMRI, elderly adults with higher levels of education not only performed better on memory tasks than their less educated peers, but they also used areas of their frontal cortex that were not used by other elderly and younger individuals (Springer et al., 2005).

> Now test your understanding of the three basic types of dependent measures by completing
> **Check Your Learning:** Practice Exercise #2 at the end of the chapter.

Multiple Measures

Although it is convenient to describe single dependent variables, most studies include more than one dependent measure. One reason to use multiple measures stems from the fact that a variable can be measured in a variety of concrete ways (recall the discussion of operational definitions in the chapter **"Fundamental Research Issues"**). In a study on the effects of an employee wellness program on health, the researchers might measure self-reported fatigue, stress, physical activity, and eating habits along with physical measures of blood pressure, blood sugar, cholesterol, and weight (see Clark et al., 2011). If the independent variable has the same effect on several measures of the same dependent variable, our confidence in the results is increased. It is also useful to know whether the same independent variable affects some measures but not others. For example, an independent variable designed to affect liking might have an effect on some measures of liking (e.g., desirability as a person to work with) but not others (e.g., desirability as a dating partner). Researchers may also be interested in studying the effects of an independent variable on several different behaviors. For example, an experiment on the effects of a new classroom management technique might examine academic performance, interaction rates among classmates, and teacher satisfaction.

When you have more than one dependent measure, the question of *order* arises. Does it matter which measures are made first? Is it possible that the results for a particular measure will be different if the measure comes earlier rather than later? The issue is similar to the order effects that were discussed in the chapter **"Experimental Design"** in the context of repeated measures designs. Perhaps responding to the first measures will somehow affect responses on the later measures, or perhaps the participants attend more closely to first measures than to later measures. There are two possible ways of responding to this issue. If it appears that the problem is serious, the order of presenting the measures can be counterbalanced using the techniques described in the chapter **"Experimental Design."** Often there are no indications from previous research that order is a serious problem. In this case, the prudent response is to present the most important measures first and the less important ones later. With this approach, order will not be a problem in interpreting the results on the most important dependent variables. Even though order may be a potential problem for some of the measures, the overall impact on the study is minimized.

Making multiple measurements in a single experiment is valuable when it is feasible to do so. However, it may be necessary to conduct a separate series of experiments to explore the effects of an independent variable on various behaviors.

Sensitivity of the Dependent Variable

The dependent variable should be sensitive enough to detect differences between groups. A measure of liking that asks "Do you like this person?" with only a simple "yes" or "no" response alternative is less sensitive than one that asks "How much do you like this person?" on a 5- or 7-point scale. With the first measure, people may tend to be nice and say yes even if they have some negative feelings about the person. The second measure allows for a gradation of liking; such a scale would make it easier to detect differences in amount of liking.

The issue of **sensitivity** is particularly important when measuring human performance. Memory can be measured using recall, recognition, or reaction time; cognitive task performance might be measured by examining speed or number of errors during a proofreading task; physical performance can be measured through various motor tasks. Such tasks vary in their difficulty. Sometimes a task is so easy that everyone does well regardless of the conditions that are manipulated by the independent variable. This results in what is called a **ceiling effect**—the independent variable appears to have no effect on the dependent measure only because participants quickly reach the maximum performance level. The opposite problem occurs when a task is so difficult that hardly anyone can perform well; this is called a **floor effect.**

The need to consider sensitivity of measures is nicely illustrated by a study examining the effect of crowding on various measures of cognitive task performance (Freedman et al., 1971). In the study, crowding did not impair performance. You could conclude that crowding has no effect on performance; however, it is also possible that the measures were either too easy or too difficult to detect an effect of crowding. In fact, subsequent research showed that the tasks may have been too easy; when subjects perform complex cognitive tasks in laboratory or natural settings, crowding does result in lower performance (Bruins & Barber, 2000; Paulus et al., 1976).

Cost of Measures

Another consideration is cost—some measures may be more costly than others. Paper-and-pencil self-report measures are generally inexpensive; measures that require trained observers or elaborate equipment can become quite costly. A researcher studying nonverbal behavior, for example, might have to use a video camera to record each participant's behaviors in a situation. Two or more observers would then have to view the tapes to code behaviors such as eye contact, smiling, or self-touching (two observers are needed to ensure that the observations are reliable). Thus, there would be expenses for both equipment and personnel. Physiological recording devices are also expensive. Researchers need resources from the university or outside agencies to carry out such research.

ADDITIONAL CONTROLS

The basic experimental design has two groups: in the simplest case, an experimental group that receives the treatment and a control group that does not. Use of a control group makes it possible to eliminate a variety of alternative explanations for the results, thus improving internal validity. Sometimes additional control procedures may be necessary to address other types of alternative explanations. Two general control issues concern participant expectations and experimenter expectations.

Controlling for Participant Expectations

Demand Characteristics

We noted previously that experimenters generally do not wish to inform participants about the specific hypotheses being studied or the exact purpose of the research. The reason for this lies in the problem of **demand characteristics** (Orne, 1962), which is any feature of an experiment that might inform participants of the purpose of the study. The concern is that when participants form expectations about the hypothesis of the study, they will then do whatever is necessary to confirm the hypothesis. For example, if you were studying the relationship between political orientation and homophobia, participants might figure out the hypothesis and behave according to what they think you want, instead of being truthful.

One way to control for demand characteristics is to use deception—to make participants think that the experiment is studying one thing when actually it is studying something else. The experimenter may devise elaborate cover stories to explain the purpose of the study and to disguise what is really being studied. The researcher may also attempt to disguise the dependent variable by using an unobtrusive measure or by placing the measure among a set of unrelated **filler items** on a questionnaire. Another approach is simply to assess whether demand characteristics are a problem by asking participants about their perceptions of the purpose of the research. It may be that participants do not have an accurate view of the purpose of the study; or if some individuals do guess the hypotheses of the study, their data may be analyzed separately.

Demand characteristics may be eliminated when people are not aware that an experiment is taking place or that their behavior is being observed. Thus, experiments conducted in field settings and observational research in which the observer is concealed or unobtrusive measures are used minimize the problem of demand characteristics.

Placebo Groups

A special kind of participant expectation arises in research on the effects of drugs. Consider an experiment that is investigating whether a drug such as Prozac reduces depression. One group of people diagnosed as depressive receives the drug and the other group receives nothing. Now suppose that the drug group shows an improvement. We do not know whether the improvement was caused by the properties of the drug or by the participants' expectations about the effect of the drug—what is called a *placebo effect*. In other words, just administering a pill or an injection may be sufficient to cause an observed improvement in behavior. To control for this possibility, a **placebo group** can be added. Participants in the placebo group receive a pill or injection containing an inert, harmless substance; they do not receive the drug given to members of the experimental group. If the improvement results from the active properties of the drug, the participants in the experimental group should show greater improvement than those in the placebo group. If the placebo group improves as much as the experimental group, all improvement could be caused by a placebo effect.

Sometimes participants' expectations are the primary focus of an investigation. For example, Marlatt and Rohsenow (1980) conducted research to determine which behavioral effects of alcohol are due to alcohol itself as opposed to the psychological impact of believing that one is drinking alcohol. The experimental design to examine these effects had four groups: (1) expect no alcohol—receive no alcohol; (2) expect no alcohol—receive alcohol; (3) expect alcohol—receive no alcohol; and (4) expect alcohol—receive alcohol. This design is called a *balanced placebo design*. Marlatt and Rohsenow's research suggests that the belief that one has consumed alcohol is a more important determinant of behavior than the alcohol itself. That is, people who believed they had consumed alcohol (Groups 3 and 4) behaved very similarly, although those in Group 3 were not actually given any alcohol.

In some areas of research, the use of placebo control groups has ethical implications. Suppose you are studying a treatment that does have a positive effect on people (for example, by reducing migraine headaches or alleviating symptoms of depression). It is important to use careful experimental procedures to make sure that the treatment does have an impact and that alternative explanations for the effect, including a placebo effect, are eliminated. However, it is also important to help those people who are in the control conditions; this aligns with the concept of beneficence that was covered in the chapter **"Ethics in Behavioral Research."** Thus, participants in the control conditions must be given the treatment as soon as they have completed their part in the study in order to maximize the benefits of participation.

Placebo effects are real and must receive serious study in many areas of research. A great deal of current research and debate focuses on the extent to which any beneficial effects of antidepressant medications, such as Prozac, are due to placebo effects (e.g., Kirsch, 2010; Wampold et al., 2005).

Controlling for Experimenter Expectations

Experimenters are usually aware of the purpose of the study and thus may develop expectations about how participants should respond. These expectations can in turn bias the results. This general problem is called **expectancy effects** or *experimenter bias* (Rosenthal, 1966, 1967, 1969).

Expectancy effects may occur whenever the experimenter knows which condition the participants are in. There are two potential sources of experimenter bias. First, the experimenter might unintentionally treat participants differently in the various conditions of the study. For example, certain words might be emphasized when reading instructions to one group but not the other, or the experimenter might smile more when interacting with people in one of the conditions. The second source of bias can occur when experimenters record the behaviors of the participants; there may be subtle differences in the way the experimenter interprets and records the behaviors.

Research on Expectancy Effects

Expectancy effects have been studied in a variety of ways. Perhaps the earliest demonstration of the problem is the case of Clever Hans, a horse with alleged mathematical and other abilities that attracted the attention of Europeans in the early 20th century (Rosenthal, 1967). The owner of the horse posed questions to Hans, who in turn would provide answers by tapping his hoof (e.g., the question "What is two times five?" would be followed by 10 taps). Pfungst (1911) later showed that Hans was actually responding to barely detectable cues provided by the person asking the question. The person would look at the hoof as Hans started to tap and then changed to look at Hans as the correct answer was about to be given. Hans was responding to these head and eye movements that went undetected by observers.

If a clever horse can respond to subtle cues, it is reasonable to suppose that clever humans can too. In fact, research has shown that experimenter expectancies can be communicated to humans by both verbal and nonverbal means (Duncan et al., 1969; Jones & Cooper, 1971). An example of more systematic research on expectancy effects is a study by Rosenthal (1966). In this experiment, graduate students trained rats that were described as coming from either "maze bright" or "maze dull" genetic strains. The animals actually came from the same strain and had been randomly assigned to the bright and dull categories; however, the "bright" rats *did* perform better than the "dull" rats! Subtle differences in the ways the students treated the rats or recorded their behavior must have caused this result. A generalization of this particular finding is called "teacher expectancy." Research has shown that telling a teacher that a pupil will bloom intellectually over the next year results in an increase in the pupil's IQ score (Rosenthal & Jacobson, 1968). In short, teachers' expectations can influence students' performance.

The problem of expectations influencing ratings of behavior is nicely illustrated in an experiment by Langer and Abelson (1974). Clinical psychologists were shown a videotape of an interview in which the person interviewed was described as either an applicant for a job or a patient; in reality, all saw the same tape. The psychologists later rated the person as more "disturbed" when they thought the person was a patient than when the person was described as a job applicant.

Solutions to the Expectancy Problem

Clearly, experimenter expectations can influence the outcomes of research investigations. How can this problem be solved? Fortunately, there are a number of ways to minimize expectancy effects. First, experimenters should be well trained and should practice behaving consistently with all participants. The benefit of training was illustrated in the Langer and Abelson (1974) study with clinical psychologists. The bias of rating the "patient" as disturbed was much less among behavior-oriented therapists than among traditional ones. Presumably, the training of the behavior-oriented therapists led them to focus more on the actual behavior of the person, so they were less influenced by expectations stemming from the label "patient."

Another solution is to run all conditions simultaneously so that the experimenter's behavior is the same for all participants. However, this solution is feasible only under certain circumstances, such as when the study can be carried out with the use of printed materials or the experimenter's instructions to participants are the same for everyone.

Expectancy effects are also minimized when the procedures are automated. As noted earlier in this chapter, it may be possible to manipulate independent variables and record responses using computers; with automated procedures, the experimenter's expectations are less likely to influence the results.

A final solution is to use experimenters who are unaware of the hypothesis being investigated. In these cases, the person conducting the study or making observations is blind regarding what is being studied or which condition the participant is in. This procedure originated in drug research using placebo groups. In a **single-blind experiment,** the participant is unaware of whether a placebo or the actual drug is being administered; in a **double-blind experiment**, neither the participant nor the experimenter knows whether the placebo or actual treatment is being given. To use a procedure in which the experimenter or observer is unaware of either the hypothesis or the group the participant is in, you must hire other people to conduct the experiment and make observations.

Because researchers are aware of the problem of expectancy effects, solutions such as the ones just described are usually incorporated into the procedures of the study. The procedures used in scientific research must be precisely defined so they can be replicated by others. This allows other researchers to build on previous research. If a study does have a potential problem of expectancy effects, researchers are bound to notice and will attempt to replicate the experiment with procedures that control for them. It is also a self-correcting mechanism that ensures that methodological flaws will be discovered. The importance of replication will be discussed further in the chapter **"Generalization."**

FINAL PLANNING CONSIDERATIONS

So far we have discussed several of the factors that a researcher considers when planning a study. Actually conducting the study and analyzing the results are time-consuming processes. Before beginning the research, the investigator wants to be as sure as possible that everything will be done right. And once the study has been designed, there are some additional procedures that will improve it.

Research Proposals

After putting considerable thought into planning the study, the researcher writes a research proposal. The proposal will include a literature review that provides a background for the study. The intent is to clearly explain why the research is being done—what questions the research is designed to answer. The details of the procedures that will be used to test the idea are then given. The plans for analysis of the data are also provided. A research proposal is very similar to the introduction and method sections of a journal article. Such proposals must be included in applications for research grants; ethics review committees require some type of proposal as well (see the chapter called **"Ethics in Behavioral Research"** for more information on Institutional Review Boards).

When planning any research project, it is a good idea to prepare a proposal, because simply putting your thoughts on paper will help you organize and systematize your ideas. In addition, you can show the proposal to friends, colleagues, professors, and other interested parties who can provide useful feedback about the adequacy of your procedures. They may see problems that you did not recognize, or they may offer ways of improving the study.

Pilot Studies

When the researcher has finally decided on all the specific aspects of the procedure, it is possible to conduct a **pilot study** in which the researcher does a trial run with a small number of participants. The pilot study will reveal whether participants understand the instructions, whether the total experimental setting seems plausible, whether any confusing questions are being asked, and so on.

Sometimes participants in the pilot study are questioned in detail about the experience following the experiment. Another method is to use the think-aloud protocol, in which the participants in the pilot study are instructed to verbalize their thoughts about everything that is happening during the study. Such procedures provide the researcher with an opportunity to make any necessary changes in the procedure before doing the entire study. Also, a pilot study allows the experimenters who are collecting the data to become comfortable with their roles and to standardize their procedures.

Manipulation Checks

A **manipulation check** is an attempt to directly measure whether the independent variable manipulation has the intended effect on the participants. Manipulation checks provide evidence for the construct validity of the manipulation. If you are manipulating anxiety, for example, a manipulation check will tell you whether participants in the high-anxiety group really were more anxious than those in the low-anxiety condition. The manipulation check might involve a self-report of anxiety, a behavioral measure (such as number of arm and hand movements), or a physiological measure. All manipulation checks, then, ask whether the manipulation of the independent variable was in fact a successful operationalization of the conceptual variable being studied. Consider, for example, a manipulation of physical attractiveness as an independent variable. In an experiment, participants respond to someone who is supposed to be perceived as attractive or unattractive. The manipulation check in this case would determine whether participants do rate the highly attractive person as more physically attractive.

Manipulation checks are particularly useful in the pilot study to decide whether the independent variable manipulation is having the intended effect. If the independent variable is not effective, the procedures can be changed. However, it is also important to conduct a manipulation check in the actual experiment. Because a manipulation check in the actual experiment might distract participants or inform them about the purpose of the experiment, it is usually wise to position the administration of the manipulation check measure near the end of the experiment; in most cases, this would be after measuring the dependent variables and prior to the debriefing session.

A manipulation check has two advantages. First, if the check shows that your manipulation was not effective, you have saved the expense of running the actual experiment. You can turn your attention to changing the manipulation to make it more effective. For instance, if the manipulation check shows that neither the low- nor the high-anxiety group was very anxious, you could change your procedures to increase the anxiety in the high-anxiety condition

Second, a manipulation check is advantageous if you get nonsignificant results—that is, if the results indicate that no relationship exists between the independent and dependent variables. A manipulation check can identify whether the nonsignificant results are due to a problem in manipulating the independent variable. If your manipulation is not successful, it is only reasonable that you will obtain nonsignificant results. If both groups are equally anxious after you manipulate anxiety, anxiety cannot have any effect on the dependent measure. What if the check shows that the manipulation was successful, but you still get nonsignificant results? Then you know at least that the results were not due to a problem with the manipulation; the reason for not finding a relationship lies elsewhere. Perhaps you had a poor dependent measure, or perhaps there really is no relationship between the variables.

Debriefing

After all the data are collected, a debriefing session is usually held. This is an opportunity for the researcher to interact with the participants to discuss the ethical and educational implications of the study. The debriefing session can also provide an opportunity to learn more about what participants were thinking during the experiment. Researchers can ask participants what they believed to be the purpose of the experiment, how they interpreted the independent variable manipulation, and what they were thinking when they responded to the dependent measures. Such information can prove useful in interpreting the results and planning future studies.

Finally, researchers may ask the participants to refrain from discussing the study with others. Such requests are typically made when more people will be participating and they may talk with one another in classes or residence halls. People who have already participated are aware of the general purposes and procedures; it is important that these individuals not provide expectancies about the study to potential future participants.

ANALYZING AND INTERPRETING RESULTS

After the data have been collected, the next step is to analyze them. Statistical analyses of the data are carried out to allow the researcher to examine and interpret the pattern of results obtained in the study. The statistical analysis helps the researcher decide whether there really is a relationship between the independent and dependent variables. The logic underlying the use of statistical tests is discussed in the chapter **"Understanding Research Results: Statistical Inference."** It is not the purpose of this book to teach statistical methods; however, the calculations involved in several statistical tests are provided in **Appendix C.**

COMMUNICATING RESEARCH TO OTHERS

The final step is to write a report that details why you conducted the research, how you obtained the participants, what procedures you used, and what you found. A description of how to write such reports is included in **Appendix A.** After you have written the report, what do you do with it? How do you communicate the findings to others? Research findings are most often submitted as journal articles or as papers to be read at scientific meetings. In either case, the submitted paper is evaluated by two or more knowledgeable reviewers who decide whether the paper is accepted for publication or presentation at the meeting.

Professional Meetings

Meetings sponsored by professional associations are important opportunities for researchers to present their findings to other researchers and the public. National and regional professional associations such as the American Psychological Association (APA) and the Association for Psychological Science (APS) hold annual meetings at which psychologists and students present their own research and learn about the latest research being done by their colleagues. Some findings are reported in verbal presentations delivered to an audience. However, poster sessions are more common; here, researchers display posters that summarize the research and the researchers are available to discuss the research with others.

Journal Articles

As we noted in the chapter **"Where to Start,"** many journals publish research papers. Nevertheless, the number of journals is small compared to the number of reports written; thus, it is not easy to publish research. When a researcher submits a paper to a journal, two or more reviewers read the paper and recommend acceptance (often with the stipulation that revisions be made) or rejection. This process is called *peer review* and it is very important in making sure that research has careful external review before it is published. As many as 90% of papers submitted to the more prestigious journals are rejected. Many rejected papers are submitted to other journals and eventually accepted for publication, but much research is never published. This is not necessarily bad; it simply means that selection processes separate high-quality research from that of lesser quality.

Many of the decisions that must be made when planning an experiment were described in this chapter. The discussion focused on experiments that use the simplest experimental design with a single independent variable. In the chapter **"Complex Experimental Designs,"** more complex experimental designs are described.

ILLUSTRATIVE ARTICLE: CONDUCTING EXPERIMENTS

When a person feels safe, they counterintuitively take more risks. This has been observed among people driving cars, kids on a playground, and bicyclists. This is a problem: The point of safety equipment is not to encourage people to behave less safely! The safety equipment used in past research was designed to be used with the activity that participants completed for the study (e.g., bike helmet with riding a bike). Would the increased risk taking occur even if the equipment was not designed for the activity?

Gamble and Walker (2016) attempted to address this question with an experimental manipulation and some clever deception by attempting to credibly convince research subjects that they were taking part in an eye-tracking experiment that required either a baseball cap or a helmet. They found that participants who wore the helmet showed higher levels of both risk taking and sensation seeking compared to those who wore the cap.

First, acquire and read the article (available at **https://tinyurl.com/vgvabkv**):

Gamble, T., & Walker, I. (2016). Wearing a bicycle helmet can increase risk taking and sensation seeking in adults. *Psychological Science, 27*(2), 289–294. https://doi.org/10.1177/0956797615620784

Then, after reading the article, consider the following:

What did they do?

1. What is the basic design of this study?
2. Is the deception used in this study ethical? Was it necessary?

What was measured?

1. Describe the manipulation of the independent variable, and identify the manipulation as straightforward or staged.

2. In this chapter we discuss three types of dependent measures: self-report, behavioral, and physiological. In the experiments presented in this paper, what types of dependent measures were used? Could other types of dependent measures have been used? Explain.

3. Do you think that the risk of overinflating a balloon equates to the risks associated with riding a bicycle? Explain why it does or why it does not.

4. These researchers did not use any manipulation checks in their experiments. How would you design a manipulation check for this experiment?

To what or whom can we generalize the results? Given the population that was studied, do you think that the results can be broadly generalized? Why or why not?

How do they know that one thing caused another?

1. Evaluate the internal validity of this study.

2. Do you believe that their conclusion is justified, given the experiment and results?

Have other researchers found similar results? How do Gamble and Walker put their results in the context of previous work on risk taking?

CRITICAL THINKING: BEING A SKILLED CONSUMER OF RESEARCH

1. Dr. Garcia has decided to conduct an experiment to see if moods impact political attitudes. She is planning on manipulating positive mood and measuring the strength of people's attitudes toward polarizing political topics (e.g., how strongly a person holds an attitude that climate change is a serious problem). She believes that people who are in a positive mood state will show more weak attitudes; they will care less about divisive issues if they are happy. First, she needs to consider the independent variable.

    a. Should she choose a straightforward manipulation or a staged manipulation? Why or why not?

    b. Identify two examples of manipulations that she could make (e.g., she could show a funny video).

    c. How should she test the strength of the manipulation?

2. Next, Dr. Garcia needs to consider her dependent variable:

    a. Identify examples of self-report and behavioral measures to recommend to Dr. Garcia.

    b. Should she include multiple DVs? Why or why not?

    c. Given the examples that you identified, describe the sensitivity of each measure. Is there potential for a floor effect? Or a ceiling effect?

3. Then, Dr. Garcia has to consider experimental controls:

     a.   What additional controls should Dr. Garcia include in the experiment to control for demand characteristics?

     b.   What additional controls should Dr. Garcia include in the experiment to control for experimenter expectancies?

4.   Finally, Dr. Garcia decides to conduct a pilot study and finds no significant difference between the experimental conditions. Should she continue with the experiment? Why or why not? What should she do next? Explain your recommendations.

Check Your Learning: Practice Exercises

Practice Exercise #1

Read each statement and then circle the appropriate letter: T (true) or F (false).	T	F
1. Staged manipulations are designed to involve participants in a situation that becomes a real experience.		
2. A staged experiment may be difficult to replicate by other researchers.		
3. Presenting participants with one of three versions of a written confession to a crime is an example of an event manipulation.		
4. In some staged manipulations, a confederate appears to be another participant in an experiment but is actually part of the manipulation.		
5. To study helping behavior, a confederate of the experimenter drops a stack of papers in front of one individual or a group of five people. The amount of time it takes for the confederate to receive help picking up the papers is the dependent variable. The manipulation employed in this experiment would be an example of a straightforward manipulation.		

Practice Exercise #2

For the following five variables, identify the general type of dependent measure:

	Self-Report Measure	Behavioral Measure	Physiological measure
1. Rating of current mood (e.g., "How happy are you?" on a scale of 1–10).			
2. Number of positive and negative words used during a couple's 10-minute interaction.			
3. Heart rate during and after giving a speech.			
4. Number of eye-blinks in a 5-second span.			
5. Number of errors on a spelling test.			

(Some answers are provided at the end of this chapter.)

CHAPTER REVIEW

Review Questions

1. What is the difference between straightforward and staged manipulations of an independent variable?
2. What are the three general types of dependent variables?
3. What is meant by the sensitivity of a dependent measure? What are ceiling effects and floor effects?
4. What are demand characteristics? Describe ways to minimize demand characteristics.
5. What is the reason for having a placebo group?
6. What are experimenter expectancy effects? What are some solutions to the experimenter bias problem?
7. What is a pilot study?
8. What is a manipulation check? How does it help the researcher interpret the results of an experiment?
9. Describe the value of a debriefing following the study.
10. What does a researcher do with the findings after completing a research project?

Study Terms

Behavioral measure

Ceiling effect

Confederate

Demand characteristics

Double-blind experiment

Electroencephalogram (EEG)

Electromyogram (EMG)

Expectancy effects (experimenter bias)

Filler items

Floor effect

Functional magnetic resonance imagery (fMRI)

Galvanic skin response (GSR)

Manipulation check

Magnetic resonance imagery (MRI)

Physiological measure

Pilot study

Placebo group

Self-report

Sensitivity

Single-blind experiment

Staged manipulation

Straightforward manipulation

Strength of manipulation

Check Your Learning: Answers

Practice Exercise #1

1. T; 2. T; 3. F; 4. T; 5. F

Practice Exercise #2

1. self-report; 2. behavioral; 3. physiological; 4. physiological; 5. behavioral

Complex Experimental Designs

Uaurelijus/Shutterstock

LEARNING OBJECTIVES

- Define *factorial design* and discuss reasons a researcher would use this design.
- Describe the information provided by main effects and interaction effects in a factorial design.
- Describe an IV × PV design.
- Discuss the role of simple main effects in interpreting interactions.
- Compare the assignment of participants in an independent groups design, a repeated measures design, and a mixed factorial design.

Thus far we have focused primarily on the simplest experimental design, in which one independent variable is manipulated and one dependent variable is measured. However, researchers often investigate problems that demand more complicated designs. These complex experimental designs are the subject of this chapter.

We begin by discussing the idea of increasing the number of levels of an independent variable in an experiment. Then we describe experiments that expand the number and types of independent variables. These changes impact the complexity of an experiment.

INCREASING THE NUMBER OF LEVELS OF AN INDEPENDENT VARIABLE

In the simplest experimental design, there are only two levels of the independent variable (IV). However, a researcher might want to design an experiment with three or more levels for several reasons. First, a design with only two levels of one independent variable cannot provide very much information about the exact form of the relationship between the independent and dependent variables. For example, **Figure 1** is based on the outcome of an experiment on the relationship between amount of "mental practice" and performance on a motor task: dart-throwing score (Kremer et al., 2009). In this study, mental practice consisted of imagining practice throws prior to an actual dart-throwing task. So, did mental practice improve dart performance? The solid line describes the results when only two levels were used—no mental practice throws and 100 mental practice throws. Because there are only two levels, the relationship can be described only with a straight line. We do not know what the relationship would be if other practice amounts were included as separate levels of the independent variable. The broken line in **Figure 1** shows the results when 25, 50, and 75 mental practice throws are also included. This result is a more accurate description of the relationship between amount of mental practice and performance. The amount of practice is very effective in increasing performance up to a point, after which further practice is not helpful. This type of relationship is termed a *positive monotonic relationship;* there is a positive relationship between the variables, but it is not a strictly positive linear relationship. An experiment with only two levels cannot yield such exact information.

FIGURE 1   Linear versus positive monotonic functions

Source: Experiment conducted by Kremer et al. (2009).

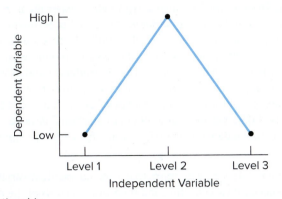

FIGURE 2   Curvilinear relationship

Note: At least three levels of the independent variable are required to show curvilinear relationships.

Recall from the chapter **"Fundamental Research Issues"** that variables are sometimes related in a curvilinear or nonmonotonic fashion; that is, the direction of relationship changes. **Figure 2** shows an example of a curvilinear relationship; this particular form is called an *inverted-U* because the wide range of levels of the independent variable produces an inverted U shape (recall our discussion of inverted-U relationships in the chapter **"Fundamental Research Issues"**). An experimental design with only two levels of the independent variable cannot detect curvilinear relationships between variables. If a curvilinear relationship is predicted, at least three levels must be used. As **Figure 2** shows, if only levels 1 and 3 of the independent variable had been used, no relationship between the variables would have been detected. Many such curvilinear relationships exist in psychology. The relationship between fear arousal and attitude change is one example—we can be scared into changing an attitude, but if we think that a message is "over the top," attitude change does not occur. In other words, increasing the amount of fear aroused by a persuasive message increases attitude change up to a moderate level of fear; further increases in fear arousal actually reduce attitude change.

Finally, researchers frequently are interested in comparing more than two groups. Suppose you want to know whether playing with an animal has beneficial effects on nursing home residents. You could have two conditions, such as a no-animal control group and a group in which a dog is brought in for play each day. However, you might also be interested in knowing the effect of a cat and a bird, and so you could add these two groups to your study. Or you might be interested in comparing the effect of a large versus a small dog in addition to a no-animal control condition. Niven (2015), for example, conducted a field experiment with three groups of callers to a customer helpline who heard different types of music while waiting on hold: instrumental only, music with neutral lyrics, and music with prosocial lyrics encouraging kindness. Caller anger was lower on days with neutral lyrics than on days with instrumental only or prosocial lyrics.

INCREASING THE NUMBER OF INDEPENDENT VARIABLES: FACTORIAL DESIGNS

Researchers recognize that in any given situation a number of variables are operating to affect behavior. So, researchers often manipulate more than one independent variable in a single experiment. Typically, two or three independent variables are operating simultaneously. This type of experimental design is a closer approximation of real-world conditions, in which independent variables do not exist by themselves.

In the chapter **"Experimental Design"** we described a hypothetical experiment in which exercise was the independent variable and mood was the dependent variable. An actual experiment on the relationship between exercise and depression was conducted by Dunn et al. (2005). In this study, participants were randomly assigned to one of two exercise conditions—a low amount or a high amount, with energy expenditure of either 7.0 or 17.5 kcal per kilogram body weight per week. The dependent variable was the score on a standard depression measure after 12 weeks of exercise. You might be wondering how often the participants exercised each week. Indeed, the researchers did wonder if frequency of exercising would be important, so they scheduled some subjects to exercise 3 days per week and others to exercise 5 days per week. Thus, the researchers designed an experiment with two independent variables—in this case, (1) amount of exercise and (2) frequency of exercise.

Factorial designs are experimental designs with more than one independent variable (or *factor*). In a factorial design, all levels of each independent variable are combined with all levels of the other independent variables. The simplest factorial design—known as a 2 × 2 (two by two) factorial design—has two independent variables, each having two levels.

An experiment by Hermans et al. (2009) illustrates a 2 × 2 factorial design. Hermans et al. studied modeling of food intake when someone is with another person who is eating. What influences whether you will model the other person's eating? In the experiment, a subject was paired with a same-sex confederate to view and rate movie trailers—they were seated in a comfortable living room environment with a bowl of M&Ms within easy reach on a coffee table. After 10 minutes of viewing, there was a break period. Two independent variables were manipulated: (1) confederate sociability and (2) confederate food intake. The sociable confederate initiated a conversation; the unsociable confederate did not initiate a conversation, responded with only brief answers if the subject said something, and avoided eye contact. The confederate also was first to reach for the M&Ms. One piece was taken in the low food intake condition; a total of 6 pieces were taken during the break. In the high food intake condition, 4 pieces were taken immediately; a total of 24 pieces were eaten by the confederate in this condition. During the break period (lasting 15 minutes), the subject could ignore the bowl of M&Ms or eat as many as desired.

This 2 × 2 design results in four experimental conditions: (1) sociable confederate–low food intake, (2) unsociable confederate–low food intake, (3) sociable confederate–high food intake, (4) unsociable confederate–high food intake. A 2 × 2 design always has four groups. **Figure 3** shows how these experimental conditions are created.

	Independent variable A: Confederate sociability	
Independent variable B: Confederate food intake	Sociable	Unsociable
Low	Sociable/ low food intake	Unsociable/ low food intake
High	Sociable/ high food intake	Unsociable/ high food intake

FIGURE 3   2 × 2 factorial design: Setup of food intake modeling experiment

The general format for describing factorial designs is

Number of levels of first IV   ×   Number of levels of second IV   ×   Number of levels of third IV

and so on. A design with two independent variables, one having two levels and the other having three levels, is a 2 × 3 factorial design; there are six conditions in the experiment. A 3 × 3 design has nine conditions.

Interpretation of Factorial Designs

Factorial designs yield two kinds of information. The first is information about the effect of each independent variable taken by itself: This is called the **main effect** of an independent variable. In a design with two independent variables, there are two main effects—one for each independent variable.

The second type of information is called an **interaction.** If there is an interaction between two independent variables, the effect of one independent variable depends on the particular level of the other variable. In other words, the effect that an independent variable has on the dependent variable depends on the level of the other independent variable. Interactions are a new source of information that cannot be obtained in a simple experimental design in which only one independent variable is manipulated.

To illustrate main effects and interactions, we can look at the results of the Hermans et al. (2009) study on food intake modeling. **Table 1** illustrates a common method of presenting outcomes for the various groups in a factorial design. The number in each cell represents the mean number of M&Ms consumed by the subjects in the four conditions.

TABLE 1   2×2 factorial design: Results of the food intake modeling

Confederate food intake (independent variable B)	Confederate sociability (independent variable A)		Overall means (main effect of B)
	Sociable	Unsociable	
Low	6.58	2.14	4.36
High	5.68	10.63	8.16
Overall means (main effect of A)	6.13	6.39	

Data based on results of Hermans et al. (2009).

Main Effects

A main effect is the effect each variable has by itself. The main effect of independent variable A, confederate sociability, is the overall effect of the variable on the dependent measure. Similarly, the main effect of independent variable B, confederate food intake, is the effect of number of M&Ms that the confederate ate on the number of M&Ms consumed by the subject.

The main effect of each independent variable is the overall relationship between that independent variable and the dependent variable. For independent variable A, is there a relationship between sociability and food intake? We can find out by looking at the overall means in the sociable and unsociable confederate conditions. These overall main effect means are obtained by averaging across all participants in each group, irrespective of confederate food intake (low or high). The main effect means are shown in the rightmost column and bottom row (called the margins of the table) of **Table 1**. The average number of M&Ms consumed by participants in the sociable confederate condition is 6.13, and the number eaten in the unsociable condition is 6.39. Note that the overall mean of 6.13 in the sociable confederate condition is the average of 6.58 in the sociable–low food intake group and 5.68 in the sociable–high food intake group (this calculation assumes equal numbers of participants in each group). You can see that overall, somewhat more M&Ms are eaten when the confederate is unsociable. Statistical tests would enable us to determine whether this is a significant main effect.

The main effect for independent variable B (confederate food intake) is the overall relationship between that independent variable, by itself, and the dependent variable. You can see in **Table 1** that the average number of candies consumed by subjects in the low food intake condition is 4.36, and the overall number eaten in the high food intake condition is 8.16. Thus, in general, more M&Ms are eaten by subjects when they were with a confederate who had consumed a high number of M&Ms (this is a modeling effect).

Interactions

These main effect means tell us that, overall, subjects eat (1) slightly more M&Ms when the confederate is unsociable and (2) considerably more when the confederate eats a large amount of candy. There is also the possibility that an interaction exists; if so, the main effects of the independent variables must be qualified. This is because an interaction between independent variables indicates that the effect of one independent variable is different at different levels of the other independent variable. That is, an interaction tells us that the effect of one independent variable depends on the particular level of the other.

We can see an interaction in the results of the Hermans et al. (2009) study. The effect of confederate food intake is different depending on whether the confederate is sociable or unsociable. When the confederate is unsociable, subjects consume many more M&Ms when the confederate food intake is high (10.68 in the unsociable condition versus 2.14 in the sociable condition). However, when the confederate is sociable, confederate food intake has little effect and in fact is the opposite of what would be expected based on modeling (6.58 in the low food intake condition and 5.68 in the high food intake condition). Thus, the relationship between confederate food intake and subject food intake is best understood by considering both independent variables: We must consider the food intake of the confederate *and* whether the confederate is sociable or unsociable.

Interactions can be seen easily when the means for all conditions are presented in a graph. **Figure 4** shows a bar graph of the results of Hermans et al. food intake modeling experiment. Note that all four means have been graphed. Two bars compare low versus high confederate food intake in the sociable confederate condition; the same comparison is shown for the unsociable confederate. You can see that confederate food intake has a small effect on the participants' modeling of M&Ms consumed when the confederate is sociable; however, when the confederate is unsociable, the participants do model the food intake of the confederate. Hermans et al. (2009) noted that they expected to observe the modeling effect primarily when the confederate is sociable; why do you think someone might actually model the food intake of the unsociable confederate instead?

The concept of interaction is a relatively simple one that you probably use all the time. When we say "it depends," we are usually indicating that some sort of interaction is operating—it depends on some other variable. Suppose, for example, that a friend has asked you if you want to go to a movie. Whether you want to go may reflect an interaction between two variables: (1) Is an exam coming up? and (2) Who stars in the movie?

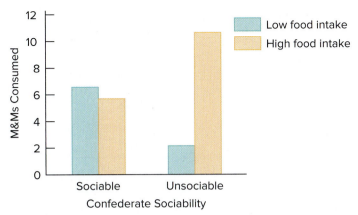

FIGURE 4   Interaction between confederate sociability and food intake

If there is an exam coming up, you will not go under any circumstance (obviously). If you do not have an exam to worry about, your decision will depend on whether you like the actors in the movie; that is, you will be much more likely to go if a favorite actor is in the movie.

You might try graphing the movie example in the same way we graphed the food intake example in **Figure 4**. The dependent variable (likelihood of going to the movie) is always placed on the vertical axis. One independent variable is placed on the horizontal axis. Bars are then drawn to represent each of the levels of the other independent variable. Graphing the results in this manner is a useful method of visualizing interactions in a factorial design.

Factorial Designs With Manipulated and Nonmanipulated Variables

One common type of factorial design includes both experimental (manipulated) and nonexperimental (measured or nonmanipulated) variables. These designs—sometimes called **IV × PV designs** (i.e., independent variable by participant variable)—allow researchers to investigate how different types of individuals (i.e., participants) respond to the same manipulated variable. These "participant variables" are personal attributes such as age, ethnicity, participant sex, personality characteristics, and clinical diagnostic category. You will sometimes see participant variables described as *subject variables* or *attribute variables*. This is only a difference of terminology.

The simplest IV × PV design includes one manipulated independent variable that has at least two levels and one participant variable with at least two levels. The two levels of the subject variable might be two different age groups, groups of low and high scorers on a personality measure, or groups of males and females. An example of this design is a study by Furnham et al. (1994). Do you ever try to study in the presence of a distraction such as a video playing on your laptop or television? Furnham et al. showed that the ability to study with such a distraction depends on whether you are more extraverted or introverted. The manipulated variable was distraction. College students read material in silence and within hearing range of a drama program. Thus, a repeated measures design was used and the order of the conditions was counterbalanced. After they read the material, the students completed a reading comprehension measure. The participant variable was extraversion: Participants completed a measure of extraversion and then were classified as extraverts or introverts. The results are shown in **Figure 5**. There was a main effect of distraction and an interaction.

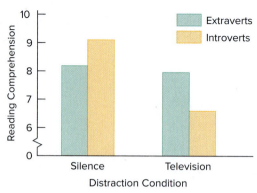

FIGURE 5   Interaction in IV × PV design

Overall, as you can see, students had higher comprehension scores when they studied in silence. In addition, there was an interaction between extraversion and distraction. Without a distraction, the performance of extraverts and introverts was almost the same. However, extraverts performed better than introverts when the TV was on. You can speculate whether similar results would be obtained today when text messages are a potential distraction.

Factorial designs with both manipulated independent variables and participant variables offer a very appealing method for investigating many interesting research questions. Such experiments recognize that full understanding of behavior requires knowledge of both situational variables and the personal attributes of individuals.

OUTCOMES OF A 2 × 2 FACTORIAL DESIGN

A 2 × 2 factorial design has two independent variables, each with two levels. When analyzing the results, researchers deal with several possibilities: (1) There may or may not be a significant main effect for independent variable A, (2) there may or may not be a significant main effect for independent variable B, and (3) there may or may not be a significant interaction between the independent variables.

Figure 6 illustrates the eight possible outcomes in a 2 × 2 factorial design. For each outcome, the means are given and then graphed using line graphs. In addition, for each graph in **Figure 6**, the main effect for each variable (A and B) is indicated by a Yes (indicating the presence of a main effect) or No (no main effect). Similarly, the A × B interaction is either present ("Yes" on the figure) or not present ("No" on the figure). The means that are given in the figure are idealized examples; such perfect outcomes rarely occur in actual research. Nevertheless, you should study the graphs to determine for yourself why, in each case, there is or is not a main effect for A, a main effect for B, and an A × B interaction.

Before you begin studying the graphs, it will help think of concrete variables to represent the two independent variables and the dependent variable. You might want to think about the example of the effect of amount and frequency of exercise on depression. Suppose that independent variable A is amount of exercise per week (A_1 is low exercise; A_2 is higher amount of exercise per week) and independent variable B is frequency of exercise (B_1 is 3 times per week and B_2 is 5 times per week). The dependent variable (DV) is the score on a depression measure, with higher numbers indicating greater depression.

The top four graphs illustrate outcomes in which there is no A × B interaction, and the bottom four graphs depict outcomes in which there is an interaction. When there is a statistically significant interaction, you

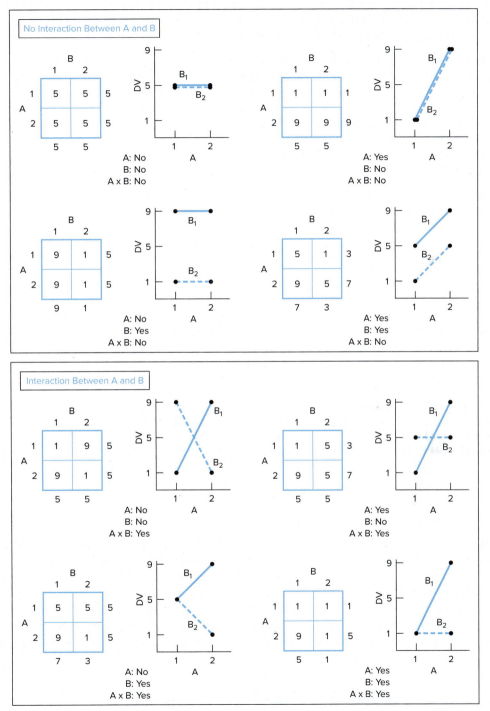

FIGURE 6   Outcomes of a factorial design with two independent variables

need to carefully examine the means to understand why the interaction occurred. In some cases, there is a strong relationship between the first independent variable and the dependent variable at one level of the second independent variable; however, there is no relationship or a weak relationship at the other level of the second independent variable. In other outcomes, the interaction may indicate that one independent variable has opposite effects on the dependent variable, depending on the level of the second independent variable.

The independent and dependent variables in **Figure 6** do not have concrete variable labels. As an exercise, interpret each of the graphs using actual variables from three different hypothetical experiments, using the scenarios suggested below. This works best if you draw the graphs, including labels for the variables, on a separate sheet of paper for each experiment. You can try depicting the data as either line graphs or bar graphs. The data points in both types of graphs are the same and both have been used in this chapter. In general, line graphs are used when the levels of the independent variable on the horizontal axis (independent variable A) are quantitative—low and high amounts. Bar graphs are more likely to be used when the levels of the independent variable represent different categories, such as one type of therapy compared with another type.

Hypothetical experiment 1: Effect of age of defendant and type of substance use during an offense on months of sentence. A male, age 20 or 50, was found guilty of causing a traffic accident while under the influence of either alcohol or marijuana.

Independent variable A: Type of offense—Alcohol versus marijuana

Independent variable B: Age of defendant—20 versus 50 years of age

Dependent variable: Months of sentence (range from 0 to 10 months)

Hypothetical experiment 2: Effect of sex and violence on recall of advertising. Participants (males and females) viewed a video on a computer screen that was either violent or not violent. They were then asked to read print ads for eight different products over the next 3 minutes. The dependent variable was the number of ads correctly recalled.

Independent variable A: Exposure to violence—Nonviolent versus violent video

Independent variable B: Participant sex—Male versus female

Dependent variable: Number of ads recalled (range from 0 to 8)

Hypothetical experiment 3: Devise your own experiment with two independent variables and one dependent variable.

Interactions and Simple Main Effects

A statistical procedure called *analysis of variance* is used to assess the statistical significance of the main effects and the interaction in a factorial design. When a significant interaction occurs, the researcher must statistically evaluate the individual means. If you take a look at **Table 1** and **Figure 4** once again, you see a clear interaction. When there is a significant interaction, the next step is to look at the **simple main effects.** A simple main effect analysis examines mean differences at *each level* of the independent variable. Recall that the main effect of an independent variable averages across the levels of the other independent variable; with simple main effects, the results are analyzed as if we had separate experiments at each level of the other independent variable.

Simple Main Effect of Confederate Food Intake

In **Figure 4**, we can look at the simple main effect of confederate food intake. This will tell us whether the difference between the low and high confederate food intake is significant when the confederate is (1) sociable and (2) unsociable. In this case, the simple main effect of confederate food intake is significant when the confederate is unsociable (means of 2.14 versus 10.63), but the simple main effect of confederate food intake is not significant when the confederate is sociable (means of 6.58 and 5.68).

Simple Main Effect of Sociability

We could also examine the simple main effect of confederate sociability; here we would compare the sociable versus unsociable conditions when the food intake is low and then when food intake is high. The simple main effect that you will be most interested in will depend on the predictions that you made when you designed the study. The exact statistical procedures do not concern us; the point here is that the pattern of results with all the means must be examined when there is a significant interaction in a factorial design.

ASSIGNMENT PROCEDURES AND FACTORIAL DESIGNS

Methods of assigning participants to conditions were discussed in the chapter **"Experimental Design."** There are two basic ways of assigning participants to conditions: (1) In an independent groups design, different participants are assigned to each of the conditions in the study and (2) in a repeated measures design, the *same* individuals participate in all conditions in the study. These two types of assignment procedures have implications for the number of participants necessary to complete the experiment. We can illustrate this fact by looking at a 2 × 2 factorial design. The design can be completely independent groups, completely repeated measures, or a **mixed factorial design**—that is, a combination of the two.

Independent Groups (between-subjects) Design

In a 2 × 2 factorial design, there are four conditions. If we want a completely **independent groups (between-subjects) design,** a different group of participants will be assigned to each of the four conditions. The food intake modeling study illustrates a factorial design with different individuals in each of the conditions. Suppose that you have planned a 2 × 2 design and want to have 10 participants in each condition; you will need a total of 40 *different* participants, as shown in the first table in **Figure 7**.

Repeated Measures (within-subjects) Design

In a completely **repeated measures (within-subjects) design,** the same individuals will participate in *all* conditions. Suppose you have planned a study on the effects of marijuana: One factor is marijuana (marijuana treatment versus placebo control) and the other factor is task difficulty (easy versus difficult). In a 2 × 2 completely repeated measures design, each individual would participate in all of the conditions by completing both easy and difficult tasks under both marijuana treatment conditions. If you wanted 10 participants in each condition, a total of 10 subjects would be needed, as illustrated in the Repeated Measures Design table in **Figure 7**. This design offers considerable savings in the number of participants required. In deciding whether to use a completely repeated measures assignment procedure, however, the researcher would have to consider the potential disadvantages of repeated measures designs.

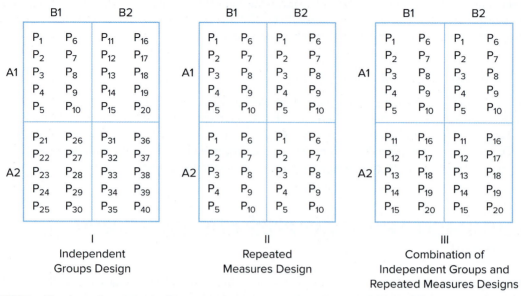

FIGURE 7   Number of participants (P) required to have 10 observations in each condition

Mixed Factorial Design Using Combined Assignment

The Furnham et al., (1994) study on distraction and extraversion illustrates the use of both independent groups and repeated measures procedures in a mixed factorial design. The participant variable, extraversion, is an independent groups variable. Distraction is a repeated measures variable; all participants studied with both distraction and silence. The third table in **Figure 7** shows the number of participants needed to have 10 per condition in a 2 × 2 mixed factorial design. In this table, independent variable A is an independent groups variable. Ten participants are assigned to level 1 of this independent variable, and another 10 participants are assigned to level 2. Independent variable B is a repeated measures variable, however. The 10 participants assigned to A_1 receive both levels of independent variable B. Similarly, the other 10 participants assigned to A_2 receive both levels of the B variable. Thus, a total of 20 participants are required.

Now complete **Check Your Learning:** Practice Exercise #1 to test your understanding of more complex assignment strategies.

INCREASING THE NUMBER OF LEVELS OF AN INDEPENDENT VARIABLE

The 2 × 2 is the simplest factorial design. With this basic design, the researcher can arrange experiments that are more and more complex. One way to increase complexity is to increase the number of levels of one or more of the independent variables. A 2 × 3 design, for example, contains two independent variables: Independent variable A has two levels, and independent variable B has three levels. Thus, the 2 × 3 design has six conditions.

Table 2 shows a 2 × 3 factorial design with the independent variables of task difficulty (easy, hard) and anxiety level (low, moderate, high). The dependent variable is performance on the task. The numbers in each of the six cells of the design indicate the mean performance score of the group. The overall means in the margins (rightmost column and bottom row) show the main effects of each of the independent variables. The results in **Table 2** indicate a main effect of task difficulty because the *overall* performance score in the easy-task group is higher than the hard-task mean. However, there is no main effect of anxiety because the mean performance score is the same in each of the three anxiety groups. Is there an interaction between task difficulty and anxiety? Note that increasing the amount of anxiety has the effect of increasing performance on the easy task but *decreasing* performance on the hard task. The effect of anxiety is different, depending on whether the task is easy or hard; thus, there is an interaction.

TABLE 2   2 × 3 factorial design

Task difficulty	Anxiety level			Overall means (main effect)
	Low	Moderate	High	
Easy	4.0	7.0	10.0	7.0
Hard	7.0	4.0	1.0	4.0
Overall means (main effect)	5.5	5.5	5.5	

This interaction can be easily seen in a graph. **Figure 8** is a line graph in which one line shows the effect of anxiety for the easy task and a second line represents the effect of anxiety for the difficult task. As noted previously, line graphs are used when the independent variable represented on the horizontal axis is quantitative—that is, the levels of the independent variable are increasing amounts of that variable (not differences in category).

FIGURE 8   Line graph of data from 3 (anxiety level) × 2 (task difficulty) factorial design

FACTORIAL DESIGNS WITH THREE OR MORE INDEPENDENT VARIABLES

We can also increase the number of variables in the design. A 2 × 2 × 2 factorial design contains three variables, each with two levels. Thus, there are 8 conditions in this design. In a 2 × 2 × 3 design, there are 12 conditions; in a 2 × 2 × 2 × 2 design, there are 16. The rule for constructing factorial designs remains the same throughout.

A 2 × 2 × 2 factorial design is constructed in **Table 3**. The independent variables are (1) instruction method (lecture, discussion), (2) class size (10, 40), and (3) class time (noon, 7:00 p.m.). If participants are randomly assigned, this would be a completely between-subjects design because all three variables would be manipulated. The dependent variable is performance on a standard test.

TABLE 3   2 × 2 × 2 factorial design

Instruction method	Class size	
	10	40
Class held at noon		
Lecture		
Discussion		
Class held at 7:00 p.m.		
Lecture		
Discussion		

Notice that the 2 × 2 × 2 design can be seen as two 2 × 2 designs, one for the classes held at noon and another for classes held at 7:00 p.m. The design yields main effects for each of the three independent variables. For example, the overall mean for the lecture method is obtained by considering all participants who experience the lecture method, irrespective of class size or class time. Similarly, the discussion method mean is derived from all participants in this condition. The *two* means are then compared to see whether there is a significant main effect: Is one of these methods superior to the other *overall*?

The design also allows us to look at interactions. In the 2 × 2 × 2 design, we can look at the interaction between (1) method and class size, (2) method and class time, and (3) class size and class time. We can also look at a three-way interaction that involves all three independent variables. Here, we want to determine whether the nature of the interaction between two of the variables differs depending on the particular level of the other variable. Three-way interactions are rather complicated; fortunately, you will not encounter too many of these in your explorations of behavioral science research.

Sometimes students are tempted to include in a study as many independent variables as they can think of. A problem with this is that the design may become needlessly complex and require enormous numbers of participants. The design previously discussed had 8 groups; a 2 × 2 × 2 × 2 design has 16 groups; adding yet another independent variable with two levels means that 32 groups would be required. Also, when there are more than three or four independent variables, many of the particular conditions that are produced by the combination of so many variables do not make sense or could not occur under natural circumstances. Finally, as the number of independent variables grows, the results become more difficult to interpret. We just saw that describing a significant three-way interaction is complicated. Interactions with more independent variables are much more difficult to describe or understand.

The designs described thus far all use the same logic for determining whether the independent variable did in fact cause a change on the dependent variable measure. In the chapter **"Single-Case, Quasi-Experimental, and Developmental Research"** we consider alternative designs that use somewhat different procedures for examining the relationship between independent and dependent variables.

Now complete **Check Your Learning:** Practice Exercise #2 at the end of the chapter to test your understanding of more complex experiments.

ILLUSTRATIVE ARTICLE: COMPLEX EXPERIMENTAL DESIGNS

We have all seen people walking while using a mobile device. Often they are talking, but they might be texting or viewing something on a smartphone screen. The authors of this illustrative article were interested in the "mini-encounters" that occur when two people pass each other on a walkway. How does mobile device use affect what happens in these encounters?

Patterson et al. (2014) conducted an experiment in which confederates varied their greeting of a stranger approaching with or without a mobile device.

First, acquire and read the article (available at **https://www.researchgate.net/publication/2642430 49_Busy_Signal_Effects_of_Mobile_Device_Usage_on_Pedestrian_Encounters**):

Patterson, M. L., Lammers, V. M., & Tubbs, M. E. (2014). Busy signal: Effects of mobile device usage on pedestrian encounters. *Journal of Nonverbal Behavior, 38*(3), 313–324. https://doi.org/10.1007/s10919-014-0182-4

Then, after reading the article, answer the following questions:

What did they do?

1. Identify the design of the experiment.
2. Which dependent variable was discarded from the analysis? Why?

What was measured?

1. Identify each independent variable. For each independent variable:
   a. What were the levels (values) of the variable?
   b. Was the variable a manipulated variable or a participant variable?
   c. How was the variable operationalized?
2. Identify each dependent variable. Describe how each dependent variable was operationalized.

What did they find?

1. Describe the results.
2. Describe the results in figure 2 in the article. Is there an interaction effect?
3. Describe at least one additional result that you found interesting or surprising.

How do they know that one thing caused another? Do you think that are any issues with the experimental design that would be a threat to drawing cause-and-effect conclusions?

To what or whom can we generalize the results? Given the population that was studied, do you think that the results can be broadly generalized? Why or why not?

CRITICAL THINKING: BEING A SKILLED CONSUMER OF RESEARCH

1. Participants were randomly assigned to conditions in a 2 × 2 between-subjects (independent groups) experiment exploring the potential impact of distraction on reaction time. In this study, two variables were manipulated: (1) a confederate in the room reading a book, either aloud or to themselves, and (2) popular music playing on a speaker (present, absent). One variable was measured: time in seconds taken to complete a Sudoku puzzle.

    a. Describe what you think the results would be if there was a main effect for reading.

    b. Describe what you think the results would be if there was also a main effect for music.

    c. Describe what you think the results would be if there was an interaction between reading and music.

    d. What assignment procedures would you recommend—completely independent groups, completely repeated measures, or a mixed factorial design? Why?

2. Research participants were randomly assigned to read one of four "resumés," which were identical except for being described as written by a 25-year-old high school graduate, a 25-year-old college graduate, a 35-year-old high school graduate, or a 35-year-old college graduate. After reviewing the resumé, participants rated the resumé for overall job qualification. The results (higher numbers indicate more qualification) showed: 25-year-old high school graduate (2.02), 25-year-old college graduate (2.05), 35-year-old high school graduate (3.82), and 35-year-old college graduate (4.90).

    a. Identify the design of this experiment.

    b. Identify the independent variable(s) and dependent variable(s).

    c. How many conditions are in the experiment?

    d. Is there a participant variable in this experiment? If so, identify it. If not, can you suggest a participant variable that might be included?

    e. Given the results, do you think that there could be any main effects, or an interaction?

Check Your Learning: Practice Exercises

Practice Exercise #1

In a series of studies designed to assess the impact of lunch nutrients and caffeine on nursing home patients' sleepiness, participants were assigned to levels of the independent variables using different strategies. For each of the strategies listed below, describe the study design and identify the assignment procedures (e.g., completely independent groups completely repeated measures, or mixed factorial design). In all three cases, the dependent measure was the score on the Stanford Sleepiness Scale 1 hour after lunch.

1. Study 1: Over the course of 2 days, participants are assigned to one of two different conditions in one variable (extra protein at lunch in the form of protein powder in the soup: yes, no), and to both conditions of another variable (caffeine with lunch: cola on day 1, caffeine-free cola on day 2).

2. Study 2: On a single day, participants are assigned to one of two levels of one variable (extra protein with lunch: yes, no), and to one of the conditions of another variable (caffeine with lunch: yes, no).

3. Study 3: Over the course of 4 days, participants are assigned to both levels of one variable (extra protein with lunch: yes, no), and to both of the conditions of another variable (caffeine with lunch: yes, no). Day 1: extra-protein/caffeine, Day 2: extra-protein/no caffeine, Day 3: no extra-protein/caffeine, Day 4: no extra-protein/no caffeine.

Practice Exercise #2

Scenario	Number of independent variables	Number of experimental conditions	Number of possible main effects	Number of possible interactions
1. Participants were randomly assigned to read a short story printed in either 12-point or 14-point font in one of three font style conditions: Courier, Times Roman, or Arial. Afterward they answered several questions designed to measure memory recall.				
2. Researchers conducted an experiment to examine age and weight biases in juror behavior.				

Participants were randomly assigned to read a scenario describing a crime committed by either a younger (25 year-old) or older (55 year-old) person who was described as overweight or average weight.

(Answers are provided at the end of this chapter.)

CHAPTER REVIEW

Review Questions

1. Why would a researcher have more than two levels of the independent variable in an experiment?
2. What is a factorial design? Why would a researcher use a factorial design?
3. What are main effects in a factorial design? What is an interaction?
4. Describe an IV × PV factorial design.
5. Identify the number of conditions in a factorial design on the basis of knowing the number of independent variables and the number of levels of each independent variable.
6. Describe 2 × 2 factorial designs in which (a) both independent variables are independent groups (between-subjects), (b) both independent variables are repeated measures (within-subjects), and (c) the design is mixed, so that one independent variable is independent groups and the other is repeated measures.

Study Terms

Factorial design

Independent groups design (between-subjects design)

Interaction

IV × PV design

Main effect

Mixed factorial design

Repeated measures design (within-subjects design)

Simple main effect

Check Your Learning: Answers

Practice Exercise #1

1. 2 (extra protein: yes, no) × 2 (caffeine: yes, no) mixed factorial design with repeated measures on caffeine.

2. 2 (extra protein: yes, no) × 2 (caffeine: yes, no) factorial design with completely independent groups.

3. 2 (extra protein: yes, no) × 2 (caffeine: yes, no) factorial design with completely repeated measures.

Practice Exercise #2

1. 2 IVs (font size and font style); 6 conditions; 2 possible main effects; 1 possible interaction

2. 3 IVs (gender, attractiveness, weight level); 8 conditions; 3 possible main effects; 4 possible interactions (3 two-way interactions and 1 three-way interaction)

Single-Case, Quasi-Experimental, and Developmental Research

FatCamera/E+/Getty Images

LEARNING OBJECTIVES

- Describe single-case experimental designs and discuss reasons to use this design.
- Describe the one-group posttest-only design.
- Describe the one-group pretest-posttest design and the associated threats to internal validity that may occur: history, maturation, testing, instrument decay, and regression toward the mean.
- Describe the nonequivalent control group design and nonequivalent control group pretest-posttest design, and discuss the advantages of having a control group.
- Distinguish between the interrupted time series design and control series design.
- Describe cross-sectional, longitudinal, and sequential research designs, including the advantages and disadvantages of each design.
- Define cohort effect.

In the classic posttest-only experimental design, participants are randomly assigned to the independent variable conditions, and a dependent variable is measured. The responses on the dependent measure are then compared to determine whether the independent variable had an effect. Because all other variables are held constant, differences on the dependent variable must be due to the effect of the independent variable. This design has high internal validity—we are very confident that the independent variable caused the observed responses on the dependent variable. You will often encounter this experimental design when you explore research in the behavioral sciences. However, other research designs have been devised to address special research problems.

This chapter focuses on three of these research designs. First we will look at the instance in which the effect of an independent variable must be inferred from an experiment with only one participant: single-case experimental designs. Second, we will describe pre-experimental and quasi-experimental designs that may be considered if it is not possible to use one of the true experimental designs. Third, we consider research designs for studying changes that occur with age.

SINGLE-CASE EXPERIMENTAL DESIGNS

Single-case experimental designs have traditionally been called *single-subject* designs; an equivalent term you may see is *small-N* designs. Much of the early interest in single-case designs in psychology came from research on operant conditioning pioneered by B. F. Skinner (e.g., Skinner, 1953). Today, research using single-case designs is often seen in applied behavior analysis in which operant conditioning techniques are used in clinical, counseling, educational, medical, and other applied settings (Kazdin, 2011, 2013).

Single-case experiments were developed from a need to determine whether an experimental manipulation had an effect on a single research participant. In a single-case design, the subject's behavior is measured over time during a **baseline** control period. A treatment period follows in which the experimental manipulation is introduced, and the subject's behavior continues to be observed. A change in the subject's behavior from baseline to treatment periods is evidence for the effectiveness of the manipulation. The problem, however, is that there could be many explanations for the change other than the experimental treatment (i.e., alternative explanations). For example, some other event may have coincided with the introduction of the treatment. The single-case designs described in the following sections address this problem.

Reversal Designs

As noted, the basic issue in single-case experiments is how to determine that the manipulation of the independent variable had an effect. One method is to demonstrate the reversibility of the manipulation. A simple **reversal design** takes the following form:

A (baseline period) → B (treatment period) → A (baseline period)

This basic reversal design is called an ABA design; it requires observation of behavior during the baseline control (A) period, again during the treatment (B) period, and also during a second baseline (A) period after the experimental treatment has been removed. (Sometimes this is called a *withdrawal design,* in recognition of the fact that the treatment is removed or withdrawn.) For example, the effect of a reinforcement procedure on a child's academic performance could be assessed with an ABA design. The number of correct homework problems could be measured each day during the baseline. A reinforcement treatment procedure would then be introduced in which the child received stars for correct problems; the stars could be accumulated and exchanged for toys or candies. Later, this treatment would be discontinued during the second baseline (A) period. Hypothetical data from such an experiment are shown in **Figure 1.** The fact that behavior changed when the treatment was introduced and reversed when the treatment was withdrawn is evidence for its effectiveness.

Figure 1 depicts a treatment that had a relatively dramatic impact on behavior. Some treatments do produce an immediate change in behavior, but many other variables may require a longer time to show an impact.

The ABA design can be greatly improved by extending it to an ABAB design, in which the experimental treatment is introduced a second time, or even to an ABABAB design that allows the effect of the treatment to be tested a third time. This is done to address two problems with the ABA reversal design. First, a single reversal is not extremely powerful evidence for the effectiveness of the treatment. The observed reversal might have been due to a random fluctuation in the child's behavior; perhaps the treatment happened to coincide with some other event, such as the child's upcoming birthday, that caused the change (and the post-birthday reversal). These possibilities are much less likely if the treatment has been shown to have an effect two or more times; random or coincidental events are unlikely to be responsible for both reversals. The second problem is ethical. As Barlow et al. (2009) point out, it does not seem right to end the design with the withdrawal of a treatment that may be very beneficial for the participant. Using an ABAB design provides the opportunity to observe a second reversal when the treatment is introduced again. The sequence ends with the treatment rather than the withdrawal of the treatment.

The logic of the reversal design can also be applied to behaviors observed in a single setting. For example, Kazbour and Bailey (2010) examined the effectiveness of a procedure designed to increase the use of designated drivers in a bar. The percentage of bar patrons either serving as or being with a designated driver was recorded over a baseline period of 2 weeks. A procedure to increase the use of designated drivers was then implemented during the treatment phase. Designated drivers received a $5 gas card, and the driver and passengers received free pizza on their way out of the bar. The pizza and gas incentive was discontinued during the final phase of the study. The percentage of bar patrons engaged in designated driver arrangements increased substantially during the treatment phase but returned to baseline levels when the incentive was withdrawn.

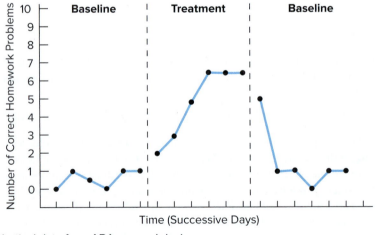

FIGURE 1   Hypothetical data from ABA reversal design

Multiple Baseline Designs

It may have occurred to you that a reversal of some behaviors may be impossible or unethical. For example, it would be unethical to reverse treatment that reduces dangerous or illegal behaviors, such as indecent exposure or alcoholism, even if the possibility exists that a second introduction of the treatment might be effective. Other treatments might produce a long-lasting change in behavior that is not reversible. In such cases, multiple measures over time can be made before and after the manipulation. If the manipulation is effective, a change in behavior will be immediately observed, and the change will continue to be reflected in further measures of the behavior. In a **multiple baseline design,** the effectiveness of the treatment is demonstrated when a behavior changes only after the manipulation is introduced. To demonstrate the effectiveness of the treatment, such a change must be observed under *multiple* circumstances to rule out the possibility that other events were responsible.

There are several variations of the multiple baseline design (Barlow et al., 2009). In the multiple baseline *across subjects,* the behavior of several subjects is measured over time; for each subject, though, the manipulation is introduced at a different point in time. **Figure 2** shows data from a hypothetical smoking-reduction experiment with three subjects. Note that introduction of the manipulation was followed by a change in behavior for each subject. However, because this change occurred across all individuals and the manipulation was introduced at a different time for each subject, we can rule out explanations based on chance, historical events, and so on.

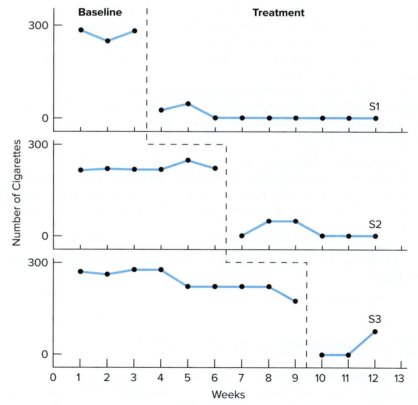

FIGURE 2   Hypothetical data from multiple baseline design across three subjects (S1, S2, and S3)

In a multiple baseline *across behaviors,* several different behaviors of a single subject are measured over time. At different times, the same manipulation is applied to each of the behaviors. For example, a reward system could be instituted to increase the socializing, grooming, and reading behaviors of a psychiatric patient. The reward system would be applied to each of these behaviors at different times. Demonstrating that each behavior increased when the reward system was applied would be evidence for the effectiveness of the manipulation.

The third variation is the multiple baseline *across situations,* in which the same behavior is measured in different settings, such as at home and at work. Again, a manipulation is introduced at a different time in each setting, with the expectation that a change in the behavior in each situation will occur only after the manipulation.

Replications in Single-Case Designs

The procedures for use with a single subject can, of course, be replicated with other subjects, greatly enhancing the generalizability of the results. Usually, reports of research that employs single-case experimental procedures do present the results from several subjects (and often in several settings). The tradition in single-case research has been to present the results from each subject individually rather than as group data with overall means. Sidman (1960), a leading spokesperson for this tradition, has pointed out that grouping the data from a number of subjects by using group means can sometimes give a misleading picture of individual responses to the manipulation. For example, the manipulation may be effective in changing the behavior of some subjects but not others. This was true in a study conducted by Ryan and Hemmes (2005) that investigated the impact of rewarding college students with course grade points for submitting homework. For half of the 10 chapters, students received points for submitting homework; however, there were no points given if they submitted homework for the other chapters (to control for chapter topic, some students had points for odd-numbered chapters only and others received points for the even-numbered chapters). Ryan and Hemmes found that, on average, students submitted more homework assignments and performed better on chapter-based quizzes that were directly associated with point rewards. However, some individual participants performed about the same regardless of condition. Because the emphasis of the study was on the individual subject, this pattern of results was quickly revealed.

Single-case designs are useful for studying many research problems and should be considered a powerful alternative to more traditional research designs. They can be especially valuable for someone who is applying some change technique in a natural environment—for example, a teacher who is trying a new technique in the classroom. In addition, complex statistical analyses are not required for single-case designs.

> Now complete **Check Your Learning:** Practice Exercise #1 to assess your understanding of single-case experimental designs.

QUASI-EXPERIMENTAL DESIGNS

Quasi-experimental designs address the need to study the effect of an independent variable in settings in which the control features of true experimental designs cannot be achieved. Thus, a quasi-experimental design allows us to examine the impact of an independent variable on a dependent variable, but causal inference is much more difficult because quasi-experiments lack important features of true experiments such as random assignment to conditions. In this section we will examine several quasi-experimental designs that might be used in situations in which a true experiment is not possible. This is most likely to occur in applied settings when an independent variable is manipulated in a natural setting such as a school, business, hospital, or an entire city or state.

There are many types of quasi-experimental designs—see Campbell (1968, 1969), Campbell and Stanley (1966), Cook and Campbell (1979), and Shadish et al. (2002). Only six designs will be described here. As you read about each design, compare the design features and problems with the randomized true experimental designs described in the chapter **"Experimental Design."** We start out with the simplest and most problematic of the designs. In fact, the first three designs we describe are sometimes called "pre-experimental" to distinguish them from other quasi-experimental designs. This is because of the problems associated with these designs. Nevertheless, all may be used in different circumstances, and it is important to recognize the internal validity issues raised by each design.

One-Group Posttest-Only Design

Suppose you want to investigate whether sitting close to a stranger will cause the stranger to move away. You might try sitting next to a number of strangers and measure the number of seconds that elapse before they leave. Your design would look like this:

Now suppose that the average amount of time before the people leave is 9.6 seconds. Unfortunately, this finding is not interpretable. You do not know whether they would have stayed longer if you had not sat down or whether they would have stayed for 9.6 seconds anyway. It is even possible that they would have left sooner if you had not sat down—perhaps they liked you!

This **one-group posttest-only design**—called a "one-shot case study" by Campbell and Stanley (1966)—lacks a crucial element of a true experiment: a control or comparison group. There must be some sort of comparison condition to enable you to interpret your results. The one-group posttest-only design with its missing comparison group has serious deficiencies in the context of designing an internally valid experiment that will allow us to draw causal inferences about the effect of an independent variable on a dependent variable.

You might wonder whether this design is ever used. In fact, you may see this type of design used as evidence for the effectiveness of a program. For example, employees in a company might participate in a 4-hour information session on emergency procedures. At the conclusion of the program, they complete a knowledge test on which their average score is 90%. This result is then used to conclude that the program is successfully educating employees. Such studies lack internal validity—our ability to conclude that the independent variable had an effect on the dependent variable. With this design, we do not even know if the score on the dependent variable would have been equal, lower, or even higher without the program. The reason such results are sometimes accepted is that we may have an implicit idea of how a control group would perform. Unfortunately, we need that comparison data.

One-Group Pretest-Posttest Design

One way to obtain a comparison is to measure participants before the manipulation (a pretest) and again afterward (a posttest). An index of change from the pretest to the posttest could then be computed. Although this **one-group pretest-posttest design** sounds fine, there are some major problems with it.

To illustrate, suppose you want to test the hypothesis that a relaxation training program will result in a reduction in cigarette smoking. Using the one-group pretest-posttest design, you would select a group of people who smoke, administer a measure of smoking, have them go through relaxation training, and then readminister the smoking measure. Your design would look like this:

If you did find a reduction in smoking, you could not assume that the result was due to the relaxation training program. This design has failed to take into account several alternative explanations. These alternative explanations are threats to the internal validity of studies using this design and include history, maturation, testing, instrument decay, and regression toward the mean.

History

History refers to any event that occurs between the first and second measurements but is not part of the manipulation. Any such event is confounded with the manipulation. For example, suppose that a famous person dies of lung cancer during the time between the first and second measures. This event, and not the relaxation training, could be responsible for a reduction in smoking. Admittedly, the celebrity death example is dramatic and perhaps unlikely. However, **history effects** can be caused by virtually any confounding event that occurs at the same time as the experimental manipulation.

Maturation

People change over time. In a brief period they become bored, fatigued, perhaps wiser, and certainly hungrier; over a longer period, children become more coordinated and analytical; and so on. Any changes that occur systematically over time are called **maturation effects.** Maturation could be a problem in the smoking reduction example if people generally become more concerned about health as they get older. Any such time-related factor might result in a change from the pretest to the posttest. If this happens, you might mistakenly attribute the change to the treatment rather than to maturation.

Testing

Testing becomes a problem if simply taking the pretest changes the participant's behavior. This is the problem of **testing effects.** For example, the smoking measure might require people to keep a diary in which they note every cigarette smoked during the day. Simply keeping track of smoking might be sufficient to cause a reduction in the number of cigarettes a person smokes. Thus, the reduction found on the posttest could be the result of taking the pretest rather than of the program itself. In other contexts, taking a pretest may sensitize people to the purpose of the experiment or make them more adept at a skill being tested. Again, the experiment would not have internal validity.

Instrument Decay

Sometimes, the basic characteristics of the measuring instrument change over time; this is called **instrument decay**. Consider sources of instrument decay when human observers are used to measure behavior: Over time, an observer may gain skill, become fatigued, or change the standards on which observations are based. In our example on smoking, participants might be highly motivated to record all cigarettes smoked during the pretest when the task is new and interesting, but by the time the posttest is given they may be tired of the task and sometimes forget to record a cigarette. Such instrument decay would lead to an apparent reduction in cigarette smoking.

Regression Toward the Mean

Sometimes called *statistical regression,* **regression toward the mean** is likely to occur whenever participants are selected because they score extremely high or low on some variable. When they are tested again, their scores tend to change in the direction of the mean. Extremely high scores are likely to become lower (closer to the mean), and extremely low scores are likely to become higher (again, closer to the mean).

Regression toward the mean would be a problem in the smoking experiment if participants were selected because they were initially found to be extremely heavy smokers. By choosing people for the program who scored highest on the pretest, the researcher may have selected many participants who were, for whatever reason, smoking much more than usual at the particular time the measure was administered. Those people who were smoking much more than usual will likely be smoking less when their smoking is measured again. If we then compare the overall amount of smoking before and after the program, it will appear that people are smoking less. The alternative explanation is that the smoking reduction is due to statistical regression rather than the effect of the program.

Regression toward the mean will occur whenever you gather a set of extreme scores taken at one time and compare them with scores taken at another point in time. The problem is actually rooted in the reliability of the measure. Recall from the chapter **"Measurement Concepts"** that any given measure reflects a true score plus measurement error. If there is perfect reliability, the two measures will be the same (if nothing happens to lower or raise the scores). If the measure of smoking is perfectly reliable, a person who reports smoking 20 cigarettes today will report smoking 20 cigarettes 2 weeks from now. However, if the two measures are not perfectly reliable and there is measurement error, most scores will be close to the true score but some will be higher and some will be lower. Thus, one smoker with a true score of 20 cigarettes per day might sometimes smoke 5 and sometimes 35; however, most of the time the number is closer to 20 than to the extremes. Another smoker might have a true score of 35 but on occasion smokes as few as 20 and as many as 50; again, most of the time the number is closer to the true score than to the extremes. Now suppose that you select two people who said they smoked 35 cigarettes on the previous day, and that both of these people are included in the group—you picked the first person on a very unusual day and the second person on a very ordinary day. When you measure these people 2 weeks later, the first person is probably going to report smoking close to 20 cigarettes and the second person close to 35. If you average the two, it will appear that there is an overall reduction in smoking.

What if the measure were perfectly reliable? In this case, the person with a true score of 20 cigarettes would always report this amount and therefore would not be included in the heavy smoker (35+ cigarettes) group at all. Only people with true scores of 35 or more would be in the group, and any reduction in smoking would be due to the treatment program. The point here is that regression toward the mean is a problem if there is measurement error.

Statistical regression occurs when we try to explain events in the "real world" as well. Sports columnists often refer to the hex that awaits an athlete who appears on the cover of *Sports Illustrated.* The performances of a number of athletes have dropped considerably after they were the subjects of *Sports Illustrated* cover stories. Although these cover stories might cause the lower performance (perhaps the notoriety results in nervousness and reduced concentration), statistical regression is also a likely explanation. An athlete is selected for the cover of the magazine because he or she is performing at an exceptionally high level; the principle of regression toward the mean states that very high performance is likely to deteriorate. We would know this for sure if *Sports Illustrated* also did cover stories on athletes who were in a slump and this became a good omen for them!

All these problems can be eliminated by the use of an appropriate control group. A group that does not receive the experimental treatment provides an adequate control for the effects of history, statistical regression, and so on. For example, outside historical events would have the same effect on both the experimental and the control groups. If the experimental group differs from the control group on the dependent measure administered after the manipulation, the difference between the two groups can be attributed to the effect of the experimental manipulation.

Given these problems, is the one-group pretest-posttest design ever used? This design may in fact be used in many applied settings. Recall the example of the evaluation of a program to teach emergency procedures to employees. With a one-group pretest-posttest design, the knowledge test would be given before and after the training session. The ability to observe a change from the pretest to the posttest does represent an improvement over the posttest-only design, even with the threats to internal validity that we identified. In addition, the ability to use data from this design can be enhanced if the study is replicated at other times with other participants. However, formation of a control group is always the best way to strengthen this design.

In any control group, the participants in the experimental condition and the control condition must be equivalent. If participants in the two groups differ *before* the manipulation, they will probably differ *after* the manipulation as well. The next design illustrates this problem.

> Now complete **Check Your Learning:** Practice Exercise #2 to test your understanding of threats to internal validity using one-group pretest-posttest designs.

Nonequivalent Control Group Design

The **nonequivalent control group design** employs a separate control group, but the participants in the two conditions—the experimental group and the control group—are not equivalent. In other words, the two groups are not the result of random assignment. The differences become a confounding variable that provides an alternative explanation for the results. This problem, called **selection differences** or *selection bias,* usually occurs when participants who form the two groups in the experiment are chosen from existing natural groups. If the relaxation training program is studied with the nonequivalent control group design, the design will look like this:

The participants in the first group are given the smoking frequency measure after completing the relaxation training. The people in the second group do not participate in any program. In this design, the researcher does not have any control over which participants are in each group. Suppose, for example, that the study is conducted in a division of a large company. All of the employees who smoke are identified and recruited to participate in the training program. The people who volunteer for the program are in the experimental group, and the people in the control group are simply the smokers who did not sign up for the training. The problem of selection differences arises because smokers who choose to participate may differ in some important way from those who do not. For instance, they may already be light smokers compared with the others and more confident that a program can help them. If so, any difference between the groups on the smoking measure would reflect preexisting differences rather than the effect of the relaxation training. Such a preexisting difference is what we have previously described as a confounding variable (see the chapter **"Fundamental Research Issues"**).

It is important to note that the problem of selection differences arises in this design even when the researcher apparently has successfully manipulated the independent variable using two similar groups. For example, a researcher might have all smokers in the engineering division of a company participate in the relaxation training program and smokers who work in the marketing division serve as a control group. The problem here, of course, is that the smokers in the two divisions may have differed in smoking patterns *prior* to the relaxation program.

Nonequivalent Control Group Pretest-Posttest Design

The nonequivalent control group posttest-only design can be greatly improved if a pretest is given. When this is done, we have a **nonequivalent control group pretest-posttest design,** one of the most useful quasi-experimental designs. It can be diagrammed as follows:

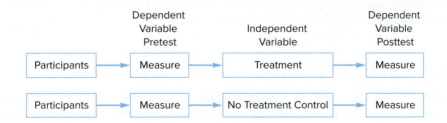

This design is similar to the pretest-posttest design described in the chapter **"Experimental Design."** However, this is not a true experimental design because assignment to groups is not random; the two groups may not be equivalent. We have the advantage, however, of knowing the pretest scores. Thus, we can see whether the groups were the same on the pretest. Even if the groups are not equivalent, we can look at *changes* in scores from the pretest to the posttest. If the independent variable has an effect, the experimental group should show a greater change than the control group (see Kenny, 1979).

An evaluation of National Alcohol Screening Day (NASD) provides an example of the use of a nonequivalent control group pretest-posttest design (Aseltine et al., 2008). NASD is a community-based program that provides free access to alcohol screening, a private meeting with a health professional to review the results, educational materials, and referral information if necessary. For the evaluation, NASD attendees at five community locations completed a baseline (pretest) measure of their recent alcohol consumption. This measure was administered as a posttest 3 months later. A control group was formed 1 week following NASD at the same locations using displays that invited people to take part in a health survey. These individuals completed the same pretest measure and were contacted in 3 months for the posttest. The data analysis focused on participants identified as at-risk drinkers; the NASD participants showed a significant decrease in alcohol consumption from pretest to posttest when compared with similar individuals in the control group.

Propensity Score Matching of Nonequivalent Treatment and Control Groups

The nonequivalent control group designs lack random assignment to conditions and so the groups may in fact differ in important ways. For example, people who decide to attend an alcohol screening event may differ from those who are interested in a health screening. Perhaps the people at the health screening are in fact healthier than the alcohol-screening participants.

One approach to making the groups equivalent on a variable such as health is to match participants in the conditions on a measure of health (this is similar to matched pairs designs, covered in the chapter **"Experimental Design"**). The health measure can be administered to everyone in the treatment condition and all individuals who are included in the control condition. Each person in the treatment condition would be matched with a control individual who possesses an identical or highly similar health score. Once this has been done, the analysis of the dependent measure can take place. This procedure is most effective when the measure used for the matching is highly reliable and the individuals in the two conditions are known to be very similar. Nonetheless, it is still possible that the two groups are different on other variables that were not measured.

Advances in statistical methods have made it possible to simultaneously match individuals on multiple variables. Instead of matching on just one variable, such as health, the researcher can obtain measures of other variables thought to be important when comparing the groups. The scores on these variables are combined to produce what is called a *propensity score* (the statistical procedure is beyond the scope of the book). Individuals in the treatment and control groups can then be matched on propensity scores—this process is called **propensity score matching** (Guo & Fraser, 2010; Shadish et al., 2002).

Interrupted Time Series Design and Control Series Design

Campbell (1969) discusses at length the evaluation of one specific legal reform: the 1955 crackdown on speeding in Connecticut. Although seemingly an event in the distant past, the example is still a good illustration of an important methodological issue. The crackdown was instituted after a record high number of traffic fatalities occurred in 1955. The easiest way to evaluate this reform is to compare the number of traffic fatalities in 1955 (before the crackdown) with the number of fatalities in 1956 (after the crackdown). Indeed, the number of traffic deaths fell from 324 in 1955 to 284 in 1956. This single comparison is really a one-group pretest-posttest design with all of that design's problems of internal validity; there are many other reasons traffic deaths might have declined. One alternative is to use an **interrupted time series design** that would exam-ine the traffic fatality rates over an extended period of time, both before and after the reform was instituted. **Figure 3** shows this information for the years 1951–1959. Campbell (1969) argues that the drop from 1955 to 1956 does not look particularly impressive, given the great fluctuations in previous years, but there is a steady downward trend in fatalities after the crackdown. Even here, however, Campbell sees a problem in interpre-tation. The drop could be due to statistical regression: Because 1955 was a record high year, the probability is that there would have been a drop anyway. Still, the data for the years extending before and after the crack-down allow for a less ambiguous interpretation than would be possible with data for only 1955 and 1956.

One way to improve the interrupted time series design is to find some kind of control group—a **control series design**. In the Connecticut speeding crackdown, this was possible because other states had not instituted the reform. **Figure 4** shows the same data on traffic fatalities in Connecticut plus the fatality figures of four com-parable states during the same years. The fact that the fatality rates in the control states remained relatively constant while those in Connecticut consistently declined led Campbell to conclude that the crackdown did indeed have some effect.

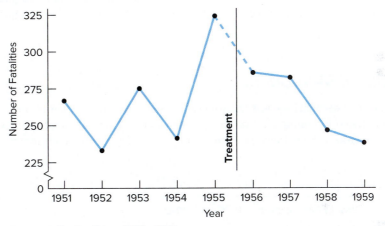

FIGURE 3   Connecticut traffic fatalities, 1951–1959

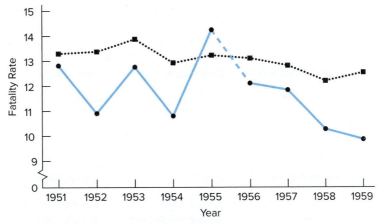

FIGURE 4   Control series design comparing Connecticut traffic fatality rate (solid color line) with the fatality rate of four comparable states (dotted black line)

Now complete **Check Your Learning:** Practice Exercise #3 to test your understanding of quasi-experimental design.

DEVELOPMENTAL RESEARCH DESIGNS

Developmental psychologists often study the ways individuals change as a function of age. A researcher might test a theory concerning changes in reasoning ability as children grow older, the age at which self-awareness develops in young children, or the global values people have as they move from adolescence through old age. In all cases, the major variable is age. Developmental researchers face an interesting choice in designing their studies because there are two general methods for studying individuals of different ages: the cross-sectional method and the longitudinal method. You will see that the cross-sectional method shares similarities with the independent groups design whereas the longitudinal method is similar to the repeated measures design. We will also examine a hybrid approach called the sequential method. The three approaches are illustrated in **Figure 5.**

Cross-Sectional Method

In a study using the **cross-sectional method,** persons of different ages are studied at only one point in time. Suppose you are interested in examining how the ability to learn a computer application changes as people grow older. Using the cross-sectional method, you might study people who are currently 20, 30, 40, and 50

Cross-Sectional Method

	Year of Birth (cohort)	Time 1: 2010
Group 1:	1955	55 years old
Group 2:	1950	60 years old
Group 3:	1945	65 years old

Longitudinal Method

	Year of Birth (cohort)	Time 1: 2010	Time 2: 2015	Time 3: 2020
Group 1:	1955	55 years old →	60 years old →	65 years old

Sequential Method

	Year of Birth (cohort)	Time 1: 2010	Time 2: 2015	Time 3: 2020
Group 1:	1955	55 years old →	60 years old →	65 years old
Group 2:	1945	65 years old →	70 years old →	75 years old

FIGURE 5   Three designs for developmental research

years of age. The participants in your study would be given the same computer learning task, and you would compare the groups on their performance.

In a study by Tymula et al. (2013) using this method, subjects in four age groups (12–17, 21–25, 30–50, 65–90) completed the same financial decision-making task. The task involved choosing among options with varying levels of risk and reward that led to an expected financial outcome for each subject. Individuals in the oldest age group made the poorest financial decisions with more inconsistent decisions and lower financial outcomes.

Longitudinal Method

In the **longitudinal method,** the same group of people is observed at different points in time as they grow older. Perhaps the most famous longitudinal study is the Terman Life Cycle Study, which was begun by Stanford psychologist Lewis Terman in 1921. Terman studied 1,528 California schoolchildren who had intelligence test scores of at least 135. The participants, who called themselves "Termites," were initially measured on numerous aspects of their cognitive and social development in 1921 and 1922. Terman and his colleagues continued studying the Termites from childhood through adulthood (see Terman, 1925; Terman & Oden, 1947, 1959).

Terman's successors at Stanford have continued to track the Termites. The study has provided a rich description of the lives of highly intelligent individuals and disconfirmed many negative stereotypes of high intelligence—for example, the Termites were very well adjusted both socially and emotionally. The data have now been archived for use by other researchers, such as Friedman and Martin (2011), who used the Terman data to study whether personality and other factors are related to health and longevity. To complete their investigations, Friedman and Martin obtained death certificates of Terman participants to have precise data on both how long they lived and the causes of death. One strong pattern that emerged was that the personality dimension of "conscientiousness" (being self-disciplined, organized) that was measured in childhood was related to longevity. Of interest is that changes in personality qualities also affected longevity. Participants who had become less conscientious as adults had a reduction in longevity; those who became more conscientious as adults experienced longer lives. Another interesting finding concerned interacting with pets. Questions about animals were asked when participants were in their sixties; contrary to common beliefs, having or playing with pets was not related to longevity.

A unique longitudinal study on aging and Alzheimer's disease called the Nun Study illustrates a different approach (Snowden, 1997). In 1991, all members of a particular religious order born prior to 1917 were asked to participate by providing access to their archived records as well as various annual medical and psychological measures taken over the course of the study. The sample consisted of 678 women with a mean age of 83. One fascinating finding from this study was based on autobiographies that all sisters wrote in 1930 (Danner et al., 2001). The researchers devised a coding system to measure positive emotional content in the autobiographies. Greater positive emotions were strongly related to actual survival rate during the course of the study. Other longitudinal studies may study individuals over only a few years. For example, a 9-year study of U.S. children found a variety of impacts—positive and negative—of early nonmaternal child care (NICHD Early Child Care Research Network, 2005).

Comparison of Longitudinal and Cross-Sectional Methods

The cross-sectional method is much more common than the longitudinal method primarily because it is less expensive and yields results immediately. Note that with a longitudinal design, it would take 30 years to study the same group of individuals from age 20 to 50, but with a cross-sectional design, comparisons of different age groups can be obtained relatively quickly.

There are some disadvantages to cross-sectional designs, however. Most important, the researcher must infer that differences among age groups are due to the developmental variable of age. The developmental change is not observed directly among the same group of people, but instead is based on comparisons among different cohorts of individuals. You can think of a **cohort** as a group of people born at about the same time, exposed to the same events in a society, and influenced by the same demographic trends such as divorce rates and family size. If you think about the hairstyles of people you know who are in their 30s, 40s, 50s, and 60s, you will immediately recognize the importance of **cohort effects**! More crucially, differences among cohorts reflect different economic and political conditions in society, different music and arts, different educational systems, and different child-rearing practices. In a cross-sectional study, a difference among groups of different ages may reflect developmental age changes; however, the differences may result from cohort effects (Schaie, 1986).

To illustrate this issue, let's return to our hypothetical study on learning to use computers. Suppose you found that age is associated with a decrease in ability such that the people in the 50-year-old group score lower on the learning measure than the 40-year-olds, and so on. Should you conclude that the ability to learn to use a computer application decreases with age? That may be an accurate conclusion; alternatively, the differences could be due to a cohort effect: The older people had less experience with computers while growing up. The key point here is that the cross-sectional method confounds age and cohort effects. (Review the discussion of confounding and internal validity at the beginning of the chapter **"Experimental Design."**) Finally, you should note that cohort effects are most likely to be a problem when the researcher is examining age effects across a wide range of ages (e.g., adolescents through older adults).

The only way to conclusively study changes that occur as people grow older is to use a longitudinal design. Also, longitudinal research is the best way to study how scores on a variable at one age are related to another variable at a later age. For example, researchers at the National Children's Study (**http://www.nationalchildre nsstudy.gov**) began collecting data in 2009 at 105 study locations across the United States. In each of those study sites, participants (new parents) are being recruited to participate in the study that will run from the birth of their child until the child is 21 years of age. The goal of the study is to better understand the interactions of the environment and genetics and their effects on child health and well-being. The alternative in this case would be to study samples of children of various ages and ask them or their parents about the earlier home environment; this *retrospective* approach has its own problems when one considers the difficulty of remembering events in the distant past.

Thus, the longitudinal approach, despite being expensive and difficult, has definite advantages. However, there is one major problem: Over the course of a longitudinal study, people may move, die, or lose interest in the study. Researchers who conduct longitudinal studies become adept at convincing people to continue, often travel anywhere to collect more data, and compare test scores of people who drop out with those who stay to provide better analyses of their results. In sum, a researcher should not embark on a longitudinal study without considerable resources and a great deal of patience and energy!

Sequential Method

A compromise between the longitudinal and cross-sectional methods is to use the **sequential method.** This method, along with the cross-sectional and longitudinal methods, is illustrated in **Figure 5.** In the figure, the goal of the study is to minimally compare 55- and 65-year-olds. The first phase of the sequential method begins with the cross-sectional method; for example, you could study groups of 55- and 65-year-olds. These individuals are then studied using the longitudinal method with each individual tested at least one more time.

Orth et al. (2010) studied the development of self-esteem over time using just such a sequential method. Using data from the Americans' Changing Lives study, Orth and his colleagues identified six different age cohorts (25–34, 35–44, 45–54, 55–64, 65–74, 75+) and examined their self-esteem ratings from 1986, 1989, 1994, and 2002. Thus, they were interested in changes in self-esteem for participants at various ages, over time. Their findings provide an interesting picture of how self-esteem changes over time: They found that self-esteem gradually increases from age 25 to around age 60 and then declines in later years. Imagine how many years it would take if this were conducted as a full longitudinal study!

Clearly, this method takes fewer years and less effort to complete than a longitudinal study, and the researcher reaps immediate rewards because data on the different age groups are available in the first year of the study. On the other hand, the participants are not followed over the entire time span as they would be in a full longitudinal investigation; that is, no one in the Orth study was followed from age 25 to 100.

We have now described most of the major approaches to designing research. In the chapters **"Understanding Research Results: Description and Correlation"** and **"Understanding Research Results: Statistical Inference"** we consider methods of analyzing research data.

> Now complete **Check Your Learning:** Practice Exercise #4 to test your understanding of developmental research designs.

ILLUSTRATIVE ARTICLE: A LONGITUDINAL STUDY

In what ways do young adolescents change as they mature into young adults? What happens when adolescents develop typical teen behaviors a bit too early?

Allen et al. (2014) examined data from a longitudinal study in which adolescents were measured at 13, 14, and 15 years old, and then again at 23 years old. They focused specifically on early-adolescent "pseudomature" behaviors like vandalism or shoplifting, romantic involvement, and focus on physical appearance. They were interested in what happens to these "cool" kids, who enjoy high status among peers in early adolescence, 10 years later.

First, acquire and read the article (available at **https://www.ncbi.nlm.nih.gov/pmc/articles/PMC4165811/**):

> Allen, J. P., Schad, M. M., Oudekerk, B., & Chango, J. (2014). What ever happened to the "cool" kids? Long-term sequelae of early adolescent pseudomature behavior. *Child Development, 85*(5), 1866–1880. https://doi.org/10.1111/cdev.12250

Then, after reading the article, consider the following:

What did they do?

1. The researchers note, "Pseudomature behavior has been cross-sectionally associated with greater popularity among peers" (p. 1867). They use this finding to support their method. How is their approach different from a cross-sectional approach? What are the strengths and weaknesses of their approach?
2. The authors had five hypotheses. Choose one, describe how the authors arrived at the hypothesis, and then describe the actual results related to the hypothesis.

3. What if the researchers had continued to follow these same participants? Do you think that the conclusions about long-term implications of early pseudomature behavior would be the same when the participants were 33 years old? 43?

What did they find?

1. Interpret table 5 in the article: Find the section of the article that is associated with table 5 and compare the written results with the information in the table.

2. Interpret figure 1 in the article: What does it tell you about popularity change over time?

What was measured? How did the researchers operationally define "pseudomature behavior"? What is your opinion of their operational definition?

To what or whom can we generalize the results? Given the nature and make-up of their sample of adolescents, how well do you think that these results can be generalized?

Have other researchers found similar results? How do the authors talk about their results in the context of results of other, similar work?

CRITICAL THINKING: BEING A SKILLED CONSUMER OF RESEARCH

1. You leave your dog alone at home while you are at work. When you are away, your dog engages in destructive activities such as pulling down curtains or strewing wastebasket contents all over the floor. You decide that playing a radio while you are gone might help. How might you determine whether this "treatment" is effective?

2. Your best friend frequently suffers from severe headaches. You have noticed that your friend consumes a great deal of diet cola, and so you consider the hypothesis that the artificial sweetener in the cola is responsible for the headaches. Devise a way to test your hypothesis using a single-case design. What do you expect to find if your hypothesis is correct? If you obtain the expected results, what do you conclude about the effect of the artificial sweetener on headaches?

3. Gilovich (1991) described an incident he had read about during a visit to Israel. A very large number of deaths had occurred during a brief time period in one region of the country. A group of rabbis attributed the deaths to a recent change in religious practice that allowed women to attend funerals. Women were immediately forbidden to attend funerals in that region, and the number of deaths subsequently decreased. How would you explain this phenomenon?

4. The captain of each precinct of a metropolitan police department selected two officers to participate in a program designed to reduce prejudice by increasing sensitivity to racial and ethnic group differences and community issues. The training program took place every Friday morning for 3 months. At the first and last meetings, the officers completed a measure of prejudice. To assess the effectiveness of the program, the average prejudice score at the first meeting was compared with the average score at the last meeting; it was found that the average score was in fact lower following the training program. What type of design is this? What specific problems arise if you try to conclude that the training program was responsible for the reduction in prejudice?

5. Many elementary schools have implemented a daily "sustained silent reading" period during which students, faculty, and staff spend 15–20 minutes silently reading a book of their choice.

Advocates of this policy claim that the activity encourages pleasure reading outside the required silent reading time. Design a nonequivalent control group pretest-posttest quasi-experiment to test this claim. Include a well-reasoned dependent measure as well. Discuss the advantages and disadvantages of using a quasi-experimental design in contrast to conducting a true experiment.

Check Your Learning: Practice Exercises

Practice Exercise #1

A youth soccer/football coach has three children who volunteered to play goalie. Coach normally spends 20 minutes each week having the three children practice being goalie and records the number of goals saved and scored during that time. The coach has just read an article on how to improve goalie performance; it requires the coach to spend 3 hours with a child outside of regular practice. All of the goalies receive the new goalie training—1 hour per week for 6 weeks; the coach starts the first goalie in week 1, the second goalie in week 2, and the last goalie in week 3. Meanwhile, all the goalies continued to practice for 20 minutes during regular practice sessions. Which of the following designs best fits this scenario? Explain your answer:

a. reversal design
b. multiple baseline across subjects
c. multiple baseline across behaviors
d. time series

Practice Exercise #2

In the third week of the fall term, a group of first-year college students were given a measure of overall adjustment to college life. A week later, students were trained on meditation/mindfulness techniques designed to help people cope with stress. Then, in the fifth week, participants were asked again to complete the measures adjustment to college life. Results showed that the intervention improved self-reported adjustment and stress.

What is the design of this study?

Describe how each of the threats to internal validity listed below could influence the results of this study:

a. history
b. maturation
c. testing
d. regression toward the mean (statistical regression)

Practice Exercise #3

In 2009 a donor provided the State of Colorado with funding to provide no-cost Long-Acting Reversible Contraception (LARC) devices at clinics throughout the state. LARC contraception methods include IUDs and implants. The funding lasted from 2009 to 2015. Researchers have now presented data supporting the effectiveness of the program. For example, the unintended pregnancy rate for 15- to 19-year-olds in 2007 and 2008, prior to the program, was 38 pregnancies per 1,000 females. The rates in subsequent years were 35 in 2009, 34 in 2010, 29 in 2011, 26 in 2012, 24 in 2013, and 21 in 2014. There were also decreases in number of abortions, births to mothers with less than high school education, and other measures (see **https://www.colorado.gov/pacific/sites/default/files/PSD_TitleX3_CFPI-Report.pdf**). Which of the following designs best fits this scenario? Explain your answer:

a. reversal design

b. interrupted time series design

c. control series design

d. one group posttest-only design

Practice Exercise #4

A community weekly newspaper in Southern California in 1975 published the names of the parents of all children born in the community's three hospitals during the previous week. For one year, a team of university researchers contacted the parents about participating in a study. If the parents agreed, they would provide data about themselves and the child once each year until 2015. Which of the following designs best fits this scenario? Explain your answer:

a. longitudinal

b. cross-sectional

CHAPTER REVIEW

Review Questions

1. What is a reversal design? Why is an ABAB design superior to an ABA design?
2. What is meant by *baseline* in a single-case design?
3. What is a multiple baseline design? Why is it used? Distinguish between multiple baseline designs across subjects, across behaviors, and across situations.
4. Why might a researcher use a quasi-experimental design rather than a true experimental design?
5. Why does the use of a control group eliminate the problems associated with the one-group pretest-posttest design?
6. Describe the threats to internal validity discussed in the text: history, maturation, testing, instrument decay, regression toward the mean, and selection differences.
7. Describe the nonequivalent control group pretest-posttest design. Why is this a quasi-experimental design rather than a true experiment?
8. Describe the interrupted time series and the control series designs. What are the strengths of the control series design as compared with the interrupted time series design?
9. Distinguish between longitudinal, cross-sectional, and sequential methods.
10. What is a cohort effect?

Study Terms

Baseline

Cohort

Cohort effects

Control series design

Cross-sectional method

History effects

Instrument decay

Interrupted time series design

Longitudinal method

Maturation effects

Multiple baseline design

Nonequivalent control group design

Nonequivalent control group pretest-posttest design

One-group posttest-only design

One-group pretest-posttest design

Propensity score matching

Quasi-experimental design

Regression toward the mean (statistical regression)

Reversal design

Selection differences

Sequential method

Single-case experimental design

Testing effects

Check Your Learning: Answers

Practice Exercise #1

b. Multiple baseline across subjects. The behavior of several subjects is measured over time. For each subject, the manipulation is introduced at a different point in time.

Practice Exercise #2

The design of this study is a one group pre-test/post-test.

a. It's possible that, instead of the intervention, a major event (e.g., a speaker who focuses on life in college, a crime on campus, something that happens at the national level) could have changed students' perceptions of their adjustment.

b. Students change over time. It's possible that, as first-year students experience increasingly more of college life, their scores change naturally, and not as the result of the intervention.

c. The adjustment scale was given twice in a three-week period. It's possible that the first administration could affect the second. For instance, after the students were first asked about their adjustment, they might have begun to think more deeply about their adjustment and then change as a result of the measure, rather than as a result of the intervention.

d. Regression toward the mean is possible if many of the participants scored particularly low on the pretest adjustment measure (lower than their true score) because of random error. When measured later on the posttest, we would expect these individuals to score closer to their true score. Therefore, they would show an improvement in adjustment with no effect of the meditation training.

Practice Exercise #3

a. Interrupted time-series design. Measurements are made over time, both before and after the "treatment" (in this case, the LARC funding) is in place.

Practice Exercise #4

a. Longitudinal. Research participants are followed over time.

Understanding Research Results: Description and Correlation

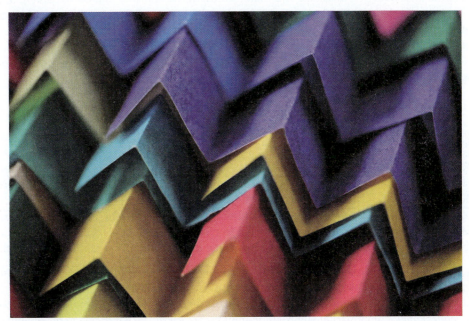

Photo ephemera/Moment/Getty Images

LEARNING OBJECTIVES

- Contrast the three ways of describing results: comparing group percentages, correlating scores, and comparing group means.
- Describe a frequency distribution, including the various ways to display a frequency distribution.
- Describe the measures of central tendency and variability.
- Define a correlation coefficient.
- Define effect size.
- Describe the use of a regression equation and a multiple correlation to predict behavior.
- Discuss how a partial correlation addresses the third-variable problem.
- Summarize the purpose of structural equation models.

In the chapter **"Fundamental Research Issues"** we identified four types of validity: *construct validity, internal validity, external validity,* and *statistical validity.* Statistical validity was defined as the accuracy of the statistical conclusions drawn from the results of a research investigation. Statistical validity is sometimes called *statistical conclusion validity.* This chapter and the chapter **"Understanding Research Results: Statistical Inference"** are critical in understanding statistical validity.

There are two ways in which statistics help us understand data collected in research investigations. First, statistics are used to describe the data. Second, statistics are used to make inferences and draw conclusions about a population on the basis of sample data. This chapter will focus on the underlying logic and general procedures for making statistical decisions. We examine descriptive statistics and correlation in this chapter. Inferential statistics are discussed in the chapter **"Understanding Research Results: Statistical Inference,"** and specific calculations for a variety of statistics are provided in **Appendix C**. These chapters will also provide an introduction to the statistical techniques that you will see presented in published studies. While some of these techniques are quite advanced, to be a skilled consumer of research you must have some knowledge of these techniques.

SCALES OF MEASUREMENT: A REVIEW

Before looking at any statistics, we need to review the concept of scales of measurement. Whenever a variable is studied, the researcher must create an operational definition of the variable and devise two or more levels of the variable. Recall from the chapter **"Measurement Concepts"** that the levels of the variable can be described using one of four scales of measurement: nominal, ordinal, interval, and ratio. The scale used determines the types of statistics that are appropriate when analyzing data. Also recall that the meaning of a particular score on a variable depends on which type of scale was used when the variable was measured or manipulated.

The levels of **nominal scale** variables have no numerical, quantitative properties. The levels are simply different categories or groups. Most independent variables in experiments are nominal—for example, as in an experiment that compares behavioral and cognitive therapies for depression. Variables such as eye color, hand dominance, college major, and marital status are nominal scale variables; left-handed and right-handed people differ from each other, but not in a quantitative way.

Variables with **ordinal scale** levels exhibit minimal quantitative distinctions. We can rank order the levels of the variable being studied from lowest to highest. The clearest example of an ordinal scale is one that asks people to make rank-ordered judgments. For example, you might ask people to rank the most important problems facing your state today. If education is ranked first, health care second, and crime third, you know the order but you do not know how strongly people feel about each problem: Education and health care may be deemed very close together in seriousness, with crime a distant third. With an ordinal scale, the intervals between items probably are not equal.

Interval scale and ratio scale variables have much more detailed quantitative properties. With an **interval scale** variable, the intervals between the levels are equal in size. The difference between 1 and 2 on the scale, for example, is the same as the difference between 2 and 3. Interval scales generally have five or more quantitative levels. You might ask people to rate their mood on a 7-point scale ranging from a "very negative" to a "very positive" mood. There is no absolute zero point that indicates an "absence" of mood.

In the behavioral sciences, it is often difficult to know precisely whether an ordinal or an interval scale is being used. However, it is often useful to assume that the variable is being measured on an interval scale, because interval scales allow for more sophisticated statistical treatments than do ordinal scales. Of course, if the measure is a rank ordering (for example, a rank ordering of professors on the basis of popularity), an ordinal scale clearly is being used.

Ratio scale variables have both equal intervals and an absolute zero point that indicates the absence of the variable being measured. Time, weight, length, and other physical measures are the best examples of ratio scales. Interval and ratio scale variables are conceptually different; however, the statistical procedures used to analyze data with such variables are identical. An important implication of interval and ratio scales is that data can be summarized using the mean, or arithmetic average. It is possible to provide a number that reflects the mean amount of a variable—for example, "the average mood of people who won a contest was 5.1" or "the mean weight of the men completing the weight loss program was 187.7 pounds."

DESCRIBING RESULTS

Scales of measurement have important implications for the way the results of research investigations are described and analyzed. Most research focuses on the study of relationships between variables. Depending on the way the variables are studied, there are three basic ways of describing the results: (1) comparing group percentages, (2) correlating scores of individuals on two variables, and (3) comparing group means.

Comparing Group Percentages

This first way of describing results is useful when a key variable is measured on a nominal scale. Suppose you want to know whether males and females differ in their interest in travel. In your study, participants who identified as males and females were asked whether they like or dislike travel. To describe your results, you will need to calculate the percentage of females who like to travel and compare this with the percentage of males who like to travel. Suppose you tested 50 females and 50 males and found that 40 of the females and 30 of the males indicated that they like to travel. In describing your findings, you would report that 80% of the females like to travel in comparison with 60% of the males. Thus, a relationship between the gender and travel variables appears to exist. Note that we are focusing on percentages because the travel variable is nominal: Liking and disliking are simply two different categories.

After describing your data, the next step would be to perform a statistical analysis to determine whether there is a statistically significant difference between the males and females, or if the differences in the sample are due to chance. Statistical significance is discussed in the chapter **"Understanding Research Results: Statistical Inference";** statistical analysis procedures are described in **Appendix C**.

Correlating Individual Scores

A second type of analysis is needed when you have an interval or ratio scale of measurement. In this circumstance, individuals are measured on two variables, and each variable has a range of numerical values. For example, we will consider an analysis of data on the relationship between location in a classroom and grades in the class: Do people who sit near the front receive higher grades?

Comparing Group Means

Much research is designed to compare the mean responses of participants in two or more groups. For example, in an experiment designed to study the effect of exposure to an aggressive adult, one group might be children who observe an adult "model" behaving aggressively and the control group might be children who do not. Each child then plays alone for 10 minutes in a room containing a number of toys, while observers record the number of times the child behaves aggressively during play. Aggression is a ratio scale variable because there are equal intervals and a true zero on the scale.

In this case, you would be interested in comparing the mean number of aggressive acts by children in the two conditions to determine whether the children who observed the model were more aggressive than the children in the control condition. Hypothetical data from such an experiment in which there were 10 children in each condition are shown in **Table 1**; the scores in the table represent the number of aggressive acts by each child. In this case, the mean aggression score in the model group is 5.20 and the mean score in the no-model condition is 3.10.

TABLE 1   Scores on aggression measure in a hypothetical experiment on modeling and aggression

Model group	No-model group
3	1
4	2
5	2
5	3
5	3
5	3
6	4
6	4
6	4
7	5
ΣX = 52	ΣX = 31
$\overline{X}$ = 5.20	$\overline{X}$ = 3.10
s^2 = 1.29	s^2 = 1.43
s = 1.14	s = 1.20
n = 10	n = 10

For all types of data, it is important to understand your results by carefully describing the data collected. We begin by constructing frequency distributions.

FREQUENCY DISTRIBUTIONS

When analyzing results, researchers often start by constructing a frequency distribution of the data. A **frequency distribution** indicates the number of individuals who receive each possible score on a variable. Frequency distributions of exam scores are familiar to most college students—they tell how many students received a given score on the exam. Along with the number of individuals associated with each response or score, it is useful to examine the percentage associated with this number.

Graphing Frequency Distributions

It is often useful to graphically depict frequency distributions. Let's examine several types of graphs: pie chart, bar graph, and frequency polygon and histogram.

Pie Charts

Pie charts divide a whole circle, or "pie," into "slices" that represent relative percentages. **Figure 1** shows a pie chart depicting a frequency distribution in which 70% of people like to travel and 30% dislike travel. Because there are two pieces of information to graph, there are two slices in this pie. Pie charts are particularly useful when representing nominal scale information. In the figure, the number of people who chose each response has been converted to a percentage—the simple number could have been displayed instead, of course. Pie charts are most commonly used to depict simple descriptions of categories for a single variable. They are useful in applied research reports and articles written for the general public. Articles in scientific journals require more complex information displays.

Bar Graphs

Bar graphs use a separate and distinct bar for each piece of information. **Figure 2** represents the same information about travel using a bar graph. In this graph, the *x* or horizontal axis shows the two possible responses. The *y* or vertical axis shows the number who chose each response, and so the height of each bar represents the number of people who responded to the "like" and "dislike" options.

FIGURE 1   Pie chart

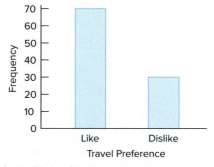

FIGURE 2   Bar graph displaying data obtained in two groups

Frequency Polygons

Frequency polygons use a line to represent the distribution of frequencies of scores. This is most useful when the data represent interval or ratio scales as in the modeling and aggression data shown in **Table 1**. Here we have a clear numeric scale of the number of aggressive acts during the observation period. **Figure 3** graphs the data from the hypothetical experiment using two frequency polygons—one for each group. The solid line represents the no-model group, and the dotted line stands for the model group.

Histograms

A **histogram** uses bars to display a frequency distribution for a quantitative variable. In this case, the scale values are continuous and show increasing amounts on a variable such as age, blood pressure, or stress. Because the values are continuous, the bars are drawn next to each other. A histogram is shown in **Figure 4** using data from the model group in **Table 1**.

What can you discover by examining frequency distributions? First, you can directly observe how your participants responded. You can see what scores are most frequent, and you can look at the shape of the dis-

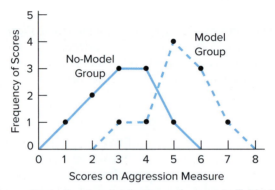

FIGURE 3   Frequency polygons illustrating the distributions of scores in **Table 1**

Note: Each frequency polygon is anchored at scores that were not obtained by anyone (0 and 6 in the no-model group; 2 and 8 in the model group).

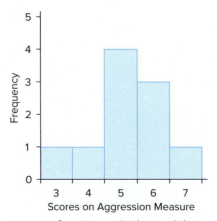

FIGURE 4   Histogram showing frequency of responses in the model group

tribution of scores. You can tell whether there are any outliers—scores that are unusual, unexpected, or very different from the scores of other participants. In an experiment, you can compare the distribution of scores in the groups.

DESCRIPTIVE STATISTICS

In addition to examining the distribution of scores, you can calculate descriptive statistics. **Descriptive statistics** allow researchers to make precise statements about the data. Two statistics are needed to describe the data. A single number can be used to describe the central tendency, or how participants scored overall. Another number describes the variability, or how widely the distribution of scores is spread. These two numbers summarize the information contained in a frequency distribution.

Central Tendency

A **central tendency** statistic tells us what the sample as a whole, or on the average, is like. There are three measures of central tendency—the mean, the median, and the mode.

The **mean** of a set of scores is obtained by adding all the scores and dividing by the number of scores. It is symbolized as $\overline{X}$; in scientific reports, it is abbreviated as M. The mean is an appropriate indicator of central tendency only when scores are measured on an interval or ratio scale, because the actual values of the numbers are used in calculating the statistic. In **Table 1**, the mean score for the no-model group is 3.10 and for the model group is 5.20. Note that the Greek letter Σ (sigma) in **Table 1** is statistical notation for summing a set of numbers. Thus, ΣX is shorthand for "sum of the values in a set of scores."

The **median** is the score that divides the group in half (with 50% scoring below and 50% scoring above the median). In scientific reports, the median is abbreviated as Mdn. The median is appropriate when scores are on an ordinal scale, because it takes into account only the rank order of the scores. It is also useful with interval and ratio scale variables, however. The median for the no-model group is 3 and for the model group is 5.

The **mode** is the most frequent score. The mode is the only measure of central tendency that is appropriate if a nominal scale is used. The mode does not use the actual values on the scale, but simply indicates the most frequently occurring value. There are two modal values for the no-model group—3 and 4 occur equally frequently. The mode for the model group is 5.

The median or mode can be a better indicator of central tendency than the mean if a few unusual scores bias the mean. For example, the median family income of a county or state is usually a better measure of central tendency than the mean family income. Because a relatively small number of individuals have extremely high incomes, using the mean would make it appear that the "average" person makes more money than is actually the case.

Variability

We can also determine how much **variability** exists in a set of scores. A measure of variability is a number that characterizes the amount of spread in a distribution of scores. One such measure is the **standard deviation,** symbolized as s, which indicates the average deviation of scores from the mean. Income is a good example. The Census Bureau reports that the median U.S. household income in 2017 was $61,372 (**https://www.census.gov/library/publications/2018/demo/p60-263.html**). Suppose that you live in a community that matches the U.S median and there is very little variation around that median (i.e., every household earns something close to $61,372); your community would have a smaller standard deviation in household income compared to another community in which the median income is the same but there is a lot more variation (e.g., where many people earn $15,000 per year and others $5 million per year). It is possible for measures of central tendency in two communities to be close with the variability differing substantially.

In scientific reports, the standard deviation is abbreviated as *SD*. It is derived by first calculating the **variance,** symbolized as s^2 (the standard deviation is the square root of the variance). The standard deviation of a set of scores is small when most people have similar scores close to the mean. The standard deviation becomes larger as more people have scores that lie farther from the mean value. For the model group, the standard deviation is 1.14, which tells us that most scores in that condition lie 1.14 units above and below the mean—that is, between 4.06 and 6.34. Thus, the mean and the standard deviation provide a great deal of information about the distribution. Note that, as with the mean, the calculation of the standard deviation uses the actual values of the scores; thus, the standard deviation is appropriate only for interval and ratio scale variables.

Another measure of variability is the **range,** which is simply the difference between the highest score and the lowest score. The range for both the model and no-model groups is 4.

> Now, go to **Check Your Learning:** Practice Exercise #1 to work on your own descriptive statistics and figures.

GRAPHING RELATIONSHIPS

Graphing relationships between variables was discussed briefly in the chapter **"Fundamental Research Issues."** A common way to graph relationships between variables is to use a bar graph or a line graph. **Figure 5** is a bar graph depicting the means for the no-model and model groups. The levels of the independent variable (no-model and model) are represented on the horizontal *x-axis*, and the dependent variable values are shown on the vertical *y-axis*. For each group, a point is placed along the *y-axis* that represents the mean for the groups, and a bar is drawn to visually represent the mean value. Bar graphs are used when the values on the *x-axis* are nominal categories (e.g., a no-model and a model condition). Line graphs are used when the values on the *x-axis* are numeric (e.g., marijuana use over time, as shown in the chapter **"Asking People About Themselves," Figure 1**). In line graphs, a line is drawn to connect the data points to represent the relationship between the variables.

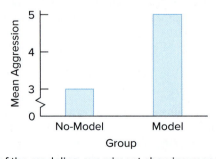

FIGURE 5   Graph of the results of the modeling experiment showing mean aggression scores

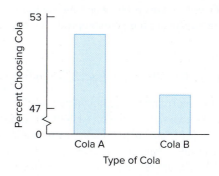

FIGURE 6   Two ways to graph the same data

Choosing the scale for a bar graph allows a common manipulation that is sometimes used by scientists and all too commonly used by advertisers. The trick is to exaggerate the distance between points on the measurement scale to make the results appear more dramatic than they really are. Suppose, for example, that a cola company (cola A) conducts a taste test that shows 52% of the participants prefer cola A and 48% prefer cola B. How should the cola company present these results? The two bar graphs in **Figure 6** show the most honest method, as well as one that is considerably more dramatic. It is always wise to look carefully at the numbers on the scales depicted in graphs.

CORRELATION COEFFICIENTS: DESCRIBING THE STRENGTH OF RELATIONSHIPS

It is important to know whether a relationship between variables is relatively weak or strong. A **correlation coefficient** is a statistic that describes how strongly variables are related to one another. You are probably most familiar with the **Pearson product-moment correlation coefficient,** which is used when both variables have interval or ratio scale properties. The Pearson product-moment correlation coefficient is called the Pearson *r.* Values of a Pearson *r* can range from 0.00 to ± 1.00. Thus, the Pearson *r* provides information about the strength of the relationship and the direction of the relationship. A correlation of 0.00 indicates that there is no relationship between the variables. The nearer a correlation is to 1.00 (plus or minus), the stronger is the relationship. Indeed, a 1.00 correlation is sometimes called a perfect relationship, because the two variables go together in a perfect fashion. The sign of the Pearson *r* tells us the direction of the relationship—that is, whether the relationship between the variables is positive or negative.

Data from studies examining similarities of intelligence test scores among siblings illustrate the connection between the magnitude of a correlation coefficient and the strength of a relationship. The relationship between scores of monozygotic (identical) twins reared together is .86 and the correlation for monozygotic twins reared apart is .74, demonstrating a strong similarity of test scores in these pairs of individuals. The correlation for dizygotic (fraternal) twins reared together is less strong, with a correlation of .59. The correlation among nontwin siblings raised together is .46, and the correlation among nontwin siblings reared apart is .24. Data such as these are important in ongoing research on the relative influence of heredity and environment on intelligence (Devlin et al., 1997; Kaplan, 2012).

There are several different types of correlation coefficients. Each coefficient is calculated somewhat differently depending on the measurement scale that applies to the two variables. As noted, the Pearson *r* correlation coefficient is appropriate when the values of both variables are on an interval or ratio scale. We will now focus on the details of the Pearson product-moment correlation coefficient.

Pearson r Correlation Coefficient

To calculate a correlation coefficient, we need to obtain pairs of observations from each subject. Thus, each individual has two scores, one on each of the variables. **Table 2** shows fictitious data for 10 students measured on the variables of classroom seating pattern and exam grade. Students in the first row receive a seating score of 1, those in the second row receive a 2, and so on. Once we have made our observations, we can see whether the two variables are related. Are the variables associated in a systematic fashion?

TABLE 2   Pairs of scores for 10 participants on seating pattern and exam scores (fictitious data)

Subject identification number	Seating	Exam score
01	2	95
02	5	50
03	1	85
04	4	75
05	3	75
06	5	60
07	2	80
08	3	70
09	1	90
10	4	70

The Pearson *r* provides two types of information about the relationship between the variables. The first is the strength of the relationship; the second is the direction of the relationship. As noted previously, the values of *r* can range from 0.00 to ±1.00. The absolute size of *r* is the coefficient that indicates the strength of the relationship irrespective of whether the coefficient is positive or negative. A value of 0.00 indicates that there is no relationship. The nearer *r* is to 1.00 (plus or minus), the stronger is the relationship. The plus and minus signs indicate whether there is a positive linear or negative linear relationship between the two variables. It is important to remember that it is the size of the correlation coefficient, not the sign, that indicates the strength of the relationship. Thus, a correlation coefficient of −54 indicates a stronger relationship than does a coefficient of +45.

Scatterplots

The data in **Table 2** can be visualized in a **scatterplot** in which each pair of scores is plotted as a single point in a diagram. **Figure 7** shows two scatterplots. The values of the first variable are depicted on the *x-axis,* and the values of the second variable are shown on the *y-axis*. These scatterplots show a perfect positive relationship (+1.00) and a perfect negative relationship (−1.00). You can easily see why these are perfect relationships:

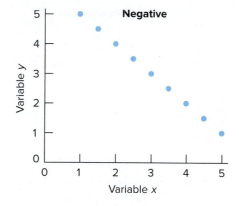

FIGURE 7   Scatterplots of perfect (±1.00) relationships

The scores on the two variables fall on a straight line that is on the diagonal of the diagram. Each person's score on one variable correlates precisely with his or her score on the other variable. If we know an individual's score on one of the variables, we can predict exactly what his or her score will be on the other variable. Such "perfect" relationships are rarely observed in reality.

The scatterplots in **Figure 8** show patterns of correlation you are more likely to encounter in exploring research findings. The first diagram shows pairs of scores with a positive correlation of +65; the second diagram shows a negative relationship, −77. The data points in these two scatterplots reveal a general pattern of either a positive or negative relationship, but the relationships are not perfect. You can make a general prediction in the first diagram—for instance, that the higher the score on one variable, the higher the score on the second variable. However, even if you know a person's score on the first variable, you cannot perfectly predict what that person's score will be on the second variable. To confirm this, take a look at value 1 on variable x (the horizontal axis) in the positive scatterplot. Looking along the vertical y-axis, you will see that two individuals had a score of 1. One of these had a score of 1 on variable y, and the other had a score of 3. The data points do not fall on the perfect diagonal shown in **Figure 7**. Instead, there is a variation (scatter) from the perfect diagonal line.

The third diagram shows a scatterplot in which there is absolutely no correlation ($r = 0.00$). The points fall all over the diagram in a completely random pattern. Thus, scores on variable x are not related to scores on variable y.

The fourth diagram has been left blank so that you can plot the scores from the data in **Table 2**. The x (horizontal) axis has been labeled for the seating pattern variable, and the y (vertical) axis for the exam score variable. To complete the scatterplot, you will need to plot the 10 pairs of scores. For each individual in the sample, find the score on the seating pattern variable; then go up from that point until you are level with that person's exam score on the y-axis. A point placed there will describe the score on both variables. There will be 10 points on the finished scatterplot.

The correlation coefficient calculated from these data shows a negative relationship between the variables ($r = -88$). In other words, as the seating distance from the front of the class increases, the exam score decreases. Although these data are fictitious, a (much smaller) negative relationship has been reported in research on this topic (Benedict & Hoag, 2004; Brooks & Rebata, 1991).

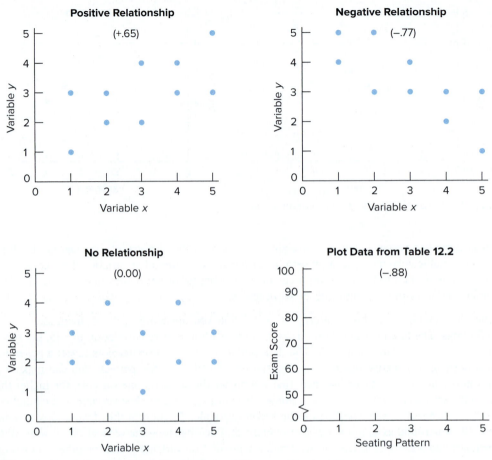

FIGURE 8   Scatterplots depicting patterns of correlation

Important Considerations

Correlation coefficients are a useful way to understand the relationship between two variables. That said, there are two important factors to consider when thinking about correlations: restriction of range and the fact that the two variables could have a non-linear relationship.

Restriction of Range

It is important that the researcher sample from the full range of possible values of both variables. If the range of possible values is restricted, the magnitude of the correlation coefficient is reduced. For example, if the range of seating pattern scores is restricted to the first two rows, you will not get an accurate picture of the relationship between seating pattern and exam score. In fact, when only scores of students sitting in the first two rows are considered, the correlation between the two variables is exactly 0.00. With a restricted range comes restricted variability in the scores and thus less variability that can be explained. **Figure 9** illustrates a scatterplot with the entire range of X values represented and with a portion of those values missing because of restriction of range.

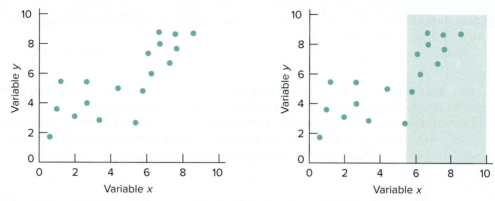

FIGURE 9 Left scatterplot—positive correlation with entire range of values. Right scatterplot—no correlation with restricted range of values

The problem of **restriction of range** occurs when the individuals in your sample are very similar on the variable you are studying. If you are studying age as a variable, for instance, testing only 6- and 7-year-olds will reduce your chances of finding age effects. Likewise, trying to study the correlates of intelligence will be almost impossible if everyone in your sample is very similar in intelligence (e.g., the senior class of a prestigious private college).

Curvilinear Relationship

The Pearson product-moment correlation coefficient (r) is designed to detect only linear relationships. If the relationship is curvilinear, as in the scatterplot shown in **Figure 10**, the correlation coefficient will not indicate the existence of a relationship. The Pearson r correlation coefficient calculated from these data is exactly 0.00, even though the two variables clearly are related.

FIGURE 10 Scatterplot of a curvilinear relationship (Pearson product-moment correlation coefficient = 0.00)

Go to **Check Your Learning:** Practice Exercise #2 to check your understanding of these important aspects of correlation coefficients.

Because a relationship may be curvilinear, it is important to construct a scatterplot in addition to looking at the magnitude of the correlation coefficient. The scatterplot is valuable because it gives a visual indication of the shape of the relationship. Computer programs for statistical analysis will usually display scatterplots and can show you how well the data fit to a linear or curvilinear relationship. When the relationship is curvilinear, another type of correlation coefficient must be used to determine the strength of the relationship.

EFFECT SIZE

We have presented the Pearson r correlation coefficient as the appropriate way to describe the relationship between two variables with interval or ratio scale properties. Researchers also want to describe the strength of relationships between variables in all studies. **Effect size** refers to the strength of association between variables. The Pearson r correlation coefficient is one indicator of effect size; it indicates the strength of the linear association between two variables. In an experiment with two or more treatment conditions, other types of correlation coefficients can be calculated to indicate the magnitude of the effect of the independent variable on the dependent variable. For example, in our experiment on the effects of witnessing an aggressive model on children's aggressive behavior, we compared the means of two groups. In addition to knowing the means, it is valuable to know the effect size. An effect size correlation coefficient can be calculated for the modeling and aggression experiment. In this case, the effect size correlation value is .69. As with all correlation coefficients, the values of this effect size correlation can range from 0.00 to 1.00 (we do not need to worry about the direction of relationship, so plus and minus values are not used).

The advantage of reporting effect size is that it provides us with a scale of values that is consistent across all types of studies. The values range from 0.00 to 1.00, irrespective of the variables used, the particular research design selected, or the number of participants studied. You might be wondering what correlation coefficients should be considered indicative of small, medium, and large effects. A general guide is that correlations around .10 are considered small, those near .30 are medium/moderate, and correlations near .50 and above are large (see Cohen, 1992, 2016).

It is sometimes preferable to report the squared value of a correlation coefficient; instead of r, you will see r^2. Thus, if the obtained $r = .50$, the reported $r^2 = .25$. Why transform the value of r? This reason is that the transformation changes the obtained r to a percentage. The percentage value represents the percent of variance in one variable that is accounted for by the second variable. The range of r^2 values can range from 0.00 (0%) to 1.00 (100%).

The r^2 value is sometimes referred to as the *percent of shared variance between the two variables*. What does this mean, exactly? Recall the concept of variability in a set of scores—if you measured the weight of a random sample of American adults, you would observe variability in that weights would range from relatively low weights to relatively high weights. If you are studying factors that contribute to people's weight, you would want to examine the relationship between weights and scores on the contributing variable. One such variable might be sex: In actuality, the correlation between sex and weight is about .70 (with, for instance, males weighing more than females). That means that 49% (squaring .70) of the variability in weight is accounted for by variability in sex. You have therefore explained 49% of the variability in the weights, but there is still 51% of the variability that is not accounted for. This variability might be accounted for by other variables, such as the weights of the biological mother and father, prenatal stress, diet, and exercise. In an ideal world, you could account for 100% of the variability in weights if you had enough information on all other variables that contribute to people's weights: Each variable would make an incremental contribution until all the variability is accounted for.

REGRESSION EQUATIONS

Regression equations are calculations used to predict a person's score on one variable when that person's score on another variable (or set of variables) is already known. They are essentially "prediction equations" that are based on known information about the relationship between the two variables. For example, after discovering that seating pattern and exam score are related, a regression equation may be calculated that predicts anyone's exam score based only on information about where the person sits in the class. The general form of a regression equation is:

$$Y = a + bX$$

where Y is the score we wish to predict, X is the known score, a is a constant, and b is a weighting adjustment factor that is multiplied by X (it is the slope of the line created with this equation). In our seating–exam score example, the following regression equation is calculated from the data:

$$Y = 99 + (-8)X$$

Thus, if we know a person's score on X (seating), we can insert that into the equation and predict what that person's exam score (Y) will be. If the person's X score is 2 (by sitting in the second row), we can predict that $Y = 99 + (-16)$, or that the person's exam score will be 83. Through the use of regression equations such as these, colleges can use SAT scores to predict college grades.

When researchers are interested in predicting some future behavior (called the **criterion variable**) on the basis of a person's score on some other variable (called the **predictor variable**), it is first necessary to demonstrate that there is a reasonably high correlation between the criterion and predictor variables. The regression equation then provides the method for making predictions on the basis of the predictor variable score only.

MULTIPLE CORRELATION/REGRESSION

Thus far we have focused on the relationship between two variables at a time. Researchers recognize that a number of different variables may be related to a given behavior (this is the same point noted above in the discussion of factors that contribute to weight). A technique called **multiple correlation** is used to combine a number of predictor variables to increase the accuracy of prediction of a given criterion or outcome variable.

A multiple correlation (symbolized as R to distinguish it from the simple r) is the correlation between a combined set of predictor variables and a single criterion variable. Taking all of the predictor variables into account usually permits greater accuracy of prediction than if any single predictor is considered alone. For example, applicants to graduate school in psychology could be evaluated on a combined set of predictor variables using multiple correlation. The predictor variables might be (1) college grades, (2) scores on the Graduate Record Exam Aptitude Test, (3) scores on the Graduate Record Exam Psychology Test, and (4) favorability of letters of recommendation. No one of these factors is a perfect predictor of success in graduate school, but this combination of variables can yield a more accurate prediction. The multiple correlation is usually higher than the correlation between any one of the predictor variables and the criterion or outcome variable.

In actual practice, predictions would be made with an extension of the regression equation technique discussed previously. A multiple regression equation can be calculated that takes the following form:

$$Y = a + b_1 X_1 + b_2 X_2 + \dots + b_n X_n$$

where Y is the criterion variable, X_1 to X_n are the predictor variables, a is a constant, and b_1 to b_n are weights that are multiplied by scores on the predictor variables. For example, a regression equation for graduate school admissions would be:

Predicted grade point average = $a + b_1$ (college grades)

$+ b_2$ (score on GRE Aptitude Test)

$+ b_3$ (score on GRE Psychology Test)

$+ b_4$ (favorability of recommendation letters)

Researchers use multiple regression to study basic research topics. For example, Ajzen and Fishbein (1980) developed a model called the "theory of reasoned action" that uses multiple correlation and regression to predict specific behavioral intentions (e.g., to attend church on Sunday, buy a certain product, or join an alcohol recovery program) on the basis of two predictor variables. These are (1) attitude toward the behavior and (2) perceived normative pressure to engage in the behavior. Attitude is one's own evaluation of the behavior, and normative pressure comes from other people such as parents and friends. In one study, Codd and Cohen (2003) found that the multiple correlation between college students' intention to seek help for alcohol problems and the combined predictors of attitude and norm was .35. The regression equation was as follows:

Intention = .29(attitude) + .18(norm)

This equation is somewhat different from those described previously. In basic research, you are not interested in predicting an exact score (such as an exam score or GPA), and so the mathematical calculations can assume that all variables are measured on the same scale. When this is done, the weighting factor reflects the magnitude of the correlation between the criterion variable and each predictor variable. In the help-seeking example, the weight for the attitude predictor is somewhat higher than the weight for the norm predictor; this shows that, in this case, attitudes are more important as a predictor of intention than are norms. However, for other behaviors, attitudes may be less important than norms.

It is also possible to visualize the regression equation. In the help-seeking example, the relationships among variables could be diagrammed as follows:

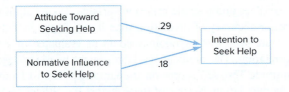

You should note that the squared multiple correlation coefficient (R^2) is interpreted in much the same way as the squared correlation coefficient (r^2). That is, R^2 tells you the percentage of variability in the criterion variable that is accounted for by the combined set of predictor variables. Again, this value will be higher than that of any of the single predictors by themselves.

THE THIRD-VARIABLE PROBLEM

Researchers face the third-variable problem in nonexperimental research when some uncontrolled third variable may be responsible for the relationship between the two variables of interest. For example, a finding that people who exercise more have lower anxiety levels could be due to a third variable such as income. High income may cause both exercise and low anxiety (see the chapter **"Fundamental Research Issues"**). When properly designed and executed, the problem does not exist in experimental research, because all extraneous variables are controlled either by keeping the variables constant or by using randomization.

A technique called **partial correlation** provides a way of statistically controlling third variables. A partial correlation is a correlation between the two variables of interest, with the influence of the third variable removed from, or "partialed out of," the original correlation. This provides an indication of what the correlation between the primary variables would be if the third variable were held constant. This is not the same as actually keeping the variable constant, but it is a useful approximation.

Suppose a researcher is interested in a measure of number of bedrooms per person as an index of household crowding—a high number indicates that more space is available for each person in the household. After obtaining this information, the researcher gives a cognitive test to children living in these households. The correlation between bedrooms per person and test scores is .50. Thus, children in more spacious houses score higher on the test. The researcher suspects that a third variable may be operating. Social class could influence both housing and performance on this type of test. If social class is measured, it can be included in a partial correlation calculation that looks at the relationship between bedrooms per person and test scores with social class held constant. To calculate a partial correlation, you need to have scores on the two primary variables of interest and the third variable that you want to examine.

When a partial correlation is calculated, you can compare the partial correlation with the original correlation to see if the third variable did have an effect. Is our original correlation of .50 substantially reduced when social class is held constant? **Figure 11** shows two different partial correlations. In both, there is a .50 correlation between bedrooms per person and test score. The first partial correlation between bedrooms per person and test scores drops to .09 when social class is held constant because social class is so highly correlated with the primary variables. However, the partial correlation in the second example remains high at .49 because the correlations with social class are relatively small. Thus, the outcome of the partial correlation depends on the magnitude of the correlations between the third variable and the two variables of primary interest.

FIGURE 11   Two partial correlations between bedrooms per person and performance

STRUCTURAL EQUATION MODELING

Advances in statistical methods have resulted in a complex set of techniques to examine models that specify a set of relationships among variables using quantitative nonexperimental methods (see Raykov & Marcoulides, 2000; Ullman, 2007). **Structural equation modeling (SEM)** is a general term to refer to these techniques. The methods of SEM are beyond the scope of this book, but you will likely encounter some research findings that use SEM; thus, it is worthwhile to provide an overview. A model is an expected pattern of relationships among a set of variables. The proposed model is based on a theory of how the variables are causally related to one another. After data have been collected, statistical methods can be applied to examine how closely the proposed model actually "fits" the obtained data.

Researchers typically present path diagrams to visually represent the models being tested. Such diagrams show the theoretical causal paths among the variables. The multiple regression diagram on attitudes and intentions shown previously is a path diagram of a very simple model. The theory of reasoned action evolved into a more complex "theory of planned behavior" that has an additional construct to predict behavior. Huchting et al. (2008) studied alcohol consumption among 247 sorority members at a private university. They measured four variables at the beginning of the study: (1) attitude toward alcohol consumption based on how strongly the women believed that consuming alcohol had positive consequences, (2) subjective norm or perceived alcohol consumption of other sorority members, (3) perceived lack of behavioral control based on beliefs about the degree of difficulty in refraining from drinking alcohol, and (4) intention to consume alcohol based on the amount that the women expected to consume during the next 30 days. The sorority members were contacted 1 month later to provide a measure of actual behavior—the amount of alcohol consumed during the previous 30 days.

The theory of planned behavior predicts that attitude, subjective norm, and behavior control will each predict the behavioral intention to consume alcohol. Intention will in turn predict actual behavior. The researchers used structural equation modeling techniques to study this model. It is easiest to visualize the results using the path diagram shown in **Figure 12.** In the path diagram, arrows leading from one variable to another depict the paths that relate the variables in the model. The arrows indicate a causal sequence. Note that the model specifies that attitude, subjective norm, and behavioral control are related to intention and that intention in turn causes actual behavior. The statistical analysis provides what are termed *path coefficients*—these are similar to the standardized weights derived in the regression equations described previously. They indicate the strength of a relationship on our familiar –1.00 to +1.00 scale.

In **Figure 12** you can see that both attitude and subjective norm were significant predictors of intention to consume alcohol. However, the predicted relationship between behavioral control and intention was not significant (therefore, the path is depicted as a dashed line). Intention was strongly related to actual behavior. Note also that behavioral control had a direct path to behavior; this indicates that difficulty in controlling alcohol consumption is directly related to actual consumption.

Besides illustrating how variables are related, a final application of SEM in the Huchting et al. study was to evaluate how closely the obtained data fit the specified model. The researchers concluded that the model did in fact closely fit the data. The lack of a path from behavioral control to intention is puzzling and will lead to further research.

There are many other applications of SEM. For example, researchers can compare two competing models in terms of how well each fits obtained data. Researchers can also examine much more complex models that contain many more variables. These techniques allow us to study nonexperimental data in more complex ways. This type of research leads to a better understanding of the complex networks of relationships among variables.

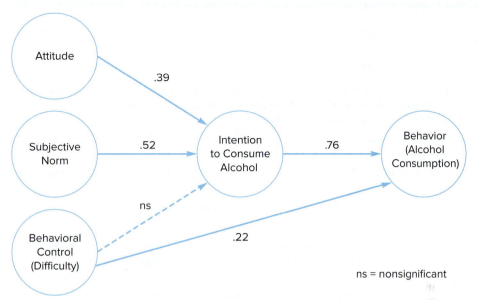

FIGURE 12   Structural model based on data from Huchting et al. (2008)

In the chapter **"Understanding Research Results: Statistical Inference"** we turn from description of data to making decisions about statistical significance. These two topics are of course related. The topic of effect size that was described in this chapter is also very important when evaluating statistical significance.

CRITICAL THINKING: BEING A SKILLED CONSUMER OF RESEARCH

1. Ask 20 students on campus how many units (credits) they are taking, as well as how many hours per week they work in paid employment. Create a frequency distribution and find the mean for each data set. Construct a scatterplot showing the relationship between class load and hours per week employed. Does there appear to be a relationship between the variables? (Note: There might be a restriction of range problem on your campus if few students work or most students take about the same number of units. If so, ask different questions, such as the number of hours spent studying and watching television each week.)

2. Think of three variables that use a nominal scale, three variables that use an ordinal scale, three variables that use an interval scale, and three variables that use a ratio scale. What would be the best way to describe each of your examples statistically and graphically?

Check Your Learning: Practice Exercises

Practice Exercise #1

1. Download the income and poverty 2017 report from the U.S. Census Bureau (**https://www.cens us.gov/library/publications/2018/demo/p60-263.html**). First, review table 1, on page 2 of the report, and answer the following questions:

    a. How did the median income of all households change between 2016 and 2017?

    b. What was the median incoming in 2017 for individuals 25 to 34 years old?

    c. What does it mean that these data are reported as medians rather than as means or modes?

2. Review figure 1 in the report and answer the following questions:

    a. What kind of figure is this?

    b. What has happened to real median household income for "all races" since 1967?

    c. How does real median household income differ between Blacks and Hispanics (of any race)?

3. Review figure 5 in the report, and answer the following questions:

    a. What kind of figure is this?

    b. Compared to people under 18, how does the poverty rate differ by sex?

    c. What does it mean that the bar represents the "median" income?

Practice Exercise #2

1. This exercise has two steps. First refer to the figure below, then select the correct answer to questions a, b, and c.

The size (value) of the coefficient indicates the strength of the relationship.
The sign (plus or minus) of the coefficient indicates the direction of the linear relationship.

    a. Which one of the following numbers could *not* be a correlation coefficient?
        −.99 +.71 +1.02 +.01 +.38

    b. Which one of the following correlation coefficients indicates the strongest relationship?
        +.23 −.89 −.10 −.91 +.77

    c. Which of the following correlation coefficients indicates the weakest negative relationship?
        −.28. +.08 −.42 +.01 −.29

2. Second, use the axes below to draw a scatterplot depicting (a) a positive linear relationship, (b) a negative linear relationship, and (c) no linear relationship.

(Answers are provided at the end of this chapter.)

CHAPTER REVIEW

Review Questions

1. What are the differences between the three ways of describing results: comparing percentages, comparing means, and correlating scores?
2. What is a frequency distribution?
3. Distinguish between a pie chart, bar graph, and frequency polygon. Construct one of each.
4. What is a measure of central tendency? Distinguish between the mean, median, and mode.
5. What is a measure of variability? Distinguish between the standard deviation and the range.
6. What is a correlation coefficient? What do the size and sign of the correlation coefficient tell us about the relationship between variables?
7. What is a scatterplot?
8. What happens when a scatterplot shows the relationship to be curvilinear?
9. What is a regression equation? How might an employer use a regression equation?
10. How does multiple correlation increase the accuracy of prediction?
11. What is the purpose of partial correlation?
12. When a path diagram is shown, what information is conveyed by the arrows leading from one variable to another?

Study Terms

Bar graph

Central tendency

Correlation coefficient

Criterion variable

Descriptive statistics

Effect size

Frequency distribution

Frequency polygons

Histogram	**Predictor variable**
Interval scales	**Range**
Mean	**Ratio scales**
Median	**Regression equations**
Mode	**Restriction of range**
Multiple correlation	**Scatterplot**
Nominal scales	**Standard deviation**
Ordinal scales	**Structural equation modeling (SEM)**
Partial correlation	**Variability**
Pearson product-moment correlation coefficient	**Variance**
Pie chart	

Check Your Learning: Answers

Practice Exercise #1

1a. Median income of all households rose 1.8%; b. $62,294; c. half of householders earned less than the median, and half earned more than the median

2a. line graph; b. it has risen; c. the median household income of Hispanics (of any race) is higher than that of Blacks

3a. bar graph; b. for people under 18, males and females had similar poverty rates, but for older people females had higher poverty rates; c. half of householders earned less than the median, and half earned more than the median

Practice Exercise #2

1.   a. +1.02; b. −.91; c. −.28

2.

(a)

(b)

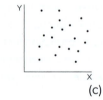

(c)

Understanding Research Results: Statistical Inference

SNP_SS/Shutterstock

LEARNING OBJECTIVES

- Explain how researchers use inferential statistics to evaluate sample data.
- Distinguish between the null hypothesis and the research hypothesis.
- Discuss probability in statistical inference, including the meaning of statistical significance.
- Describe the *t* test and explain the difference between one-tailed and two-tailed tests.
- Describe the *F* test, including systematic variance and error variance.
- Describe what a confidence interval tells you about your data.
- Distinguish between Type I and Type II errors and discuss the factors that influence the probability of a Type II error.
- Discuss the reasons a researcher might obtain nonsignificant results.
- Define *power* of a statistical test.
- Describe the criteria for selecting an appropriate statistical test.

In the chapter **"Understanding Research Results: Description and Correlation"** we examined ways of describing the results of a study using descriptive statistics and a variety of graphing techniques. In addition to using descriptive statistics to describe the data, researchers use inferential statistics to draw more general conclusions about their data. In short, inferential statistics allow researchers to (a) assess just how confident they are that their results reflect what is true in the larger population and (b) assess the likelihood that their findings would still occur if their study was repeated over and over. In this chapter, we examine inferential statistics.

In order to determine whether a study is accurate, true, or valid, we must understand and trust its statistical methodology. Recall from the chapter **"Fundamental Research Issues"** the four types of validity: construct validity, internal validity, external validity, and statistical validity. This chapter and the chapter **"Understanding Research Results: Description and Correlation"** are meant to introduce the concept of statistical validity, support your thinking about this kind of validity, and help you evaluate existing studies in the literature in terms of their statistical validity. These chapters are also meant to help you design the analysis for your own study.

SAMPLES AND POPULATIONS

Inferential statistics are necessary because the results of a given study are based only on data obtained from a single sample of research participants. Researchers rarely, if ever, study entire populations; their findings are based on sample data. In addition to describing the sample data, we want to make statements about populations. Would the results hold up if the experiment were conducted repeatedly, each time with a new sample?

In the hypothetical experiment described in the chapter **"Understanding Research Results: Description and Correlation,"** aggression scores were obtained in model and no-model conditions. Results from this hypothetical study are shown in **Table 1**. The mean aggression score in the model condition was 5.20, and the mean aggression score in the no-model group mean was 3.10. These means are different: Children who observe an aggressive model subsequently behave more aggressively than children who do not see an aggressive model. **Inferential statistics** are used to determine whether the results match what would happen if we were to conduct the experiment again and again with multiple samples. In essence, we are asking whether we can infer that the difference in the *sample means* shown in **Table 1** reflects a true difference in the *population means*.

TABLE 1 **Aggression score data from a hypothetical experiment on modeling and aggression**

	Model group	No-model group
Mean $(\bar{X})$	5.20	3.10
Standard deviation (s)	1.14	1.20
Variance (s^2)	1.29	1.43
n	10	10

You may recognize the issue of samples and populations from presentations of survey results. A news story might report that a sample of people in your state found that that 55% prefer the Democratic candidate for an office and that 45% favor the Republican candidate. The report then says that these results are accurate to within 3 percentage points, with a 95% confidence level. This means that the researchers are very (95%) confident that, if they were able to study the entire population rather than a sample, the actual percentage who preferred the Democratic candidate would be between 58% and 52% and the percentage preferring the Republican would be between 48% and 42%. In this case the researcher could predict with a great deal of certainty that the Democratic candidate will win, because there is no overlap in the projected population values. Note, however, that even when we are very (in this case, 95%) sure, we still have a 5% chance of being wrong.

Inferential statistics allow us to arrive at such conclusions on the basis of sample data. In our study with the model and no-model conditions, are we confident that the means are sufficiently different to infer that the difference would be obtained in an entire population?

INFERENTIAL STATISTICS

Much of the previous discussion of experimental design centered on the importance of ensuring that the groups are equivalent in every way except the independent variable manipulation. Equivalence of groups is achieved by experimentally controlling all other variables or by randomization. The assumption is that if the groups are equivalent, any differences in the dependent variable must be due to the effect of the independent variable.

This assumption is usually valid. However, it is also true that the difference between any two groups will almost never be zero. In other words, there will be some difference in the sample means, even when all of the principles of experimental design are rigorously followed. This happens because we are dealing with samples, rather than populations. Random or chance error will be responsible for some difference in the means, even if the independent variable had no effect on the dependent variable.

So, differences in sample means reflect actual difference in the population means (i.e., the effect of the independent variable), but they also reflect some random error. Inferential statistics allow researchers to make inferences about the true difference in the population on the basis of the sample data. Specifically, inferential statistics give the probability that the difference between means reflects random error rather than a real difference.

NULL AND RESEARCH HYPOTHESES

Statistical inference begins with a statement of the null hypothesis and a research (or alternative) hypothesis. The **null hypothesis** is simply that the population means are equal—the observed difference is due to random error. The **research hypothesis** is that the population means are, in fact, not equal. The null hypothesis states that the independent variable had no effect; the research hypothesis states that the independent variable did have an effect. In the aggression modeling experiment, the null and research hypotheses are:

H_0 (null hypothesis): The population mean of the no-model group is equal to the population mean of the model group.

H_1 (research hypothesis): The population mean of the no-model group is not equal to the population mean of the model group.

The logic of the null hypothesis is this: If we can determine that the null hypothesis is incorrect, then we accept the research hypothesis as correct. Acceptance of the research hypothesis means that the independent variable had an effect on the dependent variable.

The null hypothesis is used because it is a very precise statement—the population means are exactly equal. This permits us to know precisely the probability of obtaining our results if the null hypothesis is correct.

Such precision is not possible with the research hypothesis, so we infer that the research hypothesis is correct only by rejecting the null hypothesis. We reject the null hypothesis when we find a very low probability that the obtained results could be due to random error. This is what is meant by **statistical significance:** A significant result is one that has a very low probability of occurring if the population means are equal. More simply, significance indicates that there is a low probability that the difference between the obtained sample means was due to random error. Significance, then, is a matter of probability.

PROBABILITY AND SAMPLING DISTRIBUTIONS

Probability is the likelihood of the occurrence of some event or outcome. We all use probabilities frequently in everyday life. For example, if you say that there is a high probability that you will get an A in this course, you mean that this outcome is likely to occur. Your probability statement is based on specific information, such as your grades on examinations. The weather forecaster says there is a 10% chance of rain today; this means that the likelihood of rain is very low. A gambler gauges the probability that a particular horse will win a race on the basis of the past records of that horse.

Probability in statistical inference is used in much the same way. We want to specify the probability that an event (in this case, a difference between means in the sample) will occur if there is no difference in the population. The question is: What is the probability of obtaining this result if only random error is operating? If this probability is very low, we reject the possibility that only random or chance error is responsible for the obtained difference in means.

Probability: The Case of ESP

The use of probability in statistical inference can be understood intuitively from a simple example. Suppose that a friend claims to have ESP (extrasensory perception) ability. You decide to test your friend with a set of five cards commonly used in ESP research; a different symbol is presented on each card. In the ESP test, you look at each card and think about the symbol, and your friend tells you which symbol you are thinking about. In your actual experiment, you have 10 trials; each of the five cards is presented two times in a random order. Your task is to know whether your friend's answers reflect random error (guessing) or whether they indicate that something more than random error is occurring. The null hypothesis in your study is that only random error is operating. In this case, the research hypothesis is that the number of correct answers shows more than random or chance guessing. (Note, however, that accepting the research hypothesis could mean that your friend has ESP ability, but it could also mean that the cards were marked, that you had somehow cued your friend when thinking about the symbols, and so on.)

You can easily determine the number of correct answers to expect if the null hypothesis is correct. Just by guessing, 1 out of 5 answers (20%) should be correct. On 10 trials, 2 correct answers are expected under the null hypothesis. If, in the actual test, more (or less) than 2 correct answers are obtained, would you conclude that the obtained data reflect random error or something more than merely random guessing?

Suppose that your friend gets 3 correct. Then you would probably conclude that only guessing is involved, because you would recognize that there is a high probability that there would be 3 correct answers *even though only 2 correct are expected under the null hypothesis.* You expect that exactly 2 answers in 10 trials would be correct in the long run, if you conducted this experiment with this subject over and over again. However, small deviations away from the expected 2 are highly likely in a sample of 10 trials.

Suppose, though, that your friend gets 7 correct. You might conclude that the results indicate more than random error in this one sample of 10 observations. This conclusion would be based on your intuitive judgment that an outcome of 70% correct when only 20% is expected is very unlikely. At this point, you would decide to reject the null hypothesis and state that the result is significant. A significant result is one that is very unlikely if the null hypothesis is correct.

A key question then becomes: How unlikely does a result have to be before we decide it is significant? A decision rule is determined prior to collecting the data. The probability required for significance is called the **alpha level.** The most common alpha-level probability used is .05. The outcome of the study is considered significant when there is a .05 or less probability of obtaining the results; that is, there are only 5 chances out of 100 that the results were due to random error in one sample from the population. If it is very unlikely that random error is responsible for the obtained results, the null hypothesis is rejected.

Sampling Distributions

You may have been able to judge intuitively that obtaining 7 correct on the 10 trials is very unlikely. Fortunately, we do not have to rely on intuition to determine the probabilities of different outcomes. **Table 2** shows the probability of actually obtaining each of the possible outcomes in the ESP experiment with 10 trials and a null hypothesis expectation of 20% correct. An outcome of 2 correct answers has the highest probability of occurrence. Also, as intuition would suggest, an outcome of 3 correct is highly probable, but an outcome of 7 correct is highly unlikely.

TABLE 2   **Exact probability of each possible outcome of the ESP experiment with 10 trials**

Number of correct answers	Probability
10	.00000+
9	.00000+
8	.00007
7	.00079
6	.00551
5	.02642
4	.08808
3	.20133
2	.30199
1	.26844
0	.10737

The probabilities shown in **Table 2** were derived from a probability distribution called the *binomial distribution;* all statistical significance decisions are based on probability distributions such as this one. Such distributions are called **sampling distributions.** The sampling distribution is based on the assumption that the null hypothesis is true; in the ESP example, the null hypothesis is that the person is only guessing and should therefore get 20% correct. Such a distribution assumes that if you were to conduct the study with the same number of observations over and over again, the most frequent finding would be 20%. However, because of the random error possible in each sample, there is a certain probability associated with other outcomes. Outcomes that are close to the expected null hypothesis value of 20% are very likely. However, outcomes farther from the expected result are less and less likely if the null hypothesis is correct. When your obtained results are highly unlikely if you are, in fact, sampling from the distribution specified by the null hypothesis, you conclude that the null hypothesis is incorrect. Instead of concluding that your sample results reflect a random deviation from the long-run expectation of 20%, you decide that the null hypothesis is incorrect. That is, you conclude that you have not sampled from the sampling distribution specified by the null hypothesis. Instead, in the case of the ESP example, you decide that your data are from a different sampling distribution in which, if you were to test the person repeatedly, most of the outcomes would be near your obtained result of 7 correct answers.

All statistical tests rely on sampling distributions to determine the probability that the results are consistent with the null hypothesis. When the obtained data are very unlikely according to null hypothesis expectations (usually a .05 probability or less), the researcher decides to reject the null hypothesis and therefore to accept the research hypothesis.

Sample Size

The ESP example also illustrates the impact of sample size—the total number of observations—on determinations of statistical significance. Suppose you had tested your friend on 100 trials instead of 10 and had observed 30 correct answers. Just as you had expected 2 correct answers in 10 trials, you would now expect 20 of 100 answers to be correct. However, 30 out of 100 has a much lower likelihood of occurrence than 3 out of 10. This is because, with more observations sampled, you are more likely to obtain an accurate estimate of the true population value. Thus, as the size of your sample increases, you are more confident that your outcome is actually different from the null hypothesis expectation.

GROUP DIFFERENCES: THE *t* AND *F* TESTS

Different statistical tests allow us to use probability to decide whether to reject the null hypothesis. In this section, we will examine the *t* test and the *F* test. The **t test** is commonly used to examine whether two groups are significantly different from each other. In the hypothetical experiment on the effect of a model on aggression, a *t* test is appropriate because we are asking whether the mean of the no-model group differs from the mean of the model group. The *F* test is a more general statistical test that can be used to ask whether there is a difference among three or more groups or to evaluate the results of factorial designs (discussed in the chapter **"Complex Experimental Designs"**).

To use a statistical test, you must first specify the null hypothesis and the research hypothesis that you are evaluating. The null and research hypotheses for the modeling experiment were described previously. You must also specify the significance level that you will use to decide whether to reject the null hypothesis; this is the alpha level. As noted, researchers generally use a significance level of .05.

t Test

The sampling distribution of all possible values of *t* is shown in **Figure 1**. (This particular distribution is for the sample size we used in the hypothetical experiment on modeling and aggression; the sample size was 20 with 10 participants in each group.) This sampling distribution has a mean of 0 and a standard deviation of 1. It reflects all the possible outcomes we could expect if we compare the means of two groups *and* the null hypothesis is correct.

To use this distribution to evaluate our data, we need to calculate a value of *t* from the obtained data and evaluate the obtained *t* in terms of the sampling distribution of *t* that is based on the null hypothesis. If the obtained *t* has a low probability of occurrence (.05 or less), then the null hypothesis is rejected.

The *t* value is a ratio of two aspects of the data, the difference between the group means and the variability within groups. The ratio may be described as follows:

$$t = \frac{\text{group difference}}{\text{within-group variability}}$$

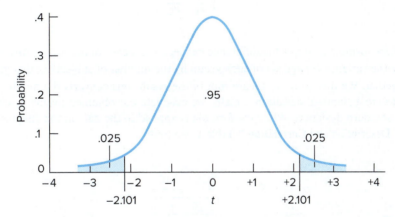

Critical Value for Two-Tailed Test with .05 Significance Level

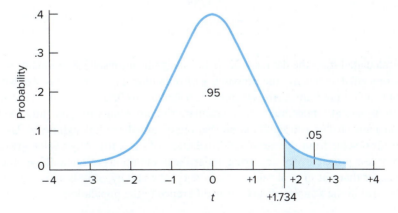

Critical Value for One-Tailed Test with .05 Significance Level

FIGURE 1   Sampling distributions of *t* values with 18 degrees of freedom

The group difference is simply the difference between your obtained means; under the null hypothesis, you expect this difference to be zero. The value of t increases as the difference between your obtained sample means increases. Note that the sampling distribution of t assumes that there is no difference in the population means; thus, the expected value of t under the null hypothesis is zero. The within-group variability is the amount of variability of scores about the mean. The denominator of the t formula is essentially an indicator of the amount of random error in your sample. Recall from the chapter **"Understanding Research Results: Description and Correlation"** that s, the standard deviation, and s^2, the variance, are indicators of how much scores deviate from the group mean.

A concrete example of a calculation of a t test should help clarify these concepts. The formula for the t test for two groups with equal numbers of participants in each group is:

$$t = \frac{\overline{X}_1 - \overline{X}_2}{\sqrt{\dfrac{s_1^2}{n_1} + \dfrac{s_2^2}{n_2}}}$$

The numerator of the formula is simply the difference between the means of the two groups. In the denominator, we first divide the variance (s_1^2 and s_2^2) of each group by the number of subjects in that group (n_1 and n_2) and add these together. We then find the square root of the result; this converts the number from a squared score (the variance) to a standard deviation. Finally, we calculate our obtained t value by dividing the mean difference by this standard deviation. When the formula is applied to the data in the chapter **"Understanding Research Results: Description and Correlation," Table 1,** we find:

$$t = \frac{5.20 - 3.10}{\sqrt{\dfrac{1.29}{10} + \dfrac{1.43}{10}}}$$

$$= \frac{2.1}{\sqrt{.1289 + .1433}}$$

$$= 4.02$$

Thus, the t value calculated from the data is 4.02. Is this a significant result? A computer program analyzing the results would immediately tell you the probability of obtaining a t value of this size with a total sample size of 20. Without such a program, there are internet resources to find a table of "critical values" of t (**htt p://davidmlane.com/hyperstat/t_table.html**) or to calculate the probability for you (**http://vassarstats.net/tab s.html**). Before going any farther, you should know that the obtained result is significant. Using a significance level of .05, the critical value from the sampling distribution of t is 2.101. Any t value greater than or equal to 2.101 has a .05 or less probability of occurring under the assumptions of the null hypothesis. Because our obtained value is larger than the critical value, we can reject the null hypothesis and conclude that the difference in means obtained in the sample reflects a true difference in the population.

Degrees of Freedom

You are probably wondering how the critical value was selected from the table. To use the table, you must first determine the **degrees of freedom** for the test (the term *degrees of freedom* is abbreviated *df*). When comparing two means, you assume that the degrees of freedom are equal to $n_1 + n_2 - 2$, or the total number of participants in the groups minus the number of groups. In our experiment, the degrees of freedom would be $10 + 10 - 2 = 18$. The degrees of freedom are the number of scores free to vary once the means are known. For example, if the mean of a group is 6.0 and there are five scores in the group, there are 4 degrees of freedom; once you have any four scores, the fifth score is known because the mean must remain 6.0.

One-Tailed Versus Two-Tailed Tests

In the table, you must choose a critical *t* for the situation in which your research hypothesis either (1) specified a direction of difference between the groups (e.g., "group 1 will be greater than group 2") or (2) did not specify a predicted direction of difference (e.g., "group 1 will differ from group 2"). Somewhat different critical values of *t* are used in the two situations: The first situation is called a one-tailed test, and the second situation is called a two-tailed test.

The issue can be visualized by looking at the sampling distribution of *t* values for 18 degrees of freedom, as shown in **Figure 1**. As you can see, a value of 0.00 is expected most frequently. Values greater than or less than zero are less likely to occur. The first distribution shows the logic of a two-tailed test. We used the value of 2.101 for the critical value of *t* with a .05 significance level because a direction of difference was not predicted. This critical value is the point beyond which 2.5% of the positive values and 2.5% of the negative values of *t* lie (hence, a total probability of .05 combined from the two "tails" of the sampling distribution). The second distribution illustrates a one-tailed test. If a directional difference had been predicted, the critical value would have been 1.734. This is the value beyond which 5% of the values lie in only one "tail" of the distribution. Whether to specify a one-tailed or two-tailed test will depend on whether you originally designed your study to test a directional hypothesis.

F Test

The **analysis of variance,** or **F test,** is an extension of the *t* test. The analysis of variance is a more general statistical procedure than the *t* test. When a study has only one independent variable with *two* groups, *F* and *t* are virtually identical—the value of *F* equals t^2 in this situation. However, analysis of variance is also used when there are more than two levels of an independent variable and when a factorial design with two or more independent variables has been used. Thus, the *F* test is appropriate for the simplest experimental design, as well as for the more complex designs discussed in the chapter **"Complex Experimental Designs."** The *t* test was presented first because the formula allows us to demonstrate easily the relationship of the group difference and the within-group variability to the outcome of the statistical test. However, in practice, analysis of variance is the more common procedure. The calculations necessary to conduct an *F* test are provided in **Appendix C.**

The *F* statistic is a ratio of two types of variance: systematic variance and error variance (hence the term *analysis of variance*). **Systematic variance** is the deviation of the group means from the grand mean, or the mean score of all individuals in all groups. Systematic variance is small when the difference between group means is small and increases as the group mean differences increase. **Error variance** is the deviation of the individual scores in each group from their respective group means. Terms that you may see in research instead of systematic and error variance are *between-group variance* and *within-group variance*. Systematic variance is the variability of scores between groups, and error variance is the variability of scores within groups. The larger the F ratio is, the more likely it is that the results are significant.

Calculating Effect Size

The concept of effect size was discussed in the chapter **"Understanding Research Results: Description and Correlation."** After determining that there was a statistically significant effect of the independent variable, researchers will want to know the magnitude of the effect. Therefore, we want to calculate an estimate of effect size. For a t test, the calculation is

$$\text{effect size } r = \sqrt{\frac{t^2}{t^2 + df}}$$

where df is the degrees of freedom. Thus, using the obtained value of t, 4.02, and 18 degrees of freedom, we find:

$$\text{effect size } r = \sqrt{\frac{(4.02)^2}{(4.02)^2 + 18}} = \sqrt{\frac{16.201}{34.201}} = .69$$

This value is a type of correlation coefficient that can range from 0.00 to 1.00; as mentioned in the chapter **"Understanding Research Results: Description and Correlation,"** .69 is considered a large effect size. For additional information on effect size calculation, see Fritz et al. (2012). The same distinction between r and r^2 that was made in the chapter **"Understanding Research Results: Description and Correlation"** applies here as well.

Another effect size estimate used when comparing two means is called Cohen's d (websites to calculate Cohen's d and convert to effect size r are available; see, e.g., **https://www.uccs.edu/lbecker/**). Cohen's d expresses effect size in terms of standard deviation units. A d value of 1.0 tells you that the means are 1 standard deviation apart; a d of .2 indicates that the means are separated by .2 standard deviation.

You can calculate the value of Cohen's d using the means (M) and standard deviations (SD) of the two groups:

$$d = \frac{M_1 - M_2}{\sqrt{\frac{(SD_1^2 + SD_2^2)}{2}}}$$

Note that the formula uses M and SD instead of $\overline{X}$ and s. These abbreviations are used in APA style (see **Appendix A**).

The value of d is larger than the corresponding value of r, but it is easy to convert d to a value of r. Both statistics provide information on the size of the relationship between the variables studied. You might note that both effect size estimates have a value of 0.00 when there is no relationship. The value of r has a maximum value of 1.00, but d has no maximum value. You may also be wondering what should be considered a small or large effect size. **Table 3** expands on the guidelines presented in the chapter **"Understanding Research Results: Description and Correlation."**

TABLE 3   Guidelines for effect size descriptions

Strength of effect size	Effect size *r*	Cohen's *d*
Small	0.10	0.20
Moderate/medium	0.30	0.50
Large	0.50	0.80

Confidence Intervals and Statistical Significance

Confidence intervals were described in the chapter **"Asking People About Themselves: Survey Research."** After obtaining a sample value, we can calculate a confidence interval. An interval of values defines the most likely range of actual population values. The interval has an associated confidence interval: A 95% confidence interval indicates that we are 95% sure that the population value lies within the range; a 99% interval would provide greater certainty but the range of values would be larger.

A confidence interval can be obtained for each of the means in the aggression experiment. The 95% confidence intervals for the two conditions are shown below.

	Obtained sample value	Low population value	High population value
Model group	5.20	4.39	6.01
No-model group	3.10	2.24	3.96

A bar graph that includes a visual depiction of the confidence interval can be very useful. The means from the aggression experiment are shown in **Figure 2**. The shaded bars represent the mean aggression scores in the two conditions. The confidence interval for each group is shown with a vertical I-shaped line that is bounded by the upper and lower limits of the 95% confidence interval. It is important to examine confidence intervals to obtain a greater understanding of the meaning of your obtained data. Although the obtained sample means provide the best estimate of the population values, you are able to see the likely range of possible values. The size of the interval is related to both the size of the sample and the confidence level. As the sample size increases, the confidence interval narrows. This is because sample means obtained with larger sample sizes are more likely to reflect the population mean. Second, higher confidence is associated with a larger interval. If you want to be almost certain that the interval contains the true population mean (e.g., a 99% confidence interval), you will need to include more possibilities. Note that the 95% confidence intervals for the two means do not overlap. This should be a clue to you that the difference is statistically significant. Indeed, examining confidence intervals is an alternative way of thinking about statistical significance. The null hypothesis is that the difference in population means is 0.00. However, if you were to subtract all the means in the 95% confidence interval for the no-model condition from all the means in the model condition, none of these differences would include the value of 0.00. We can be very confident that the null hypothesis should be rejected.

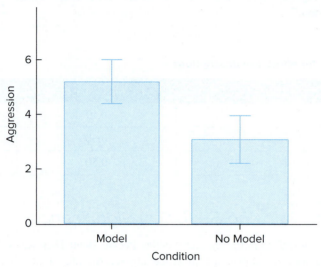

FIGURE 2   Mean aggression scores from the hypothetical modeling experiment including the 95% confidence intervals

Statistical Significance: An Overview

The logic underlying the use of statistical tests rests on statistical theory. There are some general concepts, however, that should help you understand what you are doing when you conduct a statistical test. First, the goal of the test is to allow you to make a decision about whether your obtained results are reliable; you want to be confident that you would obtain similar results if you conducted the study over and over again. Second, the significance level (alpha level) you choose indicates how confident you wish to be when making the decision. A .05 significance level says that you are 95% sure of the reliability of your findings; however, there is a 5% chance that you could be wrong. There are few certainties in life! Third, you are most likely to obtain significant results when you have a large sample size because larger sample sizes provide better estimates of true population values. Finally, you are most likely to obtain significant results when the effect size is large, that is, when differences between groups are large and variability of scores within groups is small.

In the remainder of this chapter, we will expand on these issues. We will examine the implications of making a decision about whether results are significant, the way to determine a significance level, and the way to interpret nonsignificant results. We will then provide some guidelines for selecting the appropriate statistical test in various research designs.

TYPE I AND TYPE II ERRORS

The decision to reject the null hypothesis is based on probabilities rather than on certainties. That is, the decision is made without direct knowledge of the true state of affairs in the population. Thus, the decision might not be correct; errors may result from the use of inferential statistics.

A decision matrix is shown in **Figure 3**. Notice that there are two possible decisions: (1) Reject the null hypothesis or (2) accept the null hypothesis. There are also two possible truths about the population: (1) The null hypothesis is true or (2) the null hypothesis is false. In sum, as the decision matrix shows, there are two kinds of correct decisions and two kinds of errors.

Correct Decisions

One correct decision occurs when we reject the null hypothesis and the research hypothesis is true in the population. Here, our decision is that the population means are not equal, and in fact, this is true in the population. This is the decision you hope to make when you begin your study.

The other correct decision is to accept the null hypothesis, and the null hypothesis is true in the population: The population means are in fact equal.

Type I Errors

A **Type I error** is made when we reject the null hypothesis but the null hypothesis is actually true. Our decision is that the population means are not equal when they actually are equal. Type I errors occur when, simply by chance, we obtain a large value of t or F. For example, even though a t value of 4.025 is highly improbable if the population means are indeed equal (less than 5 chances out of 100), this *can* happen. When we do obtain such a large t value by chance, we *incorrectly* decide that the independent variable had an effect.

The probability of making a Type I error is determined by the choice of significance or alpha level (alpha may be shown as the Greek letter alpha, α). When the significance level for deciding whether to reject the null hypothesis is .05, the probability of a Type I error (alpha) is .05. If the null hypothesis is rejected, there are 5 chances out of 100 that the decision is wrong. The probability of making a Type I error can be changed by either decreasing or increasing the significance level. If we use a lower alpha level of .01, for example, there is less chance of making a Type I error. With a .01 significance level, the null hypothesis is rejected only when the probability of obtaining the results is .01 or less if the null hypothesis is correct.

	True State in Population	
	Null Hypothesis Is True	Null Hypothesis Is False
Reject the Null Hypothesis	Type I Error (α)	Correct Decision $(1 - \beta)$
Accept the Null Hypothesis	Correct Decision $(1 - \alpha)$	Type II Error (β)

FIGURE 3   Decision matrix for Type I and Type II errors

Type II Errors

A **Type II error** occurs when the null hypothesis is accepted although in the population the research hypothesis is true. The population means are not equal, but the results of the experiment do not lead to a decision to reject the null hypothesis.

Research should be designed so that the probability of a Type II error (this probability is called beta, often designated by the Greek letter β) is relatively low. The probability of making a Type II error is related to three factors. The first is the significance (alpha) level. If we set a very low significance level to decrease the chances of a Type I error, we increase the chances of a Type II error. In other words, if we make it very difficult to reject the null hypothesis, the probability of incorrectly accepting the null hypothesis increases. The second factor is sample size. True differences are more likely to be detected if the sample size is large. The third factor is effect size. If the effect size is large, a Type II error is unlikely. However, a small effect size may not be significant with a small sample.

The Everyday Context of Type I and Type II Errors

The decision matrix used in statistical analyses can be applied to the kinds of decisions people frequently must make in everyday life. For example, consider the decision made by a juror in a criminal trial. As is the case with statistics, a decision must be made on the basis of evidence: Is the defendant innocent or guilty? However, the decision rests with individual jurors and does not necessarily reflect the true state of affairs: that the person really is innocent or guilty.

The juror's decision matrix is illustrated in **Figure 4**. To continue the parallel to the statistical decision, assume that the null hypothesis is the defendant is innocent (i.e., the dictum that a person is innocent until proven guilty). Thus, rejection of the null hypothesis means deciding that the defendant is guilty, and acceptance of the null hypothesis means deciding that the defendant is innocent. The decision matrix also shows that the null hypothesis may actually be true or false. There are two kinds of correct decisions and two kinds of errors like those described in statistical decisions. A Type I error is finding the defendant guilty when the person really is innocent; a Type II error is finding the defendant innocent when the person actually is guilty. In our society, Type I errors by jurors generally are considered to be more serious than Type II errors. Thus, before finding someone guilty, the juror is asked to make sure that the person is guilty "beyond a reasonable doubt" or to consider that "it is better to have a hundred guilty persons go free than to find one innocent person guilty."

The decision that a doctor makes to operate or not operate on a patient provides another illustration of how a decision matrix works. The matrix is shown in **Figure 5**. Here, the null hypothesis is that no operation is necessary. The decision is whether to reject the null hypothesis and perform the operation or to accept the null hypothesis and not perform surgery. In reality, the surgeon is faced with two possibilities: Either the surgery is unnecessary (the null hypothesis is true) or the patient will die without the operation (a dramatic case of the null hypothesis being false). Which error is more serious in this case? Most doctors would believe that not operating on a patient who really needs the operation—making a Type II error—is more serious than making the Type I error of performing surgery on someone who does not really need it.

One final illustration of the use of a decision matrix involves the important decision to marry someone. If the null hypothesis is that the person is "wrong" for you, and the true state is that the person is either "wrong" or "right," you must decide whether to go ahead and marry the person. You might try to construct a decision matrix for this particular problem. Which error is more costly: a Type I error or a Type II error?

True State

	Null Is True (Innocent)	Null Is False (Guilty)
Reject Null (Find Guilty)	Type I Error	Correct Decision
Accept Null (Find Innocent)	Correct Decision	Type II Error

Decision

FIGURE 4   Decision matrix for a juror

True State

	Null Is True (No Operation Needed)	Null Is False (Operation Is Needed)
Reject Null (Operate on Patient)	Type I Error	Correct Decision
Accept Null (Do Not Operate)	Correct Decision	Type II Error

Decision

FIGURE 5   Decision matrix for a doctor

CHOOSING A SIGNIFICANCE LEVEL

Researchers traditionally have used either a .05 or a .01 significance level in the decision to reject the null hypothesis. If there is less than a .05 or a .01 probability that the results occurred because of random error, the results are said to be significant. However, there is nothing magical about a .05 or a .01 significance level. The significance level chosen merely specifies the probability of a Type I error if the null hypothesis is rejected. The significance level chosen by the researcher usually is dependent on the consequences of making a Type I versus a Type II error. As previously noted, for a juror a Type I error is more serious than a Type II error; for a doctor, however, a Type II error may be more serious.

Researchers generally believe that the consequences of making a Type I error are more serious than those associated with a Type II error. If the null hypothesis is rejected, the researcher might publish the results in a journal, and the results might be reported by others in textbooks or in newspaper or magazine articles. Researchers do not want to mislead people or risk damaging their reputations by publishing results that are not reliable and so cannot be replicated. Thus, they want to guard against the possibility of making a Type I error by using a very low significance level (.05 or .01). In contrast to the consequences of publishing false results, the consequences of a Type II error are not seen as being very serious.

Thus, researchers want to be very careful to avoid Type I errors when their results may be published. However, in certain circumstances, a Type I error is not serious. For example, if you were engaged in pilot or exploratory research, your results would be used primarily to decide whether your research ideas were worth pursuing. In this situation, it would be a mistake to overlook potentially important data by using a very conservative significance level. In exploratory research, a significance level of .25 may be more appropriate for deciding whether to do more research. Remember that the significance level chosen and the consequences of a Type I or a Type II error are determined by what the results will be used for.

INTERPRETING NONSIGNIFICANT RESULTS

Although "accepting the null hypothesis" is convenient terminology, it is important to recognize that researchers are not generally interested in accepting the null hypothesis. Research is designed to show that a relationship between variables does exist, not to demonstrate that variables are unrelated.

More important, a decision to accept the null hypothesis when a single study does not show significant results is problematic, because negative or nonsignificant results are difficult to interpret. For this reason, researchers often say that they simply "fail to reject" or "do not reject" the null hypothesis. The results of a single study might be nonsignificant even when a relationship between the variables in the population does in fact exist. This is a Type II error. Sometimes, the reasons for a Type II error lie in the procedures used in the experiment. For example, a researcher might obtain nonsignificant results by providing incomprehensible instructions to the participants, by having a very weak manipulation of the independent variable, or by using a dependent measure that is unreliable and insensitive. Rather than concluding that the variables are not related, researchers may decide that a more carefully conducted study would find that the variables are related.

We should also consider the statistical reasons for a Type II error. Recall that the probability of a Type II error is influenced by the significance (alpha) level, sample size, and effect size. Thus, nonsignificant results are more likely to be found if the researcher is very cautious in choosing the alpha level. If the researcher uses a significance level of .001 rather than .05, it is more difficult to reject the null hypothesis (there is not much chance of a Type I error). However, that also means that there is a greater chance of accepting an incorrect null hypothesis (i.e., a Type II error is more likely). In other words, a meaningful result is more likely to be overlooked when the significance level is very low.

A Type II error may also result from a sample size that is too small to detect a real relationship between variables. A general principle is that the larger the sample size is, the greater the likelihood of obtaining a significant result. This is because large sample sizes give more accurate estimates of the actual population than do small sample sizes. In any given study, the sample size may be too small to permit detection of a significant result.

A third reason for a nonsignificant finding is that the effect size is small. Very small effects are difficult to detect without a large sample size. In general, the sample size should be large enough to find a real effect, even if it is a small one.

The fact that it is possible for a very small effect to be statistically significant raises another issue. A very large sample size might enable the researcher to find a significant difference between means; however, this difference, even though statistically significant, might have very little *practical* significance. For example, if an expensive new psychiatric treatment technique significantly reduces the average hospital stay from 60 to 59 days, it might not be practical to use the technique despite the evidence for its effectiveness. The additional day of hospitalization costs less than the treatment. There are other circumstances, however, in which a treatment with a very small effect size has considerable practical significance. Usually this occurs when a very large population is affected by a fairly inexpensive treatment. Suppose a simple flextime policy for employees reduces employee turnover by 1% per year. This does not sound like a large effect. However, if a company normally has a turnover of 2,000 employees each year and the cost of training a new employee is $10,000, the company saves $200,000 per year with the new procedure. This amount may have practical significance for the company.

The key point here is that you should not accept the null hypothesis just because the results are nonsignificant. Nonsignificant results do not necessarily indicate that the null hypothesis is correct. However, there must be circumstances in which we can accept the null hypothesis and conclude that two variables are, in fact, not related. Frick (1995) describes several criteria that can be used in a decision to accept the null hypothesis. For example, we should look for well-designed studies with sensitive dependent measures and evidence from a manipulation check that the independent variable manipulation had its intended effect. In addition, the research should have a reasonably large sample to rule out the possibility that the sample was too small. Further, evidence that the variables are not related should come from multiple studies. Under such circumstances, you are justified in concluding that there is in fact no relationship.

> Next, head to **Check Your Learning:** Practice Exercise #1 to try your own null hypothesis testing.

CHOOSING A SAMPLE SIZE: POWER ANALYSIS

You will also need to determine your sample size. How many participants will you need in your study? In general, increasing your sample size increases the likelihood that your results will be statistically significant, because larger samples provide more accurate estimates of population values (see the chapter **"Asking People About Themselves: Survey Research," Table 2**). Most researchers take note of the sample sizes in the research area being studied and select a sample size that is typical for studies in the area. A more formal approach is to select a sample size on the basis of a desired probability of correctly rejecting the null hypothesis. This probability is called the **power** of the statistical test. It is obviously related to the probability of a Type II error:

$$Power = 1 - p \text{ (Type II error)}$$

We previously indicated that the probability of a Type II error is related to significance level (alpha), sample size, and effect size. Statisticians such as Cohen (1988) have developed procedures for determining sample size based on these factors. **Table 3** shows the total sample size needed for an experiment with two groups and a significance level of .05. In the table, effect sizes range from .10 to .50, and the desired power is shown at .80 and .90. Smaller effect sizes require larger samples to be significant at the .05 level. Higher desired power demands a greater sample size; this is because you want a more certain "guarantee" that your results will be statistically significant. Researchers usually use a power between .70 and .90 when using this method to determine sample size. Several computer programs have been developed to allow researchers to easily make the calculations necessary to determine sample size based on effect size estimates, significance level, and desired power.

TABLE 3   Total sample size needed to detect a significant difference for a *t* test

Effect size *r*	Power = .80	Power = .90
.10	789	1052
.20	200	266
.30	88	116
.40	52	68
.50	26	36

Note: Effect sizes are correlations, based on two-tailed tests.

If a researcher is studying a relationship with an effect size correlation of .20, a fairly large sample size is needed for statistical significance at the .05 level. An inappropriately low sample size in this situation is likely to produce a nonsignificant finding.

THE IMPORTANCE OF REPLICATIONS

Throughout this discussion of statistical analysis, the focus has been on the results of a single research investigation. What were the means and standard deviations? Was the mean difference statistically significant? If the results are significant, you conclude that they would likely be obtained over and over again if the study were repeated. We now have a framework for understanding the results of the study. Be aware, however, that scientists do not attach too much importance to the results of a single study. A rich understanding of any phenomenon comes from the results of numerous studies investigating the same variables. Instead of inferring population values on the basis of a single investigation, we can look at the results of several studies that replicate previous investigations (see Cohen, 1994). The importance of replications is a central concept in the chapter **"Generalization."**

SIGNIFICANCE OF A PEARSON *r* CORRELATION COEFFICIENT

Recall from the chapter **"Understanding Research Results: Description and Correlation"** that the Pearson *r* correlation coefficient is used to describe the strength of the relationship between two variables when both variables have interval or ratio scale properties. However, there remains the issue of whether the correlation is statistically significant. The null hypothesis in this case is that the true population correlation is 0.00–the two variables are not related. What if you obtain a correlation of .27 (plus or minus)? A statistical significance test will allow you to decide whether to reject the null hypothesis and conclude that the true population correlation is, in fact, greater than 0.00. The technical way to do this is to perform a *t* test that compares the obtained coefficient with the null hypothesis correlation of 0.00. The procedures for calculating a Pearson *r* and determining significance are provided in **Appendix C.**

STATISTICAL ANALYSIS SOFTWARE

Although you can calculate statistics with a calculator using the formulas provided in the chapter **"Understanding Research Results: Description and Correlation,"** and **Appendix C,** most data analysis is carried out via specially designed statistical software. Sophisticated statistical analysis software packages make it easy to calculate statistics for any data set. Descriptive and inferential statistics are obtained quickly, the calculations are accurate, and information on statistical significance is provided in the output. Statistical software also facilitate graphic displays of data.

Some of the major statistical programs include SPSS, SAS, SYSTAT, and freely available R. Other programs may be used on your campus. Many people do most of their simple statistical analyses using a spreadsheet program such as Microsoft Excel. You will need to learn the specific details of the computer system used at your college or university. No one program is better than another; they all differ in the appearance of the output and the specific procedures needed to input data and have the program perform the test. However, the general procedures for doing analyses are quite similar in all of the statistics programs.

The first step in doing the analysis is to input the data. Suppose you want to input the data from the chapter **"Understanding Research Results: Description and Correlation," Table 1,** the modeling and aggression experiment. Data are entered into columns. It is easiest to think of data analysis as a matrix with rows and columns. Data for each research participant are the rows of the matrix. The columns contain each participant's scores on one or more measures, and an additional column may be needed to indicate a code to identify which condition the individual was in (e.g., Group 1 or Group 2). A data matrix in SPSS for Windows is shown in **Figure 6.** The numbers in the "group" column indicate whether the individual is in Group 1 (model) or Group 2 (no model), and the numbers in the "aggscore" column are the aggression scores from the chapter **"Understanding Research Results: Description and Correlation," Table 1.**

Other programs may require somewhat different methods of data input. For example, in Excel, it is usually easiest to set up a separate column for each group, as shown in **Figure 6.**

The next step is to provide instructions for the statistical analysis. Again, each program uses somewhat different steps to perform the analysis; most require you to choose from various menu options. When the analysis is completed, you are provided with the output that shows the results of the statistical procedure you performed. You will need to learn how to interpret the output. **Figure 6** shows the output for a *t* test using Excel.

When you are first learning to use a statistical analysis program, it is a good idea to practice with some data from a statistics text to make sure that you get the same results. This will ensure that you know how to properly input the data and request the statistical analysis.

The appropriate statistical tests are shown as the output in **Figure 6.**

SELECTING THE APPROPRIATE STATISTICAL TEST

We have covered several types of designs, and the variables that we study may have nominal, ordinal, interval, or ratio scale properties. How do you choose the appropriate statistical test for analyzing your data? Fortunately, there are a number of online guides and tutorials, such as **https://www.socialresearchmethods.net/selstat/ssstart.htm** and **https://wise.cgu.edu/wise-tutorials/tutorial-choosing-the-correct-statistical-test/**; SPSS even has its own Statistics Coach to help with the decision.

We cannot cover every possible analysis. Our focus will be on variables that have either (1) nominal scale properties—two or more discrete values, such as male and female—or (2) interval/ratio scale properties with

	group	aggscore
1	1	3
2	1	4
3	1	5
4	1	5
5	1	5
6	2	1
7	2	2
8	2	2
9	2	3
10	2	3
11	1	5
12	1	6
13	2	3
14	2	4
15	2	4

Data Matrix in SPSS for Windows

	A	B
1	Model	No Model
2	3	1
3	4	2
4	5	2
5	5	3
6	5	3
7	5	3
8	6	4
9	6	4
10	6	4
11	7	5
12		
13		

Excel Method of Data Input

t Test: Two-Sample Assuming Equal Variances

	Model	No Model
Mean	5.200	3.100
Variance	1.289	1.433
Observations	10.000	10.000
Pooled Variance	1.361	
Hypothesized Mean Difference	0.000	
df	18.000	
t Stat	4.025	
P(T<=t) one-tail	0.000	
t Critical one-tail	1.734	
P(T<=t) two-tail	0.001	
t Critical two-tail	2.101	

Output for a t test using Excel

FIGURE 6   Sample input and output using data from the chapter **"Understanding Research Results: Description and Correlation," Figure 1** (modeling experiment)

many values such as reaction time or rating scales (also called continuous variables). We will not address variables with ordinal scale values.

Research Studying Two Variables (Bivariate Research)

In these cases, the researcher is studying whether two variables are related. In general we would refer to the first variable as the independent variable (IV) and the second variable as the dependent variable (DV). However, because it does not matter whether we are doing experimental or nonexperimental research, we could just as easily refer to the two variables as Variable X and Variable Y or Variable A and Variable B.

IV	DV	Statistical test
Nominal *Right-handed; left-handed*	Nominal *Vegetarian—yes/no*	Chi-square
Nominal (2 groups) *Right-handed; left-handed*	Interval/ratio *Grade point average*	*t* test
Nominal (3 groups) *Study time (low, medium, high)*	Interval/ratio *Test score*	One-way analysis of variance
Interval/ratio *Optimism score*	Interval/ratio *Sick days last year*	Pearson correlation

Research with Multiple Independent Variables

In the following situations, we have more-complex research designs with two or more independent variables that are studied with a single outcome or dependent variable.

IV	DV	Statistical test
Nominal (2 or more variables)	Interval/ratio	Analysis of variance (factorial design)
Interval/ratio (2 or more variables)	Interval/ratio	Multiple regression

These research design situations have been described in previous chapters. There are, of course, many other types of designs. Designs with multiple variables (multivariate statistics) are described in detail by Tabachnick and Fidell (2013). Procedures for research using ordinal level measurement may be found in books by Siegel and Castellan (1988) and Corder and Foreman (2009).

Next, go to **Check Your Learning:** Practice Exercise #2 and match the independent/dependent variable combination to the correct statistical test.

CRITICAL THINKING: BEING A SKILLED CONSUMER OF RESEARCH

1. In an experiment, one group of research participants is given 10 pages of material to proofread for errors. Another group proofreads the same material on a computer screen. The dependent variable is the number of errors detected in a 5-minute period. A .05 significance (alpha) level is used to evaluate the results.

   a. What statistical test would you use?
   b. What is the null hypothesis? The research hypothesis?
   c. Given the hypothesis, what is the Type I error? The Type II error?
   d. What is the probability of making a Type I error?
   e. When Professor Rodríguez conducted the proofreading study, the average number of errors detected in the print and computer conditions was 38.4 and 13.2, respectively; this difference was not statistically significant. When Professor Seuss conducted the same experiment, the means of the two groups were 21.1 and 14.7, but the difference was statistically significant. Explain how this could happen.

2. A researcher investigated attitudes toward individuals in wheelchairs. The question was: Would people react differently to a person they perceived as being temporarily confined to the wheelchair than to a person they perceived as having a permanent disability? Participants were randomly assigned to two groups. Individuals in one group each worked on various tasks with a confederate in a wheelchair; members of the other group worked with the same confederate in a wheelchair, but this time the confederate wore a leg cast. After the session was over, participants filled out a questionnaire regarding their reactions to the study. One question asked, "Would you be willing to work with your test partner in the future on a class assignment?" with "yes" and "no" as the only response alternatives. What would be the appropriate significance test for this experiment? Can you offer a critique of the dependent variable? If you changed the dependent variable, would it affect your choice of significance tests? If yes, how?

Check Your Learning: Practice Exercises

Practice Exercise #1

A simple random sample of the inhabitants of the Island of Broccoli was selected. There are 5,000 inhabitants, and the sample was 100 inhabitants. Everyone who was identified in the sample agreed to be studied (Broccolivians are very agreeable people). Two pieces of data were collected from each person in the sample: the presence or absence of the "Broccoli gene" (**https://www.livescie nce.com/39578-why-some-hate-broccoli.html**), which determines whether broccoli tastes bitter to the person (Lipchock et al., 2013), and general evaluation of broccoli on a scale of 1 to 10.

1. First, answer these questions:
   a. How many members are in the population?
   b. How many members are in the sample?

2. Next, given the hypothesis—people without the "broccoli gene" will like broccoli more than people with the gene—answer the following questions:

a. What statistical test should be used to test the hypothesis? Why?

b. Given the hypothesis, should we use a one-tailed or two-tailed test? Why?

3. Now, answer these questions related to statistical significance and error:

a. You conduct the statistical test (alpha = .05) and conclude there is a significant difference in broccoli preference between those with and without the gene. Describe what the Type I error would be in this case.

b. You conduct the statistical test (alpha = .05) and conclude there is not a significant difference in broccoli preference between those with and without the gene. Describe what the Type II error would be in this case.

Practice Exercise #2

For each of the independent variable–dependent variable combinations below, indicate the appropriate statistical test procedure: 1. *F* test (analysis of variance). 2. *t* test. 3. Chi-square test. 4. Pearson correlation coefficient. 5. Multiple regression.

Independent variable(s)	Dependent variable(s)	Statistical test procedure
Age (under 21; over 21)	Number of alcoholic beverages in past 2 weeks	
Age in years	Number of alcoholic beverages in past 2 weeks	
Age in years; Exercise hours per week	Number of alcoholic beverages in past 2 weeks	
Enrollment in college (yes; no)	Any alcohol use in past month (yes; no)	
Age (under 21; over 21); Enrollment in college (yes; no)	Number of alcoholic beverages in past 2 weeks	

(Answers are provided at the end of this chapter.)

CHAPTER REVIEW

Review Questions

1. Distinguish between the null hypothesis and the research hypothesis. When does the researcher decide to reject the null hypothesis?

2. What is meant by statistical significance?

3. What factors are most important in determining whether obtained results will be significant?

4. Distinguish between a Type I and a Type II error. Why is your significance level the probability of making a Type I error?

5. What factors are involved in choosing a significance level?

6. What influences the probability of a Type II error?

7. What is the difference between statistical significance and practical significance?

8. Discuss the reasons a researcher might obtain nonsignificant results.

Study Terms

Alpha level	Probability
Analysis of variance (*F* test)	Research hypothesis
Confidence interval	Sampling distribution
Degrees of freedom	Statistical significance
Error variance	Systematic variance
F test	*t* test
Inferential statistics	Type I error
Null hypothesis	Type II error
Power	

Check Your Learning: Answers

Practice Exercise #1

1a. 5,000; b. 100; 2a. t test, the dependent variable is an interval scale; b. one tailed, the hypothesis states a direction—that the average broccoli score would be higher as opposed to just 'different'; 3a. when there is no difference in the population, a Type I error would be incorrectly concluding that the difference observed in the sample is true in the population; 3b. when there is a difference in the population, a Type II error would be incorrectly concluding that there is no difference in the population.

Practice Exercise #2

Independent variable(s)	Dependent variable(s)	Statistical test procedure
Age (under 21; over 21)	Number of alcoholic beverages in past 2 weeks	2. *t* test
Age in years	Number of alcoholic beverages in past 2 weeks	4. Pearson correlation coefficient
Age in years; Exercise hours per week	Number of alcoholic beverages in past 2 weeks	5. Multiple regression
Enrollment in college (yes; no)	Any alcohol use in past month (yes; no)	3. Chi-square
Age (under 21; over 21) Enrollment in college (yes; no)	Number of alcoholic beverages in past 2 weeks	1. *F* test

14 Generalization

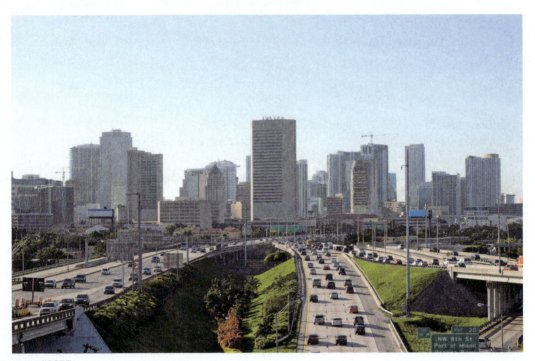

©Jonathang/123RF

LEARNING OBJECTIVES

- Discuss the issues created by generalizing research results to other populations, including potential problems with using college students as research participants.
- Discuss issues to consider regarding generalization of research results across various human identities (e.g., sex and gender, race and ethnicity) and cultures.
- Describe the potential problem of generalizing to other experimenters and suggest possible solutions.
- Discuss the importance of replications, distinguishing between exact replications and conceptual replications.
- Distinguish between narrative literature reviews and meta-analyses.

In this chapter, we will consider the issue of generalization of research findings. When a single study is conducted with a particular sample and procedure, can the results be generalized to other populations of research participants, or to other ways of manipulating or measuring the variables? Recall from the chapter **"Fundamental Research Issues"** that internal validity refers to the accuracy of conclusions drawn about cause and effect. **External validity** is the extent to which findings may be generalized.

GENERALIZING TO OTHER POPULATIONS

Even though a researcher may randomly assign participants to experimental conditions, rarely are participants randomly selected from the general population. Individuals who participate in psychological research are usually selected because they are available, and the most available population consists of college students—or more specifically, first- and second-year students enrolled in the introductory psychology course to satisfy a general education requirement. They may also be from a particular college or university, may be volunteers, or may be mostly males or mostly females. So, are our research findings limited to these types of subjects, or can we generalize our findings to a more general population? After considering these issues, we will examine the larger issue of culture and how research findings can be generalized to different cultural groups.

College Students

Smart (1966) found that college students were studied in over 70% of the articles published between 1962 and 1964 in the *Journal of Experimental Psychology* and the *Journal of Abnormal and Social Psychology*. Later, Sears (1986) reported finding similar percentages in 1980 and 1985 in a variety of social psychology journals; Arnett (2008) found that 67% of the articles in the 2007 volume of the *Journal of Personality and Social Psychology* used college student samples. Because research using college students is research on a highly restricted population—generally first- and second-year students taking the introductory psychology class—the subjects tend to be young and to possess the characteristics of emerging adults: a sense of self-identity that is still developing, social and political attitudes that are in a state of flux, a high need for peer approval, and unstable peer relationships. Furthermore, they are college students, which means that they are intelligent and have other characteristics associated with academic success (e.g., cognitive abilities, test-wiseness). So, what we learn from such studies might apply only to a highly select and unusual group, and not to "people in general." Indeed, Peterson (2001) found that students, as a group, are more homogeneous than nonstudent samples. That is, students are more similar to each other than adults are similar to other adults in the general population.

Research by Henry (2008) illustrates how the use of college students may affect the external validity of research on prejudice. In his sample of articles from 1990 to 2005, an increasing percentage of studies used college students as participants. Further, in looking at the actual results of studies on prejudice that compared college students with adults, he reported a variety of differences among adults and college students. For example, college students were less conservative and rated women and ethnic minorities more favorably. If we are to understand something about prejudice in humans, we need to also study people who are not college-students!

Volunteers

In most cases, ethics dictate that researchers must ask people to volunteer to participate in their research. At many colleges, introductory psychology students are required either to volunteer for research or to complete an alternative project. If you are studying populations other than college students, you are even more dependent on volunteers—for example, asking people living in an apartment complex to participate in a study of neighborliness, or conducting research on the internet in which people must go to your Web page and then agree to participate in the study, or conducting a telephone survey of county residents to determine health care needs. In all these cases, external validity of the findings may be limited because the data from volunteers may be different from what would be obtained with a more general sample. For instance, neighborliness is likely associated with volunteering!

Research indicates that volunteers differ in various ways from nonvolunteers. In their comprehensive study on the topic, Rosenthal and Rosnow (1975) reported that volunteers tend to be more highly educated, of a higher socioeconomic status, more in need of approval, and more social.

Finally, it seems that different kinds of people volunteer for different kinds of experiments. In colleges, there may be a sign-up board with the titles of many studies listed or a Web page that manages research participants and volunteer opportunities for the university. People drawn to a study titled "Problem Solving" might be significantly different from people who are drawn to a study titled "Interaction in Small Groups" or one titled "Feeling Anxious?" Available evidence indicates that the title on a call for participants does influence who signs up (Hood & Back, 1971; Silverman & Margulis, 1973).

Online Research Participants

Another important consideration arises when asking participants to volunteer for online surveys and experiments. Researchers can find potential participants through online survey design services. Psychologists are increasingly using Amazon Mechanical Turk or mTurk (**https://www.mturk.com**; Buhrmester et al., 2011; Chandler, 2017; Jacquet, 2011), a website for recruiting people to work on many types of tasks including participating in research for a specified payment. This sort of sampling strategy has important implications for external validity. Although the online sample is more diverse than the typical college student sample, there are still generalization issues because internet users represent a unique demographic, although this is changing over time. It is estimated that 90% of U.S. adults use the internet, and the share of Americans who say that they own a smartphone has increased from 35% in 2011 to 81% in 2019 (Pew Research Center Internet & Technology, 2019). The Pew Research Center's Internet and American Life Project (Pew Internet, 2010) found that living in an urban/suburban area, being college educated, being younger, and having a higher income are all related to reporting more time online. Thus, by asking for volunteers for an online survey, researchers are sampling from a particular demographic that may not generalize well to the population of interest.

Sex, Gender, Race, and Identity

Humans have multiple identities, and those identities can have an impact on how they react to, respond to, and comply with research projects. Among our most central identities are sex, gender, race, and ethnicity. These are themselves important areas for research. They are also important when we evaluate the external validity of research. The American Psychological Association (2017) published a framework for researchers to help support competent multicultural research in the context of identities.

Sex and Gender

Our collective understanding of sex and gender has evolved rapidly, as has the language around these topics. Although the terms *sex* and *gender* are frequently used interchangeably, it is important to remember that the term *sex* generally refers to a biological classification and *gender* generally refers to a sociocultural classification.

Sex differences refer to biological differences. Although *sex* generally refers to being biologically male or female, people may have variations on sex chromosomes, as is the case with intersex individuals. The term *gender* is used to focus on social roles, groups, and identities associated with sex in a given culture and the term *gender identity* refers to a person's own personal and psychological identity related to sex. Of course, there is significant diversity in gender identity—for example, transgender individuals whose gender identity does not match their sex at birth, or people who identify as non-binary (neither male nor female). The term *cisgender* refers to people for whom their biological sex matches their gender identity. The key, here, is to understand that the concepts of sex, gender, and gender identity are interrelated and complex.

Understanding this complexity is important because the history of psychology is full of examples of research in which only cisgender males or only cisgender females were studied (Denmark et al., 1988). For example, research on achievement motivation only studied male subjects, and researchers asking about contraception typically studied only females. In the past, many researchers did not even report the number of males and females in the description of their study. Even if they did collect data on participant sex or gender, they did not report whether the results applied to both males and females. Therefore, in many cases it is not clear whether the results of specific studies can be generalized to all humans or only to specific human subgroups.

Ultimately, researchers should not exclude sex or gender categories when recruiting or studying participants. If a researcher has a research question and would like to generalize to all humans, then they need to make sure that their samples are representative of all humans and this includes differences in sex, gender, and gender identity.

Race and Ethnicity

Classifying people by race is very complicated. The history of psychology is full of examples of research in which only people who are white were studied (Guthrie, 2004). At a time when race was considered to be only a biological feature of humans, as few as three categories were used (Black; Caucasian/White; Asian). The U.S. Census is required by law to have five categories for a race question: White, Black or African American, American Indian or Alaska Native, Asian, and Native Hawaiian or Other Pacific Islander. Many people objected that these categories do not reflect the diversity of racial self-identification. Therefore the 2010 U.S. census experimented with a new question that identified 15 categories: White; Black, African American, or Negro; American Indian or Alaska Native; Asian Indian; Japanese; Chinese; Filipino; Korean; Vietnamese; Native Hawaiian; Samoan; Guamanian or Chamorro; Other Pacific Islander; Other Asian (**https://www.censu s.gov/prod/cen2010/briefs/c2010br-02.pdf**). It also allowed respondents to choose as many categories as they like. The new question is much closer to the categories people use as they describe themselves in a way that may include some combination of race, ethnicity, and nationality and may include multiracial self-identification as well. An advantage of the new system is that more respondents complete the race question.

The construct of race is made more complex by the independent concept of ethnicity. The 2010 U.S. census asked if respondents identify as "Hispanic, Latino, or Spanish origin." If so, respondents are asked to select a specific Hispanic, Latino, or Spanish ethnic group: Mexican, Mexican American, or Chicano; Puerto Rican; Cuban; another Hispanic Latino, or Spanish origin category such as Argentinian, Colombian, Dominican. A new question was proposed for the 2020 census, but it will not be implemented (**https://www.npr.org/2018/0 1/26/580865378/census-request-suggests-no-race-ethnicity-data-changes-in-2020-experts-say**).

Asking about race and ethnicity is very important in the census and in surveys in which the data are going to be used for making policy decisions for such things as housing and education. For issues of external validity, we are most interested in the ways that research findings generalize to people from different racial and ethnic identities. This is an important issue for researchers who study the psychology of race, ethnicity, and culture.

Location

The location where participants are recruited can also have an impact on a study's external validity. Participants in one locale may differ from participants in another locale. For example, students at the University of California, Los Angeles, may differ from students at a nearby state university, who in turn may differ from students at a community college. People in Iowa may differ from people in New York City. Thus, a finding obtained with the students in one type of educational setting or in one geographic region may not generalize to people in other settings or regions. In fact, studies have explored how personality traits like extraversion (the tendency to seek social stimulation) and openness to new experiences vary across geographic areas. Rentfrow et al. (2008) looked at geographic differences in personality traits among citizens of various U.S. states and found extraversion to vary by state. People in midwestern states tended to be more extraverted than people in northeastern states, and people in western states tended to be more open to new experiences. Thus, a study conducted in one location may not generalize well to another, particularly if the variables in question are related to location in some way.

Culture

Whether theories and research findings generalize across cultures is a critically important issue. Some observers of current psychological research have been very critical of the types of samples employed in behavioral research. Based on analyses of published research by Arnett (2008) and others, Henrich et al. (2010) contend that psychology is built on the study of WEIRD (Western, Educated, Industrialized, Rich, Democratic) people. In many cases, research samples consist primarily of college students from the United States, other English-speaking countries, and Europe. Ultimately, researchers wish to discover aspects of human behavior that have universal applications but in fact cannot generalize beyond their limited samples. At its heart this is a critique of the external validity of behavioral research: Does our human behavioral research generalize to all humans, or is it really a study of the WEIRD?

Clearly, if psychologists want to understand human behavior, they must understand human behavior across and among cultures (Henrich et al., 2010; Miller, 1999). Miller (1999) described research on self-concept by Kitayama et al. (1997) to illustrate the benefits of incorporating culture into psychological theory. Traditional theories of self-concept are grounded in the culture of the United States and Western Europe; the "self" is an individualistic concept where people are independent from others and self-enhancement comes from individual achievements. Kitayama and his colleagues take a broader, cultural perspective: In contrast to the U.S. meaning of self, in other cultures the "self" is a collective concept in which self-esteem is derived from relationships with others. Often, Japanese engage in self-criticism, which can be seen as relationship-maintaining, whereas Americans work to maintain and enhance self-esteem—thus, very different activities contribute to a positive self-concept in the two cultures (Kitayama et al., 1997). This is a very common theme in research that incorporates culture in psychological processes: "The significance of self-esteem, however, may be much more specific to a culture than has typically been supposed in the literature" (p. 1262).

Much of this cultural research centers on identifying similarities and differences that may exist in personality and other psychological characteristics, as well as ways that individuals from different cultures respond to the same environments (Matsumoto, 1994). Research by Kim et al. (2008) provides another example of the limits of external validity across cultural groups. This research focused on how people from different cultures use social support to cope with stress. In reviewing the research on the topic, they concluded that Asians and Asian Americans might benefit from different styles of social support as compared with European Americans. For example, Asian Americans are more likely to benefit from support that does not involve the sort of intense disclosure of personal stressful events and feelings that is the hallmark of support in many European American groups. Rather, they suggest that Asians and Asian Americans may benefit more from support that comes with the comforts of proximity (being with close friends) rather than sharing.

These examples all focused on differences among cultures. Many studies also find similarities across cultures. Evolutionary psychologists, for instance, often conduct studies in different cultural groups because they are looking for similarities across cultures in order to see if a particular behavior or attitude can be tied to our evolutionary past. For example, Singh et al. (2010) wanted to see if a particular aspect of beauty that is tied to greater reproductive success—namely, waist-to-hip ratio (e.g., the ratio for a 25-inch waist and 35-inch hips is .71), which is related to sex hormones and thus fertility—would be seen as attractive across cultures. Diverse groups from Africa, Samoa, Indonesia, and New Zealand evaluated photographs of females with small and large waist-to-hip ratios. The researchers found that indeed, low waist-to-hip ratio among females was seen as more attractive across all these groups. In this example, the results obtained in one culture do generalize to other cultures.

Finally, we should emphasize that behavioral research across the globe has increased dramatically and researchers everywhere now have more direct access to this literature. To illustrate, the PsycINFO database now includes over 2,200 journals published in multiple countries and languages, with new journals added regularly (**https://www.apa.org/pubs/databases/psycinfo/coverage**). It is becoming much easier to examine the role that culture plays in human behavior.

Nonhuman Animals

We noted in the chapter **"Ethics in Behavioral Research"** that about 7% of psychological research is conducted with nonhuman animals. Almost all of this research is done with rats, mice, and birds. Most research with other species is conducted to study the behavior of those animals directly, in order to gather information that may help with the survival of endangered species and increase our understanding of our bonds with nonhuman animals such as dogs, cats, and horses (**https://www.apa-hai.org/human-animal-interaction**).

The basic research that psychologists conduct with nonhuman animals is usually done with the expectation that the findings can be generalized to humans. This research is important because the research problems that are addressed require procedures such as long-term observation that could not be done with human samples. We do expect that we can generalize, because our underlying biological and behavioral patterns are shared. In fact, the value of studying nonhuman animals has been demonstrated by research that does apply to humans. These applications include the biological bases of memory, food preferences, sexual behavior, choice behavior, and drug addictions. The American Psychological Association's brochure on animal research is available at **https://www.apa.org/research/responsible/research-animals.pdf**.

In Defense of College Students

It is easy to criticize research on the basis of subject characteristics, yet criticism by itself does not mean that results cannot be generalized. Although we need to be concerned about the potential problems of generalizing from unique populations such as college students (Sears, 1986), we should also keep several things in mind when thinking about this issue. First, criticisms of the use of any particular type of subject, such as college students, in a study should be backed with good reasons for expecting that a relationship would not be found with other types of subjects. College students, after all, *are* human, and researchers should not be blamed for not worrying about generalization to a particular type of subject if there is no good reason to. Moreover, college student populations are increasingly diverse and increasingly representative of the society as a whole (although college students will always be characterized by having the ability and motivation to pursue a college degree). Second, replication of research studies provides a safeguard against the limited external validity of a single study. Studies are replicated at other colleges using different mixes of students, and many findings first established with college students are later found to apply to other populations, such as children, aging adults, and people in other countries. It is also worth noting that internet samples are increasingly used in many types of studies. Although such studies raise their own issues of external validity, they frequently complement studies based on college student samples.

GENERALIZING ACROSS METHODS

The person who actually conducts the experiment is the source of another external validity problem. In most research, only one experimenter is used, and rarely is much attention paid to the personal characteristics of the experimenter (McGuigan, 1963). The main goal is to make sure that any influence the experimenter has on subjects is constant throughout the experiment. There is always the possibility, however, that the results are generalizable only to certain types of experimenters.

Some of the important characteristics of experimenters have been discussed by Kintz and his colleagues (1965). These include the experimenter's personality and gender and amount of practice in the role of experimenter. A warm, friendly experimenter will almost certainly produce different results than will a cold, unfriendly experimenter. Participants also may behave differently with male and female experimenters. It has even been shown that rabbits learn faster when trained by experienced experimenters (Brogden, 1962)! The influence of the experimenter may depend as well on the characteristics of the participants. For example, participants seem to perform better when tested by an experimenter of the other sex (Stevenson & Allen, 1964).

One solution to the problem of generalizing to other experimenters is to use two or more experimenters. A fine example of the use of multiple experimenters is a study by Rubin (1975), who sent several male and female experimenters to the Boston airport to investigate self-disclosure. The experimenters revealed different kinds of information about themselves to both male and female travelers and recorded the passengers' self-disclosures in return. One interesting result was that women tended to reveal more about themselves to male experimenters, and men tended to reveal more about themselves to female experimenters.

Pretests and Generalization

Researchers are often faced with the decision of whether to give a pretest. Intuitively, pretesting seems to be a good idea. The researcher can be sure that the groups are equivalent on the pretest, and it is often more satisfying to see that individuals changed their scores than it is to look only at group means on a posttest. A pretest also enables the researcher to assess mortality (attrition) effects when it is likely that some participants will withdraw from an experiment. If you give a pretest, you can determine whether the people who withdrew are different from those who completed the study.

Pretesting, however, may limit the ability to generalize to populations that did not receive a pretest (see Lana, 1969). Simply taking the pretest may cause subjects to behave differently than they would without the pretest. Recall from the chapter **"Experimental Design"** that a Solomon four-group design (Solomon, 1949) can be used in situations in which a pretest is desirable but there is concern over the possible impact of taking the pretest. In the **Solomon four-group design,** half of the participants are given the pretest; the other half receive the posttest only. That is, the same experiment is conducted with and without the pretest. Mortality effects can be assessed in the pretest conditions. Also, the researcher can examine whether there is an interaction between the independent variable and the pretest: Are posttest scores on the dependent variable different depending on whether the pretest was given? Sometimes researchers find that it is not feasible to conduct the study with all four groups in a single experiment. In this case, the first study can include the pretest; the study can be replicated later without the pretest.

Generalizing from Laboratory Settings

Research conducted in a laboratory setting has the advantage of allowing the experimenter to study the impact of independent variables under highly controlled conditions. In this sort of highly controlled environment, the internal validity of the research is the primary consideration. But does the artificiality of the laboratory setting limit the ability to generalize what is observed in the laboratory to real-life settings? Consider, for instance, a carefully controlled laboratory study of college student learning in which participants are invited into a room, shown a "lecture" on a screen, and then asked to recall different facts from the lecture. While this sort of experiment may provide an opportunity to manipulate variables to test their impact on "learning," it is what we would call a simulated classroom rather than the actual lived experience of students in a classroom, with real grades on the line, an interactive lecturer, several students talking to each other, and another distractingly watching YouTube! On the other hand, it would be difficult to run a study with clear and clean findings tying an independent variable to a dependent variable given the "noise" of the live classroom.

Mook (1983) articulated one response to the artificiality issue: Generalization to real-life settings is not relevant when the purpose of the study is to investigate causal relationships under carefully controlled conditions. Mook is concerned that a "knee-jerk" criticism of laboratory research on the basis of external validity is too common. Good research is what is most important.

Another response to the laboratory artificiality criticism is to examine the results of field experiments. Recall from the chapter **"Fundamental Research Issues"** that in a field experiment, the researcher manipulates the independent variable in a natural setting—a factory, a school, or a street corner, for example.

Anderson et al. (1999) asked whether laboratory and field experiments that examine the same variables do produce the same results. To answer this question, they found 38 pairs of studies for which a laboratory investigation had a field experiment counterpart. The studies were drawn from a variety of research areas, including aggression, helping, memory, leadership style, and depression. Results of the laboratory and field experiments were very similar—the effect size of the independent variable on the dependent variable was very similar in the two types of studies. Thus, even though lab and field experiments are conducted in different settings, the results are complementary rather than contradictory. When findings are replicated using multiple methods, our confidence in the external validity of the findings increases.

SUPPORTING GOOD EXTERNAL VALIDITY

It may seem as if no research can possibly be generalizable! In some ways this is true. Furthermore, it can be very difficult to understand the extent to which a study is generalizable; external validity is an aspect of a study that we try to assess, but cannot truly know. How, then, can we support good external validity? There are a few ways that external validity can be supported.

The key means of supporting external validity is related to a study's methodology. Using a census or a random sample will always produce better external validity than using a nonrandom sample. This, of course, is not always possible. Here we will explore a few other ways in which external validity can be supported.

Generalization as a Statistical Interaction

The problem of generalization can be thought of as an interaction in a factorial design (see the chapter **"Complex Experimental Designs"**). An interaction occurs when a relationship between variables exists under one condition but not under another, or when the nature of the relationship is different in one condition than in another. Thus, if you question the generalizability of a study that used only males, you are suggesting that there is an interaction between sex and the independent variable. Suppose, for example, that a study examines the relationship between crowding and aggression among males and reports that crowding is associated with higher levels of aggression. You might then question whether the results are generalizable to females.

Figure 1 shows four potential outcomes of a hypothetical study on crowding and aggression that tested both males and females. In each graph, the relationship between crowding and aggression for males has been maintained. In Graph A, there is no interaction—the behavior of males and females is virtually identical. Thus, the results of the original all-male study could be generalized to females. In Graph B, there is also no interaction; the effect of crowding is identical for males and females. However, in this graph, males are more aggressive than females. Although such a difference is interesting, it is not a factor in generalization because the overall relationship between crowding and aggression is present for males and females.

Graphs C and D do show interactions. In both, the original results with males cannot be generalized to females. In Graph C, there is no relationship between crowding and aggression for females. In Graph D, the interaction tells us that a positive relationship between crowding and aggression exists for males but that a negative relationship exists for females. As it turns out, Graph D describes the results of several studies on this topic (cf. Freedman et al., 1972).

Researchers can address issues of external validity that stem from the use of different populations by including subject type as a variable in the study. By including variables such as gender, age, or ethnic group in the design of the study, the results may be analyzed to determine whether there are interaction effects like the ones illustrated in **Figure 1.**

The Importance of Replications

Replication of research is a way of overcoming any problems of generalization that occur in a single study. There are two types of replications to consider: exact replications and conceptual replications.

Exact Replications

An **exact replication** is an attempt to precisely replicate the procedures of a study to see whether the same results are obtained. A researcher who obtains an unexpected finding will frequently attempt a replication to make sure that the finding is reliable. If you are starting your own work on a problem, you may try to replicate a crucial study to make sure that you understand the procedures and can obtain the same results. Often, exact replications occur when a researcher builds on the findings of a prior study. For example, suppose you are intrigued by Singh et al.'s (2010) research on waist-to-hip ratio that was mentioned previously. Singh reports that males rate females with a ratio of .70 as most attractive. In your research, you might replicate the procedures used in the original study and expand on the original research. For example, you might study this phenomenon with males similar to those in the original sample as well as males from different cultures or age groups. When you replicate the original research findings using very similar procedures, your confidence in the external validity of the original findings is increased.

The "Mozart effect" provides us with an interesting example of the importance of replications. In the original study by Rauscher et al. (1993), college students listened to 10 minutes of a Mozart sonata. These students then showed better performance on a spatial-reasoning measure drawn from the Stanford-Binet Intelligence Scale than students exposed to a relaxation tape or simple silence. This finding received a great deal of attention in the press as people quickly generalized it to the possibility of increasing children's intelligence by having them listen to Mozart sonatas. In fact, one state governor began producing Mozart CDs to distribute in maternity wards, and entrepreneurs began selling Mozart kits to parents over the internet. Over the next few years, however, there were many failures to replicate the Mozart effect (see Steele et al., 1999). We noted above that failures to replicate may occur because the exact conditions for producing the effect were not used. In this case, Rauscher and Shaw (1998) responded to the many replication failures by precisely describing the conditions necessary to produce the Mozart effect. However, Steele et al. (1999) and McCutcheon (2000) were unable to obtain the effect even though they followed the recommendations of Rauscher and Shaw.

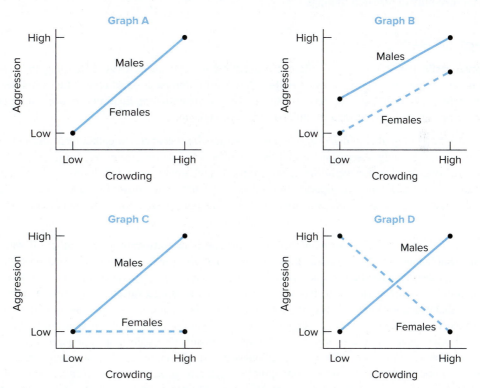

FIGURE 1   Outcomes of a hypothetical experiment on crowding and aggression

Note: The presence of an interaction indicates that the results for males cannot be generalized to females.

Research on the Mozart effect continues. Some recent findings suggest that the effect is limited to music that also increases arousal, and that it is this arousal that can cause better performance following exposure to the music (Thompson et al., 2001). Bangerter and Heath (2004) present a detailed analysis of the development of the research on the Mozart effect.

A single failure to replicate does not reveal much, though; it is unrealistic to assume, on the basis of a single failure to replicate, that the previous research is necessarily invalid. Failures to replicate share the same problems as nonsignificant results, discussed in the chapter **"Understanding Research Results: Statistical Inference."** A failure to replicate could mean that the original results are invalid, but it could also mean that the replication attempt was flawed. For example, if the replication is based on the procedure as reported in a journal article, it is possible that the article omitted an important aspect of the procedure. For this reason, it is usually a good idea to write to the researcher to obtain detailed information on all of the materials that were used in the study.

Several scientific societies are encouraging systematic replications of important scientific findings. The journal *Perspectives on Psychological Science* (published by the Association for Psychological Science) is sponsoring the publication of Registered Research Replications (**https://www.psychologicalscience.org/index.php/re plication**). Multiple groups of researchers will undertake replications of important studies using procedures that are made public before initiating the research. When completed, all of the replications will be described in a single report. In addition to the Psychological Science initiative, the online journal *PLOS ONE* (*Public Library of Science*) has developed the Reproducibility Initiative to encourage independent replication of research in the clinical sciences (Pattinson, 2012). Such developments should lead to greater understanding of the generalizability of research findings.

Conceptual Replications

A **conceptual replication** is the use of different procedures to replicate a research finding. In a conceptual replication, researchers attempt to understand the relationships among abstract conceptual variables by using new, or different, operational definitions of those variables. Conceptual replications are even more important than exact replications in furthering our understanding of behavior.

In most research, a key goal is to discover whether a relationship between conceptual variables exists. In the original Mozart effect study, researchers examined the effect of *exposure to classical music* on *spatial reasoning*. These are conceptual variables; in the actual study, specific operational definitions of the variables were used. *Exposure to classical music* was operationalized as 10 minutes of exposure to the Mozart Sonata for Two Pianos in D Major. *Spatial reasoning* was operationalized as performance on a particular spatial reasoning measure.

In a conceptual replication, the same independent variable is operationalized in a different way, and the dependent variable may be measured in a different way, too. Conceptual replications are extremely important in the social sciences because the variables used are complex and can be operationalized in many ways. Complete understanding of any variable involves studying the variable using a variety of operational definitions. A crucial generalization question is whether the relationship holds when other ways of manipulating or measuring the variables are studied. Sometimes the conceptual replication may involve an alternative stimulus (e.g., a different Mozart sonata, or a selection by a different composer) or an alternative dependent measure (e.g., a different spatial reasoning task). Or as we previously noted, the same variables are sometimes studied in both laboratory and field settings. When conceptual replications produce similar results, our confidence in the generalizability of relationships between variables is greatly increased.

This discussion should also alert you to an important way of thinking about research findings. The findings represent relationships between conceptual variables but are grounded in specific operations. You may read

Open Science and Replication

In 2012, the Open Science Collaboration launched an effort to understand the replicability of behavioral research. "Reproducibility," they noted, "is a defining feature of science." To study reproducibility, the leaders of the Open Science Collaboration initiated a large-scale project to conduct replications of 100 studies published in three psychology journals. Researchers from around the globe joined in to complete the studies. The results were published with the title "Estimating the Reproducibility of Psychological Science" (Open Science Collaboration, 2015). The results were disappointing: Depending on the criteria used to define a successful replication, 36% to 47% of the replications projects were successful. That is, when other scientists tried to replicate studies from the past, less than half were successful. As you can imagine, this attracted a great deal of media attention with newspaper and Web-based features describing the "replication crisis" facing psychology.

How should this result be interpreted? As with any failure to replicate, there are numerous possible explanations. One is that too many journal articles in psychology are reporting results that cannot be replicated—a Type I error. We should note that the replication study included articles primarily in social or cognitive psychology published in just three journals. We should also note that the cognitive psychology articles were more likely to be replicated than were the social psychology articles. Of course, even before the report from the Open Science group there had been concerns about problems replicating many recent studies on unconscious priming that were being published in social psychology journals (Kahneman, 2012). There are other explanations. Gilbert et al. (2016) noted, along with Kahneman (2014), that replications are most likely to be successful when the original author is involved. Some of the Open Science replications were given prior approval by the original researcher, and these had more successful replications (Gilbert et al., 2016). In addition, original research results with greater effect sizes were more often replicated. It may be that statistically significant findings with small effect sizes need replication research with large sample sizes and attention paid to the smallest details of methodology. Finally, the Open Science replications attempted exact replications—it may be that the unsuccessful replications were particularly tied to the context of the subject populations, the independent variable manipulation, or the dependent measures (Gilbert et al., 2016; Open Science Collaboration, 2015).

We hope, along with Anderson et al. (2016), that the reproducibility project motivates researchers to attempt to replicate more studies and discover the factors that lead to reproducible research findings. Moreover, *you* can help resolve this "crisis" by doing good science. By conducting well-designed research and writing detailed, well-written research reports, you can play a critical role in addressing the crisis. When research reports are sufficiently detailed so as to make studies easy to replicate—and much of what we have described in this book is related to you learning how to do just that—findings can be replicated. You can participate in the open science movement. By making data sets publicly accessible, and publishing in journals that have wide access, you support replications. In science, answers to questions and problems are found in the data.

The Collaborative Replications and Education Project (CREP) (**https://osf.io/wfc6u/**) is a project designed to support undergraduate students and their mentors in the completion of replication projects. it is housed within the Open Science Framework, which is a free and open-source software project designed to facilitate open collaboration in science. As an example of CREP's work, seven teams of researchers conducted replications of a study by Forest and Wood (2012). The summary and analysis of those replications was published by Leighton et al. (2018).

How can you get involved? CREP has a straightforward process to select the study, plan your replication, execute your replication, and submit a report: **https://osf.io/wfc6u/wiki/home/**

about the specific methods employed in a study conducted 20 years ago and question whether the study could be replicated today. You might also speculate that the methods used in a study are so unusual that they could never generalize to other situations. These concerns are not as serious when placed within the context of conceptual replications, because although operational definitions can change over time, the underlying conceptual variable often remains more consistent. Admittedly, a specific method from a study conducted at one time might not be effective today, given changes in today's political and cultural climate. A conceptual replication of the manipulation, however, might demonstrate that the relationship between the conceptual theoretical variables is still present. Similarly, the narrow focus of a particular study is less problematic if the general finding is replicated with different procedures.

Evaluating Generalizations via Literature Reviews and Meta-analyses

Researchers have traditionally drawn conclusions about the external validity of research findings by conducting literature reviews. In a **literature review,** a reviewer reads a number of studies that address a particular topic and then writes a paper that summarizes and evaluates the literature. The literature review provides information that (1) summarizes what has been found, (2) tells the reader which findings are strongly supported and which are only weakly supported in the literature, (3) points out inconsistent findings and areas in which research is lacking, and (4) discusses future directions for research.

Sometimes a review will be a narrative in which the author provides descriptions of research findings and draws conclusions about the literature. The conclusions in a narrative literature review are based on the reviewer's subjective impressions. Another technique for comparing a large number of studies in an area is **meta-analysis** (Borenstein et al., 2009). In a meta-analysis, the researcher combines the actual results of a number of studies. The analysis consists of a set of statistical procedures that employ effect sizes to compare a given finding across many different studies. Instead of relying on judgments obtained in a narrative literature review, you can draw statistical conclusions from this material. The statistical procedures need not concern you. They involve examining several features of the results of studies, including the effect sizes and significance levels obtained. The important point here is that meta-analysis is a method for determining the reliability of a finding by examining the results from many different studies.

Stewart and Chambless (2009) conducted a meta-analysis of research on the effectiveness of cognitive-behavioral therapy (CBT) for anxiety disorders. Both a traditional literature review and a meta-analysis begin with a body of previous research on a topic; in this case, Stewart and Chambless located 56 studies using CBT with adults diagnosed with an anxiety disorder (including panic disorder, social anxiety, post-traumatic stress disorder, generalized anxiety disorder, and obsessive-compulsive disorder). Studies that included an additional medication treatment were excluded. The researchers performed a statistical analysis of the results of these studies and concluded that CBT was effective in treating all of the types of anxiety disorders. In a traditional literature review, it can be difficult to provide the type of general conclusion that was reached with the meta-analysis because it is necessary to integrate information from many studies with different experimental designs, disorders, and measures of anxiety.

One of the most important reasons a meta-analysis can lead to clear conclusions is that meta-analytic studies focus on effect size (recall that an effect size represents the extent to which two variables are associated). A typical table in a meta-analysis will show the effect size obtained in a number of studies along with a summary of the average effect size across the studies. More important, the analysis allows comparisons of the effect sizes in different types of studies to allow tests of hypotheses. For example, Miller and Downey (1999) analyzed the results of 71 studies that examined the relationship between weight and self-esteem. **Table 1** shows a few of the findings. The effect size r averaged across all studies was $-.18$: Heavier weight is associated with lower self-esteem. However, several variables moderate the relationship between weight and self-esteem. Thus, the effect size is larger when the weight variable is a report of self-perceived rather than actual weight, and the relationship between weight and self-esteem is somewhat larger for females than for males. Finally, the effect is greater among individuals with a high socioeconomic background.

TABLE 1   Some meta-analysis findings for weight and self-esteem

Variable	Effect size r
Overall relationship	−.18
Weight measure	−.12
Actual weight	−.34
Self-perceived weight	
Gender	−.23
Females	−.19
Males	
Socioeconomic status (SES)	−.16
Low SES	−.19
Middle SES	−.31
High SES	

Source: Adapted from Miller and Downey (1999).

Both narrative reviews and meta-analyses provide valuable information and in fact are often complementary. A meta-analysis allows statistical, quantitative conclusions, whereas a narrative review identifies trends in the literature and directions for future study—a more qualitative approach. A study by Bushman and Wells (2001) points to an interesting way in which knowledge of meta-analysis can improve how we interpret information for literature reviews.

The reviewers in their study were undergraduates who were provided with both titles and information about the findings of 20 studies dealing with the effect of attitude similarity on attraction. Sometimes the titles were salient with respect to the findings ("Birds of a Feather Flock Together") and others were nonsalient ("Research Studies Who Likes Whom"). Salient titles are obviously easier to remember. When asked to draw conclusions about the findings, naive reviewers with no knowledge of meta-analysis overestimated the size of the similarity–attraction relationship when provided with salient titles. Other reviewers were given brief training in meta-analysis; these reviewers drew accurate conclusions about the actual findings. That is, they were not influenced by the article title. Thus, even without conducting a meta-analysis, a background in meta-analysis can be beneficial when reviewing research findings.

Now, test your knowledge of meta-analyses with **Check Your Learning:** Practice Exercise #1.

USING RESEARCH TO IMPROVE LIVES

In a presidential address to the American Psychological Association, George Miller (1969) discussed "psychology as a means of promoting human welfare" and spoke of "giving psychology away." Miller was addressing the broadest issue of generalization: taking what we know about human behavior and allowing it to be applied by many people in all areas of everyday life. Zimbardo's (2004) presidential address to the American Psychological Association described many ways in which Miller's call to give psychology away is being honored. The impact of psychological research can be seen in areas such as health (programs to promote health-related behaviors related to stress, heart disease, and sexually transmitted diseases), law and criminal justice (providing data on the effects of 6-person versus 12-person juries and showing how law enforcement personnel can improve the accuracy of eyewitness identification), education (providing methods for encouraging academic performance or reducing conflict among different ethnic groups), and work environments (providing workers with more control and improving how people interact with computers and other machines in the workplace). In addition, psychologists are using the internet to provide the public with information on parenting, education, mental health, and many other topics—for example, the websites of the American Psychological Association and the Association for Psychological Science (**https://www.apa.org**; **https://www.psychologicalscience.org**), national mental health resource websites (**https://www.mentalhealth.gov/** and **https://www.samhsa.gov/**), and many individual psychologists who are sharing their expertise with the public.

We have discussed a few of the ways research can improve people's lives. Despite all the potential problems of generalizing research findings that we have highlighted in this chapter—and other important critiques of research methods—the fact remains that science provides us with the best way to understand our world and our behavior.

ILLUSTRATIVE ARTICLE: GENERALIZING RESULTS

Driving around in a 4,000-pound automobile is a dangerous thing. Motor vehicle accidents are among the leading preventable causes of death in the United States every year. Distraction is one of the most common causes of automobile accidents, and talking to another person is a very common distraction.

In an effort to observe the impact of conversation on driving, Drews et al. (2008) conducted a study using a driving simulator that tracks errors committed by drivers. The researchers varied the type of conversation. In one condition, participants had a conversation with a passenger; in another condition, participants talked on a cell phone. There was also a no conversation, control condition. As you would expect, having any conversation resulted in more driving errors. However, the number of driving errors was highest in the cell phone condition.

For this exercise, acquire and read the article (available at **https://www.apa.org/pubs/journals/releases/xap-14-4-392.pdf**):

Drews, F., Pasupathi, M., & Strayer, D. (2008). Passenger and cell phone conversations in simulated driving. *Journal of Experimental Psychology: Applied, 14*(4) 392–400. https://doi.org/10.1037/a0013119

After reading the article, consider the following:

What was measured? How did the researchers measure driving errors?

What did they do?

1. Describe how well you think the sample of participants in this study generalizes to other groups of people.
2. In this study, participants were told to have a conversation about a time when "their lives were threatened." Do you think that the results of this study would be different if the conversation were about something else? How so? Why?

How do they know that one thing caused another? Evaluate the internal validity of this study. Explain your answer.

To what or whom can we generalize the results?

1. Do you think that the findings from this study would generalize to other cultures? Do you think that samples of college students in Mexico, Italy, and Germany would generate similar results? Why or why not?
2. Evaluate the external validity of this study. Explain your answer.
3. How well do you think the driving simulator generalizes to real-world driving? What would you change to improve the generalizability of the simulator?

CRITICAL THINKING: BEING A SKILLED CONSUMER OF RESEARCH

If you conducted a study using a sample of participants from your college or university, in what ways do you think the sample would:

  a. differ from the population of the city that your college/university is in?

  b. differ from the population of the state, or the population of the country?

  c. differ from other college student samples by gender, race, and/or ethnicity?

  d. differ from other college student samples by other factors (e.g., regional, cultural, social class)?

Check Your Learning: Practice Exercises

Practice Exercise #1

Fraundorf et al. (2019) conducted a meta-analysis of 232 previously conducted studies on aging and recognition memory (i.e., recognizing something that has been previously encountered: words, faces, pictures). They concluded that younger adults showed superior performance on recognition tasks compared with older adults. The article title was *Aging and Recognition Memory: A Meta-analysis*. Now address the following:

1. What does it mean that Fraundorf et al. (2019) conducted a meta-analysis; in other words, what do you know about this article just from the title and our brief description?
2. What conclusions were drawn from the meta-analysis?
3. In what ways is your confidence in a conclusion about a finding different when based on a meta-analysis instead of based on the results of a single investigation?

(Answers are provided at the end of this chapter.)

CHAPTER REVIEW

Review Questions

1. What is external validity?
2. Why should a researcher be concerned about generalizing to other populations?
3. How can the fact that most studies are conducted with college students, volunteers, and individuals from a limited location and culture potentially impact external validity?
4. How does the use of the internet to recruit subjects and collect data impact external validity?
5. What is the source of the problem of generalizing to other experimenters? How can this problem be solved?
6. Why is it important to pretest a problem for generalization? Discuss why including a pretest *may* affect the ability to generalize results.
7. Distinguish between an exact replication and a conceptual replication. What is the value of a conceptual replication?
8. What is a meta-analysis?

Study Terms

Conceptual replication

Exact replication

External validity

Literature review

Meta-analysis

Replication

Solomon four-group design

Check Your Learning: Answers

Practice Exercise #1

1. It means that they combined the actual results from many published studies to generate their conclusions.

2. They found that older adults, compared to younger adults, were less effective at recognizing stimuli such as words, faces, or pictures to which they had been previously exposed.

3. Because meta-analysis combines the results from many studies, a conclusion that is drawn from the meta-analysis should be stronger than a conclusion based on a single study. You should be more confident that the result will be able to be replicated.

Appendix A

Reporting Research

INTRODUCTION

Communicating science is one of the most important jobs of the scientist. The main ways this is accomplished are by researchers writing detailed research reports and attending scientific conferences to give talks and present posters describing their results. This appendix focuses on writing research reports, but we will also summarize guidelines for preparing a poster or talk for a professional meeting. This appendix also includes a sample paper that illustrates the stylistic features of a research report.

We will consider the specific rules that should be followed in organizing and presenting research results. These rules are a great convenience for both the writer and the reader. They provide structure for the report and a uniform method of presentation, making it easier for the reader to understand and evaluate the report. Specific rules vary from one discipline to another. A rule for presenting research results in psychology may not apply to the same situation in, for example, sociology research. Also, the rules may vary depending on whether you are preparing the report for a class, a thesis, or submission to a journal. Fortunately, the variation is usually minor, and the general rules of presentation are much the same across disciplines and situations.

The format presented here for writing research reports is drawn from the seventh edition of the *Publication Manual of the American Psychological Association* (APA, 2020b). APA style is used in many journals in psychology, child development, family relations, and education. If you are concerned about specific rules for a particular journal, consult a recent issue of that journal. APA has also published a book titled *Concise Guide to APA Style* (APA, 2020a). You may purchase the *Publication Manual* through your college bookstore, at retail bookstores, or directly from the American Psychological Association. Useful online resources for APA style include **https://www.apastyle.org** and Purdue's Online Writing Lab at **https://owl.english.purdue.edu/owl/resource/560/01/**. Other recommended sources for preparing papers are Gernsbacher (2018), Rosnow and Rosnow (2012), Sternberg and Sternberg (2016), Kazdin (1995), and Schwartz, Landrum, and Gurung (2017).

The APA manual identifies types of articles that students and professionals might prepare:

- Five types of empirical studies—three of which are described in the chapter **"Where to Start,"** including qualitative articles, quantitative articles, mixed-methods articles, replication articles, and meta-analyses.
- Literature reviews describe past research in a specific area of psychology. These reports integrate research findings, evaluate the current status of research on the topic, and point to new directions for research.
- Theoretical articles emphasize the status of existing theory and may propose changes in a theory or development of a new theory.
- Methodological articles focus on methods of conducting research and analyzing data.

In this appendix, we will describe only procedures for reporting empirical studies. Further, we will simplify the discussion by focusing primarily on articles that present the results of a single study rather than multiple studies.

WRITING YOUR REPORT

Writing well is important. A poorly written report that is difficult to understand is of no value (and almost certainly will bring you a poor grade!). Also, a good paper will not contain typos, misspellings, or grammatical errors. In this section, we will cover some fundamentals of good writing and will include solutions to some of the key issues that students face when writing their first scientific paper.

Clarity

Clarity in writing is essential. Be precise and clear in presenting ideas, and think about your intended audience. It is helpful to write your paper as if it were addressed to an audience that is unfamiliar with your general topic and the methods you used to study the topic. Eliminate jargon that most readers will not comprehend. Sometimes a researcher will develop an abbreviated notation for referring to a specific variable or procedure. Such abbreviations may be convenient when communicating with others who are directly involved in the research project, but they are confusing to the general reader. However, you should assume that the reader has a general familiarity with statistics and hypothesis testing. Statistical outcomes can usually be presented without defining terms such as the *mean, standard deviation,* or *significance.* These are only general guidelines, however. Rosnow and Rosnow (2012) point out that when your intended audience is your instructor, you should pay close attention to what he or she has to say about expectations for the paper!

The entire report should have a coherent structure. Ideas should be presented in an orderly, logical progression to facilitate understanding. If you write your report as if it were addressed to someone who is being introduced to your ideas and research findings for the first time, you will be more likely to communicate clearly with the reader.

One method of producing a more organized report is to use an outline. Many writers plan a paper by putting their thoughts and ideas into outline form. The outline then serves as a writing guide. This method forces writers to develop a logical structure before writing the paper. Other writers prefer to use a less structured approach for the first draft. They then try to outline what has been written. If the paper does not produce a coherent outline, the organization needs to be improved. Word-processing programs usually have an outline feature to help you organize your paper; find this feature using the program's help menu.

Paragraphs should be well organized. It is a good idea for a paragraph to contain a topic sentence. Other sentences within a paragraph should be related to the topic sentence and develop the idea in this sentence by elaborating, expanding, explaining, or supporting the idea in the topic sentence. Also, avoid one-sentence paragraphs. If you find such paragraphs in your paper, expand the paragraph, move the idea in another paragraph, or simply delete the sentence.

After completing the first draft of your paper, let it sit for a day or so before you reread it. Carefully proofread the paper, paying attention to grammar and spelling. Some grammatical considerations are described here; you can also use a word processor to check your spelling and grammar. After you make changes and corrections, you may want to get feedback from others. Find one or more people who will read your report critically and suggest improvements. Students may have access to advice from a university writing center. Professionals often benefit from hiring a copyeditor. Be prepared to write several drafts before you have a satisfactory finished product.

Acknowledging the Work of Others

It is extremely important to clearly separate your own words and ideas from those obtained from other sources. Recall our discussion of plagiarism in the chapter **"Ethics in Behavioral Research."** If you use a passage drawn from an article or book, make sure the passage is presented as a direct quotation. There is nothing wrong with quoting another author as long as you acknowledge your source. Never present another person's idea as your own. This is plagiarism and is inexcusable. You should cite your sources even if you are not using direct quotations. Indicating that your paper draws on the works of others actually strengthens your paper.

Sometimes writers are tempted to fill a paper with quotes from other sources or to quote another paper at great length (e.g., several paragraphs or more). This practice is distracting and counterproductive. Be direct and use your own descriptions and interpretations while acknowledging your sources. If you have any questions about how to properly include material from source articles in your own paper, consult your instructor.

Active Versus Passive Voice

Many writers rely too much on the passive voice in their reports, perhaps because they believe that the passive voice makes their writing seem more "scientific." Consider the following sentences:

> It was found by Yee and Johnson (1996) that adolescents prefer . . .
> Participants were administered the test after a 10-minute rest period.
> Participants were read the instructions by the experimenter.

Now try writing those sentences in a more active voice. For example:

> Yee and Johnson (1996) found that adolescents prefer . . .
> Participants took the test after a 10-minute rest period.
> I read the instructions to the participants.

Prose that seems stilted using the passive voice is much more direct when phrased in the active voice.

Although APA style allows the author to use "I" (or "we" when there are multiple authors), many authors are still uncomfortable with the use of the first person pronoun and refer to themselves in the third person. They might say "The experimenter distributed the questionnaires" instead of "I distributed the questionnaires" or "This researcher contacted the head administrators at five community mental health centers" instead of "I contacted the head administrators at five community mental health centers." Thus, when reading research papers, you should not be surprised to see this form of wording.

Avoiding Biased Language

The APA publication manual describes several ways of reducing bias. One of the most important is to be specific when describing the participants in your study. The APA manual allows the use of either *participants* or *subjects* when describing humans who take part in psychological research. In addition, it is appropriate to describe participants as *respondents* in survey research. You may also use specific descriptors such as *children*, *patients*, *clients*, and so on if these terms more accurately describe the participants in your study. Moreover, you should make sure to provide specific information about your participants. Descriptors such as *toddlers* or *teenagers* or *young adults* are not sufficiently specific; you should also provide exact age ranges.

You must also be sensitive to the possibility that your writing might convey a bias, however unintentional, regarding gender, sexual orientation, or ethnic or racial group. As a general principle, be as specific as possible when referring to groups of people. For example, referring to the participants in your study as "Korean Americans and Vietnamese Americans" is more specific and accurate than describing them as "Asians." Also, be sensitive to the use of labels that might be offensive to members of certain groups. In practice, this means that you refer to people using the terms that these people prefer. Also, avoid implicit labeling, as in, for example, "The lesbian sample, in contrast to the sample of normal women" or "We tested groups of autistics and normals." The phrasing in these examples suggest that lesbians and people with autism are "abnormal." Such phrasings could be written along the lines of "We tested people with autism and without autism."

The APA manual has numerous examples of ways of being sensitive to gender, racial and ethnic identity, age, sexual orientation, and disabilities. The term *gender* refers to social roles and identities associated with being male and female. Thus, gender is the proper term to use in a phrase such as "gender difference in average salary." The term *sex* refers to biological classification. Take care when using gender pronouns. Do not use *he, his, man, man's,* and so on when referring to multiple genders or gender identities. Sentences can usually be rephrased or specific pronouns deleted to avoid linguistic biases. For example, "The worker is paid according to his productivity" can be changed to "The worker is paid according to productivity" or "Workers are paid according to their productivity." In the first case, *his* was simply deleted; in the second case, the subject of the sentence was changed to plural. Do *not* try to avoid sexist language by simply substituting *s/he* whenever that might appear convenient.

There are certain rules to follow when referring to racial and ethnic groups. In APA style, the names of these groups are capitalized and never hyphenated—for example, Black, White, African American, Latino or Latinx, Asian, Asian American. The manual also reminds us that the terms that members of racial and ethnic groups use to describe themselves may change over time, and there may be a lack of consensus about a preferred term. Currently, for example, both *Black* and *African American* are generally acceptable. Depending on a number of factors, participants may prefer to be called Hispanic, Latino/Latina, Latinx, Chicano/Chicana, Mexican American, or Puerto Rican. You are urged to use the term most preferred by your participants.

The APA publication manual includes a great deal of information and numerous examples to encourage sensitivity in writing reports. The best advice is to review your papers for possible problems at least once prior to writing your final draft. If you have any questions about appropriate language, consult the manual and colleagues whose opinions you respect.

Some Grammatical Considerations

Transition Words and Phrases

One way to produce a clearly written research report is to pay attention to how you connect sentences within a paragraph and connect paragraphs within a section. The transitions between sentences and paragraphs should be smooth and consistent with the line of reasoning. Some commonly used transition words and phrases and their functions are described in this section.

Adverbs

Adverbs can be used as introductory words in sentences. However, you must use them to convey their implied meanings.

Adverb	*Implied meaning*
(Un)fortunately	It is (un)fortunate that . . .
Similarly	In a similar manner . . .
Certainly	It is certain that . . .
Clearly	It is clear that . . .

One adverb that is frequently misused as an introductory or transition word is *hopefully. Hopefully* means "in a hopeful manner," *not* "it is hoped that . . ."

Incorrect: Hopefully, this is not the case.

Correct: I hope this is not the case.

Words Suggesting Contrast

Some words and phrases suggest a contrast or contradiction between what was written immediately before and what is now being written:

Between sentences	*Within sentences*
By contrast,	whereas
On the other hand,	although
However,	but

The words in the left list refer to the previous sentence. The words in the right list connect phrases within a sentence; that is, they refer to another point in the same sentence.

Words Suggesting a Series of Ideas

The following words and phrases suggest that information after the transition word is related or similar to information in the sentence:

First	In addition	Last	Further
Second	Additionally	Finally	Moreover
Third	Then	Also	Another

Words Suggesting Implication

These words and phrases indicate that the information following the transition word is implied by or follows from the previous information:

Therefore   If . . . then

It follows that   Thus

In conclusion   Then

When you use transition words, be sure that they convey the meaning you intend. Sprinkling them around to begin sentences leads to confusion on the reader's part and defeats your purpose.

Troublesome Words and Phrases

"That" Versus "Which"

That and *which* are relative pronouns that introduce subordinate clauses and reflect the relationship of the subordinate clause to the main clause. *That* clauses are called restrictive clauses and are essential to the meaning of the sentence; *which* clauses are nonrestrictive and simply add more information. Note the different meanings of the same sentence using *that* and *which:*

The mice that performed well in the first trial were used in the second trial.

The mice, which performed well in the first trial, were used in the second trial.

The first sentence states that only mice that performed well in the first trial were used in the second. The second sentence states that all the mice were used in the second trial and they also happened to perform well in the first trial.

"While" Versus "Since"

While and *since* are subordinate conjunctions that also introduce subordinate clauses. To increase clarity in scientific writing, the APA manual suggests that *while* and *since* should be used only to refer to time. *While* is used to describe simultaneous events, and *since* is used to refer to a subsequent event:

The participants waited together while their personality tests were scored.

Since the study by Elder (1974), many studies have been published on this topic.

The APA manual suggests other conjunctions to use when linking phrases that do not describe temporal events. *Although, whereas,* and *but* can be used in place of *while,* and *because* should be substituted for *since.*

Incorrect: While the study was well designed, the report was poorly written.

Correct: Although the study was well designed, the report was poorly written.

"Effect" Versus "Affect"

A common error in student reports is incorrect use of *effect* and *affect. Effect* is a noun that is used in scientific reports to mean "what is produced by a cause," as in the sentence: "The movie had a strong effect on me." *Affect* can be a noun or a verb. As a noun it means emotion, as in "The patient seemed depressed but she displayed very little affect." As a verb it means "to have an influence on," as in "The listeners' responses were affected by the music they heard."

Incorrect: The independent variable effected their responses.

Correct: The independent variable affected their responses.

Incorrect: The independent variable had only a weak affect on the participants' behavior.

Correct: The independent variable had only a weak effect on the participants' behavior.

Singular and Plural

The following words are often misused. The left list shows singular nouns requiring singular verb forms. The right list contains plural nouns that must be used with plural verbs.

Singular	**Plural**
datum	data
stimulus	stimuli
analysis	analyses
phenomenon	phenomena
medium	media
hypothesis	hypotheses
schema	schemas
appendix	appendices
criterion	criteria

Probably the most frequently misused word is *data.*

Incorrect: The data *was* coded for computer analysis.
Correct: The data *were* coded for computer analysis.

Some Spelling Considerations

Here are words that are frequently misspelled and technology terms identified in the APA manual:

questionnaire
database
email
URL
internet
website
webpage
the web
home page
smartphone
username
ebook
Wi-Fi

FORMATTING YOUR REPORT

You will eventually have to prepare a printed copy of your paper. In APA style, the paper should be *entirely double-spaced.* The margins for text should be set to 1 inch on all four sides of the page. APA style also dictates that text should not be "justified" on the right-hand margin. That is, text should be left-aligned with justification turned off—this is sometimes referred to as "ragged right" formatting.

Page headers—the information that appears at the top of each page including the running head and page number—are set approximately .5 inch from the top of the page. All pages are numbered. Paragraphs are indented .5 inch (use the tab function or paragraph-specific formatting, not the space bar). Make sure that hyphenation is turned off: There should not be hyphenated word breaks at the end of a line.

Be sure to take advantage of the features of your word-processing application, including double-spacing text, centering (for equations and so on), and spell-check. Use the tabs and table functions to format text correctly; do not use the space bar to format text or tables.

You will need to place a page header and/or page number at the top of each page. Don't type this yourself at the top of every page—instead, use the header/footer feature of your word-processing application.

Use the same font throughout your paper. You may select a serif font or sans serif font. Serif fonts have short lines at the ends of the strokes that form the letters; sans serif literally means "without serif" and so does not have serif lines. Here are examples:

This is Times New Roman serif text.

This is Arial sans serif text.

Serif fonts recommended in the APA publication manual include 12-point Times New Roman, 11-point Georgia, or 10-point Computer Modern. San serif fonts include 11-point Arial, 11-point Calibri, or 10-point Lucinda Sans Unicode.

There should be one space following a period or a colon. If you find yourself inserting two spaces, you can always perform a "search and replace" when you have completed the paper. Search for two spaces and replace with a single space. Exceptions to this rule include United States (expressed as U.S.) and initials used to identify an individual (such as H.M.).

You will need to use italic and boldface fonts correctly. Use the italics feature of your word processor to create italics for (a) titles and volume numbers of periodicals, (b) titles of books, (c) some headings in your paper, (d) most statistical terms, (e) anchors of a scale, such as 1 (*strongly disagree*) to 5 (*strongly agree*), (f) emphasis of a particular word or phrase when first mentioned in the paper, and (g) words used as words, as in "Authors now routinely use the word *participants*." Pay attention to the use of italics in the examples used throughout this appendix. Boldface font is used for some of the headings of your paper (examples are shown below).

APA style uses a "hanging indent" for the reference list at the end of your paper. Here is an example:

Goldstein, N. J., Cialdini, R. B., & Griskevicius, V. (2008). A room with a viewpoint: Using social norms to motivate environmental conservation in hotels. *Journal of Consumer Research, 35*(3), 472–482. https://doi.org/10.1086/586910

Note that the first line of a reference begins flush with the left margin, but subsequent lines are indented .5 inch (you might want to think of the old "hangman" game to remember why this is called a hanging indent). Do not try to create a hanging indent using the space bar. This takes time and can cause problems when printing. Use the hanging indent feature of your word processor for correct, reliable formatting. It is very easy to learn how to do this through your Help menu or a search on your browser.

Professional and Student Paper Formats

The APA *Publication Manual* (2020) makes a distinction between professional and student papers. Professional papers are prepared for submission to a journal for possible publication. Student papers are prepared for submission to an instructor for a course requirement. A thesis or dissertation is also a student paper in that it may have a set of special preparation rules even though it may use the general format of APA style. Student papers for a class may be a report of a research study, a review of the literature on a specific topic, an annotated bibliography, or any number of other assigned writing projects.

We will focus on writing a professional paper using APA style. Many instructors will require students to use this format for class papers. However, we will note a few of the specific student paper suggestions that are detailed in the APA manual. When you are getting ready to prepare your own report, be sure to check the particular requirements of your instructor or college.

ORGANIZATION OF THE REPORT

As you start to prepare your own report, you are probably already familiar with the major parts of a paper prepared using APA style. A paper prepared using APA style has several major parts (see **Figure 1**):

- Title page that includes the title, author name and affiliation, and author note
- Abstract
- Body of the paper, including Introduction, Method, Results, and Discussion
- References
- Footnotes (if any)
- Tables and figures

We will consider the parts of the paper in the order prescribed by APA style. Recall from the chapter **"Where to Start"** the figure that depicts the structure of a standard empirical article.

Refer to the **Sample Paper** at the end of this appendix as you read the material that follows.

Title Page

Title

The first page of the paper is the title page. It is a separate page and is numbered page 1. The title should be fairly short (usually no more than 12 words) and should inform the reader of the nature of your research. A good way to do this is to include the names of your variables in the title. For example, the following titles are both short and informative:

Effect of Anxiety on Mathematical Problem Solving

Memory for Faces Among Elderly and Young Adults

Sometimes a subtitle, following a colon, will help convey the nature of your research or even add a bit of "flair" to your title, as in

Cognitive Responses in Persuasion: Affective and Evaluative Determinants

Comparing the Tortoise and the Hare: Gender Differences and Experience in Dynamic Spatial Reasoning Tasks

Another method of titling a paper is to pose the question that the research addresses. For example,

Do Rewards in the Classroom Undermine Intrinsic Motivation?

Does Occupational Stereotyping Still Exist?

One further consideration in the choice of a title is that computer literature searches are most likely to include your article if the title includes words and phrases that people are most likely to use when conducting the search. This consideration also applies to the abstract.

Note that the title is centered, boldface, and typed in upper- and lowercase (called title case). It is positioned in the top half of the page but is not at the very top of the page.

Author and Affiliation

The author's name and affiliation are provided just below the title. This is sometimes called the byline. The name usually includes the full first name, middle initial, and last name. Some people adopt a professional

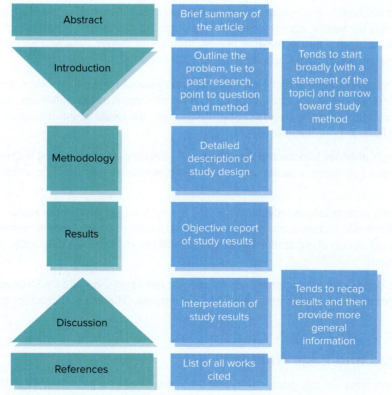

FIGURE 1   Major sections of a research article

name that has a first initial and full middle name. Do not use your initials only. The author name should not include any other descriptive information such as professional title (e.g., Dr.) or degree (e.g., M.A.).

The author's institutional affiliation where the research was conducted is typed below the byline. The affiliation will list the name of your department (or major) and the name of your college or university. Use the complete name of your college without abbreviations or shortened names. If in doubt, check how the college or university name is presented on its official website. If there are two or more authors, the order is determined by the relative contribution of each author to the research.

Following are examples of bylines with affiliation, first for one author:

Amanda S. Reynolds

Department of Psychology, New Mexico State University

Here is an example when there are two authors:

Jorge Orozco and Olivia R. Dunham

School of Communications, University of Houston–Clear Lake

The APA manual also includes examples for other authorship possibilities with more authors, authors with multiple affiliations, and authors with no affiliation.

Author Note

The author note is included in professional papers. It is typed in the lower half of the title page, provides information on contacting the author, acknowledging the assistance of others, and specifying any funding sources that supported the research. Student research papers, theses, and dissertations will probably not require an author note; the **Sample Paper** in this appendix therefore does not include one.

Begin the author note by typing **"Author Note"** in bold and centered several lines below the last author affiliation. The first paragraph (with first line indented) gives detailed department affiliations of the authors. Here you specify that an author is in the Department of Psychology, the Department of Human Development, or a special research laboratory or institute.

A second paragraph provides information on changes of affiliation of any authors, if this is needed. Most commonly, an author publishing a master's thesis from one institution may describe a new affiliation in this paragraph.

The next paragraph contains acknowledgments and any special information that the author wishes to include with the paper. This would include sources of grant support, names of colleagues who assisted with the study in some way, and any details about authorship (e.g., that authors are listed alphabetically because their contributions were equal).

A final paragraph begins with "Correspondence concerning this article should be addressed to . . ." followed by the mailing address of the person designated for that purpose. The email address for correspondence is included as well.

Running Head and Page Number

The last task in preparing the title page is to create a running head and page number in the header area of your page. The header is located between the page edge and the top margin, and the information that you type there will be printed at the top of the page. Use your word processor's Help feature or an internet search to learn how to create a header; do not manually type the information at the top of each page of your paper. Your word processor may have a Header/Footer menu choice to facilitate this.

First you must decide on the wording of the running head, which should be a brief (up to 50 characters, including spaces) summary of your title. Thus, a title such as "Aging and Memory for Pictures of Faces" might use MEMORY FOR FACES as the running head. It will be printed on each page of your paper. In a published paper, it is printed at the top (or head) of the pages. It helps the reader identify your paper. Also, the title page with names is usually removed when the paper is sent for masked review; this allows the paper to be identified even if the pages become mixed with other papers.

The running head is typed in all capital letters against the left margin and will look like this:

MEMORY FOR FACES

The APA manual student paper guidelines do not require a running head. You will need to have a page number, however. Again, check your instructor requirements.

You need to activate the automatic page numbering feature of your word processing application. Move your cursor to the right margin of the header and insert the automatic page number command that will cause page numbers to appear throughout your paper.

When the title page is complete, insert a page break to begin the second page. Do not simply press the Enter key multiple times, or your page numbers may be incorrect.

Student Title Page

This section summarizes the elements of the student paper title page described in the APA manual. There is no running head. You will need to include the following information. Remember that your entire paper will be double-spaced. Refer to the example in **Figure 2**.

- Page number that continues on all pages
- Title of your paper (bold) followed by two double-spaced lines
- Your name
- Affiliation and department
- Course number and name
- Instructor name (check if instructor has a preferred form such as Dr. Kenneth Mio or Professor May)
- Assignment due date in format used in your location (e.g., December 5, 2020)

Abstract

The abstract is a brief summary of the research report and is usually 150 to 250 words in length, depending on the rules specified by the publication or your college. The purpose of the abstract is to introduce the article, allowing readers to decide whether the article appears relevant to their own interests. The abstract should provide enough information so that the reader can decide whether to read the entire report, and it should make the report easier to comprehend when it is read. An abstract is not included in APA student paper guidelines. However, your instructor may require an abstract in your class.

Although the abstract appears at the beginning of your report, it is easiest to write the abstract last. Read a few abstracts and you will get some good ideas for how to condense a full-length research report down to 8

1

Memory for Text and Text + Image Advertisements

Samuel B. Fuller

Department of Psychology, Darwin College

PSYC 200: Research Methods

Dr. Rosa Aguire

May 1, 2020

FIGURE 2   Example title page for APA style student paper

or 10 information-packed sentences. A very informative exercise is to write an abstract for a published article and then compare your abstract to the one written by the original authors.

Abstracts generally include a sentence or two about each of the four main sections in the body of the article. First, from the Introduction section, state the problem under study and the primary hypotheses. Second, from the Method section, include information on the characteristics of the participants (e.g., number, age, sex, and any special characteristics) and a brief summary of the procedure (e.g., self-report questionnaires, direct observation, repeated measurements on several occasions). Third, from the Results section, describe the pattern of findings for major variables. This is typically done by reporting the direction of differences without relying on numerical values. APA guidelines recommend including statistical significance levels, yet few authors comply (Ono, Phillips, & Leneman, 1996). Rely on guidelines provided by your instructor. Finally, the abstract will include implications of the study taken from the Discussion section. Informative comments about the findings are preferred to general statements such as "the implications of the study are addressed" (Kazdin, 1995).

The abstract is typed on a separate page and is numbered page 2. The word "Abstract" is centered at the top of the page with boldface type.

The abstract is always typed as a single paragraph with no paragraph indentation.

When you have completed the abstract page, insert a page break to take you to the third page of your paper.

Keywords in Professional Papers

Keywords associated with the article are also included on the abstract page. Keywords help other researchers find your article when conducting searches. Provide three to five words that you might use to search for an article on your topic using PsycINFO.

Two lines below the abstract, indent for a new paragraph. Type "Keywords:" using italics and then list your keywords, all in lower case with no period.

   Keywords: word1, word2, word3

Body of the Paper

Begin the third page by typing the complete title of your paper, centered on the first line. Do not include your name or affiliation (this allows a masked review in which the reader cannot identify the author). You are now ready to type the body of your paper. For most research reports, the body of the paper will have four sections: Introduction, Method, Results, and Discussion. These are organized through the use of headings.

Introduction

The Introduction section begins after the boldface title at the top of the page. It is not labeled "Introduction"—instead, you (and your readers) understand that the first part of the body of the paper is the Introduction. The Introduction has three components, although formal subsections introduced by headings are rarely used. The components are (1) the problem under study, (2) the literature review, and (3) the rationale and hypotheses of the study. After reading the Introduction, the reader should know why you decided to do the research and how you decided to go about doing it. In general, the Introduction progresses from broad theories and research findings to specific details and expectations of the current research.

Gernsbacher (2018) notes that the Introduction should begin with a hook that will grab the attention of the reader as you describe the problem under study. In one or two paragraphs, give the reader an appreciation of the broad context and significance of the topic being studied. The hook may start with something familiar to the reader, such as an incident from the news or a common situation in everyday life, that then leads to the purpose of the study. Stating what problem is being investigated is worthwhile; it helps readers, even those who are unfamiliar with the topic, understand and appreciate why the topic was studied in the first place.

Following the opening statement, the Introduction provides a description of past research and theory. This is called the *literature review.* An exhaustive review of past theory and research is not necessary. (If there are major literature reviews of the topic, you would of course refer the reader to the reviews.) Rather, you want to describe only the research and theoretical issues that are clearly related to your study. State explicitly how this previous work is logically connected to your research problem. This tells the reader why your research was conducted and shows the connection to prior research.

The final part of the Introduction tells the reader the rationale of the current study. Here you state what variables you are studying and what results you expect. The links between the research hypotheses, prior research, and the current research design are shown by explaining why the hypotheses are being examined by the study.

Method

As noted above, the body of the paper is organized using headings. The Method section begins immediately after you have completed the Introduction (on the same page, if space permits). The heading for this section is the word "Method," centered on the line using boldface type, as follows:

Method

The Method section provides the reader with detailed information about how your study was conducted. Ideally, there should be enough information in the Method section to allow a reader to replicate your study.

The Method section is typically divided into a number of subsections. Both the order of the subsections and the number of subsections vary in published articles. Decisions about which subsections to include are guided by the complexity of the investigation. The sample paper in this appendix uses three subsections: *Participants, Design and Materials,* and *Procedure.* Some of the most commonly used subsections are discussed next.

Overview

If the experimental design and procedures used in the research are complex, a brief overview of the method should be presented to help the reader understand the information that follows.

Participants

A subsection on the participants (or subjects or respondents) is always necessary. The number and nature of the participants should be described. Age, sex, ethnicity, and any other relevant characteristics should be described. Special characteristics of participants are described, such as firstborn children, adolescent children of alcoholics, student teachers, or police officers. State explicitly how participants were recruited and what incentives for participation might have been used. The number of individuals in each experimental condition also can be included here. Finally, you should state that the procedures were approved by your IRB.

Apparatus, Materials, or Measures

A subsection labeled Apparatus, Materials, or Measures may be necessary to describe special equipment or materials used in the experiment. The apparatus, materials, or measures should be described in sufficient detail to allow other researchers to replicate the study. For example, if your project used the CESD-R (Center for Epidemiological Studies Depression Scale, Revised; https://cesd-r.com/) to measure depression, provide a citation, describe the number of items, and provide evidence of reliability and validity.

Procedure

The Procedure subsection tells the reader what instructions were given to the participants, how the independent variables were manipulated, and how the dependent variables were measured. The methods used to control extraneous variables also should be described. These include randomization procedures, counterbalancing, and special means that were used to keep a variable constant across all conditions. Finally, the method of debriefing should be described. If your study used a nonexperimental method, you would still provide details on exactly how you conducted the study and the measurement techniques you used.

It is up to you to decide how much detail to include here. Use your own judgment to determine the importance of a specific aspect of the procedure and the amount of detail that is necessary for the reader to clearly understand what was done in the study. Include any detail that might be important in a replication of the study.

Other Subsections

Include other subsections if they are needed for clear presentation of the method. For example, a subsection on testing materials might be necessary instead of an Apparatus subsection. Other sections are customized by the authors to suit their study. If you glance through a recent issue of a journal, you will find that some studies have only two subsections and others have many more subsections. This reflects the varying complexity of the studies and the particular writing styles of the researchers.

Results

In the Results section, present the results as clearly as possible. The Results section is a straightforward description of your analyses. Although it is tempting to explain your findings in the Results section, save that discussion for the next section of the paper.

Be sure to state the alpha (probability) level that you used in making decisions about statistical significance: This will usually be .05 or .01 and requires only a simple sentence such as "An alpha level of .05 was used for statistical analyses."

Present your results in the same order in which your predictions are stated in the Introduction section of the paper. If a manipulation check was made, present it before you describe the major results.

The content of your Results section will vary according to the type of statistical test performed and the number of analyses you conducted. However, every Results section includes some basic elements. If applicable, describe any scoring or coding procedures performed on the data to prepare them for analysis. This is particularly important when coding qualitative data. (Sometimes data transformations are included in a subsection of the Method section.) State which statistical test was performed on the data (t test, F test, correlation, etc.). Justify the selection of a particular statistical comparison to address your hypothesis. Be sure to summarize each finding in words as well as to include the results of statistical tests in the form of statistical phrases. The APA manual includes guidelines for reporting statistics that were recommended by an APA Task Force on Statistical Inference (Wilkinson et al., 1999). One major recommendation is to report exact probability values that are routinely provided by computer programs used to perform statistical analyses. In the past, most researchers reported probabilities as "less than" the standard probabilities shown in statistical tables, for example, $p < .10$, $p < .05$, or $p < .01$. It is now possible to report exact probabilities of the null hypothesis being correct, for example, $p = .09$, $p = .03$, or $p = .02$. This change allows readers to apply their own standards of statistical significance when evaluating the study.

Another recommendation is to report effect size. The manual recognizes that there are currently many indicators of effect size associated with different statistical procedures; the primary concern is to have an effect size in the published article (see the chapter **"Understanding Research Results: Description and Correlation"** for a review of effect size).

A related APA guideline is to report statistical values (e.g., mean, standard deviation, t, F, or chi-square) using two decimal places. When you are reporting statistical significance, probabilities are rounded to two or three decimals (e.g., $p = .03$ or $p = .034$). If you are consistently using two decimals, any value less than .01 should be reported as $p < .01$. For three decimals, values less than .001 are reported as $p < .001$. Your instructor may specify a decimal place rule for your papers.

The results should be stated in simple sentences. For example, the results of the modeling and aggression experiment described in the chapter **"Understanding Research Results: Description and Correlation"** might be expressed as follows:

> As predicted, children who viewed the aggressive model were significantly more aggressive than children in the no-model condition, $t(18) = 4.03$, $p < .01$. The mean aggression score in the model group was 5.20 ($SD = 1.14$) and the no-model mean was 3.10 ($SD = 1.20$). The effect size r associated with this finding was .69.

These brief sentences inform the reader of the general patterns of the results, the obtained means, statistical significance, and effect size. You should note the wording of the phrase that includes the symbol for the t test, degrees of freedom, and significance level (probability).

If the results are relatively straightforward, they can be presented entirely in sentence form. If the study involved a complex design, tables and figures may be needed to clarify presentation of the results.

Tables and Figures

Tables are generally used to present large arrays of data. For example, a table might be useful in a design with several dependent measures; the means of the different groups for all dependent measures would be presented in the table. Tables are also convenient when a factorial design has been used. For example, in a $2 \times 2 \times 3$ factorial design, a table could be used to present all 12 means.

Figures are used when a visual display of the results would help the reader understand the outcome of the study. Figures may be used to illustrate a significant interaction or show trends over time. When preparing a figure, you will need to decide whether to present the information as a pie chart, a bar graph, or a line graph. Pie charts are used when showing percentages or proportions. The entire pie represents 100% and is divided into slices. In this way, the whole is divided into separate groups or responses. Bar graphs are used when describing the responses of two or more groups—for example, the mean aggression score of a model and a no-model group in an experiment. Line graphs are used when both the independent and dependent variables have quantitative properties, for example, the average response time of two groups on days 1, 2, 3, 4, and 5 of an experiment. Nicol and Pexman (2010a, 2010b) provide detailed information on creating figures, tables, and other visual displays of data.

In APA style, tables and figures are not presented in the main body of the manuscript. Instead they are placed at the end of the paper. Each table and figure appears on a separate page. A table or figure is noted in the text by referring to a table or figure number and describing the content of the table or figure. Never make a reference to the placement of the figure because the placement is determined by the typesetter. In the Results section, make a statement such as "As shown in Figure 2, the model group . . ." or "Table 1 presents the demographic characteristics of the survey respondents." Describe the important features of the table or figure; don't rely on mere cross-references, such as "See Figure 3."

Do not repeat the same data in more than one place. An informative table or figure supplements, and does not duplicate, the text. Using tables and figures does not diminish your responsibility to clearly state the nature of the results in the text of your report.

When you are writing a student research paper, it may be more convenient to place each figure and table within the main body of the paper. Because rules about the placement of tables and figures may vary, check on the proper format before writing your report.

Discussion of the Results

It is usually *not* appropriate to discuss the implications of the results in the Results section. However, the Results and Discussion sections may be combined if the discussion is brief and greater clarity is achieved by the combination.

Discussion

The Discussion section is the proper place to discuss the implications of the results. One way to organize the Discussion is to begin by summarizing the original purpose and expectations of the study, then to state whether the results were consistent with your expectations. If the results do support your original ideas, you should discuss how your findings contribute to knowledge of the problem you investigated. You will want to consider the relationship between your results and past research and theory. If you did not obtain the expected results, discuss possible explanations. The explanations would be quite different, of course, depending on whether you obtained results that were the opposite of what you expected or the results were not significant.

It is often a good idea to include your own criticisms of the study. Many published articles include limitations of the study. Try to anticipate what a reader might find wrong with your methodology. For example, if you used a nonexperimental research design, you might point out problems of cause and effect and possible extraneous variables that might be operating. Sometimes there may be major or minor flaws that could be corrected in a subsequent study (if you had the time, money, and so on). You can describe such flaws and suggest corrections. If there are potential problems in generalizing your results, state the problems and give reasons why you think the results would or would not generalize.

The results will probably have implications for future research. If so, you should discuss the direction that research might take. It is also possible that the results have practical implications—for example, for childrearing or improving learning in the classroom. Discussion of these larger issues is usually placed at the end of the Discussion section. Finally, you will probably wish to have a brief concluding paragraph that provides "closure" to the entire paper.

References

The list of references begins on a new page with the word "References" in bold and centered at the top. The list of references must contain complete citations for all sources mentioned in your report. Do not omit any sources from the list of references; also, do not include any sources that are not mentioned in your report. The exact procedures for citing sources within the body of your report and in your list of references are described later in this appendix in the section **"Citing and Referencing Sources."** Follow the examples in recent publications.

Appendix

An appendix is rarely provided in manuscripts submitted for publication. The APA *Publication Manual* notes that an appendix might be appropriate when necessary material would be distracting in the main body of the report. Examples of appendices include a sample of a questionnaire or survey instrument, a complex mathematical proof, or a long list of words used as stimulus items. An appendix (or several appendices) is much more appropriate for a student research project or a thesis. The appendix might include the entire questionnaire that was used, a new test that was developed, or other materials employed in the study. Check with your instructor concerning the appropriateness of an appendix for your paper. If an appendix is provided, it begins on a new page with the word "Appendix" centered at the top.

Footnotes

Footnotes, if used, are not typed in the body of the text. Instead, all footnotes in the paper are typed on a separate page at the end of the paper. Avoid using footnotes unless they are absolutely necessary. They tend to be distracting to readers, and the information can and should be integrated into the body of the paper.

Tables

For professional papers, each table should be on a separate page. APA style requires placement of the table at the end of the paper, but for a class you may be asked to place your tables on separate pages within the body of the paper or even within the text of the paper. In preparing your table, allow enough space so that the table does not appear cramped on a small portion of the page. Define areas of the table using typed horizontal lines (do not use vertical lines). Give some thought to the title so that it accurately and clearly describes the content of the table. You may wish to use an explanatory note in the table to show significance levels or the range of possible values on a variable. Before you make up your own tables, examine the tables in a recent issue of one of the journals published by the American Psychological Association as well as the examples in the *Publication Manual* and in Nicol and Pexman (2010b), and the sample paper in this appendix. Formats are provided for many types of tables, for example, tables of means, correlation coefficients, multiple regression analyses, and so on. For example, here is a table of correlations:

Table 1

Correlations Between Dependent Measures

Measure	1	2	3	4
1. Attractiveness	–	.52	.35	.29
2. Extraversion		–	.11	.23
3. Conscientiousness			–	.49
4. Starting salary				–

Note that the title of the table is typed in italics. Also, the areas of the table are separated by horizontal lines.

Figures

Figures consist of graphic displays of information including results depicted in graphs (e.g., a line graph or bar graph), drawings, or photographs. In APA style for professional papers, figures are placed after any tables in your paper. However, when preparing a student report or thesis, you may be asked to include figures within the body of the paper.

Although it is sometimes tempting to draw a graph by hand, you will find it much easier to use a computer program to create graphs. Most spreadsheet, word processing, and statistical analysis programs have graphing features. Independent and predictor variables are placed on the horizontal axis; dependent and criterion variables are placed on the vertical axis. Both the horizontal and vertical axes must be labeled. Figures should be easy to read and should fit on the page along with the figure caption. Use a sans serif typeface such as Arial or Helvetica. Select font sizes no larger than 14 point and no smaller than 8 point. The figure number and figure caption appear below each figure. Refer to the figure in the sample paper in this appendix, the *APA Publication Manual*, and Nicol and Pexman (2010a) for examples.

Remember that the purpose of a figure is to increase comprehension of results by having a graphic display of data. If the graph is cluttered with information, it will confuse the reader and will not serve its purpose. Plan your graphs carefully to make sure that you are accurately and clearly informing the reader. If you become interested in the topic of how to display information in graphs and charts, Tufte's (1983, 1990, 1997, 2006) books are recommended. Tufte explores a variety of ways of presenting data, factors that lead to data clarity, and ways that graphs can deceive the reader.

Summary: Order of Pages

To summarize, the organization of your paper is as follows:

1. Title page, including Author Note if required (page 1)
2. Abstract (page 2)
3. Body of paper (start on page 3)
   a. Title at top of page 3 followed by the Introduction (no heading)
   b. Method (boldface type and centered)
   c. Results (boldface type and centered)
   d. Discussion (boldface type and centered)
4. References (start on new page)
5. Footnotes (start on new page if included)
6. Tables, with table captions (each table on a separate page)
7. Figures, with figure captions (each figure on a separate page)
8. Appendix (start on new page if included)

You should now have a general idea of how to structure and write your report. The remainder of this appendix focuses on some of the technical rules that may be useful as you prepare your own research report.

THE USE OF HEADINGS

The body of the paper in APA style is organized through the use of headings. There are five levels of heading. Most commonly, you will use the first three levels. The five levels of heading are shown below:

Level 1:

Centered Heading, Bold, Title Case

Level 2:

Flush Left, Bold, Title Case

    The text begins indented on a new line.

Level 3:

Flush Left, Bold, Italics, Title Case

    The text is indented as a new paragraph. More paragraphs may follow.

Level 4:

    Indented, Bold, Title Case, Ends with a Period. This heading is used after a Level 3 heading and will usually not be needed in papers reporting a single study. See the APA manual for information on reporting the results of two or more studies in a single paper.

Level 5:

    Indented, Bold, Italicized, Ends with a Period. This additional heading will probably not be needed in student papers.

The paper title is used for the introduction section. The headings for the other main sections of the paper—Method, Results, Discussion—are centered using boldface type; these are Level 1 headings. Each of these sections can be further divided into subsections using Level 2 headings. If needed, Level 3 headings allow you to provide an organizational structure for any subsections. **Figure 3** shows an example of the use of headings in the body of your paper.

CITING AND REFERENCING SOURCES

Researchers often use citation management software like Zotero (open source software available at https://www.zotero.org) to collect, store, and organize references. If you integrate your citation management software with a popular word-processing application, it will also help you cite an article in-text and create an APA-styled bibliography.

Citation Style

Whenever you refer to information reported by other researchers, you *must* accurately identify the sources. APA journals use the author–date citation method: The author name(s) and year of publication are inserted at appropriate points. The citation style depends on whether the author names are part of the narrative or are in parentheses.

Title of Paper

The title is a Level 1 Heading. The text for the Introduction section begins after the title. Your first paragraphs introduce your research. You may or may not wish to organize the Introduction using subsections.

Level 2 Heading for a Subsection

Text would continue here.

Level 2 Heading for Another Subsection

Text begins here for the second subsection.

Method

Begin the Method, Results, and Discussion sections with a centered and boldface Level 1 heading. Further subsections will have Level 2 and Level 3 headings as shown below.

Participants

Describe your participants and sampling procedures here.

Procedure

This is your description of how the study was conducted. Level 3 paragraph headings may be useful. These are only examples.

Stimuli

Here you might describe the stimuli that participants were given in various conditions. Note that this is a Level 3 heading.

Dependent Measures

Describe the measures that were made after participants were presented with the stimuli. This is another Level 3 heading.

Results

An introduction to the results would go here.

Perceived Competence (Example of a Level 2 Heading)

This subsection would be a description of results for the first dependent measure.

Perceived Attractiveness (Example of a Level 2 Heading)

Here you would present the results for the second dependent variable.

Discussion

You may wish to divide the discussion into subsections. Begin with a discussion of the ways that your results supported or did not support your predictions. Explain what you found and relate your findings to past research. You may include additional subsections. The following are only examples.

Limitations

Future Research

Possible Applications

FIGURE 3   Example of headings in the body of a paper

One Author

When the author's name is part of the narrative, include the publication date in parentheses immediately after the name:

Markman (1991) found that marital discord can lead to constructive resolution of conflict.

When the author's name is not part of the narrative, the name and date are cited in parentheses at the end of an introductory phrase or at the end of the sentence:

In one study (Markman, 1991), couples learned to discuss . . .

Couples have lower rates of divorce and marital violence after problem-solving intervention (Markman, 1991).

Two Authors

When the work has two authors, both names are included in each reference citation. The difference between narrative and parenthetical citations is in the use of the conjunction "and" and the ampersand "&" to connect authors' names. When the names are part of a sentence, use the word "and" to join the names of two authors. When the complete citation is in parentheses, use the "&" symbol:

Harris and Marmer (1996) reported that fathers in poor families are less involved with their adolescent children than fathers in non-poor families.

Fathers in poor families are less likely to spend time with their adolescent children than fathers in non-poor families (Harris & Marmer, 1996).

Three or More Authors

When a report has three or more authors, cite the first author's surname followed by the abbreviation et al. ("and others") along with the publication date. The abbreviation may be used in narrative and parenthetical citations:

Abernathy et al. (1995) also examined the relationship between smoking and self-esteem in adolescent males.

For males, there is no relationship between smoking and self-esteem, suggesting gender-specific motivations for initiating smoking in adolescence (Abernathy et al., 1995).

Another question about subsequent citations is whether to include the publication date each time an article is referenced. Within a paragraph, you do *not* need to include the year in subsequent citations as long as the study cannot be confused with other studies cited in your report.

Citation within a paragraph

In a study of reaction times, Yokoi and Jones (2006) reported . . .
Yokoi and Jones also reported that . . .

When subsequent citations are in another paragraph or in another section of the report, the publication date should be included.

References with No Author

When an article has no author (e.g., some newspaper or magazine articles), cite the first two or three words of the title in quotation marks, followed by the publication date:

Citation in reference list

Parental smoking kills 6,200 kids a year, study says. (1997, July 15). *Orange County Register,* p. 11.

Citation in text

In an article on smoking ("Parental Smoking," 1997), data obtained from . . .

Multiple Works within the Same Parentheses

A convenient way to cite several studies on the same topic or several studies with similar findings is to reference them as a series within the same parentheses. When two or more works are by the same author(s), report them in order of year of publication, using commas to separate citations:

Mio and Willis (2003, 2005) found . . .

Past research (Mio & Willis, 2003, 2005) indicates . . .

When two or more works by different authors are cited within the same parentheses, arrange them in alphabetical order and separate citations with semicolons:

Investigations of families in economic distress consistently report that girls react with internalization problems whereas boys respond with externalization problems (Conger et al., 1994; Flanagan & Eccles, 1993; Lempers et al., 1989).

Reference List Style

The APA *Publication Manual* (2020) provides reference formatting guidelines for more than 100 different sources including journal articles, books, book chapters, conference presentations, Wikipedia entries, YouTube videos, tweets, song lyrics, and webpages, among many others. Only a few of these are presented here. When in doubt about how to construct a reference, consult the APA manual. The general format for a reference list is as follows:

- The references are listed in alphabetical order by the first author's last name. Do not categorize references by type (i.e., books, journal articles, and so on). Note that commas and periods are followed by one space in APA style.
- Elements of a reference (authors' names, article title, publication data) are separated by periods.
- The first line of each reference is typed flush to the left margin; subsequent lines are indented. This is called a "hanging indent":

Bushman, B. (2006). Effects of warning and information labels on attraction to television violence in viewers of different ages. *Journal of Applied Social Psychology, 36*(9), 2073–2078. https://doi.org/10.1111/j.0021-9029.2006.00094.x

Each reference begins on a new line (think of each reference as a separate paragraph). Most word-processing applications will allow you to easily format the paragraph with a hanging indent so you do not have to manually insert spaces on the second and subsequent lines. Using Microsoft Word, for example, set the paragraph style for your references using the hanging indent option; you can also manually create a hanging indent with Ctrl-t.

Page Numbers

APA recommends using the en-dash symbol between page numbers rather than a simple hyphen. To type an en dash in Microsoft Word for Windows, choose Symbol from the Insert menu, click the Special Characters tab, highlight En Dash, and click Insert. Because you will be using the en dash often, create a shortcut key (such as Alt-1) for quick insertion of en dashes. To type an en dash on a Mac, press Option-hyphen (not the hyphen on the numeric keypad). Check with your instructor to determine if using an en dash is necessary in your papers.

Inclusion of a URL or DOI

The new edition of the *Publication Manual* has incorporated changes that reflect the fact that we only rarely access printed sources; instead, we are much more likely to access sources using websites and library or publisher databases. It is therefore often necessary to provide readers with additional information on the source that you used.

The URL is used when your source was a website. This is the full website address of the location and file name of the document as it appears in your web browser. Examples will be provided below. An important rule about typing the URL (location) of the document you are citing concerns insertion of line breaks. It is acceptable to have the URL carry over to a second line if it will not fit on a single line. However, never insert a hyphen, because this is not part of the address. Instead, let your word processor wrap the URL to the next line by its own line-break rules.

The DOI (Digital Object Identifier) was devised by publishers to provide a unique and consistent method of identifying and locating electronic sources of information. The DOI takes the form doi:10.xxxx/xxxxxxxxx or https://doi.org/xxxx/xxxxxxxxx. The DOI always begins with 10 followed by a period. What follows next is a "prefix" that identifies the publishing organization, a slash, and then a "suffix" that the publisher assigns to the article.

You will see the DOI when you access research articles using databases such as PsycINFO. The DOI also appears on the first page of the full-text version of the article, no matter where it appears (e.g., a printed journal article or a downloaded version that might be available in either PDF or HTML format). The *APA Publication Manual* now recommends including the DOI in the reference if it is available.

Format for Journal Articles

Most journals are organized by volume and year of publication (e.g., volume 60 of *American Psychologist* consists of journal issues published in 2005). A common confusion is whether to include the journal issue number in addition to the volume number. The rule is simple: If the issues in a volume are paginated consecutively throughout the volume, *do not* include the journal issue number. If each issue in a volume begins with page 1, the issue number should be included.

In the reference list, both the name of the journal and the volume number are italicized. Also, only the first letter of the first word in article titles is capitalized (except for proper nouns and the first word after a colon or question mark).

Following are examples:

>   ***One author—no issue number, no DOI provided***
>   Newby, T. J. (1991). Classroom motivation strategies: Strategies of first-year teachers. *Journal of Educational Psychology, 83*(2), 195–200.
>   ***Two authors—use of issue number, no DOI provided***
>   Greenwald-Robbins, J., & Greenwald, R. (1994). Environmental attitudes conceptualized through developmental theory: A qualitative analysis. *Journal of Social Issues, 50*(3), 29–47.

Three to twenty authors—DOI provided

Hammen, C., Brennan, P. A., & Le Brocque, R. (2011). Youth depression and early childrearing: Stress generation and intergenerational transmission of depression. *Journal of Consulting and Clinical Psychology, 79*(3), 353-363. https://doi.org/10.1037/a0023536

21 or more authors—DOI provided

Note that only names of the first 19 authors and the last author are provided. The ellipses are used to indicate that there are more authors not named.

Anders, A., Bitter, B., Cape, C., Deal, D., Egan, E., Forest, F., Gordan, G., Haley, H., Itin, I., Jade, J., King, K., Lash, L., Moore, M., Noone, N., Ortiz, O., Pan, P., Quick, Q., Rami, R., Song, S., . . . Zappa, Z. (2019). Some articles have many authors. *Journal of Popular Psychology, 12*(1), 34-45. https://doi.org/10.1000/a0000001

Format for Books

When a book is cited, the title of the book is italicized. Capitalize only the first word of the title, proper nouns, and the first word after a colon or question mark. Include the name of the publisher (location of publisher is no longer required).

One-author book

Nisbett, R. E. (2003). *The geography of thought: How Asians and Westerners think differently . . . and why.* Free Press.

Book retrieved from a website

James, W. (1929). *The varieties of religious experience*: A study in human nature. Modern Library. Retrieved from http://books.google.com/ books?id=Qi4XAAAAIAAJ&printsec=frontcover&dq=william+james&cd=1#v=onepage&q&f=false

One-author book—second or later edition

Regan, P. C. (2008). *The mating game: A primer on love, sex, and marriage* (2nd ed.). Sage.

Edited book

Dass-Brailsford, P. (Ed.). (2010). *Crisis and disaster counseling: Lessons learned from Hurricane Katrina and other disasters.* Sage.

Format for Articles/Chapters in Edited Books

For edited books, the reference begins with the names of the authors of the article, not the book. The title of the article follows. The name(s) of the book editor(s), the book title, the inclusive page numbers for the article, and the publisher of the book follow, in that order. Only the book title is italicized, and only the first letters of the article and book titles are capitalized. Here are some examples:

One editor

Goldstein, N. J., & Cialdini, R. B. (2009). Normative influences on consumption and conservation behaviors. In M. Wänke (Ed.), *Social psychology of consumer behavior* (pp. 273-296). Psychology Press.

Two editors

Bartlett, A. (2010). Gender, crime, and violence. In A. Bartlett & G. McGauley (Eds.), *Forensic mental health: Concepts, systems, and practice* (pp. 53-65). Oxford University Press.

Chapter from book in multivolume series

Stors, T. J. (2006). Stressful experience and learning across the lifespan. In S. T. Fiske, A. E. Kazdin, & D. L. Schachter (Eds.), *Annual review of psychology: Vol. 57* (pp. 55–85). Annual Reviews, Inc. https://doi.org/10.1146/annurev.psych.57.102904.190205

Format for "Popular" Articles

The reference styles shown below should be used for articles from popular magazines and newspapers appearing in print or on websites. As a general rule, popular press articles are used sparingly (e.g., when no scientific articles on a topic can be found, or to provide an example of an event that is related to your topic).

Magazine—continuous pages

Begley, S. (1995, March 27). Gray matters. *Newsweek, 125,* 48–54.

Magazine—retrieved from website

Cullen, L. T. (2006, Jan. 6). How to get smarter, one breath at a time. *Time.* Retrieved from http://www.time.com/time/magazine/article/0,9171,1147167-2,00.html

Newspaper—retrieved from website

Parker-Pope, T. (2010, May 10). The science of a happy marriage. *New York Times.* Retrieved from http://well.blogs.nytimes.com/2010/05/10/tracking-the-science-of-commitment/

Newspaper—discontinuous pages

Cole, K. C. (1995, May 1). Way the brain works may play role in bias, experts say. *Los Angeles Times,* pp. Al, A18.

No author—retrieved from website

Substitute the title for the author in the reference:

Driver error to blame for truck's plunge from bridge-tunnel. (2017, February 19). Retrieved from https://wina.com/news/064460-driver-error-to-blame-for-trucks-plunge-off-cbbt/

The citation in the body of the paper uses the first few words of the title in quotation marks along with the year:

Road rage can in fact have serious consequences ("4-year old shot," 2011).

Format for Papers and Posters Presented at Conferences

Occasionally you may need to cite an unpublished paper or poster that was presented at a professional meeting. Provide the year and month of the conference as well as the name and location of the conference.

Conference paper

Gates, K., & Rovine, M. (2009, April). Modeling mother-infant interactions as dynamic processes. *Paper presented at the meeting of the Society for Research on Child Development,* Denver, CO.

Poster presentation

Storm, B. C., & White, H. A. (2009, May). ADHD and retrieval-induced forgetting: Evidence for a deficit in inhibitory control. *Poster presented at the annual convention of the Association for Psychological Science,* Boston, MA.

Secondary Sources

Sometimes you need to cite an article, book, or book chapter that you read about through a textbook, an abstract, or a book review. Although it is always preferable to read primary sources, sometimes you may have to cite a secondary source when the primary source cannot be found in a timely manner (with internet searches, this is becoming less likely!).

Suppose you wish to cite an article that you read about in a book. When you refer to the article in your paper, you need to say that it was cited in the book. In the following example, a paper by Conway and Pleydell-Pearce is the secondary source:

> Conway and Pleydell-Pearce (as cited in Woll, 2002) suggested that autobiographical memory . . .

In the reference list at the end of the paper, simply provide the reference for the primary source you used (in this case, the 2002 book by Woll).

Sometimes you may need to cite the abstract of an article that you found in a search of PsycINFO or another database. Although it is preferable to find the original article, the original article may not be available online or at any nearby libraries or is published in a foreign language with only the abstract available in English. Here is an example:

> King, Y., & Parker, D. (2008). Driving violations, aggression and perceived consensus. *European Review of Applied Psychology, 58*(1), 43–49. Abstract retrieved from PsycINFO database. (Accession No. 2007-19875-005)

In this example, the complete reference is given. However, you also provide the crucial information that you have only examined the abstract of the article and you found the abstract through a search of the PsycINFO database. The accession number is provided with the abstract.

Citing Specific Web Documents/Pages

Many webpages were written just for the web and should not be considered journal articles *or* books. For example, a document prepared by David Kenny provides information on mediating variables. Here you would cite the title of the document and retrieval information. To cite this document, your text might read as follows:

> Kenny (2018) describes a procedure for using multiple regression to examine causal models that include mediating variables.

This document's entry in the reference list would be:

> Kenny, D. A. (2018). *Mediation.* Retrieved from http://davidakenny.net/cm/mediate.htm

Note that the reference includes the author, a date that was provided in the document, and a title. Some web documents do not include a date; in this case, simply substitute n.d. in parentheses to indicate that there is no date. However, documents that may be regularly updated should include the date that you accessed the website. This will make it clear to others that you may have accessed a different version than the one that is currently available. Here is an example of how to do that using the Kenny reference:

> Kenny, D. A. (2018). *Mediation.* Retrieved March 6, 2019, from http://davidakenny.net/cm/mediate.htm

ABBREVIATIONS

Abbreviations are not used extensively in APA-style papers. They can be distracting because the reader must constantly try to translate the abbreviation into its full meaning. However, APA style does allow for the use of abbreviations that are accepted as words in the dictionary (specifically, Webster's *Collegiate Dictionary*). These include IQ, REM, ESP, and AIDS.

Certain well-known terms may be abbreviated when it would make reading easier, but the full meaning should be given when first used in the paper. Examples of commonly used abbreviations are:

MMPI	Minnesota Multiphasic Personality Inventory
STM	short-term memory
CS	conditioned stimulus
RT	reaction time
CVC	consonant-vowel-consonant
ANOVA	analysis of variance

Statistical terms are sometimes used in their abbreviated or symbol form. These are always italicized in a manuscript. For example,

M	mean
SD	standard deviation
Mdn	median
df	degrees of freedom
n	number of individuals in a group or experimental condition
N	total number of participants or respondents
p	probability (significance) level
SS	sum of squares
MS	mean square
F	value of F in analysis of variance
r	Pearson correlation coefficient
R	multiple correlation coefficient

The following scientific abbreviations for various measurement units are frequently used:

cm	centimeter
g	gram
hr	hour
in	inch
kg	kilogram
km	kilometer
m	meter
mg	milligram
min	minute
ml	milliliter
mm	millimeter
ms	millisecond
s	second

Finally, certain abbreviations of Latin and Middle English terms are regularly used in papers, although the APA manual states that they should be used only in parenthetical material. Some of these abbreviations and their meanings are given below:

cf.	compare	(from Latin *confer*)
e.g.,	for example,	(from Latin *exempli gratia*)
etc.	and so forth	(from Latin *et cetera*)
i.e.,	that is,	(from Latin *id est*)
viz.,	namely,	
vs.	versus	

REPORTING NUMBERS AND STATISTICS

Virtually all research papers report numbers: number of participants, number of groups, the values of statistics such as *t*, *F*, or *r*. Should you use numbers (e.g., *43*), or should you use words (e.g., *forty-three*)? The general rule is to use words when expressing the numbers zero through nine but to use numbers for 10 and above. There are some important qualifications, however.

If you start a sentence with a number, you should use words even if the number is 10 or larger (e.g., *Eighty-five student teachers participated in the study*). Starting a sentence with a number is often awkward, especially with large numbers. Therefore, you should try to revise the sentence to avoid the problem (e.g., *The participants were 85 students enrolled in teaching-credential classes*).

When numbers both above and below 10 are being compared in the same sentence, use numerals for both (e.g., *Participants read either 8 or 16 paragraphs*). However, this sentence contains an appropriate mix of numbers and words: *Participants read eight paragraphs and then answered 20 multiple-choice questions.* The sentence is correct because the paragraphs and the questions are different entities and so are not being compared.

When reporting a percentage, always use numerals followed by a percent sign except when beginning a sentence. This is true regardless of whether the number is less than 10 (e.g., *Only 6% of the computer games appealed to females.*) or greater than 10 (e.g., *When using this technique, 85% of the participants improved their performance*).

Always use numbers when describing ages (e.g., *5-year-olds*), points on a scale (e.g., *a 3 on a 5-point scale*), units of measurement (e.g., *the children stood 2 m from the target*), sample size (e.g., *6 girls and 6 boys were assigned to each study condition*), and statistics (e.g., *the mean score in the no-model group was 3.10*). An odd but sensible exception to the word–number rule occurs when two different types of numbers must appear together. An example is: *Teachers identified fifteen 7-year-olds as the most aggressive.* This sentence avoids an awkward juxtaposition of two numbers.

For a multiplication sign, use either a lowercase x or the multiplication symbol used by your word processor. This is true whether you are describing a mathematical operation or a factorial design (e.g., *a 2 × 2 design*). For a minus sign, go to Symbol and select the minus sign (note that the Symbol menu shows both an en dash and a minus sign—they are not the same). More generally, Word has an easy way to insert mathematical symbols: Insert > Equation brings up an equation input box and a set of symbols including addition, subtraction, multiplication, and division. You can choose to use a single symbol or type an entire equation. You should also use the multiplication symbol when describing a factorial design (e.g., *a 2 × 3 design*).

Finally, you need to know about presenting statistical results within your paper. As noted previously, statistical terms are abbreviated and typed with italics (e.g., M, r, t, F). In addition, when reporting the results of a statistical significance test, provide the name of the test, the degrees of freedom, the value of the test statistic, and the probability level. Here are two examples of sentences that describe statistical results:

> As predicted, participants in the high-anxiety condition took longer to recognize the words ($M = 2.63$, $SD = .42$) than did the individuals in the low-anxiety condition ($M = 1.42$, $SD = .36$), $t(20) = 2.54$, $p = .02$.

> Job satisfaction scores were significantly correlated with marital satisfaction, $r(50) = .48$, $p < .01$.

Recall that exact probabilities are reported using two or three decimal places. However, the computer printout may not indicate very small probabilities so you should use the < (less than) symbol for probabilities less than .01, as follows: $p < .01$. Many researchers prefer to report probabilities using three decimal places (e.g., $p = .037$) because the major statistical software applications provide that level of precision. In that case, use $p < .001$ with very small probabilities.

Pay attention to the way statistics are described in the articles you read. You will find that you can vary your descriptions of results to best fit your data and presentation, as well as vary your sentence constructions.

Finalizing Your Paper

Before printing your final copy, use your spelling and grammar checker; then give the paper one last look to find any possible errors.

PAPER AND POSTER PRESENTATIONS

Students present their research findings in many different ways: in class, at regional and national meetings of psychology organizations, and at conferences specifically designed to highlight student research. Advice on preparing paper and poster presentations is available in books (e.g., Nicol & Pexman, 2010a) and on a variety of websites (e.g., **http://colinpurrington.com/tips/academic/posterdesign**; **http://www.apa.org/science/about/psa/2010/04/presentation.aspx**; **http://www.apa.org/convention/poster-instructions.pdf**; **http://www.psychologicalscience.org/index.php/members/apssc/undergraduate_update/fall-2010/standing-in-front-of-your-poster-a-guide-for-new-presenters**).

Remember: (1) Prepare your presentation in advance to allow time for practice, (2) time is limited, and (3) have handouts available with a summary of your research and contact information including email address. Your presentation may take the form of a talk to an audience or a poster presentation in which individuals may read the poster and engage in conversation with you.

Oral Presentations

Paper presentations are only about 10 to 12 minutes long, and people in attendance receive lots of information in many sessions of the meeting. The major thing to remember, then, is that you should attempt to convey only a few major ideas about why and how you conducted your research. You can avoid describing the details of past research findings, discussing exactly how you did your data analysis, or listing every step in your procedure. Remember that your audience wants the "big picture," so make sure that you do not use technical jargon. Instead, use clear language to convey the reason you conducted the research, the general methods used, and the major results. You should try to provide a summary at the end, along with the conclusions you have reached about the meaning of the results.

It is a good idea to write the presentation in advance but not to read it to your actual audience. You can use the written version for practice and timing. Remember that many people in the audience would like a written summary to which they can refer later. Therefore, bring copies of a summary that includes your name, the title of the presentation, when and where it was presented, and how you can be contacted.

Posters

A poster session consists of a fairly large number of presenters who are provided with space to display poster material. During the poster session, members of the audience may stop to read the poster, and some may have questions or comments. The chance to have conversations about your research with people who find your work interesting is the most valuable feature of a poster session.

The conference organizers will provide information on the amount of space available for each poster. Typical dimensions are 4 feet high (1.22m) and 6 to 8 feet wide (1.83–2.44m); the poster itself is typically 30 to 36 inches high (76–91cm) and 40 to 48 inches wide (102–123cm). The poster materials will usually be divided up into areas of (1) title, name, affiliation, (2) abstract, (3) introduction information, (4) method, (5) results, along with tables and figures, and (6) conclusions. Examples of poster layouts are provided in **Figures 4** and **5**. The actual construction of the poster may consist of a series of separate pages or a single professionally printed poster using large-format printing technology.

Your college may have template files for constructing posters. A template is already formatted for a title, author, text, tables, and figures; it is ready for you to place your information without worrying about the technical aspects of designing the poster. If your college does not provide one, templates can be found on the web—for an example, see **https://colinpurrington.com/tips/academic/posterdesign#templates.**

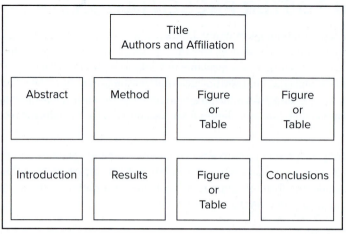

FIGURE 4   A sample poster

FIGURE 5   Sample poster template

African American College Student: ©pixelheadphoto digitalskillet/Shutterstock

Businesswoman with client in office: ©Jupiterimages/Getty Images

Avoid providing too much detail—often a bulleted list of major points will be most effective. One or two easy-to-read figures can also be very helpful. There are probably no more than two major points that you would like someone to remember after viewing your poster. Make sure those points are obvious. The font that you use should be large enough to be read from a distance (usually the text will be 26- to 32-point font). Color can be used to enhance the attractiveness of the display. Remember to bring copies of a summary that includes the date and location of the conference as well as your contact information.

CRITICAL THINKING: BEING A SKILLED CONSUMER OF RESEARCH

The way in which behavioral scientists communicate is intentional. Everything from the width of the margin to the way in which the work of others is referenced is done for a reason. Learning about APA formatting may seem like a task without reason, but it is actually developed over time to enhance communication by providing a common style—it is easier to read manuscripts and provide peer reviews of papers that are formatted consistently. But more than that, APA style represents important features of how behavioral scientists think: There are deeper reasons for APA style being what it is. Madigan et al. (1995) published a paper titled "The Language of Psychology: APA Style as Epistemology (available at **https://pdfs.semanticscholar.org/c7a2/270cd3fe06ba86b475fba6c32bd4a528d d37.pdf**)":

> Madigan, R., Johnson, S., & Linton, P. (1995). The language of psychology: APA style as epistemology. *American Psychologist, 50*(6), 428–436. https://doi.org/10.1037/ 0003-066X.50.6.428

After reading the article, respond to the following:

1. Describe each of the five characteristics of APA style as described by Madigan et al.
2. Describe how each of these five characteristics of APA style represents the "core values and epistemology of the discipline" (p. 428).
3. Given Madigan et al. and your discussion of the article, discuss how reducing bias in language (APA, 2020b, pp. 130–149) represents one of the "core values and epistemology of the discipline" (p. 428).

SAMPLE PAPER

The remainder of this appendix consists of a typed manuscript of a paper that was published in a professional journal. This is intended to be a useful guide when you write your own reports in APA style. Read through the manuscript, paying particular attention to the general format, and make sure you understand the rules concerning page numbering, section headings, reference citation, and the format of figures. Writing your first research report is always a challenging task. It will become easier as you read the research of others and gain practice by writing reports of your own.

Dr. Janet Polivy from the University of Toronto graciously gave permission to adapt the paper to illustrate elements of APA style. The comments at the side alert you to features of APA style that you will need to know about when writing your own papers. Be aware, though, that every paper will include slightly different types of information depending on the particular topic, method, and results. Your paper will follow the general guidelines of APA style, but many of the details will be determined by the needs of your study.

You may note that the title of this paper is longer than the 12 words recommended by APA style (many journals do not enforce the word length rule). A briefer title might be *Effects of Perceived Portion Size on Eating and Emotion*. A problem with this shorter title is that a search for articles with *restrained eaters* in the title would not find this article; a few extra words can often be useful to future researchers.

If you would be interested in viewing other samples of papers in APA style, there are several good ones that may be located with an internet search. Make sure the ones you use specify seventh edition of the APA manual.

GETTING A BIGGER SLICE

1

Getting a Bigger Slice of the Pie: Effects on
Eating and Emotion in Restrained and Unrestrained Eaters

Janet Polivy, C. Peter Herman, and Rajbir Deo
Department of Psychology, University of Toronto

The running head is a shortened version of the title (up to 50 characters, including spaces).

All pages are numbered consecutively, starting with the title page. Page numbers are flush right, on the same line as the running head. Running head is flush left and page number is flush right in header area of the page.

The title is usually no more than 12 words centered and boldface.

Title, author(s), and affiliation are centered and appear in the upper half of the page.

The Author Note, if required, would begin about here. Student papers usually do not require an author note.

GETTING A BIGGER SLICE   2

Abstract

We investigated the influence of perceptions of the portion size of food on subsequent eating by restrained and unrestrained eaters. In the present study, all participants were served a same-sized slice of pizza. For one-third of participants, their slice appeared larger than the slice being served to another ostensible participant, another third perceived their slice as smaller, and the final third did not see a second slice. All participants then proceeded to "taste and rate" cookies in an ad lib eating opportunity. A significant interaction reflected the fact that when the pizza slice was perceived as large, restrained eaters tended to eat more cookies whereas unrestrained eaters tended to eat less cookies. Emotion data suggest that the differential responses of restrained and unrestrained eaters to the belief that they have overeaten relative to another eater influenced their subsequent dissimilar ad lib eating behavior.

The running head identified on the title page should be carried forward on every subsequent page. It should remain flush left in all uppercase letters.

There is no paragraph indentation in the abstract.

Abstract begins on a new page with the word **"Abstract"** centered and bold.

The abstract is generally 150–250 words in length.

Keywords appear below the abstract in a professional paper. A student paper usually does not need keywords.

Getting a Bigger Slice of the Pie: Effects on Eating and Emotion in Restrained and Unrestrained Eaters

We often eat one food followed by another (e.g., main course and then dessert). How much we eat of the later food probably depends to a large extent on our intake of the earlier food. In the laboratory, we refer to the earlier food as a "preload." The effects of food preloads on subsequent eating are complex: Chronic dieters or restrained eaters generally respond quite differently than nondieters or unrestrained eaters do. Whereas unrestrained eaters typically compensate by eating less after a larger preload than after a smaller one, restrained eaters often "counter-regulate," eating more after a large preload than after a small preload or after no preload at all (Adams & Leary, 2007; Herman et al., 1987; Polivy, et al., 1988; Polivy et al., 1986). Presumably, the larger preload is more likely to sabotage the restrained eater's diet for that day, undermining motivation for continued restraint and unleashing disinhibited eating (possibly potentiated by chronic perceived deprivation). If the preload is actually large and fattening, it is likely to produce disinhibited eating by restrained eaters (Herman et al., 1987; McCann et al., 1992; Polivy et al., 1986, 1988), but disinhibition may be observed even when the restrained eater is merely led to believe that the preload is high in calories or otherwise forbidden (Polivy, 1976; Spencer & Fremouw, 1979) or when the restrained eater draws that implication from the nature of the food itself (Knight & Boland, 1989).

Previous studies have manipulated the perceived size of the preload (holding actual size or caloric content constant) by either telling participants that the preloads are high in calories (Polivy, 1976; Spencer & Fremouw, 1979) or by implication. For example, Knight and Boland (1989), served iso-caloric preloads of milkshake or a cottage cheese and fruit mixture. Restrained eaters displayed disinhibition only when served milkshake, because they regard milkshake as inherently more caloric than the salad-like cottage cheese and fruit mixture.

Punctuation such as periods and commas appear inside the quotes. Punctuation such as question marks, exclamation marks, colons, and semicolons that are not part of the quote appear outside the quotes.

Standard form: Citation of two authors, parenthetically (Author & Author, Year).

Standard form: Citation of three or more authors: (Author et at., Year)

When several references are cited together, alphabetize, and separate with a semicolon.

Standard form: Citation of a single author, parenthetically (Author, Year).

GETTING A BIGGER SLICE   4

More recently, Pliner and Zec (2007) showed that thinking about a preload as a meal (rather than as a snack) makes people perceive the preload as higher in calories and affects eating accordingly.

The present study was designed to further extend the exploration of the effects of perceived preload/portion size on eating and, moreover, to do this in a more externally valid meal setting. In order to understand the source of these effects, we included measures of affective responses, as it has been shown that affect influences eating differently for restrained and unrestrained eaters (Polivy & Herman, 1999), and eating, especially eating what is seen as a large amount, affects emotions differently in restrained and unrestrained eaters (Polivy & Herman, 2005).

We hypothesized that even with the preload/meal held constant, restrained eaters who regard the portion as larger will subsequently eat more than will those who regard it as normal sized or small, because the "large" portion is more likely to break their diets and lead to disinhibited eating. We also predicted that unrestrained eaters will eat less after a perceived large portion than after what they perceive to be a normal-sized meal, and less after a portion perceived as normal sized than after one perceived as small. In the present study, all participants received an identical, standard light lunch meal, but some were led to perceive the portion they received as large and some were led to perceive the portion as small simply by means of social comparison (or more accurately, perceptual contrast). If someone gets a larger portion than yours, your own portion may appear to be "small," whereas, if someone gets a portion that is smaller than yours, your own portion may appear to be "large."

Method

Participants

The participants were 106 female undergraduate students enrolled in an introductory psychology class at a large university. The participants were recruited via an experimental database, where they could sign up for a study entitled "Market Taste Test Study." Each experimental session lasted 1 hr; participants received credit toward a course requirement for their participation.

Annotation boxes (left margin):

Standard form for citation of two authors, in text: Name and Name (Year).

Level 1 heading The Method section begins immediately after the Introduction (no new page). The word "Method" is centered and **boldface**.

Level 2 heading Subsection headings such as "Participants" are **boldface**, typed flush to the left margin, and set alone on the line.

Use numerals to express numbers 10 and above.

Use numerals to express numbers that are immediately followed by a unit of measurement (in this case, hr for hour). Also abbreviate min (minute), s (second), ms (millisecond). Do not abbreviate day, week, month, year.

GETTING A BIGGER SLICE   5

Materials

Food

Extra-large uncut cheese pizza was ordered from a local pizza chain for each day of experimentation. The slices were reheated in a microwave oven before they were served to the participants. Any leftover pizza was stored in a freezer for use on another day. Frozen cookie dough (from a manufacturer who supplies "fresh-baked" cookies to local restaurants) was stored in a freezer and used to bake bite-sized cookies regularly throughout the week. Three different types of cookies were baked as needed: oatmeal raisin, chocolate chip, and double chocolate chip.

Questionnaires

Pre- and post-pizza rating scales were completed by all participants immediately after the manipulation and again after the pizza but before the cookie taste test. The pizza rating scales included a section from the PANAS (Positive and Negative Affect Schedule; Watson, Clark, & Tellegen, 1988), which was designed to measure the participants' negative affect. Participants described their negative emotional states such as "guilty" and "angry" using rating scales ranging from 1 for *very slightly or not at all* to 5 for *extremely*. Other questions assessed hunger and various aspects of the pizza that they were about to eat or had just eaten using a 9-point Likert-type scale. These questions included a manipulation check that asked participants to rate the portion size (rating from 1 for *too small* to 5 for *just right* to 9 for *too big*). The questions were answered before and after eating the pizza (with wording changed appropriately). In addition, participants were asked at the end of the study to what extent they had noticed any difference in the size of the pizza slices ("How did your slice of pizza compare to the slice received by the other person in the study?" Response options were *smaller*, *the same*, and *larger*).

Restraint Scale

The 10-item Herman and Polivy Revised Restraint Scale (Herman, Polivy, & Silver, 1979) was used to determine restraint status. Participants who scored 15 or less on the restraint scale were classified as unrestrained eaters, whereas participants who scored above 15 were classified as restrained eaters.

This section describes the measures and materials used to conduct the study. They make up a sort of "ingredients" list for the study.

Level 3 heading

Define unfamiliar acronyms when they are first used.

The anchors of scales (e.g., *very slightly or not at all*) are *italicized*.

GETTING A BIGGER SLICE   6

Procedure

Female participants were recruited for this study through a psychology experimental website advertisement that specified that the participants must have no food allergies, must not be lactose intolerant, and should refrain from eating for up to 3 hr prior to their experimental session.

Each participant was informed that she would be given a light vegetarian cheese-pizza lunch in order to ensure that each participant had the same taste experience and same level of fullness before completing taste ratings for market research. She was told that she would be sampling various food products that were being proposed for the market by a large food company that targeted the university-student population. The participant was also informed that she would be completing some questionnaires to assess her mood and other variables to ensure that these factors were not influencing her food ratings. Furthermore, the participant was told that she would be discussing her food ratings with another female participant in a brief discussion at the end of their session. She then signed the consent form.

Participants were randomly assigned to one of three pizza-slice conditions: smaller slice, larger slice, and no information. Regardless of which condition the participant was in, she always received a standard slice of pizza (1/6 of the pizza), but the size of the "other participant's" slice was varied. Each pizza was cut into six pieces consisting of four standard-sized slices (1/6 of the pizza), one larger slice (1/3 larger than a standard-sized slice), and one smaller slice (1/3 smaller than the standard slice). In order to ensure that each slice was consistently cut for all pizzas used in the study, the appropriate sized slices were drawn onto a piece of paper and cut out to be used as templates for all pizzas. Thus, in the "smaller" condition, the participant received a standard-sized slice of pizza, while the "other female participant" was supposedly receiving the slice 1/3 larger than the standard slice. Similarly, participants in the "larger" condition received the standard slice of pizza, while the "other female participant" appeared to be receiving the slice

---

This section describes exactly how the study was conducted.

Numbers less than 10 are expressed as words.

GETTING A BIGGER SLICE   7

1/3 smaller than the standard slice. In the "no information" control condition,
participants were given a standard-sized slice of pizza, with no indication of the
"other female participant's" slice.

When the experimenter presented the participant with the pizza slices, the pizza
slices were placed on a tray with a glass of water next to each slice and brought into
the experimental room. Each participant in the "smaller" condition was presented with
her standard-sized slice of pizza next to the 1/3 larger slice belonging to the "other
female participant," which was identified as such as it was situated further away from
her. Each participant in the "larger condition" saw her standard-sized slice along
with the "other" female participant's smaller slice. In the "no information" control
condition, the participant was presented only with her standard-sized slice, along
with a glass of water. The experimenter then left the room, leaving the slices in the
room and explaining that she had to retrieve a questionnaire for the participants. The
experimenter left the room for exactly 1 min, allowing a sufficient amount of time for
the participant to observe the slices and perceive the differences in their sizes. When
the experimenter returned, the participant's slice and water were placed on the table in
front of her and the pre-pizza rating scale was handed to the participant. She was asked
to complete the questionnaire before eating her pizza slice. The experimenter then left
the room with the "other participant's" slice.

The participant was given 7 min to complete the preeating questionnaire and
to eat her entire pizza slice (supposedly to ensure equal fullness in all participants),
after which time the experimenter returned to the experimental room and handed
the participant another set of questionnaires (to maintain the cover story). These
questionnaires included the post-pizza scales. The participant was instructed
to ring a bell when she had completed the questionnaires. At that time, the
experimenter returned with three heaping (preweighed) plates of each of three
types of cookie and another glass of water, plus three cookie-rating sheets (one
for each cookie type). Tasting these cookies was ostensibly the principal purpose

> Numbers that are immediately followed by a unit of measurement are expressed as numerals, as are numbers that represent time.

GETTING A BIGGER SLICE 8

of the experiment, but the cookies were actually provided as a measure of ad lib consumption. In order to measure how many cookies the participants ate, the cookies were weighed prior to the experimental session and again after the "taste-test task." A heaping amount of each cookie type (oatmeal raisin, chocolate chip, and double chocolate chip) was placed onto one of three separate plates and the weight of each plate was measured and recorded. The three plates of cookies were placed on the table in front of the participant, with oatmeal-raisin cookies always being first, chocolate-chip cookies second, and double chocolate-chip cookies third. The participant was instructed that she would now be participating in the taste-test portion of the study, wherein she would sample three different types of cookies that were about to be released on the market by a large food company that marketed its snack foods to the university-aged population. The participant was instructed to begin with the oatmeal-raisin cookies and take as many cookies as she required to be very sure of her taste ratings of the cookies. She was told to sample the oatmeal-raisin cookies first, followed by the chocolate-chip cookies, and finally the double chocolate-chip cookies. It was emphasized that once she had completed the ratings for one cookie type, she was not to go back and resample the previous cookie type and she was not to change her ratings once she had moved on to a "new taste." The water was provided to permit the participant to "cleanse her palate" as she moved from cookie to cookie. Moreover, the participant was reminded to be sure of her ratings since she would be comparing her food ratings with the "other female participant" at the end of the session. Finally, the participant was informed that once she was finished making her ratings, there were plenty of cookies and she was free to have as many more of any type as she liked, as long as she did not change any ratings. After the instructions were clear to the participant, the experimenter left the room for 10 min.

The experimenter reentered the room with the final set of questionnaires to be completed (including the restraint scale). The cookie plates were removed from the

GETTING A BIGGER SLICE   9

room, where they were reweighed without the participants' knowledge, in order to measure how many grams of cookies the participant had consumed. When the participant had completed the last set of questionnaires, her height and weight were measured and recorded. The participant was debriefed as to the purpose of the study. She was also asked if she had noticed the size difference in the pizza slices that had been presented, when she last ate, and what she ate at that time. She was thanked and asked some questions about the experiment so that she could receive credit for her psychology course before being dismissed. The study was thus conducted in accordance with ethical principles and had full institutional ethical review and approval.

Results

Participant Characteristics

A series of 2 (restrained versus unrestrained) × 3 (control, "small slice," "large slice") ANOVAs indicated the usual restraint main effect on BMI, $F(1,98) = 9.77$, $p = .002$, with restrained eaters having higher BMIs ($M = 24.27$) than unrestrained eaters ($M = 21.63$). There was no effect of condition and no significant interaction; as well, there were no restraint or condition differences in preeating hunger.

Manipulation Checks

On the pre- and post-pizza questionnaires, participants were asked about the quantity of pizza that they had been served. A 2 (restrained versus unrestrained) × 3 (control, "small slice," "large slice") ANOVA on each of these questions yielded only main effects for condition, preeating $F(2,97) = 5.25$, $p = .008$, and posteating $F(2,100) = 8.16$, $p < .001$. In both analyses, the "small" slice was rated as close to 5 (which corresponded to "just right") ($Mpre = 5.22$; $Mpost = 5.43$), the control/no information slice was seen as bigger than the small one ($Mpre = 5.69$; $Mpost = 6.03$), and the "large" slice was seen as bigger than either of the others ($Mpre = 6.33$; $Mpost = 6.80$). All differences were significant at the .05 level.

The Results section begins immediately following the Method section. The word "Results" is centered and **boldface**.

When the outcome of a statistical test is presented, the name of the test is italicized and followed by the degrees of freedom in parentheses. The *p* refers to the probability of obtaining the results if the null hypothesis is correct.

Generally, exact probabilities are shown except when *p* < .001. Sometimes it is appropriate to use "ns" to indicate that a result is nonsignificant.

Statistical symbols, such as *M* for the mean, are italicized.

GETTING A BIGGER SLICE   10

Cookie Intake

A 2 (Restraint: restrained, unrestrained) × 3 (Condition: control, "small

slice," "large slice") ANOVA on the amount of cookies eaten (in grams)

yielded no main effects of restraint or condition; however, there was a significant

interaction, $F(2,100) = 3.51$, $p = .034$, $\eta^2 = 0.066$. Post hoc t tests indicated

that whereas neither restrained nor unrestrained participants in the "small

slice" condition differed from those in the control condition or from each

other, restrained and unrestrained eaters in the "large slice" condition differed

significantly from each other, $t(100) = 2.98$, $p = .005$. In addition, although not

significant, restrained eaters in the "large slice" condition ate marginally more

than did restrained eaters in the control condition, $t(100) = 1.82$, $p = .075$, and

unrestrained eaters in the "large slice" condition ate marginally less than did

unrestrained eaters in the control condition, $t(100) = 1.66$, $p = .10$ (see Table 1 for

all means and standard deviations).

Negative Affect

A 2 × 3 ANOVA on total negative affect before eating the pizza (but after

the manipulation of perceived portion size) yielded no significant main effects,

but there was a significant interaction between restraint and condition, $F(2,100) =$

3.40, $p = .037$, $\eta^2 = 0.066$ (see Figure 1). The only significant differences found

in the post hoc t tests were between the "small" versus "large" conditions for

the unrestrained eaters, with those receiving the large slice feeling more negative

emotion than those receiving the small slice, $t(100) = 2.25$, $p = .026$, and between

restrained and unrestrained eaters in the "small" condition, $t(100) = 2.03$,

$p = .045$, with restrained eaters feeling more negative affect than did unrestrained

eaters. The analysis comparing restrained and unrestrained participants in the

"large" slice condition indicated a trend in the opposite direction, $t(100) = 1.49$,

$p = .14$, as did the analysis comparing "small" versus "large" for restrained eaters,

$t(100) = 1.41$, $p = .17$. The negative affect ratings made after eating the pizza were

GETTING A BIGGER SLICE   11

no longer significantly different. Also, there were no significant effects on hunger

ratings either before or after eating the pizza.

Discussion

Participants clearly perceived the size of their portion of pizza differently as a

function of whether they saw a comparison slice and what they saw in the comparison.

When they saw their slice next to a larger one, they perceived their slice as smaller

than did those who did not see a comparison slice; and when they saw their slice

next to a smaller slice they perceived it as larger than did participants who saw only

their own slice. The change in perception occurred despite the fact that not only were

all participants given the same-sized slice, but this size is the standard slice sold on

campus and at all other outlets of the major pizza chain that supplied the pizza.

Based simply on these different perceptions of the identical portion,

participants went on to eat different amounts, as shown by the significant

interaction between restraint and condition. Those who saw their pizza slice

as smaller ate the same amount of cookies as did those who did not have a

comparison (regardless of restraint status), but the cookie intake of those who

thought that they had eaten a larger slice of pizza was affected by this perception

(in different ways depending on restraint status). That the effect was more a

matter of the "large slice" condition changing intake somewhat (relative to

control) than of the "small slice" condition changing intake (relative to control)

was probably due to the fact that in the "small slice" condition, the slice was seen

as close to—indeed, slightly more than—"just right," but the "large slice" was

seen as significantly larger than "just right." In other words, it was the pizza in the

"large slice" condition that was seen as unusually large, rather than the pizza in

the "small slice" condition being seen as unusually small.

The direction of the effect in the "large slice" condition depended on restraint

status, as was reflected in the significant interaction. Restrained and unrestrained

eaters ate the same amount of cookies in the control and "small slice" conditions,

The Discussion section is used to list and comment upon the implications of the results of the study. The Discussion section immediately follows the Results section. The word "Discussion" is centered and **boldface**.

Quotation marks are placed after the period.

GETTING A BIGGER SLICE   12

but unrestrained eaters tended to eat less in the "large slice" condition, whereas restrained eaters tended to eat more in the "large slice" condition. (Restrained eaters ate significantly more than did unrestrained eaters in the "large slice" condition.) In other words, unrestrained eaters compensated by eating less cookies if they thought that they had eaten a lot of pizza, whereas restrained eaters counter-regulated and ate more cookies when they thought that they had already overeaten on pizza. This pattern corresponds to the effect obtained in previous research when preload size was actually manipulated or when perceived preload size was manipulated by telling participants that the preloads varied in caloric value (Polivy, 1976) or by implying that the preloads differed in caloric value because they were either "forbidden" or "allowed" foods (e.g., Knight & Boland, 1989). While subtle manipulations such as the smell of food have been shown to induce restrained eaters to eat more (Fedoroff et al., 1997, 2003; Jansen & Van den Hout, 1991), the present study involved arguably the subtlest manipulation yet. Nothing was said about size or caloric value of the preload, and the identical preload/meal was used in all conditions; only a visual comparison to someone else's smaller portion acted to render one's own portion relatively large, with predictable effects on subsequent intake. Moreover, the present "preload" was actually a meal ("light lunch") rather than extraneous eating. However, even simply perceiving one's meal as "larger than just right" seems to have been enough to push eating in opposite directions for restrained versus unrestrained eaters. Eating was thus more strongly influenced by social comparison and the perception this fostered (I'm eating more than she is) than by actual portion size.

     The fact that restrained eaters ate somewhat more in the "large slice" condition is what we have come to expect from the literature in which restrained eaters typically overeat after a large preload (or a preload perceived as large). That they did not eat less in the "small slice" condition than in the control condition was consistent with the finding that restrained eaters' eating is

APA strongly encourages writers to use past tense when reporting procedures and results.

"dichotomous": they ate either a small, reasonable amount, when they were not disinhibited (i.e., when the preload was not seen as large, or they were not disinhibited by food cues, negative emotion, or other factors) or they ate a large amount when they became disinhibited (i.e., when the preload—or in the present case, meal—was large or perceived as large). In the present study, the "large slice" condition was perceived as a large preload/meal whereas the other two conditions were seen as appropriate sized.

The unrestrained eaters on the other hand did not compensate for receiving the smaller piece of pizza by eating more cookies, even though they perceived the smaller portion as smaller than the other portions. They did, however, rate the small slice as "just right" in size. They may possibly have simply responded to their internal signals of satiety and thus ate the same amount of cookies as did the unrestrained eaters who got no comparative information (and also saw their slice as close to the "right" size). Of course, unrestrained eaters in the large slice condition presumably had the same satiety signals, but unrestrained eaters may be more prepared to eat less (after a preload/meal that they consider to be large) than to eat more (after a preload/meal that they consider to be "just right").

Not surprisingly, because all participants were actually given and ate the same amount of pizza, there were no group or condition differences in hunger either before or after eating the pizza. There were, however, some potentially interesting differences in the extent of negative affect experienced upon realizing that one had been given a larger or smaller portion of pizza. For unrestrained eaters, getting a large slice made them more dysphoric, but for restrained eaters, dysphoria was higher when they received a smaller slice. Although small, these opposite emotional reactions may speak to the differential psychology of the restrained and unrestrained eaters. Unrestrained eaters may be responding to the prescriptive norm of not appearing to eat excessively (Herman et al., 2003), and feel worse if they think that they are violating the norm. Restrained eaters, on the other hand, may actually be more upset with being allowed to maintain their diets (by eating the smaller piece); apparently they feel somewhat better when "forced" by the experimenter to eat "more," break their diets, and indulge themselves with additional cookies. This interpretation comports with the assumption that fundamentally, people want to eat as much as possible, but are constrained by considerations of social propriety (not eating excessively so as not to look like a "pig") or their self-imposed dietary agendas (Herman et al., 2003). When forced by someone else to transgress against their diets, restrained eaters may well experience what we have called the "what the hell effect" (Herman & Polivy, 1984) and feel relieved to be pushed off their diets and allowed to unleash their eating.

The present study shows that the mere perception that one's meal was excessively large acts the same as a gratuitous preload to disinhibit eating in restrained eaters. The data also show that restrained and unrestrained eaters alike judge the amount that they are served in comparison to what those around them are eating. Such perceptions about the social context or meaning of one's portion apparently outweigh feelings of hunger in influencing the amount eaten, particularly if one sees oneself as having overeaten relative to others. Restrained eaters, when they perceive themselves as having eaten excessively compared to others, continue to eat liberally rather than curtail their intake. This indulgence undermines their stated dietary goals, but the fact that they feel worse when they do not (get to) overindulge provides a hint as to why dieters so often find themselves breaking their diets.

GETTING A BIGGER SLICE   15

References

Adams, C., & Leary, M. (2007). Promoting self-compassionate attitudes toward eating among restrictive and guilty eaters. *Journal of Social & Clinical Psychology, 26*(10), 1120–1144. https://doi.org/10.1521/jscp.2007.26.10.1120

Fedoroff, I., Polivy, J., & Herman, C. P. (1997). The effect of pre-exposure to food cues on the eating behavior of restrained and unrestrained eaters. *Appetite, 28*(1), 33–47. https://doi.org/10.1006/appe.1996.0057

Fedoroff, I., Polivy, J., & Herman, C. P. (2003). The specificity of restrained versus unrestrained eaters' responses to food cues: General desire to eat, or craving for the cued food? *Appetite, 41*(1), 7–13. https://doi.org/10.1016/S0195-6663(03)00026-6

Jansen, A., & Van den Hout, M. (1991). On being led into temptation: "Counterregulation" of dieters after smelling a preload. *Addictive Behaviors, 16*(5), 247–253. https://doi.org/10.1016/0306-4603(91)90017-C

Herman, C. P., & Polivy, J. (1984). A boundary model for the regulation of eating. *Psychiatric Annals, 13*(12), 918–927.

Herman, C. P., Polivy, J., & Silver, R. (1979). Effects of an observer on eating behavior: The induction of "sensible" eating. *Journal of Personality, 47*(1), 85–99. https://doi.org/10.1111/j.1467-6494.1979.tb00616.x

Herman, C. P., Polivy, J., & Esses, V. M. (1987). The illusion of counter-regulation. *Appetite, 9*(3), 161–169. https://doi.org/10.1016/S0195-6663(87)80010-7

Herman, C. P., Roth, D., & Polivy, J. (2003). Effects of the presence of others on food intake. A normative interpretation. *Psychological Bulletin, 129*(6), 873–886. https://doi.org/10.1037/0033-2909.129.6.873

Knight, L., & Boland, F. (1989). Restrained eating. An experimental disentanglement of the disinhibiting variables of calories and food type. *Journal of Abnormal Psychology, 98*(4), 412–420. https://doi.org/10.1037/0021-843X.98.4.412

References begin on a new page. The word "References" is centered at the top of the page and boldface.

A comma always follows the first author's initial, even if only two authors are listed.

APA style recommends including the DOI (Digital Object Identifier) if it is available.

APA recommends using the en-dash symbol between page numbers rather than a simple hyphen.

Each reference begins on a new line and is considered a paragraph.

The paragraph is a hanging indent, in which the first line is flush to the left margin and subsequent lines are indented.

GETTING A BIGGER SLICE   16

McCann, K. L., Perri, M. G., Nezu, A. M., & Lowe, M. R. (1992). An
     investigation of counterregulatory eating in obese clinic attenders.
     International Journal of Eating Disorders, 12(2), 161–169. https://doi.
     org/10.1002/1098-108X(199209)12:2<161::AID-EAT2260120206>3.0.CO;2-A

Pliner, P., & Zec, D. (2007). Meal schemas during a preload decrease subsequent
     eating. *Appetite, 48*(3), 278–288. https://doi.org/10.1016/j.appet.2006.04.009

Polivy, J. (1976). Perception of calories and regulation of intake in restrained and
     unrestrained subjects. *Addictive Behaviors, 1*(3), 237–243. https://doi.
     org/10.1016/0306-4603(76)90016-2

Polivy, J., Heatherton, T. F., & Herman, C. P. (1988). Self-esteem, restraint, and
     eating behavior. *Journal of Abnormal Psychology, 97*(3), 354–356. https://doi.
     org/10.1037/0021-843X.97.3.354

Polivy, J., & Herman, C. P. (1999). Distress and eating: Why do dieters overeat?
     International Journal of Eating Disorders, 26(2), 153–164. https://doi.
     org/10.1002/(SICI)1098-108X(199909)26:2<153::AID-EAT4>3.0.CO;2-R

Polivy, J., & Herman, C. P. (2005). Mental health and eating behaviours: A
     bi-directional relation. *Canadian Journal of Public Health, 96*(3), 43–48.

Polivy, J., Herman, C. P., Hackett, R., & Kuleshnyk, I. (1986). The effects of self-
     attention and public attention on eating in restrained and unrestrained subjects.
     Journal of Personality and Social Psychology, 50(6), 1203–1224.
     https://doi.org/10.1037/0022-3514.50.6.1253

Spencer, J. A., & Fremouw, W. J. (1979). Binge eating as a function of restraint and
     weight classification. *Journal of Abnormal Psychology, 88*(3), 262–267.
     https://doi.org/ 10.1037/0021-843X.88.3.262

Watson, D., Clark, L. A., & Tellegen, A. (1988). Development and validation of
     brief measures of positive and negative affect: The PANAS scale. *Journal
     of Personality and Social Psychology, 54* (6), 1063–1070. https://doi.org/10.1037/
     0022-3514.54.6.1063

Titles of books and journals are *italicized*, as are the volume numbers of journals.

Note that "&" is used for multiple authors throughout the Reference section.

Note capitalization: First word and first word following a colon, plus any proper nouns.

When the same set of authors is included multiple times, the entries are ordered by date, from oldest to newest.

No period following doi.

GETTING A BIGGER SLICE   17

Table 1

Amount of Cookies Eaten (in grams) in the Pizza Size Conditions

	Larger slice			Control/no info			Smaller slice		
Restraint	*M*	*SD*	*n*	*M*	*SD*	*n*	*M*	*SD*	*n*
Unrestrained eaters	50.39	6.83	25	67.89	8.05	18	61.20	7.12	23
Restrained eaters	84.36	9.13	14	59.94	9.86	12	62.12	9.13	14

Note. The number of participants (*n*) in the unrestrained eaters group is higher than the number in the restrained group when using the standard cutoff score on the Restraint Scale.

The first line of the table is the table number and is typed in boldface.

The next double-spaced line should include the table title, which should be *italicized*, with all major words capitalized. No period is required.

Only the first words of headings within the table are capitalized. Sections of the table are separated by horizontal lines. Do not use vertical lines.

A note below the table is optional. The note may provide additional information such as an explanation of abbreviations or specific group differences.

A horizontal line should separate column headers from data presented in the table.

Include another horizontal line below the last row of information.

GETTING A BIGGER SLICE   18

Figure 1

Total Negative Affect Before Eating Pizza But After Seeing It

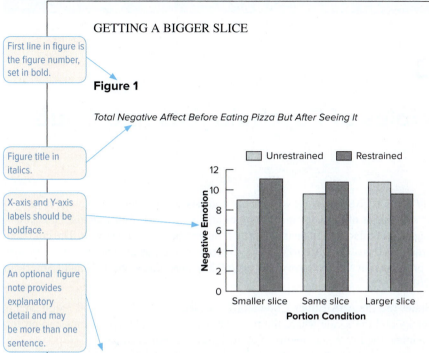

Note. Post hoc *t* tests show a significant difference between the restrained and unrestrained eaters who were given the smaller slice. Unrestrained eaters getting the small slice felt better than those given the larger slice; restrained eaters given the small slice felt marginally worse than those given the large slice.

Appendix B

Ethical Principles of Psychologists and Code of Conduct

The APA *Ethical Principles of Psychologists and Code of Conduct* consists of five General Principles and 10 Standards. We have included summaries of the General Principles and *Standard 8: Research and Publication*, which is most relevant to designing, conducting, evaluating, and producing behavioral research. The complete document, including standards that focus on other roles of psychologists, such as clinical practitioner, may be found at with a complete print version at **https://www.apa.org/ethics/code/ethics-code-2017.pdf** (American Psychological Association, 2017).

Researchers in the United States use the APA Ethics Code along with federal regulations and requirements of their own college or university and the locale where the research is conducted. Other nations and professional societies have also developed their own statements of ethical practice. For example:

Canadian Psychological Association *Code of Ethics*: **https://www.cpa.ca/aboutcpa/committees/ethics/codeofethics/**

British Psychological Society *Code of Ethics and Conduct*: **https://www.bps.org.uk/news-and-policy/bps-code-ethics-and-conduct**

American Educational Research Association *Code of Ethics*: **http://www.aera.net/Portals/38/docs/About_AERA/CodeOfEthics(1).pdf**

Society for Research in Child Development *Ethical Standards in Research*: **http://www.srcd.org/about-us/ethical-standards-research**

GENERAL PRINCIPLES

General Principles are aspirational; they are intended to guide and inspire psychologists toward the very highest ethical ideals of the profession.

Principle A: Beneficence and Nonmaleficence: Psychologists strive to benefit those with whom they work and take care to do no harm.

Principle B: Fidelity and Responsibility: Psychologists establish relationships of trust with those with whom they work.

Principle C: Integrity: Psychologists seek to promote accuracy, honesty, and truthfulness in the science, teaching, and practice of psychology.

Principle D: Justice: Psychologists recognize that fairness and justice entitle all persons to access to and benefit from the contributions of psychology and to equal quality in the processes, procedures, and services being conducted by psychologists.

Principle E: Respect for People's Rights and Dignity: Psychologists respect the dignity and worth of all people, and the rights of individuals to privacy, confidentiality, and self-determination.

Source: APA Ethical Principles of Psychologists and Code of Conduct (American Psychological Assocation, 2017).

STANDARD 8: RESEARCH AND PUBLICATION

Standard 8 (Research and Publication) describes the ethical standards related to designing, conducting, evaluating, and producing behavioral research. The full standard can be found HERE. A brief summary of relevant sections of this standard are included below.

8.01 Institutional Approval: "Psychologists provide accurate information about their research proposals and obtain approval prior to conducting the research. They conduct the research in accordance with the approved research protocol."

8.02 Informed Consent to Research: Research subjects are informed about the nature of any study that they are participating in and provide consent for participation.

8.06 Offering Inducements for Research Participation: When conducting research, psychologists do not offer excessive incentives, which are coercive.

8.07 Deception in Research: "Psychologists do not conduct a study involving deception unless they have determined that the use of deceptive techniques is justified by the study's significant prospective scientific, educational or applied value and that effective nondeceptive alternative procedures are not feasible."

8.08 Debriefing: Psychologists debrief research participants.

8.09 Humane Care and Use of Animals in Research: "(a)Psychologists acquire, care for, use, and dispose of animals in compliance with current federal, state and local laws and regulations, and with professional standards."

8.10 Reporting Research Results: "Psychologists do not fabricate data." Psychologists correct significant errors in published data.

8.11 Plagiarism: "Psychologists do not present portions of another's work or data as their own."

8.12 Publication Credit: Psychologists take credit only for work to which they have substantially contributed and work to assign authorship in ways that align with individual contributions.

8.14 Sharing Research Data for Verification: "Psychologists do not withhold the data on which their conclusions are based from other competent professionals who seek to verify the substantive claims through reanalysis and who intend to use such data only for that purpose, provided that the confidentiality of the participants can be protected and unless legal rights concerning proprietary data preclude their release."

Source: American Psychological Assocation (2017).

Appendix C
Statistical Tests

The purpose of this appendix is to provide the formulas and calculational procedures for analysis of data. Not all possible statistical tests are included, but a variety of tests are given that should be appropriate for many of the research designs you might use.

We will examine both descriptive and inferential statistics. Before you study the statistics, however, you should review the properties of measurement scales described in the chapter **"Measurement Concepts."** Remember that there are four types of measurement scales: nominal, ordinal, interval, and ratio. Nominal scales have no numerical properties, ordinal scales provide rank-order information only, and interval and ratio scales have equal intervals between the points on the scale. In addition, ratio scales have a true zero point. You will also recall from the chapter **"Understanding Research Results: Statistical Inference"** that the appropriate statistical analysis is determined by the type of design and by the measurement scale that was used in the study. As we proceed, the discussion of the various statistical tests will draw to your attention the relevant measurement scale restrictions that apply.

The examples here use small and simple data sets so the calculations can be easily done by hand using a calculator. You will probably use a computer program such as SPSS, SAS, R, or Excel for your analyses. However, a review of the underlying calculations will help you understand the output from these computer programs.

DESCRIPTIVE STATISTICS

With a knowledge of the types of measurement scales, we can turn to a consideration of statistical techniques. We can start with two ways of describing a set of scores: central tendency and variability.

Measures of Central Tendency

A measure of central tendency gives a single number that describes how an entire group scores as a whole, or on the average. Three different central tendency measures are available: the mode, the median, and the mean.

The Mode

The mode is the most frequently occurring score. **Table 1** shows a set of scores and the descriptive statistics that are discussed in this section. The most frequently occurring score in these data is 5. No calculations are necessary to find the mode. The mode can be used with any of the four types of measurement scales. However, it is the only measure of central tendency that can be used with nominal scale data. If you are measuring gender and find there are 100 females and 50 males, the mode is "female" because this is the most frequently occurring category on the nominal scale.

TABLE 1 **Descriptive statistics for a set of scores**

Score	Descriptive statistic
1	Mode = 5
2	Median = 5
4	
4	
5	$\overline{X} = \dfrac{\sum X}{N} = 4.5$
5	
5	
6	Range = 6
6	
7	$S^2 = \dfrac{\sum \left(X - \overline{X} \right)^2}{N - 1} = \dfrac{\sum X^2 - N \overline{X}^2}{N - 1} = \dfrac{233 - 202.5}{9} = 3.388$

$$\sum X = 45$$
$$\sum X^2 = 233 \qquad S = \sqrt{S^2} = 1.84$$
$$N = 10$$

The Median

The median is the score that divides the group in half: 50% of the scores are below the median and 50% are above the median. When the scores have been ordered from lowest to highest (as in **Table 1**), the median is easily found. If there is an odd number of scores, you simply find the middle score. (For example, if there are 11 scores, the sixth score is the median, because there are 5 lower and 5 higher scores.) If there is an even number of scores, the median is the midpoint between the two middle scores. In the data in **Table 1**, there are 10 scores, so the fifth and sixth scores are the two middle scores. To find the median, we add the two middle scores and divide by 2. Thus, in **Table 1,** the median is

$$\frac{5 + 5}{2} = 5$$

The median can be used with ordinal, interval, or ratio scale data. It is most likely to be used with ordinal data, however. This is because calculation of the median considers only the rank ordering of scores and not the actual size of the scores.

The Mean

The mean is based on more information about the scores than either the mode or the median. However, it is appropriate only for interval or ratio scale data.

The mean is the sum of the scores in a group divided by the number of scores. The calculational formula for the mean can be expressed as

$$\overline{X} = \frac{\Sigma X}{N}$$

where $\overline{X}$ is the symbol for the mean. In this formula, X represents a score obtained by an individual, and the Σ symbol indicates that scores are to be summed or added. The symbol ΣX can be read as "sum of the Xs" and simply is an indication that the scores are to be added. Thus, ΣX in the data from **Table 1** is

$$1 + 2 + 4 + 4 + 5 + 5 + 5 + 6 + 6 + 7 = 45$$

The N in the formula symbolizes the number of scores in the group. In our example, $N = 10$. Thus, we can now calculate the mean:

$$\overline{X} = \frac{\Sigma X}{N} = \frac{45}{10} = 4.5$$

Measures of Variability

In addition to describing the central tendency of the set of scores, we want to describe how much the scores vary. That is, how much spread is there in the set of scores?

The Range

The range is the highest score minus the lowest score. In our example, the range is 6. The range is not a very useful statistic, however, because it is based on only two scores in the distribution. It does not take into account all of the information that is available in the entire set of scores.

The Variance and Standard Deviation

The variance and a related statistic called the standard deviation use all the scores to yield a measure of variability. The variance indicates the degree to which scores vary about the group mean. The formula for the variance (symbolized as s^2) is

$$s^2 = \frac{\Sigma \left(X - \overline{X} \right)^2}{N - 1}$$

where $\left(X - \overline{X} \right)^2$ is an individual score, X, minus the mean, $\overline{X}$, and then squared. Thus $\left(X - \overline{X} \right)^2$ is the squared deviation of each score from the mean. The Σ sign indicates that these squared deviation scores are to be summed. Finally, dividing by $N - 1$ gives the mean of the squared deviations. The variance, then, is the mean of the squared deviations from the group mean. (Squared deviations are used because simple deviations would add up to zero. $N - 1$ is used in most cases for statistical purposes because the scores represent a sample and not an entire population. As the sample size becomes larger, it makes little difference whether N or $N - 1$ is used.)

The data in **Table 1** can be used to illustrate calculation of the variance. $\Sigma\,(X - \overline{X})^2$ is equal to

$$(1 - 4.5)^2 + (2 - 4.5)^2 + (4 - 4.5)^2 + (4 - 4.5)^2 + (5 - 4.5)^2 + (5 - 4.5)^2$$
$$+ (5 - 4.5)^2 + (6 - 4.5)^2 + (6 - 4.5)^2 + (7 - 4.5)^2 = 30.50$$

The next step is to divide $\Sigma\,(X - \overline{X})^2$ by $N - 1$. The calculation for the variance, then, is

$$S^2 = \frac{\Sigma\left(X - \overline{X}\right)^2}{N - 1} = \frac{30.50}{9} = 3.388$$

A simpler, and equivalent, calculational formula for the variance is

$$S^2 = \frac{\Sigma X^2 - N\overline{X}^2}{N - 1}$$

where ΣX^2 is the sum of the squared individual scores, and $\overline{X}^2$ is the mean squared. You can confirm that the two formulas are identical by computing the variance using this simpler formula. (Remember that ΣX^2 tells you to square each score and then sum the squared scores.)

The standard deviation is the square root of the variance. Because the variance uses squared scores, the variance does not describe the amount of variability in the same units of measurement as the original scale. The standard deviation (s) corrects this problem. Thus, the standard deviation is the average deviation of scores from the mean.

STATISTICAL SIGNIFICANCE AND EFFECT SIZE

This section describes several statistical significance tests. These tests are used to determine the probability that the outcome of the research was due to chance. All use the logic of the null hypothesis discussed in the chapter **"Understanding Research Results: Statistical Inference."** We will consider two significance tests in this section: the chi-square test and the analysis of variance or F test.

Chi-Square (χ^2)

The chi-square (Greek letter chi, squared) test is used when dealing with nominal scale data. It is used when the data consist of frequencies—the number of subjects who fall into each of several categories.

Chi-square can be used with either experimental or nonexperimental data. The major requirement is that both variables are studied using nominal scales.

Example

Suppose you want to know whether there is a relationship between gender and hand dominance. To answer this question, you sample 50 males and 50 females and ask whether they are right-handed, left-handed, or ambidextrous (use both hands with equal skill). Your data collection involves classifying each person as male or female and as right-handed, left-handed, or ambidextrous.

Fictitious data for such a study are presented in **Table 2.** The frequencies labeled as "O" in each of the six cells in the table refer to the *observed* number of male and female subjects who fall into each of the three hand-dominance categories. The frequencies labeled "E" refer to frequencies that are *expected* if the null hypothesis is correct. It is important that each subject falls into only one of the cells when using chi-square (that is, no subject can be counted as both male and female or both right- and left-handed).

TABLE 2   Data for hypothetical study on hand dominance: Chi-square test

Sex of subject	Hand dominance			Row totals
	Right	**Left**	**Ambidextrous**	
Male	$O_1 = 15$ $E_1 = 25$	$O_2 = 30$ $E_2 = 20$	$O_3 = 5$ $E_3 = 5$	50
Female	$O_4 = 35$ $E_4 = 25$	$O_5 = 10$ $E_5 = 20$	$O_6 = 5$ $E_6 = 5$	50
Column totals	50	40	10	$N = 100$

Computations:	Cell number	$\dfrac{(O - E)^2}{E}$	
	1	4.00	
	2	5.00	
	3	0.00	
	4	4.00	
	5	5.00	
	6	0.00	
	$\Sigma =$	18.00	

$$\chi^2 = \Sigma \frac{(O - E)^2}{E}$$

$$= 18.00$$

The chi-square test examines the extent to which the frequencies that are actually observed in the study differ from the frequencies that are expected if the null hypothesis is correct. The null hypothesis states that there is no relationship between sex and hand dominance: Males and females do not differ on this characteristic.

The formula for computing chi-square is

$$\chi^2 = \sum \frac{\left(O - E\right)^2}{E}$$

where O is the *observed* frequency in each cell, E is the *expected* frequency in each cell, and the symbol Σ refers to summing over all cells. The steps in calculating the value of χ^2 are these:

Step 1: Arrange the observed frequencies in a table such as **Table 2.** Note that in addition to the observed frequencies in each cell, the table presents row totals, column totals, and the total number of observations (*N*).

Step 2: Calculate the expected frequencies for each of the cells in the table. The expected frequency formula is

$$E = \frac{\text{row total} \times \text{column total}}{N}$$

where the row total refers to the row total for the cell, and the column total refers to the column total for the cell. Thus, the expected frequency for cell 1 (male right-handedness) is

$$E_1 = \frac{50 \times 50}{100} = 25$$

The expected frequencies for each of the cells are shown in **Table 2** below the observed frequencies.

Step 3: Calculate the quantity $(O - E)^2/E$ for each cell. For cell 1, this quantity is

$$\frac{\left(15 - 25\right)^2}{25} = \frac{100}{25} = 4.00$$

Step 4: Find the value of χ^2 by summing the $(O - E)^2/E$ values found in step 3. The calculations for obtaining χ^2 for the example data are shown in **Table 2.**

Significance of Chi-Square

The significance of the obtained χ^2 value can be evaluated by consulting a table of critical values of χ^2. The critical χ^2 values indicate the value that the *obtained* χ^2 must equal or exceed to be significant at the .10 level, the .05 level, and the .01 level. A table of critical χ^2 values is easy to obtain (e.g., **http://www.itl.nist.gov/div8 98/handbook/eda/section3/eda3674.htm**).

To be able to use the table of critical values of χ^2 as well as most other statistical tables, you must understand the concept of *degrees of freedom* (*df*). The critical value of χ^2 for any given study depends on the degrees of freedom. Degrees of freedom refers to the number of scores that are free to vary. In the table of categories for a chi-square test, the number of degrees of freedom is the number of cells in which the frequencies are free to vary once we know the row totals and column totals. The degrees of freedom for chi-square is easily calculated:

$$df = (R - 1)(C - 1)$$

where R is the number of rows in the table and C is the number of columns. In our example in **Table 1,** there are two rows and three columns, so there are 2 degrees of freedom. In a study with three rows and three columns, there are 4 degrees of freedom, and so on.

In a table of critical χ^2 values, find the correct degrees of freedom and then determine the critical value of χ^2 necessary to reject the null hypothesis at the chosen significance level. With 2 degrees of freedom, the obtained χ^2 value must be *equal to* or *greater than* the critical value of 5.991 to be significant at the .05 level. There is only a .05 probability that a χ^2 of 5.991 would occur if only random error is operating. Because the obtained χ^2 from our example is 18.00, we can reject the null hypothesis that there is no relationship between sex and hand dominance. (The chi-square was based on fictitious data, but it would be relatively easy for you to determine for yourself whether there is in fact a relationship.)

There is an easy alternative method of determining if your obtained χ^2 is significant: Use an application that provides the exact null hypothesis probability of your χ^2 value. Such an application is located at **http://vass arstats.net/tabs.html#csq.** Simply input your obtained χ^2 value and degrees of freedom and the output is the probability.

Effect Size for the Chi-Square Statistic

Measures of effect size indicate the strength of association between variables. Results range from 0.00, which indicates no relationship, to 1.00. Correlations above .50 are considered to show very strong relationships. In much research, expect correlations between about .15 and .40. Correlations between about .10 and .20 are weaker, but can be statistically significant with large sample sizes. They can also be important for theoretical and even practical reasons.

The chi-square (χ^2) test was described previously. In addition to determining whether there is a significant relationship, you want an indicator of effect size to tell you the strength of association between the variables. For the sex difference in hand dominance example, a statistic called Cramer's V (or phi) is appropriate. The V coefficient is computed after obtaining the value of chi-square. The formula is

$$V = \sqrt{\frac{\chi^2}{N(k - 1)}}$$

In this formula, N is the total number of cases or subjects and k is the smaller of the rows or columns in the table (thus, in our example with three columns [hand dominance] and two rows [sex], the value of k is 2, the lower value).

The value of V for the sex and hand dominance example in **Table 2** is

$$V = \sqrt{\frac{18}{100(2 - 1)}} \ = \ \sqrt{.18} \ = .42$$

Because the significance of the chi-square value has already been determined, no further significance testing is necessary.

Concluding Remarks

The chi-square test is extremely useful and is used frequently in all of the behavioral sciences. The calculational formula described is generalizable to expanded studies in which there are more categories on either of the variables. One note of caution, however: When both variables have only two categories, so that there are only two rows and two columns, the formula for calculating chi-square changes slightly. In such cases, the formula is

$$\chi^2 = \sum \frac{(\ |\ O - E\ | \ - .5)^2}{E}$$

where $|O - E|$ is the absolute value of $O - E$, and .5 is a constant that is subtracted for each cell.

Analysis of Variance (F Test)

The analysis of variance, or F test, is used to determine whether there is a significant difference between groups that have been measured on either interval or ratio scales. The analysis of variance may be used with either independent groups or repeated measures designs. Procedures for calculating F for both types of designs are presented.

Analysis of Variance: One Independent Variable

To illustrate the use of the analysis of variance, let's consider a hypothetical experiment on physical distance and self-disclosure. You think that people will reveal more about themselves to an interviewer when they are sitting close to the interviewer than they will when sitting farther away. To test this idea, you conduct an experiment on interviewing. Participants are told that interviewing techniques are being studied. Each participant is seated in a room; the interviewer comes into the room and sits at one of three distances from the participant: close (2 feet, or .61 meter), medium (4 feet, or 1.22 meters), or far (6 feet, or 1.83 meters). The distance chosen by the interviewer is the independent variable manipulation. Participants are randomly assigned to the three distance conditions, and the interviewer's behavior is constant in all conditions. The interview consists of a number of questions, and the dependent variable is the number of personal, revealing statements made by the participant during the interview.

Fictitious data for such an experiment are shown in **Table 3.** Note that this is an independent groups (between-subjects) design with five participants in each group. The calculations of the systematic variance and error variance involve computing the *sum of squares* for the different types of variance.

TABLE 3   Data for hypothetical experiment on distance and self-disclosure: Analysis of variance

Distance (A)		
Close ($A1$)	Medium ($A2$)	Far ($A3$)
33	21	20
24	25	13
31	19	15
29	27	10
34	26	14
T_{A1} = 151	T_{A2} = 118	T_{A3} = 72
n_{A1} = 5	n_{A2} = 5	n_{A3} = 5
$\overline{X}_{A1}$ = 30.20	$\overline{X}_{A2}$ = 23.60	$\overline{X}_{A3}$ = 14.40
$\sum X_{A1}^2$ = 4623	$\sum X_{A2}^2$ = 2832	$\sum X_{A3}^2$ = 1090
T_{A1}^2 = 22801	T_{A2}^2 = 13924	T_{A3}^2 = 5184

$$SS_{TOTAL} = \sum X^2 - \frac{G^2}{N} = (4623 + 2832 + 1090) - \frac{(151 + 118 + 72)^2}{15}$$
$$= 8545 - 7752.07 = 792.93$$

$$SS_A = \sum \frac{T_a^2}{n_a} - \frac{G^2}{N} = \left[\frac{(151)^2}{5} + \frac{(118)^2}{5} + \frac{(72)^2}{5}\right] - 7752.07$$
$$= 8381.80 - 7752.07 = 629.73$$

$$SS_{ERROR} = \sum X^2 - \sum \frac{T_a^2}{n_a} = 8545 - 8381.80 = 163.20$$

Sum of Squares

Sum of squares stands for the *sum of squared deviations from the mean*. Computing an analysis of variance for the data in **Table 3** involves three sums of squares: (1) SS_{TOTAL}, the sum of squared deviations of each individual score from the grand mean; (2) SS_A, the sum of squared deviations of each of the group means from the grand mean; and (3) SS_{ERROR}, the sum of squared deviations of the individual scores from their respective group means. The "A" in SS_A is used to indicate that we are dealing with the systematic variance associated with independent variable A.

The three sums of squares are deviations from a mean. (Recall that we calculated such deviations earlier when discussing the variance in a set of scores.) We could calculate the deviations directly with the data in **Table 3,** but such calculations are hard to work with, so we will use simplified formulas for computational purposes.

The computational formulas are

$$SS_{TOTAL} = \sum X^2 - \frac{G^2}{N}$$

$$SS_A = \sum \frac{T_a^2}{n_a} - \frac{G^2}{N}$$

$$SS_{ERROR} = \sum X^2 - \sum \frac{T_a^2}{n_a}$$

You might note here that $SS_{TOTAL} = SS_A + SS_{ERROR}$. The actual computations are shown in **Table 3**.

SS_{TOTAL}

The formula for SS_{TOTAL} is

$$\Sigma X^2 - \frac{G^2}{N}$$

ΣX^2 is the sum of the squared scores of all subjects in the experiment. Each of the scores is squared first and then added. Thus, for the data in **Table 3**, ΣX^2 is $33^2 + 24^2 + 31^2$ and so on until all of the scores have been squared and added. If you are doing the calculations by hand or with a pocket calculator, it may be convenient to find the ΣX^2 for the scores in each group and then add these up for your final computation. This is what I did for the data in the table. The G in the formula stands for the grand total of all of the scores. This involves adding up the scores for all subjects. The grand total is then squared and divided by N, the total number of subjects in the experiment. When computing the sum of squares, you should always keep the calculations clearly labeled, because you can simplify later calculations by referring to these earlier ones. Once you have computed SS_{TOTAL}, you can calculate SS_A.

SS_A

The formula for SS_A is

$$\sum \frac{T_a^2}{n_a} - \frac{G^2}{N}$$

The T_a in this formula refers to the total of the scores in Group a of independent variable A. (T_a is a short-hand notation for ΣX in each group. Recall the computation of ΣX from our discussion of the mean. The T_a symbol is used to avoid having to deal with too many Σ signs in our calculation procedures.) The a is used to symbolize the particular group number; thus, T_a is a general symbol for T_1, T_2, and T_3. Looking at our data in **Table 3,** $T_1 = 151$, $T_2 = 118$, and $T_3 = 72$. These are the sums of the scores in each of the groups. After T_a has been calculated, $T^2{}_a$ is found by squaring T_a. Now, $T^2{}_a$ is divided by n_a, the number of subjects in Group a. Once the quantity $T^2{}_a/n_a{}^a$ has been computed for each group, the quantities are summed as indicated by the Σ symbol.

Note that the second part of the formula, G^2/N, was calculated when SS_{TOTAL} was obtained. Because we already have this quantity, it need not be calculated again when computing SS_A. After obtaining SS_A, we can now compute SS_{ERROR}.

SS_{ERROR}

The formula for SS_{ERROR} is

$$\sum X^2 \; - \; \sum \frac{T_a^2}{n_a}$$

Both of these quantities were calculated above in obtaining SS_{TOTAL} and SS_A. To obtain SS_{ERROR}, we merely have to find these quantities and perform the proper subtraction.

As a check on the calculations, we can make sure that $SS_{TOTAL} = SS_A + SS_{ERROR}$.

The next step in the computation of the analysis of variance is to find the *mean square* for each of the sums of squares. We can then find the value of F. The necessary computations are shown in an analysis of variance summary table in **Table 4.** Constructing a summary table is the easiest way to complete the computations.

TABLE 4   Analysis of variance summary table

Source of variance	Sum of squares	df	Mean square	F
A	SS_A	$a-1$	SS_A / df_A	$MS_A\ /\ MS_{ERROR}$
Error	SS_{ERROR}	$N-a$	$SS_{ERROR}\ /\ df_{ERROR}$	
Total	SS_{TOTAL}	$N-1$		
A	629.73	2	314.87	23.15
Error	163.20	12	13.60	
Total	792.93	14		

Mean Squares

After obtaining the sum of squares, it is necessary to compute the mean squares. Mean square stands for the *mean of the sum of the squared deviations from the mean* or, more simply, the mean of the sum of squares. The mean square (*MS*) is the sum of squares divided by the degrees of freedom. The degrees of freedom are determined by the number of scores in the sum of squares that are free to vary. The mean squares are the variances that are used in computing the value of *F*.

From **Table 4** you can see that the mean squares that concern us are the mean square for *A* (systematic variance) and the mean square for error (error variance). The formulas are

$$MS_A = SS_A \,/\, df_A$$
$$MS_{ERROR} = SS_{ERROR} \,/\, df_{ERROR}$$

where $df_A = a - 1$ (the number of groups minus one) and $df_{ERROR} = N - a$ (the total number of subjects minus the number of groups).

Obtaining the *F* Value

The obtained *F* is found by dividing MS_A by MS_{ERROR}. If only random error is operating, the expected value of *F* is 1.0. The greater the *F* value, the lower the probability that the results of the experiment were due to chance error.

Significance of *F*

To determine the significance of the obtained *F* value, it is necessary to compare the obtained *F* to a critical value of *F*. A table of critical values of *F* for significance levels of .05 and .01 may be found at **http://www.it l.nist.gov/div898/handbook/eda/section3/eda3673.htm.** To find the critical value of *F*, locate on the table the degrees of freedom for the numerator of the ratio (the systematic variance) and the degrees of freedom for the denominator of the *F* ratio (the error variance). The intersection of these two degrees of freedom on the table is the critical *F* value.

The appropriate degrees of freedom for our sample data are 2 and 12 (see **Table 4**). The critical *F* value is 3.89 for a .05 level of significance. For the results to be significant, the obtained *F* value must be equal to or greater than the critical value. Because the obtained value of *F* in **Table 4** (23.15) is greater than the critical value, we conclude that the results are significant and reject the null hypothesis that the means of the groups are equal in the population. A calculator to obtain an exact probability could also be used (e.g., **http://vassar stats.net/tabs.html#f**).

Effect Size for the F *Statistic*

After computing an analysis of variance and evaluating the significance of the *F* statistic, you need to examine effect size. *Eta* is a type of correlation coefficient that can be calculated easily. The formula is

$$eta = \sqrt{\frac{\text{between group (systematic) variance}}{\text{total variance}}}$$

In the experiment on interpersonal distance and disclosure previously described, the SS_A was 629.73, and the SS_{TOTAL} was 792.93. The value of eta then would be

$$eta = \sqrt{\frac{629.73}{792.93}}$$
$$= .89$$

This is a very high correlation, reflecting the fact that the data were all generated for ease of computation.

Concluding Remarks

The analysis of variance for one independent variable with an independent groups design can be used when there are two or more groups in the experiment. The general formulas described are appropriate for all such designs. Also, the calculations are the same whether the experimental or the correlational method is used to form the groups. The formulas are also applicable to cases in which the number of subjects in each group is not equal (although you should have approximately equal numbers of subjects in the groups).

When the design of the experiment includes more than two levels of the independent variable (as in our example experiment, which had three groups), the obtained F value does not tell us whether any two specific groups are significantly different from one another. One way to examine the difference between two groups in such a study is to use the formula for SS_A to compute the sum of squares and the mean square for the two groups (the df in this case is $2 - 1$). When doing this, the previously calculated MS_{ERROR} should be used as the error variance term for computing F. More complicated procedures for evaluating the difference between two groups in such designs are available, and easily calculated with statistical software.

Analysis of Variance: Two Independent Variables

In this section, we will describe the computations for analysis of variance with a factorial design containing two independent variables. The formulas apply to an $A \times B$ factorial design with any number of levels of the independent variables. The formulas apply only to a completely independent groups design with different subjects in each group, and the number of subjects in each group must be equal. Once you understand this analysis, however, you should have little trouble understanding the analysis for more complicated designs with repeated measures or unequal numbers of subjects. With these limitations in mind, let's consider example data from a hypothetical experiment.

The experiment uses a 2×2, IV $\times$ PV, factorial design. Variable A is the type of instruction used in a course, and variable B is the intelligence level of the students. The students are classified as of either "low" or "high" intelligence on the basis of intelligence test scores and are randomly assigned to one of two types of classes. One class uses the traditional lecture method; the other class uses an individualized learning approach with frequent testing over small amounts of material, proctors to help individual students, and a stipulation that students master each section of material before going on to the next section. The information presented to students in the two classes is identical. At the end of the course, all students take the same test, which covers all of the material presented in the course. The score on this examination is the dependent variable.

Table 5 shows fictitious data for such an experiment, with five subjects in each condition. This design allows us to evaluate three effects—the main effect of A, the main effect of B, and the $A \times B$ interaction. The main effect of A is whether one type of instruction is superior to the other; the main effect of B is whether high-intelligence students score differently on the test than do low-intelligence students; the $A \times B$ interaction examines whether the effect of one independent variable is different depending on the particular level of the other variable.

TABLE 5 Data for hypothetical experiment on the effect of type of instruction and intelligence level on exam score: Analysis of variance

	Intelligence (B)		
	Low ($B1$)	**High ($B2$)**	
Traditional lecture ($A1$)	75	90	
	70	95	
	69	89	
	72	85	
	68	91	
	$T_{A1B1} = 354$	$T_{A1B2} = 450$	$T_{A1} = 804$
	$\sum X^2_{A1B1} = 25094$	$\sum X^2_{A1B2} = 40552$	$n_{A1} = 10$
	$n_{A1B1} = 5$	$n_{A1B2} = 5$	$\overline{X}_{A1} = 88.90$
	$\overline{X}_{A1B1} = 70.80$	$\overline{X}_{A1B2} = 90.00$	
Individualized method ($A2$)	85	87	
	87	94	
	83	93	
	90	89	
	89	92	
	$T_{A2B1} = 434$	$T_{A2B2} = 455$	$T_{A2} = 889$
	$\sum X^2_{A2B1} = 37704$	$\sum X^2_{A2B2} = 41439$	$n_{A2} = 10$
	$n_{A2B1} = 5$	$n_{A2B2} = 5$	$\overline{X}_{A2} = 88.90$
	$\overline{X}_{A2B1} = 86.80$	$\overline{X}_{A2B2} = 91.00$	
	$T_{B1} = 788$	$T_{B2} = 905$	
	$n_{B1} = 10$	$n_{B2} = 10$	
	$\overline{X}_{B1} = 78.80$	$\overline{X}_{B2} = 90.50$	

The computation of the analysis of variance starts with calculation of the sum of squares for the following sources of variance in the data: SS_{TOTAL}, SS_A, SS_B, $SS_{A \times B}$, and SS_{ERROR}. The procedures for calculation are similar to the calculations performed for the analysis of variance with one independent variable. The numerical calculations for the example data are shown in **Table 6.** We can now consider each of these calculations.

TABLE 6   Computations for analysis of variance with two independent variables

$$SS_{TOTAL} = \sum X^2 - \frac{G^2}{N} = (25094 + 40552 + 37704 + 41439)$$

$$- \frac{(354 + 450 + 434 + 455)^2}{20}$$

$$= 144789 - 143312.45$$

$$= 1476.55$$

$$SS_A = \frac{\sum T_a^2}{n_a} - \frac{G^2}{N} = \frac{(804)^2 + (889)^2}{10} - 143312.45$$

$$= 143673.70 - 143312.45$$

$$= 361.25$$

$$SS_B = \frac{\sum T_b^2}{n_b} - \frac{G^2}{N} = \frac{(788)^2 + (905)^2}{10} - 143312.45$$

$$= 143996.90 - 143312.45$$

$$= 684.45$$

$$SS_{A \times B} = \frac{\sum T_{ab}^2}{n_{ab}} - \frac{G^2}{N} - SS_A - SS_B = \frac{(354)^2 + (450)^2 + (434)^2 + (455)^2}{5}$$

$$- 143312.45 - 361.25 - 684.45$$

$$= 144639.40 - 143312.45 - 361.25 - 684.45$$

$$= 281.25$$

$$SS_{ERROR} = \sum X^2 - \frac{\sum T_{ab}^2}{n_{ab}} = 144789 - 144639.40$$

$$= 149.60$$

SS$_{TOTAL}$

The SS_{TOTAL} is computed in the same way as the previous analysis formula. The formula is

$$SS_{TOTAL} = \sum X^2 - \frac{G^2}{N}$$

where ΣX^2 is the sum of the squared scores of all subjects in the experiment, G is the grand total of all of the scores, and N is the total number of subjects. It is usually easiest to calculate ΣX^2 and G in smaller steps by calculating subtotals separately for each group in the design. The subtotals are then added. This is the procedure followed in **Tables 5** and **6.**

SS_A

The formula for SS_A is

$$SS_A = \frac{\sum T_a^2}{n_a} - \frac{G^2}{N}$$

where $\sum T_a^2$ is the sum of the squared totals of the scores in each of the groups of independent variable A, and n_a is the number of subjects in each level of independent variable A. When calculating SS_A, we consider only the groups of independent variable A without considering the particular level of B. In other words, the totals for each group of the A variable are obtained by considering all subjects in that level of A, irrespective of which condition of B the subject may be in. The quantity of $G^2{-}/N$ was previously calculated for SS_{TOTAL}.

SS_B

The formula for SS_B is

$$SS_B = \frac{\sum T_b^2}{n_b} - \frac{G^2}{N}$$

SS_B is calculated in the same way as SS_A. The only difference is that we are calculating totals of the groups of independent variable B.

$SS_{A \times B}$

The formula for $SS_{A \times B}$ is

$$SS_{A \times B} = \frac{\sum T_{ab}^2}{n_{ab}} - \frac{G^2}{N} - SS_A - SS_B$$

The sum of squares for the $A \times B$ interaction is computed by first calculating the quantity $\sum T_{ab}^2$. This involves squaring the total of the scores in each of the ab conditions in the experiment. In our example experiment in **Table 5,** there are four conditions; the interaction calculation considers *all* of the groups. Each of the group totals is squared, and then the sum of the squared totals is obtained. This sum is divided by n_{ab}, the number of subjects in each group. The other quantities in the formula for $SS_{A \times B}$ have already been calculated, so the computation of $SS_{A \times B}$ is relatively straightforward.

SS_{ERROR}

The quantities involved in the SS_{ERROR} formula have already been calculated. The formula is

$$SS_{ERROR} = \sum X^2 - \frac{\sum T_{ab}^2}{n_{ab}}$$

These quantities were calculated previously, so we merely have to perform the proper subtraction to complete the computation of SS_{ERROR}.

At this point, you may want to practice calculating the sums of squares using the data in **Table 5.** As a check on the calculations, make sure that $SS_{TOTAL} = SS_A + SS_B + SS_{A \times B} + SS_{ERROR}$.

After obtaining the sums of squares, the next step is to find the mean square for each of the sources of variance. The easiest way to do this is to use an analysis of variance summary table like **Table 7.**

TABLE 7   Analysis of variance summary table: Two independent variables

Source of variance	Sum of squares	df	Mean square	F
A	SS_A	$a - 1$	SS_A/df_A	MS_A/MS_{ERROR}
B	SS_B	$b - 1$	SS_B/df_B	MS_B/MS_{ERROR}
A × B	$SS_{A \times B}$	$(a-1)(b-1)$	$SS_{A \times B}/df_{A \times B}$	$MS_{A \times B}/MS_{ERROR}$
Error	SS_{ERROR}	$N - ab$	SS_{ERROR}/df_{ERROR}	
Total	SS_{TOTAL}			
A	361.25	1	361.25	38.64
B	684.45	1	684.45	73.20
A × B	281.25	1	281.25	30.08
Error	149.60	16	9.35	
Total	1476.55	19		

Mean Square

The mean square for each of the sources of variance is the sum of squares divided by the degrees of freedom. The formulas for the degrees of freedom and the mean square are shown in the top portion of **Table 7,** and the computed values are shown in the bottom portion of the table.

Obtaining the *F* value

The *F* value for each of the three sources of systematic variance (main effects for *A* and *B*, and the interaction) is obtained by dividing the appropriate mean square by the MS_{ERROR}. We now have three obtained *F* values and can evaluate the significance of the main effects and the interaction.

Significance of *F*

To determine whether an obtained *F* is significant, we need to find the critical value of *F* from **http://vassa rstats.net/textbook/apx_d.html.** For all of the *F*s in the analysis of variance summary table, the degrees of freedom are 1 and 16. Let's assume that a .01 significance level for rejecting the null hypothesis was chosen. The critical *F* at .01 for 1 and 16 degrees of freedom is 8.53. If the obtained *F* is larger than 8.53, we can say that the results are significant at the .01 level. By referring to the obtained *F*s in **Table 7,** you can see that the main effects and the interaction are all significant. I will leave it to you to interpret the main effect means and to graph the interaction. If you do not recall how to do this, you should review the material in the chapter **"Complex Experimental Designs."**

Analysis of Variance: Repeated Measures (Within Subjects)

The analysis of variance computations considered thus far have been limited to independent groups (between-subjects) designs. This section considers the computations for analysis of variance of a repeated measures (within-subjects) design with one independent variable.

Fictitious data for a hypothetical experiment using a repeated measures design are presented in **Table 8.** The experiment examines the effect of a job candidate's physical attractiveness on judgments of the candidate's competence. The independent variable is the candidate's physical attractiveness; the dependent variable is judged competence on a 10-point scale. Participants in the experiment view two videotapes of different females performing a mechanical aptitude task that involved piecing together a number of parts. Both females do equally well, but one is physically attractive and the other is unattractive. The order of presentation of the two tapes is counterbalanced to control for order effects.

TABLE 8 Data for hypothetical experiment on attractiveness and judged competence: Repeated measures analysis of variance

Subjects (or subject pairs)	Condition (*A*)		T_S	T_s^2
	Unattractive candidate (A_1)	Attractive candidate (A_1)		
#1	6	8	14	196
#2	5	6	11	121
#3	5	9	14	196
#4	7	6	13	169
#5	4	6	10	100
#6	3	5	8	64
#7	5	5	10	100
#8	4	7	11	121

Subjects (or subject pairs)	Condition (A)		T_S	T_s^2
	Unattractive candidate (A_1)	Attractive candidate (A_1)		
	T_{A1} = 39	T_{A2} = 52	$\sum T_S^2$ = 1067	
	$\sum X_{A1}^2$ = 201	$\sum X_{A2}^2$ = 352		
	n_{A1} = 8	n_{A2} = 8		
	$\overline{X}_{A1}$ = 4.88	$\overline{X}_{A2}$ = 6.50		

$$SS_{Total} = \Sigma X^2 - \frac{G^2}{N} = (201 + 352) - \frac{(39 + 52)^2}{16}$$
$$= 553 - 517.56$$
$$= 35.44$$

$$SS_A = \frac{\Sigma T_a^2}{n_a} - \frac{G^2}{N} = \frac{(39)^2 + (52)^2}{8} - 517.56$$
$$= 528.13 - 517.56$$
$$= 10.57$$

$$SS_{SUBJECTS} = \frac{\Sigma T_s^2}{n_s} - \frac{G^2}{N} = \frac{1067}{2} - 517.56$$
$$= 533.50 - 517.56$$
$$= 15.94$$

$$SS_{ERROR} = SS_{TOTAL} - SS_A - SS_{SUBJECTS} = 35.44 - 10.57 - 15.94$$
$$= 8.93$$

The main difference between the repeated measures analysis of variance and the independent groups analysis described earlier is that the effect of subject differences becomes a source of variance. There are four sources of variance in the repeated measures analysis of variance, and so four sums of squares are calculated:

$$SS_{TOTAL} = \sum X^2 - \frac{G^2}{N}$$

$$SS_A = \frac{\Sigma T_a^2}{n_a} - \frac{G^2}{N}$$

$$SS_{SUBJECTS} = \frac{\Sigma T_s^2}{n_s} - \frac{G^2}{N}$$

$$SS_{ERROR} = SS_{TOTAL} - SS_A - SS_{SUBJECTS}$$

The calculations for these sums of squares are shown in the lower portion of **Table 8**. The quantities in the formula should be familiar to you by now. The only new quantity involves the calculation of $SS_{SUBJECTS}$. The term T_s^2 refers to the squared total score of each subject—that is, the squared total of the scores that each subject gives when measured in the different groups in the experiment. The quantity ΣT_s^2 refers to the sum of these squared totals for all subjects. The calculation of $SS_{SUBJECTS}$ is completed by dividing ΣT_s^2 by n_s and then subtracting by G^2/N. The term n_s refers to the number of scores that each subject gives. Because our hypothetical experiment has two groups, $n_s = 2$, the total for each subject is based on two scores.

An analysis of variance summary table is shown in **Table 9.** The procedures for computing the mean squares and obtaining F are similar to our previous calculations. Note that the mean square and F for the subjects' source of variance are not computed. There is usually no reason to know or care whether subjects differ significantly from one another. The ability to calculate this source of variance does have the advantage of reducing the amount of error variance—in an independent groups design, subject differences are part of the error variance. Because there is only one score per subject in the independent groups design, it is impossible to estimate the influence of subject differences.

TABLE 9   **Analysis of variance summary table: Repeated measures design**

Source of variance	Sum of squares	df	Mean square	F
A	SS_A	$a-1$	SS_A/df_A	MS_A/MS_{ERROR}
Subjects	$SS_{SUBJECTS}$	$s-1$	–	
Error	SS_{ERROR}	$(a-1)(s-1)$	SS_{ERROR}/df_{ERROR}	
Total	SS_{TOTAL}	$N-1$		
A	10.57	1	10.57	8.26
Subjects	15.94	7	–	
Error	8.93	7	1.28	
Total	35.44	15		

You can use the summary table and the table of critical F values to determine whether the difference between the two groups is significant. The procedures are identical to those discussed previously.

Analysis of Variance: Conclusion

The analysis of variance is a very useful statistical procedure that can be extended to any type of factorial design, including those that use both independent groups and repeated measures in the same design. The method of computing analysis of variance is much the same regardless of the complexity of the design. A section on analysis of variance as brief as this cannot hope to cover all of the many aspects of such a general statistical technique. However, you should now have the background to compute an analysis of variance and to understand the more detailed discussions of analysis of variance in advanced statistics texts.

Pearson Product-Moment Correlation Coefficient

The Pearson product-moment correlation coefficient (r) is used to find the strength of the relationship between two variables that have been measured on interval or ratio scales.

Example

Suppose you want to know whether travel experiences are related to knowledge of geography. In your study, you give a 15-item quiz on North American geography, and you also ask how many states and Canadian provinces participants have visited. After obtaining the pairs of observations from each participant, a Pearson r can be computed to measure the strength of the relationship between travel experience and knowledge of geography.

Table 10 presents fictitious data from such a study along with the calculations for r. The calculational formula for r is

$$r = \frac{N\Sigma XY - \Sigma X\Sigma Y}{\sqrt{N\Sigma X^2 - (\Sigma X)^2}\sqrt{N\Sigma Y^2 - (\Sigma Y^2)}}$$

where X refers to a subject's score on variable X, and Y is a subject's score on variable Y. In **Table 10**, the travel experience score is variable X, and the geography knowledge score is variable Y. In the formula, N is the number of paired observations (that is, the number of participants measured on both variables).

TABLE 10   Data for hypothetical study on travel and knowledge of geography: Pearson r

Subject identification number	Travel score (X)	Knowledge score (Y)	XY
01	4	10	40
02	6	15	90
03	7	8	56
04	8	9	72
05	8	7	56
06	12	10	120
07	14	15	210
08	15	13	195
09	15	15	225
10	17	14	238

Subject identification number	Travel score (X)	Knowledge score (Y)	XY
	$\Sigma X \;=\; 106$	$\Sigma Y \;=\; 116$	$\Sigma XY \;=\; 1302$
	$\Sigma X^2 \;=\; 1308$	$\Sigma Y^2 \;=\; 1434$	
	$(\Sigma X^2) \;=\; 11236$	$(\Sigma Y^2) \;=\; 13456$	

$$\text{Computation: } r \;=\; \frac{N\Sigma XY - \Sigma X \Sigma Y}{\sqrt{N\Sigma X^2 - (\Sigma X)^2}\;\;\sqrt{N\Sigma Y^2 - (\Sigma Y)^2}}$$

$$= \frac{10(1302) - (106)(116)}{\sqrt{10(1308) - 11236}\;\;\sqrt{10(1434) - 13456}}$$

$$= \frac{13020 - 12296}{\sqrt{13080 - 11236}\;\;\sqrt{14340 - 13456}}$$

$$= \frac{724}{\sqrt{1844}\;\;\sqrt{844}}$$

$$= \frac{724}{1276.61}$$

$$= .567$$

The calculation of r requires a number of arithmetic operations on the X and Y scores. ΣX is simply the sum of the scores on variable X. ΣX^2 is the sum of the squared scores on X (each score is first squared and then the sum of the squared scores is obtained). The quantity $(\Sigma X)^2$ is the square of the sum of the scores: The total of the X scores (ΣX) is first calculated and then this total is squared. It is important not to confuse the two quantities, ΣX^2 and $(\Sigma X)^2$. The same calculations are made, using the Y scores, to obtain ΣY, ΣY^2, and $(\Sigma Y)^2$. To find ΣXY, each participant's X score is multiplied by the score on Y; these values are then summed for all subjects. When these calculations have been made, r is computed using the formula for r given above.

At this point, you may wish to examine carefully the calculations shown in **Table 10** to familiarize yourself with the procedures for computing r. You might then try calculating r from another set of data, such as the seating pattern and exam score study shown in the chapter **"Understanding Research Results: Description and Correlation," Table 2.**

Significance of *r*

The null hypothesis is that the population correlation coefficient is in fact 0.00. To test this hypothesis, you can consult a table of critical values of r or use a simple calculator application to provide the probability of obtaining your correlation value if the null hypothesis is true. Let's use the calculator at **http://vassarstats.n et/tabs.html#r.** Here you input your obtained r (.567) and the total number of paired observations (10). The output shows the degrees of freedom ($N - 2$) and the p value associated with $r = .567$. In this case, $p = .087$ (2-tailed). If the alpha for significance is .05, we cannot reject the null hypothesis. If using a table of critical values of r, you would find that the .05 critical value is .632; because the obtained correlation coefficient is .567, you would conclude that the correlation is not significant.

Notice that we do not reject the null hypothesis in this case, even though the magnitude of r is fairly large. Recall the discussion of nonsignificant results from the chapter **"Understanding Research Results: Statistical Inference."** It is possible that you would obtain a significant correlation if you used a larger sample size or more sensitive and reliable measures of the variables.

Glossary

alpha level The probability of incorrectly rejecting the null hypothesis that is used by a researcher to decide whether an outcome of a study is statistically significant (most commonly, researchers use a probability of .05).

alternate forms reliability Assessment of reliability by administering two different forms of the same measure to the same individuals at two points in time.

alternative explanation Part of causal inference; a potential alternative cause of an observed relationship between variables.

analysis of variance *See F* test.

APA Ethics Code The American Psychological Association code of general ethical principles. Including: beneficence and nonmaleficence; fidelity and responsibility; integrity; justice, and; respect for people's rights and dignity. The code was last updated in 2017.

applied research Research that addresses questions that have immediate practical implications.

archival research The use of existing sources of information for research. Sources include statistical records, survey archives, and written records.

attrition The loss of subjects who decide to leave an experiment. *See* mortality.

bar graph A visual presentation that uses bars to depict frequencies of responses, percentages, or means in two or more groups.

baseline In a single case design, the subject's behavior during a control period before introduction of the experimental manipulation.

basic research Research that addresses fundamental questions about behavior.

behavioral measures Measures that require participants to engage in a specific behavior.

Belmont Report The Belmont Report, published in 1979 by the National Commission for the Protection of Human Subjects of Biomedical and Behavioral Research, is an important foundational document guiding ethical research with human subjects. It includes three basic principles: beneficence, respect for persons (autonomy), and justice.

between-subjects design An experiment in which different subjects are assigned to each group. Also called independent groups design or between-persons design.

carryover effect A problem that may occur in repeated measures designs if the effects of one treatment are still present when the next treatment is given.

case study A descriptive account of the behavior, past history, and other relevant factors concerning a specific individual.

ceiling effect Failure of a measure to detect a difference because it was too easy (*also see* floor effect).

central tendency A single number or value that describes the typical or central score among a set of scores.

closed-ended questions Questions with response options provided for the research participants to choose from.

cluster sampling A probability sampling method in which existing groups or geographic areas, called clusters, are identified. Clusters are randomly sampled and then everyone in the selected clusters participates in the study.

coding system A set of rules used to categorize observations.

cohort A group of people born at about the same time and exposed to the same societal events; cohort effects are confounded with age in a cross-sectional study.

cohort effects In developmental research using a cross-sectional approach, differences among age groups attributed to social, cultural, economic, or political differences rather than to the effect of age.

conceptual replication A type of replication of research using different procedures for manipulating or measuring the variables.

concurrent validity The construct validity of a measure is assessed by examining whether groups of people differ on the measure in expected ways.

confederate A person posing as a participant in an experiment who is actually part of the experiment.

confidence interval An interval of values within which there is a given level of confidence (e.g., 95%) where the population value lies.

confidentiality When data collected from subjects is identifiable such that names or other identifying information is attached to responses or measurements, the data are only accessible to people with permission.

confounding variable A variable that is not controlled in a research investigation. In an experiment, the experimental groups differ on both the independent variable and the confounding variable.

construct validity The extent to which an operational definition of a variable accurately reflects underlying theoretical variable. Applies to both measured and manipulated variable. In the context of measurement, the degree to which a measurement device accurately measures the theoretical construct it is designed to measure.

content analysis Systematic analysis of records.

content validity An indicator of construct validity of a measure in which the content of the measure is compared to the universe of content that defines the construct.

control series design An extension of the interrupted time series quasi-experimental design in which there is a comparison or control group.

convenience sampling Selecting subjects because they are easy to obtain (a convenient or haphazard manner), usually on the basis of availability, and not with regard to having a representative sample of the population; a type of nonprobability sampling. Also known as "haphazard" sampling.

convergent validity An assessment of the construct validity of a measure via examination of the extent to which scores on the measure are related to scores on other measures of the same construct or similar constructs.

correlation coefficient An index of how strongly two variables are related to each other.

counterbalancing A method of controlling for order effects in a repeated measures design by either including all orders of treatment presentation or randomly determining the order for each subject.

covariation of cause and effect Part of causal inference; observing that a change in one variable is accompanied by a change in a second variable.

criterion variable The variable/score that is predicted based upon an individual's score on another variable (the predictor variable). Conceptually similar to a dependent variable.

Cronbach's alpha An indicator of internal consistency reliability assessed by examining the average correlation of each item (question) in a measure with every other question.

cross-sectional method A developmental research method in which persons of different ages are studied at only one point in time; conceptually similar to an independent groups design.

curvilinear relationship A relationship in which changes in the values of the first variable are accompanied by both increases and decreases in the values of another variable.

debriefing Explanation of the purposes of the research that is given to participants following their participation in the research.

deception In a research study, intentionally providing misinformation to or withholding information from a participant.

Declaration of Helsinki An ethical code of conducted developed by the World Medical Association in 1964 that is broader in its application than the Nuremberg Code. It requires that published journal research conform to its ethical principles.

degrees of freedom A concept used in tests of statistical significance; the number of observations that are free to vary to produce a known outcome; abbreviated *df*.

demand characteristics Cues that inform the subject how he or she is expected to behave.

dependent variable The variable that is the subject's response to, and dependent on, the level of the manipulated independent variable.

descriptive statistics Statistical measures that describe the results of a study; descriptive statistics include measures of central tendency (e.g., mean), variability (e.g., standard deviation), and correlation (e.g., Pearson *r*).

discriminant validity An assessment of the construct validity of a measure by means of examining the extent to which scores on the measure are not related to scores on conceptually unrelated measures.

double-blind experiment An experimental method originating in drug research wherein research participants and experimenters are unaware of participant status in the experimental or control conditions. *See* single-blind experiment, expectancy effects.

effect size The extent to which two variables are associated. In experimental research, the magnitude of the impact of the independent variable on the dependent variable.

electroencephalogram (EEG) A measure of the electrical activity of the brain.

electromyogram (EMG) A measure of the electrical activity of muscles, including muscle tension.

empiricism Use of objective, verifiable observations to answer questions and draw conclusions.

error variance Random variability in a set of scores that is not the result of the independent variable. Statistically, the variability of each score from its group mean.

exact replication A type of replication of research using the same procedures for manipulating and measuring the variables that were used in the original research.

exempt review research Research can undergo an exempt review by the IRB in one of several exempt categories, including: educational settings without adverse effect on learning opportunities, cognitive tests and surveys, benign behavioral interventions, and secondary data.

expectancy effects The impact an experimenter's expectations can have on the outcome of a research study. Also called experimenter bias.

expedited review A review required for research that is minimal risk research, but does not match the exempt research categories.

experimental control Eliminating the influence of an extraneous variable on the outcome of an experiment by keeping the variable constant in the experimental and control groups.

experimental method A method of determining whether variables are related, in which the researcher manipulates the independent variable and controls all other variables either by randomization or by direct experimental control.

external validity The degree to which the results of an experiment may be generalized.

extraneous variables Variables in a study other than the variables being investigated. *Also see* third variable.

***F* test (analysis of variance)** A statistical significance test for determining whether two or more means are significantly different. *F* is the ratio of systematic variance to error variance.

face validity The degree to which a measurement device appears to accurately measure a variable.

factorial design A design in which all levels of each independent variable are combined with all levels of the other independent variables. A factorial design allows investigation of the separate main effects and interactions of two or more independent variables.

falsifiability The principle that a good scientific idea or theory should be capable of being shown to be false when tested using scientific methods.

fatigue effect Deterioration in participant performance with repeated testing.

field experiment An experiment that is conducted in a natural setting rather than in a laboratory setting.

filler items Items included in a questionnaire measure to help disguise the true purpose of the measure.

floor effect Failure of a measure to detect a difference because it was too difficult (*also see* ceiling effect).

fMRI (functional magnetic resonance imagery) A method of measuring blood flow to areas of the brain as a way to provide an image of electrical activity in different areas of the brain while the subject is alert.

focus group An interview strategy wherein multiple respondents are encouraged to interact in a group interview.

fraud Fabrication of data.

frequency distribution An arrangement of a set of scores from lowest to highest that indicates the number of times each score was obtained.

frequency polygon A graphic display of a frequency distribution in which the frequency of each score is plotted on the vertical axis, with the plotted points connected by straight lines.

galvanic skin response (GSR) The electrical conductance of the skin, which changes when sweating occurs.

graphic rating scale A rating scale that uses a graphical representation of a numerical dimension.

histogram Graphic representation of a frequency distribution using bars to represent each score or group of scores.

history effect As a threat to the internal validity of an experiment, refers to any outside event that is not part of the manipulation that could be responsible for the results.

hypothesis A statement of the way in which variables are predicted to be related.

IACUC Institutions that conduct research with certain nonhuman animals must have an Institutional Animal Care and Use Committee (IACUC). The IACUC is composed of at least one scientist, one veterinarian, and a community member and is charged with reviewing animal research procedures and ensuring that all regulations are adhered to.

independent groups design An experiment in which different subjects are assigned to each group. Also called between-subjects design or between-persons design.

independent variable The variable that is manipulated to observe its effect on the dependent variable.

inferential statistics Statistics designed to determine whether results based on sample data are generalizable to a population.

informed consent In research ethics, the principle that participants in an experiment be informed in advance of all aspects of the research that might influence their decision to participate.

Institutional Review Board (IRB) An ethics review committee established to review research proposals. The IRB is composed of scientists, nonscientists, and legal experts.

instrument decay As a threat to internal validity, the possibility that a change in the characteristics of the measurement instrument, including human observers, is responsible for the results.

integrity Acting to promote accuracy, honesty, and truthfulness.

interaction Situation in which the effect of one independent variable on the dependent variable changes, depending on the level of another independent variable.

internal consistency reliability Reliability assessed with data collected at one point in time with multiple measures of a psychological construct. A measure is reliable when the multiple measures provide similar results.

internal validity The certainty with which results of an experiment can be attributed to the manipulation of the independent variable rather than to some other, confounding variable.

interrater reliability An indicator of reliability that examines the agreement of observations made by two or more raters (judges).

interrupted time series design A design in which the effectiveness of a treatment is determined by examining a series of measurements made over an extended time period both before and after the treatment is introduced. The treatment is not introduced at a random point in time.

interval scale A scale of measurement in which the intervals between numbers on the scale are all equal in size.

interviewer bias Intentional or unintentional influence exerted by an interviewer in such a way that the actual or interpreted behavior of respondents is consistent with the interviewer's expectations.

item-total correlation The correlation between scores on individual items with the total score on all items of a measure.

IV × PV design A factorial design that includes both an experimental independent variable (IV) and a nonexperimental participant variable (PV).

Latin square A technique to control for order effects without having all possible orders.

limited review An IRB review that includes benign behavioral interventions for which sensitive data are collected from adult participants under circumstances where participates would need to be identified.

literature review A written summary and evaluation of the existing literature on a specific topic.

longitudinal method A developmental research method in which the same persons are observed repeatedly as they grow older; conceptually similar to a repeated measures design.

main effect The direct effect of an independent variable on a dependent variable.

manipulation check A measure used to determine whether the manipulation of the independent variable has had its intended effect on a subject.

matched pairs design A method of assigning subjects to groups in which pairs of subjects are first matched on some characteristic and then individually assigned randomly to groups.

maturation effect As a threat to internal validity, the possibility that any naturally occurring change within the individual is responsible for the results.

mean A measure of central tendency, obtained by summing scores and then dividing the sum by the number of scores.

measurement error The degree to which a measurement deviates from the true score value.

median A measure of central tendency; the middle score in a distribution of scores that divides the distribution in half.

meta-analysis An analytics technique that allows researchers to draw statistical conclusions from multiple studies of a single research question.

minimal risk the risks of harm to participants are no greater than risks encountered in daily life or in routine physical or psychological tests.

mixed factorial design A design that includes both independent groups (between-subjects) and repeated measures (within-subjects) variables.

mode A measure of central tendency; the most frequent score in a distribution of scores.

mortality The loss of subjects who decide to leave an experiment. Mortality is a threat to internal validity when the mortality rate is related to the nature of the experimental manipulation.

MRI (magnetic resonance imagery) The use of magnetic fields and radio waves to scan body structures, including the brain, to create images.

multiple baseline design Observing behavior before and after a manipulation under multiple circumstances (across different individuals, different behaviors, or different settings).

multiple correlation A correlation between one variable and a combined set of predictor variables.

naturalistic observation Descriptive method in which observations are made in a natural social setting. Also called field observation.

nay-saying A response set in which a respondent consistently disagrees with a set of questions. *See also* yea-saying.

negative linear relationship A relationship in which increases in the values of the first variable are accompanied by decreases in the values of the second variable.

nominal scale A scale of measurement with two or more categories that have no quantitative (numerical) properties. Variables with nominal scale properties are sometimes termed *qualitative* or *categorical* variables.

nonequivalent control group design A quasi-experimental design in which nonequivalent groups of subjects participate in the different experimental groups, and there is no pretest.

nonequivalent control group pretest-posttest design A quasi-experimental design in which nonequivalent groups are used, but a pretest allows assessment of equivalency and pretest-posttest changes.

nonexperimental method Use of measurement of variables to determine whether variables are related to one another. Also called correlational method.

nonprobability sampling Type of sampling procedure in which one cannot specify the probability that any member of the population will be included in the sample.

null hypothesis The hypothesis, used for statistical purposes, that the variables under investigation are not related in the population, that any observed effect based on sample results is due to random error.

Nuremberg Code The legal document that resulted from the trials of Nazi doctors and scientists that outlines 10 rules of research designed to prevent future research atrocities. The Nuremberg Code is an important foundational document for ethical research.

one-group posttest-only design A quasi-experimental design that has no control group and no pretest comparison; a very poor design in terms of internal validity.

one-group pretest-posttest design A quasi-experimental design in which the effect of an independent variable is inferred from the pretest-posttest difference in a single group.

open-ended questions Questions that give research participants the opportunity to provide free-form responses in their own words.

operational definition Definition of a concept that specifies the method used to measure or manipulate the concept.

order effect In a repeated measures design, the effect that the order of introducing treatment has on the dependent variable.

ordinal scale A scale of measurement in which the measurement categories form a rank order along a continuum.

panel study Research in which the same sample of subjects is studied at two or more points in time, usually to assess changes that occur over time.

paraphrasing plagiarism Paraphrasing another person's ideas without attribution. Compare with *word-by-word plagiarism.*

partial correlation The correlation between two variables with the influence of a third variable statistically controlled for.

participant observation A technique of observing a situation wherein the observer takes an active role in the situation.

participant (subject) variable A characteristic of the research participant such as gender, age, personality, or ability.

Pearson product-moment correlation coefficient A type of correlation coefficient used with interval and ratio scale data. In addition to providing information on the strength of relationship between two variables, it indicates the direction (positive or negative) of the relationship.

peer review The process of judging the scientific merit of research through review by other scientists with the expertise to evaluate the research.

physiological measures Measures of physiological activity (e.g., heart rate, brain cell activity).

pie chart Graphic display of data in which frequencies or percentages are represented as "slices" of a pie.

pilot study A small-scale study conducted prior to conducting an actual experiment; designed to test and refine procedures.

placebo group In drug research, a group given an inert substance to assess the psychological effect of receiving a treatment.

plagiarism Misrepresenting another's work as your own.

population The defined group of individuals from which a sample is drawn (also termed *population of interest*).

positive linear relationship A relationship in which increases in the values of the first variable are accompanied by increases in the values of the second variable.

posttest-only design A true experimental design in which the dependent variable (posttest) is measured only once, after manipulation of the independent variable.

power The probability of correctly rejecting the null hypothesis.

practice effect Improvement in participant performance with repeated testing.

prediction A statement of the expected outcome of a research investigation.

predictive validity The construct validity of a measure is assessed by examining the ability of the measure to predict a future behavior.

predictor variable A variable that is used to make a prediction of an individual's score on another variable (the criterion variable). Conceptually similar to an independent variable.

pretest-posttest design A true experimental design in which the dependent variable is measured both before (pretest) and after (posttest) manipulation of the independent variable.

principle of beneficence Ethical principle of the Belmont Report and APA Code that researchers should maximize the well-being of participants while minimizing harm or distress.

principle of fidelity and responsibility "Psychologists establish relationships of trust with those with whom they work. They are aware of their professional and scientific responsibilities to society and to the specific communities in which they work." (APA Ethics Code)

principle of integrity "Psychologists seek to promote accuracy, honesty and truthfulness in the science, teaching and practice of psychology. In these activities psychologists do not steal, cheat or engage in fraud, subterfuge or intentional misrepresentation of fact." (APA Ethics Code)

principle of justice Ethical principle of the Belmont Report and APA Code that researchers adhere to fairness in the selection of participants so that any risks to not apply to one social group but not another; similarly, any benefits should be applied in a fair and just manner to people of different social groups.

principle of respect for persons (autonomy) Ethical principle of the Belmont report and APA Code that researchers respect the autonomy of individuals to make informed decisions about whether to participate in research. Moreover, persons with impaired autonomy deserve special protection. Participants can expect to be treated with respect in conduct of the research.

privacy In the context of research, privacy refers to participants' ability to maintain control of the information they provide and behaviors that may be observed.

probability The likelihood that a given event (among a specific set of events) will occur.

probability sampling Type of sampling procedure in which one is able to specify the probability that any member of the population will be included in the sample.

program evaluation Research designed to assess procedures (e.g., social reforms, innovations) that are designed to produce certain changes or outcomes in a target population.

propensity score matching A method of pairing individuals for assignment to a treatment and control condition based upon a combination of scores on participant variables.

pseudoscience The use of seemingly scientific terms and demonstrations to substantiate claims that have no basis in scientific research.

psychobiography A type of case study in which the life of an individual is analyzed using psychological theory.

PsycINFO A digital database of abstracts of articles in psychology, indexed by topic, updated weekly and maintained by the American Psychological Association.

purposive sampling A type of convenience sampling conducted to obtain predetermined types of individuals for the sample.

quasi-experimental design A type of design that approximates the control features of true experiments to infer that a given treatment did have its intended effect.

quota sampling A sampling procedure in which the sample is chosen to reflect the numerical composition of various subgroups in the population. A convenience sampling technique is used to obtain the sample.

random assignment Use of a random "chance" procedure (such as a random number generator or coin toss) to determine which condition an individual will participate in.

randomization Controlling for the effects of extraneous variables by ensuring that the variables operate in a manner determined entirely by chance.

range A measure of variability. The difference between the highest score and the lowest score.

rating scale A measure used to assign scores along some numerical dimension (such as, indicate current level of hunger).

ratio scale A scale of measurement in which there is an absolute zero point, indicating an absence of the variable being measured. An implication is that ratios of numbers on the scale can be formed (generally, these are physical measures such as weight or timed measures such as duration or reaction time).

reactivity A problem of measurement in which the measure changes the behavior being observed.

regression equation A mathematical equation that allows prediction of one behavior when the score on another variable is known.

regression toward the mean Also called statistical regression; the principle that extreme scores on a variable tend to be closer to the mean when a second measurement is made.

reliability The degree to which a measure is consistent.

repeated measures design An experiment in which the same subjects are assigned to each group. Also called within-subjects design or within-persons design.

replication Repeating a research study to determine whether the results can be duplicated.

research hypothesis The hypothesis that the variables under investigation are related in the population—that the observed effect based on sample data is true in the population.

research question A description of the broad topic of study, in question form.

respect for People's Rights and Dignity (APA) Ethical researchers respect the dignity and worth of all people, and their rights to privacy, confidentiality, and self-determination.

response rate The percentage of people selected for a sample who actually completed a survey.

response set A pattern of responses to questions on a self-report measure that is not related to the content of the question.

restriction of range A problem when scores on a variable are limited to a small subset of their possible values; this makes it more difficult to identify relationships of the variable to other variables of interest.

reversal design A single-case design in which the treatment is introduced after a baseline period and then withdrawn during a second baseline period. It may be extended by adding a second introduction of the treatment. Sometimes called a "withdrawal" design.

sample The members of a population selected to participate in a research investigation.

sampling distribution Theoretical distribution of the frequency of all possible outcomes of a study conducted with a given sample size.

sampling error The potential deviation from the true population value of a value obtained using sample data (e.g., a sample mean).

sampling frame The individuals or clusters of individuals in a population who might actually be selected for inclusion in the sample.

scatterplot Graphic representation of each individual's scores on two variables. The score on the first variable is found on the horizontal axis and score on the second variable is found on the vertical axis.

selection differences Differences in the type of subjects who make up each group in an experimental design. One way such differences can arise is by allowing participants to choose which group they will be assigned to.

self-reports Measures that require participants to describe themselves (e.g., their own characteristics, past or planned behaviors, reactions to stimuli).

semantic differential scale A type of rating scale used to measure participants' cognitive understanding of a concept (such as a topic or behavior). Scale items differentiate three dimensions—evaluation, activity, and potency.

sensitivity The ability of a measure to detect differences between groups.

sequential method A combination of the cross-sectional and longitudinal design to study developmental research questions.

simple main effect In a factorial design, the effect of one independent variable at a particular level of another independent variable.

simple random sampling A sampling procedure in which each member of the population has an equal probability of being included in the sample.

single blind experiment An experimental method originating in drug research wherein research participants do not know whether they are in the experimental group or the control group. *See* double-blind experiment, expectancy effects.

single-case experimental designs Experimental designs that allow cause-and-effect inferences based on data from one or a small number of research participants. Also called single-subject design and small-N design.

social desirability A response set in which respondents answer questions to present themselves favorably.

Solomon four-group design Experimental design in which the experimental and control groups are studied with and without a pretest.

split-half reliability A reliability coefficient determined by the correlation between scores on half of the items on a measure with scores on the other half of a measure.

staged manipulation Manipulation of the independent variable, using complex situations, often simulating real-life social interactions. Also called event manipulation.

standard deviation The average deviation of scores from the mean (the square root of the variance).

statistical significance Rejection of the null hypothesis when an outcome has a low probability of occurrence (usually .05 or less) if, in fact, the null hypothesis is correct.

statistical validity The accuracy of or the statistical conclusions drawn from the results of a research investigation (sometimes called *statistical conclusion validity*)

straightforward manipulation Manipulation of the independent variable through the use of direct stimulus presentations, types of instructions, and other simple procedures.

stratified random sampling A probability sampling method in which a population is divided into subpopulation groups called strata; individuals are then randomly sampled from each of the strata.

strength of manipulation The potential amount of impact of the independent variable on the dependent variable.

structural equation modeling Statistical techniques that are used to evaluate a proposed set of relationships among variables.

survey research Research method in which people are asked questions using telephone, written questionnaires, interviews, or Internet.

systematic observation Observations of one or more specific variables, usually made in a precisely defined setting.

systematic variance Variability in a set of scores that is the result of the independent variable; statistically, the variability of each group mean from the grand mean of all subjects.

***t*-test** A statistical significance test used to compare differences between means.

temporal precedence Part of causal inference; the cause occurs before the effect.

test-retest reliability A reliability coefficient determined by the correlation between scores on a measure given at one time with scores on the same measure given at a later time.

testing effect A threat to internal validity in which taking a pretest changes behavior without any effect on the independent variable.

theory A systematic, coherent, and logical set of ideas about a particular topic or phenomenon that serves to organize and explain data and generate new knowledge.

third variable In descriptions of the relationship between two variables, a third variable is any other variable that is extraneous to the two variables of interest. True experiments control for the possible influence of third variables.

third-variable problem An observed relationship (correlation) between two variables may be due to correlations between each of the two variables and a third variable. True experiments control for the possible influence of third variables.

true score An individual's actual score on a variable being measured, as opposed to the score the individual obtained on the measure itself.

Type I error An incorrect decision to reject the null hypothesis when it is true.

Type II error An incorrect decision to accept the null hypothesis when it is false.

variability The amount of dispersion of scores about some central value.

variable Any event, situation, behavior, or individual characteristic that varies—that is, has at least two values.

variance A measure of the variability of scores about a mean; the mean of the sum of squared deviations of scores from the group mean.

within-subjects design An experiment in which the same subjects are assigned to each group. Also called repeated measures design or a within-persons design.

word-for-word plagiarism A writer commits word-for-word plagiarism when he or she copies a section of another person's work word for word without placing those words within quotation marks to indicate that the segment was written by somebody else, and without citing the source of the information. This is contrasted with *paraphrasing plagiarism.*

yea-saying A response set in which a respondent consistently agrees with a set of questions. Also called acquiescence. *See also* nay-saying.

References

Abel, E. L., & Kruger, M. L. (2010). Smile intensity in photographs predicts longevity. *Psychological Science, 21,* 542–544. https://doi.org/10.1177/0956797610363775

Ajzen, I. (1991). The theory of planned behavior. *Organizational Behavior and Human Decision Processes, 50,* 179–211.

Ajzen, I., & Fishbein, M. (1980). *Understanding attitudes and predicting social behavior.* Prentice-Hall.

Akhtar, S., Justice, L. V., Morrison, C. M., & Conway, M. A. (2018). Fictional first memories. *Psychological Science, 29*(10), 1612–1619. https://doi.org/10.1177/0956797618778831

Akins, C. K., Panicker, S., & Cunningham, C. L. (2005). *Laboratory animals in research and teaching: Ethics, care, and methods.* American Psychological Association. https://doi.org/10.1037/10830-000

Albright, L., & Malloy, T. E. (2000). Experimental validity: Brunswik, Campbell, Cronbach, and enduring issues. *Review of General Psychology, 4*(4), 337–353. https://doi.org/10.1037/1089-2680.4.4.337

Allen, J. P., Schad, M. M., Oudekerk, B., & Chango, J. (2014). What ever happened to the "cool" kids? Long-term sequelae of early adolescent pseudomature behavior. *Child Development, 85*(5), 1866–1880. https://doi.org/10.1111/cdev.12250

Alter, A. L., Stern, C., Granot, Y., & Balcetis, E. (2016). The "bad is black" effect: Why people believe evildoers have darker skin than do-gooders. *Personality and Social Psychology Bulletin, 42*(12), 1653–1665. https://doi.org/10.1177/0146167216669123

American Psychological Association (2020a). Concise guide to APA style (7th ed.).

American Psychological Association (2020b). *Publication Manual of the American Psychological Association* (7th ed.). https://doi.org/10.1037/0000165-000

American Psychological Association (2017). *Multicultural guidelines: An ecological approach to context, identity, and intersectionality.* Retrieved from: https://www.apa.org/about/policy/multicultural-guidelines.pdf

American Psychological Association (2017). Ethical principles of psychologists and code of conduct. Retrieved from https://www.apa.org/ethics/code/ethics-code-2017.pdf

Anderson, C. A., Lindsay, J. J., & Bushman, B. J. (1999). Research in the psychological laboratory: Truth or triviality? *Current Directions in Psychological Science, 8,* 3–9.

Anderson, C. J., Bahnik, Š., Barnett-Cowan, M., Bosco, F. A., Chandler, J., Chartier, C. R., & . . . van der Hulst, M. (2016). Response to comment on "Estimating the reproducibility of psychological science." *Science, 351*(6277), 1037-c. https://doi.org/10.1126/science.aad9163

APA Task Force on Violent Media. (2015). *Technical report on the review of the violent video game literature.* Retrieved from https://www.apa.org/pi/families/violent-media.aspx

Arnett, J. J. (2008). The neglected 95%: Why American psychology needs to become less American. *American Psychologist, 63,* 602–614.

Aronson, E., Brewer, M., & Carlsmith, M. (1985). Experimentation in social psychology. In G. Lindzey & E. Aronson (Eds.), *Handbook of social psychology* (3rd ed.). Random House.

Asch, S. (1956). Studies of independence and conformity: A minority of one against a unanimous majority. *Psychological Monographs, 709* (Whole No. 416).

Aseltine, Jr., R. H., Schilling, E. A., James, A., Murray, M., & Jacobs, D. G. (2008). An evaluation of National Alcohol Screening Day. *Alcohol & Alcoholism, 43*(1), 97–103.

Bakeman, R. (2000). Behavioral observation and coding. In H. T. Reis & C. M. Judd (Eds.), *Handbook of research methods in social and personality psychology* (pp. 138–159). Cambridge University Press.

Bakeman, R., & Brownlee, J. R. (1980). The strategic use of parallel play: A sequential analysis. *Child Development, 51,* 873–878.

Bandura, A. (1977). Self-efficacy: Toward a unifying theory of behavioral change. *Psychological Review, 84*(2), 191–215. https://doi.org/10.1037/0033-295X.84.2.191

Bangerter, A., & Heath, C. (2004). The Mozart effect: Tracking the evolution of a scientific legend. *British Journal of Social Psychology, 43,* 605–623.

Barlow, D. H., Nock, M. K., & Hersen, M. (2009). *Single case experimental designs: Strategies for studying behavior change* (3rd ed.). Allyn & Bacon.

Barry, A. E., Howell, S. M., Riplinger, A., & Piazza-Gardner, A. K. (2015). Alcohol use among college athletes: Do intercollegiate, club, or intramural student athletes drink differently? *Substance Use & Misuse, 50*(3), 302–307. https://doi.org/10.3109/10826084.2014.977398

Benedict, M. E., & Hoag, J. (2004). Seating location in large lectures: Are seating preferences or location related to course performance? *Journal of Economic Education, 35,* 215–231.

Blanchflower, D. G., & Oswald, A. J. (2008). Is well-being U-shaped over the life cycle? *Social Science & Medicine, 66*(8), 1733–1749.

Blass, T. (2004). *The man who shocked the world: The life and legacy of Stanley Milgram.* Basic Books.

Bodenlos, J. S., & Wormuth, B. M. (2013). Watching a food-related television show and caloric intake: A laboratory study. *Appetite, 61,* 8–12. https://doi.org/10.1016/j.appet.2012.10.027

Borchgrevink, C. P., Cha, J., & Kim, S. (2013). Hand washing practices in a college town environment. *Journal of Environmental Health, 75*(8), 18–24.

Borenstein, M., Hedges, L. V., Higgins, J. P. T., & Rothstein, H. R. (2009). *Introduction to meta-analysis.* Wiley.

Bortnik, K., Henderson, L., & Zimbardo, P. (2002). The Shy Q, a measure of chronic shyness: Associations with interpersonal motives and interpersonal values. Retrieved November 10, 2002, from http://www.shyness.com/documents/2002/SITAR2002poster_handout.pdf

Bowman, L. L., Levine, L. E., Waite, B. M., & Gendron, M. (2010). Can students really multitask? An experimental study of instant messaging while reading. *Computers & Education, 54,* 927–931. https://doi.org/10.1016/j.compedu.2009.09.024

Bröder, A. (1998). Deception can be acceptable. *American Psychologist, 53,* 805–806.

Brogden, W. J. (1962). The experimenter as a factor in animal conditioning. *Psychological Reports, 11,* 239–242.

Brooks, C. I., & Rebata, J. L. (1991). College classroom ecology: The relation of sex of student to classroom performance and seating preference. *Environment and Behavior, 23,* 305–313.

Brothers, T., & Traxler, M. J. (2016). Anticipating syntax during reading: Evidence from the boundary change paradigm. *Journal of Experimental Psychology: Learning, Memory, and Cognition, 42*(12), 1894–1906. https://doi.org/10.1037/xlm0000257

Brown, A. S., & Rahhal, T. A. (1994). Hiding valuables: A questionnaire study of mnemonically risky behavior. *Applied Cognitive Psychology, 8,* 141–154.

Brown, C. (2016). *The evidence-based practitioner: Applying research to meet client needs.* F. A. Davis.

Bruins, J., & Barber, A. (2000). Crowding, performance, and affect: A field experiment investigating mediational processes. *Journal of Applied Social Psychology, 30,* 1268–1280.

https://doi.org/10.1111/j.1559-1816.2000
.tb02520.x

Buchanan, E. A., & Hvizdak, E. E. (2009).
Online survey tools: Ethical and
methodological concerns of human research
ethics committees. *Journal of Empirical
Research on Human Research Ethics, 4*(2),
37–48. https://doi.org/10.1525/
jer.2009.4.2.37

Buchanan, T., & Williams, J. E. (2010). Ethical
issues in psychological research on the
internet. In S. D. Gosling & J. A. Johnson
(Eds.), *Advanced methods for conducting
online behavioral research* (pp. 255–271).
American Psychological Association.

Buhrmester, M., Kwang, T., & Gosling, S. D.
(2011). Amazon's Mechanical Turk: A new
source of inexpensive, yet high-quality, data?
Perspectives on Psychological Science, 6(1),
3–5. https://doi.org/10.1177/
1745691610393980

Burger, J. M. (2009). Replicating Milgram:
Would people still obey today? *American
Psychologist, 64*(1), 1–11. https://doi.org/
10.1037/a0010932

Bushman, B., Wang, M., & Anderson, C.
(2005). Is the curve relating temperature to
aggression linear or curvilinear? Assaults
and temperature in Minneapolis
reexamined. *Journal of Personality and Social
Psychology, 89*(1), 62–66.

Bushman, B. J., & Wells, G. L. (2001). Narrative
impressions of the literature: The availability
bias and the corrective properties of
meta-analytic approaches. *Personality and
Social Psychology Bulletin, 27,* 1123–1130.

Buss, D. M. (2011). *Evolutionary psychology: The
new science of the mind* (4th ed.). Allyn &
Bacon.

Butler, L. P., Schmidt, M. F. H., Tavassolie,
N. S., & Gibbs, H. M. (2018). Children's
evaluation of verified and unverified claims.
*Journal of Experimental Child Psychology,
176*(1), 73–83. https://doi.org/10.1016/
j.jecp.2018.07.007

Byrne, G. (1988, October 7). Breuning pleads
guilty. *Science, 242,* 27–28.

Cacioppo, J. T., & Tassinary, L. G. (1990).
Inferring psychological significance from
physiological signals. *American Psychologist,
45*(1), 16–28.

Campbell, D. T. (1968). Quasi-experimental
design. In D. L. Gillis (Ed.), *International
encyclopedia of the social sciences* (Vol. 5).
Macmillan and Free Press.

Campbell, D. T. (1969). Reforms as
experiments. *American Psychologist, 24,*
409–429.

Campbell, D. T., & Stanley, J. C. (1966).
*Experimental and quasi-experimental designs
for research.* Rand McNally.

Carroll, M. E., & Overmier, J. B. (Eds.). (2001).
*Animal research and human health:
Advancing human welfare through behavioral
science.* American Psychological
Association.

Chambless, D. L., Sanderson, W. C., Shoham,
V., Bennett, S. B., Pope, K. S.,
Crits-Christoph, P., . . . & McCurry, S.
(1996). An update on empirically validated
therapies. *Clinical Psychologist, 49,* 5–18.

Chandler, J. (2017). Pulling back the curtain:
Using Mechanical Turk for research.
https://www.mathematica.org/commentary/
crowdsourcing-samples

Chang, H., & Beilock, S. L. (2016). The math
anxiety–math performance link and its
relation to individual and environmental
factors: A review of current behavioral and
psychophysiological research. *Current
Opinion in Behavioral Sciences,* 1033–1038.
https://doi.org/10.1016/j.cobeha.
2016.04.011

Chastain, G. D., & Landrum, R. E. (Eds.).
(1999). *Protecting human subjects:
Department subject pools and institutional
review boards.* American Psychological
Association.

Clark, K. B., & Clark, M. P. (1947). Racial
identification and preference in Negro
children. In T. M. Newcomb & E. L. Hartley

(Eds.), *Readings in social psychology.* Holt, Rinehart & Winston.

Clark, M. M., Warren, B. A., Hagen, P. T., Johnson, B. D., Jenkins, S. M., Werneburg, B. L., & Olsen, K. D. (2011). Stress level, health behaviors, and quality of life in employees joining a wellness center. *American Journal of Health Promotion, 26,* 21–25. https://doi.org/10.4278/ajhp.090821-QUAN-27

Clay, R. A. (2010). Psychology's voice is heard. *APA Monitor, 41*(7), 22.

Codd, R. T., III, & Cohen, B. N. (2003). Predicting college student intention to seek help for alcohol abuse. *Journal of Social and Clinical Psychology, 22,* 168–191.

Cohen, J. (1988). *Statistical power analysis for the behavioral sciences.* Erlbaum.

Cohen, J. (1992). A power primer. *Psychological Bulletin, 112*(1), 155–159. https://doi.org/10.1037/0033-2909.112.1.155

Cohen, J. (1994). The earth is round ($p < OS$). *American Psychologist, 49,* 997–1003.

Cohen, J. (2016). A power primer. In A. E. Kazdin (Ed.), *Methodological issues and strategies in clinical research,* 4th ed. (pp. 279–284). American Psychological Association. https://doi.org/ 10.1037/14805-018

Coile, D. C., & Miller, N. E. (1984). How radical animal activists try to mislead humane people. *American Psychologist, 39,* 700–701.

Coltheart, V., & Langdon, R. (1998). Recall of short word lists presented visually at fast rates: Effects of phonological similarity and word length. *Memory & Cognition, 26,* 330–342.

Cook, T. D., & Campbell, D. T. (1979). *Quasi-experimentation: Design and analysis issues for field settings.* Houghton Mifflin.

Cooper, J., Blackman, S. F., & Keller, K. T. (2016). *The science of attitudes.* Routledge/Taylor & Francis Group.

Corder, G. W., & Foreman, D. I. (2009). *Non-parametric statistics for non-statisticians:*

A step-by-step approach [E-reader Version]. Wiley. Retrieved from http://onlinelibrary.wiley.com/book/10.1002/9781118165881

Cramer, S., Mayer, J., & Ryan, S. (2007). College students use cell phones while driving more frequently than found in government study. *Journal of American College Health, 56,* 181–184. https://doi.org/10.3200/JACH.56.2.181-184

Credé, M., Roch, S. G., & Kieszczynka, U. M. (2010). Class attendance in college: A meta-analytic review of class attendance with grades and student characteristics. *Review of Educational Research, 80,* 272–295.

Curtiss, S. R. (1977). *Genie: A psycholinguistic study of a modern-day "wild child."* Academic Press.

Danner, D. D., Snowden, D. A., & Friesen, W. V. (2001). Positive emotions in early life and longevity: Findings from the Nun Study. *Journal of Personality and Social Psychology, 80,* 804–813.

Denmark, F., Russo, N. P., Frieze, I. H., & Sechzer, J. A. (1988). Guidelines for avoiding sexism in psychological research: A report of the Ad Hoc Committee on Nonsexist Research. *American Psychologist, 43,* 582–585.

Devlin, B., Daniels, M., & Roeder, K. (1997). The heritability of IQ. *Nature, 388*(6641), 468–471.

Dill, C. A., Gilden, E. R., Hill, P. C., & Hanslka, L. L. (1982). Federal human subjects regulations: A methodological artifact? *Personality and Social Psychology Bulletin, 8,* 417–425.

Dillman, D., Smyth, J., & Christian, L. (2014). *Internet, mail, and mixed-mode surveys: The tailored design method* (4th ed.). Wiley.

Dittrich, L. (2016). *Patient H. M.: A story of memory, madness, and family secrets.* Random House.

Drews, F., Pasupathi, M., & Strayer, D. (2008). Passenger and cell phone conversations in simulated driving. *Journal of Experimental*

Psychology: Applied, 14, 392–400. https://doi.org/10.1037/a0013119

Dunbar, A., Kubrin, C. E., & Scurich, N. (2016). The threatening nature of "rap" music. *Psychology, Public Policy, and Law, 22*(3), 280–292. https://doi.org/10.1037/law0000093

Duncan, S., Rosenberg, M. J., & Finklestein, J. (1969). The paralanguage of experimenter bias. *Sociometry, 32,* 207–219.

Dunn, A. L., Trivedi, M. H., Kampert, J. B., Clark, C. G., & Chambliss, H. O. (2005). Exercise treatment for depression. *American Journal of Preventive Medicine, 28*(1), 1–8.

Eagan, K., Stolzenberg, E. B., Bates, A. K., Aragon, M. C., Suchard, M. R., & Rios-Aguilar, C. (2015). *The American freshman: National norms fall 2015.* Los Angeles: Higher Education Research Institute, UCLA. Retrieved from https://www.heri.ucla.edu/monographs/TheAmericanFreshman2015.pdf

Fiske, S. T., & Taylor, S. E. (1984). *Social cognition.* Random House.

Flavell, J. H. (1996). Piaget's legacy. *Psychological Science, 7,* 200–203.

Forest, A. L., & Wood, J. V. (2012). When social networking is not working: Individuals with low self-esteem recognize but do not reap the benefits of self-disclosure on Facebook. *Psychological Science, 23*(3), 295–302. https://doi.org/10.1177/0956797611429709

Fowler, F. J., Jr. (2014). *Survey research methods* (5th ed.). Sage.

Frank, M. G., & Gilovich, T. (1988). The dark side of self- and social perception: Black uniforms and aggression in professional sports. *Journal of Personality and Social Psychology, 54,* 74–85.

Fraundorf, S. H., Hourihan, K. L., Peters, R. A., & Benjamin, A. S. (2019). Aging and recognition memory: A meta-analysis. *Psychological Bulletin, 145*(4), 339–371. https://doi.org/10.1037/bul0000185

Freedman, J. L., Klevansky, S., & Ehrlich, P. R. (1971). The effect of crowding on human

task performance. *Journal of Applied Social Psychology, 1,* 7–25.

Freedman, J. L., Levy, A. S., Buchanan, R. W., & Price, J. (1972). Crowding and human aggressiveness. *Journal of Experimental Social Psychology, 8,* 528–548.

Frick, R. W. (1995). Accepting the null hypothesis. *Memory and Cognition, 25*(1), 132–138. https://doi.org/10.3758/BF03210562

Friedman, H. S., & Martin, L. R. (2011). *The longevity project.* Hudson Street Press.

Fritz, C. O., Morris, P. E., & Richler, J. J. (2012). Effect size estimates: Current use, calculations, and interpretation. *Journal of Experimental Psychology: General, 141*(1), 2–18. https://doi.org/10.1037/a0024338

Funk, F., & Todorov, A. (2013). Criminal stereotypes in the courtroom: Facial tattoos affect guilt and punishment differently. *Psychology, Public Policy, and Law, 19*(4), 466–478. https://doi.org/10.1037/a0034736

Furnham, A., Gunter, B., & Peterson, E. (1994). Television distraction and the performance of introverts and extroverts. *Applied Cognitive Psychology, 8,* 705–711.

Gallup, G. G., & Suarez, S. D. (1985). Alternatives to the use of animals in psychological research. *American Psychologist, 40,* 1104–1111.

Gamble, T., & Walker, I. (2016). Wearing a bicycle helmet can increase risk taking and sensation seeking in adults. *Psychological Science, 27*(2), 289–294. https://doi.org/10.1177/0956797615620784

García-Vera, M. P., Sanz, J., & Gutiérrez, S. (2016). A systematic review of the literature on posttraumatic stress disorder in victims of terrorist attacks. *Psychological Reports, 119*(1), 328–359. https://doi.org/10.1177/0033294116658243

Gardner, G. T. (1978). Effects of federal human subjects' regulations on data obtained in environmental stressor research. *Journal of Personality and Social Psychology, 34,* 774–781.

Gardner, L. E. (1988). A relatively painless method of introduction to the psychological literature search. In M. E. Ware & C. L. Brewer (Eds.), *Handbook for teaching statistics and research methods.* Erlbaum.

Garvin, A. W., & Damson, C. (2008). The effects of idealized fitness images on anxiety, depression and global mood states in college age males and females. *Journal of Health Psychology, 13,* 433–437.

Gernsbacher, M. A. (2018). Writing empirical articles: Transparency, reproducibility, clarity, and memorability. *Advances in Methods and Practices in Psychological Science, 1*(3), 403–414. https://doi.org/10.1177/2515245918754485

Gilbert, D. T., King, G., Pettigrew, S., & Wilson, T. D. (2016). Comment on "Estimating the reproducibility of psychological science." *Science, 351*(6277), 1037. https://doi.org/10.1126/science.aad7243

Gilovich, T. (1991). *How we know what isn't so: The fallibility of human reason in everyday life.* Free Press.

Golder, S. A., & Macy, M. W. (2011). Diurnal and season mood vary with work, sleep, and daylength across diverse cultures. *Science, 333*(6051), 1878–1881. https://doi.org/10.1126/science.1202775

Goldstein, N. J., Cialdini, R. B., & Griskevicius, V. (2008). A room with a viewpoint: Using social norms to motivate environmental conservation in hotels. *Journal of Consumer Research, 35,* 472–482. https://doi.org/10.1086/586910

Golub, S. A., Gilbert, D. T., & Wilson, T. D. (2009). Anticipating one's troubles: The costs and benefits of negative expectations. *Emotion, 9,* 227–281. https://doi.org/10.1037/a0014716

Goodstein, D. (2000). How science works. https://www.nap.edu/read/13163/chapter/4

Graesser, A. C., Cai, Z., Louwerse, M. M., & Daniel, F. (2006). Question Understanding Aid (QUAID): A web facility that tests question comprehensibility. *Public Opinion Quarterly, 70*(1), 3–22. http://doi.org/10.1093/poq/nfj012

Graesser, A. C., Kennedy, T., Wiemer-Hastings, P., & Ottati, V. (1999). The use of computational cognitive methods to improve questions on surveys and questionnaires. In M. G. Sirkin, D. J. Hermann, S. Schechter, N. Schwarz, J. M. Tanur, & R. Tourangeau (Eds.), *Cognition and survey methods research* (pp. 199–216). Wiley.

Graham, K., Tremblay, P. F., Wells, S., Pernanen, K., Purcell, J., & Jelley, J. (2006). Harm, intent, and the nature of aggressive behavior: Measuring naturally occurring aggression in barroom settings. *Assessment, 13,* 280–296. https://doi.org/10.1177/1073191106288180

Grant, A. M., & Schwartz, B. (2011). Too much of a good thing: The challenge and opportunity of the inverted U. *Perspectives on Psychological Science, 6,* 61–76.

Greenwald, A. G. (1976). Within-subjects designs: To use or not to use? *Psychological Bulletin, 83,* 314–320.

Gross, A. E., & Fleming, I. (1982). Twenty years of deception in social psychology. *Personality and Social Psychology Bulletin, 8,* 402–408.

Groves, R. M., Fowler, J. J., Couper, M. P., Lepkowski, J. M., Singer, E., & Tourangeau, R. (2009). *Survey methodology* (2nd ed.). Wiley.

Guiding principles for mail and internet surveys. (2012). Retrieved from https://www.une.edu/sites/default/files/Microsoft-Word-Guiding-Principles-for-Mail-and-Internet-Surveys_8-3.pdf

Guo, S., & Fraser, M. W. (2010). *Propensity score analysis: Statistical methods and applications.* Sage.

Guthrie, R. V. (2004). *Even the rat was white: A historical view of psychology* (2nd ed.). Pearson Education.

Guyer, J. J., Fabrigar, L. R., & Vaughan-Johnston, T. I. (2019). Speech rate, intonation, and pitch: Investigating the bias and cue effects of vocal confidence on persuasion. *Personality and Social Psychology Bulletin, 45*(3), 389–405. https://doi.org/10.1177/0146167218787805n

Guzzo, K. B., & Hayford, S. R. (2018). Adolescent reproductive and contraceptive knowledge and attitudes and adult contraceptive behavior. *Maternal and Child Health Journal, 22*(1), 32–40. https://doi.org/10.1007/s10995-017-2351-7

Hamby, S. L., & Koss, M. P. (2003). Shades of gray: A qualitative study of terms used in the measurement of sexual victimization. *Psychology of Women Quarterly, 27,* 243–255.

Harris, R. (2002). Anti-plagiarism strategies for research papers. Retrieved September 10, 2002, from http://www.virtualsalt.com/antiplag.htm

Henle, M., & Hubbell, M. B. (1938). "Egocentricity" in adult conversation. *Journal of Social Psychology, 9,* 227–234.

Henrich, J., Heine, S., & Norenzayan, A. (2010). The weirdest people in the world? *Behavioral and Brain Sciences, 33*(2–3), 61–83. https://doi.org/10.1017/S0140525X0999152X

Henry, P. J. (2008). College sophomores in the laboratory redux: Influences of a narrow data base on social psychology's view of the nature of prejudice. *Psychological Inquiry, 19,* 49–71.

Hermans, R. C., Engels, R. C., Larsen, J. K., & Herman, C. P. (2009). Modeling of palatable food intake: The influence of quality of social interaction. *Appetite, 52*(3), 801–804. https://doi.org/10.1016/j.appet.2009.03.008

Hermans, R., Herman, C., Larsen, J., & Engels, R. (2010). Social modeling effects on snack intake among young men: The role of hunger. *Appetite, 54,* 378–383.

Herrmann, S. D., Adelman, R. M., Bodford, J. E., Graudejus, O., Okun, M. A., & Kwan, V. Y. (2016). The effects of a female role model on academic performance and persistence of women in STEM courses. *Basic and Applied Social Psychology, 38*(5), 258–268. https://doi.org/10.1080/01973533.2016.1209757

Hertwig, R., & Ortmann, A. (2008). Deception in social psychological experiments: Two misconceptions and a research agenda. *Social Psychology Quarterly, 71*(3), 222–227.

Hoerger, M., & Currell, C. (2012). Ethical issues in Internet research. In S. J. Knapp, M. C. Gottlieb, M. M. Handelsman, & L. D. VandeCreek (Eds.), *APA handbook of ethics in psychology, Vol 2: Practice, teaching, and research.* (pp. 385–400). American Psychological Association. https://doi.org/10.1037/13272-018

Holden, C. (1987). Animal regulations: So far, so good. *Science, 238*(4829), 880–882. https://doi.org/10.1126/science.3672130

Hölzel, B. K., Carmody, J., Vangel, M., Congleton, C., Yerramsetti, S. M., Gard, T., & Lazar, S. W. (2011). Mindfulness practice leads to increases in regional brain gray matter density. *Psychiatry Research: Neuroimaging Section, 191,* 36–43.

Hood, T. C., & Back, K. W. (1971). Self-disclosure and the volunteer: A source of bias in laboratory experiments. *Journal of Personality and Social Psychology, 17,* 130–136.

Hostetler, A. J. (1987, May). Fraud inquiry revives doubt: Can science police itself? *APA Monitor, 1,* 12.

Huchting, K., Lac, A., & LaBrie, J. W. (2008). An application of the Theory of Planned Behavior to sorority alcohol consumption. *Addictive Behaviors, 33,* 538–551.

Humphreys, L. (1970). *Tearoom trade.* Aldine.

Jacquet, J. (2011). The pros and cons of Amazon Mechanical Turk for scientific surveys. http://blogs.scientificamerican.com/guilty-planet/2011/07/07/the-pros-cons-of-amazon-mechanical-turk-for-scientific-surveys/

Jones, R., & Cooper, J. (1971). Mediation of experimenter effects. *Journal of Personality and Social Psychology, 20,* 70–74.

Judd, C. M., Smith, E. R., & Kidder, L. H. (1991). *Research methods in social relations* (6th ed.). Holt, Rinehart & Winston.

Kahneman, D. (2012, Sept. 26). A proposal to deal with questions about priming effects. http://www.nature.com/polopoly_fs/7.6716.1349271308!/suppinfoFile/Kahneman%20Letter.pdf

Kahneman, D. (2014). A new etiquette for replication. *Social Psychology*, 45(4), 310–311.

Kamin, L. G. (1974). *The science and politics of IQ*. Wiley.

Kaplan, J. S. (2012). The effects of shared environment on adult intelligence: A critical review of adoption, twin, and MZA studies. *Developmental Psychology, 48,* 1292–1298.

Kazbour, R. R., & Bailey, J. S. (2010). An analysis of a contingency program on designated drivers at a college bar. *Journal of Applied Behavior Analysis, 43*(2), 273–277.

Kazdin, A. E. (1995). Preparing and evaluating research reports. *Psychological Assessment, 7,* 228–237.

Kazdin, A. E. (2011). *Single-case research designs: Methods for clinical and applied settings* (2nd ed.). Oxford University Press.

Kazdin, A. E. (2013). *Behavior modification in applied settings* (7th ed.). Waveland Press.

Kenny, D. A. (1979). *Correlation and causality.* Wiley.

Khurana, A., Bleakley, A., Ellithorpe, M. E., Hennessy, M., Jamieson, P. E., & Weitz, I. (2019). Media violence exposure and aggression in adolescents: A risk and resilience perspective. *Aggressive Behavior*, 45(1), 70–81. https://doi.org/10.1002/ab.21798

Kim, H., Sherman, D., & Taylor, S. (2008). Culture and social support. *American Psychologist, 63*(6), 518–526. https://doi.org/10.1037/0003-066X

Kimmel, A. (1998). In defense of deception. *American Psychologist, 53,* 803–805.

Kintz, N. L., Delprato, D. J., Mettee, D. R., Persons, C. E., & Schappe, R. H. (1965). The experimenter effect. *Psychological Bulletin, 63,* 223–232.

Kirsch, I. (2010). *The emperor's new drugs: Exploding the antidepressant myth.* Basic Books.

Kitayama, S., Markus, H. R., Matsumoto, H., & Norasakkunkit, V. (1997). Individual and collective processes in the construction of the self: Self-enhancement in the United States and self-criticism in Japan. *Journal of Personality and Social Psychology, 72,* 1245–1267.

Klonsky, E. D., & May, A. M. (2015). The Three-Step Theory (3ST): A new theory of suicide rooted in the "ideation-to-action" framework. *International Journal of Cognitive Therapy, 8*(2), 114–129. https://doi.org/10.1521/ijct.2015.8.2.114

Korn, J. H. (1997). *Illusions of reality: A history of deception in social psychology.* SUNY Press.

Korn, J. H. (1998). The reality of deception. *American Psychologist, 53,* 805.

Krahé, B., & Möller, I. (2010). Longitudinal effects of media violence on aggression and empathy among German adolescents. *Journal of Applied Developmental Psychology, 31*(5), 401–409. https://doi.org/10.1016/j.appdev.2010.07.003

Kremer, P., Spittle, M., McNeil, D., & Shinners, C. (2009). Amount of mental practice and performance of a simple motor task. *Perceptual and Motor Skills, 109,* 347–356.

Lana, R. E. (1969). Pretest sensitization. In R. Rosenthal & R. L. Rosnow (Eds.), *Artifacts in behavioral research.* Academic Press.

Lane, S. D., Cherek, D. R., Tcheremissine, O. V., Lieving, L. M., & Pietras, C. J. (2005). Clinical research acute marijuana effects on human risk taking. *Neuropsychopharmacology, 30,* 800–809. https://doi.org/10.1038/sj.npp.1300620

Langer, E. J., & Abelson, R. P. (1974). A patient by any other name. . . : Clinical group difference in labeling bias. *Journal of Consulting and Clinical Psychology, 42,* 4–9.

Larson, J., Newell, K., Topham, G., & Nichols, S. (2002). A review of three comprehensive premarital assessment questionnaires. *Journal of Marital and Family Therapy, 28,* 233–239.

Latané, B., Williams, K., & Harkins, S. (1979). Many hands make light the work: The causes and consequences of social loafing. *Journal of Personality and Social Psychology, 37,* 822–832.

Lee, S., W. Kim, M., Mcdonough, I., Mendoza, J., & Kim, M. (2017). The effects of cell phone use and emotion-regulation style on college students' learning. *Applied Cognitive Psychology, 31*(3), 360–366. https://doi.org/10.1002/acp.3323

Lee, S. S., Schwarz, N., Taubman, D., & Hou, M. (2010). Sneezing in times of a flu pandemic: Public sneezing increases perception of unrelated risks and shifts preferences for federal spending. *Psychological Science, 21,* 375–377. https://doi.org/10.1177/0956797609359876

Leighton, D. C., Legate, N., LePine, S., Anderson, S. F., & Grahe, J. (2018). Self-esteem, self-disclosure, self-expression, and connection on Facebook: A collaborative replication meta-analysis. *Psi Chi Journal of Psychological Research, 23*(2), 98–109. https://doi.org/10.24839/2325-7342.JN23.2.98

Levin, J. R. (1983). Pictorial strategies for school learning: Practical illustrations. In M. Pressley & J. R. Levin (Eds.), *Cognitive strategy research: Educational applications* (pp. 213–238). Springer-Verlag.

Levine, R. V. (1990). The pace of life. *American Scientist, 78,* 450–459.

Levy, K. N., & Kelly, K. M. (2010). Sex differences in jealousy: A contribution from attachment theory. *Psychological Science, 21,* 168–173.

Lilienfeld, S., Lynn, S., & Lohr, J. (Eds.). (2004). *Science and pseudoscience in clinical psychology.* Guilford Press.

Lipchock, S. V., Mennella, J. A., Spielman, A. I., & Reed, D. R. (2013). Human bitter perception correlates with bitter receptor messenger RNA expression in taste cells. *American Journal of Clinical Nutrition, 98*(4), 1136–1143. https://doi.org/10.3945/ajcn.113.066688

Lofland, J., Snow, D. A., Anderson, L., & Lofland, L. H. (2006). *Analyzing social settings: A guide to qualitative observation and analysis* (4th ed.). Wadsworth.

Loftus, E. (1979). *Eyewitness testimony.* Harvard University Press.

Luria, A. R. (1968). *The mind of a mnemonist.* Basic Books.

Mace, J. H., McQueen, M. L., Hayslett, K. E., Staley, B. J. A., & Welch, T. J. (2019). Semantic memories prime autobiographical memories: General implications and implications for everyday autobiographical remembering. *Memory & Cognition, 47*(2), 299–312. https://doi.org/10.3758/s13421-018-0866-9

Madigan, R., Johnson, S., & Linton, P. (1995). The language of psychology: APA style as epistemology. *American Psychologist, 50*(6), 428–436. https://doi.org/10.1037/0003-066X.50.6.428

Marlatt, G. A., & Rohsenow, D. R. (1980). Cognitive processes in alcohol use: Expectancy and the balanced placebo design. In N. K. Mello (Ed.), *Advances in substance abuse* (Vol. 1). JAI Press.

Matsumoto, D. (1994). *Cultural influences on research methods and statistics.* Brooks/Cole.

Mazer, J. P., Murphy, R. E., & Simonds, C. J. (2009). The effects of teacher self-disclosure via Facebook on teacher credibility. *Learning, Media and Technology, 34,* 175–183. https://doi.org/10.1080/17439880902923655

McCutcheon, L. E. (2000). Another failure to generalize the Mozart effect. *Psychological Reports, 87,* 325–330.

McFarland, C., Cheam, A., & Buehler, R. (2007). The perseverance effect in the debriefing paradigm: Replication and extension. *Journal of Experimental Social Psychology, 43,* 233–240. https://doi.org/10.1016/j.jesp.2006.01.010

McGuigan, F. J. (1963). The experimenter: A neglected stimulus. *Psychological Bulletin, 60,* 421–428.

Mehl, M. R., Vazire, S., Holleran, S. E., & Clark, C. S. (2010). Eavesdropping on happiness: Well-being is related to having less small talk and more substantive conversations. *Psychological Science, 21,* 539–541. https://doi.org/10.1177/0956797610362675

Melzack, R. (2005). The McGill Pain Questionnaire: From description to measurement. *Anesthesiology, 103,* 199–202.

Meston, C. M., & Buss, D. M. (2007). Why humans have sex. *Archives of Sexual Behavior, 36,* 477–507. https://doi.org/10.1007/s10508-007-9175-2

Midanik, L. T., & Greenfield, T. K. (2008). Interactive voice response versus computer-assisted telephone interviewing (CATI) surveys and sensitive questions: The 2005 National Alcohol Survey. *Journal of Studies of Alcohol and Drug, 69*(4), 580–588.

Milgram, S. (1963). Behavioral study of obedience. *Journal of Abnormal and Social Psychology, 67,* 371–378.

Milgram, S. (1964). Group pressure and action against a person. *Journal of Abnormal and Social Psychology, 69,* 137–143.

Milgram, S. (1965). Some conditions of obedience and disobedience to authority. *Human Relations, 18,* 57–76.

Milgram, S., (1974). *Obedience to authority: An experimental view.* Harper & Row.

Miller, A. G. (1986). *The obedience experiments: A case study of controversy in social science.* Praeger.

Miller, C. T., & Downey, K. T. (1999). A meta-analysis of heavyweight and self-esteem. *Personality and Social Psychology Review, 3,* 68–84.

Miller, G. A. (1969). Psychology as a means of promoting human welfare. *American Psychologist, 24,* 1063–1075.

Miller, J. G. (1999). Cultural psychology: Implications for basic psychological theory. *Psychological Science, 10,* 85–91.

Miller, N. E. (1985). The value of behavioral research on animals. *American Psychologist, 40,* 423–440.

Moher, D., Liberati, A., Tetzlaff, J., & Altman, D. G. (2009). Preferred reporting items for systematic reviews and meta-analyses: The PRISMA statement. *PLoS Medicine, 6*(7), e1000097. https://doi.org/10.1371/journal.pmed.1000097

Montee, B. B., Miltenberger, R. G., & Wittrock, D. (1995). An experimental analysis of facilitated communication. *Journal of Applied Behavior Analysis, 28,* 189–200.

Mook, D. G. (1983). In defense of external invalidity. *American Psychologist, 38,* 379–387.

Murray, B. (2002). Research fraud needn't happen at all. *APA Monitor, 33*(2). Retrieved July 31, 2002, from http://www.apa.org/monitor/feb02/fraud.html

National Commission for the Protection of Human Subjects of Biomedical and Behavioral Research. (April 18, 1979). *The Belmont Report: Ethical principles and guidelines for the protection of human subjects of research.* Retrieved from https://www.hhs.gov/ohrp/regulations-and-policy/belmont-report/read-the-belmont-report/index.html

NICHD Early Child Care Research Network (Eds.). (2005). *Child care and child development.* Guilford Press.

Nicol, A. A. M., & Pexman, P. M. (2010a). *Displaying your findings: A practical guide for creating figures, posters, and presentations* (6th ed.). American Psychological Association.

Nicol, A. A. M., & Pexman, P. M. (2010b). *Displaying your findings: A practical guide for creating tables* (6th ed.). American Psychological Association.

Nisbett, R. E., & Ross, L. (1980). *Human inference: Strategies and shortcomings of social judgment.* Prentice-Hall.

Nisbett, R. E., & Wilson, T. D. (1977). Telling more than we can know: Verbal reports on mental processes. *Psychological Review, 84,* 231-259.

Niven, K. (2015). Can music with prosocial lyrics heal the working world? A field intervention in a call center. *Journal of Applied Social Psychology, 45*(3), 132-138. https://doi.org/10.1111/jasp.12282

O'Brien, E. (2019). Enjoy it again: Repeat experiences are less repetitive than people think. *Journal of Personality and Social Psychology, 116*(4), 519-540. https://doi.org/10.1037/pspa0000147

Oczak, M. (2007). Debriefing in deceptive research: A proposed new procedure. *Journal of Empirical Research on Human Research Ethics, 2,* 49-59.

Ono, H., Phillips, K. A., & Leneman, M. (1996). Content of an abstract: De jure and de facto. *American Psychologist, 51,* 1338-1340.

Open Science Collaboration. (2012). An open, large-scale, collaborative effort to estimate the reproducibility of psychological science. *Perspectives on Psychological Science, 7*(6), 657-660. https://doi.org/10.1177/1745691612462588

Open Science Collaboration (2015). Estimating the reproducibility of psychological science. *Science, 349*(6251), 716-1-716-8. https://doi.org/10.1126/science.aac4716

Opris, D., Pintea, S., García-Palacios, A., Botella, C., Szamosközi, S., & David, D. (2012). Virtual reality exposure therapy in anxiety disorders: A quantitative meta-analysis, *Depression and Anxiety, 29*(2), 85-93.

Orne, M. T. (1962). On the social psychology of the psychological experiment: With particular reference to demand characteristics and their implications. *American Psychologist, 17,* 776-783.

Orth, U., Trzesniewski, K. H., & Robins, R. W. (2010). Self-esteem development from young adulthood to old age: A cohort-sequential longitudinal study. *Journal of Personality and Social Psychology, 98,* 645-658. https://doi.org/10.1037/a0018769

Osgood, C. E., Suci, G. J., & Tannenbaum, P. H. (1957). *The measurement of meaning.* Urbana: University of Illinois Press.

Patterson, M. L., Lammers, V.M., & Tubbs, M.E. (2014). Busy signal: Effects of mobile device usage on pedestrian encounters. *Journal of Nonverbal Behavior, 38*(3), 313-324. https://doi.org/10.1007/s10919-014-0182-4

Pattinson, D. (2012). PLOS ONE launches Reproducibility Initiative. Retrieved from http://blogs.plos.org/everyone/2012/08/14/plos-one-launches-reproducibility-initiative/

Paulus, P. B., Annis, A. B., Seta, J. J., Schkade, J. K., & Matthews, R. W. (1976). Crowding does affect task performance. *Journal of Personality and Social Psychology, 34,* 248-253.

Pawlenko, N. B., Safer, M. A., Wise, R. A., & Holfeld, B. (2013). A teaching aid for improving jurors' assessments of eyewitness accuracy. *Applied Cognitive Psychology, 27,* 190-197.

Perry, G. (2013). *Behind the shock machine: The untold story of the notorious Milgram psychology experiments.* New Press.

Peterson, D. A. M., Biederman, L. A., Andersen, D., Ditonto, T. M., & Roe, K. (2019). Mitigating gender bias in student evaluations of teaching. *PLOS ONE, 14*(5), e0216241. https://doi.org/10.1371/journal.pone.0216241

Peterson, K., Sharps, P., Banyard, V., Powers, R. A., Kaukinen, C., Gross, D., ... & Campbell, J. (2018). An evaluation of two dating violence prevention programs on a college campus. *Journal of Interpersonal Violence,*

33(23), 3630–3655. https://doi.org/10.1177/0886260516636069

Peterson, R. A., (2001). On the use of college students in social science research: Insights from a second-order meta-analysis. *Journal of Consumer Research, 28*(3), 450–461.

Petty, R. E., Wheeler, S. C., & Tomala, Z. L. (2003). Persuasion and attitude change. In T. Millon & M. J. Lerner (Eds.), *Comprehensive handbook of psychology* (pp. 353–382). Wiley.

Pew Internet. (2010). *Demographics of internet users.* Retrieved from http://www.pewinternet.org/Static-Pages/Trend-Data/Whos-Online.aspx

Pew Research Center (2015). Teens, Social Media & Technology Overview 2015. Retrieved from https://www.pewinternet.org/2015/04/09/teens-social-media-technology-2015/

Pew Research Center Internet & Techology (2019). Fact Sheets. https://www.pewresearch.org/internet/fact-sheet/

Pfungst, O. (1911). *Clever Hans (the horse of Mr. von Osten): A contribution to experimental, animal, and human psychology* (C. L. Rahn, Trans.). Holt, Rinehart & Winston. (Republished 1965.)

Piaget, J. (1952). *The origins of intelligence in children.* International Universities Press.

Pigliucci, M. (2010). *Nonsense on stilts: How to tell science from bunk.* University of Chicago Press.

Plous, S. (1996a). Attitudes toward the use of animals in psychological research and education: Results from a national survey of psychologists. *American Psychologist, 51*, 1167–1180.

Plous, S. (1996b). Attitudes toward the use of animals in psychological research and education: Results from a national survey of psychology majors. *Psychological Science, 7*, 352–363.

Popper, K. (2002). *The logic of scientific discovery.* Routledge.

Ramírez-Esparza, N., Mehl, M. R., Alvarez-Bermúdez, J. & Pennebaker, J. W. (2009). Are Mexicans more sociable than Americans? Insights from a naturalistic observation study. *Journal of Research in Personality, 43,* 1–7.

Ramirez, G., & Beilock, S. L. (2011). Writing about testing worries boosts exam performance in the classroom. *Science, 331*(6014), 211–213.

Rauscher, F. H., & Shaw, G. L. (1998). Key components of the Mozart effect. *Perceptual and Motor Skills, 86,* 835–841.

Rauscher, F. H., Shaw, G. L., & Ky, K. N. (1993). Music and spatial task performance. *Nature, 365,* 611.

Ravizza, S. M., Uitvlugt, M. G., & Fenn, K. M. (2017). Logged in and zoned out: How laptop internet use relates to classroom learning. *Psychological Science, 28*(2), 171–180. https://doi.org/10.1177/0956797616677314

Raykov, T., & Marcoulides, G. A. (2000). *A first course in structural equation modeling.* Erlbaum.

Rentfrow, P., Gosling, S., & Potter, J. (2008). A theory of the emergence, persistence, and expression of geographic variation in psychological characteristics. *Perspectives on Psychological Science, 3,* 339–369. https://doi.org/10.1111/j.1745-6924.2008.00084.x

Reverby, S. M. (2011). "Normal exposure" and inoculation syphilis: A PHS "Tuskegee" doctor in Guatemala, 1946–1948. *Journal of Policy History, 23,* 6–28. https://doi.org/10.1017/S0898030610000291

Reverby, S. M. (Ed.). (2000). *Tuskegee's truths: Rethinking the Tuskegee syphilis study.* University of North Carolina Press.

Rhoades, G., & Stocker, C. M. (2006). Can spouses provide knowledge of each other's communication patterns? A study of self-reports, spouses' reports, and observational coding. *Family Process, 45,*

499–511. https://doi.org/10.1111/
j.1545-5300.2006.00185.x

Rhodes, N., Roskos-Ewoldsen, D., Eno, C. A., &
Monahan, J. L. (2009). The content of
cigarette counter-advertising: Are perceived
functions of smoking addressed? *Journal of
Health Communication, 14*(7), 658–673.
https://doi.org/10.1080/10810730903204262

Rideout, V. J., Foehr, U. G., & Roberts, D. F.
(2010). *Generation M²: Media in the lives of
8- to 18-year-olds.* Henry J. Kaiser Family
Foundation. Retrieved from
http://kaiserfamilyfoundation.files.wordpress
.com/2013/04/8010.pdf

Ring, K., Wallston, K., & Corey, M. (1970).
Mode of debriefing as a factor affecting
subjective reaction to a Milgram-type
obedience experiment: An ethical inquiry.
*Representative Research in Social Psychology,
1,* 67–68.

Riordan, C. A., & Marlin, N. A. (1987). Some
good news about some bad practices.
American Psychologist, 42, 104–106.

Roberson, M. T., & Sundstrom, E. (1990).
Questionnaire design, return rates, and
response favorableness in an employee
attitude questionnaire. *Journal of Applied
Psychology, 75,* 354–357.

Robinson, J. P., Athanasiou, R., & Head, K. B.
(1969). *Measures of occupational attitudes
and occupational characteristics.* Ann Arbor,
MI: Institute for Social Research.

Robinson, J. P., & Martin, S. P. (2009). Social
attitude differences between internet users
and non-users: Evidence from the General
Social Survey. *Information, Communication
& Society, 12* (4), 508–524. https://doi.org/
10.1080/13691180902857645

Robinson, J. P., Rusk, J. G., & Head, K. B.
(1968). *Measures of political attitudes.*
Institute for Social Research.

Robinson, J. P., Shaver, P. R., & Wrightsman, L.
S. (1991). *Measures of personality and social
psychological attitudes* (Vol. 1). Academic
Press.

Robinson, J. P., Shaver, P. R., & Wrightsman, L.
S. (Eds.). (1999). *Measures of political
attitudes.* Academic Press.

Rodriguez-Seijas, C., Eaton, N. R., & Pachankis,
J. E. (2019). Prevalence of psychiatric
disorders at the intersection of race and
sexual orientation: Results from the
National Epidemiologic Survey of Alcohol
and Related Conditions-III. *Journal of
Consulting and Clinical Psychology, 87*(4),
321–331. https://doi.org/10.1037/
ccp0000377

Rosen, C. C., Simon, L. S., Gajendran, R. S.,
Johnson, R. E., Lee, H. W., & Lin, S.-H.
(Joanna). (2019). Boxed in by your inbox:
Implications of daily e-mail demands for
managers' leadership behaviors. *Journal of
Applied Psychology, 104*(1), 19–33.
https://doi.org /10.1037/apl0000343

Rosenthal, R. (1966). *Experimenter effects in
behavior research.* Appleton-Century-Crofts.

Rosenthal, R. (1967). Covert communication in
the psychological experiment. *Psychological
Bulletin, 67,* 356–367.

Rosenthal, R. (1969). Interpersonal
expectations: Effects of the experimenter's
hypothesis. In R. Rosenthal & R. L. Rosnow
(Eds.), *Artifacts in behavioral research.*
Academic Press.

Rosenthal, R., & Jacobson, L. (1968). *Pygmalion
in the classroom: Teacher expectation and
pupils' intellectual development.* Holt,
Rinehart & Winston.

Rosenthal, R., & Rosnow, R. L. (1975). *The
volunteer subject.* Wiley.

Rosnow, R. L., & Rosnow, M. (2012). *Writing
papers in psychology* (9th ed.). Wadsworth
Cengage Learning.

Ruback, R. B., & Juieng, D. (1997). Territorial
defense in parking lots: Retaliation against
waiting drivers. *Journal of Applied Social
Psychology, 27,* 821–834.

Rubin, Z. (1975). Disclosing oneself to a
stranger: Reciprocity and its limits. *Journal
of Experimental Social Psychology, 11,*
233–260.

Ryan, C. S., & Hemmes, N. S. (2005). Effects of the contingency for homework submission on homework submission and quiz performance in a college course. *Journal of Applied Behavior Analysis, 38,* 79–88. https://doi.org/10.1901/jaba.2005.123-03

Schachter, S. (1959). *The psychology of affiliation.* Stanford University Press.

Schaie, K. W. (1986). Beyond calendar definitions of age, time, and cohort: The general developmental model revisited. *Developmental Review, 6,* 252–277.

Schmiedeberg, C., Huyer-May, B., Castiglioni, L., & Johnson, M. D. (2017). The more or the better? How sex contributes to life satisfaction. *Archives of Sexual Behavior, 46*(2), 465–473. https://doi.org/10.1007/s10508-016-0843-y

Schultz, W. (Ed.). (2005). *Handbook of psychobiography.* Oxford University Press.

Schwartz, B. M., Landrum, R. E., & Gurung, R.A.R. (2017). *An easy guide to APA style* (3rd ed.). Sage.

Schwarz, N. (1999). Self-reports: How the questions shape the answers. *American Psychologist, 54,* 93–105.

Schwarz, N., Knauper, B., Oyserman, D., & Stich, C. (2008). The psychology of asking questions. In E. Desiree de Leeuw, J. J. Hox, & D. A. Dillman (Eds.), *International handbook of survey methodology* (pp. 18–34). Taylor & Francis.

Schwinn, T. M., Schinke, S. P., Hopkins, J., Keller, B., & Liu, X. (2018). An online drug abuse prevention program for adolescent girls: Posttest and 1-year outcomes. *Journal of Youth and Adolescence, 47*(3), 490–500. https://doi.org/10.1007/s10964-017-0714-4

Scribner, S. (1997). Studying literacy at work: Bringing the laboratory to the field. In E. Torbach, R. J. Falmagne, M. B. Parlee, L. M. W. Martin, & A. S. Kapelman (Eds.), *Mind and social practice: Selected writings of Sylvia Scribner.* Cambridge University Press.

Sears, D. O. (1986). College sophomores in the laboratory: Influences of a narrow data base on social psychology's view of human nature. *Journal of Personality and Social Psychology, 51,* 515–530.

Shadish, W. R., Cook, T. D., & Campbell, D. T. (2002). *Experimental and quasi-experimental designs for generalized causal inference.* Houghton Mifflin.

Shepard, R. N., & Metzler, J. (1971). Mental rotation of three-dimensional objects. *Science, 171,* 701–703.

Sidman, M. (1960). *Tactics of scientific research.* Basic Books.

Sieber, J. E. (2009). Evidence-based ethical problem solving (EBEPS). *Perspectives on Psychological Science, 4*(1), 26–27. https://doi.org/10.1111/j.1745-6924.2009.01087.x

Sieber, J. E., Iannuzzo, R., & Rodriguez, B. (1995). Deception methods in psychology: Have they changed in 23 years? *Ethics and Behavior, 5,* 67–85.

Siegel, S., & Castellan, N. J. (1988). *Nonparametric statistics for the behavioral sciences.* McGraw-Hill.

Silverman, L., & Margulis, S. (1973). Experiment title as a source of sampling bias in commonly used "subject-pool" procedures. *Canadian Psychologist, 14,* 197–201.

Simmons, J. P., Nelson, L. D., & Simonsohn, U. (2013). Life after P-Hacking. Paper presented at the Meeting of the Society for Personality and Social Psychology, New Orleans, LA, January 17–19, 2013. Available at SSRN: https://ssrn.com/abstract=2205186 or http://doi.org/10.2139/ssrn.2205186

Singh, D., Dixson, B., Jessop, T., Morgan, B., & Dixson, A. (2010). Cross-cultural consensus for waist–hip ratio and women's attractiveness. *Evolution and Human Behavior, 31*(3), 176–181. https://doi.org/10.1016/j.evolhumbehav.2009.09.001

Skinner, B. F. (1953). *Science and human behavior.* Macmillan.

Smart, R. (1966). Subject selection bias in psychological research. *Canadian Psychologist, 7,* 115-121.

Smith, C. P. (1983). Ethical issues: Research on deception, informed consent, and debriefing. In L. Wheeler & P. Shaver (Eds.), *Review of personality and social psychology* (Vol. 4). Sage.

Smith, R. J., Lingle, J. H., & Brock, T. C. (1978). Reactions to death as a function of perceived similarity to the deceased. *Omega, 9,* 125-138.

Smith, S. M., & Shaffer, D. R. (1991). Celerity and cajolery: Rapid speech may promote or inhibit persuasion through its impact on message elaboration. *Personality and Social Psychology Bulletin, 17,* 663-669.

Smith, S. S., & Richardson, D. (1983). Amelioration of harm in psychological research: The important role of debriefing. *Journal of Personality and Social Psychology, 44,* 1075-1082.

Smith, S. S., & Richardson, D. (1985). On deceiving ourselves about deception: A reply to Rubin. *Journal of Personality and Social Psychology, 48,* 254-255.

Snowden, D. A. (1997). Aging and Alzheimer's disease: Lessons from the Nun Study. *Gerontologist, 37,* 150-156.

Solomon, R. L. (1949). An extension of control group design. *Psychological Bulletin, 46,* 137-150.

Springer, M. V., McIntosh, A. R., Winocur, G., & Grady, C. L. (2005). The relation between brain activity during memory tasks and years of education in young and older adults. *Neuropsychology, 19,* 181-192.

Stabell, A., Eide, H., Solheim, G. A., Solberg, K. N., & Rustoen, T. (2004). Nursing home residents' dependence and independence. *Journal of Clinical Nursing, 13,* 677-686.

Steele, K. M., Bass, K. E., & Crook, M. D. (1999). The mystery of the Mozart effect: Failure to replicate. *Psychological Science, 10,* 366-369.

Stephan, W. G. (1983). Intergroup relations. In D. Perlman & P. C. Cozby (Eds.), *Social psychology.* Holt, Rinehart & Winston.

Sternberg, R. J., & Sternberg, K. (2016). *The psychologist's companion: A guide to scientific writing for students and researchers* (6th ed.). Cambridge University Press.

Stevenson, H. W., & Allen, S. (1964). Adult performance as a function of sex of experimenter and sex of subject. *Journal of Abnormal and Social Psychology, 68,* 214-216.

Stewart, R. E., & Chambless, D. L. (2009). Cognitive–behavioral therapy for adult anxiety disorders in clinical practice: A meta-analysis of effectiveness studies. *Journal of Consulting and Clinical Psychology, 77,* 595-606.

Stone, V. E., Cosmides, L., Tooby, J., Kroll, N., & Knight, R. T. (2002). Selective impairment of reasoning about social exchange in a patient with bilateral limbic system damage. *Proceedings of the National Academy of Sciences, 99* (17), 11531-11536. Retrieved November 1, 2002, from http://www.pnas.org/cgi/content/full/99/17/11531

Storer, H. L., Casey, E., & Herrenkohl, T. (2016). Efficacy of bystander programs to prevent dating abuse among youth and young adults: A review of the literature. *Trauma, Violence, & Abuse, 17*(3), 256-269. https://doi.org/10.1177/1524838015584361

Sue, D. W., Capodilupo, C. M., Torino, G. C., Bucceri, J. M., Holder, A. M. B., Nadal, K. L., & Esquilin, M. (2007). Racial microaggressions in everyday life: Implications for clinical practice. *American Psychologist, 62*(4), 271-286. https://doi.org/10.1037/0003-066X.62.4.271

Sue, V. M., & Ritter, L. A. (2012). *Conducting online surveys* (2nd ed.). SAGE Publications. https://doi.org/10.4135/9781506335186

Szabo, A., & Underwood, J. (2004). Cybercheats: Is information and communication technology fueling academic dishonesty? *Active Learning in Higher Education, 5,* 180–199.

Tabachnick, B. G., & Fidell, L. S. (2013). *Using multivariate statistics* (6th ed.). Allyn & Bacon.

Tauber, S. K., Witherby, A. E., Dunlosky, J., Rawson, K. A., Putnam, A. L., & Roediger, H. L., III. (2018). Does covert retrieval benefit learning of key-term definitions? *Journal of Applied Research in Memory and Cognition, 7*(1), 106–115. https://doi.org/10.1016/j.jarmac.2016.10.004

Terman, L. M. (1925). *Genetic studies of genius:* Vol. 1. *Mental and physical traits of a thousand gifted children.* Stanford University Press.

Terman, L. M., & Oden, M. H. (1947). *Genetic studies of genius:* Vol. 4. *The gifted child grows up: Twenty-five years' follow-up of a superior group.* Stanford University Press.

Terman, L. M., & Oden, M. H. (1959). *Genetic studies of genius:* Vol. 5. *The gifted group in mid-life: Thirty five years' follow-up of the superior child.* Stanford University Press.

Thomas, G. V., & Blackman, D. (1992). The future of animal studies in psychology. *American Psychologist, 47,* 1678.

Thompson, W. F., Schellenberg, E. G., & Husain, G. (2001). Arousal, mood, and the Mozart effect. *Psychological Science, 12,* 248–251.

Tipping expert. (2013). Retrieved from http://tippingresearch.com

Tufte, E. R. (1983). *The visual display of quantitative information.* Graphics Press.

Tufte, E. R. (1990). *Envisioning information.* Graphics Press.

Tufte, E. R. (1997). *Visual explanations: Images and quantities, evidence and narrative.* Graphics Press.

Tufte, E. R. (2006). *Beautiful evidence.* Graphics Press.

Tymula, A., Belmaker, L., Ruderman, L., Glimcher, P. W., & Levy, I. (2013). Like cognitive function, decision making across the life span shows profound age-related changes. *PNAS Proceedings of the National Academy of Sciences of the United States of America, 110*(42), 17143–17148. https://doi.org/10.1073/pnas.1309909110

U.S. Department of Health and Human Services (HHS). (1998). OHRP Expedited Review Categories (1998). https://www.hhs.gov/ohrp/regulations-and-policy/guidance/categories-of-research-expedited-review-procedure-1998/index.html

U.S. Department of Health and Human Services (HHS). (2001). Protection of human subjects. Retrieved from http://www.hhs.gov/humansubjects/guidance/45cfr46.htm

U.S. Department of Health and Human Services (HHS). (2018). 45 CFR 46 Protection of Human Subjects. Retrieved from https://www.hhs.gov/ohrp/regulations-and-policy/regulations/45-cfr-46

U.S. Office of Science and Technology Policy. 2013. Expanding public access to the results of federally funded research. Retrieved from https://obamawhitehouse.archives.gov/sites/default/files/microsites/ostp/ostp_public_access_memo_2013.pdf

Ullman, J. B. (2007). Structural equation modeling. In B. G. Tabachnick & L. S. Fidell, *Using multivariate statistics* (5th ed.). Allyn & Bacon.

van den Bosch, A., Bogers, T. & de Kunder, M. (2016). Estimating search engine index size variability: A 9-year longitudinal study. *Scientometrics, 107,* 839. https://doi.org/10.1007/s11192-016-1863-z

Vasquez, E. A., Pedersen, W. C., Bushman, B. J., Kelley, N. J., Demeestere, P., & Miller, N. (2013). Lashing out after stewing over public insults: The effects of public provocation, provocation intensity, and rumination on triggered displaced aggression. *Aggressive Behavior, 39,* 13–29. https://doi.org/10.1002/ab.21453

Verfaellie, M., & McGwin, J. (2011). The case of Diederik Stapel. Retrieved from http://www.apa.org/science/about/psa/2011/12/diederik-stapel.aspx

Viney, W., King, D., & Berndt, J. (1990). Animal research in psychology: Declining or thriving? *Journal of Comparative Psychology, 104,* 322–325. https://doi.org/10.1037/0735-7036.104.4.322

Wampold, B. E., Minami, T., Tierney, S., Baskin, T. W., & Bhati, K. S. (2005). The placebo is powerful: Estimating placebo effects in medicine and psychotherapy from randomized clinical trials. *Journal of Clinical Psychology, 61,* 835–854. https://doi.org/10.1002/jclp.20129

Webb, E. J., Campbell, D. T., Schwartz, R. D., Sechrest, R., & Grove, J. B. (1981). *Nonreactive measures in the social sciences* (2nd ed.). Houghton Mifflin.

Wilkinson, L., & the Task Force on Statistical Inference. (1999). Statistical methods in psychology journals: Guidelines and explanations. *American Psychologist, 54,* 594–604.

Winograd, E., & Soloway, R. M. (1986). On forgetting the location of things stored in special places. *Journal of Experimental Psychology: General, 115,* 366–372.

Wolpe, J. (1982). *The practice of behavior therapy* (3rd ed.). Pergamon.

Yechiam, E., Ashby, N. J. S., & Hochman, G. (2019). Are we attracted by losses? Boundary conditions for the approach and avoidance effects of losses. *Journal of Experimental Psychology: Learning, Memory, and Cognition, 45*(4), 591–605. https://doi.org/10.1037/xlm0000607

Yin, R. K. (2014). *Case study research: Design and methods* (5th ed.). Sage.

Zimbardo, P. G. (2004). Does psychology make a significant difference in our lives? *American Psychologist, 59,* 339–351.

Zitek, E. M., Jordan, A. H., Monin, B., & Leach, F. R. (2010). Victim entitlement to behave selfishly. *Journal of Personality and Social Psychology, 98,* 245–255.

Index

A

abbreviations, 34, 258, 293, 320–321
abstract, 27, 28, 303–305, 327
accomplice. *See* confederate
accuracy, reliability of measures and, 101
acquiescence response set, 131
active versus passive voice, 294
activity rating, 133
alpha level, 253
alternate forms reliability, 99
alternative explanations, 9, 84
Amazon Mechanical Turk (MTurk), 137, 276
American Psychological Association (APA)
    animal research ethics, 279, 345
    databases, 39. *See also* PsycINFO
    Ethics Code, 49–50, 58, 344–345
    Guidelines for Ethical Conduct in the Care and Use of Nonhuman Animals, 62, 279
    professional meetings, 181–182
    Publication Manual of the American Psychological Association, 29, 286, 292
    Standard 8: Research and Publication, 345
    Stress in America reports, 127
    style. *See* research reports
    website as resource, 29–30
analysis of variance (*F* test), 196, 257, 353–365
    conclusion, 365
    effect size for *F* statistic, 357–358
    one independent variable, 354–357, 354t
    repeated measures (within subjects), 363–365, 363t–364t, 365t
    two independent variables, 358–363, 359t, 360t, 362t
anecdotal evidence, 4
animal research
    ethics and, 61–62
    generalizing to human populations, 279
    multiple levels of independent variable, 189
    Standard 8: Research and Publication, 345

APA. *See* American Psychological Association (APA)
appendices, 310
applied research, 12–14
archival research, 120–122
    statistical records, 121
    survey archives, 121–122
    written and mass communication records, 122–123
Aristotle, 4
articles. *See* journal articles; paper and poster presentations; research reports
Asch conformity experiment, 171, 171f
Association for Psychological Science (APS), 284
    Perspectives on Psychological Science, 284
    professional meetings, 181–182
    website as resource, 29–30, 288
attitudinal survey questions, 129
attribute variables. *See* participant variables
attrition, 155
author and affiliation, 301–302
author-date citation method, 312–315
authority, 3, 4
author note, 302
autism spectrum disorder (ASD), 25
autonomy
    as ethical principle, 49
    informed consent and, 54–55

B

Bakeman, Roger, 118
balanced placebo design, 177
bar graphs, 231, 231f
baseline, 207
basic research, 11–12
behavior
    describing, 7–8, 8f
    determining causes, 8–9, 10f

explaining, 9

predicting, 8

understanding. *See* scientific understanding
   of behavior

behavioral measures, 174

behavioral research, common risks, 51–52

behavioral science goals, 7–10

   causes of behavior, 8–9, 10f

   description of behavior, 8, 8f

   explanation of behavior, 9

   prediction of behavior, 8

behavioral survey questions, 129

Belmont Report, 48–49, 58

beneficence principle, 49, 344

   as Belmont Report principle, 49

   risk-benefit analysis and, 50–52

between-group variance, 257

between-subjects design, 157

bias

   convenience sampling and, 142, 145–146

   experimenter's, 178–179

   illusory correlation, 4

   interviewer's, 137

   in language, 109, 294–295

   measurement concepts and, 109

   selection, 214

   in survey questions, 128–130

binomial distribution, 253

bivariate research, 269

books, format for reference list, 317

Boolean operators, 36–37

Brown v. Board of Education, 3

Brownlee, John, 118

Burt, Cyril (Sir), 63

C

carryover effect, 158–159

case studies, 119–120

cause and effect

   covariation, 9, 10f

   direction of, 80–81

   internal validity and, 84

ceiling effect, 176

central tendency, 233, 346–348

children, ethical research with, 54

chi-square (X^2), 350–353, 350t–351t

cisgender, 277

citation style, 312–315

classical conditioning, 23

closed-ended questions, 131–132

cluster sampling, 142, 143t

coding systems, 118

Cohen's *d*, 258–259t

Cohen's kappa, 100

cohort, 220

cohort effects, 220

Collaborative Replications and Education
   Project (CREP), 286

college students as study subjects, 145–146, 275,
   280

common sense, as source of research ideas,
   21–22

communication, facilitated, 6

communication records, written and mass,
   122–123

computer-assisted telephone interview (CATI)
   system, 138

conceptual replications, 284–285

conclusions, erroneous, 4

concurrent validity, 103, 104t

conduct validity, measurement indicators,
   104t–105t

confederate, 170–171

conferences. *See* professional meetings

confidence interval, 139–140

   sample size and, 140

   statistical significance and, 259, 260f

confidentiality, 52

confounding variable, 82, 152

construct validity, 75, 89

   defined, 101–102

   indicators, 102–104

introduction, 73
construct validity of measures, 101–104
    concurrent validity, 103
    content validity, 102
    convergent validity, 103
    discriminant validity, 103–104
    face validity, 102
    indicators, 104t–105t
    predictive validity, 103
content analysis, 122
content validity, 102, 104t
control series design, 217, 217f
convenience sampling, 142, 143t, 145–146
convergent validity, 103, 104t
correlational method, 80
correlation coefficients, 78, 98–99, 235–240. *See also* Pearson product-moment correlation
coefficient (*r*)
    curvilinear relationship, 239–240, 240f
    defined, 235
    restriction of range, 238–239, 239f
    scatterplots, 236–237, 237f, 238f, 239f
counterbalancing, 159–160, 160f
covariation, 84
covariation of cause and effect, 9, 10f
criterion, 102
criterion variable, 241
Cronbach's alpha, 100
cross-sectional method, 218–220
culture, 278–279
curvilinear relationship, 76, 77, 189f
    considerations in relationships, 239–240, 240f
    independent variables and, 188, 189f
    inverted-U, 77, 189

D

data
    description and interpretation, 115–116
    scientific approach and, 5
    sharing for verification, 345

data accessibility, 121
databases, 33. *See also* PsycINFO
    strategies for searching, 37f–38f
    Web of Science and Scopus, 38–39
debriefing, 57–58, 181, 345
deception, 55–57, 345
decision matrix, 260, 261f, 263f
Declaration of Helsinki, 48
degrees of freedom (*df*), 256–257, 352
demand characteristics, 176–177
demographics, sex, gender, race, and identity, 276–278
demographic survey questions, 129
dependent variables
    experimental method and, 82
    independent variables and, 85
    measuring, 173–176
description and correlation, 227–248. *See also* research results
descriptive statistics, 233–234, 346–349
    central tendency, 233
    measures of central tendency, 346–348
    measures of variability, 348–349
    variability, 234–235
developmental research designs, 206, 218–221, 281f
    cross-sectional method, 218–220
    longitudinal method, 219–220
    sequential method, 220–221
digital object identifier (DOI), 34, 316
dignity, respecting study subject's, 50
direction of cause and effect, 80–81, 81f
discriminant validity, 103–104, 104t–105t
discussion section, 29–30, 309, 336
distress, as research risk, 51–52
double-barreled questions, 130
double-blind experiment, 179

E

EAR, 118–119
edited books, format for reference list, 317–318

effect size, 240–241
  calculating, 258–259, 259t
  for chi-square statistic, 352–353
  defined, 240
  for *F* statistic, 357–358
  meta-analysis and, 286–287, 287t
  sample size and, 266t
electroencephalogram (EEG), 174
electromyogram (EMG), 174
Electronically Activated Recorder (EAR),
  118–119
empirical research articles, 27–32, 292
empiricism, 4–5
equipment concerns, 118–119
errors
  measurement, 97–98
  Type I and Type II, 260–264, 260f
error variance, 257
*Ethical Principles of Psychologists and Code of
  Conduct. See* American Psychological
  Association (APA), Ethics Code
ethics, 46–71
  APA Ethics Code, 49–50, 58, 344–345
  autonomy issues, 54–55
  Belmont Report principles, 48–49
  debriefing, 57–58, 345
  deception, 55–57
  Declaration of Helsinki, 48
  fraud, 63–64
  historical context of standards, 48–49
  illustrative article, 67–68
  informed consent, 52–57
  Institutional Review Boards (IRBs), 58–61
  Milgram's obedience experiment, 46–47,
    51, 55–56, 57, 67
  misrepresentation by researcher, 62–65
  nonhuman animal research subjects,
    61–62, 345
  Nuremberg Code, 48
  plagiarism, 64–65
  risk-benefit analysis, 50–52, 66–67, 66f

ethnicity, 277–278
evaluation rating, 133
event manipulation. *See* staged manipulation
exact replication, 282–284
exempt review research, 59, 60f
expectancy effects, 178–179
expedited review, 59–60, 60f
experimental control, 83
experimental design, 151–166. *See also*
  quasi-experimental designs; research design;
  single-case experimental designs
  assigning participants to experimental
    conditions, 157–163
  basic experiments, 153–156
  confounding and internal validity, 152
  developmental research design, 218–221
  illustrative article, 163
  independent groups design, 157
  matched pairs design, 162–163
  repeated measures design, 157–161
  single-case, 206–210
experimental design, complex, 187–205
  assignment procedures and factorial
    designs, 197–198
  factorial designs, 189–194
  illustrative article, 201–202
  increasing number of independent variable
    levels, 188–189, 188f, 189f, 198–199
  interactions and simple main effects,
    196–197
  2 × 2 outcomes, 194–196, 195f
experimental method, 82–84
  additional considerations, 86–89
  defined, 80
  experimental control and, 83
  internal validity and, 84
  multiple methods, 88–89
  randomization and, 83–84
  unanswerable questions, 87–88
experimenter bias, 178–179
experimenters
  controlling for expectations, 178–179

misrepresentation by, 62–65

two or more, 280

experiments, conducting, 167–186

  additional controls, 176–179

  analyzing and interpreting results, 181

  communicating research to others, 181–182

  final planning considerations, 179–181

  illustrative article, 182–183

  manipulating independent variable, 168–173

  measuring dependent variable, 173–176

  selecting participants, 168

ex post facto design, 87

exposure therapy, 14

external validity

  defined, 73, 86, 89, 275

  evaluating, 286–287

  generalization and, 86, 275–282

  replication, 282–286

  supporting, 282–287

extraneous variables, 81

F

F test, 254, 257. *See also* analysis of variance

face-to-face interviews, 137

FACES scale, variables in, 74–75

face validity, 102, 104t

facilitated communication, 6, 25

factorial designs, 189–194, 190f

  assignment procedures and, 197–198

  interpreting, 191–193

  manipulated and nonmanipulated variables, 193–194, 194f

  three or more independent variables, 200–201

  2 × 3 design, 198–199, 199t, 199f

  2 × 2 outcomes, 194–196, 195f

falsifiability, 5

fatigue effect, 158

fidelity and responsibility principle, 49–50, 344

field experiments, 86–87. *See also* naturalistic observation

figures, 308–309, 311, 343

filler items, 177

floor effect, 176

focus groups, 138

footnotes, 310. *See also* references; sources, citing and referencing

formatting, survey, 135

fraud, 63–64

frequency distributions, 230–233

frequency polygons, 232, 232f

functional MRI (fMRI), 174

G

galvanic skin response (GSR), 174

gender, 277

gender identity, 277

generalization, 274–291

  across methods, 280–281

  evaluating via literature reviews and meta-analysis, 286–287, 287t

  external validity and, 282–287

  illustrative article, 288–289

  from laboratory setting, 281

  to other populations, 275–280

  pretests and, 280–281

  replications and, 282–286

  as statistical interaction, 282, 283f

Google Scholar, 39–40

Graham v. Florida, 3

grammatical considerations, 295–298

graphic rating scale, 132

graphs and charts

  frequency distributions, 231–233

  graphing relationships, 234–235, 234f, 235f

  histograms, 232–233, 232f

  scatterplots, 236–237, 237f, 238f, 239f

greater than minimal risk, 59

group differences, statistical inferences and, 254–260
  confidence intervals and statistical significance, 259, 260f
  degrees of freedom (*df*), 256–257
  effect size calculation, 258–259, 259t
  F test, 257
  one-tailed versus two-tailed tests, 257
  statistical significance overview, 260
  t test, 254–256, 255f
group means, comparing, 229–230, 230t
group percentages, comparing, 229

H

Helsinki Declaration, 48
high-frequency scale, 134–135
histograms, 232–233, 232f
history effects, 212
hypothesis, 20–21, 21f
  defined, 20
  demand characteristics and, 177
  discussion and, 29–30
  multiple methods of testing, 88–89
  null, 251–255, 261f, 262–263
  research, 251–252
  theory and, 23

I

ideas, sources, 21–25
  common sense, 21–22
  observation, 22–23
  past research, 24–25
  practical problems, 22
  theories, 23–24
  versus theories, 23–24
illusory correlation, 4
illustrative articles
  complex experimental designs, 201–202
  conducting experiments, 146–147, 182–183
  experimental design, 163

generalizing results, 288–289
laptops in class, 40–41
longitudinal study, 221–222
measurement concepts, 109
observational methods, 123–124
replication of Milgram, 67–68
scientific understanding of behavior, 15–16
studying behavior, 90
independent groups (between-subjects) design, 157, 197
independent variables
  basic experiments and, 153–155
  defined, 82, 85
  increasing number of levels, 188–189, 198–199
  increasing number of variables. *See* factorial designs
  internal validity and, 152
  manipulating, 168–173
  manipulation checks and, 180–181
  measuring, 173–176
  research with multiple, 269
  three or more, 200–201, 200t
individual scores, correlating, 229
inferential statistics, 250–251. *See also* statistical inference
informants, 29
informed consent, 52–57, 345
  autonomy issues, 54–55
  form, 53–54, 53f–54f
  withholding information and, 55–56
Institutional Animal Care and Use Committee (IACUC), 62
Institutional Review Boards (IRBs), 58–61, 60f, 345
  decision tree, 60f
  exempt review research, 59
  expedited review, 59–61
  full review, 61
  limited review, 61
instrument decay, 213
integrity principle, 50, 344

interaction, 191, 191t, 192–193, 193f
interactive voice response (IVR) technology, 138
internal consistency reliability, 99–100, 101f
internal validity
    confounding variable and, 152
    considerations, 86
    defined, 73, 89
    experimental method and, 84
internet. *See also* databases; websites
    archival research, 120–122
    citations from sources, 316, 319
    false claims and, 7
    online participants, 276
    searches, 39
interrater reliability, 100, 101f
interrupted time series design, 216–217
interval scales, 106–107, 107t, 228
interviewer bias, 137
interviews, 137–138
introduction section, 28, 305–306
intuition, 3–4
inverted-U relationship, 77, 189
IRBs. *See* Institutional Review Boards (IRBs)
items, 98
item-total correlations, 100

J

journal articles, 25–32. *See also* research reports
    empirical research articles, 27–32
    format for reference list, 316–317
    literature reviews, 25–26
    meta-analyses, 26
    publishing research results, 182
    theory articles, 26–27
journals, 32–33
    exploring past research, 32–40
    peer reviewed, 35
    psychology, 30t–32t
justice principle, 49–50, 345

K

keywords, 305

L

laboratory setting, generalization from, 281
Latin square, 160, 160f
limited review, 60f, 61
linear relationships, 81–83, 77f
literature reviews, 25–26, 292
    defined, 25
    evaluating generalizations via, 286–287
    in proposal, 179
literature review section, 27
loaded survey questions, 130
location of participants, 278
longitudinal method, 219–222

M

mail surveys, 136
main effect, 191–192, 191t
manipulation checks, 180–181
manipulation of independent variables, 168–173
    cost of manipulation, 173
    setting stage, 169
    strength of manipulation, 172–173, 172f
    types of manipulations, 169–171
margin of error. *See* sampling error
mass communication records, written records
    and, 122–123
matched pairs design, 162–163
maturation effects, 212
mean, 233, 347–348
mean squares, 357, 362
measurement concepts, 96–112
    conduct validity indicators, 104t–105t
    construct validity of measures, 101–104
    illustrative article, 109
    reactivity of measures, 105
    reliability of measures, 97–101, 98f
    variables and measurement scales, 105–108

measurement error, 97–98

measurement scales, 107t–108t, 228–229. *See also* rating scales
  importance of, 108
  interval and ratio scales, 106–107, 107t
  nominal scales, 105–106, 107t
  ordinal scales, 106, 107t
  variables and, 105–108

measures, dependent variables, 173–176
  costs, 176
  multiple measures, 175
  sensitivity, 175–176
  types of measures, 173–174

measures, reliability, 97–101, 98f

median, 233, 347

meta-analysis
  defined, 26
  data accessibility and, 121
  evaluating generalizations via, 286–287, 287t

methodological issues, 118–119

method section, 29, 306–307, 329

Milgram, Stanley, 46–47, 47f, 51, 55–56, 57, 67

Milgram's obedience experiment, 46–47, 51, 55–56, 57, 67
  debriefing, 57
  deception and, 55–56
  risks, 51

Miller, George, 288

minimal risk research, 59–61, 60f

misrepresentation, 62–65

mixed factorial design, 197–198, 198f

mode, 233, 346

Monitoring the Future project, 127, 128f

monotonic function, 77

mortality, 155

Mozart effect, 283–284

MRI (magnetic resonance imagery), 174

multiple baseline designs, 209–210, 209f

multiple correlation/regression, 241–243

N

naturalistic observation, 114–117
  data description and interpretation, 115–116
  defined, 115
  limitations, 117
  participation and concealment, 116–117

nay-saying, 131

negative linear relationship, 76, 77f

negatively worded questions, 130

nominal scales, 105–106, 107t, 228

nonequivalent control group design, 214–215

nonequivalent control group pretest-posttest design, 215–216

nonexperimental method, 79–85
  causal possibilities, 81f
  defined, 79
  direction of cause and effect, 80–81
  third-variable problem, 81–82

nonmaleficence, 49, 344

nonmonotonic function, 77

nonprobability sampling, 140, 142–143, 143t–144t

nonreactive measures, 105

no relationship variables, 78, 77f, 83

nonsignificant results, interpreting, 264–265

nonverbal scales, 133

null hypothesis, 251

Nuremberg Code, 48

O

objectives, defining, 129

observation as source of research ideas, 22–23

observational methods, 113–125
  archival research, 120–122
  case studies, 119–120
  illustrative article, 123–124
  naturalistic, 114–117
  quantitative and qualitative approaches, 114, 116
  systematic, 117–119

one-group posttest-only design, 211

one-group pretest-posttest design, 212–214

one-tailed tests, 257

online databases, 33. *See also* Google Scholar; internet; PsycINFO

online surveys, 136–137

open-ended questions, 131–132

Open Science Collaboration, replication and, 285–286

open science and data accessibility, 121

operational definition, 74–75

oral presentations, 323

order effect, 158

ordinal scales, 106, 107t, 228

outlines, 293

P

page headers, 302–303, 326

page numbers, for reference list, 315–316

panel study, 139

paper and poster presentations, 318, 323–325

paraphrasing plagiarism, 65

partial correlation, 243, 243f

participant observation, 116

participants, 29, 294. *See also* populations, generalizing to other
    assigning to experimental conditions, 157–163
    college students, 145–146, 275, 280
    controlling for expectations, 176–177
    groups or individuals, 136
    language for identifying, 294–295
    online research, 276
    protecting. *See* informed consent; Institutional Review Boards (IRBs)
    selecting, 168
    terminology to describe, 29, 294
    volunteers, 276

participant variables, 87, 193

passive voice, versus active voice, 294

path coefficients, 244

Pavlov, Ivan, 23

Pearson product-moment correlation coefficient (r), 236–237, 236t, 239
    defined, 235
    example, 365–368, 366t–367t
    measurement reliability and, 98–99
    significance, 266
    when to use, 235

peer review, 5, 35, 182

percent of shared variance between two variables, 240

personal attributes. *See* participant variables

Perspectives on Psychological Science, 284

physical harm, as research risk, 51

physiological measures, 174

Piaget, Jean, 87–88

pie charts, 231, 231f

pilot studies
    conducting, 180
    manipulation checks and, 180
    testing survey, 135

placebo groups, 177

plagiarism, 64–65, 65f
    acknowledging others' work and, 294, 345
    paraphrasing, 65
    Standard 8 ethics and, 345
    word-for-word, 64

PLOS ONE (Public Library of Science), 284

popular articles, format for reference list, 318

population, 139

populations, generalizing to other
    college students, 275
    cultures, 278–279
    defending, 280
    location and, 278
    nonhuman animals, 279
    online participants, 276
    sex, gender, race, and identity, 276–278
    volunteers, 276

population sampling. *See* statistical inference, samples and populations positive linear relationship, 76, 77f

positive monotonic relationship, 188, 188f

poster presentations, 318, 323–324, 324f

posttest-only design, 153–154, 155–156, 156f

potency rating, 133

power analysis, 265–266

power of statistical test, 265

practice effect, 158

prediction, 20–21, 21f

predictive validity, 103, 104t

predictor variable, 241

pre-experimental design. *See* quasi-experimental designs

presentations, paper and poster, 318, 323–325, 324f

pretest-posttest design, 154–156, 1516f

pretests, generalization and, 280–281

privacy, 55–56

probability

    inferential statistics and, 251

    statistical significance and, 251–252

    sampling distributions and, 252–254, 253t

probability sampling, 141–142, 143t

problems, practical, as source of research ideas, 22

professional meetings

    format for citing papers and posters, 318

    presenting research results, 181–182

program evaluation, 13

propensity score matching, 216

proposals, 179–180

pseudoscience, 6–7

psychobiology, 120

psychology journals, 30t–32t

PsycINFO, 33

    conducting search, 33–38

    output example, 35–36

    strategies for searching, 37f–38f

public policy, 3

Publication Manual of the American Psychological Association, 292

purposive sampling, 142, 143t–144t

Q

QUAID (Question Understanding Aid), 131

qualitative approach, 114, 116

quantitative approach, 114, 116

quasi-experimental designs, 206, 210–217

    defined, 210

    interrupted time series design and control series design, 216–217, 217f

    nonequivalent control group design, 214–215

    nonequivalent control group pretest-posttest design, 215–216

    one-group posttest-only design, 211

    one-group pretest-posttest design, 212–214

    propensity score matching, 216

questionnaires, 136–137

questions, 20–21, 21f

    closed- vs. open-ended, 131–132

    constructing, 128–131

    responses, 131–135

    sequence, 135

    wording, 129–130

quota sampling, 142, 144t

R

race, 277–278

random assignment, 157

randomization, 83–84

random variability, 78–79

range, 234, 348

rating scales, 132–133

ratio scales, 106–107, 107t, 229

reactivity, 105, 119

reference list style, 315–319

references. *See also* footnotes; sources, citing and referencing

    elements, 34f

    description, 309

    hanging indent style, 299–300

order in report, 311
reference list style, 315–319
Registered Research Replications, 284
regression equations, 241
regression toward the mean, 213–214
reliability coefficient, 99
reliability issues, 119
reliability of measures, 97–101, 98f
    accuracy and, 101
    defined, 97
    internal consistency reliability, 99–100, 101f
    interrater reliability, 100, 101f
    test-retest reliability, 99, 100, 100f
repeated measures design, 157–161
    advantages and disadvantages, 158–159
    counterbalancing, 159–160
    defined, 157
    factorial designs and, 197, 198f
    independent groups vs. repeated measures, 161
    time intervals between treatments, 161
replications, 282–286
    conceptual, 284–285
    exact, 282–284
    importance to statistical inference, 266
    of Milgram, 67–68
    Open Science and, 285–286
    in single-case designs, 210
research
    archival, 120–122
    basic and applied, 11–14
    basic vs. applied, 14–15
    consuming, 2–3, 7
    common risks, 51–52
    exploring others', 32–40
    form for description, 53f
    improving lives through, 288
    past, as source of research ideas, 24–25

research design. *See also* experimental design; quasi-experimental designs; research design; single- case experimental designs
    bivariate research, 269
    multiple independent variables, 269
researchers
    controlling for expectations, 178–179
    misrepresentation by, 62–65
    two or more, 280
research hypothesis, 251
research issues, 72–95
    evaluating research, 89
    experimental methods, additional considerations, 86–89
    illustrative article, 90
    nonexperimental vs. experimental methods, 79–85
    operational definitions of variables and, 74–75
    relationships between variables, 76–79
    validity and, 73, 89
    variables, 73–74
research proposals, 179–180
research questions. *See* questions
research reports, 292–343. *See also* journal articles
    abbreviations, 320–321
    citing and referencing sources, 312–319, 340–341
    formatting, 299–300
    headings, 312, 313f
    introduction, 292–293
    major sections, 28f, 301f
    reporting numbers and statistics, 321–322
    sample paper, 325–343
    student's, 300, 303
    writing, 293–298
research reports, organization, 300–311
    abstract, 303–305
    appendix, 310
    body, 305–309
    figures, 311

footnotes, 310

references, 309

summary, 311

tables, 310

title page, 300–303

research results, 227–248

correlation coefficients, 235–240

describing, 229–230

descriptive statistics, 233–234

effect size, 240–241

frequency distributions, 230–233

graphing relationships, 234–235, 234f, 235f

measurement scales, 228–229

multiple correlation/regression, 241–243

nonsignificant results, 264–265

regression equations, 241

reporting, 345

statistical inference. *See* statistical inference

structural equation modeling, 244–245, 245f

third-variable problem, 243, 243f

respect for persons principle

APA Ethics code and, 50, 345

informed consent and, 52–53

respondents. *See* participants

response rate, 145

response set, 128

responsibility principle, 49–50

restriction of range, 238–239, 239f

results section, 29, 307–309, 334

retrospective approach, 220

reversal design, 207–208, 208f

risk-benefit analysis, 50–52, 53f–54f

Roper v. Simmons, 3

Ruggiero, Karen, 63

running heads, 302–303, 326–327

S

samples, 139, 144–145

sample size

choosing, 168, 265–266, 266t

nonsignificant results and, 264

from population, 140

probability and sampling distributions, 254

sampling distributions, 253–254, 253t, 255f

sampling error, 139

sampling frame, 144

sampling issues, 119

sampling techniques, 140–144

advantages and disadvantages, 143t–144t

nonprobability sampling, 141, 142–143

probability sampling, 141–142

scales. *See* FACES scale; measurement scales; rating scales

scatterplots, 236–237, 237f, 238f, 239f

scientific approach, 5

scientific understanding of behavior, 1–18

authority, 4

basic and applied research, 11–14

causes of behavior, 8–9, 10f

description of behavior, 8, 8f

empiricism, 5

evaluating research critically, 2–3, 7

explanation of behavior, 9

goals of behavioral science, 7–10

illustrative article, 15–16

intuition and anecdotal evidence, 4

prediction of behavior, 8

questioning research methods, 7

research methods, reasons for learning, 2–3

scientific approach, 5

ways of knowing, 3–7

Scopus, 38–39

Scribner, Sylvia, 115

secondary sources, referencing, 319

selection differences, 153, 214

self-report measures, 173

semantic differential scale, 133

sensitivity of dependent variable, 175–176

sequential method, 220–221

setting the stage, 168–169

sex and gender, 277

simple main effects, 196–197

simple random sampling, 141, 143t

simplicity of survey questions, 130

single-blind experiment, 179

single-case experimental designs

    defined, 207

    multiple baseline designs, 209–210, 209f

    replicating, 210

    reversal designs, 207–208, 208f

skepticism, 5–7

small-N designs. *See* single-case experimental designs

social desirability, 128

software, statistical analysis, 267

Solomon four-group design, 155–156, 156f, 281

sources

    anatomy of reference, 34f

    citation style, 312–315

    citing and referencing, 312–319, 340–341

    failure to acknowledge. *See* plagiarism

    reference list style, 315–319, 340–341

    secondary, 319

    websites and databases, 316, 319

spatial reasoning, 284

Spearman-Brown split-half reliability coefficient, 100

split-half reliability, 100

staged manipulations, 170–171

standard deviation, 233, 348–349

Standard 8: Research and Publication, 345

Stapel, Diederik, 63

statistical inference, 249–273

    group differences, 254–260

    interpreting nonsignificant results, 264–265

    null and research hypotheses, 251–252

    probability and sampling distributions, 252–254, 253t

    replications, 266

samples and populations, 250–251, 250t

sample size, 254, 265–266, 266t

selecting appropriate test, 267–269

significance level, 263–264

statistical analysis software, 267, 268f

Type I and Type II errors, 260–264, 260f

statistical interaction, generalization as, 282, 283f

statistical records, 121

statistical regression. *See* regression toward the mean

statistical significance

    confidence intervals and, 259, 260f

    defined, 252

    overview, 260

statistical significance, effect size and, 349–368

    analysis of variance (F test), 353–365

    chi-square (X^2), 350–353

statistical tests, 346–368

    descriptive statistics, 346–349

    F test, 257

    one-tailed versus two-tailed tests, 257

    power of, 265

    selecting, 267–269

    statistical significance and effect size, 349–368

    t test, 254–256, 255f

statistical validity, 73, 89, 228

statistics, reporting, 321–322

straightforward manipulations, 169–170

stratified random sampling, 141, 143t

strength of manipulation, 172–173, 172f

stress, as research risk, 51–52

structural equation modeling, 244–245, 245f

study participants. *See* participants

subject variables. *See* participant variables

subjects. *See* participants

subsections, 306–307, 329

sum of squares, 354–356, 356t

survey archives, 121–122

survey research, 126–150

administering surveys, 136–138

constructing questions, 128–131

convenience sampling, 145–146

defined, 127

evaluating samples, 144–145

finalizing instrument, 135

graph, 128f

illustrative article, 146–147

objectives, 129

population sampling, 139–140. *See also* statistical inference, samples and populations

reasons for conducting, 127–128

responses, 131–135

sampling techniques, 140–144

studying design changes over time, 138–139

wording of questions, 129–131

systematic observation, 117–119

coding systems, 118

defined, 117

methodological issues, 118–119

systematic review, 26

systematic variance, 257

T

tables, 308–309, 310, 342

telephone interviews, 138

temporal precedence, 9, 84

terminology, psychological, 33

testing effects, 212–213

test-retest reliability, 99, 100, 100f

theories, as source of research ideas, 23–24

theory articles, 26–27

Thesaurus of Psychological Index Terms, 33

third variable, 87

third-variable problem, 81–82, 81f

title, 300–301

title page, 300–303, 304f, 326

transition words and phrases, 295–297

troublesome words and phrases, 297–298

true score, 97

t test, 254–256, 255f

two-tailed tests, 257

Type I errors, 260–261, 261f, 262–264

Type II errors, 260, 261f, 262–264

U

uncertainty, reducing, 78–79, 79t

unobtrusive measures, 105

V

validity, 73

concurrent, 103, 104t

construct, 73, 75, 89, 101–104, 228

content, 102, 104t

convergent, 103, 104t

discriminant, 103–104, 104t–105t

external, 73, 84, 86, 89, 228, 275

face, 102, 104t

internal, 73, 90, 95, 228

predictive, 103, 104t

statistical, 73, 89, 228

summary of types, 89

variability, 233–234, 348–349

variables, 73–79

ability to manipulate, 87

confounding, 82, 152

construct validity and, 78

extraneous, 81

factorial designs with, 193–194, 194f

manipulating. *See* manipulation of independent variables

measurement scales and, 105–108

operational definitions, 74–75

participant, 87

random variability, 78–79

relationships between, 76–79, 77f

third-variable problem, 81–82, 81f, 243

two, research studying, 269

See also dependent variables; independent variables; *and entries for specific variables*

variance, 234, 348–349

W

Web of Science, 38–39

websites

citing specific documents/pages, 319

electronic search resources, 39–40

including URLs in citation, 316

WEIRD (Western, Educated, Industrialized, Rich, Democratic), 278

withdrawal design, 207

within-group variance, 257

within-subjects design. *See* repeated measures design

Wong-Baker FACES Pain Rating Scale, variables in, 74–75

word-for-word plagiarism, 64

written and mass communication records, 122–123

written reports. *See also* journal articles; research reports

active versus passive voice, 294

avoiding plagiarism, 294

clarity, 293–294

grammatical considerations, 295–298

X

X^2. *See* Chi-square (X^2)

Y

yea-saying, 131

APA 7th Edition
FORMATTING CHECKLIST

Style Checklist for Entire Document

- ☐ Serif fonts: 12-point Times Roman; 11-point Georgia; 10-point Computer Modern
- ☐ San serif fonts: 11-point Arial; 11-point Calibri; 10-point Lucinda Sans Unicode
- ☐ Double-space the entire paper (exception: block quotes).
- ☐ 1-inch margins.
- ☐ Running head: regular font, placed on top right of every page.
- ☐ Page numbers: regular font, placed on top right of each page.
- ☐ Text paragraphs: have first line indented ½ inch.
- ☐ One space following each period or colon.

Title Page

- ☐ Title: Generally no more than 12 words, centered in the upper half of the page, **boldface**, title case (typed in upper and lower case).
- ☐ Author: First name, middle initial(s), last name(s). Omit titles.
- ☐ Author affiliation: department and university.

Abstract

- ☐ "Abstract" centered, top of page, **boldface** font styling.
- ☐ First line flush left (not indented).
- ☐ 150"250 words (typically).
- ☐ "Keywords," if needed, are included as an indented section at the end of the abstract.

Introduction

- ☐ Manuscript title, centered, top of page, **boldface** font styling. This must be at the top of a page.

Method

- ☐ **"Method"** centered and **boldface.** This does not need to be at the top of a page.

- ☐ Sub-sections typically include **Participants** or **Subjects, Materials, Procedure.** These subheadings should be **boldface,** flush left, on a line by themselves.

Results

- ☐ **"Results"** centered and **boldface.** Does not need to be at the top of a page.

Discussion

- ☐ **"Discussion"** centered and **boldface.** This does not need to be at the top of a page.

Reference Page

- ☐ "References" centered, top of new page, in **boldface.**
- ☐ Alphabetical order by first author"s last name.
- ☐ Double-spaced.
- ☐ First line of each entry flush left, subsequent lines indented (hanging indent).

Tables

- ☐ Included at the end of the document, after references.
- ☐ Each table on its own page.
- ☐ **"Table X"** flush left, on its own line, **boldface.**
- ☐ Title of table flush left, italicized, title case.
- ☐ Column headings capitalized.
- ☐ Horizontal lines separate the headers from the content. No vertical lines are used on tables.
- ☐ Double-spaced.

Figures

- ☐ Included at the end of the document, after references and tables.
- ☐ Each figure on its own page.
- ☐ **"Figure X"** flush left, on its own line, **boldface.**
- ☐ Title of figure flush left, italicized, title case.